Campaign Journal

Also by Elizabeth Drew

Washington Journal: The Events of 1973–1974
American Journal: The Events of 1976
Senator
Portrait of an Election: The 1980 Presidential Campaign
Politics and Money: The New Road to Corruption

Campaign Journal

THE POLITICAL EVENTS OF
1983–1984

Elizabeth Drew

MACMILLAN PUBLISHING COMPANY

NEW YORK

Macmillan Publishing Company
866 Third Avenue, New York, N.Y. 10022
Collier Macmillan Canada, Inc.

Library of Congress Cataloging in Publication Data
Drew, Elizabeth.
Campaign journal.
Includes index.
1. United States—Politics and government—1981–
2. Presidents—United States—Election—1984.
I. Title.
E876.D74 1985   324.973′0927   84-12204
ISBN 0-02-533510-3

Macmillan books are available at special discounts for bulk purchases for sales promotions, premiums, fund-raising, or educational
use. Special editions or book excerpts can also be created to specifi-
cation. For details, contact:
Special Sales Director
Macmillan Publishing Company
866 Third Avenue
New York, New York 10022

10 9 8 7 6 5 4 3 2 1

Printed in the United States of America

Again, for William Shawn

Acknowledgments

Some years ago, I had the wonderful fortune of being invited by William Shawn to write for *The New Yorker*—and became the recipient of that alchemy of kindly, exacting support for which he is renowned. His understanding of writers, and of writing, is an amazing thing. He often knows where you are headed before you do, and helps to get you there; he gives writers that much-needed oxygen—confidence. Along the way, I have published six books under his guidance, and it is more than appropriate that this is the second one dedicated to him.

I am extremely grateful to a number of other people who helped make this book possible. John Bennet, a gifted editor and good friend, guided almost all the chapters of this book into print at *The New Yorker*—and he did so with a skill, steadiness, and humor that eased the way through a highly pressurized time. There were many others at *The New Yorker* who worked very hard to help get the work into print, and they, too, have my thanks. My assistant, Kathy Glover, was her usual bright, loyal, and hard-working self, and was of tremendous help, in many ways. Two former associates, Laura Waltz and Christine Haynes Myers, pitched in to help get the book produced, and I am grateful for and moved by their continuing loyalty and support. Hillel Black, of Macmillan, has given this book, as he gave my last one, his enthusiastic support, and has also shown me great kindness. And Sterling Lord, my agent and friend, has been a wise and steadfast counselor. My husband, David Webster, lived through this project, which is more than should be asked of anyone, but he also shared it with me and contributed to it in countless ways.

Finally, I am also grateful to all those people involved in the election, and others who observed it wisely, who took the time to talk to me about it, and teach me about the endlessly interesting and always somewhat mysterious subject of politics.

E.D.

Introduction

The Presidential election of 1984 was both an unusual one and an important one in several respects—not all of them so obvious. The outcome may have been one-sided, but it was not inevitable, and the election bespoke a number of important things about our politics and about what was going on in our country at the time. As a writer for *The New Yorker* I was asked to write a journal of the election and the surrounding events—a contemporary account, with periodic entries, of what was happening and why. Through a combination of on-the-scene reporting, interviewing the candidates, their advisers, and others wise about what was happening, and my own reflection and experience, I was to provide as clear a picture as I could of what was taking place—as it was taking place. The surprising twists and turns are presented here as they happened, and as I saw them, without tidying up or hindsight.

While this election stands on its own as an important and interesting one, it will also affect our country, and our politics, not just in the near term but for years to come. Therefore, we need to understand all that we can about it.

Elizabeth Drew
Washington, D.C.
November 28, 1984

1983

I

In the future, those looking back on the Reagan Administration will be struck by two things: how quickly what was termed "the Reagan revolution" was over, and how evident the seeds of its destruction were all along. This is not to say that Reagan will not run for reelection (a subject of endless, albeit fruitless, speculation in Washington), or even, given a bit of luck, be reelected. But his conquest was over by August of his first year in office, and the story of the Reagan Administration since then has been one of improvisation and reaction to outside forces (especially those within his own party) in an attempt to retake the high ground. By misinterpreting his mandate (with the help of a large number of commentators) and operating at the far end of the ideological spectrum, the President squandered his advantage. By pushing through his own economic program in the early months, instead of taking the opportunity to compromise with the Democrats, he may have committed the greatest tactical blunder of his Administration. The many Republicans who had misgivings followed fashion rather than their instincts. In August of 1981, Republicans, according to their own accounts, went home for the recess "in a state of euphoria"—their President was sweeping all before him—and returned in September "in a state of panic." The public was upset about interest rates. The drive to reduce the deficits through tax increases was on; Republicans began putting distance between themselves and their briefly invincible leader. A program that didn't add up in the Presidential campaign didn't add up when it was submitted to Congress, and emerged (after Democrats and the White House bid up its price) even more mathematically askew. Since September of 1981, the White House has engaged in one maneuver after another to try to regain command of the agenda. Last year's State of the Union Message, with its drum-rolling introduction of "the New Federalism," was designed to do

3

that, and it met with a notable, and predictable, lack of success. (Presidents often resort to speeches to "turn things around"— rarely with success. A great deal is expected from Reagan—by Reagan and his aides, as well as by others—because of his reputation as an effective speaker.) This year, the President's aides were aware that the stakes were very high, and that Reagan held a weaker hand than ever before. Washington, with its animal instinct for flows of power, had taken note. Reagan's popularity, never as high as it was generally assumed to be in Washington, was clearly on a downward slide; the 1982 elections, in which the President was more involved than several of his aides thought wise (especially in retrospect), had not gone well for the Republicans.

"Watch the State of the Union address with real care," one of the President's advisers said to me not long after the 1982 elections. "If the President tries to paper over the problems, then we're in real trouble." In early January, a White House aide described himself as "anxious now, because it could go either way." The question that was now on the table was, as the White House aide said, "whether Reagan can govern." It was this question that caused the White House people to go into something of a panic as the new year got under way. It was this question that led to the news stories, which were based on conversations with White House aides, about "disarray." What in fact was going on was strikingly like what had been going on a year earlier, only this time writ larger. The prospective deficits were now more than twice as large as those that had so alarmed the President's aides and congressional Republicans the year before. Aides, having shot their bolt a year earlier, had to be more indirect in trying to maneuver the President toward their idea of reality. Their instruments were Republican congressional leaders—and the press. The Republicans were brought to the White House, and distress signals were sent through the press. The "leaks" that so disturbed the President were essentially purposeful anxious talk on the part of his aides. And even the term "leaks" itself was misapplied. A leak is the giving out of a specific piece of information, authorized or otherwise; a leak is about a policy proposal, an internal discussion, an event that is supposed to stay hidden from view. What was emerging from the White House earlier this year was not so much these sorts of leaks as the public fretting of the President's associates. Such airing of internal stress had irritated the President for quite a while, but the phenomenon, and the President's reaction to it, reached a new pitch this January. (The last straw, according to a Presidential aide, was a lead story in early January in the Los Angeles *Times* with the headline "REAGAN AIDES FRUSTRATED BY HIS RIGIDITY.") There followed the attempt to crack down on contacts with the press, but while some aides became, at least temporarily, more circumspect ("I'll talk to you in a month"), the public fretting went right on. Every Administration in memory has struggled with the problem of talkative aides and has tried, in vain, to silence them, but there was something different about the nature of the talk that came out of the Reagan White House. It reflected not simply the traditional battles among aides and between aides and other Administration officials but also an attitude of despair on the part of the aides toward the President they were serving, and it conveyed a lack of respect. It was not leaks of information but the talk of the President's "stubbornness" and the picture of him as out of it that caused the President to try to crack down.

The problem of portraying Reagan as being in charge has, it is often forgotten, bedevilled his aides and managers for a long time—when he was governor of California, during his Presidential campaign, during the Presidential transition period, and even in his first weeks in office. (Thus, in those early days his aides staged frantic "day in the life of" features about Reagan.) The sense that Reagan drops in and out of his job, is intellectually lazy, has long been regarded by some of his associates as one of his most serious vulnerabilities. When things are going well, it is not so much of a problem; when they are not, it can be murderous. (That's why, in August of 1981, there was near-apoplexy within the White House over the failure of Edwin Meese, the President's counsellor, to wake him during the dogfight between American and Libyan planes over the Gulf of Sidra.) Privately, few White House aides take great pains any longer to maintain that the President works particularly hard at the job; when questioned, they draw a favorable contrast with the obsessive work habits of Jimmy Carter. (They do not acknowledge that there could be something in between.) Despite the efforts of his aides, Reagan's passivity and his hazy command of the facts—which the good-guy shrugs and the smiling imperturbability seemed to underscore—have, bit by bit, impressed themselves upon the public. And once such impressions register they are hard to erase. The definitive sign of a shift in public attitude occurred when *Time*, which had treated Reagan generously and contributed to his apotheosis in the first year, ran a cover story in December that called into question his grasp of his job. What was happening to Reagan had happened to other Presidents, with respect to other characteristics. Gradually, an attribute sinks into the public consciousness—placed there not by "the media," as Presidents usually suppose, but by the President's own behavior. To the extent that there is such a collective creature, "the media" tend to follow public fashion, are reluctant to get crosswise with the public mood, to go beyond the limits of what is deemed acceptable. In fact, Reagan was given a pretty good ride by the media—in part because of his charm, and in part because of his presumed popularity. Reagan's working style had long perturbed members of Congress who sought to cooperate with him, and gradually their stories filtered out through Washington. They spoke of the irrelevant anecdotes, of the difficulty of engaging him on issues. An important Senate Republican said recently, "I just don't think he works very hard." A leading House Republican said to me, "The President makes a real effort with Congress, but not a pointed one. He doesn't really engage with his staff—they talk past each other. His lack of involvement with details is a real detriment to this Administration." He paused and then added, "Dealing with Reagan can be very nerve-racking."

To a large extent, as some of the President's associates now realize, the President created a trap for himself by adopting the role of the last true believer. His aides, who study the polls feverishly, say that this apparent steadiness of purpose brings the President good marks for "leadership" and "consistency." They also maintain that his standing firm puts him in a strong bargaining position when it comes time to compromise with Congress. The trap is that this approach suggests a picture of a man who is out of touch with reality—being pushed and nudged and importuned by his own aides. (A recent Washington *Post*/ABC News poll found that fifty-five per cent of the respondents felt that Reagan's advisers make "most of the important decisions in the White House." Congress noticed.) It leaves his aides and would-be congressional allies to bear the burden of arguing for a more moderate course. If taxes are raised or defense spending is cut, Reagan can say, "They made me do it." The risks for him of such an approach are that it suggests a non-leader, and that he may be written off as politically irrelevant. One aide conceded when we talked in early January that the President was running the risk of appearing to be stubborn, out of touch, worn down by the arguments of others. A number of people here, including some within the White House, think that Reagan has paid a price—a heavy one—for his wily-fox approach.

The tipoff came when key Republicans began paddling away from the President this year even before he delivered the State of the Union address. On the Sunday before the speech, Senate Majority Leader Howard Baker, Republican of Tennessee, gave a bravura performance on *Meet the Press*, paying his respects to the President but talking about the program the President was about to submit as if it were just another piece of paper. Baker, who will run for President as soon as Reagan doesn't, took aim at some parts of the President's program—the level of defense expenditures and the idea of a contingency, or "trigger," tax to deal with deficits three years hence. The trigger tax is a kind of look-Ma-no-hands approach to raising taxes, and was the most that the President's aides could talk him into. Baker's view was that it was too hypothetical to be convincing. A little over a week after the speech, Robert Dole, Republican of Kansas and chairman of the Senate Finance Committee, who initiated last year's tax increase, said that there was "no support" on the committee for the President's tax proposal and that he was working on an alternative. And Reagan's domestic and military priorities—his continuing to shrink domestic programs while expanding the military budget, his selective indignation about "fraud and waste" (he finds it in the food-stamp program but not in the Pentagon)—were destined not to sit well with many Republicans, to say nothing of Democrats. In no time, there were bipartisan efforts to do more to help the unemployed. A number of Republicans concluded a year ago that no more should be taken from the poor. Many of them consider the Administration's vendetta against the Legal Services program (thus far resisted by Congress) to be, in the word of one Senate Republican, "dumb." The most that some key Republicans could say when the President submitted his new program was that they would "not reject it out of hand." The White House portrayed this as a major achievement. The Republicans were polite but intent on making revisions across the board. So by yielding as little ground as possible Reagan failed to do the two things that he needed to do: take command of the agenda, and make a convincing case that he had the budget deficits under control. Once again, he left the hard part to Congress.

A powerful motivating force behind the Republicans' behavior is, of course, survival. The 1984 elections, congressional as well as Presidential, are under way. Republican senators begin the day aware that nineteen of the thirty-three Senate seats up in 1984 are held by Republicans, and that their party came uncomfortably close to losing the Senate in 1982. These things, says a Senate leadership aide, "have compelled the Republicans to focus on 1984 very intently." Fund-raising events were being held even before the Senate got down to doing business this year. In deciding how they will vote, the Republicans will be making cold-blooded calculations about how closely they want to be identified with Reagan as well as about how their votes will affect their ability to raise campaign funds. And while Reagan is trying to govern, the next contest for the Republican nomination—be it in 1984 or 1988— will be going on. In fact, it has been going on for some time. To follow the action, it is important to understand that the race is already on among Jack Kemp, Republican representative from New York and chief apostle of the supply-side economic theory, and a moderate Republican (Baker or Dole or someone else) and Vice-President George Bush, who will try to maintain his credentials with both Reagan and the moderates. When Senator Paul Laxalt, Republican of Nevada, said on *Face the Nation* recently that if Reagan didn't run the nomination would not automatically go to Bush but would be "totally up for grabs," this was generally assumed throughout Washington to mean that Laxalt is interested. But since Bush may not be seen to have any views of his own until he is liberated by Reagan—he has been an exemplary Vice-President in this respect—the overt struggle is between Kemp and the moderates, with some figures on the far right making threatening noises. Kemp will keep up the drumfire on what he terms Reagan's abandonment of supply-side theory (no tax increases should have been countenanced last year or this), thus putting himself in a position to argue that his theory cannot be said to have failed, since it was never tried. Dole, who has no use for Kemp or his theory, takes frequent potshots at the theory and, through that, at

Kemp. All over Washington, Republican politicians and political managers and political activists are maneuvering for the big fight, which they know will occur sooner or later.

There was a certain piquancy to President Reagan's talk, in his State of the Union Message, of the wonders of high technology and the promise it holds for solving the nation's economic problems, and to his rushing off to Boston to view some microchips the following day. In this, he was following the fad started by a group of Democrats—the "Atari Democrats"—in the House and the Senate. The trouble is, Silicon Valley isn't hiring these days. Moreover, at a seminar in Washington before Christmas, the news was broken to the Atari Democrats that computers could actually end up costing people their jobs.

The State of the Union speech was perhaps the most difficult one the President has had to give. This may account for his uncharacteristically halting and, it seemed, defensive delivery of it—Reagan is usually seamless in speaking from a prepared text, his manner confident. He is at home with broad themes and optimism. This time, he had to proceed from unaccustomed territory—a corner. Even Reagan, according to his associates, has come to admit that his economic program has not worked as well as expected—at least, not in the short run. (He is said to still believe that it will be successful, and not to trust the economists' predictions of a weak recovery or large future deficits.) So he had to adopt a sombre tone that is not typical of him and that he is not comfortable with. And, given the trouble his program is in, and the need to maintain some control over the agenda on Capitol Hill and not be on the defensive, he felt compelled to lay out a list of proposals having to do with training, education, and so on—and his speech took on the laundry-list character of those of so many of his predecessors. "It was not the kind of speech that Reagan likes to give," said one of his advisers. "And therefore it was a difficult speech for him to deliver." And diluted Reaganism loses not only its flavor but its sense of purpose. One of the President's advisers said, "The thing that drove the campaign and the first two years was a clearly articulated set of goals—goals that now can't be reached."

Some of the President's advisers knew that his proposed cut in the scheduled defense increase would be considered too small, and suspect, on Capitol Hill, but according to one of them, it was difficult to get him to go even as far as he did. They foresaw that the size of the defense budget was likely to meet resistance, and feared that this would place Reagan not in the position of negotiating from strength with Capitol Hill but on the sidelines.

The Administration's economic projection—of about three-percent growth in 1983—is considered too low even by people who have been critical of the Administration's previous, optimistic predictions. According to some sources, one reason the projection is low is that the Administration is resorting to a form of the political economics that many Administrations have practiced: in this case, adjusting the numbers so that if things turn out better, so much the merrier. Moreover, it was widely understood within the Administration that it dared not come forward yet again with unbelievable optimistic assumptions—"Rosy Scenario" (the optimistic assumptions behind the President's original economic program) had been disgraced. Another theory is that the Administration is deliberately seeking a recovery that is slower than has usually occurred after recessions, so as not to reignite inflation. Still another theory, which has some foundation, is that Martin Feldstein, the new chairman of the Council of Economic Advisers, was afraid the Administration would insist on projections that were unrealistically positive, so he offered his colleagues excessively negative ones, expecting to strike a bargain—and his offer was accepted.

The flight into illusion about the true nature of the budget deficits has caused the government to come up with a whole new vocabulary. In talking about the large deficits that will occur in the next year and the year after that, people now use the term "out years"—as in "out-year deficits"—which makes them seem farther away. The Office of Management and Budget refers to the cut in the growth of the defense budget as a "decrement." There can, of course, be an "out-year decrement." Then, there is the talk about the "glide path" the budget is on—that is, the deficits are unfortunate, but the situation is acceptable if the deficits are on the right "glide path." And now everything is "structural." "Structural" is a very popular and useful term. Some years ago, the concept of "structural" unemployment—unemployment no one knew what to do about—gained general acceptance. Now, according to the

Reagan Administration, the group that promised the balanced budget, there are "structural deficits."

The extraordinary deficits have also called forth a talent for euphemism. In the Presidential campaign, Reagan said that his economic policy would lead to a balanced budget in fiscal 1983, and in his first year in office he said it would occur in fiscal 1984. Now the Administration is predicting budget deficits through at least fiscal 1988, which gets us into the "out-out years." In this year's budget message, which projects a deficit of a hundred and eighty-nine billion dollars for fiscal 1984, the Administration explains, "The policy adjustments to the inherited 1981 budget implemented over the past two budget cycles have been somewhat more successful in reducing the out-year (1985–1988) tax claim on GNP than originally anticipated."

It is with reason that Reagan's aides have tried to screen his public statements since he took office, just as they did during his campaign. It's not merely the misstatements (confusing Brazil with Bolivia when he was in Brazil, or referring to Samuel Doe, the Liberian head of state, who was visiting the White House, as "Chairman Moe"). There's also the problem of Reagan's own impolitic views slipping out. And so when Reagan, during his trip to Boston on the day after his State of the Union address, offered his thought that the corporate-income tax should be abolished, one could almost hear a collective clap of hands to foreheads emanating from the White House. This was the General Electric-after-dinner-speech Reagan, whom his aides have tried over the years, with only partial success, to suppress. The corporate-income-tax view had caused a couple of crises in the 1980 campaign. It is a view that does have some economic respectability, but it is an impolitic thing for Reagan to suggest, especially these days. I asked one of Reagan's advisers what his reaction was when he heard the news of the remarks about the corporate-income tax. He responded, "I died."

The large, bitter battle that has been going on within the Administration over arms-control policy came to the surface only briefly when Eugene Rostow, the head of the Arms Control and Disarmament Agency, was fired, and, in fact, Rostow's firing was only a small indication of the battle. In this case, the Administration's efforts to suggest that the issue was one of personality were not entirely misleading. Rostow is described both by those who agree with him and by those who do not as a difficult man. An arms-control advocate who once served in the Johnson Administration, where Rostow was in the State Department, told me, "It's never a surprise that anyone would fire Gene Rostow. He's affable, but you can't work with him. People in the Johnson Administration made it a point to keep issues away from him." That even Rostow, who had been an arms-control conservative before joining the Reagan Administration, came to believe that the Administration should be more flexible in its approach to arms control is telling, and it did add to his vulnerability. His policy opponents had been gunning for him for some time. The nominee to replace him, Kenneth Adelman, was not likely to unsettle them.

The real point is that the Administration still—after two years—has no structure for serious, ongoing exploration of arms-control options. The civilians in the Pentagon who oppose arms-control agreements have been the predominant force. In addition, they, along with their allies on the staffs of a few right-wing senators, plus a few allies placed in the State Department, have been able to stymie the nominations of several people who might take a more flexible approach to arms control. They are unrelenting in their efforts and are skilled at bureaucratic infighting and at using the press. When the Administration, after a big internal battle, settled on the "zero-zero" approach to nuclear weapons in Europe—an approach opposed by then Secretary of State Alexander Haig—they leaked to friendly columnists the story of the struggle, with suggestions that Haig (of all people) was a bit soft. (Haig's view was that the zero-zero approach—asking the Soviet Union to disman-tle all its intermediate-range nuclear missiles in exchange for an American pledge not to proceed with the deployment of inter-mediate-range missiles in Western Europe—would be difficult to move away from if, as he considered likely, it proved impossible to achieve, and this would cause more problems with our European allies.) That episode has made others in the government leery of discussing arms-control options in interagency meetings. The re-sult has been a Balkanization of our own government, with little groups putting as much energy into planning against each other as into planning how to deal with the Soviet Union. Even Paul Nitze, the United States negotiator for the intermediate-range-

nuclear-weapons talks, who, like Rostow, is an arms-control conservative, managed to run afoul of some Administration officials
by exploring with his Soviet counterpart something other than the
zero-zero option. Negotiators customarily explore alternatives to
the official negotiating position, but Nitze went too far for the
group back home. It is reported that, contrary to what the Administration has been saying, the United States was the first to reject
the potential deal. Whatever the case, some here say that even if
the Soviet Union did turn down the possible agreement, the
United States should have indicated a willingness to continue to
explore it. Nitze, like Rostow, had opposed the SALT II agreement,
covering strategic weapons, which was negotiated by the Carter
Administration, and some Reagan Administration officials may
have assumed that he was, like them, an orthodox opponent of
arms control. (Some arms-control liberals assumed that he was.)
But Nitze is a serious man, and a proud man, who thinks that an
agreement can and should be reached. That the hopes of arms-
control liberals rest with him indicates how far the ground has
shifted.

One problem with the making of arms-control policy in the
Reagan Administration is that no one has been in charge. Haig,
who did have some understanding of the subject, was distracted
by other battles, and then gone. (He was fired in June of last year.)
William Clark, the national-security adviser, is graded by several
Administration officials as a pleasant man with no particular
knowledge and no particular intellectual depth—or interest in
filling the gaps. Like the man he serves, he is said to be intellectually lazy. Beyond that, according to some Administration officials, his deep sense of loyalty to Reagan, his protectiveness of
him, leads him to react as he thinks the President would, without
troubling the President to go into the question. Thus, he often
comes down on the most conservative end of the argument, figuring that's what Reagan would do.

That leaves Secretary of State George Shultz. When the furor
broke over the firing of Rostow, the Administration made a big
thing of saying that Shultz would be in charge of arms control.
Shultz himself turned up at a State Department press briefing—
something he had not done before—to say, "We have the situation
firmly in control," and the following day Reagan held an im-
promptu press conference to assure one and all that everything

was under control. Some Administration officials felt that this was not a good idea—that it would have the opposite of the desired effect. But the Administration was in a bit of a panic. ("How much of a firestorm do you think the Rostow thing will cause?" a White House aide had asked me earlier that week. "Firestorm" is the word that was used in 1973 to describe the reaction to Nixon's firing of Archibald Cox, the Special Prosecutor.) Shultz has become the repository of people's hopes on a number of issues. His physical presence has something to do with it: he is a large, Buddha-like figure who moves and speaks deliberately. He is calm, experienced, nonideological, and sensible—all reassuring traits. And he has a tendency not to show his hand. People are inclined to impute to him views they hope he holds. The fact that his views on arms control were unknown did not discourage anyone from assuming that they would be sound ones. But Shultz cannot just automatically take charge of arms control; he will have to work at the subject—with which he is not familiar—and enter into the continuous battle within the Administration. Until now, he has concentrated most on economics (his field), and he had the credentials to extricate the Administration from its self-defeating struggle with the Europeans over the construction of a natural-gas pipeline between the Soviet Union and Western Europe. There was the war in Lebanon and the Middle East peace initiatives. Then he spent a great deal of time sitting in Administration meetings on the budget; and then he was preparing for his trip to China. He has not yet had much time to deal with Central America, and so, while the post-Haig rhetoric is quieter, the policy, which a number of people within the Administration find vexing, has not changed. And Shultz has had little time for arms control.

The Administration did come to see that it had a public-relations problem with arms control—and so, characteristically, it turned to a public-relations man to deal with the problem. Peter Dailey, the current Ambassador to Ireland, who had handled advertising for the Reagan Presidential campaign, was put in charge of a committee. But public relations alone will not solve the problem, of course. Reagan's theatrical gesture of offering to meet the Soviet leader, Yuri Andropov, to sign an agreement on Reagan's terms was not destined to be convincing. It is widely accepted in Europe that the Soviet Union may want to retain some missiles to offset those of the British and the French, and also American aircraft stationed in Europe that are equipped with nuclear weapons. The Soviet Union has had intermediate-range missiles in place for more than two decades. Even within our own government, at high levels, there is a view that the United States should demonstrate more flexibility. Unless there is some substantive movement on arms control, the European alliance is in trouble. And we might end up with another form of zero-zero: no U.S. missiles in Europe and no reduction by the Soviet Union. The fact is that there are some in the Administration who would not mind such an outcome. Some are really concerned less about installing nuclear weapons in Europe than about having an issue against the Europeans, who they feel have become impudent. They believe that much of Europe has become, as they misleadingly term it, "Finlandized." The ultimate irony is that a number of people here, on both sides of the arms-control debate, are not enthralled by the idea of installing nuclear missiles in Europe. The decision to install them was taken by the Carter Administration after the fiasco over placing neutron warheads in Germany. The proposed installation of the missiles was seen as a way of calming European anxiety over the Soviet placement of new, more powerful missiles in Eastern Europe and of uniting the alliance. One point of the exercise was to show that the alliance could actually act like an alliance. (However, the missiles will be not NATO weapons but American ones, under American control.) There was, according to someone involved in the decision, no real strategic rationale for the number of missiles to be placed (five hundred and seventy-two). And it was understood at the time that the weapons were to become part of the SALT III negotiations—the approval of the SALT II arms-control agreement the Carter administration reached with the Soviet Union being taken for granted. "It was a lousy decision," one Carter Administration official says of the move to install intermediate-range weapons in Europe. These weapons, several people point out, would be vulnerable; moreover, they are now a source of disunity in the alliance. Some key Administration officials say that an agreement on strategic weapons is even more remote. One Administration official says, "A number of people here don't think the deployment makes sense, but we're stuck with it."

Ronald Reagan often gives the impression that he still thinks in terms of movie scenes. Some of the anecdotes he tells sound like scenes in a movie. One imagines him visualizing them. Some of his seemingly offhand remarks have the ring of having been thought out and rehearsed. His "There you go again" to Carter in the 1980 Presidential debate is one example. And it may be remembered that what was taken by many to be the seminal event of the contest for the Republican nomination was the debate in Nashua, New Hampshire, when Reagan invited the other Republican candidates to take part in what had been scheduled as a one-to-one debate with Bush, and Bush objected. Reagan carried the event by saying angrily, "I am paying for this microphone, Mr. Green." (Jon Breen was the editor of the Nashua *Telegraph*, which had arranged the debate.) Now *State of the Union*, a Spencer Tracy-Katharine Hepburn movie made in 1948, is becoming something of a cult film in Washington. Tracy plays an idealistic businessman who is seeking the Republican Presidential nomination and begins to yield to the pressures of his backers to sell out to the various interests. In a nationwide broadcast launching his campaign, his wife (Hepburn), though upset by his abandoning his uncompromising approach, begins to read a treacly statement prepared by his managers. Tracy, horrified to see that his wife, like him, has compromised, strides to the microphone and says that he has had enough. Amid the uproar, Tracy angrily says to the producer, and to the nation at large, "Don't you shut me off. I am paying for this broadcast."

II

While it is generally accepted that the Democratic contest for the
Presidential nomination was under way by February—four contenders formally announced their candidacies in the course of the
month—there is a certain artificiality to the setting of any date for
the beginning of the contest. The announcement is but one step
in a process that has been long under way. And while it is common
wisdom now to say that the current contest is uncommonly
lengthy, its length is not really unusual. For many years now, candidates have been out on the road for a long, long time, and—
would-be nominees have noticed—those who have logged the
most miles have often prevailed. It is probably no accident that
our last three newly elected Presidents—Nixon, Carter, Reagan—
were free to do little but run for the nomination long before they
received it. Hamilton Jordan's famous memorandum to Jimmy
Carter on how to go after the 1976 nomination was written in
1972, and its implementation began in January of 1973. (Carter
announced his candidacy in December of 1974—two months earlier than the formal start of this election's group.) Carter, having
noticed that George McGovern could have made more of the Iowa
precinct caucuses early in 1972, was getting acquainted with the
folks in Iowa early in 1975. McGovern had announced his Presidential candidacy in January, 1971, and had been considering the
race ever since 1968, when he made a brief run for the nomination. Edmund Muskie was presumed to be a Democratic candidate—a presumption that he gave every appearance of sharing—
from the time he made his wing-chair Election Eve television address in November, 1970. (That turned out to be the high point of
his campaign.) John F. Kennedy's race for the 1960 nomination
began with his run for the Vice-Presidential spot in 1956, and,
according to Theodore Sorensen, his closest aide, the planning
was well under way by the spring of 1959—and Kennedy had only

four real primary contests. And, while this year's Democratic candidates began making their announcements in February—Alan Cranston, Gary Hart, Walter Mondale, Reubin Askew did so—the campaign had been under way long before. Others—John Glenn, Fritz Hollings, Dale Bumpers, and who-knows-else—are expected to announce soon. The planning for Mondale's campaign began just after Carter's defeat in 1980.

So the longevity of the campaign is not really new. What is new is the amount of attention paid to it by the press so early in the game—and in this the candidates and the press are willing co-conspirators. For the candidates, the press coverage is crucial to their efforts to get themselves known and to convince would-be contributors and supporters that they are on the move and have a chance. There is a sort of backward-reeling logic to the whole thing. A candidate must start early because other candidates start early. The press is paying more attention earlier because it realizes that the early moves of the candidates may have significance and it wants to have been there, and, in truth, because it enjoys the sport. In this, it tends to reflect the somewhat schizophrenic attitude of the public, which (1) complains that the process is too long and (2) is keenly interested in who's going to win.

The other important thing that is new is the nature of the effort that it is assumed must be made early. In an attempt to abbreviate the process, and also deal with some other questions, the Democratic Party in 1981 established the Commission on Presidential Nominations, headed by Governor James Hunt, of North Carolina. The Hunt Commission recommended that the state primaries and caucuses all occur within a three-month "window"— between the second Tuesday in March and the second Tuesday in June. Exemptions were granted for Iowa and New Hampshire, which find it profitable to hold their contests early. (Iowa was permitted to hold its caucuses on February 27th, and New Hampshire its primary on March 6th.) The Commission also adopted some rule changes, including a "winner take more" allocation of the delegates, that worked to the advantage of primary and caucus winners. The states will submit their plans to a compliance commission this spring; if a state is ultimately not in compliance, its delegates might not be seated at the national Convention. There is a possibility that the whole idea of the "window" might collapse—if New Hampshire finds itself holding its primary on the same date that Vermont holds a nonbinding contest, it may insist on going earlier, in which case so will Iowa, and perhaps also Maine and some others. New Hampshire and Maine have suggested that they are less interested in having their small number of delegates seated than in the benefits of an early primary: tourism, publicity, and the potential for future Presidential favor. So the candidates and the press may find themselves once again freezing in Iowa in January as some hundred thousand Democrats prepare to cast their caucus votes. But the major fact is that the result of the Democratic Party's effort to shorten the Presidential-selection process was to increase the pressures on the candidates not only to get out there early but to build organizations and raise large amounts of money early. Perhaps this would have occurred in any event as each candidate tried to top the others' efforts. But the change in the scheduling of the primaries and caucuses in 1984 has backed into the nature of the contest the year before. The precise calendar will not be known for some time, but as of now the effect is that the contests will be earlier and more closely bunched. The new calendar will make it a different kind of campaign. In 1976, after Jimmy Carter "won" the January Iowa caucuses (actually, the "uncommitted" slate won, but Carter received more votes than the other candidates), he had five weeks to gather money and recruits to go on to win the New Hampshire primary and bask in the press attention. After New Hampshire, he had two weeks before the next important contest, in Florida, and then a week before the next one, in Illinois. His was a guerrilla movement that was able to concentrate on a few states at a time, borrowing money to tide it over from contest to contest. Under the current schedule, there will be eight days between Iowa and New Hampshire, and a large number of primaries in the Southern and industrial states will follow a week later. This time, therefore, victories in Iowa and New Hampshire could count for far less; the candidates must be ready for the other states. Thus, the campaign has been "nationalized"—it will take place on many fronts concurrently. It is now possible that fifty-one percent of the delegates, representing twenty-six states scattered all over the country, will be selected by March 27th. If the "window" holds, this will have taken place within twenty-nine days. (In 1980, this point was not reached until four weeks later—after three months of contests.) Mark Siegel, a political consultant and a leading authority on the Party rules, says, "With so many states deciding simultaneously, the strategy of relying on one early state to propel you toward the nomination becomes highly implausible, and the ability of a candidate to compete effectively in many places at the same time becomes the key to success." The pollster Patrick Caddell and others have warned that in its attempt to solve one problem the Democratic Party may have created another: it may have moved the Party perilously close to what is in effect a national primary, which is a singularly poor idea, because it does not permit extended consideration and reconsideration of the candidates, and could become a one-shot media event. Caddell argues that the new system does not protect the Party from a temporarily fashionable candidate, and even suggests that victories in Iowa and New Hampshire could provide more propulsion than before, allowing less time for voter scrutiny of the victors. Thomas Mann, the executive director of the American Political Science Association, who served as a technical adviser to the Hunt Commission, also believes that "front-loading"—the holding of so many contests early—distorts the process to ill effect. "If our system has any advantage," Mann says, "it is that it affords us time to give the candidates scrutiny. These changes take us in the wrong direction." Actually, nobody knows what the effect of the changes will be; what happens will depend heavily on the nature of the contest itself, the way candidates affect each other, and how the public reacts to them. But the "front-loading," if it should ultimately occur, could turn out to be very significant.

The real point is that the calendar itself is political. The candidates and the Party powers try to influence the timing of the state contests to meet their own exigencies. (A group of Southern primaries was set for the same day early in 1980 to help Jimmy Carter.) The Mondale forces want the contests as closely bunched as possible, figuring that this would prevent another candidate from getting much mileage out of Iowa or New Hampshire, and play into Mondale's strength, which is national organization. Glenn and Cranston tried to have the contests in their states—Ohio and California—which have customarily come at the end, moved up, in order to give them an early boost, and the Mondale forces tried to head these moves off. Both Glenn and Cranston failed. In the case of Ohio, Glenn apparently failed to do his homework, and, as it happens, the governor, Richard Celeste, is close to Mondale, and so is Tim Hagan, the leader of the Cuyahoga County (Cleveland) Democratic organization. Despite Cranston's efforts, California, which will send twenty per cent of the votes needed to win the nomination, will select its delegates in June. This is considered a blow to Cranston. Michigan has moved its caucus to an earlier date, and this, too, suits the Mondale camp's strategy. Yet there are some Party figures who are toying with the idea of trying to slow down the process, because they don't want the nomination locked up too soon. One theory floating about is that, with all the early exposure, the current crop of candidates will seem shopworn by late this year, and the public will be wondering if there isn't anything better. Not everyone agrees that later in the year would be too late to start.

The Democratic Party's effort to abbreviate the process, and also deal with some other delegate-selection questions, began as an attempt to deal with what was seen to be public tedium and the lack of involvement of Party professionals. An implicit purpose was to ward off long-shot candidacies, such as Jimmy Carter's. (Party reform commissions tend to deal with what is seen as the most recent problem.) But no such exercise takes place in a vacuum, and the outcome of the efforts of the Hunt Commission was a set of rules that were expected to benefit the candidacies of Edward Kennedy and Walter Mondale. The outcome was a victory for the representatives of the two men, who had successfully sought to design a race that favored those most able to mount a large, national campaign early and those who did best in the primaries. It was also a victory for organized labor, which wanted a big hand in deciding who was selected, and wanted a consensus candidate. Both the Kennedy and the Mondale forces assumed that Kennedy had an automatic base of thirty-some per cent of the Party; the Kennedy people figured that in a several-candidate field he could prevail, while the Mondale camp sought to reduce the field to two people quickly—Kennedy and Mondale—figuring that in such a race Mondale would prevail. With Kennedy out, the rules are presumed to favor Mondale, who now starts with the largest base.

Another new development that is changing the nature, if not the length, of the Presidential race is the number of pseudo events that are occurring before the official race begins. If a state's political leaders want attention from the candidates—and state political leaders do tend to—they simply stage a preliminary event in which the candidates are invited to participate: a "straw poll;" a fund-raising dinner (often a "Jefferson-Jackson Day" dinner, which is a floating event held by state Democratic Parties any time of the year); a state Party convention. Most dare not refuse, even though no one really has any idea what effect these unofficial events will have on the official contests. But they often yield unofficial polls, which are presumed to affect the picture of how a candidate is doing (and thus to affect the contributors and the activists). There is also, of course, the possible endorsement this year of a Democratic candidate by the A.F.L.-C.I.O. The vagaries and the chemistry of the campaign itself, the events that can change everything, cannot be foreseen. Nor can the degree to which the outcome may be affected by the number of candidates in the field and the way they take votes from each other. (Carter "won" New Hampshire with twenty-nine per cent of the vote; that is, seventy-one per cent of those who voted in the New Hampshire primary preferred someone else.) People who draw after-the-fact great-meaning-of-it-alls are inclined to overlook the extent to which a nomination contest was affected by a squeaking victory in New Hampshire (or even a loss that was interpreted as a victory, as Eugene McCarthy's was in 1968), or by an accident, or by the timing of the Michigan caucus.

One effect of both the nationalization and the acceleration of the campaign is that there will be a lot of feedback into the early states of what is happening elsewhere. The Mondale camp's theory is that if, say, Gary Hart is doing well at organizing in Iowa (as he is said to be) and he comes in fourth in a straw poll elsewhere, it will affect things in Iowa. So the pseudo events cannot be discounted. Eugene Eidenberg, the former director of the Democratic National Committee, says, "The scorn heaped on candidates for overreacting to a Jefferson-Jackson Day dinner misses the point of the campaign. A campaign is a process; it's like a train getting up a head of steam. The process is to reach out to a number of skeptical, uncommitted, reasonably active people and convince them that your nomination is inevitable, through a series of reinforcing events. It's a new form of the old bandwagon."

While the Democratic nomination could be settled unusually early, there is another possibility that some people contemplate: a brokered Convention. The brokered Convention has been a part of political fantasy for a long time—the Democrats haven't even had a second ballot since 1952. Yet some people have been thinking that, given a certain set of events, the nomination contest could result in a hung jury. Moreover, this time there will be a large contingent of Party officials at the Convention, arriving technically unpledged, though they may have made a commitment to a candidate. One motive behind this change was to tie the Party's elected officials more closely to the Convention; many had been staying away, wanting to avoid identification with the platform that the "amateur" activists wrote and not wishing to have to choose one colleague over another. Another motive was to make the Convention more "responsible"—both in its writing of the platform and in its choosing of a candidate—by having a larger proportion of people present who have to deal with the practicalities of politics (that is, get elected). Not for them, the theory went, the exotic candidate, the highly ideological candidate, the candidate from out of the blue. (The Mondale forces figured that the elected politicians would prefer Mondale to Kennedy.) More than one person in Washington permits himself to dream of being anointed by a Convention that could not agree upon any of the entered candidates.

Mondale is currently believed to be in the strongest position to win the nomination—a consensus that rests not just on the fact that he leads the others in the polls but also on the fact that his organization has laid the groundwork carefully. It is the thesis of the Mondale campaign that the more the contest is nationalized, as it has been, and accelerated, as it has been, the better off Mondale is. Therefore, Mondale's people have been encouraging the idea that it is that kind of campaign, attempting to force the other candidates to compete on Mondale's terms. (A collapse of the "window"—early Iowa caucuses, an early New Hampshire primary, which someone else might win, or come close in—is not in Mondale's interests.) The theory is that he will be the best at raising the money, building the organization, and lasting the distance. The more the process is accelerated, the thinking goes, the more the other candidates will come under scrutiny early, and the thesis is that Mondale is the best prepared to withstand the scrutiny—that he is the best long-distance runner. This narrows the other candidates' options, and puts pressure on them to perfect their routines at a much earlier point than before. Few reporters took much notice of Carter as he travelled about in 1975, trying out his themes. Now the candidates have been forced onstage, and there is less time to test their lines, less margin for making mistakes. (Some of Carter's former aides believe that if he had been subject to this much scrutiny this soon, he wouldn't have made it to the nomination.) When it began to be known in August of 1979 that Edward Kennedy might indeed challenge Carter, that was considered the last possible moment for him to get moving, and the most serious problem his campaign had at the outset was that it lacked a rationale. So now, a year before the first official events, the candidates are busily touching up their self-portraits, working out their rationales, rehearsing their responses to the predictable questions, lining up the supporters and the money, and, behind the smiling façade of brotherhood ("I'm going to run a positive campaign"), drawing their knives against each other.

The list of those who have announced their candidacies or will do so shortly does not include all those who would like to have the nomination and are thinking of making their moves later. The dream of becoming President doesn't die hard; it doesn't die at all. Morris Udall says, "The only cure for Presidentialitis is embalming fluid." Udall is one of those who are having trouble letting go of the dream. He came close enough in 1976 to defeating Jimmy Carter in New Hampshire (with enough justification for thinking that if some other candidates hadn't been in the race he'd have won), and came close enough or actually defeated him in enough other states, to still rehearse the war in his mind and in conversation. Though Udall toyed with entering the nomination contest for 1984, and then, for a variety of reasons, decided not to, he does entertain the idea of a brokered Convention turning to him. The reasons for not entering included health—Udall has Parkinson's disease, and he and his advisers concluded that they would have to spend much of their time explaining the nature of the disease. And, because of the disease, and arthritis, Udall moves slowly and with obvious difficulty. Many of the cadre who helped him in 1976—a long time ago—have moved on. Moreover, had he run, Udall, a man to whom much respect and affection flows, would have found himself knocked about as one of the crowd, subjected to the indignities and scorn that are inflicted on all Presidential candidates, even as we eagerly seek to know who'll win. (But once a new President reaches the White House, of course, the apotheosis begins.) The dream also lives for George

McGovern, who still thinks of entering the race later this year if the current candidates stumble. Robert Strauss has gone through bouts of Presidentialitis in the past couple of years but has seemed to conclude that, qualified as he may consider himself to be, he is not the type to make the run for it; yet he still gives off signs that he would just love to be nominated. In the meantime, Strauss dispenses advice to and raises money for various candidates, taking care to keep himself in good standing in various camps. There is talk of several people's running as favorite sons, or entering the contest later. And, inevitably, there is the talk about whether Kennedy is really out of the race—the kind of talk that has arisen around Kennedy since 1968, when his brother Robert was shot. Kennedy's withdrawal last December was made largely for the reasons he stated then: his children, and particularly his youngest son, Patrick, were opposed to his making another race—were fearful for his life. But there were other reasons as well: his own ambivalence, which had also preceded his entry into the 1968 campaign; the certainty that Chappaquiddick was not yet behind him; the awareness that, being newly divorced, he would have no privacy; the knowledge that there are many years left to him in which to run. Kennedy is a great tease, and clearly doesn't mind either the speculation or the candidates' pursuing his blessing (and hoping thereby to inherit his following), but his friends believe he is to be taken at his word that he is out of the race for good this time.

As the various candidates work on their rationales, one thing that makes the exercise harder than it has been in a good many years is that there is no great issue dividing the Democrats. James Johnson, Mondale's acting campaign chairman, says, "There is less factionalism in the Democratic Party than at any time since 1964." The movement toward a consensus became apparent when the Party met at its midterm conference in Philadelphia last year. The candidates largely talk to the same experts, and their stated goals are quite similar: they will all call for a slowdown in the military buildup, a fairer tax system, and a cutback in the tax cuts still scheduled to occur. They will all emphasize more money for education and for training in science. (We will be hearing often about how many more scientists per capita Japan turns out than the United States does.) They will all try to avoid talking about things that could be characterized as "big-spending" programs, but will talk about rearranging the emphases, within budgetary constraints. They will be talking about stimulating new industries and "restructuring" old ones, and about business-labor-government partnerships. They will be talking about arms control. They will be talking about the "inequity" of the Reagan Administration's domestic program and about its record on environmental issues. The fact is that, for all its heterogeneity, the Democratic Party enjoys an unaccustomed consensus—shaped both by the times and by the actions of the Reagan Administration (just as the Republicans in 1980 formed their consensus in reaction to the Carter Administration). There will be differences of degree among the candidates, and a few substantive differences—in fact, the candidates will strive to create differences. Not all of them support the domestic-content bill backed by the United Auto Workers, which would require that all cars sold in the United States contain a certain percentage of United States parts and labor—a proposal that many say would set off a new trade war and would not really solve the automobile industry's problems. (Mondale, Glenn, Cranston, and Hollings support it; Hart, Bumpers, and Askew do not.) Some quirky issues may arise along the way—they usually do—but the rationales and the self-portraits will probably have more to do with style than with substance.

It is a commonplace in the talk about Presidential politics these days to assume that if Reagan runs again, and if there is a recovery in the economy and Reagan achieves some sort of arms-control agreement with the Soviet Union, the Democratic nomination won't be worth much. The Democratic candidates themselves say that such conditions might make victory more difficult but far from impossible. They say that even if there is a recovery unemployment will still be high and memories of unemployment fresh. (The defection of blue-collar voters from the Democratic Party was critical to Reagan's victory.) They count on the fact that environmentalists, who include many independents and moderate Republicans, will be up in arms about the Reagan Administration, and that blacks will continue the pattern, which emerged in the off-year elections of 1981, of voting in unprecedented numbers. There is also the "Who knows?" factor: the possible scandal, the important slip of the tongue, evidence of Reagan's lack of grip on the job, the unpredictable event. The experienced politician realizes that there are only so many calculations one can make; after that the fates take over. Besides, it is not exactly unheard of to lose an attempt for the Presidency only to win at a later date. And there is always the chance of ending up as the Vice-Presidential nominee.

I have been talking with some of the candidates, seeing how they assess their situations at this point, checking the state of their self-portraits. They are in various stages of formulating their rationales, but all of them are eager to present themselves as winners. And all of them are coping with the series of hurdles that the press places before them—the tests that it has decided they must meet: this one can't speak well; that one is too skinny (Alan Cranston is actually trying to gain weight); that one doesn't have a good organization. Once a hurdle is surmounted, a new one is hauled out and put in place. That keeps the campaign interesting.

That Alan Cranston, who the consensus had it was a most improbable candidate, is farther along in building an organization and raising money than the consensus would have expected should really be no surprise. Cranston is a cheerfully dogged politician: he actually loves to campaign and do the scut-work of politics; he has no difficulty in asking people for money, and has been doing it with considerable success for years. He is a denial of the idea that a liberal can't be politically tough. Every Presidential race has at least one "Why not?" candidate; Cranston is a "Why not?" candidate. He figures that he is as smart as the rest, as able as the rest. Moreover, he has a special motivation: as a Californian, he has had plenty of time to develop a disdain for Reagan. Cranston's strategy is to try to identify himself more closely than the others with the nuclear-freeze movement, in the hope of attracting a cadre of committed activists. The other candidates will, of course, try to prevent that—all of them having endorsed the idea of a joint U.S.-Soviet freeze on nuclear weapons (some have signed freeze proposals that had diametrically opposite philosophical bases), and all of them making the case for arms control. Cranston's idea is that if the major (or currently major) candidates are clumped in the center, taking votes away from each other, he might get through on the left rail. Like Hart, Cranston has to try to convince the press of two things: (1) that he can win, but (2) that, because of his low name recognition, he should not be expected to show up well in the polls until next year. That is, he and Hart must try to keep expectations high and low at the same time. Cranston says, "Those of us without the name recognition matching Mondale and Glenn can't expect to make great progress on that score until after Iowa and New Hampshire. So I don't expect any change in the polls until after those first two primaries. The polls now are name recognition; you don't need it everywhere, but you need it in those early key states. With time and attention and energy, you can acquire it in key areas."

When I talked with Cranston in February, in his Senate Minority Whip's office, tucked into the labyrinth under the Capitol Dome, he listed his advantages as he sees them, including his strength in California—"almost twenty percent of the votes needed for the nomination and election." He added, smiling, "That's better than Minnesota or Colorado." Cranston has been showing a penchant for the needle in this campaign; he is wont to tell people that he does not have the name recognition of some of the others because he was not Jimmy Carter's Vice-President or an astronaut. When Cranston won a straw poll at a state Party convention in Sacramento in January, this was generally ascribed to a home-state wish not to embarrass one's own senator. But Cranston worked hard to win that vote, and is just as determined to win the test in California next year. (However, California's failure to decide to hold its nomination contest early reduced the advantage of that primary for Cranston.) Cranston pointed out that when he was reelected to the Senate in 1980 he ran ahead of Reagan in California and 1.6 million votes ahead of the Carter-Mondale ticket. Cranston said, "I know my message is attracting a great deal of support. My announcement statement expressed the view that a President should focus on one or two questions or else he wastes his time and power. Otherwise, as time slips away, he leaves the White House without accomplishing anything of enduring importance. I believe the power of the President's mind and the office should be focussed on the two key issues of the time: the arms race, before it destroys us, and the economy." Cranston acknowledged that the focus on the arms race is part of his political strategy, "but," he added, "it fits my own passions and concerns." While he says that he will stress these two issues, he also talks about the others on the Democrats' agenda: education, training, science ("This year, Japan will graduate twice as many engineers as we, even though they have half the number of people"), productivity, a new Reconstruction Finance Corporation (most of the candidates have adopted Felix Rohatyn's idea for this). Then, unasked, Cranston anticipated one of the hurdles that have been placed before him: he is sixty-eight. "One other matter is energy," he said. For a moment, I thought he was talking about the substantive issue, but he quickly set me straight. "I've got more of that than anyone, and I think that will pay off," he said. Cranston, a sprinter who runs in track meets, continued, "I have covered more ground than anyone; I'll bet that in the last year I covered more than Mondale. You watch who gets worn down in the course of this year." He laughed when he said this—a dig at Mondale, who in 1974 pulled out of the Presidential race because he said he didn't have the burning desire that it takes to run. Cranston said, "I happen to enjoy it. If you don't, it can be a terrible drag. Since I have stamina, I think my age can be an advantage. With age comes wisdom, and your values and principles become stronger." Then Cranston spoke what have become the stock lines he uses to deal with this hurdle: "I'm younger than Reagan." Reagan is seventy-two. "I'll always be younger than Reagan. I'll be younger than Reagan in '84. I happen to be a few days younger than Yuri Andropov, whom I look forward to negotiating with."

Cranston has a confident nature, and he seems determined to simply run the other candidates into the ground. His political career is based on an inability to accept the consensus that the odds are against him. There is a certain smiling relentlessness about him. As a senator, and then as the Democratic Whip, he has never minded making the calls at whatever hour to round up the votes. At this point, this early point, Cranston seems to be making more progress per investment of time than any of the others who are striving to be the alternative to Mondale: in raising money, in building an organization, in getting endorsements, in reaching Democrats who bring intensity to their politics. "For a year, I studied the practicality of running," he says. "I wasn't sure at the outset that I could get anywhere by talking about arms control in the South. I found that I could. George Wallace told me, 'You'd better talk about it; we're spending ourselves silly, and might blow ourselves up.' "

Of the presumed major candidacies, John Glenn's seems at this point to be having the most difficulty finding its rationale and its footing. The rationale that others have applied to Glenn's can-

didacy is that he is an authentic American hero with an
Eisenhoweresque visage; a middle-roader; a soothing presence.
All this may be true, but Glenn doesn't seem to know what to do
with it as yet. Glenn's formal entry into the campaign has been
deliberately delayed, his aides say, in order to give the other candidates more time to be chewed up by the process and the scrutiny,
and in order to make a smooth start. (His formal entry is now
contemplated for April.) But in fact Glenn has had trouble getting
his campaign organization in order, and, for all the talk of Glenn's
potential as a candidate, some of the best political organizers—
freelancers—took a look at the Glenn setup and walked away. This
point is not a minor one having to do simply with the technicalities
of political organizing. One of the most important aspects of a
Presidency, as we have seen time and again, is the President's taste
in people, his ability to attract and utilize talented people. And
there is a pattern of campaign staffs moving into the White
House.

Glenn's rationale appears to be his persona. (Someone who
watches politics closely said to me recently, "I don't know what he
does. I don't associate him with any active verbs.") Glenn still has
trouble delivering a speech that will stir an audience, but on television he appears calm and reassuring, which could be far more
important. He has a stock line about how he is not seeking the
Presidency to satisfy his ego: "I've had the ticker-tape parades."
This, of course, serves to remind people of the ticker-tape parades. And his advisers appear to be planning to use the ticker-
tape aura, plus the persona, to put him across.

An encounter with Glenn is pleasant, and an interview agreeable—but vaguely dissatisfying. The feeling is that one is dealing
with a man who has worked out his paragraphs but not with
someone who has a searching mind that is grappling with hard
questions. The issue of Glenn's intelligence has been raised: he
was intelligent enough to become an astronaut, but that requires
one kind of intelligence and politics another. It is true, as Glenn
likes to point out, that he won in Ohio in 1980 by over a million
and a half votes (albeit against a non-entity) while Reagan was
carrying the state by nearly half a million votes. A number of
politicians who have observed Glenn at close range say that what
he lacks is political feel: the sense of how to make a series of moves
that take you where you want to go; the "peripheral vision" that a

politician needs—the ability to sense what may be coming at you from all angles. Glenn is a bit of a political loner. He has a non-political side that makes him appealing as an individual but lacking in certain political skills: the ability to negotiate, to be flexible enough, to recognize that your opponent on one issue today may be your ally on another one tomorrow. A President needs to be a good politician, to have a zest for working out the political equations, to sense what's coming, to have a feel for implications. The coming tests will indicate whether Glenn has these characteristics in sufficient quantity.

When I spoke with Glenn, in late February, in his office, in the Dirksen Senate Office Building, he was relaxed and low-keyed. He went through his paragraphs. "It's almost un-American that we see opportunities reduced rather than expanded," he said. "I am running for a cause, not for ego, though my ego is as big as anyone's. But I've had the ticker-tape parades. On the international scene, we should be pushing arms control; we should be pushing trade policy. We have a changing international situation and we see all this going on and we're not reacting to it." He cited his own background, including not only the space program but also business ("I had four businesses, one of which went bankrupt, so I know both sides of the business world"). He pointed out that he had been in the Senate for eight years, six of them on the Foreign Relations Committee. But Glenn will have a problem in the area of foreign policy. He now urges the approval of the SALT II arms-control agreement, which was reached by the Carter Administration but never came to a vote in the Senate, in large part because of surrounding events; the chimeric Soviet "brigade" in Cuba and then the Soviet invasion of Afghanistan, coupled with substantial opposition within the Senate, caused the Senate Democratic leaders and President Carter to set the treaty aside in 1980, an election year. The treaty's supporters believed that if it had been brought to the Senate floor at the right time, with sufficient effort, it could have been passed. The fact that John Glenn expressed grave doubts about the treaty and voted against it in the Foreign Relations Committee contributed significantly to its fate. Glenn said at the time that he was concerned about the treaty's verifiability, because of the loss of some monitoring stations in Iran, but says that now he is satisfied that new verification facilities have been established. At the time that Glenn was voicing his complaints, Harold Brown, then the Secretary of Defense, and representatives of the Joint Chiefs of Staff did their mightiest to assure Glenn that the new facilities would be available when they were necessary.

In my talk with Glenn, he spoke of the necessity of improving the training of scientists, of providing more education, of scaling back the Reagan tax cuts (he would eliminate the third year of the three-year tax cut and the indexing of tax rates to inflation which is to follow). However, he supported passage of the Reagan tax-cut bill when it went through the Senate. He spoke of the need to design a defense policy that fits a well-thought-out foreign policy—"not just what the last salesman talked to you about." Glenn has opposed the MX missile. (Before conservative audiences, however, Glenn says, "I strongly reject the notion that we should balance the budget largely by making wholesale cuts in defense spending.") Glenn is small-town, Protestant, Ohio; he might easily have been a Republican. While his political style may lack edge, it is completely natural for him to link what he says must be done with some old-fashioned "verities"—the importance of an educated citizenry, the expansion of opportunities. He is good-humored about the hurdles that have been placed before him. The first was that he is a dull speaker, as was apparent when he thudded in giving the keynote address to the 1976 Democratic Convention. Glenn says that he has overcome this, but there is evidence to the contrary. He says that his organization will be seen to be in place. I asked him the question that is on a number of people's minds about him—whether he is seasoned enough to withstand the trials of a national campaign. Glenn replied, "Oh, it's of a different magnitude for everyone. No one has really been through it or has any great insight that any one of us doesn't have. I've been in some past programs that required some stick-to-itiveness. It's of a different magnitude from what you run into in a Senate campaign; it's the same thing except more intense. The amount of detail on the issues that the press expects, and the national demands—is that a major hurdle? I guess yes."

Gary Hart, who is forty-five, has developed a rationale: that it is time for a new generation of leaders (he, of course, is of the new generation), and that he is the "issues" candidate.* His approach

*As will be seen, it was later learned that Hart was in fact a year older.

seems to be to present himself as the John F. Kennedy of the nineteen-eighties—attractive, young, fresh. Perhaps he always did so, but it is noticeable now that he stands with one hand in his pocket—J.F.K. style. And recently he announced that Theodore Sorensen would be his national co-chairman. Hart is intelligent and thoughtful, and has been conscientiously addressing himself to issues and new approaches for some time now. However, given the consensus within the Democratic Party, it is difficult for him to distinguish himself substantively from his competitors to any great extent. So he refers frequently to the fact that he put out "issues papers" for the Democratic candidates last year, and frequently claims to have been the first to propose a certain idea; he often says that his Presidency would be "innovative and experimental." It is true that Hart has now developed furthest the idea of "military reform"—the idea that military weapons should not be more costly or complicated than necessary—but he is far from the only one to have espoused it. And there are certain ambiguities in Hart's approach. He likes to say that what separates him from the other candidates is that his proposals are more "specific" than theirs, but—perhaps aware from his experience as the manager of McGovern's 1972 campaign that specificity can kill a candidate— he has already backed off from at least one major specific. He used to propose a consumption tax, which would tax spending— but there are many complications with this idea, and Hart now says that he might support something along the lines of the "Fair Tax," a much simplified progressive tax espoused by Senator Bill Bradley, Democrat of New Jersey, and Representative Richard Gephardt, Democrat of Missouri. Hart stresses the point that he is an independent politician, and cites some votes he has cast. And in his announcement speech he said he would try to break the grip of the "narrow, negative agendas and special-interest government in Washington." In an apparent swipe at Mondale, who enjoys the support of several of the Democratic constituency groups, Hart said, "A President who owes his election to narrow interests risks an Administration that is owned by them. . . . A President must do more than negotiate, bargain, and compromise with an array of interests." But under questioning by reporters afterward he indicated that he did not consider labor, blacks, or ethnic groups to be "narrow, special interests." He has said that he would welcome the endorsement of the A.F.L.-C.I.O., of the National Education Asso-

ciation, of environmental groups, of women's groups, of blacks.
His stated refusal to take money from political-action committees
(PACs) for his campaign was part of his effort to indicate his independence of the interest groups. When Hart made his announcement, he assumed that he would get the jump on Mondale, who,
unlike Hart, had been making campaign financing a major issue.
But a Washington *Post* reporter immediately called the Mondale
camp, which said it would take the same position. The Mondale
camp was tickled that it got into Hart's lead; the Hart camp was
not. Such things become very important in campaigns. In fact,
Reubin Askew had announced that he would not take PAC money
before the other two did, but this was not reported in the Washington papers, so no one heard the tree fall. This often happens in
campaigns: the candidate makes a statement, the statement isn't
reported, and then the candidate is criticized for not having spoken out. Actually, PACs don't contribute much money in primaries—they are reluctant to choose sides. As between Mondale
and Hart, Mondale probably gave up the most, since he stands a
good chance of getting the endorsements of the N.E.A and the
A.F.L.-C.I.O. The major contribution of these groups, however,
will be manpower, not money.

Over lunch recently, Hart stressed that he had talked in his
speech of "narrow interests," not "special interests." He said, "I
don't think there's any contradiction between decrying the narrow
interests, the increasing fractionalization and the increasing tendency of certain groups to target their contributions, and dis-
tinguishing those groups that are able to see beyond their particular interests; labor has always been concerned with health and
housing. The danger isn't women or labor; it's the growing
number of national associations of this and national associations of
that." How this separates him from Mondale is unclear. Hart, like
Glenn, is a bit of a loner in the Senate. He can be quite charming
and agreeable, but there is a certain coolness in his style that goes
beyond reserve; he keeps some part of himself back even from
those few of his colleagues who know him well. And while politicians accept opportunism as an ingredient of their profession,
many of Hart's colleagues feel that he has this characteristic in
what may be excessive measure. They find his elbows a bit too
sharp. Even for a politician, he seems to be inclined to the maneuver—how one gets the edge here or there—so that even his em-

phasis on substantiveness, on issues and issues papers, comes across, correctly or not, as a bit of a maneuver. The way he has positioned himself on military questions is a case in point. Hart went to divinity school and then law school after he graduated from college, and thus did no military service. And he was, of course, the manager of McGovern's "dovish" Presidential campaign. Then, after he entered the Senate, in 1975, he joined the Armed Services Committee, and in December of 1980, he took the unusual step of obtaining a commission in the Naval Reserve. (Because of his age and lack of previous service, he had to receive a special waiver from the Navy.) During his campaign for reelection in 1980, he appeared in an ad driving a tank. Hart worked hard to push approval of the SALT II agreement and still espouses it, and he will stress in the campaign his credentials on arms control. However, last year Hart turned down the leaders of the nuclear-freeze movement when they asked him to be the sponsor of a congressional resolution. (They then went to Kennedy, who agreed to.) Hart explains that by that time he had offered his own proposal, called STOP, which called for the United States and the Soviet Union to pursue negotiations to reduce the number of nuclear arms and find ways to prevent their use. There were several pro-arms-control Democrats who had misgivings about the freeze proposal, and Hart believed that it might prevent the necessary development or modification of weapons systems. Hart stresses his participation in arms-control convocations last year, and says that he now endorses the freeze "as part of a broader and more comprehensive package."

In describing the 1984 race, Hart said, "My sense is that this is a different nomination race and will be a different general election. The left-right difference will be less important than the forward-backward difference. The question is whether to go forward with a new generation of purposes and ideas, with someone willing to be innovative and experimental, or whether to rely on past programs. I think the nomination will get down to a future-past race. It may not be described that way, but that's what will be going on." Hart offered an analogy to John Kennedy in 1960: "He was criticized by the Adlai Stevenson-Eleanor Roosevelt wing as too conservative, and by the Lyndon Johnson wing as too liberal, but the real point about his campaign is that it was the future. It wasn't a specific attitude about him, but it was thematic. The difference between 1984 and 1960 is that although the most important thing is to give them themes, themes will not be enough."

Hart has been working hard at building an organization, and that is something he knows how to do. "By late spring," he said, "we'll have a Hart for President committee in every state." He said, "I'm reaching across the spectrum to all age groups, interests, ideologies." And he added, "The core group is in its twenties to mid-forties, generally middle- to upper-middle-income—teachers, paraprofessionals of all races. I'm beginning to inherit a post-Great Society generation of black and Hispanic leaders who have a feeling of political independence that hasn't been described yet." He said, "I think somewhere in the first thirty days of the campaign I have to emerge as one of the two or three serious contenders—that will motivate contributors and our workers and supporters in the states—and I think that in the first forty-five days the race will narrow to two people." Hart has not done particularly well at the all-candidate pageants that have taken place so far, but he seems unfazed. (A straw poll that will be taken April 9th at a state convention in Springfield, Massachusetts, will be considered highly important, and Hart has worked hard in the state.) He just goes on building his organization. The question that remains about Hart is whether he will be able to provide the spark that will give that organization something to work with.

Dale Bumpers, Democratic senator from Arkansas, is the wild card, the unpredictable element, in the campaign. If he runs—he has been somewhat ambivalent, but he probably will—he has the potential to upend the calculations of the others. He is a man of great personal appeal: real, humane, whole, and down-to-earth. He conveys the sense that he is speaking from conviction, and, though no political naïf, not simply from calculation. When he talks about being upset about a certain issue, one has the sense that he really is upset about it, not just using it. He has taken difficult political stands: as governor of Arkansas, he raised taxes; as a senator from Arkansas, he has opposed (vehemently) Senate moves to strip the courts of jurisdiction over school busing and prayer in the schools. He has managed to formulate his arguments in a way that persuades a constituency that would not be inclined to agree. The big question about Bumpers is how he would do in the national arena, where he has never been tested. It

is also to be seen how disciplined and orderly—and deep—his
thinking is, the extent of his range. Bumpers is an intelligent man,
familiar with the issues, and he sees himself as not so much an
innovator as a motivator, and he sees the ability to move people—
to lead—as being at the heart of the Presidency. What interests a
number of people here about the potential of a Bumpers candidacy is that he might, through a combination of personal mag-
netism and political shrewdness, get across as the appealing unconventional candidate. Some political professionals think that
with the right moves Bumpers just might get himself at least in the
top tier of the candidates. Through a combination of a compelling
speaking style and a strong message, he has done well at the
candidate parades thus far, and has some able political professionals ready to go to work for him.

Bumpers has actually been thinking about running for the Presidency for a long time. Bumpers and Jimmy Carter were elected
governors of their states in the same year, 1970—as was Reubin
Askew. There had been little affection on the part of either Askew
or Bumpers toward Carter (all rivals as the symbol of "the New
South"); in fact, there was little on the part of any of Carter's
fellow-governors, which should have been a sign of problems to
come. But Carter made more of the opportunity quickly. Bumpers
and Askew believed in their hearts that they were better men.
Bumpers thought about running for the Presidency after he was
elected to the Senate, in 1974, but realized that Carter was already
well under way. Bumpers, who is popular with the Washington
press corps, noticed that he was among those "mentioned" as
possible candidates in 1984, and began to take the matter seriously some time ago. His hesitation in entering had to do with
figuring out whether there was still time; with whether he really
wanted to put himself through the gruelling pace; and with figuring that he had better think through what kind of Presidency he
wanted to offer before he got into the race, and think through
some of the things he wanted to say, and how to say them, because
there would be no time to do so afterward. Besides, the longer he
waited, the fresher he would seem by comparison with the others.
But he was also being advised that even if he did plan to run an
unconventional candidacy—a candidacy whose success was predi-
cated on simply sweeping others away at a few important events—
he could wait only so long.

I talked with Bumpers in his office, in the Dirksen Senate Office Building, in February, to get the drift of his thinking at that point. He said, "We've had too many failed Presidencies. One of the primary reasons, I think, is that people have wanted it too badly. When people say to me 'Do you want to be President?,' that's a hard question to answer in twenty-five seconds or less. My answer is 'I don't want to be President unless I can assume office unfettered and unbeholden to the point where I can govern.' If we've reached the point where you have to go through a quiz and make every right answer for every PAC, then you can't have an effective Presidency. It isn't so much, in my opinion, who's going to say the freshest thing in this campaign, or who comes up with 'new solutions.' It's the person who demonstrates the best sense of history and of the political process, of what's wrong and what to do about it. There's so much public cynicism these days, and I really believe the cynicism is there because of the process, not because of the issues we vote on up here from day to day."

On the subject of the role of the Democratic Party's interest groups—Bumpers could be expected to challenge Mondale for being insufficiently independent—Bumpers said, "I want labor's endorsement, and I want blacks and I want Hispanics and I want the teachers, but if you have to commit to a host of conflicting things in order to achieve that, then there isn't any point to being President. I have to believe that there is a common thread that is acceptable and unifying to almost all constituencies; that thread is patriotism—not in the sense of waving the flag but of a patriotic concern about the country. I believe that anybody who can articulate that concern well can draw on it as a tremendous resource to get some things done in this country. You can't convince someone standing on an assembly line that the President's tax program is fair to him; he knows it isn't. You can't convince him that there isn't someone walking these halls with a pocketful of money trying to influence what we do; he knows there is, and he's dead right."

I asked Bumpers what he would do when he appeared before such groups as the A.F.L.-C.I.O. and the N.E.A.

He replied, "I would tell them that their interests lie in the national good—that they are not incompatible."

He continued, "There are other candidates in the race who feel as strongly about the Reagan Administration as I do. There will be a whole host of issues that we'll agree on. But that's not what people will be making their choice on. They'll be making it on a whole different level. If I didn't believe that, I wouldn't be in this thing."

By any standard measurement, Walter Mondale is in the lead for the nomination as of now, and most people who have looked at the situation closely believe that the nomination will be his. The reasons for caution on the point are several: people don't like to be caught out in having made a false prediction; the press loves a horse race and is inclined to create one if none exists; and the dynamics of campaigns make nothing a certainty. Mondale has a number of things working in his favor: he has built the best campaign organization and coterie of advisers (drawing upon his years in public life); he has given a lot of thought to hard questions over a long period; he can make a case that he is best prepared to be President; he is a seasoned national politician and is less likely than others to commit the fatal gaffe (or series of gaffes). He is a man of genuine humor, and has developed an effective speaking style. (He does better before live audiences than on television, which causes him to tighten up.) He has shown a capacity for raising money, and he is in good standing with the Democratic constituency groups that will field manpower in the primary contests. He is not likely to make the mistake that Edmund Muskie did when he was the front-runner, in 1972—the mistake of assuming that an individual politician's endorsement automatically delivers votes. Moreover, Muskie had to run in a party still riven over Vietnam, one in which there was a McGovern on the left and a George Wallace running a rightish populist campaign and a Hubert Humphrey soaking up much of Muskie's support. Mondale faces no such situation. Some people here think that the analogy to Mondale's situation (people persist in finding analogies, even if there aren't any) is the Nixon campaign of 1968. Nixon, who, like Mondale, had been out there collecting chits for years, came into the contest well armed and cut such a wide swath down the middle that no one else really had a chance.

But Mondale, as the front-runner (he has led in the polls since Kennedy pulled out), is under a lot of pressure. He receives the most press scrutiny, and the other candidates play off him. And he does have certain problems: though he is well known as a public figure, he still lacks definition as a public figure; he will have to make it clear that his candidacy does not represent, as others will try to charge, a return to "the old ways;" though he can give a roof-raising speech, full of humor and passion, he still has to overcome a widespread impression that he isn't very exciting; he will have to get it across that he is something more than the sum total of the Democratic Party's interest groups—that he can govern. The Mondale camp has taken some steps to indicate that his will not be a cautious campaign, that Mondale will take risks; but not all of these moves have turned out quite as planned. The decision to refuse PAC money was taken in part because Mondale has made campaign-finance reform one of his issues and in part to indicate that he is not a captive of the interests. He spoke at a dinner sponsored by a homosexual-rights organization last September, to show that he was willing to do so. (He had left the stage at an event in San Francisco in 1977 when some gay activists took over.) To be sure, homosexual-rights groups are seen to be increasingly politically active, but Mondale's appearance was widely written off in the press as simply another move to gain the support of an interest group rather than seen as the act of courage it was intended to be seen as. His involvement in the Chicago mayoralty race this year was another move to show that he was not all caution—and one that somewhat misfired. The idea was to show, by his support of Richard M. Daley, the son of the late Mayor, that he was willing to go against the Chicago political machine, headed by Mayor Jane Byrne. Daley had worked closely with the Carter-Mondale organization in 1980, after Byrne had first said she would endorse Carter and then turned around and endorsed Kennedy. (The Carter-Mondale ticket carried the state primary handily.) There was an old bond, and an interest in seeing Byrne out of office, so Mondale and his people encouraged Daley in his challenge to Byrne, and made a commitment to support him. The problem was that the candidacy of Harold Washington, a black congressman, was not foreseen, and when Washington won, capitalizing on the split between Byrne and Daley, he and several of his black allies were unforgiving. (Had Mondale backed off after Washington came in, this undoubtedly would have been attacked as a sign of weakness.) So Mondale, who has as good a record as anyone in supporting issues of concern to blacks, has had to work to repair the damage. Black leaders are divided over whether to run a black candidate for President, on the theory that this would increase their leverage—Jesse Jackson is eager to run—or whether this risks taking votes away from the candidate who has been most sympathetic to their cause. (Andrew Young and Coretta Scott King favor Mondale.)

Another thicket that Mondale has had to work his way through is how to handle his relationship with Carter. There had been much discussion in the press to the effect that Mondale's association with Carter would be one of his political burdens. Then, when Mondale gave an interview in which he replied to questions about some of his differences with Carter during his Vice-Presidency, this was put down in some quarters as rank opportunism— sometimes by the same people who were critical of his association with Carter in the first place. The plain fact is that most of the differences Mondale listed—and others—were known in the course of the Carter Administration. And Mondale had been talking about some of them for some time: his opposition to the "mechanical" money-supply approach of Paul Volcker, who had been appointed Chairman of the Federal Reserve Board by Carter; his opposition to the MX missile. And one of the differences—that Mondale opposed the imposition of an embargo on the sale of grain to the Soviet Union after the invasion of Afghanistan—was made known by Carter himself in his recent book. Mondale says time and again that he is proud to have served in the Carter Administration, proud of many things it did, and certain that it will stand up well in history. Mondale and his adviser James Johnson say that Mondale could not go through a Presidential campaign refusing to talk about the positions he took as Vice-President. Mondale professed some irritation about this subject when I talked with him recently, in his law office in Washington. He said, "When I was Vice-President, I think I understood properly what my role was: to advise the President, to offer private criticism, and to support the President and carry out tasks I was given to do. And it included supporting positions I didn't agree with. I knew going in that there was a limit morally: that if there was something I could not support morally, I wouldn't do so. Now I'm running for President, and people have a right to know me and how I stand on important questions. If people ask me where I stood on some things, how can I refuse to answer? People have a right to know where I stood on tough issues and, if there were differences, what those differences were. I've said that I am proud to have served as Carter's Vice-President, and I am. I thought this through: there was no honorable way I could seek the Presidency without answering questions about the Vice-Presidency."

Mondale's most thorough attempt to define himself was in his announcement speech, into which he put a great deal of effort. Because Mondale is the front-runner, the speech is worth going into. Mondale says that the speech defines his thinking at this stage, and that he will be making speeches further defining some of his ideas—for example, on restructuring the economy. In the speech, delivered in St. Paul, Minnesota, Mondale described his roots in small communities of Minnesota, and the philosophy of community and family which was part of his growing up, and the progressive traditions of his state. And then, to show that he is as modern in his thinking as the rest, he talked of the need to meet new challenges: through economic growth (including high technology; restructuring basic industries; entrepreneurship; job retraining; and new relations between business and labor) and through a new emphasis on education and education standards, as well as on science and foreign languages. In foreign policy, he talked of the importance of having military effectiveness but also economic strength, energy independence, moral authority—through emphasis on human rights and a willingness to "see the world as it really is." (Mondale has spoken often of what he sees as the misguided policy on the part of the Reagan Administration in El Salvador: an unwillingness to understand other people's history, an excessive dependence on military solutions to political problems and readiness to paint everything in East-West terms.) He talked of the importance of restoring our international competitiveness. (His rhetoric on trade has sometimes had the flavor of "Yellow Peril" protectionism—this appeals to labor audiences—but he has cooled the tone recently. Again, Mondale's effort to show that he was "tough" misfired somewhat.) In his announcement speech, he talked about the importance of arms control, which he has been stressing for some time, and of blocking the spread of nuclear weapons. And then he asked for something else: "I ask the American people to give their best"—stronger families, tougher discipline, cooperation, sacrifice. And he called for "realism": "There is a long haul ahead. Politicians must stop peddling quick fixes." He attacked the Reagan Administration's economic and environmental policies, and called for social justice—a subject that has been at the heart of his concerns for years. ("To earn public trust, our government must be on the side of the vulnerable.") He offered a specific plan for reforming campaign financing. He stressed his readiness for the job and, in a clear snipe at Reagan, said, "The American people understand that we also need a President who knows what he's doing." His long experience and training, the idea that he is equipped for the Presidency—this is one of Mondale's major themes, and thus he concluded, "I have the experience. I know where the talent is. I know the White House. I know how to shape a government. I know how to manage. I know the Congress. I know how to defend this country. I know how to search for peace. I know who our friends are. I'm onto our enemies. I know our people. And I know myself: I am ready. I am ready to be President of the United States."

In our recent conversation, he told me, "I've tried very hard to make a case about where I want the country to go. I want a mandate, not just a victory. My kickoff speech was my attempt to define my mandate. You know, it's not speaking style, though that's a factor. It's what you say, how people feel about you—whether in a period of distrust, and even cynicism, you can restore trust. Without that, you're not going to win a mandate, and victory without a mandate is hell." Mondale's experience in serving in a White House under a President from whom public support had ebbed is a sharp and painful memory. "Also, you're not going to sustain yourself emotionally through the next two years without talking about the things that you really believe in, that you really want to do. You can't just do it by hackwork. It's what you're saying to people and that people are listening—that's the main point."

I asked Mondale about the question of whether he was too closely tied to the interest groups to be able to govern—how he could avoid the trap of the special-interest state. (Carter campaigned saying, "I owe the special interests nothing," and making promises to them all the while, and was soon swallowed up in the special-interest state.)

"That comes back to what I've just been talking about," Mondale replied. "If I win a mandate—and if that's what my announcement speech started, and I am perceived as having been authorized to get there—I can govern. If I win only with the special-interest groups, then all I can do is broker. If I really want to get something done about education and science, then I have to get some appropriations changed, and some structures changed, and I also have to get some people out there working harder. If I can get the trust, then I can lead. While government does a lot through appropriations and structures, fifty per cent of it is motivation—of teachers and administrators and the rest. In education, I'd be pressing for tough standards. I'd be trying very hard to move the whole educational process to another level of productivity. I am seeking the Presidency of the United States. I don't want to be the President of the A.F.L.-C.I.O. or the Chamber of Commerce." (There's not much chance of the latter.) He continued, "If I get the mandate that I began to define, I can go to all my friends and say, 'This is what I asked to do. This is what the public supports. This is what I need to do to get from here to there. This is the outline of my plans and my priorities.' That makes me President of the United States."

Some of Mondale's critics say that he is weak—not one for making tough decisions, offending potential supporters, doing something very difficult. If this is true, it will come across in the long campaign. I asked Mondale whether he would be willing to say no to a request from the groups that supported him.

"Sure," he replied. "All groups are the same: we tend to make up a list of all the things that will be ideal for us. A lot of it will be valid; some of it will be too much. I'd be saying what my priorities are amid competing demands, within a tight budget. Another thing to keep in mind is that these groups are not monolithic. The idea of brokerage—that you can gather together the strings and run this country—is not true. That comes back again to the mandate. A President of the United States is not just a technician; he's a political leader. Unless he's seen as strong, he can't lead, can't negotiate with enemies, can't deal with friends. A President must lead; he must also listen—and the notion might dawn on him occasionally that he's wrong. The notion of leadership is to keep the country with you on broad policies and national objectives."

I asked Mondale if he found any difficulties in being the front-runner.

He has a stock, jokey answer that goes "I've tried all the other positions; I prefer this one." He has a serious answer as well: "First, it is helpful in that it gives me an opportunity to be heard. Second, if I'm going to take the heat of the Presidency I have to stand the heat of being the front-runner."

III

The recent political weather for the Reagan Administration has been much like this uncharacteristic spring in Washington: a few rays of sunshine and then another storm. The Administration, in fact, appears to have fallen into a pattern of gluing itself together only to fly apart once again. The agenda and the news, despite the White House's strenuous efforts to define and control them, keep slipping out of control—for which an increasingly frustrated President places a great deal of the blame on the press. Relatively good news about the economy and a Presidential speech designed to indicate flexibility on arms control tended to get washed away by less positive developments—brought about mainly by the Administration's own actions. Most Presidents get frustrated with the press, sometimes justifiably so, and all Administrations try to control the national agenda, often to no avail. All Administrations end up engaging in a certain amount of crisis management—or "damage limitation"—but the Reagan White House has been spending an unusual amount of time and energy on such exercises this spring. Like much of Washington, the White House has seemed to be suffering from a kind of overload, from too many subjects to cope with: Central America, the Middle East, arms control, the budget, the MX missile, the economy, the environment, China, race. One White House aide said to me, in a bit of understatement, "Part of the problem is that we're not in as much control of the national agenda as we'd like to be." Reagan's frustration, and even anger, stem from his own firm view of the world—a view that is often not shared by many of those around him and, increasingly, within his own party. And from the outset the Reagan White House has gone through phases of straining to present to the public a picture of internal unity only to have the tensions and the dissension come into public view. This spring, the dissension and the bad news have been all of a piece.

45

The President's aides feverishly study the polls, and it often seems that events—developments in Central America, or in relations with the Soviet Union or Congress, or in environmental policy or the economy—are viewed as more important for their political implications than for themselves. In April, the aides put out polls and counterpolls dealing with the political effect of the President's series of speeches having to do with arms and the Soviet Union: his speech in Orlando on March 8th, before the National Association of Evangelicals, in which he inveighed, in the name of religion, against the Soviet Union ("an evil empire") and the nuclear-freeze movement; his televised address designed to gain support for his military budget, which ended with a coda calling for the development of defensive weapons systems in outer space (and immediately became known as his "Star Wars" speech); and his speech suggesting that he would be more flexible in the talks with the Soviet Union on the deployment of intermediate-range nuclear weapons in Europe. (In Orlando, the President also attacked secularism and, in the name of religion, government regulation and "social engineers," at the same time that he defended his Administration's regulations requiring that parents be informed if their teenage daughters are receiving birth-control prescriptions from federally subsidized clinics—"the squeal rule"— and a twenty-four-hour hot line in hospitals to report failures to make efforts to keep handicapped newborn infants alive. Though these are obviously sensitive issues, on which people may disagree—both regulations have been struck down by federal judges—the President does not seem to recognize his own contradictions.) These speeches, followed by the President's approach to dealing with the Republicans on the Senate Budget Committee— who responded by handing him a major defeat—divided the President's advisers as never before. One adviser said to me, "Focusing on defense the way we did was probably the third most serious blunder we have made in the two years-plus we've been here." The two other serious blunders, he said, were the Administration's proposals, early in 1981, to revise Social Security, and its inability to extricate itself from the problem through the 1982 election; and a cluster of issues involving race, including the failure to endorse an extension of the Voting Rights Act until it was a foregone conclusion in Congress, and the move to reverse the policy forbidding tax exemptions for private schools that discriminate.

That move was bad enough to begin with, and was further bungled as the Administration tried to recover. Both of these earlier mistakes, the adviser said, involved the question of "fairness"— one of the points on which the Administration is most vulnerable. An analysis done for the Reagan White House indicated that the fairness issue hurt the Republicans in the 1982 elections more than the economic issue or the arms-control issue did. Presidents often run into their most serious difficulties with the public when initial misgivings about them are reinforced. During the 1980 election, Richard Wirthlin, Reagan's pollster, advised the Reagan campaign of the importance of Reagan's coming across as "non-ideological" and "peace-oriented." Besides fairness, another issue on which Reagan has been on shaky political ground since 1980 is dealing with the Soviet Union. Questions about Reagan's instincts and his capacity in this area plagued his campaign for the Presidency, and they have plagued his Presidency, and some of his advisers feel that his recent actions have underscored them. One adviser says, "Any time you show Reagan on television talking about missiles, it doesn't help."

The very fact that the President's defense speech instantly became known as his "Star Wars" speech indicates what went wrong. The coda became the focal point, and it was quickly known in Washington that few of the President's aides were even aware of this planned excursion until shortly before it was taken, and that several of those who were thought it a poor idea, on both tactical and substantive grounds. Tactically, it diverted attention from the President's plea for his defense budget, and also made it appear that Reagan might be off on a new and different kind of arms race. Substantively, many people who have lived in the world of defense theory, where the idea of constructing a system in outer space to destroy missiles has been around for some time, simply do not find it plausible. Even some of Reagan's most hard-line defense officials tried to dissuade him from talking about it in the speech. The President offered the vision of a world in which offensive weapons would be made obsolete and unnecessary. After the logical flaw in his reasoning had been pointed out—that unless both the United States and the Soviet Union developed such defensive systems simultaneously, a destabilizing situation could ensue—Reagan, in an interview with some reporters, ventured the thought that an American President might offer to give the technology to the Soviet Union, a proposition that the Soviet Union was unlikely to accept at face value. And Caspar Weinberger, the Secretary of Defense, in various appearances, zigged and zagged on the question of whether such a defensive system could work against low-flying cruise missiles and bombers. When I asked one Administration official how thought through the President's proposal had been, he replied, "I'd put it somewhere between a cocktail napkin and a menu." (He was referring, of course, to the famous "Laffer curve," the theoretical underpinning of supply-side economics, which its author, Arthur Laffer, first drew on a cocktail napkin.) When the Presidential commission appointed to come up with a plan for the disposition of the MX missile met on the day after the speech, Alexander Haig said jokingly to his fellow commission members, a number of whom were baffled as to why the President had made the proposal, and in such dramatic terms, "Don't worry, gentlemen. It's just another of the President's fireball speeches."

People familiar with defense theory have been privy to some defensive-system proposals that they find fairly wacky. The President seemed to be going along a path laid out by Edward Teller, whose ideas are greeted with somewhat less skepticism, at least in terms of the technology. But one Presidential adviser said to me that the doctrine was absurd: Would we ever give up the offense, he asked, on the ground that the defense was sufficient? And if we would not, he said, the nuclear balance would be totally de-stabilized. He complained that there had been talk for a year of the President's giving *the* defense speech that would turn the country around on defense spending, "and then, within days, we got 'Star Wars' covers on *Time* and *Newsweek*. We'd changed the subject." Another Presidential adviser, with many years' experience in defense matters, said to me shortly after the speech, "I've been in defense long enough not to believe that there is any sure Maginot Line." He added that he feared that the President's proposal would complicate things for the worse both with our European allies and in START, the strategic-arms-reduction talks with the Soviet Union. And then he sighed and said, "But now we'll all have to go out and defend the President."

This defense ran along two lines. One was that there is no reason to assume that such a system is not technically feasible; after all, people said we couldn't get to the moon, either. The logic of this argument is that since some things that seemed technically impossible have turned out to be doable, *everything* that seems technically impossible is doable. But, as one defense expert (not a pejorative term) pointed out to me, the moon, unlike space satellites and missiles, was not an evasive target, and was not shooting back. About a billion dollars is going into defense research now—an amount that most people consider enough under the circumstances. And even if the technological problems were overcome there remained the policy questions. The fundamental question that Reagan posed—Wouldn't it be better to have a world in which the great powers could rely on defenses, and not point offensive weapons at each other?—has a simple appeal. It is the sort of question that makes those who raise doubts risk being labelled tired and negative thinkers. The same thing was true of supply-side economics: Wouldn't it be nice if we could cut taxes, and thus set off an economic boom and balance the budget in three years?

The series of speeches and the setback dealt the President by the Senate Budget Committee—which, though it is controlled by Republicans, reduced his proposed increase in defense spending from ten per cent to five per cent—set off yet another round of knife-wielding within the White House and raised new questions about the Administration's competence in dealing not only with Capitol Hill but also with the Soviet Union. The questions all stemmed from a fundamental division within the Administration over how to handle these matters and, more revealing, how to try to guide the President. The way the Administration walked into its defeat in the Senate Budget Committee tells quite a bit. From conversations with White House aides and Senate Republicans, one can see just how awry things had gone—and why. There was a failure of understanding within some parts of the White House not only of the dynamics of Capitol Hill but also of the effect of the President's actions and proposals on the public. The President, encouraged in his beliefs and his analysis of the world outside by William Clark, his national-security adviser, and by Weinberger, failed to understand that the string was running out on support for the size of his defense buildup. In the President's view, the increased resistance to giving him whatever he asked for in military funds was attributable, he often told his associates, to "the drumbeat of the press." (When Larry Speakes, the White House spokesman, told reporters that the cause of the setback in the Senate Budget Committee was "a steady drumbeat of negative thought, mainly emanating from you and your colleagues in the press corps," he was simply and accurately reflecting the President's sentiments.) When Reagan spoke on arms control to the Los Angeles World Affairs Council, on March 31st, he said, "I just think that the press must recognize it, too, has a responsibility for the welfare of the nation." This proposition—which, though it is subject to varying interpretations, is unarguable—met with inevitable applause. One senior official said to me in exasperation shortly before the committee voted, "This thing has been brewing for a year. Not enough people noticed that the Republicans on the Hill weren't saying the same things as the chief spokesmen here. They really thought it was the 'drumbeat of the press,' Democrats who want to cut back defense drastically, and one or two heretics in our own party. There was no understanding of the growing disaffection. The problem within the security community is there's a fantasy-based perception of what's going on on Capitol Hill and what's going on in the public debate. You know when you aren't viable; they don't. When you aren't viable, you figure out how to move the others—or how to move yourself."

One very interesting aspect of how the Administration has handled the defense issue is that the President is given misleading information. This goes a long way toward explaining how Reagan ended up asking for a ten-per-cent increase in defense spending this year—a higher percentage than he had ever said he would seek—and why the Administration dug in despite all the warning signs. Weinberger reinforces the President's own views by presenting the most alarmist picture of the Soviet threat. And Clark, who shares the President's predispositions and guides him to where he thinks the President wants to be, constantly reinforces him with adjurations not to bend, not give, be tough, not cave. On defense matters, Clark defers to Weinberger. The President is given a catechism that goes, "Defense expenditures aren't contributing to the deficits, because in 1963 defense expenditures constituted forty-five per cent of the budget, whereas now they constitute only twenty-nine per cent." In 1963, however, the Medicare and Medicaid programs, not to mention many others, didn't exist, and, even leaving that aside, the percentage-of-the-budget statistic doesn't prove much. But the real distortions come in what Reagan is told about what has happened to his own defense budget. It starts with the proposition that the Carter defense budget was "weak"—that it ignored the strategic threat, kept military pay too low, and allowed military readiness to deteriorate. (The last is something that both Congress and the Pentagon chronically allow to go on; it is much more exciting to put money into new weapons than to maintain old ones. As for the strategic threat, Reagan and his allies are wont to say that during the nineteen-seventies no improvements were made on any of the three legs of the strategic triad, though in fact all three were modernized.) By the second year of its term, the Carter Administration, which had kept the defense budget even with inflation, was committed to an annual three-per-cent real growth (over inflation) in defense spending—the subject of a major fight within the Democratic Party. In 1980, in the wake of the disastrous mission to rescue the American hostages in Iran, and a change in the national mood, and in the face of a national election, Congress raised the increase in the defense budget for fiscal 1981 to about seven per cent—an increase that Carter didn't resist. Before the Carter Administration left office, in 1981, it submitted a lame-duck budget calling for an annual increase of five per cent over five years. When the Reagan Administration came in, it said that the fiscal 1981 defense budget was too low and requested a supplemental appropriation that raised it by another five per cent, for a total increase of twelve per cent. It also said that the Carter budget proposal of a five-per-cent increase for 1982 was too low, and raised that by seven per cent, for a total of another twelve per cent in real growth. Thus, the defense budget grew by nearly twenty-five per cent in real terms between 1980 and 1982, and it was on top of that that the Reagan Administration proposed to raise it by seven per cent a year for the four years following. (This figure of seven per cent offered by the Administration had no basis in policy. A key official said to me at the time, "It doesn't represent a thought-out plan.") Therefore, the base on which the Administration began was actually quite high. And, because of a drop in inflation, the Administration ended up last year having asked for more than seven per cent for fiscal 1983 (about eight and a half per cent). Congress made some cuts in that increase, and the Administration made slight cuts in its fiscal 1984 defense budget. More important, inflation collapsed, thus lowering the actual amount that would have to be spent to reach a certain

percentage over inflation. (The Carter budget assumed that inflation would be a third higher than the Reagan Administration's
assumptions, so the Reagan defense dollars are worth one-third
more.) Therefore, while the real rates of growth in the defense
budget have been at least what they were intended to be, the
actual, or nominal, dollar amounts required to meet these goals
are lower. Reagan's security advisers take the dollar figures and tell
him that large cuts have been made in the increases he proposed
over the Carter budget, and that he is being driven back to the
levels of the Carter budget. In other words, the President has been
persuaded by his advisers that his defense budget has been cut by
more than it has been. In the President's mind, this apparently
means the "weak" budget of the early Carter years, and not the
five-per-cent increase that Carter proposed upon leaving office.
The last thing Reagan wants to hear is that his defense budget is
not much larger than Carter's. In fact, in terms of constant dollars
(after inflation) the continuing increase in the Reagan defense
budget is larger than the one the Reagan Administration itself
first proposed for the period from 1982 through 1986. And then,
this year, the Administration ended up asking for a ten-per-cent
increase in its defense budget for fiscal 1984. (Actually, in the
course of the Presidential campaign Reagan's advisers, desperately
trying to cobble together an economic program that would support the President's rhetoric—an exercise that led to the so-called
"mirrors" speech in Chicago in September of 1980—said that Reagan would propose defense increases of five per cent, a figure that
Congress was already considering, and that ultimately increased
for that year.)

Congress's restiveness about the size of the Reagan defense
buildup was apparent by last year. After extensive negotiations
between the White House and Republican congressional leaders,
Congress lowered the defense budget for the fiscal years 1983
through 1985. Then the President enraged his own congressional
leaders by announcing that he would go along with the cut for the
1983 fiscal year but not for the future years. Senate Majority
Leader Howard Baker, Republican of Tennessee, said he felt "very
keenly" that the Administration should stand by the agreement,
and was described by his aides as "just furious." Pete Domenici,
Republican of New Mexico, the chairman of the Senate Budget
Committee, said that the Administration's position was "unjustifia-

ble, unreasonable," and that "it makes things very difficult up here." This was a clear signal that the President and his security advisers ignored.

In proposing to restore some of the cuts made by Congress last year, the Administration ended up with its request for a ten-percent increase this year; the proposed increase for the following year is eleven per cent. And so Congress, including several members of the President's own party, rebelled. They do not accept the notion that there is not great waste in the Pentagon, and many of them, including Senator Barry Goldwater, Republican of Arizona, who is a defender of the military, cite examples of useless, excessively complicated, or redundant programs. A great many Republicans feel, moreover, that cuts in programs for the poor have gone about far enough, and that the Reagan proposals for further ones should be rejected; and they are reluctant to make changes in entitlement programs—programs such as Medicare, which help the middle class—without also making some reductions in defense. They are also worried about the looming deficits (currently at about two hundred billion dollars and hovering around that for two more years, even if the Reagan program were to be adopted, and threatening to reach three hundred billion by fiscal 1988 under present arrangements) and their potential effect on interest rates and economic recovery; and they don't accept the thesis that the defense budget doesn't have anything to do with those deficits.

The mishandling of Congress this year was of impressive proportions. The President's national-security advisers apparently fail to understand the extent to which Congress, for all the rough-and-tumble, proceeds according to understandings and faith that word will be kept. Thus, it was a major blunder for the President to ask Domenici to delay the Senate Budget Committee's consideration of the defense budget for three weeks (until after the Easter recess) when it appeared that the committee would vote for an increase of only five or six per cent, and to indicate that he would compromise, and then to stand firm when Congress reconvened. (Just before the recess, the House, with the Democrats now in true control, approved a budget that cut the growth in defense to only four per cent, allocated more money for jobs programs, and called for a tax increase of thirty billion dollars.) It was to influence the committee that the President gave what became the "Star Wars" speech; the theory was that over the recess members of Congress would be importuned by their constituents to support the President. Domenici agreed to the postponement with great reluctance, and over the objections of some of his Republican colleagues. Even Charles Grassley, Republican of Iowa, who is very conservative, remarked, "I think the President is wrong." Grassley may not be considered the brightest light on Capitol Hill, but he had been a firm supporter of the President, and his reaction should have been a sign of trouble. Slade Gorton, Republican of Washington, who is a moderate, said, "Every time the President has intervened in the budget process, he has been wrong." Domenici is an earnest, industrious, and respected senator who has been trying, in the face of substantial difficulties, to work things out. For the White House to saw off the limb behind him is not wise. Grassley was irritated because, among other reasons, the Pentagon would not permit a briefing of the Budget Committee by Franklin Spinney, a Pentagon cost analyst who was becoming known as a critic of the Pentagon's procurement policies and was one of several voices, including that of the super-conservative Heritage Foundation, saying that the true long-run cost of the weapons buildup was being underestimated. (An increasing proportion of the defense budget is for procurement, and this makes the budget more difficult for Congress to cut: the commitment to the weapons is made, and the contracts are let, and a large number of people, including politicians representing districts and states where the contractors are, have an interest in keeping the project going.) When Grassley drove over to the Pentagon himself to see Spinney, he was prevented by Spinney's superior from doing so. Eventually, Spinney was allowed to testify before a joint meeting of the Senate Armed Services and Budget Committees.

Weinberger's response to the questions raised by Spinney and other critics—of waste in procurement practices, of the purchase of weapons systems that are needlessly, or even self-defeatingly, complicated—is that these matters had been taken care of, and that Spinney's analysis was "historical." One Republican senator said to me, "Weinberger's reply is a non-reply; it's not what responsible individuals expect from other responsible individuals." Mark Andrews, Republican of North Dakota, who sits on the Defense Subcommittee of the Senate Appropriations Committee as well as on the Budget Committee, complains, "We can't get accurate figures from the Defense Department. Maybe they need those new wings for the Air Force, but they haven't justified it, or answered our legitimate questions." When senators and their staffs do their own digging and come up with their own numbers, they are told that their numbers are wrong. One Republican on the Budget Committee says of the Administration's handling of its defense-budget request, "They didn't go through the budget and how they arrived at their program." He added, "This is not a year when you can get what the President wants." The Administration, at least in this area, also seems to fail to understand the system by which a lot of members of Congress often make up their minds on issues. Andrews says of his and his colleagues' dealings with the Administration on the defense budget, "We were saying, 'This is a lot of money to put in there on blind faith.' When those of us on the Appropriations Committee, or our staffs, can't get the information—you know how it works around here. It's 'Check with your buddy.' We go to a friend and say, 'Hey, what about these figures? Are they O.K.?' Those of us on the subcommittee can't get the information." Members feel that when they do offer specific weapons cuts they are not taken seriously. Weinberger is inclined to talk in terms of: Where would you like us to reduce our presence? In a conversation I had with him at the Pentagon on the morning that the Budget Committee was to vote, he said, "Should we give up the defense of the Caribbean? Should we give up the defense of the continental United States? Should we pull out of NATO? Should we give up Korea? Should we give up Japan? Should we give up the oil fields?"

The meeting on April 5th in the White House Cabinet Room between the President and other Administration officials and the Republicans on the Senate Budget Committee, plus Senate Majority Leader Baker, was, by several accounts, a disaster. (As a matter of fact, virtually the whole government was at the meeting, which lasted nearly two hours: the President, the Vice-President, the Secretaries of State, Defense, and the Treasury, the national-security adviser, and various other aides.) When some members of the Budget Committee, among them Grassley and Andrews, suggested that the defense request was too high, the President expressed annoyance, and Weinberger told them that they weren't informed. It has become a cliché to say that Reagan is an amiable man, but there is some evidence that this idea has been carefully cultivated. Increasingly, the impression grows that he is a man with an amiable side who understands the value of his public persona as an amiable man—that much of the time he's acting. Reagan's public charm is enormous and disarming. His persona is a powerful political weapon. But members of the House and the Senate who have had differences with him in meetings tell of another side of him. Stories emerge of a man easily moved to anger and, at times, rough language and off-color imagery. One Republican senator says, "I haven't seen that amiable side. I have felt he's a great actor—when he's standing there shaking hands he does a great stage smile." When it was suggested by some Budget Committee members that money should be saved on defense and put into domestic programs, the President said, with obvious irritation, that the press had manufactured the idea that there was waste in the Pentagon programs. He went on to talk of waste in domestic programs, and said that he knew of a case of a woman in California who had two Mercedeses and a Rolls-Royce and was receiving food stamps. (This is a variation on Reagan's often used examples of the "welfare queen" in Chicago and the man who bought an orange with food stamps and vodka with the change.) Andrews said to me after the meeting, "I went away with the question: Who gives the President the information, and does he get the information we get, or is he getting puffery? I have the feeling that if he spent more of his time making sure he's getting the whole story he might make better decisions." He added, "I'm a hawk. I've been a hawk all my life. But you don't have to be a damn fool to be a hawk. That's what a lot of us are saying."

According to White House aides, the President, having finally become persuaded, on the day the Budget Committee voted, that defeat was at hand, was willing to compromise on an increase of seven and a half per cent if Weinberger would agree. The aides say that Weinberger was told this before noon but gave no response until late that afternoon, when he said that he might settle for seven and nine-tenths per cent. So a few minutes before the vote the President called Domenici, asked him to delay the vote for a day, and offered to settle for an increase of seven and nine-tenths per cent. But Domenici, by then thoroughly irritated, and knowing he could not muster the votes for that, replied that the offer was too little and too late. Moreover, he felt that the proposal was too vague—a hastily offered number with no explanation. I asked one Presidential assistant what had finally persuaded the President to give at all. He replied, "Five per cent." (Weinberger later suggested that the President simply ignore the budget process altogether, but an alarmed David Stockman, director of the Office of Management and Budget, succeeded in heading that off by arguing—in a document prepared for the Cabinet and quickly leaked to the newspapers—that this would produce deficits of two hundred billion dollars "as far as the eye can see.") The President's loss of influence on Capitol Hill was further demonstrated when he was unable to get a majority on the Budget Committee for his proposed "contingency" tax, to begin in fiscal 1986. Democrats, as well as some Republicans, wanted to vote to raise taxes more, and sooner, and some conservative Republicans didn't want to vote to raise them at all. (More than a little political positioning was involved here.) In order to get any budget resolution out of the committee, Domenici and some other Republicans voted with the Democrats to raise taxes by thirty billion dollars. The Administration was then faced with the perplexing problem of how to recoup on the Senate floor. Officials reasoned that Congress was unlikely to be persuaded to cut domestic programs any further (the Budget Committee had increased the Administration's figure for domestic spending by eleven billion dollars), while moves to increase the amount for defense or reduce the tax increase would raise the proposed deficit. Thus, the President was caught in the arithmetical fallacy that his program had contained from the outset.

How did the Administration miscalculate so badly? The legislative-strategy group, headed by James Baker, the White House Chief of Staff, is not given much of a say regarding the military budget, as opposed to other areas. One White House aide told me shortly before the committee voted, "The national-security operation under Bill Clark is a much more autonomous unit than any other around here, and, essentially, if Clark and Weinberger are determined not to move us off ten per cent I don't see how we move off ten per cent." He continued, "With any other department, I could refer to notes and tell you exactly how we got to the budget number we arrived at. Defense was handled on a different track in this budget cycle." On the day before the Senate Budget Committee voted, a number of White House aides were in a grim mood. "We are about to walk into a brick wall," one said to me.

Another said, "The nuances of good faith aren't understood around here." One said that there was a morbid joke going around the White House to the effect that "if our intelligence about the adversary—the Senate Republican caucus—is as bad vis-à-vis the Soviets and the Chinese, we've got a big problem."

Except that it may be no joke. A number of serious people here—people who can be characterized as hard-liners and have experience in dealing with the Soviet Union—have grown increasingly worried about the Administration's approach to the Soviets. One man at a high level in the Administration said, "The rhetoric is too hot." He added that he believed the Administration should have tried to deal with Yuri Andropov soon after he succeeded Leonid Brezhnev as General Secretary of the Communist Party, in November of last year. William Hyland, a specialist on Soviet affairs who served on the National Security Council staff and in the State Department during the Nixon and Ford Administrations, says, "At bottom, I don't think Reagan has a Soviet policy. The reason there is so much confusion is that there is no policy." While these people have no illusions that Andropov is of a charitable bent, they ask what conclusions the Soviet Union is to draw from a speech like the one the President gave in Orlando, or his declaration that the United States should go all out to build a defensive system. Hyland says, "Those speeches help persuade the Soviets that Reagan's basic views are still there. When they have to make a close-call decision on arms control, they have to ask, 'Does he mean it?' And then they'll remember the Orlando speech." There are varying degrees of optimism—but in general, at this point, there is not a great deal of it—about whether the Administration will reach an arms-control agreement on either intermediate-range or strategic nuclear missiles. Some people are raising questions not only about whether the Administration has any intention of reaching an agreement—or, more precisely, can overcome those within it who do not want one—but also about whether it has the wit to do so. The idea that the Administration is taking non-negotiable positions has gained strength, and not just among those who could be expected to be critical. Although Richard Pipes, the former top Soviet expert on the National Security Council staff, and an extreme hard-liner—he said in one interview that because of their economic problems the Russians would eventually have to face the choice of reforming their Communist system or going to war, and in another that there was a forty-per-cent chance of nuclear war—has returned to Harvard, he has left disciples behind on the N.S.C. staff.

Clark is not adjudged by anyone in the foreign-policy field I can find, or by others who deal with him at somewhat close range— except, presumably, the President—to have much grasp of foreign policy. Clark, a California rancher who had served Reagan when he was governor of California and whom Reagan had named to the California Supreme Court (though he never completed his undergraduate studies and dropped out of law school—he later attended law school at night and passed the bar exam), was brought in by Reagan in 1981 to serve as Deputy Secretary of State in order to try to keep the peace between Alexander Haig and the White House. When he was put in charge of the National Security Council, early in 1982, after Richard Allen had to resign (ostensibly over a matter of accepting watches and perhaps a check from some Japanese, but also because of the continuing feuding between State and the White House), the appointment was widely hailed. Clark's ignorance of foreign policy, which was apparent in his confirmation hearings, was forgiven for quite a while in favor of his calm presence and on the assumption that he'd learn. Clark is tall, quiet, genial, and composed. He has a youthful and benign appearance—ruddy cheeks, large brown eyes, and thick dark hair—and he speaks softly and works hard. A soothing style goes a long way in Washington—for a while, at least. A quiet demeanor is frequently—and sometimes mistakenly—taken for wisdom. And Clark managed to convey an impression that he was not particularly interested in power. Slowly, quietly, he established himself as a formidable force within the White House. But people who have known him for some time do not describe him as a man of any great depth. For some time, a few of his colleagues have been complaining privately about his lack of knowledge of his field, which is combined with his apparent confidence in his management skills. Sometimes, I have been told, he will make a decision for the sake of reaching a decision, without having any particular substantive basis for making it. Finally, after the "Star Wars" speech and the debacle on Capitol Hill, the frustration of other Presidential advisers began to spill over in public. And thus the Reagan White House went through yet another round of internal warfare, on which it appears to spend an inordinate amount of time, even as Administrations go. Despite the smiling façade presented to the public, the "triumvirate" of top aides—James Baker; Michael Deaver, the Deputy Chief of Staff; and Edwin Meese, the counsellor to the President—had never worked very well. Among other things, authority was too dispersed, and getting decisions made was too difficult, and much time and energy went into these people's, and their staffs', struggles with each other. The addition of Clark, who is very close to Reagan, only made things worse. One Presidential adviser says, "The only thing more unstable than a three-party system is a four-party system." But one senses from talking with people at the White House that the others fear Clark because of his relationship with Reagan and because of their concern that if it came to a showdown Clark would prevail. Thus, though Baker and Meese are said to have had misgivings about the "Star Wars" section of the President's speech, they didn't object strenuously. And thus, when the tensions did spill over, some White House aides anxiously tried to smooth things out. One White House aide said to me, smiling nervously, "We're all hiding under our desks around here—from each other." And he went on to talk—in a manner that suggested he was trying to convince himself—of how this would all blow over, and the team would be put back together. But others were still blaming Clark for encouraging Reagan in his various sallies against the Soviet Union, and for the White House's apparent political tone deafness. Both Weinberger and Clark were blamed for the fiasco on Capitol Hill. On the night the President gave his "Star Wars" speech, a group of scientists and Presidential advisers were gathered in the White House to watch the speech on television. Afterward, Clark said to the assembled group, "This thing is going to turn the country around, because the people know what's right." A couple of weeks later, when it was clear that the speech had not helped the President with Congress, a Presidential adviser said to me of Clark, "The funny thing is, he thinks that's what happened. I could understand the enthusiasm at the moment, but there's no basis for that now."

Perhaps the most significant thing about the renewed warfare within the Administration—it never really ceases, it just flares into view from time to time—and the recent foreign-policy developments is what they say about the President and about his Administration. Such disputes would not go on under a strong, interested President; this is one price of Reagan's passivity. Another is that there are now serious questions about the Administration's competence in handling foreign policy.

Between Clark and George Shultz, the Secretary of State, on the conduct of foreign policy Clark appears to have got the upper hand. For one thing, he has the advantage of propinquity. (George Ball once remarked, "Nothing propinques like propinquity.") Clark is also peculiarly sheltered from public scrutiny of his views or his knowledge. He shuns on-the-record interviews and, as head of the National Security Council, does not appear before Congress. But the picture of him and Reagan discussing foreign policy and national-security matters is not an entirely reassuring one.

It was perhaps inevitable that Shultz, too, having been the vessel of so many hopes, began to fall out of fashion, with questions increasingly being raised about what, exactly, he had been doing. When Shultz took the job, some of his friends wondered whether a man of his stability and instincts—he is a conservative but no ideologue—could survive in his new context. The answer seemed to be that he could survive by establishing his authority within the Administration—something he is now criticized for having failed to do but, given the constellation he is a part of, perhaps he was unable, even if willing, to do. He has been travelling the world (the Far East, Mexico, and now, despite his own misgivings, the Middle East, to try to rescue the President's Mideast plan), but he has not seemed to place himself in charge of foreign policy. And his much-advertised taking command of arms-control policy still hasn't occurred. It was considered a bit embarrassing when it came to light that Shultz had had no say in the selection of Kenneth Adelman as the new head of the Arms Control and Disarmament Agency. This was a product of Clark. (Other top White House aides also had no role in it, and the White House failed to consult key senators.) While the Administration did manage to get Adelman confirmed by the Senate, despite the negative recommendation of the Senate Foreign Relations Committee—which found him too lacking in stature and experience in the field, and also, at least at first, too disdainful of the committee's good opinion—it was a costly victory.

Weinberger's behavior is the subject of much speculation here. Weinberger is a pleasant, civilized man—the sort of man, the columnist Mary McGrory once wrote, "you would like to see coming up the front walk if you had trouble in the house." He is an intelligent man and a lawyer, and has the reputation of being a problem solver, a man with a cool and rational mind. But something has happened to him since he took over his job at the Pentagon. He has become rigid and dogmatic, and gives the appearance of being a man obsessed. A White House aide says, "I've never been in a meeting with Cap where he didn't argue and fight for every little thing; he digs in like a badger." Weinberger no longer gives what appear to be thoughtful responses but, rather, automatic ones, delivered rapid-fire in a tenor monotone. He appears locked in, trapped, beleaguered. The strain shows; of all the members of the Reagan Administration, Weinberger seems to have suffered the greatest physical toll. His face is strikingly pale and lined now; he looks shrunken. He seems preoccupied, and the pleasantness and civility seem to take more effort. One explanation, offered by an Administration source not particularly friendly to Weinberger, is that he accepted at the outset what the Joint Chiefs of Staff told him, and then could not be budged by others. Another explanation, offered by several who know him, is that he feels that he has an especially acute insight into the Soviet threat, and will not be budged. Some suggest that he associates himself with the Winston Churchill of "the wilderness years" of the nineteen-thirties, when Churchill was virtually alone in warning of Britain's need to prepare militarily for the imminent danger. He seems to see himself as alone, desperately defending the nation against the disbelievers. In the conversation at the Pentagon on the day the Budget Committee voted, Weinberger said, "So all of these discussions . . . Is the President going to lose, will it be a defeat for him if it's eight per cent instead of eight and a quarter—that not only trivializes the whole thing but it seems to me to miss the central point, which is not what percentage you get or who wins or loses. From our point of view, the country loses, the world loses, if we are not able to sustain the kind of drive we need."

The Reagan Administration's deepening role in Central America is attributed to Clark, but it is a development in which several people have had a hand. At the outset, White House aides tried to hush up Haig, who was talking of drawing lines in the dust in Central America, and of "going to the source"—Cuba—even though Haig was understood to be representing the President's general attitude. They wanted the issue off the front pages, both to keep the focus on the President's economic program and to head off fears that the United States was embarking on a military adventure. At the end of 1981, a White House aide said to me of El Salvador, "It's a problem. We've got too far out on it. We have to adjust; we can't make it work." The Reagan Administration has shown an inclination toward covert action from the outset, having apparently learned little from history. History, says Hyland—specifically, the history of the adventure in Angola, in the course of which Congress terminated funds for covert activities—should have taught future policymakers that covert actions tend not to stay covert, and that public opinion, unless a good case is made, tends not to be sympathetic. Moreover, as several people have pointed out, Central America—and particularly Nicaragua, where the United States is supplying aid to people trying to overthrow the Sandinista regime—is the area in which American intervention, given the history of American intervention, is most likely to backfire. (The sophistry that the United States is only trying to "harass" the regime and "interdict" weapons going to rebels in El Salvador is not very persuasive.) These people find it incredible that the United States should be joining arms in Nicaragua with Somozistas—the allies of the former dictator, Anastasio Somoza— as do many former opponents of the Somoza government who have broken with the Sandinista regime. They argue that the Reagan Administration has taken steps that have served to strengthen the grip and the militancy of the Sandinista government (named after a General Sandino, a Nicaraguan revolutionary who fought American Marines in Nicaragua in the late nineteen-twenties and early thirties). Haig is busy letting it be known that he warned against covert action at the outset. However, Weinberger opposed the kind of move that Haig wanted to make and still believes would have worked: taking some military action against Cuba. Middle-level officials in the State Department who actually have some expertise in Latin-American affairs are depressed. And at higher levels there has been internal dissension over policy. When Thomas Enders, the Assistant Secretary of State for Inter-American Affairs, who had taken a hard line, suggested in February that there might be negotiations with the rebels in El Salvador while aid to the government continued, he was subjected to a preemptive strike in the newspapers by Clark and Jeane Kirkpatrick, the Ambassador to the United Nations. Mrs. Kirkpatrick went off to Central America, and her report to the President upon her return led the Administration to ask for more military aid for El Salvador. In general, the N.S.C. takes a harder line than State on how to deal with Central America. Clark is said to feel quite comfortable about his own judgments on the subject. People here who dissent from the Administration policy—including some former career officials who worked on the area under previous Administrations, as well as some Democrats—say that they share some of the Administration's fears about the area, but not its diagnosis or its proposed solution. Developments that there had long been reason to fear have been coming about—a reaction against oligarchical and repressive regimes, which others who do not wish us well were sure to take advantage of. But these dissenters have been arguing that, as Senator Christopher Dodd, Democrat of Connecticut, puts it, the Administration sees the problem too much through the prism of the Soviet Union and its clients, and too little in terms of the indigenous factors that the Russians and the Cubans are exploiting. They have been arguing for more emphasis on diplomatic solutions and negotiations and less on military solutions, and more attention to what the non-Communist governments in the area are saying—emphases to which the President paid homage in his televised address before a joint session of Congress. In fact, one senses that, despite the forcefulness with which the various arguments are put, people here are in quite a quandary about Central America, and that there is very little certainty about what will "work."

The rationale behind the President's address was not simply to help him present his case to the public and get his way with an increasingly resistant Congress but also to set Congress up in case of reverses in the region. At the time, things were seen to be going badly for the government of El Salvador. When I asked one senior White House aide, shortly before the speech, what the pluses and minuses of the exercise were, he replied that the President did run a real risk of being rebuffed on some of his requests, and there was the danger that if the speech did not strike the right tone it might add to Reagan's "warmonger"—his term—problem. (He added that he doubted whether the latter would occur, because the President wouldn't "be talking about missiles and mega-tonnage and throw-weight.") He said that the President would not be talking about sending troops. He continued, "the record needs to be made clear about what we think needs to be done, so that when the time comes to say who lost El Salvador, or why another Central American government went Communist, the American people will know whom to blame." He added, "It would be a shame if we lost another country to Communism on our watch." (Reagan is fond of saying that the Soviet Union has not "expanded into an extra square inch since we've been here," and the "not on our watch" syndrome is a powerful one that has affected the actions of several previous Administrations.) This aide said that people in the border states—states with a lot of electoral votes—were particularly concerned about Central America. (The Administration offers a picture of Communist governments all the way up to the border.) Democrats realized that they were being set up—that the President would define the problem his way and offer his own solution and attempt to place the blame on them if anything should go wrong. And they realize that he is good at putting the question his way.

So much happened so quickly this spring that the uproar over the Environmental Protection Agency, culminating in the resignation of its administrator, Anne Gorsuch Burford, on March 9th, receded quickly into the background. But not without doing its share of damage to the Administration, which—in some quarters, at least—had all along underestimated the depth of public feeling about the environment. Mrs. Burford was really only a symptom of a deeper problem. In a way, it was an injustice to her to put her in the job. The E.P.A. has to administer one of the most complex and sensitive sets of laws of any agency in the government: laws touching on subjects that people feel very strongly about—clean air, clean water, solid waste, nuclear waste, toxic-waste dumps, noise. Some of the laws the E.P.A. has to administer are poorly drafted, and almost all of them call for sophisticated, often scientifically based, and politically sensitive judgments. The agency, having been established in 1970, was relatively new and was still finding its way through this maze when the Reagan Administration put Anne Gorsuch in charge. (She later married Robert Burford, who heads the Interior Department's Bureau of Land Management.) She had been a staff attorney for the Mountain Bell Telephone Company, and, along with Burford, a member of the Colorado state legislature and part of a group so ideologically determined to overturn government regulations that it was known as "the House crazies." (Robert Burford was Speaker of the House.) In 1980, Mrs. Gorsuch helped to kill a state bill dealing with hazardous-waste dumps. Another of the "crazies" was appointed regional director of the E.P.A. in Denver. He recently resigned in the face of charges that he had reversed his staff on environmental findings and failed to pursue cleanups of toxic-waste dumps. All these people were allied with James Watt, now the Secretary of Interior, who at that time headed the Mountain States Legal Foundation, which filed a number of suits against environmental laws—including a suit against the E.P.A. brought at the behest of the Colorado legislators. And these people were also part of a circle that was closely tied to Joseph Coors, the brewer, who backed a number of right-wing causes, including the Mountain States Legal Foundation. Coors was a major fund raiser for Reagan, and was later a member of his kitchen cabinet, helping to select the new Administration's personnel. (A former lobbyist for the Coors company against the Colorado toxic-waste-dump bill was later brought into the enforcement division of the E.P.A.) This was a group, then, that had made something of a career of railing against the federal government. So Mrs. Burford (then Gorsuch), like Watt, arrived in town blinkered by ideology, filled with hostility toward the new milieu, and combative. There was an attitude, shared in some other parts of the Administration, that laws that were not agreed with would not be enforced. Watt, at least, had served in the Interior Department before, and also on Capitol Hill, and knew a bit about his field. Mrs. Burford was utterly unprepared for the job—in a field that was more complex, and perhaps even more controversial, than Watt's. She spurned advice from predecessors and from professional bureaucrats who would have been glad to help her. For the first several weeks she was in Washington, she quartered herself in an office in the Interior Department, down the hall from Watt's, rather than spend time among her new colleagues. She failed to establish a network of support—on Capitol Hill or in the press. "Networking" is simply one of the ingredients for functioning in Washington, and it goes on on a bipartisan basis; if one has established something of a network one has built in a bit of protection, and it is a fact that if the press likes a person that person is more likely to get a bit of a break. When Mrs. Burford got in trouble, she was virtually without allies. And her administration of the E.P.A. was characterized by lack of competence and by failure to understand the sensitivity of the subjects the agency was dealing with. It was also characterized by failure to understand the importance of even appearances of conflicts of interest. (A certain lack of understanding of ethical niceties seems to run throughout the Reagan Administration.) Reasonable people can agree that there was a need for adjustments in the way some of the E.P.A.'s laws had been written or administered in earlier years. The field is one that, by definition, must adjust according to new information, and in which there is room for various interpretations, and there must be some trial and error.

But Mrs. Burford went at her job with the apparent view that government per se is bad, and her approach was to slash away. She never gave the impression that her goal was to protect the public health and safety. The invocation of executive privilege on E.P.A. documents subpoenaed by Congress may have been ordered by the Administration—that action led her to be cited for contempt of Congress—and she did have a point in feeling that she had to deal with too many congressional committees (a problem a number of government officials face), but her collision with Congress was induced largely by the attitude she struck at the outset. The mismanagement and politicization, in which the White House participated, of the Superfund—a fund to provide for the cleanup of toxic-waste sites—represented a colossal failure to understand public reaction. It is one thing, and quite a common thing, for Administrations to allocate federal bounty—housing projects, roads, military contracts—according to political exigencies; but to fool around with the disposition of funds to clean up toxic-waste dumps, as the Reagan Administration did, is quite another. People won't fear disease and death if they don't get a new federal highway, but toxic-waste dumps—in the aftermath of Love Canal and Times Beach, Missouri—do set off public fears. (Love Canal, in upstate New York, was the site of a toxic-waste dump, and had to be evacuated; Times Beach residents were relocated after it was discovered that the community's roads had been sprayed with the poisonous dioxin.) Unlike earlier generations, we do not fear such things as typhoid fever or diphtheria; our fears have to do with the effects of chemicals, and therefore the E.P.A. is an agency whose policies touch public nerves very deeply.

The toxic-dump controversy tossed up one of those figures who temporarily absorb our attention and then disappear from sight again. Suddenly Rita Lavelle, a blond, plumpish woman who was the director of the hazardous-waste cleanup program, and whom Mrs. Burford eventually got the President to fire, became a familiar figure; we studied her calendar, filled with dates to dine at Washington's most expensive restaurants with representatives of companies accused of dumping toxic wastes. Miss Lavelle said later that she had never read the E.P.A.'s code of ethics, which forbids employees to accept meals from industry executives, because no one had ever told her there was one. There was also a question of whether she had perjured herself before congressional committees on the matter of sitting in on meetings involving the cleanup of the Stringfellow Acid Pits, in California— even the name is unnerving—which her former employer used as a dump. (A congressional committee has just voted to recommend that the House cite her for contempt for refusing to answer a subpoena to testify.) And then, just as suddenly as she had come to our attention, like Dita Beard (of I.T.T. fame), she would go away. Eventually, the President's aides decided that Mrs. Burford was an excessive liability and that the E.P.A. controversy had to be put to an end, and, through various nudges and leaks to the press, they got her to resign. The President said he believed that she had been the victim of environmentalists and the press.

One significant thing about the E.P.A. mess was that in order to salvage the situation the Administration turned to William Ruckelshaus, who had been the first administrator of the E.P.A., under Nixon. Ruckelshaus is the sort of mainstream Republican who would have been anathema to the Reagan Administration at the outset. (To boot, his wife, Jill, is an ardent feminist, and marched in Detroit in 1980 to protest the Republican platform on abortion and the Equal Rights Amendment.) Another significant thing was that even some White House officials were surprised by the good reaction to the Ruckelshaus appointment. But Ruckelshaus, a man with an established reputation for integrity, will have no easy time of it, because of what has gone before. Every move he makes to change the laws or the administration of them will be the more controversial because of the background against which he must proceed. If he or someone like him had been chosen at the outset, things would have been quite different, and the Administration might have achieved more changes.

For now, the attention will swing back to Watt, who provided some welcome levity when he banned the Beach Boys—a relatively middle-aged and melodic group—from the Fourth of July celebrations on the Mall, because they would attract the "wrong element," and substituted Wayne Newton, the Las Vegas entertainer, on the theory that he would be more wholesome. Watt also inadvertently helped the White House—for the first time, in the view of some Presidential advisers—by providing the President, Mrs. Reagan, and Michael Deaver with an opportunity to come out four-square for the Beach Boys. Even George Bush spoke out for them. And the White House tried, with some success, to make a joke of it. Though a number of the President's aides believe Watt to be a serious liability because of the way he has gone about his job—and were only too happy to drop banana peels in front of him in the Beach Boys incident—it is not clear that the President has yet become attuned to the environmental sensitivities his Administration has aroused. He proclaims himself a protector of the environment; but his old instincts led him to remark recently that there are now in the United States "as much forests as there were when Washington was at Valley Forge" and, two days after Mrs. Burford resigned, that he didn't think environmental activists "will be happy until the White House looks like a bird's nest."

As April neared its close, the President's aides were aware, and began to acknowledge privately, that his authority on Capitol Hill was slipping. It is frequently suggested that Presidential authority inevitably slips in the third year of a term, but this is not necessarily true. If members of the President's own party feel that it's in their interest to go along with him, they will. The erosion of Presidential authority is often self-induced. One reason, obviously, that Republicans tended to strike out on their own more was that they received such a fright in the 1982 elections—losing twenty-six House seats and, while just holding their own in the Senate, very nearly losing five seats there. Moreover, in 1984 the mathematics work against the Republicans—more Republicans than Democrats are up for reelection in the Senate—just as they worked against the Democrats in 1980 and 1982. Politicians are an unsentimental lot when it comes to the question of survival. But even some of the President's aides recognized that another reason for the new independence on Capitol Hill was that key Republicans, including the leadership in both Houses, had gone along with the President's

economic program in the first year despite their own deep misgivings. Now they were simply less likely to follow the leader—to
extend the line of credit that new Presidents usually receive. Furthermore, one White House aide suggested to me, some Republicans were starting to think that the President was a lame duck, and
a few, of course, were fixing to run for President if Reagan didn't
seek reelection. Therefore, the President's top aides began to indicate publicly that they believed the President would run, and to
urge him privately to make a decision known. One reason was that
they were anxious to get a campaign organization under way. Another was that they were trying to push his decision into being a
fait accompli. But still another was that they were seeking to shore
up his strength.

At bottom, despite their worries about other subjects, the President's aides are resting their hopes for the President's reelection
on an economic recovery. The recovery that is now taking place is
of modest strength, and a number of people here have uncertainties about its duration. Interest rates are still high (they appear to
have come down some, but, when adjusted for inflation, have
done so little if at all), and at this point Congress is showing little
zeal for raising taxes, whatever the budget resolution may say.
(The Senate's recent caving in to the pressure stirred up by the
banking industry, and reversing last year's provision to require
withholding of interest and dividends, has further demoralized
those members of Congress who believe that more taxes should be
raised.) And even a number of liberal economists have been saying
that a repeal or a reduction of the third year of the cut in income-
tax rates, due to take effect on July 1st—a proposition that would
have to be included in any tax measure raising as much as thirty
billion dollars—might stall the recovery. In addition, this round of
tax cuts would be of more help to the middle class than those of
the past two years, and was therefore politically safer among many
Democrats.

The Administration is a divided camp over what to say about
the economy. One group wants to make cautious predictions—in
order to maintain credibility, in order to keep the heat on Congress (and the President) to get the budget deficits down, and
because that represents what they believe. The other, which consists of the few remaining supply-siders in the government and
some officials of a political bent, wants to give cheerful prognoses,

on the theory that this may be good politics and may also be self-fulfilling. So the first estimate of growth for 1983—three per cent—was deliberately low, and the second, made in late March, of four and seven-tenths per cent, was excessively high. As things turned out, the growth in the first quarter was about three per cent. Inflation, of course, is way down from what it was when Reagan came to office—a side effect of the recession. But the minor fluctuations in the percentages by which growth may occur are less significant than the nature of the recovery itself. It is, compared with past recoveries, slow; most recoveries produce growth of six to seven per cent in the first year or two. The view here is that the Administration (or part of it) is deliberately trying to keep the recovery slow, so as not to set off another round of inflation. Because of the high interest rates, and the worldwide recession, American exports continue to be low. And industrial investment is low—lower, in fact, than it was during the Carter years. So to the extent that there is a recovery from the deepest recession since the Depression—a recession deeper than the one Reagan called a "depression" during the 1980 campaign—it will be characterized by slow growth and high unemployment, and will have no resemblance to what the Reagan economic plan was supposed to bring about. This recovery now relies on consumer spending, or demand-side growth, as opposed to the supply-side theory, which premised remarkable growth on individual savings and business investment that were to be the result of tax cuts. Thus, if there is a recovery it will be, of all things, a Keynesian one. That is what the Administration is counting on.

The current weight of opinion in Washington, for what it's worth, is that Reagan will run for reelection; but for every argument that he will there is an equally convincing argument that he won't. In any event, if he does he will define the economic recovery as he likes. At that point, his talent, which is considerable, for defining the question his way would be put to its greatest test.

IV

At some future time, historians may look back and wonder how it was that politicians and policymakers made a decision to proceed with the development of a weapon that they knew had lost its original rationale, might escalate the arms race, and could put their own country's military force at greater risk. Congress's recent decision to approve going forward with the MX—for "missile experimental," a large, ten-warhead, land-based missile—was, at one level, predictable: Congress is traditionally loath to deny a President a weapons system. But, given the MX's bizarre history, the convoluted reasoning that went into its most recent justification, the serious misgivings of those who were most responsible for helping the weapon win congressional approval, and the potential consequences of their action, the story is an unusual one. It is a story of well-intentioned people acting out of a combination of their own sense of what it means to be "responsible;" their own sense of what they needed to do to "position" themselves politically or lay the groundwork for political advancement; and political fear. Almost none of those who made the President's victory possible thought that the missile was, in itself, a good idea.

While many of these people acted out of enduring political motivations, any important political decision has to also be understood in its context. The MX decision came at a time when many politicians feared they might soon be confronted with the "Who lost China?" issue in two new forms: Who "lost" Central America?; and, Who killed a weapons system a President said he needed for national security and for reaching an arms-control agreement? Behind many people's actions was the fear of a President with a clear talent for stating the case his way. The decision also came at a time when the subject of nuclear weaponry was an especially acute one politically, leaving those who did not naturally land on one side or the other of a particular question to seek what they consid-

72

ered politically safe ground. In this instance, the Reagan Administration was clever enough to provide them with it. On the one
hand was an Administration that was engaged in an arms buildup
of unprecedented magnitude, and whose zeal for arms control
was in doubt, and on the other was a movement that had arisen in
reaction to that Administration's policies and centered on a call for
a freeze in the production of nuclear weapons. It was the politicians searching for some middle ground—painstakingly trying to
pick their way through nuclear politics—who gave the President
his victory on the MX. The Administration used as its instruments
a commission that was made up of cooperative members of the
defense establishment and was "bipartisan" (a term uttered in
reverential tones); appeals to political ego; and a definition of the
issue that created its own rationale—that the question of going
ahead with the MX was one of national "will." The MX drove the
rationale, rather than the other way around—the rationale kept
changing. After the key politicians entered into a remarkable bargain with an Administration they essentially did not trust, allowing
it to proceed with a weapon they essentially did not approve of,
they, too, offered a series of rationales. They said—and fervently
hoped—that they had put themselves in a position to influence the
President's arms-control policy. But most of them were clearly uncomfortable with the bargain they had struck, and aware that,
whatever the short-run political consequences, they had taken an
action that history would judge.

There had, after all, been earlier fateful steps in the history of
the arms race—steps that some of the policymakers who took
them came to regret. And the justifications for those earlier steps
have had recent echoes. The decision to develop MIRVs (for "multiple independently targeted reentry vehicles") was made during
the Johnson Administration, and the decision to deploy them was
made early in the Nixon Administration. The deployment was
opposed by a large number of senators and representatives, who
urged a moratorium until an arms-control agreement banning
MIRVs might be reached. The Nixon Administration's response
was that MIRVs were needed to offset potential Soviet advantages,
and that only by planning to deploy MIRVs might the United States
get the Soviet Union to agree to withhold development of a similar
weapon. The rationale was that the MIRV would be a "bargaining
chip." But, according to Gerard Smith, this country's chief SALT I

negotiator, the United States' offer to ban MIRVs was "halfhearted" (he says the military wanted no ban at all), and the Soviet Union was so far behind the United States in developing MIRVs that it did not want to be prevented from catching up. The result was that both sides deployed MIRVs. This is now seen as one of the most destabilizing steps in the arms race. It led Henry Kissinger, who approved their deployment, to remark later, "I wish I had thought through the implications of a MIRVed world." Now Kissinger is among those who are trying to wrestle the MIRV out of existence.

The next great "advance" in the arms race, which also led to a new instability, was the development of the cruise missile—a small missile that can be launched from land, sea, or air—which was given the go-ahead during the Ford Administration. It had been offered to an at first unenthusiastic military as a solace for the SALT I agreement, and it, too, was touted as a "bargaining chip." Now the United States is deploying cruise missiles, and the Soviet Union is taking countermeasures, and there is widespread agreement among arms experts that cruise missiles—especially once they are deployed on submarines—will be nearly impossible to detect, and therefore to bring under an arms agreement. (By 1976, when Kissinger was trying to reach a new arms-control agreement, the Pentagon was reluctant to give up the cruise, and it was off limits as a bargaining chip. Kissinger remarked, "I didn't realize the Pentagon would fall in love with cruise missiles.") Both the MIRVs and the cruise missiles had been justified on political as much as military grounds: they would demonstrate our will to go forward with new weapons; they would cause the Soviet Union to give something up at the bargaining table. The MX was justified on the same grounds.

How is it, then, that it became a test of this country's "will" for it to go forward with a weapon for which there was very little other justification? In one sense, something like the MX was bound to come along, as each service continually tries to "improve" the weapons systems it already has. In this case, something that eventually became the MX had been discussed by the Air Force since the mid-sixties, and its justifications along the way were several, and changeable. At first, it was discussed as a larger, more accurate missile, at the same time that building a new, MIRVed Minuteman missile was under study. The new large missile would have many more warheads and, because of its improved guidance system, would be able to destroy "hard targets"—the very strong Soviet missile silos and command and control centers, which the Minuteman could not destroy. The Soviet Union has large, heavy missiles that are seen as theoretically capable of destroying Minuteman silos. But the theory behind this country's strategic planning has been that it had, over all, sufficient strength to deter a Soviet attack. Moreover, the United States has been taking other steps to make its warheads more powerful and accurate. A new missile was also sought as a solution to the presumed vulnerability of the entire land-based missile system—the "window of vulnerability"—and was to be invulnerable to a Soviet attack. The two different purposes of the new missile—that it was to be a more powerful offensive weapon, capable of hitting more Soviet targets (the emphasis given it by the Strategic Air Command); and that it was to be an invulnerable weapon (the purpose emphasized by Pentagon officials in Washington)—fed directly into the recent confusion over the rationale for the MX. Moreover, there was a strain of thought that since the Soviet Union was developing large, heavy missiles the United States should develop them as well. The United States had so far chosen not to do so, on the theory that it didn't need to—that, using miniature components, it could pack the same capability into a smaller missile, which would have greater accuracy. The heavy missile enjoyed support not only in the Air Force but also on Capitol Hill, where Senator Henry Jackson, Democrat of Washington, and an influential member of the Armed Services Committee, was vigorously pushing for one. (Thought was also given to developing a missile that could be used on land or at sea, but the Air Force and the Navy each wanted its own new missile. Also, the push for a huge missile ruled out a common one.) A member of the committee's staff, realizing that the two philosophies behind the new missile—that it should be large, and that it should be survivable—didn't necessarily mesh, came up with a proviso, which Congress approved, saying that money could not be spent developing a new large missile unless a survivable basing mode was found for it. From the time that the Minuteman II, a single-warhead missile, was first deployed, in 1965, there was talk of its becoming vulnerable to attack—by what was also a variable. During the fight in Congress in 1969 over whether to deploy an anti-ballistic missile system (ABM), Defense

Secretary Melvin Laird argued that the system was necessary because this country's land-based missiles were probably vulnerable to the Soviet SS-9, a large single-warhead missile. (At that point, the MIRV was also justified as a countermeasure to the Soviet ABM.) After the Senate approved the ABM by one vote, the Nixon Administration negotiated a treaty with the Soviet Union limiting each side to two ABM sites, and this was later amended to allow for just one, both sides having grown unenthusiastic about the efficacy of such systems. (The American system, near Grand Forks, North Dakota, was abandoned less than a year after its completion.)

The potential vulnerability of landbased missiles also led to a search for ways not just to defend them—which was the theory of the ABM—but also to make them survivable, through various schemes for not keeping them trapped in fixed silos. So the Air Force embarked on an endless series of studies of new ways to deploy land-based missiles and came up with thirty-four plans: putting them at the center of a wheel-shaped system and sending them out to one of the several spokes; transporting them in and dropping them from airplanes (the C-5A cargo plane); hanging them underneath dirigibles; putting them on trains; placing them in orbit; carting them around on trucks; and placing them in long tunnels. The tunnel idea lasted for quite some time. Then an elementary flaw occurred to someone: a tunnel would conduct the effect of a blast anywhere along it. The tunnel idea was what the Carter Administration inherited. The Carter Administration then moved toward the idea of a loop that contained twenty-three shelters; the missile would move periodically around the loop, and hide in one of the shelters. The plan was to place two hundred missiles in forty-six hundred potential shelters. This scheme became known as the "race track." Toward the end of the Carter Administration, it was modified slightly, and the modified system was officially known as the multiple protective shelters, or MPS. It was the race-track idea, however, that stuck in the public debate, and was subject to ridicule, because of its apparent gimcrackery. In June, 1979, Carter gave it his approval, mainly because he felt under pressure to do so in order to win Senate approval of the SALT II agreement. The Joint Chiefs of Staff had warned that they could not support the SALT agreement unless there was a land-based system with guaranteed survivability. The Chairman of the

Joint Chiefs had favored the tunnel, which evolved into the loop. A Pentagon official told me at the time that the race-track idea had been hurriedly developed. "The engineering was done at lightning speed and might rise up to spite us," the official said. "It took only four to six weeks to get this exact configuration." The Air Force had lobbied hard for it within the Administration and on Capitol Hill, partly because Air Force officials felt that if they had lobbied harder for the B-1 bomber Carter would not have succeeded in getting that killed. So Carter and his Defense Secretary, Harold Brown, made the political decision to go ahead with the MX in some form of multiple-shelter system, despite their reservations about the idea. A former Carter Administration official now says, "The MX is the illegitimate child of SALT." Predictably, the opponents of SALT were not mollified, and opposed the treaty anyway.

But even during the Carter Administration Western interests— ranchers, miners, environmentalists, politicians—were complaining about the prospect of a multiple-shelter system on Western public lands. Their objections had to do with everything from aesthetics to the use of water to the use of land for which some of these interests had other things in mind. (The "sagebrush rebellion" and some part of the anti-MX sentiment were closely related.) Air Force officials delivered themselves of such statistics as that the system would use less water than it takes to water the golf courses of Las Vegas. Normally pro-defense politicians, including Senator Barry Goldwater, Republican of Arizona, let it be known that they did not want missile-protection systems in their areas. The shelter system was to be based on public lands in Utah and Nevada. Others who shared this sentiment were Senator Paul Laxalt, Republican of Nevada, the chairman of the Reagan 1980 campaign and perpetually described as the President's closest friend on Capitol Hill; and Senator Jake Garn, Republican of Utah. So Reagan campaigned against the multiple-shelter system, and shortly after entering office, appointed a commission to come up with a new basing system for the MX. The commission, which was headed by Charles Townes, a Nobel physicist who teaches at Berkeley, and was composed mainly of scientists and technical people as well as defense strategists, reported in July. It said that it had some doubts about the long-term wisdom of a multiple-shelter plan but recommended that a modified, smaller version of one go forward (a hundred missiles in a hundred silos), which could be expanded into a multiple-shelter "shell game" system in case nothing else worked out. It suggested that for the long term such alternatives as carrying the MX on aircraft or putting them in deep underground bases be studied. But because Reagan had campaigned against the idea of a multiple-shelter ground-based system and his Western friends were opposed to any such thing, the Reagan Administration instead recommended placing the missiles in existing silos. (This was the plan that Reagan was embarrassingly unable to explain to the press when it was announced in October, 1981.) The Administration also said that it would study other long-term basing plans, including placing the missiles on cargo planes (this plan came to be called Big Bird), using deep underground missile basing (which came to be called DUMB), and using some kind of ABM defense (which would have required abrogating the ABM treaty). In time, all these plans went away. Secretary of Defense Caspar Weinberger, who is close to Townes, still believes that the idea of placing the missiles on planes is a good one, but he does not have much company. (The Air Force was among those who opposed it; among other things, it presents targeting problems and is very expensive. There was also some concern about public reaction if one of the planes carrying an MX happened to crash.) Congress concluded that the Administration hadn't really solved the problem of how to base the missile so that it would be survivable, and in the summer of 1982 told the Administration to try again, and to report by December.

By this time, a constituency was developing in the Air Force and among the highly placed civilians in the Pentagon for a plan to protect the silos by placing them so close together that the incoming Soviet missiles would blow each other up, by a process known as "fratricide." The fratricide theory had been around for some time, and now enjoyed a new vogue. A second, and largely unspoken, rationale for such a system was that it would provide the basis for some sort of anti-ballistic-missile system. The ABM treaty is still in effect, but a number of defense strategists would like to be rid of it. A new Townes Commission was formed in May of 1982 to study the idea of a closely spaced basing system, which acquired the name Dense Pack. The commission's report, which was not made public, was that the Dense Pack idea was promising, but that there were problems with it, including the fact that the Soviet

Union might find a way to counter it, and that it was a very complicated business. In late November, the President recommended
that one hundred MX missiles be deployed in Wyoming in a
Dense Pack formation. Officials knew that the proposal for the
new basing system hadn't been sufficiently prepared. It was to be
presented to the lame-duck Congress in late November, following
the elections, which had not exactly been a triumph for the Administration. And it emerged in testimony on Capitol Hill that
three of the five members of the Joint Chiefs of Staff opposed the
Dense Pack idea, and that even Townes had reservations. The
Administration nonetheless, with some misgivings, submitted the
Dense Pack plan to Capitol Hill in December, as was required by
law. It ran into a cross fire of questions—even the name had a
certain absurd ring to it—and was voted down. The House voted
245 to 176 to deny money to procure the MX, on the ground that
a sensible basing mode had still not been found, but it did approve
money to develop the missile and a basing mode, and stipulated
that money could not be spent—"fenced it off"—until Congress
approved of a basing system. The Senate voted 56 to 42 to establish tight procedures for future congressional action to release the
money that had been fenced off. (Those with misgivings about the
MX itself voted against the procedures.) Jackson, in cooperation
with the Administration, worked out a procedure by which Congress had to act within forty-five days of receiving another recommendation for a basing mode from the President. There was a
feeling on Capitol Hill that this was the Administration's last
chance, and it was understood that the Administration would appoint yet another commission. The procedure, in which the
House concurred (it was part of an umbrella "continuing resolution," covering spending for a number of government agencies,
and Congress was eager to get out of town), was a very unusual
one. It wrote the terms of a resolution approving the releasing of
the money for a basing mode and for developing and flight-testing the MX which was to be voted on by the next Congress: a
simple, one-line resolution stating that the House or the Senate
(the law allowed the lawmakers to fill in the blank on that matter)
"approves the obligation and expenditure of funds appropriated
in Public Law [another blank] for MX missile procurement and
full-scale engineering development of a basing mode for the MX
missile." (The public-law number could not be known until the

resolution actually became law.) In their rush, the drafters mistakenly put in the word "procurement," and this led to some confusion over exactly what was being voted on this year. The law also specified that the resolution could not be amended or delayed. It was never clear when the House voted in December how many were voting against the MX under any circumstances and how many were simply voting against the Dense Pack basing system. The Administration decided that this time it would appoint an MX commission that would deal with not just the technical but also the political realities.

The role of the new commission, the President's Commission on Strategic Forces, which was formally established in early January, was not to decide whether there should be an MX but how to fashion an MX proposal that Congress would approve. Robert McFarlane, deputy to William Clark, the head of the National Security Council, was in charge of putting together the commission. The Administration had already taken a fancy to the idea of establishing bipartisan commissions, having set one up in 1981 to deal with the sticky political problem of how to reduce the cost of the Social Security program. But whereas the Social Security commission represented a wide array of points of view, the new MX commission was a different sort of thing. McFarlane said to me recently, "I believed there was a bipartisan consensus within the community—the family—that we had to have the MX or it would demonstrate an inability on the part of the United States to solve problems." The members chosen for the new panel were people who shared that point of view. There are, of course, members of "the community"—including a number of scientists, three former Secretaries of Defense, two former directors of the Central Intelligence Agency, and former military officials—not to mention informed people outside it, who are not of the opinion that the United States needs the MX, and even feel that deployment of it is a bad idea. But though the commission was ostensibly charged with conducting a thorough review of strategic forces, it was not in the cards that it would recommend against the MX. The purpose of the commission was to turn Congress around. It followed that the commission must be "bipartisan," containing both Democratic and Republican respectables from the defense and public-policy community. The members of the commission were people who either had supported the MX or could be counted on to give it their support.

Then the White House officials made a shrewd, and crucial, decision. They decided that the best way to assure that Congress would approve the commission's product was to involve certain key members of Congress—members whose opinion would sway other members—in the commission's deliberations. And certain key members were, for their own reasons, willing to cooperate. Thus, the deal that the President ultimately made with Congress in order to get its approval of the MX was actually in the making from the outset: it was, as the expression goes, "precooked." The exercise began with the choice by McFarlane of two ideal people to carry it out: Brent Scowcroft, a retired Air Force lieutenant-general who had been Henry Kissinger's deputy when Kissinger ran the National Security Council, and then was placed in charge of the N.S.C., succeeding Kissinger, and later became a member of Carter's General Advisory Committee on Arms Control; and James Woolsey, who was an adviser to the SALT talks and a member of the N.S.C. staff during the Nixon Administration, and was Under-Secretary of the Navy during the Carter Administration. Woolsey is an old friend of McFarlane's and a defense conservative. Scowcroft, who was chosen as chairman of the commission, had been a mentor of McFarlane's for some time, and had excellent credentials for his new task. He was in good standing among mainstream Republicans and among a broad swath of Democrats as well. People of both parties viewed him as the perfect N.S.C. head: the quiet, mild, fair implementer, whose ego did not get in the way of doing his job, or of other people. He was not one for pushing policies of his own. People of both parties had compared him favorably as N.S.C. head with his predecessor, Kissinger, and his successor, Zbigniew Brzezinski. Scowcroft is a public servant, an honorable public servant, whose instinctive loyalty is to the Commander-in-Chief. He faithfully and competently gets the job done. McFarlane said to me, "Brent has said they were looking at something that was militarily sensible and how that relates to arms control and what we can succeed with—what is politically viable. We just had to win this one." McFarlane served in the Marines for twenty years and worked as a White House Fellow in the early nineteen-seventies, and therefore with Scowcroft. Woolsey helped McFarlane select other people for the commission. (Scowcroft and

Woolsey had served together on the first Townes Commission.) The list of the commission's members and its "senior counsellors" is a compilation of former officials and others who could be counted on to support a consensus and to be persuasive with Congress. Among them were William Clements, the Deputy Secretary of Defense in the Nixon and Ford Administrations (Clements had pushed the cruise missile); John Deutch, a scientist and Under-Secretary of the Department of Energy in the Carter Administration; Alexander Haig; Richard Helms, former director of the Central Intelligence Agency; John Lyons, a vice-president of the A.F.L.-C.I.O. and the chairman of its committee on defense issues, and president of the Bridge, Structural, and Ornamental Iron Workers; William Perry, the Under-Secretary of Defense for Research and Engineering during the Carter Administration; Thomas Reed, Special Assistant to the President for National Security Affairs in the Reagan Administration, who resigned from the White House (but not the commission) after he was charged with inside stock dealings; Levering Smith, a retired vice-admiral who was involved in the development of several weapons systems; and Nicholas Brady, an investment banker who in 1982 did a brief tour as an interim senator from New Jersey and in 1980 had been the state co-chairman of the Bush campaign. (George Bush had a hand in selecting some of these people.) The "senior counsellors" were four former Secretaries of Defense—Harold Brown, Melvin Laird, Donald Rumsfeld, and James Schlesinger—along with Kissinger; John McCone, a former director of the C.I.A.; and Lloyd Cutler, a Washington lawyer who had served as a Special Counsel in the Carter White House. Not a boat rocker or, of course, an MX opponent in the group; and some members were to prove quite valuable when it came time to sell the commission's report on Capitol Hill. Anything with the imprimatur of Harold Brown and William Perry was bound to make an impression on Democrats, though among some people conversant with defense issues both men are respected more for their analytical powers and ability to explicate complex matters than for their political or policy judgment. But probably no one was as politically valuable as Woolsey, who was, as it happens, an old, close friend of Les Aspin, a Democratic congressman from Wisconsin and a highly influential House member on defense matters. Aspin, who had built a reputation as a defense critic, was now looking for a way to support getting on

with the MX, and putting the issue behind him, and he and Woolsey, working together from the outset of the Scowcroft Commission's deliberations, found the way.

Les Aspin, forty-four, is a large, exuberant man, a former defense
intellectual—he was among Robert McNamara's "whiz kids"—who
was elected to Congress at the age of thirty-two and immediately
went on the Armed Services Committee. He made something of a
reputation for himself by frequently issuing clever press releases
criticizing such things as military pensions, assignment practices,
and subsidized veterinary care for servicemen's pets—rather than
strategic matters, dealing with the bigger picture. Now graying
and developing a slight paunch, Aspin in recent years has grown
more cautious: some attribute this to the fact that he had a fright
in the 1980 election, as his district grew more hawkish. And in the
past year or so he has been trying to bridge the divide within his
own party on the issue of nuclear politics. At the Democratic Party
Conference held in Philadelphia last June, he helped draft a resolution to blur the question of whether the Party supported the
idea of a nuclear freeze. When the freeze movement was recruiting congressional support last year, Aspin's own initial view was
that, rather than back a freeze resolution, the Democrats should
support the reintroduction of the SALT II agreement, and he made
a strong case for this approach. Then, whatever his misgivings, he
supported a freeze resolution when it came before the House last
August (when it lost by two votes) and again this year, when, after
much amending, it passed. Aspin was, in fact, an active participant
in developing the strategy for the freeze debate earlier this year,
once some adjustments he wanted in the resolution had been
made. Last year, he voted against the MX in its Dense Pack wrap-
pings, and in 1980 he had voted to delay development of the MX.
This year, Aspin is for the first time chairman of an Armed Services subcommittee—on Military Personnel and Compensation.
One House Democrat says, "Being chairman of a defense subcommittee means you are now dealing with a constituency out there—
the Pentagon. It means being able to deliver favors to your colleagues, but in order to do that you've got to have the support of
the Pentagon. The same thing is true in other areas, like agriculture: they need you and you need them, and you help each
other." Aspin is seen by some of his colleagues as wanting the

approval of the community of defense intellectuals; and the less charitable of his colleagues suggest that a strong motivation for Aspin is that he wants to be Secretary of Defense someday. To reach such a goal, one cannot have been simply a critic of the Pentagon. It is a fact that a sizable portion of the Washington population—more sizable all the time, it seems—consists of people "positioning" themselves for a high job in some future Administration. Positioners tend not to be terribly daring or to take highly controversial positions or to get on the wrong side of a constituency that will have a strong say in their future.

In any event, Aspin was ready to play a role in helping the Administration get the MX approved. Woolsey and Aspin had worked together in the Pentagon as systems analysts during the McNamara years, and have remained friends since, frequently playing squash or tennis together. Aspin told me recently, "We started to talk even before the commission was announced. Every other panel or commission that had looked at this thing was just looking at the narrow military-basing question, and then would try to sell it to the public, with disastrous results. So Woolsey and I thought of two things: one was you ought to start with the politics—what's possible to pass—and then, two, among the possible things to pass, what makes sense militarily."

I asked Aspin why he was looking for a way to get an MX system approved.

He replied, "My thinking was that this issue had been around a long time and it wasn't going to get settled—it wouldn't really be defeated and it wouldn't be fully deployed—and my feeling was that when both sides have gone at each other for a long time it gets time to cut a deal. And even if you had the votes to defeat the MX, a year later something happens—the Soviets invade Afghanistan—and they'd say, 'You see, we don't have a land-based missile,' and the MX would come back, and would cost more. That's what happened with the B-1 bomber—it just kept coming back."

According to Aspin, Woolsey, who essentially wrote the Scowcroft report, had the outlines of the eventual compromise in mind as early as January. The idea was to recommend that a limited number of MX missiles be deployed and that the country then move to the deployment of single-warhead missiles. While the idea of the single-warhead missile has been identified with Representative Albert Gore, Jr., Democrat of Tennessee and son of the former senator from Tennessee, and Gore showed great political entrepreneurship with it, it had actually been around for some time and had been discussed in defense circles and much written about. Recently, Henry Kissinger blessed the idea. And Scowcroft and Woolsey had pushed the idea with the first Townes Commission, in 1981. The theory is that by, in effect, de-MIRVing land-based missiles, and having many single-warhead missiles deployed, either side would have greater difficulty destroying the other's land-based missiles. An arms-control agreement that limited the ratio of each side's warheads to the other's launchers would, the theory goes, prevent either one from having a sufficient number of warheads to destroy all those of the other side. Moreover, a single-warhead missile, which came to be called Midgetman, would be a less inviting target than one that contained several warheads. Woolsey explained to me that the commission could not recommend simply skipping the MX and proceeding to the single-warhead missile, because there remained technical problems to be worked out about the single-warhead missile and such a missile might not come on line until the early nineteen-nineties. If the MX were simply scrapped, he said, the land-based-missile force would not be modernized for several more years, and that would cause a delay in providing an incentive for the Soviet Union to negotiate. The last point was a highly debatable one, as shall be seen. Moreover, it was generally understood that the Air Force was far more enthusiastic about the MX than about the single-warhead missile, and the theory was that it had to be given the one in order to induce it to develop, however reluctantly, the other. Weinberger, too, is not keen on going ahead with the Midgetman. The priority for the Air Force and for important high-level Pentagon officials is a large land-based missile with "hard-target kill capability." And there were the others, including Jackson, who were determined that the United States have such a missile. And the President himself was committed to going ahead with deploying the MX, to which he had given the name Peacekeeper. (The origin of that, it turns out, was that Peacekeeper was the name of a gun that William Clark's grandfather, a U.S. marshall, had used to "preserve the peace" in his California frontier community.)

In late January, Woolsey and Scowcroft began a series of meetings with Aspin on Sunday afternoons—at Woolsey's house, at

Aspin's house—to talk about what the effect would be on the House floor of various possible commission proposals. They talked about how many MX missiles should be recommended— the multiple-shelter system and Dense Pack basing had contemplated two hundred missiles—and concluded that something like a hundred and fifty or a hundred might be more politically acceptable. Aspin volunteered to "run the traps" with a few people. So he went to Thomas Foley, Democrat of Washington and the House Majority Whip. Foley, fifty-four, is a moderate, and is a bridge between the older and younger Democrats; he is also close to Jackson on defense and on other matters, both men coming from the same state, where defense contractors are an important part of the economy. Aspin thought that Foley would be the key to getting the support of, or at least neutralizing, other members of the House Democratic leadership. Foley told Aspin he thought that some combination of an MX deployment and a recommendation to proceed with a single-warhead missile might win enough Democratic votes for the MX. Aspin and Foley then went to House Speaker Thomas P. O'Neill, who, while he did not agree to back their proposal, advised them that if they wanted to get the matter settled in the House once and for all they should find a proposal that a majority of both parties would support. O'Neill had his own complicated equation to solve on the MX: he is from Massachusetts, where anti-nuclear sentiment is strong, yet construction of the MX would bring a substantial number of jobs to his area; moreover, his own troops were divided. In the end, he opposed the MX, but since the House leadership was divided on the question there was no Party effort to defeat the weapon. This was what Aspin had been hoping for. While the commission proceeded with its deliberations, Aspin held a number of meetings on the Hill, to which he invited some of his Democratic colleagues to talk things out with Scowcroft and Woolsey. As the commission got close to writing the report, House members were also invited to breakfast meetings at Blair House. Gore was consulted, and came away feeling that he had impressed on the commission the importance of going ahead with the single-warhead missile and of stressing arms control. One of the results of the meetings with members of Congress was that the commission became convinced of the importance of stressing arms control in its report, and Scowcroft carried this message to the White House. And so the Scowcroft Commission produced a report that was designed to be acceptable to various constituencies: Democrats on Capitol Hill, the White House, and the Pentagon. This is why the report had such an odd shape.

Having found no other politically acceptable way to base the missile, the commission in its report, released on April 11th, recommended that a hundred MX missiles be placed in Minuteman silos—the theoretical vulnerability of which had led to the long search for another way to base the MX in the first place. Some commission members believed that the shell-game shelter system still made the most sense, but this was, of course, unacceptable to the White House. The report talked vaguely of some "impressive" possibilities for hardening the silos. The commission had considered suggesting that the missiles be protected by an anti-ballistic-missile system, but decided that it wasn't worth the fuss of suggesting the abrogation or renegotiation of the ABM treaty. To justify placing the MX in fixed silos, the commission dismissed the hypothetical "window of vulnerability"—the possibility that the Soviet Union could destroy all our land-based missiles in a single strike. The window of vulnerability had been a popular argument among critics of the SALT II treaty, including Reagan, and proponents of deploying the MX. It had always been a dubious proposition, resting on the assumption that the Soviets would, with perfect accuracy and timing, destroy all the land-based missiles at once, and that the United States would not respond to the Soviet attack in any way. Some people argued that the window was real; others that it might not be real but since there was a perception that it was it had to be treated as if it were. The commission described the MX as a transitional weapon, and recommended the deployment of Midgetman single-warhead missiles, and it stressed the importance of arms control. (The commission was not specific, but one thousand was the number generally under consideration.) In addition to recommending the deployment of the MX, the commission threw a sop to the Pentagon by giving Weinberger the leeway he had sought over whether the Midgetman would be proceeded with. The commission also couched its recommendations on arms control in terms that Pentagon officials would find useful. Having proposed proceeding with the MX, albeit in a vulnerable basing system, the commission offered a number of rationales, some of them quite imaginative. It said that deployment of the MX, since it would give the United States a hard-target kill capability, might induce the Soviet Union to negotiate and also to shift its land-based system to a force of single-warhead missiles. One of its more imaginative rationales was that the booster for the MX might come in handy for space shots. But the most important reason for deploying the MX, the commission said, was that we must demonstrate to our allies and our adversaries that we "have the will" to proceed. The Scowcroft report thus has its own internal logic when viewed in the universe in which the commission had to function; outside that universe, its logic was seriously questioned.

The critics' arguments ran along several lines. One was that the strongest argument for the MX missile had been that it was to be invulnerable, but now it was being placed in vulnerable, fixed silos, and since it would have ten warheads, rather than the Minuteman's three, it would be the most inviting of targets. (In fact, even though the MX was designed to fit a Minuteman silo, there are a number of technical problems involved in placing it there which have not been resolved.) This, then, it was argued, would lead to instability, because it would be a further inducement to the United States to launch the missile if it was believed that an attack was on the way—that is, to adopt a policy of "launch on warning," one of the most controversial areas of nuclear doctrine. The Scowcroft Commission did not pretend that the MX would be survivable in the basing mode it recommended. Therefore, the argument of the critics went, the Soviets would have to be more concerned than ever that the United States was moving toward a policy of a "first strike," and they would adjust their policy accordingly, and the world would be on more of a hair trigger than ever. Moreover, since the MX would have hard-target kill capability its primary utility would be as a first-strike weapon. Since the Soviet Union has a far higher proportion of its nuclear missiles on land than the United States has (about seventy-five per cent, as compared with about twenty-five per cent), the Soviet Union would have more to fear from a first strike. The Scowcroft Commission's theory was that a hundred MX missiles would not be seen as sufficient to give the United States an effective first-strike capability. The critics said that there was no way the Soviet Union could be certain that the United States would stop with a hundred

MX missiles, and that, in fact, once they were in production the pressure to deploy still more of them was likely to increase. Even some of those who ended up supporting the MX feared that a hundred of them, combined with other weapons, would give the United States a first-strike capability. Deterrence and stability, the critics of the Scowcroft Commission's report argue, have rested on each side's knowing that the other could not destroy its nuclear arsenal. It is, in fact, this thinking that lies behind the impetus to build single-warhead missiles, and thus the Scowcroft Commission is at philosophical odds with itself. Therefore, the MX is viewed by critics as "destabilizing," and as actually detracting from our national security.

It is also seen as yet another stepup in the arms race. One argument that was made for going ahead with the MX was that it would be a "bargaining chip," but what was meant by this was vague, and subject to various interpretations. Sometimes it was said that a decision to deploy the MX would "force the Soviet Union to come to the bargaining table," but that overlooked the fact that the Soviet Union was already there. (Reagan, when he announced his approval of the commission report, said, "Unless we modernize our land-based missile systems, the Soviet Union will have no real reason to negotiate meaningful reductions.") Sometimes it was suggested that the MX would force the Soviet Union to give up something important, such as some of its own heavy missiles, but both Weinberger and Thomas Reed stated that the United States had no intention of not going ahead with the MX. In mid-May, Weinberger said on ABC's *Good Morning America*, "The question is not whether or not it's a bargaining chip. Nobody ever suggested that it was a bargaining chip. It's part of our necessary modernization." Reed said, "A bargaining chip is what we'll do if the Soviets don't come to the table." The understood implication was that the Administration would build the MX and then threaten to build more. The whole discussion was marked by more than a little confusion as to what a bargaining chip is: somehow the idea has developed that if the United States decides to go ahead with a certain weapon the Soviet Union will implore us not to do so and will offer to give up in return something it already has. In fact, this has never happened. (The MIRV and the cruise were "bargaining chips.") Proponents of the bargaining-chip theory argue that the ABM treaty is an example of its working, but others who have studied the ABM negotiations say that the treaty was reached because neither side was actually very keen on going ahead with an ABM system and the Nixon Administration knew that the backing for the ABM in Congress was shaky. They say that it was the very willingness of the United States to give up the ABM that made reaching an agreement possible. Opponents of the MX argue that the most likely Soviet response to deployment of an MX is deployment of a similar missile of its own, which is now in the testing stage, and is therefore farther along than the MX is. (While the Soviets do have large, heavy missiles, theirs are propelled by liquid fuel, which makes them harder to maintain; the MX, like the Minuteman, relies on solid fuel.) As for the argument that the MX might be an inducement to the Soviets to bargain seriously, MX opponents say that other "improvements" in our arsenal, either recently made or under way, provide a sufficient inducement. They cite the building of the B-1 bomber and the development of the Stealth; the equipping of Minuteman missiles with a more accurate and powerful warhead (the Mark 12A); developing new submarine-launched ballistic missiles (the Trident IIs, or D-5s), which will also be more accurate and powerful—capable, in fact, of destroying hard targets; and the deployment of cruise missiles, which also can destroy hard targets. A more subtle argument made by the Scowcroft Commission and its supporters in Congress is that the MX will give the United States "leverage" over the Soviet Union, by forcing it to reconfigure its strategic forces in a way that puts less reliance on large land-based missiles. The critics' response to this is that the other new weapons coming on line are sufficient to encourage such a change.

When I asked Woolsey about the criticism that the commission report seemed self-contradictory, he replied, "The report seeks to compromise a bunch of views and accepts partially a number of arguments, so I'm not surprised that that appears to be the case. It's an effort to put together several pieces of the puzzle, and an attempt to say that people who have talked about strategic weapons in different ways each in part have some legitimacy in what they're saying."

Some of the commissioners' and others' testimony about the new recommendations showed how shaky the proposition was. Scowcroft and Brown admitted that the new basing system was driven more by political than by military considerations, and that a "shell game" would have been preferable. "I think we are facing a situation where we have to proceed from where we are now," Brown said. "I think there is no way to go back." The testimony of Weinberger and of the Joint Chiefs of Staff elicited that a shell-game system would provide more survivability for the new missiles and, furthermore, that the United States might be moving to a policy of "launch under attack." The situation prompted Senator John Tower, Republican of Texas and Chairman of the Armed Services Committee, to say, "If anything, the MX program is a textbook case of how not to manage an important national-security issue."

And there was an abundance of past testimony on the part of the Scowcroft Commission's defenders (and even some of its authors) that suggested the degree to which they had either changed their minds or accommodated the new political realities. Much of this testimony was given when Congress was considering the President's short-lived plan, announced in October, 1981, to place the MX in existing silos.

Weinberger: "I would feel that simply putting it into existing silos would not answer two or three of the concerns that I have: namely, that [the location of] these are well known and are not hardened sufficiently, nor could they be, to be of sufficient strategic value to count as a strategic improvement of our forces."

Jackson: "My main criticism—and I criticized the Carter Administration—is that in the nineteen-eighties Minuteman and Titan are vulnerable in those silos. . . . We have given the Soviets a better target to shoot at."

Perry: "My concern is that if we had this very accurate, very threatening missile in unprotected silos, and if they do not go to a survivable system themselves . . . that simply increases the hair trigger . . . on both sides. . . . I agonized over that and said on balance I would not go ahead with that because I don't believe we will come up with a survivable basing mode that is acceptable."

Woolsey wrote: "The Administration's decision to deploy MX in existing silos, hardened or not, provides little more than a fig leaf, and that, at best, for only a short time."

Brown: "The October 2 decision adopts an admittedly very vulnerable basing system. . . . There is talk of further hardening of existing silos for a much-truncated MX force, but since the MX will not be available until 1986, that further hardening, if it is at all feasible, will not be available before the Soviets can install a new generation of guidance systems. The Soviets, using technology that they have already developed, will surely be able by that time to improve the accuracy of their ICBMs further, so that in the case of a nuclear war the hardened MX silos will find themselves in the fireball and in the crater left by the nuclear explosion of Soviet warheads; the silos would not survive such an experience."

The sendoff of the Scowcroft report was a carefully staged affair, with thought having been given to just what various key figures would say, and also to the timing of the release. Aspin was of the view that it was very important that no one seem overly pleased with the report, so that neither Congress nor the Pentagon would be leery of it. He says that he advised Weinberger ahead of time not to appear too cheerful about the report: "I said to Cap and others, 'Don't crow when this comes out; we need you to grouse. Say this isn't very good, but, etc., etc.' " On April 19th, when the President announced his approval of the report, Aspin did his bit by agreeing to a request by White House officials that he go out on the White House lawn to make a statement to the press. Aspin says, "I went out on the White House lawn and said that the report's not great, but it's probably the best we can get." Weinberger told a congressional hearing, "No one is saying this is a perfect solution." When the report was released, Harold Brown, for his part, said that the "proposals deserve bipartisan support even though they are not ideal and do not provide an immediate solution to the problem of ICBM vulnerability." He also said he made his recommendation "with an appreciation that more politically astute decisions in the past could well have produced a better solution." Brown, along with Scowcroft, also made a number of television appearances on behalf of the report. To have Harold Brown, the brilliant scientist and former Democratic Secretary of Defense, championing the report was critical to giving it the needed bipartisan aura and to making it acceptable for Democrats to support it. Brown and Woolsey were also important salesmen on Capitol Hill. According to some Democrats, Woolsey told them privately that Reagan might be reelected for another term, and that backing him on the MX might be the best way to influence his arms-control policy. A Democratic aide says, "The disarming thing was you had people like Harold Brown saying privately, 'You're right—it's no more survivable than the Minuteman.' They give you that up front, and they also say that, working on the assumption we're not going to launch on warning, it gives you only marginal strategic value. But they say we're not talking about much military value—that it's a test of this nation to make and implement a decision that the Soviets do not want to see made and implemented." He adds, "The way you succeed in getting a program like this through is you define it as narrowly as possible from a military point of view and as widely as possible from a symbolic point of view." Another Democratic aide says, "Without the Scowcroft Commission, we'd never have the MX. If Weinberger had said he wanted to put the MX in Minuteman silos, he'd have been laughed off the Hill. But you had Brent Scowcroft and Harold Brown—who advise Democrats—saying it, and you had a bipartisan commission of genuine experts. It was a beautiful move."

Aspin had also advised the White House that the MX should not be the first defense issue before the Congress this year. Aspin's thinking was, he says, "everyone was looking to cut money for defense; if the Scowcroft report was up first it would sink. We had a vote on the budget resolution, and people could vote to cut the defense budget there, and the Senate vote on Adelman"— Kenneth Adelman, whom Reagan had nominated to replace Eugene Rostow as director of the Arms Control and Disarmament Agency—"and all the doves could vote against him, and the House could vote on the freeze." And then Aspin pointed out a great truth about congressional behavior: "I said people will then have voted three dove votes. The usual pattern of this place is that people begin to get a little uncomfortable if they've gone too far one way and start looking for a way to pop back the other way." Aspin says that he gave this advice to Scowcroft, to people in the Pentagon, and to Reed. As a result, he says, there was an intentional delay in getting the Scowcroft report to the President and another delay before the President made his recommendation to Congress and the forty-five-day approval period stipulated by the resolution adopted last December began to run. Says Aspin, "We wanted it to come up a little bit after the freeze vote."

The legislating of a call for the President to negotiate a bilateral freeze on the testing, production, and deployment of new nuclear-

weapons systems was more difficult than its sponsors had anticipated, and this affected the politics of the MX. The freeze idea
turned out to be more viable as a political expression than as a
piece of legislation. When the freeze resolution came before the
House, its sponsors had difficulty answering hard questions about
how, exactly, it would work. Even some legislators who are arms-
control liberals were troubled by efforts to translate the freeze
idea into law: either it had to be amorphous or it had to dictate to
the President the specific terms of an agreement he must reach.
Moreover, there was the question of whether it was preferable for
the President to be involved in inevitably lengthy negotiations over
the terms of a freeze or to get on with arms-reduction talks. Members of the House who are careful students of arms control were
bothered by these questions, but, given the political strength of
the freeze movement, and being confronted with the question of
whether they wanted to "send a message" to the President on arms
control, they went along. The House freeze debate dragged on for
seven weeks, and in the end, after much amending, the House on
May 4th approved a freeze resolution that could be interpreted in
several ways. And, just as Aspin had predicted, a number of people who had supported the freeze were eager to cast a vote that
would blur the picture and protect them from the charge of being
"unilateral disarmers." The vote on the MX gave them a chance to
do that. Many members of Congress prefer not to take difficult
positions, and go to great lengths to avoid doing so. They like to
find the opportunity to vote one way and then another on controversial questions—to fuzz things over. The fact that it might seem
inconsistent to vote for a freeze on nuclear weapons and then vote
to develop the MX actually played into the hands of those who
wished to cover themselves politically. An aide to the House leadership said to me, "The MX provides the first opportunity for that
group to try to recast the attitudes about them and explain what
they think the vote on the nuclear freeze means—and interpret it
somewhat differently from the way the others have." Another
House Democratic aide said, "These are people who had doubts
about the freeze. They aren't doves who became hawks; they went
with the freeze and then wanted to get back to the center."

Meanwhile, Aspin, through a series of meetings on the Hill, some
of them in Foley's office, had put together a group of moderate

House Democrats who were prepared to support the MX, but some of them wanted something to show for their support—an indication that they had wrung concessions from the Administration. The principal members of Aspin's group were Foley; Gore; Norman Dicks, of Washington; Vic Fazio, of California; Dan Glickman, of Kansas; and Richard Gephardt, of Missouri. These were youngish members with reputations for legislative ability. This group's backing of the MX would provide protective cover for other Democrats—and also some moderate Republicans—who wanted, for whatever reasons, to support it. The issue that was put to others in these meetings was not whether the MX was a good idea but, as one participant recalls, "We've got this overture from these guys from the Scowcroft Commission; they're reaching out to us. Do you think it's do-able to put together a core group of people to avoid the political disaster of a Donnybrook over the MX?" Eventually, Jim Wright, of Texas, the House Majority Leader; Bill Alexander, of Arkansas, the Chief Deputy Whip; and Gillis Long, the chairman of the Democratic Caucus, all supported the MX. Thus, O'Neill became the only member of the leadership not to do so. Aspin had approached other relatively junior members with good credentials among their colleagues, but two of the most important of these—Thomas Downey, of New York, and Les AuCoin, of Oregon—turned him down, and helped lead the fight against the MX. Of all of Aspin's group, the two who, besides Aspin, played the most important roles were Gore and Dicks. The challenge for them, as for the Administration, was to find a way to define a vote for the MX as a vote for the "package" recommended by the Scowcroft report: the MX, the Midgetman, and a new push for arms control. The problem was that the resolution that had been drafted by the previous Congress didn't allow for any package. But the package, everyone understood, was the only thing that could get the House to approve the MX. Aspin and Foley had attended some strategy sessions at the White House— along with House Republican leaders, White House aides, and Weinberger—to try to figure out a way to transform the resolution into a package, and had concluded that there wasn't any. They decided, says Aspin, "to go with the straight resolution and, through a lot of fireworks, make it a vote on the Scowcroft package."

There ensued an elaborate quadrille, involving an exchange of

letters among some key legislators and the President, in which the
President gave the public assurances that the legislators felt they
needed in order to support the MX. These things don't just happen, of course. The Administration was well aware that the letters
were coming, and the legislators as well as Administration officals
were involved in drafting what became the President's response.
The exchange would work to everyone's benefit: the President
would draw these people into a commitment to support the MX,
and these people would have something to show for their support.
How much they actually got is the subject of some questioning, not
only among their colleagues but also among themselves.

Gore was especially anxious to nail down a Presidential commitment to proceed with the development of the Midgetman missile,
and the President—or the Administration—was anxious to nail
down Gore's vote for the MX. Gore, who is thirty-five, is a large,
dark-haired, solemn man who, like Aspin, was tagged "a comer"
as soon as he was elected to Congress. He is now planning to run
in 1984 for the Senate seat being vacated by Majority Leader
Howard Baker. It is difficult for a young House member to get
much notice, but Gore chose one of the the surer routes: he
picked a few good issues, worked hard at them, and methodically
made a name for himself. The single-warhead missile was one of
his issues. He made speeches about it, wrote articles about it, made
contact with journalists about it, and eventually, as the idea came
into fashion, he more than anybody else in public life was identified with it. In a conversation we had in his office on May 23rd, the
day before the House was to vote on whether to release funds for
the MX, Gore said of his meetings with the Scowcroft Commission, "I told them, 'If you come back with another fancy hardware
scheme, you can forget it; this thing is gone.' The only way you can
have a dialogue with Congress and get a consensus approach is to
address the over-all strategic context within which this missile is to
play a role, and to address the goal of stability." Gore also met with
every member of the Administration he could, and with the Administration's arms negotiators, pressing his views upon them, and
he pressed them upon his colleagues. He recognized that without
arms control the value of the single-warhead missile would be
sharply diminished, because one side could simply keep deploying missiles until it had a sufficient number to knock the other
side's out.

A number of people think that there will be second thoughts about the Midgetman missiles. Not only are there unresolved technical questions about how to deploy them, and questions about whether they should be made mobile (Gore says they do not have to be, but the Scowcroft Commission suggests that there would be advantages in doing so), but questions about their cost. The Congressional Budget Office has estimated that they could cost more than a hundred billion dollars over twenty years, and require fifty thousand people to man and maintain them. There will be questions about where to deploy them. (There has been talk of their being deployed on trucks, perhaps disguised as moving vans, but this would require a flotilla of trucks, carrying power generators and people to maintain the missile; there is talk of placing them in hard silos, which have yet to be developed, and placing them in a mobile basing mode in the ground—but that gets back to the race track.) One defense expert points out that not only have the Soviets tested a single-warhead missile but they also have far more territory to deploy single-warhead missiles in. "I don't think people have noticed that yet," he says. A number of people, including Scowcroft, realize that mobile single-warhead missiles will be harder to count than fixed launchers are. One defense expert says, "Wait till the hard-liners get started. They'll say the Soviets have a missile in every garage; they'll say prove they don't have that. We've been through that before. That's what the missile gap was about." He concluded, as did some others I talked to, that if the Midgetman is deployed, at some future time arms controllers may look back and wonder why they thought it was such a good idea.

Gore, like a lot of other people, was concerned about the Administration's attitude toward arms control. Gore told me on the day before the vote, "We could end up with people saying that the moderates in Congress have had the rug pulled out from under them." The worry was that, whatever the President said about his desire for reaching an arms-control agreement with the Soviet Union, and no matter how sincere he may be in this, his own bureaucracy would prevent one from occurring. In the strategic-arms-reduction talks, or START, the President had begun with what was widely recognized as a non-negotiable position. In effect, it asked the Soviet Union to give up a great deal in the area of its greatest advantage, the large land-based missiles, without the

United States' making equivalent concessions. Moreover, there were other terms of the proposed agreement that appeared to make reaching an agreement impossible. And it was by now widely understood in Washington that though these were just opening positions, the greatest resistance to changing them was coming from the Pentagon, and that probably the most important person on arms control in the Administration was not the President, not Secretary of State George Shultz, not Clark, not even Weinberger, but Richard Perle, the Assistant Secretary of Defense for International Security Policy. Perle, more than anyone else, has been the architect of the Administration's arms-control positions thus far, and he is one of the smartest, most persistent, most bureaucratically skilled members of this Administration or any other in memory. Perle, who is forty-one, worked for Jackson for many years, and helped him oppose or defeat every arms-control agreement that came along. Perle is an utterly pleasant man, of medium build and dark complexion, with a soothing voice and a public style of reasonableness. He says things that sound totally reasonable until they are examined further. A Capitol Hill aide who has worked on defense matters says, "He uses words like 'Shouldn't we be equal?' and you say yes and then you find out he's using those words to prevent an agreement that would be reasonable and balanced." Perle is knowledgeable, clever, and formidable: a number of officials of several Administrations have had their careers derailed by Perle and his allies. He expresses woundedness at any suggestion that he is less than sincere about reaching an arms-control agreement, but the plain fact is that many people believe that he does not want one, or that the only kind he would find acceptable is not negotiable, which amounts to about the same thing. And those people are also aware that, whatever the President says, Perle is in a good position to put sand in the gears.

These people are also worried about Edward Rowny, the retired Army lieutenant-general who heads the American delegation to the START talks. During the Nixon and Ford Administrations, Rowny was understood to have provided a "back channel" from the arms-control talks to Perle and Jackson; the Carter Administration nonetheless made him a member of its SALT team, under the illusion that he'd be helpful, and eventually Rowny resigned and denounced the SALT II agreement. And they are not impressed with Adelman, whom they consider too inexperienced and insufficiently independent of the other policymakers.

Perle had his own meetings with the Scowcroft Commission members—he and Woolsey are old associates—and in a recent conversation he told me that he was quite satisfied with the commission's report. He said that there were some widespread misconceptions about what the commission actually said. It was not correct, Perle said, "that Scowcroft has discounted or dismissed the window of vulnerability." He said it was also wrong to believe that the commission was "calling for a fundamental change in our arms-control policy—I can't find that anywhere." And he found the commission's endorsement of the MX "quite broad and deep." Whatever certain members of Congress may believe, Perle conceded that the Midgetman was not yet part of the Administration's strategic policy. On arms control, Perle finds an endorsement of his own approach in the commission's recommendation that arms-control limitations and reductions be couched "in terms of equal levels of warheads of roughly equivalent yield," rather than in terms of the number of launchers each side has. This gets to the heart of one of the key issues about arms-control policy—one over which the Administration itself has been deeply divided, and one in which the moderate Democrats who supported the MX got themselves, to their great discomfort, involved. The Scowcroft recommendation was made in the context of "the long run," and of encouraging both sides to move toward the deployment of small, single-warhead missiles. But at the moment both sides have multiple-warhead missiles, and the commission did endorse the deployment of the MX. What Perle has been seeking over the years is an accord that reduces the Soviet advantage in "throw-weight"—the lifting power of its missiles—while arms-control agreements negotiated by Nixon, Ford, and Carter have accepted the idea of offsetting this Soviet advantage by limiting the number of warheads allowed on each missile, and relying on the United States' advantages in submarines and bombers. (The Ford negotiations at Vladivostok were never completed, because of the opposition stirred up back home by Jackson and Perle and because Ford was facing a nomination challenge by Reagan.) An arms-control proposal that called for equal throw-weight for the United States and the Soviet Union—which Perle was seeking—would be calling for a radical reconfiguration of the Soviet forces and has been widely considered non-negotiable. Perle also found other grounds for objecting to the Vladivostok approach, and to the SALT II agreement, and he is expected to inject a number of issues into the Administration's arms-control deliberations. The concept of counting not launchers, as the two SALT agreements did, but warheads has a certain plausibility, until one gets down to the details. The SALT agreements counted launchers because there was no sure way to count warheads. (Actually, SALT II indirectly counted warheads, by assuming that each missile contained the maximum number it could carry; and it indirectly limited warheads by limiting the number each missile could hold.) The problem with simply counting warheads is that it runs into questions of verification (Perle would prefer the sort of intrusive verification that it is widely presumed would not be acceptable to the Soviets, and perhaps not to the United States military) and of rules for counting (how to count spares, and so on). There is also the real problem of how to verify the numbers of the single-warhead missile and the cruise. Perle has been engaged in a long-running battle with State Department officials, whom he accuses of pushing Reagan back toward the SALT concept; the State Department officials' reasoning is that the SALT process settled a number of questions about definitions and rules for counting, and so on, and that going this route would therefore make reaching an agreement easier. The Scowcroft Commission, containing as it did officials of the Carter Administration, also had kind words for the SALT II approach. (On June 8th, the President announced a change in the Administration's START position, but the only stated difference was an increase in the proposed limit on launchers from eight hundred and fifty to an undetermined number. Supporters of Midgetman thought that that was to accommodate their idea, but there were other possibilities: the original number was generally agreed to have been too low in proportion to the number of warheads that were to be permitted—five thousand— and thus could put each side's launchers at risk. Moreover, the proposed increase could also be explained by the fact that the Air Force had been assuming that it would have two hundred MX missiles, and if there were to be fewer of them more launchers would be needed to achieve the same number of warheads. The new proposal still sought to have the Soviet Union give up much of its advantage in land-based missiles. In essence, it left throw-weight to be limited by indirect means—by limiting what it could be used for—which is what the Administration position has been all along. Earlier, a direct limit on throw-weights was something to be done at a second stage, and Perle had been trying to make this an immediate demand. The battle within the Administration was by no means over. There remained many skirmishes over the details of the proposals, and the instructions to the negotiators, and it is in these seemingly small details that arms-control policy is made. The President's announcement was accompanied by soothing rhetoric about "flexibility" and "stability." Gore found this reassuring; Aspin and Dicks seemed less certain.) By drawing them in, the President was paving the way not only to getting the MX but to claiming that his arms-control policy was "bipartisan."

Albert Gore and his colleagues were aware of the argument going on within the Administration, and were determined to influence its outcome. On Monday, May 23rd, Aspin arranged for Perle to meet for lunch in the Capitol with a group including Gore, Dicks, Foley, Fazio, Glickman, and himself to discuss strategy for the House floor debate that began that day. Gore took the opportunity to warn Perle that if the Administration's new START position, then under review within the Administration, was seen to be excessively rigid and non-negotiable, the result could be the defeat of the MX. And he told Perle that his position on throw-weight would be seen as excessively hard-line. Gore told me later that afternoon that he saw congressional approval of the MX as "a step-by-step approach"—that Congress would have further opportunities later to deny funds for the weapon. He said, "We say if they don't seem sincere in their proposals, then the MX won't be approved." Thus, the moderate Democrats who agreed to go along with the MX injected themselves into the Administration's policymaking on arms control, and, in effect, took responsibility for it.

In their letter to the President, which was drafted by Gore and sent on May 2nd, the House Democratic moderates—who were joined by Joel Pritchard, a moderate Republican from Washington—praised the President for his endorsement of the Scowcroft report but asked for assurances that proceeding with the MX would be consistent with the goal of reaching stability, and that "a major effort will be promptly undertaken to bring sharper focus to the proposed single-warhead ICBM, and to allay concerns that it cannot be realized in a reasonable period of time." Many people on Capitol Hill were concerned that the Air Force would delay development of the Midgetman so as to assure the deployment of the MX, just as it was believed to be delaying the development of the Stealth bomber so that the B-1 could be deployed. (Scowcroft himself told a group of congressmen that "the Defense Department is a little like a glacier. It has been moving down the big ICBM road for a long time; there is no great love for the small missile in large elements both of my former service and [the office] of the Secretary.") The congressmen also stipulated in their letter that a decision on their part to approve the development and flight-testing of the MX would be distinct from approval to procure or deploy it. Many members of Congress believed, however, that once the contracts to develop the MX were let, and the production lines were open, the constituency for the MX would have expanded—labor was already supporting it—and it would become all the more difficult to terminate. "This is *the* vote on the MX," Thomas Downey said to me. Moreover, it was expected that the Air Force would begin to talk about the costliness of the Midgetman. The House Democratic moderates also requested a continuation of the Scowcroft Commission, or something like it; this would, the theory went, serve as a conduit to the Administration, and at once act as a prod to the Administration and provide political protection for those who continued to support the MX. Leaving aside the fact that the Scowcroft Commission does not represent the spectrum of views even among defense "experts," and that a number of its members displayed a certain pliability, the idea of a continuing commission along these lines is a strange one and, to many minds, a bad one. It injects into the policymaking process a body with no real authority. But a continuing commission was a convenient out for some people in a tight spot, and an improvisation that could prove a very poor precedent. (The President on June 8th told the congressmen that the Scowcroft Commission, or something like it, would continue for a while, but not for the two-year period, into 1985, the congressmen wanted.)

The President's letter of response, sent on May 11th, had a number of authors, including Gore, and its terms were negotiated between the members of Aspin's group—Gore and Dicks in particular—and the Administration. At the Administration end, Perle and other Administration officials as well as the White House staff were involved in composing the response. The President stated that he was reviewing his START proposals with a view to integrating the Scowcroft Commission recommendations—actually, the

START proposals were under review anyway—and he made some pledges whose firmness depended on who was doing the interpreting. The President's letter found in the Scowcroft report approval of deployment of the Peacekeeper—he said nothing about making it a bargaining chip or a transitional weapon, or about step-by-step decisions on whether to deploy it—together with the single-warhead missile. He assured the legislators that the United States did not seek a first-strike capability. His pledge to assure deployment of the Midgetman—"We will promptly undertake a major effort to bring the proposal of a small, single-warhead ICBM to fruition on a high priority basis"—does not appear to be everything the Midgetman's backers desired, but Gore said he saw this as a commitment to proceed with the missile. Gore also took pride in a change he was able to get in a sentence that was added to the President's letter at the last minute by the Pentagon. The Pentagon's sentence said, "As you know, the Scowcroft Commission noted that the central elements of our START proposal are consistent with and supportive of the Commission's findings." Gore was pleased that he was able to get the words "the central" deleted.

I asked Gore if he would support the MX by itself.

"It's not that simple," he replied. "I voted against it before there was a Scowcroft Commission because it was presented in isolation. It did not exist within a strategic context that encompassed an arms-control approach and a sensitive weapons-procurement plan. Its role in that context is as a transition toward a more stable relationship between the United States and the Soviet Union."

A number of Gore's and Dicks' Democratic colleagues derided the President's letter as vague and meaningless. One of them said to me, not for attribution, that he didn't think even the letter's recipients believed the letter said anything. Barney Frank, Democrat of Massachusetts, said, "It's the kind of letter we send to people: 'Thank you for your good suggestion. I find it very interesting, and I'll look into it.' " One Democrat wondered aloud whether getting a pledge, if that's what it was, from the President to build a thousand small missiles if he was permitted to build a hundred large ones with ten warheads each was really such a good bargain. A number of Democrats said that their colleagues had obtained the letter from Reagan simply to "have something to wave" when they explained their vote.

A House Democrat told me, "They got pantsed. It's so embarrassing." Gore was aware of the views of some of his colleagues about the letter. "A lot of people looked at the language in the letter and concluded we'd been snookered," Gore told me. "But the language was carefully drafted to move the President down the arms-control path and to achieve a sensible result. Whether or not we have succeeded remains to be seen. It's a big chance we're taking."

I asked him to describe the nature of the chance.

He shifted in his chair, and said, "That the Administration is really not serious. I believe they are, but I'm not certain they are." He paused, and continued, "I believe they are—I really do. But I'm concerned that the Office of the Secretary of Defense—Weinberger and his group—could eventually win out. I don't think they will. I don't think they will. But there is that chance. If it occurs, then I think the MX will be killed and the opportunity to construct a consensus on strategic policy will be lost, for quite a while."

Dicks betrayed a similar nervousness when I talked with him later that afternoon, just off the House floor. Dicks, who is forty-two, is a large, beefy man with curly dark-blond hair; he is a former football star, and remains highly competitive, even as members of Congress go. He used to work for former Senator Warren Magnuson, of Washington, and reflects his state's pro-defense politics. He is a member of the Defense Appropriations Subcommittee and from that position looks after the contractors in his state. Like Gore, Dicks worked to get the freeze resolution modified before it came to the House floor, but, unlike Gore, he played a major role in supporting the freeze during the House debate. Dicks' active backing of the freeze resolution was an uncharacteristic position for him to take, and afterward he remarked to one of his colleagues, "I'm getting identified as a freezie and I've got to get back." In our talk off the House floor, Dicks, looking quite uncomfortable, said to me, "We're taking this thing very seriously. We see a major responsibility to our colleagues—the moderates who are supporting the MX—to impress upon the Administration the necessity of having a credible arms policy in START." Dicks, like Gore, had met in recent days with Kenneth Dam, the Deputy Secretary of State, and he was shortly to meet again with Perle. (Shultz, who was supposed to take charge of arms-control policy when Rostow was fired, had been travelling in the Middle East and was otherwise engaged.) "Many of our colleagues don't trust some of these people," Dicks said.

I asked him if he did.

He replied, "I'm going to put it this way. I think the President wants an arms agreement. My problem is with the people who have historically opposed arms control. When you talk to them, they say their problem is that the agreements have legitimized the arms race"—this is what Perle says. "They don't share the same level of confidence that we have in arms control," Dicks continued. "If we kill the MX unilaterally, the Soviets won't give us anything. In contrast to what some of my colleagues think, I think it will have a very great effect on the Soviet Union if we kill the MX. If it senses that the President doesn't have the support of the Congress, how can we get an arms-control agreement—particularly one that gets at the Soviet superiority in land-based missiles?" Dicks went on to say that he believed that the Administration's arms-control opening position for the negotiations was "a nonstarter." Dicks, like Gore, emphasized the step-by-step nature of his approval of the MX. He and Gore and Aspin planned to add to the defense-authorization bill, which would be coming up later and would authorize money for procurement of the MX, amendments that would tie deployment of the MX to development of the Midgetman. After that, they point out, there would be the defense-appropriations bill, and another opportunity to "hold the Administration's feet to the fire." Dicks said, "We have said that if they change their mind we reserve the right to change ours. We see our responsibility as not ending with this resolution, or with the authorization bill."

I asked Dicks if he thought his group had forced a change in the Administration's attitude toward arms control.

He replied, "I think the President has a definite change of attitude." As for the rest of the Administration, he said, "I think we have made some progress in that area. I'd be hard pressed to quantify it. I want to see changes take place. Until then, I won't be comfortable. I'm not comfortable now."

One complication for those House Democrats who were corresponding with Reagan was that Reagan was also engaged in correspondence with some senators, and the assurances he gave them appeared to be in contradiction to the assurances he gave the House members. On the Senate side, the fashionable new idea was for something that came to be called a "build-down." Essentially, the idea was that for every new warhead each nation deployed, two would have to be retired. The idea had an appealing simplicity—until it was examined closely. It had been taken up by William Cohen, Republican of Maine, and Sam Nunn, Democrat of Georgia, both of them defense conservatives but not all-out hawks, and both of them up for reelection in 1984. Cohen and Nunn had opposed the MX in its Dense Pack formation, and had also opposed placing it in fixed silos. Now they were prepared to support the MX in fixed silos, but they wanted something, or the appearance of something, in return. Early this year, they had introduced a resolution calling for the President to negotiate a build-down, and offered it as an alternative to the freeze; in short order, the resolution had forty-three co-sponsors. There were obvious flaws in the proposal. It assumed that fewer warheads would necessarily be more stabilizing than more of them. It did not take into account that the new warheads might be in weapons that were more destabilizing than the ones that were being removed, and that therefore fewer weapons per se did not necessarily guarantee more stability. (Richard Perle likes to point out that there are eight thousand fewer warheads deployed than there were in 1967. The reduction is a result of a steady process of retiring old warheads as the forces were modernized. Perle says, "Ironically, it's been roughly a two-for-one build-down.") A world in which the two superpowers held few but more destabilizing weapons could be the most dangerous of all. The theory behind the Midgetman, by contrast, was to achieve stability. Moreover, the resolution did not make distinctions between the sizes of warheads. It did not discourage the deployment of MIRVed weapons. It did not begin to suggest how the warheads would be counted or verified. But the senators overlooked all these problems as they rushed to sign their names to the resolution, and the President called Cohen to commend him on his good idea. Cohen, Nunn, and Charles Percy, Republican of Illinois and chairman of the Senate Foreign Relations Committee, also wrote to the President, at about the same time the House members did, and they raised similar concerns, and also asked for a commitment to a build-down. The President responded with a letter that was identical to the one he sent the House members except that it added a multi-hedged promise to study the build-down idea. (The Administration had at first planned to send both sides the same letter, which would have included reasons that he thought the build-down was a bad idea. The House members, who were protective of their own good idea, were happy enough to agree to such a letter, but the senators, understandably, were not.) So the President was bowing in the direction of both deploying more missiles (the Midgetman) in the name of stability and removing more warheads (the build-down) at the same time that he was seeking to deploy one thousand warheads on one hundred MX missiles. But under the build-down, literally applied, if a hundred MX missiles were deployed this would require removal of two thousand warheads, or roughly the entire Minuteman force; otherwise, warheads would have to be removed from submarines or bombers, which are less vulnerable. If a thousand Midgetmen were also deployed, still more submarine and bomber missiles would have to be retired. As the President was preparing to respond to the senators, Perle told reporters that the Administration was "trying to find a way to extract what is positive from that [build-down] proposal without binding our modernization program beyond what is reasonable." After Nunn received the President's letter, he told reporters, "We are satisfied the President has endorsed build-down as part of arms negotiations with the Soviets." Senator Dale Bumpers, Democrat of Arkansas, characterized the senators' letter to Reagan asking him to affirm his commitment to arms control as a plea to "say it like you mean it," and Reagan's response as meaningless. Given that the subject was changes in the Administration's strategic policies, these exchanges of letters occurred with remarkable speed. At the time, I asked one high Administration official how it could be that the policy implications of the letters had been "staffed out" by the Administration. He replied, "They weren't."

I asked Nunn what he thought he had extracted from the President.

He replied, "I think they've agreed to the concept of a build-down—that there is a price to be paid for modernization, in reduced warheads. They haven't fleshed out the details. I haven't insisted on details. I'm working on it, and know the Administration is doing some thinking about this. I'll be doing a lot of thinking, and so will Cohen and others." Nunn said he realized, of course, that "the paradox is that the MX is destabilizing, of which we want less."

A few days after the President sent his letters to Capitol Hill, Weinberger, in his appearance on *Good Morning America*, was asked if the letters signalled any new bargaining position on the part of the President. He replied, "Well, I don't really understand, and never have understood, what it is additionally that is wanted from the President. The President has been the leading advocate of arms reduction, drastic arms reductions, down to the point of equality and that would be fully verifiable from the beginning. And he has reiterated that. And that is exactly the position he's always had." The moderates who were prepared to support the MX were unnerved.

At Dicks' suggestion, the President invited twenty-five moderate House members who were either committed to voting for the MX or undecided to dinner at the White House on the night before the House was to vote. According to some who were there, it was not an altogether successful event. The President, the Vice-President, and the Secretaries of State and Defense were scattered among the tables, as were the members of the Scowcroft Commission. The President called upon Scowcroft, who made what were described as incisive comments, and then he called upon George Shultz, who, one House member at the dinner said, "demonstrated once again that he hadn't had time to master the issue." Scowcroft and McFarlane quietly assured some worried House members that they had things in hand, that there was no need to be concerned about Shultz's comments. Then Gore asked the President to encourage those House members who were still undecided to support the MX. "I've been working with you," Gore said to the President, "but, frankly, some members of your Administration have been a little slow to grasp the internal logic of the new START position." He went on to say that the country has to turn away from a nuclear-war-fighting capability and eliminate the capability of both the United States and the Soviet Union to gain an advantage from a first strike. Gore told Reagan that he believed he was headed in the right direction, and would end up in the right place, and he urged him to reject those voices in his Administration who advocate equal throw-weight, because that would be considered non-negotiable in the Congress. Gore concluded by asking the President to state his views on the principles on which a new position on START should be based.

The President's response was less than reassuring. According to people who were there, Reagan talked for eight or nine minutes in a rambling fashion, and, according to one House member, "he didn't betray any understanding of what the principles involved were." When Reagan was asked about the build-down by Elliott Levitas, Democrat of Georgia, Reagan referred the question to Scowcroft. Levitas commented to a colleague the following day, "I almost wish I hadn't gone." Robert Matsui, Democrat of California, was so upset after the dinner that he called one of his colleagues to talk about it, and the next day he voted against the MX. One member who was for the MX told some of his colleagues privately that he had decided not to go to the White House dinner, because he didn't want to hear Reagan talk about arms control, for fear he would change his mind.

By the time the House voted on the MX, the opponents knew that they would be defeated. Their hope was to hold down the margin of defeat and to regroup for the next battle. They were hoping that when the House considered the defense-authorization bill it would accept an amendment to delete funds for the procurement of the MX and hold the commitment of funds to research and development.

The House debate on the resolution to release the funds for research and development and flight-testing of the MX had an edge to it that was unusual, and the bitterness showed in the members' conversations on and off the floor. Even the joking had a forced quality. The Democrats who were leading the fight for the MX and those who were leading the fight against it were old friends, who were accustomed either to working together or to disagreeing on an issue and shaking hands. But in this case there was a mistrust of motives and a resentment that all the efforts to show good fellowship could not erase. Downey said to me, "You have these good and decent men who are making decisions that are in my opinion a tragedy of the largest order." He continued, "This is not like a decision to approve the Tennessee-Tombigbee Dam. What you have here is a series of decisions that will lead both sides to adopt launch-on-warning policies, because both sides' weapons will be in jeopardy. This is another threshold decision in the arms race." Downey, a youthful-looking man of thirty-four, said wearily, "Some of these people were for the freeze, and now they're for the MX. It's the same old game: everyone seeks the middle ground. There isn't any." Downey has defense contractors in his district and used to serve on the Armed Services Committee, but he has found, he says, that he can take anti-defense-spending positions and explain them to his constituents. In the floor debate, Downey said, "Of the thirty-five or so homes that it had in the past, we have managed to find in our infinite wisdom the most dangerous and the most destabilizing," and continued, "Never has a more flawed weapons system meant so many different things to so many different people." He said, "Oh, you are dreaming, my colleagues, if you think that the MX is going to get you Midgetman. You are sadly, sadly mistaken." He mocked the build-down idea and rebutted the argument made by Aspin that the MX was the way to make the Soviets get serious about arms control. Downey said, "They come to the table because we threaten two hundred and sixty million Russians." He closed by reading from a recent speech by George Kennan: "What is needed here is only the will—the courage, the boldness, the affirmation of life—to break out of the evil spell that has been cast upon us, to declare our independence of the nightmares of nuclear danger, and to turn our minds and our hearts to better things."

Dicks and Gore, in their floor speeches, showed their uneasiness. Dicks agreed with a comment made by Pritchard that it was "a close call and a difficult one." Dicks said, "I want to say something to my friends who I know feel very opposed to the MX missile. I do not take this lightly." He said that his group feels that "we have not just a responsibility here today but an ongoing responsibility that we must convince Richard Perle and Richard Burt"—the Assistant Secretary of State for European Affairs— "and Caspar Weinberger that they must act in good faith with this Congress as well." Aspin intervened to explain why the MX was receiving more support than before: "This is a very different package. . . . It is a combination of an MX, a small missile, a new arms control. . . . This is not a single deal. This is not an agreed program that we all agree on or disagree on, and one vote here and that is the end of it. It has got to be an ongoing process." This was part of Aspin's effort to, as he had put it, throw some fireworks, to create the impression that the House was voting on "a package." Others tried to dismiss the idea that they were voting on a package.

Joseph Addabbo, Democrat of New York, and chairman of the Defense Appropriations Subcommittee, a stout man with a high-pitched voice, waved the single piece of paper containing the brief resolution in the air, crying, "There is no package in this resolution. . . . Do not kid yourselves. That is what you are voting for this afternoon—the procurement of MX missiles and the deployment of MX missiles."

"Mr. Chairman," Gore said. "This is not an easy vote. It is a very close question." And he said, "The truth of the matter is that those who look at it carefully will realize that whichever side wins, there is a likelihood that the winning side will regret the fact that they did win." Gore asked the House, "Do the opponents of this resolution *really* believe, do they *really* believe, that we are going to make arms-control agreement more likely if we eliminate this program? I'm not certain of the answer, but I cannot believe that they are that certain of the answer as well." Gore was correct; there was a great deal of uncertainty among many of the House members about the consequences of what they were doing that day. Gore issued a warning to the Administration: his vote for the MX was not a vote for procurement of the weapon. If there was not evidence of progress on the Administration's arms-control position between then and the voting on the authorization bill or the appropriations bill, Gore warned, he might not support the MX, or he might vote to scale down the number of missiles being approved. Gore had already told the Administration that when the authorization bill came before the House he would offer an amendment to reduce the number of MX missiles to be purchased, in part to make certain the United States did not obtain a first-strike capability. This would not delay the production schedule for the MX, so the Administration was not really opposed to the move.

After Gore spoke, Les AuCoin rose to make some unusually caustic remarks. "We're not dealing with a faucet here," he said. "There has been no strategic weapon that has ever reached this stage of funding that has ever been permanently cancelled." AuCoin continued, "I am amazed at those Democrats who have entered into this bargain with the Administration. . . . The President gets an MX missile, and the country gets a statement of sincerity about arms control. . . . If that is a bargain, all I can say is, to my colleagues on this side of the aisle who have entered into it, I am just pleased they are not negotiating with the Soviet Union."

The comments of some members off the floor were also harsh. James Shannon, Democrat of Massachusetts, said, "There are some guys around here who will take any position they need to take to become players on a big issue." He went on, "The driving force for a lot of guys here is not consistency but their profile on defense. You get a lot of Democrats worried about having looked 'weak' on defense in 1980 who feel that the pendulum has swung back but don't have confidence that that's going to last, and, having voted for the freeze, they want to cover their other front. And this process allows them to do it."

The House vote to release the funds for the MX was 239 to 186; the opponents lost by about twenty more votes than they had expected to. The next day, the Senate voted 59 to 39 to release the funds. Senate Minority Leader Robert Byrd, Democrat of West Virginia, was among those who supported the MX—a source of bitterness among Senate Democrats, since most of them opposed it. And Byrd had put Nunn in charge of a task force to formulate a Party policy on the MX for the Senate Democrats; under the circumstances, the task force never came up with a position. The Senate Democrats were, in fact, in disarray throughout the debate: some MX opponents had hoped to bring up a resolution after the vote on the MX—calling for a mutual United States–Soviet Union moratorium on flight-testing MX-type weapons—but they could never agree on exactly what to propose, and Majority Leader Howard Baker blocked their attempt, and so the Democrats gave up until after the Memorial Day recess. On the day after the Senate vote, nineteen Republicans wrote to Reagan warning that their vote to support the MX might be reversed later unless progress was made on arms control. One of them, Nancy Kassebaum, of Kansas, had told reporters that she had supported the MX because she was in trouble for her opposition to the Administration's policy in Central America.

The brave talk among members of both parties occurred in something of a vacuum. The President had not yet gone to work on the next votes. People who were warning that they might withhold their votes were not yet being presented with the inevitable arguments that they must not undermine the President's negotiating position. After the voting, there was some speculation that Aspin and his colleagues had in fact succeeded in gaining leverage over the Administration's arms-control policy through making their support of the MX conditional. But this view tended to underestimate the adeptness and determination of the Administration; in its work on this issue, it had demonstrated uncommon skill and political sophistication. It had played successfully on congressmen's sense of "responsibility," their vanity, and their fear. Some people who supported the MX might cast future votes to indicate to the Administration, and to their constituents, that they hadn't surrendered completely, but the odds were that in the long run, one way or another, there would be an MX. The very political calculations that had driven so many members to give Reagan what he wanted in this round suggested that that was the case.

On the night of the House vote, Aspin, appearing on the *CBS Evening News*, said, "If we don't give him this package, then comes November, 1984, the Democrats are running against him, and we say, 'You didn't produce an arms-control agreement,' and he turns around and says, 'Of course not. I could have gotten one, but you didn't give me the tools that I needed to get one.' "

I asked Leon Panetta, Democrat of California and a moderate who worked with Aspin last year on presenting a bipartisan budget to the House but who opposed the MX, what he thought of Aspin's political reasoning.

He replied, "From a substance point of view, that's a hell of a way to make decisions up here. If all we're going to do is worry about what the President is going to say, we might as well pack our bags. We have to make the argument to the public. If we decide everything that way, then we might as well give the President everything he wants. In terms of politics, we're not going to be able to mollify this guy. Historically, he's always come at us, and he will."

On the day after the House vote, Les AuCoin, a soft-spoken man, was still bitter, and his remarks in a conversation I had with him reflected the depth of the split within the Democratic Party. Referring to his comment on the House floor, he said, "I was thinking these clowns would give away the Midwest for a shoeshine and a smile. I think I spoke for a lot of mainstream Democrats who are very bitter. And what they're bitter about is the presumption on the part of members they had respected that somehow they could give Ronald Reagan religion on arms control. It's preposterous. And, even more, the idea that an Administration has to be bargained into sincerity about arms control—what kind of Administration is that, and what kind of bargain is it that relatively junior members of Congress can get them to say, 'Now we will be good'? Besides, there is no strategic system that has ever been funded that has ever been permanently cancelled. The fallacy is that Al Gore and Norm Dicks and Les Aspin, despite their obvious skill, are not strong enough to turn off the system when a massive missile like that develops an industrial and political constituency. It can't be done."

Some Democrats were obviously bitter because the moderates' action had increased their own political vulnerability on the MX. I asked AuCoin if it wasn't the case that some Democratic opponents of the MX were playing politics as well—that they were following what they believed to be anti-defense public sentiment. Some said the Democrats should oppose the MX to keep possession of the "peace issue." And a number of Democrats had said to me that they believed that "the people" were against the MX.

AuCoin pointed out that he was the first Democrat to be elected from his district, and that Reagan had carried it by a very large margin in 1980.

Then why, I asked, were so many Democrats afraid?

AuCoin replied, "I don't put a great deal of stock in the fear factor. There is a great tendency in this place to try to have it both ways. When you have a Ronald Reagan in league with a Les Aspin, then you find cover. That enables you to talk to conservatives and liberals. The safe, middle ground is less taxing, less of a chore."

Two days after the House vote, I had lunch with Aspin in the Members' Dining Room in the Capitol. He was, as usual, enthusiastic, but from time to time there was an unaccustomed note of hesitancy in his conversation. He said that he believed that the President had really come to accept the Scowcroft package but that he was less certain about the rest of the Administration. He said he was concerned that the Air Force might derail the deal: "The President might not be in office in 1985, and Weinberger won't be Secretary of Defense forever. But the Air Force goes on forever. Somehow, we have to figure out how to get them committed."

Aspin went on to say, "Where does this thing go from here? I don't know. This is an attempt at something I've never seen attempted before. We've seen deals put together by the executive and the legislature and by Democrats and Republicans, but it's always come together at one moment—a vote, a piece of legislation the President doesn't veto, and that's it. The Social Security reforms this year were one example; there are hundreds of them. But nothing like this—a deal that has to stick over ten years. If this new direction happens, we'll put a hundred MX missiles into the ground, starting in 1986; we'll begin to deploy some single-warhead missiles in the late nineteen-eighties or early nineteen-nineties, and we'll have an arms-control approach based on these two things coming into the arsenal. For all this to survive, you have to have the agreement of four or five Congresses down the line, and not just the President who is elected in 1984, who might be Reagan, but also the President who is elected in 1988, who is not going to be Reagan. So where it goes from here will be a very interesting story."

We talked about the political calculation he had made. "It became clear that the economy and the nuclear issue would be the two main issues in 1984," Aspin said. "It seemed to me that if Scowcroft came up with a bipartisan package and the President accepted that, the Democrats would not be in good shape if it was voted down. It was clear that most Democrats would vote against it. But if enough voted for it, and Reagan got it, the headline would say 'Reagan Gets MX.' If not, the headline would be 'Democrats Block MX.' Reagan could have used that as an excuse. Now that he has the tools he needs, the Administration is in a bit of a hot seat. It has to produce an agreement. I think that the politics of this are such that it would not have been in the long-term interest of the Democratic Party to have killed that weapon."

I asked him if he thought the Democrats could not have made the case against the MX.

He replied, "Sure, I think the Democrats could make the case that it's a silly weapon. But the issue is arms control, and if we gave him the argument that he had appointed a bipartisan commission and was willing to go a new direction in arms control but the Democrats wouldn't let it happen, I don't think there is a good political argument against that. We can't rerun the story and see whether he could have got an agreement anyway."

I asked Aspin if he would have supported the MX if there hadn't been a package.

He replied quickly, "No way. It's stupid without the package. But the knee-jerk reaction is that you give it all away when you let him win on something. Sometimes, by giving him something you can keep the issue, and keep the pressure on him to produce."

The question is raised, I said to Aspin, that even if he is correct in his political analysis, is that a good enough reason to vote for what could be a destabilizing weapon?

He was silent for a few moments. Then he said, "I don't know."

V

As the men around President Reagan tell it, things were coming
along nicely until, out of the blue, the matter of "filched," or
"pilfered," or whatever, briefing papers from the Carter White
House during the 1980 campaign whanged into their well-laid
plans. The economy was recovering, and this, they say, was resulting in a sharp and dramatic improvement in the way people
viewed the President—especially compared to last January, when,
according to one of the President's advisers, the polls were "fairly
dismal." The unexpected almost always does occur in the course of
a political campaign (whether or not the President is on one, his
aides are). But no one was prepared for this particular oddity.
Even how it arose was strange. The first reaction of the President's
people, and of Reagan himself, was to assume that the whole thing
would blow over quickly, and thus the President made what his
advisers now recognize as a big mistake: he did not appear to take
it seriously, and even uttered a phrase—"much ado about
nothing"—that could be, and was, turned back on him. Several of
his advisers realized that his June 28th press conference, which
was largely taken up by questions on the briefing papers, was a
disaster; once again, the President failed to convey an impression
that he took the subject seriously, or that he was on top of it—thus
emphasizing one of Reagan's greatest vulnerabilities. Within a relatively short time, the advisers began to realize that the issue
would not go away soon and to sense that, no matter how it turned
out, the President would be damaged.

Washington, as well, reacted to the story minimally at first, but
then pounced on it as not only a potentially big one but also a
welcome diversion. The story had its comic along with its serious,
even potentially sinister, aspects, and it made for better rumor
swapping and reading than, say, Central America or the budget.
Washington shortly became overwhelmed with rumors, and it was

hard to get down the street without hearing at least a few. People admitted that they reached for the morning papers with a new interest. Once the story got going in the press, competitive instincts were kindled. The bureau chief of one important paper cut short his vacation to return to Washington, and some reporters' vacations were cancelled.

But despite all the hubbub, and the fact that the story seemed to fly off on a number of tangents, some of them seemingly inconsequential, it was clear from an early stage that the questions at the heart of the matter were far from trivial. If in fact the Reagan people, in preparing Reagan for the 1980 debate with Carter, used papers that had been prepared for Carter, then the debate, a major event in the election, was a fraud. If in fact the Reagan people did not hesitate to use papers obtained from the Carter White House, this was at the least a serious ethical breach. Campaigns do try to learn of each other's plans, their poll data, their purchases of time for television advertising, and the like, of course, but there does not seem to be any precedent for the use of a large number of documents obtained, by whatever means, from the other camp—not to mention from the White House. Moreover, a debate is a thing unto itself: it is a sporting event, in which each candidate is expected to come armed with his own material and try to trip up the other one. (It is this sporting aspect, intensified by the press, that turns the debates into something they oughtn't to be, but that is another subject.) If one side knows what the other is going to do, it is not a fair fight. Few people here suggest that Carter would have defeated Reagan in the debate if Reagan had not had surreptitious aid: Reagan is a skilled debater, and Carter would have looked like the tense, bleached rabbit that he did that night anyway (though it can never be known whether Reagan would have made some major mistake, or appeared more ill at ease). But it is true that the stakes were very high and that the debate was a key event—if not the key event—of the election. That there was only one debate (another problem, and also another subject) heightened its importance. At the time, Richard Wirthlin, Reagan's pollster, told me, "Given the political environment, the election is going to hang or fall on that debate." Another question was whether there was a systematic attempt to obtain information from within the Carter White House, some of it highly sensitive and perhaps classified. Was there, in fact, a literal intelligence operation mounted against the Carter White House? There was also the question, of course, of whether any crimes were committed, but in a way this seemed of lesser rank than the questions about whether there had been yet another perversion of the political process. It was these questions that kept the story going, loopy as it sometimes seemed to be. A side drama, but a drama that had both human interest and large implications in terms of the shape and nature of the Reagan Administration, was the impact of the controversy on some of the most important figures in that Administration.

The briefing-papers story, in retrospect, ballooned rather quickly—in less than a month it grew from a minor item in the New York *Times* and the Washington *Post* into a major item on the television networks. The first newspaper mention of it, in the *Times* and the *Post*, occurred on June 9th: both papers referred to a passage in *Gambling with History*, a new book by Laurence Barrett, of *Time*, which said that before the debate a member of the Reagan campaign staff had "an unusual prize: briefing material that the other side was using." Barrett had written: "Apparently a Reagan mole in the Carter camp had filched papers containing the main points the President planned to make when he met Reagan for the debate." (Barrett also wrote that the Reagan people were pleased that the papers "had included every important item Carter used on the air except one: his reference to his daughter, Amy, in connection with nuclear arms control.") Jody Powell, Carter's former press secretary, had begun to receive calls about the item in the Barrett book, but no major story had appeared. So Powell, now a columnist, wrote a column about it, which appeared, among other places, in the following Sunday's *Post*. Three days later, Patrick Caddell, Carter's former pollster, went on the *Today* program to talk about the debate issue. Then, for a while, the story was out there, hanging in suspension, with former Carter aides anxiously trying to keep it alive, encouraging some interested reporters to work on it and seeking to interest congressional Democrats in it. (Peter Rodino, Democrat of New Jersey and chairman of the House Judiciary Committee, who presided over the impeachment proceedings against Richard Nixon, was not interested.) Then the *Post* reported that Reagan campaign aides did recall receiving "several hundred pages of anticipated questions and answers from a Carter briefing book before the debate." James Baker, the White House chief of staff, who had handled the arrangements for the debate for the Reagan campaign, remembered what was described in the *Post* as "a black notebook about three inches thick, with about three hundred pages in it," and another former Reagan campaign aide remembered an unbound "wad of double-spaced question and answer pages." To this moment, it remains unclear whether the Reagan people received the final briefing book prepared for Carter, which contained points about strategy as well as substance—and which fit Baker's description—or earlier versions of it, without the strategy, as the Reagan people maintain. Nor is it clear what moral difference it makes. (Actually, David Rubenstein, the Carter White House aide who was in charge of preparing the briefing book, says that even his preliminary drafts of questions and answers had strategy points in them.) Meanwhile, the staff of a hitherto obscure subcommittee—the Human Resources Subcommittee of the House Post Office and Civil Service Committee—which is headed by a hitherto unknown congressman, Donald Albosta, a Democrat from the central part of southern Michigan, had taken an interest. The subcommittee has jurisdiction over the Ethics in Government Act.

And, as occasionally happens, one small move set in motion big events. Albosta in mid-June sent off letters to Baker; to David Gergen, now the communications director of the White House, who had worked with Baker on the debate arrangements; to David Stockman, the director of the Office of Management and Budget, who had impersonated Carter during Reagan's rehearsals for the debate; and to William Casey, the director of the Central Intelligence Agency, who had been the director of the Reagan 1980 campaign. Their apparently contradictory replies—Baker wrote that he remembered that he had been given "a large looseleaf bound book (I believe in a black binder) that was thought to have been given to the Reagan camp by someone with the Carter campaign," and that it was his "best recollection" that Casey had given it to him "with the suggestion that it might be of use to the Debate Briefing Team;" Casey wrote that he had "no recollection" of any papers "as described in Mr. Barrett's account"—set off an explosion. Stockman, in his letter to the subcommittee, recalled "a thick, unbound set of pages" dealing with policy issues which, he explained, he had previously called "useful" because it had helped him prepare to play Carter in the debate rehearsals. Actually, Baker, though he talked about a "black binder," did say that he had "no recollection" of seeing or receiving "any debate strategy or sensitive debating points" prepared for Carter. Thus it is entirely possible that Casey, without giving the matter much thought, passed along to Baker some material that was not the final debate book prepared for Carter and recently released by Caddell but an earlier version of the final debate book. (Casey, in his denial, said, "I can assure you that the campaign management never contemplated, directed or authorized any effort to obtain information of this kind nor, to my knowledge, did the campaign ever use or have the kind of information described in Mr. Barrett's book.") According to some people at the White House, Casey and Baker discussed the letters they would be sending to the subcommittee, and it was clear that the disparity between their replies would cause a big problem. But neither man was willing to budge. Then, on July 6th, the *Times* published a story based on an interview with Casey, who had dropped around to the *Times* Washington bureau to give his side of the story, apparently out of concern that his failure of recollection wasn't going over well, and that he might be on the way to becoming a fall guy. And another explosion hit Washington. Casey's denial had a certain porousness ("It would be totally uncharacteristic and quite incredible that I would hand anybody a book I knew to be from the Carter campaign and say this might be helpful to the debate"), and his defenders later said the question was whether he *"knowingly"* passed along the papers, but what mesmerized Washington about the interview was that it appeared to be a declaration of war on Baker. "I wouldn't tolerate it," Casey said of receiving any such papers. "I wouldn't touch it with a ten-foot pole." Moreover, he said, the debate team was "remiss" in not telling the campaign hierarchy about the papers. Baker, aware that he was in a big fight, made no further comment, but columnists known to be friendly to the respective parties carried on the feud on their behalf, and Washington solemnly weighed the statements the two men had made, and, like spectators at a coliseum, looked forward to what they assumed would be a fight to the finish. (Along the way, the controversy acquired the name "Debategate," which was unfortunate and inaccurate. The term began early as a nervous joke among some Carter people, at a time they themselves wondered whether

the story would go anywhere. The suffix "gate" has been indiscriminately applied to all manner of scandals and scandalettes
since the great one of 1973–74, whereas each is a thing unto itself,
and of its own degree of importance.)

Meanwhile, Stockman allowed that he had been the source of
Barrett's anecdote about the "filched" papers, and it was reported
that Stockman had bragged to a luncheon of the Optimist Club, in
Cassopolis, Michigan, on the day of the debate that he had been
helped in preparing Reagan for the debate by using a "pilfered
copy of the briefing book he [Carter] was going to use," and predicted what both candidates would say. The original story about
what Stockman told the Optimist Club appeared on the day after
the debate in a paper called the Elkhart *Truth*—and was ignored
until recently. When these new stories broke, Stockman was there-
upon believed to be in deep trouble, his primary sin apparently
being that he talks too much. He had survived in his job after his
confessions of private doubts about the Reagan economic program had been published in *The Atlantic* in December, 1981—and
after what was described at the time as a trip to the President's
"woodshed"—but he was as if on probation. Stockman does in fact
have a little-boy quality to him, the infectious charm of the enthusiastic wunderkind who never quite grew up. His has been a life of
brilliance, and unsteadiness: the brightest boy wherever he went,
who gained important sponsors along the way, but never seemed
rooted. He enthusiastically embraced one totality after another.
His course has taken him from a farm in St. Joseph, Michigan, to
Michigan State, where he was involved in radical student politics
during the Vietnam War; to Harvard Divinity School, where he
drifted toward "neo-conservative" politics and the social sciences;
to the staff of a liberal-to-moderate Republican congressman
(John Anderson); to being elected, at twenty-nine, a Republican
congressman from Michigan, who attracted attention almost at
once; to becoming, at thirty-four, Reagan's budget director and
one of the most powerful people in the country. It is utterly in
character that Stockman now says that he told the local leaders of
Cassopolis (pop. 2,000)—the hardware-store dealer, the town
banker, and others—about the debate because he wanted to titil-
late them and also wanted them to think that he was in the big
time. Stockman tells people that he does not remember the episode but that if it was in the paper that he said these things he

must have said them. And he tells people that it is regrettable that he used the word "pilfered," because in fact he assumed that the material had been leaked by someone in the Carter White House. While Stockman has recently told people that "filched" was Barrett's word, his own spokesman had confirmed earlier that Stockman used the word in talking to Barrett. Stockman also says that the reason he had called the material "useful" was that it was useful in the sense that he had interrupted his own campaigning for his House seat and had one day to prepare for the Reagan rehearsals, and that he didn't want to make a fool of himself before the Reagan high command. But, he says, the documents were not sufficiently significant to give him moral qualms.

There have been a number of contradictions by Reagan people about the nature of the domestic material they had. Whatever such material they did have has not been released. They are saying that they did not have—or do not recollect having—the final briefing book prepared for Carter, and Stockman sometimes refers to having a collection of papers, but the Elkhart *Truth* quotes him as saying that he had used a "pilfered copy of the briefing book he [Carter] was going to use." And Baker did refer to a "black binder." Maybe what Baker received in the "black binder" was then removed from it. Maybe what all this amounts to is a loose use of language; maybe not. Sometimes Stockman says that what he had was Carter issue boilerplate, but he has also said that he saw "Carter questions and answers" having to do with certain subjects—the economy, energy, the environment, and others. The Carter people maintain that this constituted material that contained strategy. Early in the controversy, Reagan told reporters, "I don't think there ever was a briefing book as such." Frank Hodsoll, who also helped prepare Reagan for the debate, has said that he remembers seeing questions and answers. (Hodsoll is now chairman of the National Endowment for the Arts.) Stockman says that the papers he used were probably tossed out by his congressional office.

The dispute over the briefing papers deepened the schisms in an already divided Administration—more divided than any in memory, which is saying quite a bit—and outsiders who had already chosen up sides jumped on this new opportunity to rid the Administration of members of the unwanted faction. The schisms within the Reagan White House were peculiarly deep because they were caused by factors that went well beyond the usual jockeying for position. In the case of the Reagan Administration, the jockeying for position is overlaid with ideological, political, and even cultural and social factors—all making for a mixture that turns ordinary power plays into tong wars. The alignment within the Reagan White House is usually described as "pragmatists" versus either "ideologues" or, depending on who is assigning the labels, "true Reaganites." But the categorizations blur things somewhat. Counted among the pragmatists are Baker; Stockman; Gergen; Richard Darman, deputy to the chief of staff; and Michael Deaver, deputy chief of staff. Counted among the ideologues are William Clark, the President's national-security adviser; Edwin Meese, counsellor to the President; and Casey. The categories aren't quite that neat, because Deaver has worked for Reagan in some capacity since 1966, when he was brought into the Governor's office in California by Clark. And Casey was a Nixon–Wall Street Republican. The pragmatists (except for Deaver) are seen by Reagan's right-wing supporters as parvenus who won't "let Reagan be Reagan": who not only seek tax increases but talk about it in the press; who do not share Reagan's (and Clark's) hard-line-foreign-policy emphasis or his enthusiasm for the size of the military buildup that is under way. Speaking of Baker, one longtime Reagan man said to me recently, "Some of us feel that Jim's too outspoken in talking to the press, that he pushes his own views, not the President's view. And there was a feeling that sometimes Jim was up on the Hill making deals that were not the deals the President sent him up there to make. The old Reaganites who never played it that way feel this way." Baker and Gergen had worked for the Presidential nomination of George Bush (Baker was Bush's campaign manager, and before that had worked for Ford's campaign), and, Bush's faithfulness to Reagan notwithstanding, anyone connected with him is suspect in the eyes of the longtime Reaganites. This has to do with not just the present but the future: moves to moderate Reagan policies are suspected of being taken not simply to help Reagan but with a view to helping Bush's political future when the opportunity arises for him to make his own run for the Presidency again, against some candidate the far right would prefer. This is a very suspicious bunch. Baker is cut out for attracting resentments: though new to the

Reagan group, he maneuvered himself into the prime position in the White House staff (at least until Clark came along); he is a handsome, wealthy man, at home with the higher social circles of both his native Houston and Washington. (None of the other top Reagan aides has such a background.) Baker is seen by the old Reaganites as using his savvy and his entrée to further himself and his own views, and to obtain the protection that such entrée brings from criticism of the Reagan Administration. This path is one that some members of every Administration try to take, and, while it has its perils, Baker has so far been particularly successful at it. Deaver is resented by at least some old Reaganites as a man who, as they see it, owes everything to his association with Reagan but fell under the spell of Baker, and was a bit too taken with Washington's social glamour. Gergen had worked for Nixon and Ford, which makes anybody suspect to the old Reaganites and right-wingers; and Darman, whom Baker brought into the White House, had, of all things, worked for Elliot Richardson.

The true Reaganites had not spent all those years struggling to take over the Republican Party, and ultimately the Presidency, in order to have their Administration taken over by "pragmatists." Thus, as the battle heated over the papers issue, Richard Viguerie, the New Right leader, who had often complained about the take-over of the Reagan Administration by "Wall Street and the Fortune 500," appeared on television to deplore the behavior of the group (headed by Baker) that had prepared Reagan for the debate. Others also took swipes at the "newcomers" who had so misserved Reagan.

Casey is perhaps the most interesting character in this whole brew. Because he mumbles (to the point where he is sometimes difficult to understand) and has a shambling style, he is often underestimated. He is a very tough man and—as recent events prove—a formidable infighter. He has had an unusual career. He was a disciple of William (Wild Bill) Donovan, the head of the Office of Strategic Services (the forerunner of the C.I.A.) during the Second World War, and came away with the respect of his O.S.S. colleagues. He made a fortune as a lawyer and investor. When questions arose about possible connections between the settlement by the Nixon Justice Department of an anti-trust case against I.T.T. and a commitment by I.T.T. to contribute four hundred thousand dollars to the 1972 Republican Convention, Casey, who was chairman of the Securities and Exchange Commission, was alleged to have sent pertinent documents out of his office and over to John Mitchell's Justice Department, where they would be protected from interested congressional committees. After Reagan named him director of the C.I.A., Casey engendered some controversy for his failure to list many of his law clients and assets and liabilities on his disclosure form during Senate proceedings on his confirmation. And he stirred up more dust by naming as the head of covert operations Max Hugel, a Runyonesque businessman who had worked in the 1980 Reagan campaign. Hugel, whose appointment shocked the old-line C.I.A. professionals, as well as outsiders who had nothing to do with the agency, eventually had to resign, over allegations of improper stock-trading practices. In the summer of 1981, there was a brief furor over Casey, involving allegations of earlier financial misconduct and lingering irritation over his appointment of Hugel, with the whole thing having the aura of a multilayered affair which events surrounding the C.I.A. usually do. Senators resentful of Casey's bluff style, ex-C.I.A. (and perhaps current C.I.A.) operatives resentful of management of their agency by "amateurs," and various people disturbed by Casey's role all got in on the act. Casey partisans came to his defense. After an investigation, the Senate Intelligence Committee in December reported that it had no basis for concluding that Casey was "unfit to serve." But he continued to make people uneasy. Recently, there was a smaller to-do over the fact that Casey continued to manage his multimillion-dollar portfolio while sitting in a position that made him privy to highly sensitive, and perhaps financially useful, information. Other top government officials had voluntarily placed their holdings in blind trusts, and some Reagan officials were embarrassed by Casey's refusal to do so. But Casey's position on this matter was consistent with his "the hell with 'em" attitude: he is a man who has done well in the world and does not choose to live by other men's rules. (A few days ago, under congressional pressure, Casey agreed to put his holdings in a blind trust; he said there was nothing wrong with the way he had handled his finances, but that he was "tired of being hassled about it.") His management of the C.I.A. has been controversial in itself. According to a number of people, he has retained the swashbuckling style of the Wild Bill Donovan do-something days, and is more inclined than several of his predecessors to use the instruments of the agency for covert purposes. Nor does he shrink from offering his policy views as well as his intelligence assessments—"He is very outspoken," says one Reagan adviser—and his policy views tend to place him with the very-hard-liners within the Reagan entourage. Many of the agency's professionals, and its alumni, find Casey's policymaking activity disturbing, because of the clouds it places on the intelligence information he offers.

That Casey ended up within the circle of the conservative Californians around Reagan was not necessarily predictable. He comes from a different world, and has little in common with them. But it was Casey who was brought in to rescue the Reagan 1980 campaign for the nomination, on the day of the New Hampshire primary, in February, when Reagan dismissed John Sears as campaign manager because of internal feuds and because campaign funds had been overspent. "Casey came in and became part of the old team," says Lyn Nofziger, who was White House director of political affairs in 1981 and then became a political consultant. "Those were the old Reaganites in the primary days." Casey's relationship with Baker has been a rocky one. According to people who know both men, Casey began as a strong backer of Baker, and ended up as his strong antagonist. Their relationship is a study of a collision between two tough, strong-willed men. People who have observed both men closely say that Casey is the tougher of the two. It was Casey who recruited Baker for the Reagan campaign—Baker had previously not been offered what he considered an important enough post, and had returned to Houston. Casey put Baker in charge of arrangements for whatever debates might occur, and, according to someone who knows them both, was a strong backer of his in the campaign and during the first year of the Administration. But then Casey grew suspicious of Baker, feeling that a number of actions Baker took were in the interest of his own political future, and that of George Bush. Matters weren't helped when rumors emanated from the White House from time to time that Baker might be named head of the C.I.A.; the rumors were presumed to come from Baker and his allies. (The C.I.A. post was one of several positions "mentioned" for Baker, as a way of both advancing his career and removing him from the right wing's line of fire.) Gradually, Casey grew increasingly outspoken in his criticism of Baker within the Reagan circle. Richard Allen, whom Baker helped maneuver out of his job as Reagan's national-security adviser and who harbors deep resentments, is, according to mutual friends, very close to Casey. Then Baker insisted on telling the House subcommittee that he recalled receiving the briefing papers from Casey. And after that there appeared in the *Post* a leak from the White House making fun of Casey's mumble, his management of his portfolio (one White House joke had it that C.I.A. really stood for "Casey Investing Again"), and his poor memory about the briefing book. By this time, it was all-out war, with several people caught uncomfortably in the middle.

The atmosphere at the White House has been tense throughout these events. One White House aide, in a conversation we had as the story was beginning to unfold, went on at some length, and with some vehemence, about what he assumed to be ethical lapses in the personal lives of the press. Another began a half-hour conversation with the statement that he did not want to talk about the briefing-papers controversy, and his next sentence was, "How long do you think this thing will go on?" And most of that conversation was taken up with the subject. The matter has been a major source of distraction at the White House; it is the sort of thing that is clearly on the minds of the principal figures even when they are talking about something else. It is the sort of thing that makes it hard to govern. The President's aides worried about his image, and about their heads. Early in the controversy, Reagan had said that the Justice Department would "monitor" the case, and shortly after that the Justice Department inquiry became a criminal investigation. Then, just after the President seemed to disappear from sight—a development that worried his image-makers—he theatrically strode into an early-morning staff meeting and ordered his aides to cooperate with the F.B.I. Some people who belong to neither camp believe that, whatever Reagan does about it— whether or not anyone is forced to resign—the breach that the controversy has caused cannot be healed. Some officials were at pains to indicate that their own skirts were clean, and indicated that if some of their brethren had to go—well, that's too bad, but that's the way things are.

The possibility that there might have been an organized intelligence-gathering operation on the part of the Reagan campaign has not been dismissed by even some of the less melodramatic people here, because of a number of known factors and some facts that have come to light. At the least, various members of the Reagan campaign busied themselves trying to obtain information of a nature that does not normally pass from camp to camp. To some extent, these people may have been, as Reagan people now say, the flotsam and jetsam that are drawn to many campaigns and try to win points by playing up their discoveries—but the Reagan campaign does seem to have attracted quite a lot of this. It is possible that those who sought information did it of their own volition, and that a lot of information came in over the transom. But something unusual was going on.

The first sign of this was when, on June 28th, the White House released a number of documents that it said had come into the possession of the Reagan campaign. The Carter people were quick to point out that some of the documents were briefing material covering foreign policy—preliminary material prepared for Carter's debate with Reagan and also some for a possible Mondale debate with Bush—and they asserted that no single person could have had access to both this material and the domestic briefing book. They said that the foreign-policy material was held within the offices of the National Security Council staff. (Some of the released material was found in the files of Gergen—under "Afghanistan"—who had at first written to the Albosta subcommittee that, in helping prepare Reagan for the debate, he "never studied nor drew upon any sensitive materials from the Carter camp." He also said that he did not recall "seeing a 'Carter debate book' or any other notebook from the Carter campaign.") Then it was reported in the *Post* that Richard Allen, Reagan's principal foreign-policy adviser in the campaign, had received some of the daily memorandums that the Carter National Security Council staff members wrote to their boss, Zbigniew Brzezinski—documents that Allen described as "innocuous" and unclassified, pertaining to such matters as staff morale. Allen also said that he had received only three of them. He said that they had come in over the transom. Why anyone would bother to send Allen three innocuous documents about N.S.C. staff morale is only one of the puzzles in this whole thing. (Brzezinski and his deputy, David Aaron, have said that the daily memorandums contained sensitive, substantive material.) Allen's behavior was of some interest, and people tried to decide whether what he was doing was simply settling scores. He went on ABC's *Nightline* on the night of July 4th to confirm that he had received some excerpts from N.S.C. staff memorandums ("I think it was probably the most innocuous material that I had ever seen") and, while he was at it, to take some swipes at Baker. Allen said that he was aware of the existence of the briefing book but added, "I thought it would be, in the first instance, highly unethical to use it." He said that "perhaps some of the people who had only recently come on board" the campaign— that is, Baker and Gergen—"may have had some fear that they were working for someone who wasn't competent on the issues." Four nights later, Carl Bernstein reported on *Nightline* that William Van Cleave, Reagan's defense-policy adviser during the campaign, said that Allen had given him Carter briefing documents to use in preparing Reagan for the debate. Allen denied this. Few were surprised when it was reported during that same week that Allen had named as the source of his documents Jerry Jennings, a former N.S.C. staff member in charge of security in the N.S.C. offices, who was, as it happens, the man who reported the discovery in Allen's safe of the envelope containing cash. Jennings, who had worked for the C.I.A. and the F.B.I., was on the National Security Council staff during the Nixon, Ford, Carter, and Reagan Presidencies and is currently executive director of the White House Office of Science and Technology Policy. Jennings' job as N.S.C. security officer entailed, among other things, seeing to it that sensitive documents were safely locked away, and he would have had access to the staff members' offices—and their safes. Jennings said that any suggestion that he was Allen's source "is untrue and absolutely ludicrous." Then, on July 9th, it was reported in the *Post* that Allen had said that he had merely been told by someone that Jennings was the source of the material, but he couldn't recall whom. (Some journalists later wondered whether they had underplayed the Jennings story, because they had assumed Allen was simply getting even.) By then, the *Times* had reported that Allen had received classified information. Someone who was in the Reagan campaign—and is presumably allied with Allen—said to me, "Dick had good contacts in the N.S.C." The *Times* also reported that an intelligence-gathering operation had been conducted by Stefan Halper, a researcher who had served on the Bush campaign and then worked in the Reagan campaign. Some former aides suggested that he was receiving information from the C.I.A. Halper later said that this was "preposterous." Halper's father-in-law, Ray Cline, who had been a deputy director of the C.I.A. and was an adviser to the Reagan campaign, responding to the *Times* on Halper's behalf, said that the idea that Halper had conducted such an exercise was a "romantic fallacy."

By this time, all manner of heretofore unknown names were popping up, and we had to come to grips with a whole new cast of characters. In this respect, it did seem for a moment like the early Watergate days. On the day that the *Times* published its story about the supposed intelligence operation, the *Post* published material from the Carter White House found after the campaign, by a collector of memorabilia, in a dumpster outside the Reagan headquarters. The material was of no great consequence, but what attracted attention was that this showed that still more material had somehow changed hands, and that a campaign volunteer, in a covering note to Meese, Robert Gray (a public-relations man who was deputy campaign manager for communications), and Casey, said the material had come from a "White House mole." Perhaps some of the people in the Reagan campaign had read too much John le Carré or were, as some Reagan people suggest, simply seeking the attention of the big shots.

But there was another possibility. It was known that the Reagan campaign was obsessed with the possibility that Carter might, shortly before the election, obtain the release of the hostages held in Iran. When Casey told a breakfast meeting of reporters at the Republican Convention, in Detroit, that the Reagan people thought there might be "an October surprise," his suggestion just seemed like good politics: any successful move by Carter would be seen as having been manipulated for the election. At the time, Casey used the term "intelligence operation" to describe the monitoring activity the campaign would conduct in order to anticipate the "surprise." One Reagan person told me recently that some of the campaign leaders saw the Cuban missile crisis of October, 1962, just before that year's congressional elections, as a parallel for what Carter might do in October, 1980. "They know what happened on what day in October, 1962," this man said, "and how the congressional elections were affected." It had already been reported that one Reagan campaign aide, Admiral Robert Garrick (Ret.), had organized a network of retired military officers to watch military bases for the movement of troops or transport planes. Garrick confirmed this. The disclosure was at once ludicrous and worrisome. When Carter attempted the rescue mission that failed, in April of 1980, the ships and helicopters were already in the area. A former Carter foreign-policy official says that a vital requirement of that or any other rescue mission was that it be carried out without any noticeable movement of troops or ships from the United States. He and others say that there were some contingency plans for another hostage-rescue attempt but that it was never seriously considered, because, among other things, the hostages had been dispersed from the American Embassy, where they had been held. Several people here think that the Garrick operation as described was so silly—a bunch of retired military officers standing watch with their binoculars—that it might have been a cover for something else. And it was never clear what these people would do if they did spot some military movement—pick up an unsecured telephone and report it to the Reagan campaign? Or what the Reagan campaign would do with such information. When I suggested to one Reagan official that even if Carter had mounted some new effort to rescue the hostages the Reagan campaign people could not have said anything until they saw how it turned out, and that there would have been plenty of time to prepare contingency statements, he replied, "But you're being logical." When Casey went to the *Times* Washington bureau, he said, "The campaign had no intelligence organization as such." He added, "Except the whole organization had their antennae out." Allen said on *Nightline*, "I would say that even though we set up an operation designed to try to anticipate what might happen, particularly with regard to the so-called October surprise, it was based entirely on open sources." Allen also said that the story about retired military officers watching military bases—which Garrick had confirmed—was "preposterous." Allen said, "I never heard anything of that sort."

A number of factors led sensible people here—people without conspiratorial minds—to consider the possibility that something more serious than a loose collection of information gatherers, some of them self-starting, was involved in the Reagan 1980 campaign. It was known during the primaries that several former C.I.A. employees had joined the campaign of Bush, who had served as C.I.A. director for a year, from January, 1976, to January, 1977. (Other Bush campaign aides used to joke about the ex-

C.I.A. people's penchant for secrecy, and their concern about the fact that the campaign didn't use burn bags.) Bush, who had served in the House and had been chairman of the Republican National Committee during Watergate, was the first such political figure to be named head of the C.I.A. The appointment made some people nervous, but he got good marks for the job he did there, and he was, according to one former C.I.A. official, one of the most popular directors. This official says, "When George was running for President, there wasn't a person in the building who didn't support him." The C.I.A. professionals had ample reason for being unhappy with Carter. The man he named as C.I.A. director, Stansfield Turner, an admiral whom Carter had admired when both men were at Annapolis, was, like Bush, one of the few C.I.A. directors who didn't come from the ranks; but, unlike Bush, he was unpopular with them. Turner removed about six hundred people from their jobs in the area of covert operations: many of these people were placed in other positions, about two hundred of them retired, and a few were fired outright. This makes for a very unhappy network. Some of these people were what one former Carter official calls "the cowboys—the ones who run around and do things." Moreover, Carter, in 1978, issued a charter designed to put reins on the activities of the F.B.I. and the C.I.A. Many of the former C.I.A. people who helped out in the Bush campaign joined the Reagan-Bush campaign after the nomination. Among the people working with Halper was Robert Gambino, who had been the C.I.A. director of security, a position that gave him access to the files of people who had received high-level security clearances. (Such files usually contain rumors as well as facts about people's personal lives.) When Gambino left the C.I.A. and immediately joined the Bush campaign, some Carter White House people were concerned, but they concluded that there was nothing they could do about it. Halper has described what Gambino was doing for him as "grunt work," such as monitoring the news media. It struck a number of people here as odd that such a formerly high-level person would be doing such routine work. It is part of the subculture of Washington, and of politics, for networks of like-minded people in and out of the bureaucracy—people involved in the fields of poverty, education, agriculture, the military, or what have you—to share information and make common cause. When this sort of thing involves the C.I.A., however, it takes on a different aspect. And it is to be remembered that Casey had old C.I.A. contacts. (Ray Cline, Halper's father-in-law, is active in the Association of Former Intelligence Officers, a group of retired C.I.A. officials which holds meetings to express its concerns about the C.I.A.) Added to all that, according to some people here, was the anger on the part of several retired military officers and other strong supporters of the military at what they considered Carter's "weakening" of America's defenses. Therefore, these groups would have taken a great interest in seeing Carter defeated. What methods they might have used, or whether they used any more than is already known, is still open to speculation. But the atmosphere in Washington was such that, at Fourth of July parties, people actually engaged in serious debate over the question of whether, if it developed that there had been an effort by the intelligence community and perhaps old military hands, using clandestine methods, to bring down Carter, the country would care.

There were still other indications that, one way or another, sensitive information was flowing into the Reagan campaign, and that several Reagan campaign officials knew about it. Among the material released by the White House was a memorandum from Wayne Valis, a campaign volunteer who is now a public-relations man, to David Gergen, which Valis described as notes "based on a Carter debate staff brainstorming session—middle level types—nothing spectacular, but interesting—from a source intimately connected to a Carter debate staff member. Reliable." He added, "I gave a copy to Jim Baker." The material is indeed not spectacular, but it is the sort of thing that is helpful. The apparent innuendo ("intimately") in the Valis memorandum was only one of several things that set off waves of rumors and allegations about the sex lives of people who worked in the Carter White House and in the Reagan campaign. Many people are part of the permanent White House apparat—they stay when an Administration packs its bags. These people were natural suspects for the Carter people when this whole episode began, but then the Reagan people as well spread rumors about who had what sorts of personal relationships with whom—in part, it seems, to buttress their argument that all that happened was that a few documents, none of them important, were slipped to Reagan people by unhappy employees of the Carter White House. (Valis told a reporter, "I have no knowledge of any Reagan aides sleeping with Carter women to get information. If anyone says I do, it's preposterous.") There was also the story in the press that Carol Darr, the deputy counsel to the Carter campaign, had been told by a friend in the Reagan campaign, Charles Crawford, that the Reagan people had access to the debate briefing material and that therefore Reagan would win the debate. Miss Darr is reported to have told her boss, Tim Smith, who has said that he did nothing about the report because he found it "preposterous." Crawford worked under Robert Gray in the campaign.

The Reagan people have been suggesting that whatever material they received came from "disgruntled" employees of the Carter White House, and perhaps this is at least to some extent the case. About twelve hundred people work in what is loosely referred to as "the White House"—in the offices in the West Wing itself and in the Executive Office Building, next door. Most of these are the people who remain from Administration to Administration, and their loyalties are more to the institution of the Presidency than to the person who happens to be President. If the President is not a particularly considerate man, as Jimmy Carter wasn't, they can become disgruntled. Some Democrats who went to work for the Carter White House also undoubtedly became disgruntled over policy; some of them may well have favored the candidacy of Edward M. Kennedy. Moreover, during the Carter Administration there was a relatively easy flow of traffic between the Executive Office Building and the West Wing (though not to the most sensitive offices of the National Security Council staff). The Reagan Administration has shut off access of E.O.B. employees to the White House. But whether whatever disgruntled people there might have been would have of their own volition spirited all these documents out and sent them over the transom to the Reagan campaign is in question.

The fact is that it would not be very difficult to penetrate a White House if one put one's mind to it. The ingredients are in place. A certain number of White House employees will be holdovers from previous Administrations, and some will be former C.I.A. employees. A certain number of sexual relationships—heterosexual and homosexual—may exist between people who want information and people who are in a position to obtain it. C.I.A.

agents are known to penetrate governments all over the world: getting information out of a White House would be no great trick for them. So there are three possibilities: that whatever material from the Carter White House landed in the Reagan campaign's hands was voluntarily sent over the transom; that various people in and around the Reagan campaign made it their business, on their own, to obtain such material; that there was an organized effort to obtain the material.

When the *Times* printed a suggestion, which was presumed to have come from Casey, that a longtime Kennedy retainer named Paul Corbin might have had something to do with the transfer of the briefing papers, a number of people assumed that this was an attempt on Casey's part to at once throw people off the trail and suggest a Kennedy tie-in to the whole episode. Corbin is a diminutive man with a wizened face and a gravel voice and a fanatic loyalty to the Kennedy family: he helped John Kennedy win the Wisconsin primary in 1960, and worked in the Justice Department for Robert Kennedy and on the Robert Kennedy campaign of 1968. (Corbin is known among the Kennedy followers as a trickster: an associate of the Kennedy family once told an interviewer, with reference to the Wisconsin primary, "If you have a job and you want to get it done, and you don't care *how* it's done, send Paul Corbin out to do it—but just understand you can never send him back to the same district.") Corbin hung around the Kennedy entourage, but few people seemed to have much idea of what he really did. (Edward Kennedy appeared to be uneasy about him, and Corbin seemed to play almost no role in Edward Kennedy's 1980 campaign.) Corbin is a man, to put it delicately, of strong feelings, and anyone who did not share his fanaticism toward Robert Kennedy was suspect (even those loyal to Robert Kennedy were often targets of Corbin's wrath). Somewhere along the way, Corbin decided to help Reagan get elected, and at this point Corbin says that all he did was provide Casey with some speech material on crime written by Adam Walinsky, a former aide to Robert Kennedy who was then chairman of the New York State Commission of Investigation and supported Lewis Lehrman in his New York gubernatorial race. But Corbin's role remains a matter of interest.

Another line of argument by the White House was that journalists, who print leaks, and even stolen documents, including the

Pentagon Papers, were hypocritical to make a fuss over the briefing papers and other documents that made their way from the Carter White House to the Reagan camp. But there were differences: Daniel Ellsberg was tried for his theft of the Pentagon Papers, and the case was dismissed after it came to light that operatives retained by the Nixon White House had raided his psychiatrist's office; and the right of the *Post* and the *Times* to publish the Pentagon Papers was upheld by the Supreme Court. There was another difference (which White House officials did concede when it was suggested to them): When a journalist publishes a leak, or information from a leaked document (never mind that many of these leaks are provided by government, even White House, officials), the reader knows that he is reading a leak. (The story says something like "Documents obtained from government officials say . . .") But the public had no way of knowing that potentially sensitive information had been obtained by the Reagan camp, and that potentially helpful information had been used in preparation for the debate.

The inescapable conclusion as of now is that something out of the ordinary occurred in the 1980 campaign. And too much appears to have happened to lay it all at the feet of disgruntled Carter workers. There were too many people in the Reagan campaign too eager to obtain information for whatever reason—and prepared to use it. All of the Reagan people insist that Reagan knew nothing about the obtaining of material from the Carter White House. They also insist that the material that came in was of no great value—but not, it seems, for want of trying. At this point, we don't really know what was obtained. Perhaps a lot of people were simply playing soldier. It is apparent that several high-level people knew that material was coming in. One puzzle is why they didn't act on what Casey said to the *Times* he would have acted on: a suspicion that they were being set up—that the material was inaccurate, or that someone would expose them as having it. "It could have destroyed the campaign," Casey said, in explaining why he wouldn't "touch it with a ten-foot pole." It is known that the Reagan campaign was extremely worried that Carter might do something about the hostages. It is clear that there was within the Reagan campaign a pattern and practice of obtaining sensitive information from within the White House. Perhaps all this activity amounts to separate pebbles; perhaps it forms a mosaic. In any event, as far as is known, this sort of activity does not represent, as some suggest, "politics as usual." Of course there have been "dirty tricks" before, and, especially in the pre-Watergate days, some high-handed activities on the part of Administrations—but that was then. As of now, there is no sign that anything quite like this has occurred before. (And if it has, should that make any difference?) There are in fact a large number of unwritten rules governing political campaigns—lines that, it is understood, should not be crossed; anything *doesn't* go. Moreover, differences in degree at some point become differences in kind. The only real question is whether these activities were encouraged or merely condoned.

By mid-July, the frenzy surrounding the story had subsided, and Washington calmed down. Journalistic fashion turned away from the story—but not completely. Now that the F.B.I. investigation was under way, it was assumed that it might be some time before there would be any big breaks, if, indeed, there were any more breaks. Some people assumed that more documents would come to light. There were various theories about why House Speaker Thomas P. O'Neill was negative about Albosta's proceeding with the issue: some thought O'Neill had doubts about Albosta's ability to handle the case (Albosta had spoken out of turn on occasion), others took O'Neill at his word that he didn't consider it good politics (the Democrats should continue to harp on the economy and "fairness;" the issue might fizzle, leaving the Democrats empty-handed, or Reagan might fire someone and be considered a hero); some had other theories. O'Neill did say that if the subject was serious enough for a congressional investigation it should be conducted by the Judiciary Committee, and Rodino's staff was in fact now monitoring events. The Carter people fretted that unless people were put under oath the truth might not come out, and they argued that a special prosecutor should be appointed. More dispassionate observers suggested that only by having a special prosecutor appointed could the Reagan Administration make a convincing case that it had indeed got to the bottom of it. A number of people were aware that the story still had a lot of loose threads, some of which might unravel quite a lot. A few people were following those threads. Others went off on their vacations.

VI

For all the expressions of shock, dismay, and concern over the news, which broke on Thursday, September 1st, of the shooting down by the Soviet Union of the Korean passenger airliner, and over the fatalities suffered by American Marines on a "peace-keeping" mission in Lebanon in the same week, it was actually not without some relief that Congress turned to these matters when it returned to Washington from its August recess. Though there was little that Congress could do about them, or perhaps because there was little it could do about them, and little was expected of it, members of Congress preferred these new subjects to the one that was on their minds when they recessed—the enormous and seemingly open-ended budget deficits. Neither the White House nor Congress had the political will to solve the deficit problem. The paralysis, and fear of its consequences, had been making many members of Congress increasingly uncomfortable. Having taken the initiative last year to raise taxes without endorsement by President Reagan until the last minute, Congress was in no mood to undertake such a politically perilous action in the face of out-right Presidential opposition this year. Therefore, a kind of circular logic was at work: Congress, it has been widely assumed in Washington, would not take significant action until interest rates shot up and/or the financial markets panicked; as long as the markets didn't panic, little would be done about something the markets were most concerned about. Washington has chronic difficulty in concentrating on very many things at once, so the foreign-policy news—for a time, at least—blotted out almost everything else and made it unfashionable. It has long been said that when domestic issues seem intractable Presidents like to turn to foreign affairs; there is an analogue in congressional behavior.

Patrick Caddell, the pollster, talked to me a few months ago about what he saw as the ever-increasing emphasis in our political system on style, verve, audacity; we are developing a political system in which substance means very little, he said. We don't debate anymore—we react. He placed a good bit of the blame on his own profession. "We force politicians to react," he said. "We make them jump; we don't let them think." One couldn't help remembering this in recent weeks. There were the news stories over the summer about the White House "repositioning itself" vis-à-vis important electoral groups—blacks, women, Hispanics, and so on. And some of the reaction to the shooting down of the Korean plane, horrible as the event was, had the aura of politicians wanting to be seen to be reacting in a certain way, rather than of authentic reaction. The self-conscious expressions of outrage had the effect of devaluing the awful event. On the day that the news broke, the politicians who were in Washington flocked to the congressional television galleries to express their indignation. (Congress was not due to reconvene until September 12th.) Some sounded as if they were reading from a thesaurus. (Robert Byrd, Democrat of West Virginia and the Senate Minority Leader: "Revolting, revulsive, repulsive.") There was no premium on keeping cool—on suggesting that, terrible as the event was, too much should not be concluded before more facts were known. Nobody ever went broke in this country by being anti-Communist. Right-wingers used the occasion to say that the Soviet Union was just as bad as they had always said it was, and to assail any attempts to deal with it. They expressed a shock that, logically, they should not have experienced. Democrats took the opportunity to try to out-flank Reagan on the right—to show that they could be as tough on the Soviet Union as anyone else. Thus, in the course of a day the "climate" was established; sitting in Washington, one could feel the fever rising.

The President, vacationing at his California ranch, got caught by the emotional pitch that was building in Washington. His first official reaction—the release of a statement by his press spokesman, Larry Speakes, in Santa Barbara, saying that the President was "very concerned and deeply disturbed" about the incident and wanted a full accounting from the Soviet Union of how it had occurred, and would be kept abreast of developments—seemed about right under the circumstances, but it was soon overwhelmed by the emotions of the day, and by the goading of reporters who were asking why the President was not returning to Washington at once. From then on, the public relations of the situation took over. The question of whether the President is on top of things is among the most sensitive ones for the Reagan White House, and his seeming out of touch during an international incident has been a symbolic problem ever since Edwin Meese failed to wake him when United States planes shot down Libyan jets over the Gulf of Sidra in August, 1981. (Reagan was in Los Angeles at that time.) Moreover, on Thursday evening CBS News showed telephoto pictures of Reagan riding his horse that day. The heated rhetoric in Washington was threatening to take the act of defining the situation away from the President. So in the course of Thursday the President gradually raised the temperature of his own rhetoric and, in stages, moved up the day of his return to Washington from Monday to Saturday to Friday. On Friday, the President was asking, in a planeside statement, "What can be the scope of legitimate mutual discourse with a state whose values permit such atrocities?" and by the time of his televised address the following Monday, Labor Day, he was referring to "the Korean airline massacre." The fact that Reagan was loath to do anything but try to whip up world opinion against the Soviet Union, and urge other nations to suspend flights into their countries by Aeroflot, the Soviet airline, brought him under attack from his own right; if, say, Jimmy Carter had followed the same course, it would have brought heated attacks from Reagan and his political and journalistic supporters. That Carter took stronger action following the Soviet invasion of Afghanistan in December, 1979, is one of history's ironies. (Among other things, he cancelled grain sales to the Soviet Union—sales that Reagan resumed in 1981 and had recently expanded in a new long-term agreement.) But Reagan, unlike Carter, had not been accused of being insufficiently muscular toward the Soviet Union. Still, his problem was that his rhetoric was out of proportion to his actions. What's more, rhetoric is policy, too, and no one could be sure what the effect of all this would be on the balance of power within the Kremlin, and on American relations with the Soviet Union, which the Reagan Administration had been noticeably trying to improve—by the grain sale, and also by a recent decision to sell oil-pipeline equipment to the Soviet Union. Both agreements had domestic political benefits, but they also conveyed the Administration's hope of arranging a summit meeting between Reagan and the Soviet leader,

Yuri Andropov, and of reaching some arms-control agreement before the 1984 election.

The consensus in Washington was that the Korean-airliner event had sharply altered the political atmosphere. When the atmosphere changes, so do "realities." Just as the SALT II arms-control agreement reached by the Carter Administration was a dead duck as a result of the atmosphere following the Soviet invasion of Afghanistan, it was assumed that criticism of the Administration's arms-control policy, and opposition to the MX missile, would not be in fashion for a time. "The atmosphere" is sometimes used as an excuse to justify an action the politicians wish to take anyway. The Senate Democratic leaders had no stomach for taking up the SALT agreement in 1980, an election year; some people who had doubts about the MX but were afraid of the political consequences of opposing it would use the atmosphere as a rationale for supporting it. (Reagan helped set the stage in his Labor Day speech when he linked—by means of a considerable stretch—the shooting down of the plane with a plea for the MX.) Thus, the Senate, on the day after Congress reconvened, approved overwhelmingly a House-Senate compromise of a military-spending-authorization bill that contained funds for the MX; only eight senators voted against it. Two days later, the House approved the compromise by a majority of more than a hundred votes. (The bill also authorized the production of nerve-gas weaponry, for the first time since 1969. The Senate had approved the nerve-gas production earlier this summer by a one-vote margin after Vice-President George Bush broke a tie. The House had rejected it.) In July, the House approved the MX in the authorization bill by only thirteen votes—far fewer than had approved it earlier in the year—and House opponents of the MX had hoped to muster enough votes to defeat it when the bill appropriating money for the military comes up later this fall (though whether they would have ultimately prevailed is dubious). Now they are simply hoping that their defeat will not be of major proportions; and consideration of the appropriations bill is being delayed until passions cool. The authorization bill increased military expenditures by about five per cent after inflation—the amount specified in the congressional budget resolution after a protracted wrangle between each chamber and the Administration, which had sought a ten-per-cent increase. (The Senate, controlled by Republicans, had voted for six per cent and the House for four per cent.)

Democrats were chagrined that the Korean-airliner episode had put them in an awkward position on the subjects of arms and arms control—at least for a while—and were generally of the view that the episode had helped Reagan politically. (No event escapes analysis of its political implications.) Polls taken for the White House pointed to the same conclusion. One Democratic senator said to me, "Reagan's come out ahead here. What he had been saying about the Soviet Union seems to have been validated. And any time you show yourself to be cool under fire, you're helped; he needed that kind of help badly." The fact that the story of the Soviet action turned out to be more complicated, as more facts were known, than the Administration had at first suggested—that there was evidence of a Soviet miscalculation, that an American reconnaissance plane was in the same area for a while, that the Soviets are known to have standing orders to shoot down planes that invade their territory—did not change the domestic politics of the situation. The climate had already been established—and political climates are, by definition, not rational. There was some difficulty on Capitol Hill in arriving at the wording of a resolution expressing Congress's wrath: the hope was to find wording that would receive unanimous support, but getting five hundred and thirty-five members of Congress to agree on anything would be something of a miracle. Various senators—citing polls and other indicia of constituent reaction—wanted to register various degrees of outrage. Senator Jesse Helms, Republican of North Carolina, who is up for reelection next year, insisted on forcing votes on propositions that would embarrass other members (as he often does)—propositions that, for example, would demand the recall of our Ambassador to the Soviet Union and the expulsion of Soviet diplomats from this country. Other senators would have to vote against Helms' amendments with the knowledge that Helms' allies would be working up mailings criticizing them for it.

The struggling of Congress over what to do about Lebanon was an example of another political principle: in difficult foreign-policy matters Congress often wants a role but not responsibility. It wanted to be consulted, and to have something to say, about the stationing of Marines in a situation where they were in obvious danger, but it didn't want to take it upon itself to decide when they should be removed. The War Powers Act of 1973, the vehicle by which Congress sought to establish its prerogatives, is an odd law that got exactly backward what Congress really wanted. It was passed in reaction to the undeclared wars in Korea and Vietnam, in an attempt to reinforce the Constitution's giving of the authority to declare war to the Congress. The theory was that under the Constitution the President, as Commander-in-Chief, has the authority to manage the armed forces but not to take the country into war without the consent of the people's representatives. One problem was that it was difficult to define "war." The result was a compromise that gave the President the right to do pretty much as he pleases for sixty days, after which, if Congress has not passed a resolution approving his action (and if there is still a world), he has to desist. The sixty-day period was to begin when troops were introduced into "hostilities" or facing "imminent involvement in hostilities." The act was a clumsy attempt to codify the uncodifiable. In the case of Lebanon, Congress was once again presented with an accomplished fact: twelve hundred Marines were sent in as a "peacekeeping force" last September in the wake of the Israeli invasion of Lebanon. At the time of the invasion, Alexander Haig, then the Secretary of State, was telling people that this presented a fine opportunity to bring peace and unity to Lebanon—a proposition that seemed illusory to some. When the Marines were stationed in Lebanon, President Reagan said that they would remain "only for a limited period" and that the United States' arrangement with the government of Lebanon "expressly rules out any combat responsibilities for the U.S. forces." When Congress went home in August, some members were already becoming anxious about the seeming indefiniteness of the Marines' stay, and about the apparent danger of their position. On August 29th (three days before the news about the Korean airliner broke), two Marines were killed, and fourteen were wounded. Two more were killed on September 6th. Now two thousand additional Marines and a naval task force are stationed offshore, and the Marines have been empowered to call in air strikes from the task force. Thus, the United States has become intricated in the Lebanese civil war, with a policy based on improvisation and hope. Congress is nervous about the policy, such as it is, but doesn't choose to reverse it. What Congress is insisting on in this instance is the right to tell the President, under the War Powers Act, that it approves of what he is doing. (It would not need the War Powers Act to do this, or to stop the Administration's actions, just as it could have voted at any

time to end the war in Vietnam by cutting off funds for it—
though such action would require the support of two-thirds of
each chamber, to override a presumed Presidential veto.) But the
Administration objected to any use of the War Powers Act. Like
Administrations before it, it dislikes congressional involvement in
the conduct of foreign policy. Moreover, it would prefer to preserve the fiction that it had not got American troops involved in
"hostilities." (Some members of Congress, of both parties, think
the Administration is skirting the law in Central America as well.)
Secretary of State George Shultz was reportedly in private agreement with some Republican leaders on Capitol Hill that the President should proceed under the War Powers Act, but William
Clark, the President's national-security adviser, and Caspar Weinberger, the Secretary of Defense, are said to have been adamantly
opposed. Weinberger and Clark have not been notably astute in
understanding the psyche of Congress. Once its institutional
pride is up, it must be appeased—even if only symbolically. At one
point, House Speaker Thomas P. O'Neill suggested that Congress
would approve, under the War Powers Act, the stationing of the
Marines in Lebanon for at least eighteen months—a period that
would last, as it happened, until after the next Presidential Inauguration. Senator Charles McC. Mathias, Republican of Maryland, proposed invoking the act and approving the presence of
the troops for six months. But since the Administration balked at
the use of the act at all, the negotiations were stymied. A number
of Democrats were upset at the length of O'Neill's offer, yet few
members of Congress want to take responsibility for voting to
remove the Marines, for fear the possible collapse of Lebanon
would be blamed on them; and there is still substantial sentiment
for putting the whole question off until after the Inauguration,
keeping it out of electoral politics. At the week's end, Senate Majority Leader Howard Baker, who had been trying for days to
persuade the White House to be more flexible, decided to introduce his own resolution under the War Powers Act.

Central America was, for the moment, virtually forgotten—
there being no immediate crisis, no particularly clear ideas on
Capitol Hill of what to do about Central America, and little ability
to focus on very many subjects at once. Shortly before the recess,
the House did vote to end the "covert" aid to the rebels in
Nicaragua, but the Senate was not expected to go along, so the

action constituted a "message"—one that the Administration did not enjoy receiving. There had been a brief uproar in late July over the disclosure that the Administration was planning to send warships to conduct maneuvers off the Central American coast, and to send some four thousand combat troops to Honduras, for "exercises" that would last five to six months. The purpose of these moves was variously described as intimidation of the Nicaraguan government, a quarantine of Nicaragua, and an attack on Nicaragua. These actions were taken without Shultz's knowledge—and this provided new grist for the aficionados of the Clark-Shultz relationship. (Shultz is widely presumed to be enjoying a bit of a resurgence these days—thanks in large part to his untypical display of anger over the Korean-airliner incident—but this underestimates Clark.) The appointment of a commission, headed by Henry Kissinger (whom Reagan had made a target during his try for the Republican nomination in 1976), to study the "underlying problems" of Central America coincided with the news of the new military action. The appointment was the subject of much speculation here, because of Kissinger's celebrity and because his motives are always the subject of speculation.

The death of Senator Henry Jackson, Democrat of Washington, on the day that the news of the Korean airliner broke, came as a blow to Washington. Even those Democrats who disagreed with his ultra-hard line on defense and arms-control policy feel the loss of Jackson deeply. Not only was there much in his career that they admired—his standing up to Joseph McCarthy, his championing of the environment and of domestic programs—but they also admired him as an honorable and effective senator. Jackson respected the Senate as an institution and worked hard at the job of legislating; the number of such people is declining. Jackson liked publicity as much as the next senator, but everyone knew that, unlike some of his contemporaries, he took the job seriously. Moreover, Jackson was a very decent man with his colleagues: political differences did not become personal with him; he contributed no rancor to Senate debates. In an institution that appears to be losing its moorings—its sense of history and of how to make things go—the loss of Jackson is major.

As for President Reagan, the speculation goes on, however

futilely, about whether he will run for reelection. The consensus remains that he will, but there is also good reason to think that he won't. Every move he makes is studied for clues to his intentions. But it only makes sense, whatever he plans (assuming he has made up his mind), for him to postpone his announcement as long as possible. His aides and associates can proceed with the reelection effort that they have already begun. Meanwhile, if Reagan is planning to run he is "Presidential" rather than another candidate, and should he not run he is not a lame duck. There is also a practical consideration: as soon as Reagan is a declared candidate, the arguments begin over which of his activities are "political," and so should be charged to his reelection effort rather than to the federal treasury. Not all of Reagan's advisers believe that the elaborate efforts in recent months to woo disaffected groups are such a good idea. It is suggested that what became known as "Hispanics Week," "Black Week" (which ended with television shots of black children standing on the White House lawn and waving to the Reagans as they departed in a helicopter for Camp David), "outreach" efforts to placate women, and so on can backfire. One adviser says that such events lead the Administration to make exaggerated claims for its record, thus undermining its credibility and providing forums for its critics. (During a trip to Minneapolis, in June, in the course of trying to establish himself as "pro-education" the President seemed to be unable to recall what his education program was.) Reagan's response to the fact that malnutrition is rising in this country, and that his own budget cuts are being blamed—the appointment of another commission, containing a number of people opposed to increases in programs providing aid to the hungry—did not help him on the "fairness" issue. The question of the "pilfered" papers from the Carter White House and unusual political espionage during the 1980 campaign has virtually receded from view, but the investigations are going forward, and some reporters are still at work on it, and there is still considerable tension within the Administration over who might be fingered. The economic recovery, which proceeded last spring at a much faster pace than the experts had predicted, appears to be calming down, and much now depends on the effect of the deficits on interest rates—a subject over which the President's chief economic advisers are publicly feuding. (Personal savings and business investment, which supply-side theory had held would be increased by the tax cuts of 1981, are below what they were before the Reagan Administration came into office.) Some of the President's advisers do not want a very strong recovery, for fear it might set off inflation, or fear of inflation. Polls conducted for the White House show the President to be getting good marks for holding down inflation and for the fact that unemployment is easing somewhat (though it is now nine and a half per cent— higher than when Reagan took office). One adviser suggests, however, that the most important thing that has occurred politically of late is that the focus on the economy, which the Administration had established as the key political and policy question for the past two and a half years, has yielded to foreign policy. This is something that the President's advisers had sought to avoid all along, but events have not proved so manageable. Flag-draped coffins coming home from Lebanon, the potential political "downside" of the Korean-airliner incident (the presumed increased difficulty in obtaining a summit conference and, perhaps, an arms-control agreement), the warships in Central America—all combine, this adviser said, to undermine the impression that the Administration sought to give of achieving "peace through strength." The more emphasis there is on these kinds of foreign-policy developments, he said, the worse it is for the Reagan Presidency.

VII

This city last week suffered an overloading of the circuits such as has not been experienced in many years—not, perhaps, since the Vietnam War. The terrible bombing on Sunday, October 23rd, of the Marine headquarters in Beirut—killing, at last count, two hundred and twenty-nine people and wounding some seventy-eight more—followed, two days later, by the news that the United States was leading an invasion to overthrow the government of the tiny Caribbean island of Grenada was more than the capital's nervous system could bear. The politicians, for the most part, had no more information than anybody else; they were going on snatches of news, on rumor, and on briefings that gave them little more information than was already in the public domain. Yet they had to sort through the debris and try to figure out what to say and do—and, as always, try to figure out the political implications. Inevitably, many politicians wanted to see how it all turned out, especially in Grenada, before they took a position. But beneath all that there was a sense of deep unease about the Reagan Administration's handling of foreign policy in general—an unease that had been growing, and came to a head over these latest events. The hard questions that people of both parties felt could no longer be avoided were about the Administration's instincts, wisdom, and competence in its handling of foreign policy. Even before the events of last week, some highly placed people within the Administration were also troubled.

When Congress, at the end of September, gave the President the right, under the War Powers Act, to keep the Marines in Lebanon for another eighteen months, it did so with more than a little anguish. In the House, Speaker Thomas P. O'Neill prevailed on enough Democrats to join with Republicans to carry the resolution, but his younger troops were restive, and actually he did not receive the votes of the majority of his party. In the Senate, Major-

ity Leader Howard Baker had to work strenuously to win the votes
of enough Republicans to make the resolution carry by a vote of
54–46. Both chambers rejected proposals by Democrats to allow
the President to keep the Marines in Lebanon for sixty days, after
which he would have to seek an extension from Congress. Yet
there were deep misgivings on both sides of the aisle about the
Marines' mission and about their safety. A number of Republicans
voted for the resolution with sorely twisted arms. (The President
signed the resolution, but said he did not recognize Congress's
right to invoke the War Powers Act.) The resolution posited a
mission that the Marines themselves could not conceivably carry
out: "To restore full control by the Government of Lebanon over
its own territory." The Christian Phalangist government of Amin
Gemayel, which the Marines are in effect protecting (rather than
being neutral "peacekeepers"), barely controls parts of Beirut, and
that's about all; Moslems, who make up the majority of the
Lebanese population, are underrepresented in the government,
and there are some sixteen militias loose in the country. It has
been no secret in Washington that Secretary of Defense Caspar
Weinberger and the Joint Chiefs of Staff opposed the stationing of
Marines in Lebanon, on the ground that they would be too vulnerable and that their mission did not have the support of the
American people. Several senators, including some close to the
Pentagon, such as Barry Goldwater and the late Henry Jackson,
had also opposed the stationing of Marines in Lebanon, arguing
that they were being placed in a situation from which they would
not be easily extricated and that their lives would be at risk.
Shortly after Baker guided the War Powers resolution through the
Senate, he wrote to Reagan saying that while he was pleased that
he had been able to get a compromise through the Senate, he
wished to remind the President that he had been concerned about
sending the Marines in the first place, and hoped that they would
be removed as soon as possible. Not long before the Marine barracks was blown up, a high official of the Administration said to
me that he was very troubled about Lebanon. "We've got to get out
of there," he said. He added that he thought the United States
would get out of Lebanon before long—it was just a matter of
figuring out a way to declare the mission accomplished.

The first reactions to the news, which broke on Sunday morning, that a truck carrying some twenty-five hundred pounds of

TNT had blown up the building where the Marines were sleeping were a combination of shock and anger: anger at the attack, and also anger that the young men, who were in Lebanon for reasons that few here found persuasive, had been left in such a vulnerable position. The United States Embassy had, after all, been blown up in April by a large van carrying explosives, and sixty-three people, including seventeen Americans, had been killed; it emerged in the course of Sunday's news that the Lebanese had warned the Americans that the Marines might be subject to a similar attack. As Sunday unfolded, the death toll rose from forty-three to a hundred and forty-six. (A second bomb blew up quarters where a smaller contingent of French troops was staying.) On Capitol Hill on Monday, Baker, who had received a large number of calls from agitated senators on Sunday, tried to hold the lid on the congressional reaction by saying that he was going to "keep my mouth shut" until there was more information, and he suggested that others do the same. Similarly, O'Neill tried to keep the events in Lebanon from causing a partisan breakdown of the shaky consensus he had so painfully put together just three weeks earlier. O'Neill was said to believe that Lebanon should not be part of election-year politics, and to share some of the President's stated views about the country's strategic value. But the rebellion among House Democrats against O'Neill was growing, and it was because he feared that a resolution calling for an early withdrawal of the Marines—say, by January 1st—might pass that he, along with some Republican leaders, urged Reagan to give a television address by the end of the week. There remained a strong element of Congress's instinct for wanting a role but not responsibility—the instinct that led it to approve the eighteen-month extension in the first place—but there was also a growing political feeling among members that they did not want to be responsible for an increasing number of deaths of Marines in Lebanon. (Seven Marines had been killed there before the truck-bomb attack.) It was a question of when the pendulum would swing to that side, and it was the fear that it was on the way to doing so that led congressional leaders to urge Reagan to give his speech.

Those who disagreed with the President's Lebanon policy nevertheless felt trapped by the same logic as the President appeared to be: whether or not the Marines should have been there in the first place—a question the President does not acknowledge, of course—the bombing made it impossible to pull them out any time soon. That would be "yielding to terrorists" and "turning tail." So the Marines would remain in Lebanon, and vulnerable, while the policymakers and politicians in Washington tried to figure out how to save face. One big question on a number of people's minds here was how literally to take the President's apparent raising of the American stake in Lebanon following the truck-bomb attack. The purpose of the American presence had been to attempt to bring order to Lebanon's sectarian troubles and to obtain the removal of foreign troops from the area—chores that were already difficult enough. When he returned early Sunday morning from what was to have been a relaxed golfing weekend in Georgia (a weekend that had already been interrupted by an eerie incident in which a man driving a truck crashed through the gates of the Augusta National Golf Club, where the President was staying, and temporarily took some of the President's aides hostage), Reagan spoke, on the White House lawn, in the rain, from what seemed to be his own deep instincts. He said that the attack in Beirut showed "the bestial nature of those who would assume power if they could have their way and drive us out of that area," and that "we must be more determined than ever that they cannot take over that vital and strategic area of the earth, or, for that matter, any other part of the earth." He was, it was presumed, referring to the Soviet Union, whose military support of Syria had come under increasing Presidential criticism. (Syria has about forty thousand troops in Lebanon.) In a television appearance the following day, Reagan declared Lebanon to be in our "vital interests" and said that the same "force" that had taken over in Ethiopia and Yemen—by which he clearly meant the Soviet Union—could not be allowed to prevail in Lebanon. This raised the question of what the sixteen hundred Marines stationed in Lebanon could do about all this.

On Sunday, Senator Charles McC. Mathias, of Maryland, a liberal Republican and a senior member of the Foreign Relations Committee, whose agreeing to the eighteen-month extension of the Marines' stay in Lebanon had been crucial to its carrying in the Senate (he had initially supported a six-month extension), was on television, looking pained. "We cannot any longer have Marines there just as a presence, just as a symbolic act—because the price of that symbolism is too high," Mathias said. The following day,

Senator Dan Quayle, Republican of Indiana and one of those Howard Baker had to work hardest to persuade to go along with the eighteen months, said in a Senate speech that "it is important that we reexamine the whole question of why we have Marines in Lebanon."

The general reaction in Congress was to follow the usual procedure: let a few members of Congress get out in front with their criticism and, if the sky doesn't fall on them, join in. Senator Edward Kennedy on Monday denounced what he termed the "negligence" that had left the Marines so exposed to danger and said that Congress should repeal the eighteen-month extension of their stay in Lebanon. Kennedy said that if there was no demonstrable progress in the reconciliation talks among the various Lebanese factions which were supposed to take place shortly, the Marines should be brought home by January 1st. Among other things, this was a way of putting pressure on Gemayel. (The talks had been hung up over problems of where to hold them—some groups did not want to meet at the Beirut airport, Gemayel-Marine territory, and there was said to be difficulty finding sufficient hotel space in Geneva. Moreover, sitting around the table would be representatives of various warring clans who had tried to kill each other off. Now the talks are scheduled to begin in Geneva this week.) Senator Sam Nunn, of Georgia, the ranking Democrat on the Armed Services Committee and a man of great influence within his party, said on television Sunday and Monday that "we ought to go back to the drawing board and say, 'Mr. President, what are the Marines doing there and under what terms would they be withdrawn?' " Nunn said that the Marines had become "hostages." He also said that his study of the map did not suggest that Lebanon is in our "vital interests." (Among the new dangers raised by the bombing incident was that the Administration would, as it was hinting, retaliate against Iran, which Weinberger instantly blamed for the deed in Beirut, in the long-running war between Iran and Iraq—a war that was already posing new risks to the Persian Gulf. And since Syria was said to be protecting the Iranian-connected sect in Lebanon, there was also talk of retaliation against Syrian forces.)

Washington was still reeling from the events in Beirut and trying to sort out its thinking when it awoke to the news on Tuesday morning that the United States had invaded Grenada. In an appearance that morning in the White House pressroom, with Eugenia Charles, the Prime Minister of Dominica, by his side, the President said that the primary purpose of the invasion was to rescue Americans on the island—some six hundred and fifty were there as students at a medical school—in the wake of a bloody coup that had occurred the previous week. Reagan said that another goal of the mission was "the restoration of democratic institutions in Grenada." He added that the United States had acted at the request of the Organization of Eastern Caribbean States (which virtually no one had heard of until that moment), headed by Mrs. Charles. Reagan, of course, was known to have been concerned about Grenada for some time. (During a television speech appealing for his large military budget last March, he had shown the nation aerial photographs of an airstrip that he said was being built with Cuban help for the purpose of stirring up more trouble in the Caribbean.) The previous leader in Grenada, Maurice Bishop, who was killed in the recent coup, had been a Marxist and an ally of Fidel Castro. Bishop had come to Washington last June in an attempt to ease relations, and had met with some high officials but not with the President or the Secretary of State. There has been an argument here about whether the Administration was forthcoming enough with Bishop—or whether more militant Marxists overthrew Bishop because he had reached out to the United States. Nevertheless, it had also been clear for quite a while that the Reagan Administration was spoiling to land a big punch against Cuba.

After the news of the Grenada invasion broke, there was a strong feeling on Capitol Hill of "What next?," yet most, but by no means all, Republicans supported the Administration's action in Grenada right away. Some Democrats held their fire until they could get more information, and until they could see how the venture turned out—whether it would be "successful" and popularly accepted—but others lashed out. Many proceeded on the realization that when Presidents punch somebody in the nose—and get away with it—the nation tends to applaud. A Senate Democratic aide said to me, "If it works, I'm prepared to call it a splendid little war." Some Democrats felt that preventing another Cuban outpost, which could be used for aggression in the area, was warranted. Some people were torn. On the other hand, Senator Daniel Patrick Moynihan, Democrat of New York and the vice-chairman of the Select Committee on Intelligence, angrily denounced the invasion as an "act of war" and said, "I don't know that you bring in democracy at the point of a bayonet." Representative Thomas Downey, Democrat of New York, said on the House floor Tuesday afternoon that he feared that "this is an Administration that shoots first and asks questions later." As a result of a press conference held by Secretary of State George Shultz that afternoon, it became clear that the decisions about Grenada had been taken over the weekend—at the golf course in Augusta and by exhausted officials Sunday night, after the bombing in Beirut. Embarrassing questions had by now arisen: Why had the President not listened to British Prime Minister Margaret Thatcher, who had advised against the invasion? (Grenada is a member of the Commonwealth.) Why had the action been taken in apparent disregard for the treaty of the Organization of American States, which forbids outside intervention in the internal affairs of other nations of the hemisphere? Why couldn't the students have simply been evacuated if they were indeed in danger and wanted to leave the island? Why did insuring the safety of the students require the overthrow of the Grenadian government?

Mrs. Thatcher's objections were based on the fact that she did not believe that the British citizens residing on the island were in danger but felt that an invasion would place them in danger; on a concern that, however unpleasant the political situation in Grenada was, it did not justify invading a sovereign state; and on concerns about the international implications—that the United States would be subject to condemnation for the sorts of actions for which it condemned the Soviet Union. She was also concerned that the invasion would make the already sensitive matter of the deployment of cruise missiles in Britain—to be jointly controlled by the United States and Britain—an even more difficult political problem. She was also said to be disturbed by what she considered to be completely inadequate consultation: Reagan did not call her until Monday afternoon, after he had already made a tentative decision to go ahead with the invasion, and only three hours after he spoke with her he ordered it to go forward. Mrs. Thatcher's Government was put in a highly embarrassing situation in Parliament—having said on Monday that the United States did not intend to invade Grenada. Later in the week, Mrs. Thatcher told a radio audience, "As a general rule, we in the Western democracies use our force to defend our way of life. We do not use it to walk into other people's countries—independent sovereign territories."

Perhaps the President's case, made in his speech, would go over domestically: that he was convinced the students would be harmed or taken hostage ("The nightmare of our hostages in Iran must never be repeated"), and that munitions that our forces discovered on the island made it "clear" that "a Cuban occupation of the island had been planned," and that Grenada was "a Soviet-Cuban colony being readied as a major military bastion to export terror and undermine democracy." There was evidently a fairly substantial intelligence failure: the Administration planners had anticipated neither the size nor the strength of the Cuban force on the island, nor did they anticipate the extent of the resistance that the United States troops met. The possibility of the attack had been well advertised. At week's end, an operation that was supposed to be swift and surgical was still going on, and Pentagon officials were saying that American forces might have to stay on Grenada "indefinitely" to prevent a Cuban return. By Friday, it emerged that six thousand American troops were participating in the Grenada invasion—twice the number that had been previously disclosed. (As of today, Sunday, sixteen American soldiers have been killed in Grenada, three are missing, and seventy-seven have been wounded.) Admiral Wesley McDonald, who was in charge of the operation, said at a Pentagon briefing on Friday that captured documents showed that "the Cubans were planning to put their government into Grenada," and that he could not rule out the establishment of an American base there. There was also a question about why only some four hundred of the eleven hundred Americans said to have been on the island were evacuated. On Saturday, the Pentagon reduced its estimate of the number of Cubans on the island from eleven hundred to between seven hundred and seven hundred and fifty. One House Democrat says he thinks that the invasion of Grenada is a "reinforcer"—it reinforces the positive views of those who are inclined to applaud this sort of action, and it reinforces the concerns of those who are worried about the Reagan Administration's conduct of foreign policy. There is the question of what Congress would have the time to do, even if it knew what to do, about these events. It is scheduled to adjourn on November 18th—less than three weeks from now—

and not to return until January 23rd. Some members are worried about what the Administration might do during that period; some are worried about the appearances of their being out of Washington for so long.

Even before the events of the past week, there had been a growing feeling in Washington that when it came to foreign policy the Administration, to put it bluntly, did not know what it was doing. United States–Soviet relations were as bad as they had been at any time since the Cold War. Even within the Administration there was a concern, at high levels, that its policies had been too confrontational, that there was an assumption that there was no point in dealing with the Soviet Union in any serious way—in finding out what was on its mind. Indications that the facts surrounding the Soviet shooting down of the Korean airliner on September 1st were not as the Administration had instantly portrayed them— that, contrary to the officials' assertions, the Soviet pilot may have actually thought he was shooting at a reconnaissance plane— seemed of no moment to the Administration. Evidence has been coming out that the President's grasp of arms-control issues is somewhat lacking: the New York *Times* printed a story, which congressional sources confirm, that in a meeting with members of Congress the President indicated that he had only recently realized that most of the Soviet Union's nuclear force, unlike that of the United States, was concentrated in heavy land-based missiles, and that his demands that the Soviets dismantle a large number of those missiles, without equivalent concessions by the United States, were seen by many as one-sided. I have been told by someone who has met with the President on arms control that he doesn't really grasp the issue of throw-weight—the lifting power of missiles—in which the Soviet Union also has an advantage, because the United States chose not to build such heavy missiles. The insistence of some of the President's arms-control advisers on reducing the Soviet throw-weight is seen as one of the obstacles, perhaps intended, to reaching an agreement. Therefore, while the President may well, as his aides insist, want an arms-control agreement, it appears that he may not be sufficiently informed to deal with his own bureaucracy. And there is a feeling within the Administration—Vice-President George Bush even indicated so out loud a few months ago—that the United States' position on the intermediate-range missiles must, as it has not so far, take the British and French missiles into account. Before the past week, concern had been growing that not only was the Administration widening the war in Central America but, protestations notwith-standing, the emphasis was on military rather than diplomatic solutions. (The week before last, the House voted to cut off funds for the "covert" war in Nicaragua. This was a blunt move, but the Administration had refused to heed warnings from Capitol Hill that it did not approve of the expansion of the effort in Nicaragua from one to "interdict" weapons going into El Salvador to one to overthrow the Sandinista regime.) The Administration's taste for covert action—said to be under way on the grandest scale in twenty years—has made a number of people on Capitol Hill, of both parties, uneasy. William Casey, the director of the Central Intelligence Agency, seems bent on taking it back to the glory days of the O.S.S., in which he served. There are widely held concerns not only about Casey's judgment but about whether there is any-one in the Administration sufficiently knowledgeable, and of a disposition, to stop him. Casey is known to have the Presi-dent's ear.

The recent foreign-policy developments also occurred against a backdrop of considerable personnel turmoil within the Admin-istration—turmoil that had an almost antic quality except that the jobs that were being shuffled around were of major importance. There have been many versions in print about what, exactly, hap-pened, but it is a fact that William Clark, the President's national-security adviser until recently, did get tired of the job and the accompanying hassle, and did suggest to the President that he might like the newly vacated job of Secretary of the Interior. James Watt had finally been forced to resign by a near-revolt within the Republican Party, which increasingly saw him as a political liability. The President remained detached. Watt's now famous comment, in September, about the makeup of an advisory panel on coal leasing ("I have a black, a woman, two Jews, and a cripple") was the last straw in a pile that had grown quite high. Clark, who had never mastered his job and had been in nearly constant battle with other key White House aides—mainly James Baker, the Chief of Staff, and Michael Deaver, the Deputy Chief of Staff and a man close to the Reagans and, increasingly, to Baker—simply wanted out. Reagan astonished nearly everyone in Washington when he announced, late in the afternoon of October 13th, that Clark was going to the Interior Department. It is also a fact that Baker and Deaver then made a move to become national-security adviser and Chief of Staff, respectively, and they came very, very close to pulling it off. Reagan actually agreed to make the changes, but then, when a group made up of Clark, Weinberger, Casey, and Edwin Meese found out about this and expressed vehement opposition, he changed his mind. The episode suggests a certain haphazard approach to decision-making by the President, and also an unusual number of internal schisms, even as White Houses go. Added to this was the outrage of Jeane Kirkpatrick, the United States Ambassador to the United Nations, whose name had been put forward by hard-liners for the National Security Council job, but who did not receive it. The new national-security adviser, Robert McFarlane, is a retired Marine professional who had served as Clark's deputy and, most recently, as special envoy to the Middle East. He was a military assistant to Henry Kissinger when Kissinger was Nixon's national-security adviser. McFarlane, who was expected to be more of an implementer and less of an ideologue than Clark, had been opposed by a number of the hardliners, apparently because of his Kissinger connection, and because—unlike Clark—he had sought a compromise with Congress on the MX missile. (It is one of the several ironies of the current situation that just before his appointment McFarlane had recommended that the Marines take an even more active role on the side of the Gemayel government.) Reagan tried to assuage Mrs. Kirkpatrick by offering her a Washington-based job as a counsellor to the President, but she saw that the job did not carry the sort of influence she sought. Mrs. Kirkpatrick and what were described as "sources close to" her then took to the Washington *Post* and *Newsweek* to vent her complaints. The *Post* quoted Mrs. Kirkpatrick as saying that Clark's departure from the N.S.C. job was "an unmitigated disaster," and she was said to be concerned that foreign policy would be dominated by "the weak and rudderless leadership" of Secretary of State Shultz and his key aides. "As Kirkpatrick sees it," *Newsweek* reported, "the Baker-Deaver-Bush school aims to package Reagan with a safe, noncontroversial foreign policy during the 1984 election campaign—to 'homogenize Reagan.' " The *Post* story ran on the front page on the morning of the Beirut bombing, and the *Newsweek* story appeared the following day. It was quite a performance, and the sort of thing that in another Administration would get someone fired—or, at least, severely reprimanded—but not in the relaxed ambience of the Reagan Administration.

The sense of things being out of control in the last week was added to by the sudden firing, on Tuesday, by Reagan of three of the six members of the Civil Rights Commission. His move not only broke the tradition of the independence of the commission but also abruptly ended negotiations with a bipartisan group of senators who were trying to compromise with the Reagan Administration on its desire for a more sympathetic commission.

On Tuesday of this past week, I spoke with Senator Mark Andrews, Republican of North Dakota, about the astounding events that were unfolding. Andrews had reluctantly voted for the eighteen-month extension, at the behest of Howard Baker. Referring to the killing of the Marines in Beirut and to the fact that their safety had been so ill provided for, he said, "I wonder if anybody's even minding the store." He continued, "The people in North Dakota are saying, 'What kind of an outfit doesn't guard kids when they're sleeping at night?' It gets back to whether the Administration knows what it's doing. Does the President have a plan? They keep putting flyweights in key positions. Nothing is happening around the disarmament table. That's not the decisiveness the American people wanted. If you're talking about farm policy or foreign policy, there's no decisiveness. We haven't had a steady policy toward the Soviet Union. There's just drift and indecision."

On Wednesday, I spoke with Senator Mathias. "I'm somewhat aghast," he said. "I'm trying to catch my breath." Mathias said that his concern about Lebanon was that there was no clearly defined mission for the Marines, and that the Administration had allowed the political process in the Middle East to become "dead in the water." He added, "Without a political process, there's nothing for the Marines to do." Referring to the long, hard negotiations he felt were necessary in the Middle East, Mathias said, "That's not Ronald Reagan's concept of a heroic Presidency, but it has to be done." Mathias, like others, said that the events in Grenada had temporarily distracted Congress from Lebanon, but he said that attention would return to it soon. As for Grenada, Mathias said that while a case could be made for the Administration's rationale, as a counsellor to the Kissinger commission on Central American policy he was distressed by the renewal at this point of the "ghosts of old American raids in the Caribbean, which come back to haunt you every day." He added, "You wonder where the sensitivity is." He also wondered, he said, why an Administration that sets so much store by linkage—seeking the cooperation of our allies on matters of importance to us—did not see that a "reverse linkage" might occur in the case of Grenada. Mathias also expressed concern about the decision-making process that led to the invasion of Grenada—calling it "the Golf Course War." He said, "I think it was very bad to discuss this on a golf course; you need a meeting with the naysayers around. They weren't on the golf course." Mathias raised the question, as others have, whether the safety and the evacuation of the students could not have been achieved by diplomatic means. As for Lebanon, Mathias said, "It's the same failing. We didn't press the political process in the Middle East, and we didn't pursue it in Grenada. Maurice Bishop provided an opening that we did not work. The common theme is that the commitment to work through the political process is yet to be seen. It's hard work; it requires great attention to detail, and *people*—and that's part of the problem."

The President's televised address on Thursday night was an awesome display of Reagan's talent: the voice and the delivery were soothing, and his contact with the viewer was intimate; the arguments had a surface plausibility; and he effectively, if manipulatively, appealed to the emotions. He addressed questions that had been raised in the course of the week with rhetorical questions of his own: "To answer those who ask if we're serving any purpose in being there, let me answer a question with a question: Would the terrorists have launched their suicide attacks against the multinational force if it were not doing its job?" Setting forth his world view, he said, "The events in Lebanon and Grenada, though oceans apart, are closely related. Not only has Moscow assisted and encouraged the violence in both countries, but it provides direct support through a network of surrogates and terrorists." He talked again of the strategic importance of Lebanon and asked, "If we turned our backs on Lebanon now, what would be the future of Israel?" (Actually, Israel, which invaded Lebanon last year in order to drive out the Palestine Liberation Organization, had grown tired of taking casualties, and in early September had withdrawn to southern Lebanon.) Reagan spoke emotionally of the deaths of the Marines in Lebanon, and asked, "Are we to tell them their sacrifice was wasted?"

On Friday and Saturday, the tensions that had been building all week on Capitol Hill spilled over into Senate debates. Howard Baker and other key Republicans decided not to fight a move by Democrats to apply the War Powers Act to the President's action in Grenada, thus limiting the troops' stay to sixty days unless Congress approves an extension. Earlier in the week, this might have appeared to be a hypothetical exercise, but, given the news out of Grenada on Thursday and Friday, that no longer seemed the case. The Senate passed the resolution on Friday by a vote of sixty-four to twenty, with Baker and a majority of other Republicans voting in favor. The House will take up a resolution applying the War Powers Act to Grenada this week. Republicans generally praised the President's speech as a triumph, and many Democrats were impressed with the latest display of Reagan's oratorical skills—and with the fact that the operation on Grenada seemed to have strong public support. Yet some Democrats spoke out, and others raised questions. Senator Daniel Inouye, Democrat of Hawaii and a member of the Intelligence Committee, said, following a special briefing of the committee, that he wanted to see "further evidence" that Americans in Grenada had been in danger. Other Intelligence Committee members—of both parties—raised questions concerning the Administration's claims about the Cuban role on the island. Moynihan said, "We simply do not know enough yet to draw any firm conclusions about Cuba's role or intentions. Nothing has been discovered so far that would show with any certainty that Cuba was planning to take over Grenada." On Friday, O'Neill, who had earlier in the week said that comment about Grenada should be withheld while the operation was under way, said that the people may support the invasion but asked, "Is it the right thing to do? No, it isn't the right thing to do." He also said, referring to Reagan, "To be perfectly truthful, his policy scares me. We can't go the way of gunboat diplomacy."

The Senate's adoption, on Friday, of the resolution applying the War Powers Act to Grenada prompted Howard Baker to offer a resolution commending the President for "swift and effective action in protecting the lives of American citizens in Grenada." Baker said the President's action there was "in the manifest best interest of this country and its security for years to come." He was rebutted by, among others, Lowell Weicker, Republican of Connecticut and a maverick, who said that the President had violated the O.A.S. charter, the War Powers Act, and the Constitution—for forbidding press coverage of the Grenada operation. Baker's move in turn prompted Senate Minority Leader Robert Byrd to offer an amendment criticizing the Administration for providing "inadequate" security for the Marines in Beirut, and calling for a transferral of the peacekeeping duties to a United Nations force or to other forces from neutral countries. All week, there had been growing bipartisan distress at officials' almost blasé assurances that the truck-bomb attack could not have been prevented. Weinberger said on television, "Nothing can work against a suicidal attack like that," and Marine Commandant Paul X. Kelley, whom Weinberger sent to Beirut following the attack, said he was "totally satisfied" with the security procedures that had been in effect before the bombing. "I think we had very adequate security measures," Kelley said. In his speech, Reagan talked as if this sort of thing could not be helped. Yet Americans had learned how to prevent such attacks in Vietnam, and the Embassy personnel in Beirut, now sheltered by the British, are far better protected than the Marines were. One factor, many senators thought, was that the Administration was insisting that the Marines were on a peacekeeping mission, and not involved in combat, and wanted to keep up the appearance that this was the case. After about four hours of debate on Friday, Baker and Byrd both backed off, but there was an unspoken bipartisan feeling in the Senate that, as one Senate Republican described it, "we've got to get those Marines the hell out of there." Kennedy and John Warner, Republican of Virginia, who sit on the Armed Services Committee, have been asking some hard questions about why the security was so poor, and are planning further inquiry. On Friday, Warner told the Senate that the investigation "in my humble judgment . . . is the most serious and poses the broadest range of issues that I personally have ever witnessed in my career." Perhaps because the Pentagon was aware that it was headed for rough waters, Weinberger on Saturday announced that the Pentagon would hold its own investigation into the matter. Also on Saturday, Baker and Byrd tentatively agreed to send a committee of inquiry to Grenada; the senators were as in the dark about what was going on there as everyone else, because of the Administration's tight censorship of the news—and they were becoming increasingly uncomfortable. Privately, a large number of senators were incredulous at the idea that a group of senators trotting about the island could find out the "facts" (as opposed to ascertaining them through careful hearings in Washington), but the Senate, like much of the government, was groping.

At the end of the week, I spoke by phone to one of the President's advisers. "It's white-knuckle time," he said. He felt that the evidence of the danger in Grenada which the President offered in his speech would be helpful, but he felt that the Administration was at very high risk in both Lebanon and the Caribbean. In both places, he said, it's not a question of where we are now but how we get out, and how soon. He recognized that the President's speech was a holding action—that its effect could be only temporary. "We find these situations easier to get into than to get out of," he said. "If we pull the Marines out of Lebanon in the next ninety days, the damage will be minimized, but if they are there next spring and summer and fall—during an election campaign—it's going to hurt us." The crux of the problem for the Administration, of course, is that misgivings about how Reagan would handle foreign policy— the fear that he might be, as the shorthand for it went, "triggerhappy"—was one of his greatest vulnerabilities in 1980. As a matter of fact, even before the events of the past week, surveys taken for the White House showed that what worried people most about the Reagan Administration was its handling of foreign policy. This ranked far above unemployment, which was next. But perhaps the White House was comforting itself with a thought offered to me by one of its officials not long ago. This man said, "It's how you manage foreign policy between April and November of next year that will matter—not what we've done in the past."

VIII

In one important respect, the race for the Democratic nomination is very far along, and in that respect it is different in nature—as it was designed to be—from any previous nomination contest. The structure of the race plays into the hands of the front-runners—as it was designed to do—and therefore the front-runners in this particular race are, at least as of now, in a different position from those in previous races; that is, there appears to be more supporting their front-runnerness. However, the current front-runners, Walter Mondale and John Glenn, are in quite different positions from each other: in fact, the composition, nature, style, and relative strengths of their campaigns and candidacies are so different that comparisons are almost impossible. But in another very important respect the race for the Democratic nomination remains unformed: the public is just beginning to tune in; and both Glenn and Mondale have some way to go in defining their candidacies—defining them, that is, in the way that they want them defined. Much of what has been going on in the past month or so has been an effort on the part of both men not only to define themselves but to define each other in the voters' minds.

The two reasons the contest seems to be so much further along in sorting out the candidates are that it was intended to be, and that the Mondale campaign has methodically and, so far, successfully taken advantage of the new shape of the contest—a shape the Mondale people had very much to do with. It was the strategy of the Mondale campaign to make the other candidates run on terms it defined: they would have to run national campaigns, thus making their ability to organize well in a state with an early contest more difficult and also less valuable than before. Events that occurred in other places—straw polls and the like—or that did not occur (the candidates' failure to catch on elsewhere) would affect their chances in the early states. Having to run national campaigns this year, and to enter straw polls to try to establish their viability, put a premium on fund-raising, and three candidates—Alan Cranston, Gary Hart, and Fritz Hollings—are in debt. Another purpose of forcing a national campaign on the other candidates was to subject them to national scrutiny early, to give no one a free ride. It was because the Mondale people feared that Glenn was getting by without being looked at very carefully—was coasting along on his celebrity as a former astronaut—that they opened fire on his record this fall.

Perhaps some combination of events will upend the current assumptions. One factor that makes any campaign unpredictable is the unknowable chemistry of the campaign itself: the interaction of the candidates with the voters and with each other, and the unforeseeable events. Another factor is math: how the candidates divide the vote—which ones draw from which others' potential supporters. It is often forgotten that in 1976 Jimmy Carter won the New Hampshire primary with twenty-nine per cent of the vote, only five percentage points ahead of Morris Udall; then there were Birch Bayh, with sixteen per cent; Fred Harris, with eleven per cent; Sargent Shriver, with nine per cent; and other candidates with a scattering of votes. It is generally accepted that Bayh, Harris, and Shriver all drew from Udall. Within the Mondale camp, there is some mixed opinion on how much to worry about the math of 1984. While Mondale could be hurt by several candidates vying for the same voters he is after (though there are conservative candidates who could pull voters from Glenn), the prevailing view seems to be, consistent with the campaign's over-all strategy, that few of the other candidates will be viable long enough to do much damage. Therefore, the thinking goes, even if the math should lead to a reversal in one of the early states the other candidates will not have enough resources to carry on for very long. The campaign-finance law itself will help to eliminate candidates: any candidate who fails to receive ten per cent of the vote in two consecutive contests he enters is cut off from federal matching funds thirty days later, and can qualify for funds once again only by getting twenty per cent of the vote in a subsequent contest.

There is as yet some uncertainty about the calendar—Iowa and New Hampshire are still struggling to maintain the momentary, and lucrative, glory of holding the first two contests, and some other states are still working out where they will come on line. But it remains the case that there will be much less time in 1984 between the Iowa caucus and the New Hampshire primary and between New Hampshire and several other states. As of now, Iowa will hold its caucus on February 20th or 27th, and the New Hampshire primary will be held on February 28th (the Democratic National Committee has not yet agreed to these dates), and then, only two weeks after New Hampshire, on March 13th, there will be eleven contests; twenty-one contests in all will be held within the eight days from March 13th to March 20th. By April 3rd, more than half of the three thousand nine hundred and thirty-three delegates will have been chosen (it takes a majority to win).

Of the eight Democrats now in the race—Reubin Askew, Alan Cranston, John Glenn, Gary Hart, Fritz Hollings, Jesse Jackson, George McGovern, and Walter Mondale—Glenn and Mondale started out with the most advantages. Both were nationally known to begin with; both have strong assets as candidates; and both represent a broad spectrum of the Party. Askew, who is running as the "different" candidate, will have more money than some of the other minor candidates come January and, it is believed, could possibly carve out a slice of the conservative vote in the early states: he has come out against the unlimited right to abortion, and against the nuclear freeze. Alan Cranston has ridden the nuclear-freeze issue—presenting himself as the candidate who cares most about arms control—with some success, but there appear now to be limits on how far he can take this. Cranston on occasion conveys a certain naïveté about dealing with the Soviet Union; he has also been criticized by some liberals for his support of the B-1 bomber and other weapons systems, and for his support of certain tax breaks for business. Moreover, Cranston is being crowded now by George McGovern who entered the race on September 13th. For McGovern, the candidacy is a way to get some attention to what he has to say; before he was a candidate he couldn't get anyone's ear. McGovern seems never to have recovered from his devastating loss to Richard Nixon in 1972; he can tell himself that he was right in his opposition to the Vietnam War, and that he was defeated by a corrupt Administration using illegal means to defeat him. So McGovern, with nothing to lose, can take uncompromising, politically unconventional positions:

even before the recent events in Lebanon and Grenada he said, "Let's get out of Central America. Bring the Marines out of that religious war in Lebanon." He has called for the United States to engage at least temporarily in a unilateral weapons freeze. (The nuclear freeze that is being widely espoused is always carefully described by its supporters as "mutual.") Thus, for those who want to make a certain kind of statement McGovern is a vehicle, and he seems to arouse a degree of sentimental support among Democratic audiences. Gary Hart has tried to present his campaign as one of the "new generation" and of "new ideas," but he hasn't seemed to have been able to catch on. One problem may be that his ideas aren't so different from those of others; moreover, ideas have to be conveyed through an appealing persona—position papers don't win campaigns. Hart's political persona does not seem to be going over—it appears too cold and withdrawn. He has recently decided on the new tack of reaching for the women's vote. At a forum on arms control at Harvard, in mid-October, he said, to great applause, "I think those of us who happen to be men ought to begin finally to listen to the women of this society." Fritz Hollings has had trouble establishing himself as a national candidate. He is trying to present himself as a fiscally responsible, reasonable man, who will keep the Democratic Party from making what he sees as its old mistakes. He is a smart man, and a witty man, but sometimes the wit spills over into meanness and is at someone else's expense; sometimes it gets Hollings himself into trouble. At the moment, the effect of the candidacy of Jesse Jackson, who entered the race on November 3rd, is the subject of much speculation and little consensus.

Throughout the year, there have been rumors of others' possibly entering the race—rumors usually fanned by those who are dissatisfied with the current field (there has seldom been a field that people haven't been dissatisfied with). Inevitably, the name of Edward Kennedy keeps floating about; others whose names have come up are Mario Cuomo, the governor of New York (but Cuomo has now endorsed Mondale), and Senator Dale Bumpers, of Arkansas, who came very close to entering the race earlier this year but then, in early April, backed off. Bumpers attributed his decision publicly to a lack of time to raise enough money and build an organization, but there seemed also to be a strong element of ambivalence on his part about running. Eugene McCarthy is talking about running. It would seem now, however, that the requirements for making the race are so formidable that, barring a set of unpredictable events, and except for some symbolic candidacy, the list is closed.

The potential candidacy of Jesse Jackson had divided black leaders from the time it was first considered. It grew out of an interest on the part of some black leaders in the idea of having a black candidate in order to press the concerns of blacks on the Democratic Party and perhaps act as a broker at the Convention—and Jackson was the person most interested in making the race. Many black leaders were opposed—some privately, some publicly. Among those publicly opposed have been Coretta Scott King, the widow of Martin Luther King, Jr., to whom Jackson was once an aide; Andrew Young, the mayor of Atlanta; Coleman Young, the mayor of Detroit; Julian Bond, a former civil-rights leader and now a member of the Georgia senate; and Benjamin Hooks, the executive director of the N.A.A.C.P. Jackson also has some prominent black supporters, among them Richard Hatcher, the mayor of Gary, Indiana, and Representative John Conyers, of Michigan. The controversy surrounding Jackson's candidacy has to do with the tactical implications of his making the race and with Jackson's personality. The concern of a number of blacks has been that Jackson's effort could be counterproductive—that by drawing votes from Mondale it could help nominate Glenn, who is more conservative. One of the earlier arguments for having a black make the race was that if there was a brokered Convention a black candidate with delegates would be in a position to make demands; but a brokered Convention, while theoretically possible, is not, on the basis of recent history, probable. There are of course other rationales as well: several blacks who back the idea of the candidacy feel that the Democratic Party has been taking their support for granted, and that the presence of a black candidate, particularly one as articulate as Jackson, will force more attention in the course of the campaign to issues of concern to blacks.

It is, in fact, the longer-term dynamic of the race which has a number of people, including several sympathetic to Jackson's making the race, worried. The rationale of the Jackson candidacy must be that he offers blacks more hope, is more attuned to their problems, than the other candidates—though he is running, he says, as the candidate of a "rainbow coalition" of blacks, Hispanics,

women, Indians, Chinese, Philippine-Americans. No one doubts
that Jackson's charismatic personality will attract a following during the campaign, whether or not he does well in winning votes or
delegates. There then comes the question of what happens next:
at the Convention, Jackson will inevitably be a center of attention
as the press seeks to learn whether he will back the nominee and
what demands he will make in exchange for his support. This is a
position that a number of people love to be in at Conventions, and
there is no reason to think that Jackson will not make the most of
it. Jackson, to carry out his rationale, will have to make some
demands that cannot be met. Then there will be the problem of
Jackson's trying to transfer the loyalty of his following—assuming
he chooses to do so—to the Democratic nominee, of whom he will
presumably have been critical. For those blacks who believe that
the defeat of Ronald Reagan is the highest priority, this is a real
worry. Jackson's candidacy may not, of course, last all the way to
the Convention, but that doesn't mean he will not be a force there.

The personality issue that a number of prominent blacks have
with Jackson is that they consider him unreliable and demagogic,
a self-promoter. Some of this feeling may well, as Jackson and
certain of his backers say, stem from jealousy and from the fact
that many established black politicians have arrived at their current prominence in the world as it is and do not want the status
quo disturbed. This sentiment does exist, but it may not be as
cynically based as the Jackson forces feel: several black mayors
have won election by putting together a coalition of blacks and
whites, and they feel that a polarizing force, which many see Jackson to be, would make such a coalition impossible. There is also a
sense on the part of a several black leaders that while a key part of
Jackson's mission is to get more blacks registered, black registration has been increasing dramatically since 1980, and a Jackson
Presidential candidacy is not necessary to keep that going. Jackson, it was argued, could have mounted a registration drive without running as a candidate. Jackson and some of those sympathetic to his making the race suggest that objections were being
raised to his candidacy—in contrast to that of, for example,
Cranston, Hart, or McGovern—because he is a black. Jackson
asks, "Where is the division sign on my forehead?" But the same
arguments would not have been made if, say, Coleman Young or
Tom Bradley, the mayor of Los Angeles, had entered the race.

Both are men with solid political credentials; Jackson is a flamboyant, if engaging, character who is running to make a point. There is no' question that Jackson's point is a serious one, and that his bringing more blacks into the political process—if he does it in a way that does not end in their disillusionment—could, as Jackson puts it, "liberalize the process." Yet there is also the question of precedent: what would happen to our political system if leaders of various causes entered the Presidential contests—within both parties—not for the purpose of winning the nomination but in order to gain the votes of a certain faction for negotiating purposes?

A number of elected black leaders have endorsed Mondale. They include Bradley, Bond, and Coleman Young, and Mondale's people believe that other black leaders are prepared to endorse him. Harold Washington, who became mayor of Chicago in a bitter election in April, has not endorsed Jackson, who played a prominent role in the Chicago contest. Jackson's role is said to have been considered not constructive by a number of people, including Mayor Washington. Jackson, who runs an organization called PUSH—People United to Serve Humanity—in Chicago, is a controversial figure there, and his saying on the night of Washington's victory in the primary, "We want it all," embarrassed the Washington people, who didn't want to drive away the white vote. Washington has said publicly that he has made no decision to support Jackson and has told a number of people privately that he expects to support Mondale. (Aside from Washington's own misgivings about Jackson, he is not enthusiastic about the idea of having Jackson, rather than himself, head the delegates from Chicago's black districts.) But the political atmosphere in Chicago these days is not unlike that of the Middle East, and Mondale already has the support of the white-dominated Cook County Central Committee, which is at war with the Mayor. Negotiating its way through this mess may be beyond the skills of the Mondale organization, which is very skilled. The Mondale camp tried, through various emissaries and in meetings with Jackson, to dissuade him from making the race. Recently, the Mondale staff did an analysis of the possible effect of Jackson's candidacy on the actual distribution of delegates in twenty-one of the states that will have held their contests by March 20th. The analysis assumed that black registration and turnout would be high, that white registration and turnout would be normal, and that Jackson would receive nearly a hundred per cent of the black vote and no white votes. It concluded that Jackson would win between fifty-eight and sixty-four delegates, out of the thirteen hundred and seventy-three to be chosen in those states. But this comforting statistical analysis does not deal with Jackson's effect on the vote percentages in these states—or with the dynamics of the race, which could show Jackson as the one stirring excitement among blacks, especially the young ones, and make him a volatile force throughout the election campaign.

I had a long talk with Jackson a couple of weeks ago. He was soft-spoken, thoughtful, and charming—and clearly, despite his public ambivalence at the time about whether he would enter, keen to get in the race. Jackson's private conversation is marked by the same sorts of rhymes that he uses in his public speech. ("From the outhouse to the White House." "From slave ship to championship.") When we talked, he said, "Society is moving from the gutter of the racial battleground to the economic common ground." He continued, "When a steel mill in Alabama closes and moves to Korea, interests converge." Jackson said that his campaign would be about redistributing political power not just within the federal context but all the way down to local elections, and he said that the other candidates, and their elected allies in the Southern states, want to preserve the status quo. "So," he said, "the Party is going to have to make some fundamental change in the negotiation, have to make room for blacks and women and Hispanics. It's fundamental, because if we get our share of power we'll get our share of health and housing. Those are programs. The candidates are focussing on employment; we had that in slavery—everybody had a job." There is no question that Jackson will enliven the dialogue in the Democratic race; he is imaginative, and he can afford to be bold. He talks of job creation through rebuilding the slums, and criticizes the labor unions for running apprenticeship programs that do not provide enough slots for blacks. He pointed out that in nine Southern states, where more than a third of the blacks live, there are no black congressmen; that Texas and Tennessee have only one black congressman each; and that there are only three Hispanic congressmen from Texas. Jackson attributes the lack of minority officeholders to roadblocks thrown in the way of minority participation: dual registration requirements (in Mississippi, people must register in both

their county and the nearest city); gerrymandering; requirements
for runoff elections, which prevent a black who wins a plurality
from being elected; and other methods of diluting the minority
vote. He said that the movement for an Equal Rights Amendment,
which he would embrace in his campaign, should be seen not as an
upper-middle-class movement but as one working for "the eman-
cipation of a lot of poor women living without a husband." He
said, "It's somewhat academic to discuss roles when only one lives
in the house." He pointed out that more than half of all poor
children live in households headed by women.

In our conversation, Jackson listed, as he does in his public
appearances, the Southern states that Reagan carried by small
margins, thus indicating that new black registration could make
the difference. He pointed out that Reagan won eight Southern
and border states, where there were almost two million unregistered blacks, by a hundred and ninety-two thousand votes. (In
his public appearances, he calls these unregistered voters "rocks
just laying around.")

I asked Jackson if he thought it mattered whether Glenn or
Mondale was nominated.

He paused, and then said, "Not fundamentally. Blacks tend to
prefer Mondale—they know him better and think his record is
better. But our focus is not from the top down but from the
bottom up. We're interested in state and local elections as well as
the Presidency. Three or four more blacks and Hispanics on the
tickets would liberalize the process." Jackson pointed out that
there are eleven million blacks registered, out of almost eighteen
million, and he said that if fourteen million blacks are registered,
and two million more Hispanics are registered, "Reagan cannot
win—and no one can ignore their demands."

I asked Jackson what he would do about encouraging his supporters to back the Democratic nominee in the general election.

He replied, "How the candidates treat us and the issues we raise
will determine our response. We must have a reciprocal relationship. The issues that are crucial to us—dual registration, inte-
grated slates, and so on—cannot be put on the back burner. Anyone who doesn't work on those takes our support for granted and
is at risk. Never again can the ticket write us off. If we have just
expanded the number of Democrats without expanding our role
in democracy, we will have failed." He added, "There are a lot of

by-products of what we're doing. We're changing the American consciousness. The minute I step on the stage with those seven guys, it's a psychological change. It'll affect not only blacks but women and Hispanics. They'll think, if he can argue about Euromissiles and industrial policy, I can do that, too."

John Glenn's candidacy took off in the polls shortly after he announced—in a picture-book ceremony, on April 21st, in his home town of New Concord, Ohio—that he was running, and by mid-May the fashionable thought in Washington was that the nomination was Glenn's, that Mondale was finished. The Mondale campaign had expected Glenn to enjoy a surge, but not so soon. Even at that time, as it happens, there was a wide disparity in what the polls showed. The major change in the relative positions of Glenn and Mondale was indicated in the polls taken by the Los Angeles *Times*, which in early April had shown Mondale ahead of Glenn by seventeen points and a month later behind him by two points. In June, the Los Angeles *Times* showed Mondale ahead again by four points, and the New York *Times*/CBS News poll showed him ahead by only two points, but other polls taken during June showed Mondale ahead by fourteen points (Gallup) and thirteen points (Harris). Glenn has not led Mondale in the polls since, and recent polls have shown Mondale anywhere from two to twenty-eight points ahead of Glenn. The Gallup poll published November 2nd showed Mondale leading Glenn by nineteen points—an increase of ten points over Gallup's September poll—and a Washington *Post*/ABC News poll just released showed Mondale leading Glenn among registered Democrats by twenty-eight points, an increase of fifteen points over its poll of a month before. The new poll included Jesse Jackson and showed him coming in third, and it showed Mondale increasing his lead over Glenn in the South and the West. McGovern came in fourth, with six per cent, and no other candidate received more than two per cent. (The disparities among the polls have to do with the samples they use and the questions they ask. The only guide, then, is the change in the standing of the candidates as measured by the same polling organization.) The polls are not predictive, of course; they are snapshots of the moment. But candidates—especially if they are ahead—set great store by them, because polls affect their ability to attract backers, to raise money, and to convey a sense that they are on the move. Until recently, the polls have consistently shown Glenn doing better against Reagan than Mondale does (the latest Gallup survey showed Mondale doing better against Reagan than does Glenn), though there are strong differences of opinion here over which man would be the more effective general-election candidate. However, the election is so far off, and so much can happen between now and then, that such speculation is essentially futile.

The straw polls that have been held this year not only have tended to favor Mondale but have helped him with his strategic objectives. These events are often written off as meaningless, but they in fact can have an important effect on the nomination contest. The 1980 election was preceded by attention-getting straw polls in Florida and Iowa, and this year a number of other states picked up the idea. A straw poll is usually held in connection with a fund-raising dinner or a state party convention, and it is a good way for a state party to raise money and get the candidates to pay attention to the state. The Mondale campaign figured that Mondale, as the front-runner, had to enter most of the straw polls to validate his position, and it also saw these contests as a way of forcing other candidates to use up their resources, and of demonstrating that they did not have real strength. Other candidates, by contrast, saw the straw polls as a way of establishing themselves. Glenn passed up some of the straw polls—his campaign preferred to save its resources for next year—but he did make either real or token efforts in a few places; sometimes the passing up occurred after an initial effort was made and the prospects did not look good. Moreover, the straw polls have reverberations in both the pre-primary and the primary periods. In the pre-primary period, victories or losses in one state affect attitudes about a candidate's chances not only in that state but elsewhere—and thus his ability to raise money and attract supporters. And they can lay the groundwork for the real contests in those states the following year. After Mondale, Cranston got the most out of the straw polls, by coming in first or second in several places. The first straw poll—in California, in January—was won, as expected, by Cranston, since this is his home state, and he had worked hard not to be embarrassed at the state convention; but Mondale came in second, and also was the most effective speaker at the state convention—showing that he could excite a Democratic audience. (Mondale had demonstrated this before, but the word that he is a dull speaker follows him, so he has to keep proving he can rouse an audience.) Glenn and Hart, who also attended the California convention, ran a poor third and fourth. (Since then, Mondale has overtaken Cranston in California polls; a Los Angeles *Times* poll published quite recently showed Mondale leading Cranston forty-three per cent to eighteen per cent, with Glenn at fourteen per cent. McGovern received eight per cent. The poll said that in a two-way race Mondale would defeat Glenn sixty-five per cent to twenty-six per cent.) In the Massachusetts straw poll, on April 9th, Mondale came in first, Cranston second, Glenn third, and Hart fourth. This was a big defeat for Hart, who was then vying with Cranston to be the third man in the race, after Mondale and Glenn. The Mondale forces suffered a setback when, much to their surprise, Mondale lost the Wisconsin straw poll, in June, to Cranston. Cranston and his supporters had simply worked harder, and Cranston won by thirty-nine per cent to Mondale's thirty-six per cent. Hart was third and Glenn was fourth. One irony of the event in Wisconsin was that the Mondale people had essentially cooked it up, in the hope that Cranston would do better there than Hart, whom they then saw as the stronger rival of the two. Hart did try hard there, and his poor showing affected his campaign elsewhere. (A poll taken by the Milwaukee *Sentinel* a week after the straw poll had Mondale coming in first, with forty-nine per cent; Glenn second, with twenty per cent; and Cranston third, with nine per cent.) Cranston then won a meaningless straw poll among a hundred and twenty-four Alabama Young Democrats attending their state convention; the only other candidate who contested this particular event was Hollings. (For good measure, Cranston had chartered a riverboat to take delegates on a cruise the night before the vote.) In September, Glenn beat Mondale at a New Jersey state party convention—Glenn appeared before the convention and Mondale did not. The Mondale people essentially did pass that one up, but still they were not happy with the outcome. There were larger stakes in a Maine state-convention straw poll, held October 1st, because Mondale made a major effort and spent quite a bit of money on it, and would be seen to be in big trouble if he lost. And Hollings also made a major effort in Maine, to try to demonstrate that he was a national candidate; in the days before the event, there were a number of news stories indicating that he

might do well, or even win—and that this would show the flim-
siness of the Mondale lead. Cranston, too, worked hard and spent
quite a bit of money in Maine. Mondale won, with fifty-one per
cent of the vote; Cranston came in second, with twenty-nine per
cent; and Hollings came in third, with eleven per cent. Glenn,
who had made an initial effort in Maine and then pulled back,
came in fourth; he did make an appearance at the convention,
and argued that he was the Democrat most likely to defeat Reagan. The Mondale campaign expects its work in Maine to carry
over into 1984 in two respects: in the course of the exercise about
a hundred campaign workers were trained there, to be then
farmed out to other states; and the Mondale people felt that they
had made such a thorough effort in Maine that it was hard to see
how any other candidate, especially Glenn, could get very far
there next year. In early October, Mondale won a straw poll at a
Jefferson-Jackson Day dinner in Des Moines, Iowa, and at the
same time a poll of Iowa Democrats by the Des Moines *Register*
showed that Mondale led Glenn, forty-six per cent to twenty-seven
per cent, and that Mondale did as well as Glenn against Reagan
(both beat him by about ten percentage points).

The last straw poll of the year took place in late October, at the
Florida state convention. Askew won, as he was expected to, since
he is a former governor of the state, but the significant news out of
the occasion was that Mondale came in second, with thirty-five per
cent, while Glenn, who also attended—and again made an initial
effort to do well—came in third, with eighteen per cent. At the
same time, a poll by three Florida newspapers showed Mondale as
the first choice of registered Democrats in Florida, with Askew
second and Glenn third. The significance of Florida is that the
South will be a major area of combat between Mondale and Glenn,
and three Southern states—Florida, Alabama, and Georgia—will
hold contests on March 13th. It has been an assumption of the
Glenn campaign that Glenn, the more moderate of the two candidates, and the one with a stronger pro-defense record, would do
better than Mondale in the South. The Mondale people have been
arguing that this is not necessarily the case: that with some black
support (even with Jackson in the race) and the support of
organized labor, Mondale could beat Glenn—and, later, Reagan—
in the South.

In some instances, the differences between the Glenn and Mon-

dale approaches to the campaign may arise more out of necessity
than either camp would admit. The so-called special-interests issue—the fact that an important part of Mondale's strategy has
been to seek the support of major interest groups in the Party—is
a case in point. There is some validity to the issue, and there is also
some phoniness to it. The valid issue is whether Mondale, having
courted and won the support of the A.F.L.-C.I.O., which endorsed
him on October 1st—the first pre-Convention endorsement ever
made by the federation—and of the large teachers' union, the
National Education Association, and having sought the support of
other major constituency groups of the Democratic Party, would
be able to govern. Implicit in this is a question about Mondale's
inner strength. The question is how he would, once in office, deal
with the groups that had given him support—whether he would
shape the compromises that must be made among the competing
interests in this country, or would be paralyzed. But governing is a
process of working out accommodations among competing interests, and another question is whether or not one is better able to
do that if one has had the support of and close relationships with
major groups. It is natural for the other candidates to try to use
the special-interests issue against Mondale—and through that to
convey that he may be weak—but the fact is that others would have
been happy to have the support of the Democratic constituency
groups. Both Cranston and Glenn tried for the A.F.L.-C.I.O. endorsement, or at least tried to block Mondale from getting it. It is
altogether possible that some adroit moves by the Glenn campaign
could have warded off the endorsements of Mondale by the
A.F.L.-C.I.O. and the N.E.A. All the candidates complied with a
request by the N.E.A. to supply videotaped addresses to its June
meeting—and they went before other interest groups, submitting
themselves to often humiliating tests of fealty. Most of the candidates have made strong pitches to environmental groups, women's
groups, and so on. (Cranston even told the National Women's
Political Caucus that as President he would withhold federal funds
for bridges and the like from states that did not endorse the Equal
Rights Amendment.) When Edward Kennedy challenged Jimmy
Carter in 1980, one of his devices was to appeal to the liberal
interest groups on the ground that Carter had not done enough
for them. Ronald Reagan routinely appears before interest groups
whose support he is seeking to maintain—signing bills and mak-

ing promises. The question is not whether a politician has appealed to the interest groups but which interest groups he has appealed to, and then how, having received their support, he deals with them.

The thesis of the Glenn campaign is that Glenn represents what most Democrats—as opposed to most Democratic activists, those who normally turn out for caucuses and primaries—are looking for, and that if the Democratic turnout is increased Glenn can win the nomination. The corollary is, as one Glenn adviser put it, that "if there is not a large enough turnout, we lose." The Mondale strategists say that the Glenn people are deluding themselves if they believe that there is a large pool of new Democratic voters who will be drawn to the more conservative candidate. The largest group of new voters that will participate, says a Mondale strategist, is made up of those most likely to vote for a liberal candidate— blacks, Hispanics, and women. Besides, he adds, Mondale has a stronger motivating force—Reagan—for bringing in his new participants than Glenn has.

Glenn's people believe that Glenn is uniquely well positioned as a candidate in 1984: that he is not too associated with the past, that his identity as an astronaut conveys the idea that he is modern and capable of dealing with the technological future, and that his centrism and moderation are what both the Democratic Party and the nation are looking for. They also recognize that there are hazards in his approach to trying to win the nomination. The Glenn people's thesis that Glenn represents what most Democrats are looking for grows out of their survey research—polling, open-ended interviews with small groups, and so on—and as they describe it one can see how the research and the campaign are being made to fit. One thing that struck the Glenn people was that their research indicated that most Democrats felt that the Reagan economic program had been necessary—that the Democrats had let things get out of hand. One important Glenn strategist says that he was, in fact, surprised by the degree to which Reagan is still held in high regard among Democrats, and he added that the more tolerant Democrats were of Reagan, the more sympathetic they were to Glenn. Another thing that struck the Glenn people was that when they asked which former President could best handle the situation in the world today the most frequent answer was John F. Kennedy (actually, this should not have been very surprising). In crass political terms, one adviser said, this helps Glenn, because of his past association with the Kennedys. John Kennedy associated himself at once with Glenn's earth-orbiting space shot, in 1962, and Glenn and his wife, Annie, soon became friends of the Kennedy family. It was the Kennedys who encouraged Glenn to go into politics, hoping that his status as a hero would help the Democrats hold a Senate seat in Ohio. Robert Kennedy, who admired people who had faced great physical challenge, also became a friend of Glenn's, and asked Glenn to campaign with him during his race for the Presidency in 1968. (Relations between Edward Kennedy and Glenn are cool.) "The Kennedy thing jumped out at us," says David Sawyer, Glenn's media adviser, "and we realized that what people connected him with were things we could connect with: the future, excellence, getting the country moving, a sense that we can do it together, goals. Kennedy said we could put a man on the moon in ten years, and we did." The Glenn campaign tries to evoke the Kennedy ethos in a number of ways. A five-minute ad that it ran on CBS in mid-October, on the night before the première, in Washington, of *The Right Stuff*, the movie about the astronauts, showed Glenn riding in a car with John Kennedy after the space flight. Glenn summons up the can-do spirit of the Kennedy era, advocating, for example, a "ten-year plan" to make all Americans literate, thus evoking Kennedy's moon program.

The Glenn people say that their research shows that Glenn is associated with positive qualities—bravery, honesty, strength, an understanding of the future, an association with technology—and that people view Mondale as a politician and as representing the past. One Glenn adviser says that the ongoing controversy between Glenn and Mondale, which began this fall, was not helpful, because it was important for Glenn to live up to the positive attributes associated with him and not be seen as another brawling politician. (The Mondale people also saw that if Glenn the hero was lured into a political brawl he would look less heroic—particularly if he didn't take it very well.) The Glenn advisers also say that their research indicates one major problem for Glenn: no one knows much about him other than the fact that he was an astronaut (many think he walked on the moon). One adviser said, "The crucial thing for us is to go out there and fill the tabula rasa about him." The problem, as the Glenn people see it, is that Glenn is not associated in the public mind with contemporary issues. They want to present Glenn as a figure of the future and Mondale as one of the past, and they see Mondale's efforts to engage Glenn in debate about his voting record in the Senate as an attempt to center the discussion on Glenn's past rather than on his vision of the future. A number of Glenn's advisers talked to me about the need to "fill in the blanks" about John Glenn in the public mind. One said, "People don't have any handle on what he's been doing for the past twenty years, or what he's all about. Our problem is to define that before anybody else does. And that's what Mondale is trying to do. His polling is as good as ours. He's trying to define for the electorate that John Glenn is a Republican; we're trying to define that he's their kind of Democrat." Another Glenn adviser said he thought that the argument had helped Glenn draw the contrast between himself as representing the new and Mondale as representing the old, but that there was a danger if the battling kept going. "If the heat stays up for very long, my guess is that Mondale will get his constituency aroused one hundred per cent," he said. "If the heat doesn't stay up too long, there's going to be a lot of his constituency available to us."

Because the Glenn people are so concerned that Glenn will be seen as simply an astronaut, and not as a man who has any connection with issues that are of importance to Democrats, they have been putting out position papers and having Glenn give speeches about education, the environment, the Middle East (this is in part to deal with Glenn's problem with Jewish voters, many of whom have found him insufficiently supportive of Israel; in the speech, Glenn proposed that the American Embassy be moved from Tel Aviv to Jerusalem—a litmus-test issue for many backers of Israel). They have devised their five-point programs on a number of subjects. One of Glenn's closest aides said to me in early November that the problem that Glenn would be seen as running as a hero, a celebrity, had dogged the campaign all along, and was more virulent than they had expected. "This period is critical to us," he said. "We always knew that this fall was when Glenn would become known to more people, and that if we failed to show that he has positions on the issues and a vision of the future and a concept of the Presidency we wouldn't make it." Therefore, the Glenn people decided to make a major effort to get Glenn on network television programs, talking substance. But another adviser said at about the

same time that they plan to attack Mondale with even more intensity as a figure of the past.

The Glenn campaign appears to have run into the substance
problem for two reasons: it has tried to have it both ways on the
matter of his celebrity as an astronaut; and Glenn has in fact been
vague on issues and in several instances has betrayed something of
a lack of grasp. The Glenn people were perfectly delighted that
The Right Stuff opened this fall. William Hamilton, Glenn's pollster,
told me, "The movie helps define him in terms of an era of history
and it associates him with that era and its positive character traits."
He added, "But it puts more pressure on us to show how he would
put those personality traits into a style of leadership for the
eighties." (According to a very good book about Glenn by Frank
Van Riper, called *Glenn: The Astronaut Who Would Be President*, one
of the most famous scenes in the movie—the one in which Glenn
tells his wife that if she doesn't want Vice-President Lyndon
Johnson in their house during Glenn's orbital shot then he should
not be there, a scene based on an episode in Tom Wolfe's book *The
Right Stuff*—does not have it quite right. It is a fact that Mrs.
Glenn, who until quite recently had a severe stuttering problem,
was terrified at the idea of having Johnson, and the press corps
accompanying him, in the house. According to Van Riper, however, the issue was not Johnson himself but the fact that the astronauts had signed over the exclusive rights to their story to *Life*,
and Johnson was insisting that the *Life* reporter who was with Mrs.
Glenn leave the house and let Johnson and his press contingent in.
Glenn confirmed to Van Riper that the issue was not Johnson's
presence but the *Life* contract. As told in Van Riper's book, Glenn
simply asked the NASA people to do whatever his wife wanted and
to stick to the terms of the agreement with *Life*. Glenn told Van
Riper, "Did I object to the Vice-President calling on Annie? No,
not at all.")

A Glenn adviser said to me, "If you gave Glenn and Mondale
the choice of either an endorsement by the A.F.L.-C.I.O. or the
movie, Mondale would pick the A.F.L.-C.I.O. endorsement and
Glenn would pick the movie." The Glenn five-minute network ad
shows Glenn in his space suit and then shows his space flight
taking off as the voice from mission control says, "Godspeed, John
Glenn." (The voice-over says, "They call him one of the true
American heroes—hurtling through space at five miles per sec-

ond, as the whole world held its breath.") Then it shows Glenn in the car with Kennedy. The Glenn people are disturbed that the press seems to have focussed on the space shot rather than on Glenn's discussion of the issues in the ad. However, one of them did say to me that though the scenes of the space shot and of Glenn with Kennedy took only twelve seconds of the actual four minutes and twenty seconds of the spot, they were the most dramatic. The ad stresses another theme: it says that "only one man is talking about the future," and reiterates that Glenn has "goals" for the future. In the ad, Glenn says, "We're just moving into a whole new time period that has tremendous advantages for the future, if we just set goals and go for it." ("Go for it" and "Thumbs up" are part of the Glenn lexicon.) The ad says that Glenn "doesn't play to the special interests, doesn't play the old political game," and stresses subjects that Glenn has tried to identify with in his campaign: education, research, a commitment to peace.

Glenn himself emphasizes his career as a Marine fighter-pilot—he was in both the Second World War and the Korean War—and as an astronaut as a political credential. His statement at a forum featuring all the candidates, in New York City, on October 6th, that he was no "celluloid candidate" was an echo of a familiar Glenn theme. He said that he had been in the Marine Corps for twenty-three years: "I went through two wars, and I know what it's like to be in combat. . . . I wasn't doing *Hellcats of the Navy*"—a movie Reagan starred in—"when I went through a hundred and forty-nine missions. That wasn't celluloid; that was the real thing. And when I sat on top of that booster down there, getting ready to go, it wasn't *Star Trek* or *Star Wars*, I can guarantee you that. It was representing the future of this country." Glenn used a similar device in his campaign against Howard Metzenbaum for the Ohio Senate seat in 1974. (He had lost a primary campaign against Metzenbaum in 1970. Now both men are in the Senate, and their relationship is notably bad.) Glenn often says that he doesn't have to watch late-night movies to see what war is like, that he knows how it feels to tell the next of kin of the death of a loved one in battle. (He talks in this vein in the five-minute ad: "I've been shot at myself. My plane was hit on twelve different occasions.") His aides say that the point of this emphasis is to show Glenn's commitment to peace. Van Riper, whose book is not unsympathetic to Glenn and was recommended to me by the Glenn staff, says that

Glenn really believed that his war record and career as an astronaut, and his decent family life, entitled him to the Senate seat and
to a chance to lead the nation, and that his own staff has warned
him not to convey this attitude in his race for the Presidency. The
book also shows Glenn, for all his easygoing, pleasant style, as a
fiercely competitive man: he went to great lengths to be chosen as
an astronaut, was highly competitive with his fellow-astronauts
(and was not very popular among them as a result), and went into
a rage and then a depression when he was not selected for the first
space flight.

Glenn has always been a bit of a loner in politics, and seems to
have little taste for the political rough-and-tumble—factors that
are relevant to the sort of President he might be. He tends to be
unforgiving of people who have opposed him in campaigns or on
issues. He is not one for palling around with his Senate colleagues—often a prerequisite for getting things done. His style in
the Senate has been to take a position—he is often slow to make up
his mind—and then wait for others to come around to it. His most
notable accomplishment as a senator was sponsorship of legislation to curb nuclear proliferation—one of the most important
issues of the age. Beyond that, his Senate career is a bit of a blur.
One of Glenn's colleagues says that an important clue to understanding him is the fact that he grew up in an essentially Republican milieu and did not much think about politics until, urged by
the Kennedys, he entered in—that this is why it is somewhat difficult to locate him. (Glenn has said that he used to be a Republican.) Two characteristics that emerge from conversations about
him with other politicians, and with his staff, are his lonerness,
and that he is a stickler for detail and tends not to see the larger
picture. An analogy to the engineer's approach of Jimmy Carter is
sometimes suggested. More than one Glenn adviser told me recently that a problem the campaign was facing was that Glenn
wanted to be deeply involved in the development of the issues he
would present. Actually, the problem may be not that he wants to
be so involved—presumably a candidate should be involved in
developing the issues he presents to the public—but that his positions on issues have not been developed by now. Several staff
members felt that Glenn was spending more time in Washington
this fall—as opposed to being on the road—than they would have
liked. "He rebelled," one adviser told me. Another said, "He's a

studier, compulsive. He wants to dot every 'i' and cross every 't.'
That's good—you don't want somebody to go off the deep end—
but, my God, it's hard to get a brochure printed."

Glenn has a lot of strengths as a media candidate—just as Mondale has weaknesses in this respect—and it is on television that most voters see the candidates. Glenn's wholesome, apple-pie face is an attractive television face. David Sawyer says, "You can put the camera right up to his face—closer than to Walter Mondale's or Ronald Reagan's—and strength comes through." Glenn has the strong physique and the bearing that people tend to associate with leadership. He appears calm and in command on television; he projects sincerity and confidence. Mondale, by contrast, still tightens up on television; his voice is reedy. Glenn's voice is warm and mellow. Still, Sawyer says, "Our greatest difficulty is, How do you convey excitement with moderation? It is more difficult to convey excitement around centrism." The hope, he says, is that people will respond to the intensity and straightness that Glenn conveys.

The Glenn people seem to have been unprepared for the enormous demands of running a national campaign—especially under the new timetable. And they were apparently unprepared for the pressures that the campaign put on Glenn. "This thing is playing out much faster than I thought it would," a key Glenn adviser said to me recently. Unlike Mondale, Glenn had to put together a campaign organization consisting of people who had not worked together before; unlike Mondale, Glenn was often going into a city, and meeting the local political leaders, for the first time. Glenn had not spent as long as Mondale marinating in the issues, and was less intellectually inclined to do so. Mondale is widely said to have the best political organization ever assembled—should he lose the nomination, its reputation for genius will end rapidly— and Mondale himself has had long years of political seasoning. A Glenn adviser said, "One of our weaknesses, and one of their strengths, is that, unlike us, they've all worked together for years, and Mondale is a consummate politician. He understands how politics works at the constituent level, at other levels. Glenn doesn't have the automatic political instincts that Mondale has." The group around Glenn has recently gone through some turmoil—the man with the most experience in political organization has left. The Glenn people say that the shakeup did not have to do, as was said in the press, with an argument over whether the emphasis of the campaign should be on organization or media, and that the result will be a tightening of the management of its organizational activities. The immediate result of the reorganization of the Glenn campaign staff is that, next to William White, the campaign manager—a forty-two-year-old Ohioan who has been with Glenn since 1969—the two most important figures in the campaign are major Washington lobbyists. One is Thomas Boggs, who is forty-three and is one of Washington's most famous lawyer-lobbyists. Boggs is one of the preeminent practitioners of the new art of winning influence among lawmakers by steering campaign funds their way. He has helped Glenn raise funds, and another of his major roles in the campaign, other than offering general advice, is to work on the five hundred and sixty-eight elected officials and Party leaders who will attend the Convention as unpledged delegates. These people can commit to a candidate before the Convention. In fact, one of the largest delegate contests will take place in January, when the House Democrats select the hundred and sixty-four House members to attend the Convention. The Senate will probably select its twenty-seven delegates in February. The Mondale people, also using Washington lobbyists, have been working for quite some time on lining up as much support among those groups as possible, and now Boggs will be making a major effort on Glenn's behalf. (As one Glenn aide explained, "These are the people he is in contact with anyway.") The other major figure in the Glenn campaign is Robert Keefe, a Washington lobbyist with longtime ties to the Democratic Party. The last two Presidential campaigns that Keefe played an important role in were those of Henry Jackson and Birch Bayh. The Glenn people say that a significant role will also be played by James Jones, a moderate-to-conservative young House member from Oklahoma, who is the chairman of the House Budget Committee.

Right now, because of the various states' filing dates, the campaigns have to be involved in, among other things, drawing up their delegate slates in Florida, Illinois, and Pennsylvania—and drawing up delegate slates involves dicey questions of allocating seats among one's various supporters, achieving racial balance, rewarding contributors, and so on. The Glenn people concede that the Mondale campaign is now in a far better position to do this than they are. Moreover, Glenn, like the other candidates, has had to spend a great deal of time on fund-raising. Since the candidates can raise funds in amounts of only up to a thousand dollars per individual contributor, and since they need to raise millions, this takes a great deal of their time. Of course, fund-raisers for the candidates aggregate, through various techniques, large sums of money. The Mondale people expect to have raised more than Glenn has by the end of this year, and to have raised more of it in small sums that will be matched by the government—which matches amounts of up to two hundred and fifty dollars. The Mondale people believe they will continue to have a substantial financial advantage over Glenn, because they have a much larger base of smaller contributors, whom they can resolicit next year. Mondale started with broader and deeper ties within the Democratic community of contributors; Glenn, after tapping his natural base of support in Ohio, has opened new sources of funding in some areas—in particular, Texas—and has had some help from Boggs and others in the District of Columbia. "The problem," a Glenn adviser said to me in mid-October, "is organizing the issues and ideas and the campaign in time."

Another thing that has clearly been worrying the Glenn camp somewhat is Glenn's lack of political surefootedness. He has already made a number of the sort of political errors that cause anxiety among campaign managers. In August, 1982, he walked right into one of politics' greatest danger zones by suggesting, at a breakfast with reporters, that Social Security might be made voluntary for younger people. This, of course, raises the question of how retired people would be supported. Sensing that he was in trouble, he backed off. Last summer, at an arms-control forum in Iowa, the candidates were asked under what circumstances they would use nuclear weapons against the Soviet Union. Glenn said that he would not "respond with hundreds of weapons" if the Soviet Union fired a single nuclear weapon at a remote area in the Western United States, but added that if there was a major nuclear attack "it would be inconceivable to me that a U.S. President wouldn't reply in kind." The latter comment drew gasps from the pro-arms-control audience, but it was on the first point that Glenn later reversed himself, saying, "I guess what I should have said is if they shoot us, we shoot back. That's it." This fall, he told the National Organization for Women, to their displeasure, "We all loafed on the E.R.A. too much." He apologized later. Even his argument in the New York City forum that he was not a "celluloid

candidate" may not have been a very good move, since it was in
rebuttal to a remark that had been made by Governor Mario
Cuomo, who was at that point making up his mind whom to
endorse. Part of the problem seems to come from a certain lack of
political feel—or "polish" as one of his advisers puts it—and part
from an uncertain grasp of substance. At the New York forum, for
example, Glenn said that America used to be a capital-intensive
country but is now a labor-intensive country—which got it backward—and he was vague in other respects.

In mid-October, Glenn's own staff was clearly concerned about
how he had handled the contretemps with Mondale. Though
Glenn had been saying that the Party would lose if it appealed to
the "special interests," he had declined an invitation by Cuomo, in
his appearance in Syracuse in late September, to specify where he
differed with Mondale on the issues. Mondale welcomed the opportunity to cite such differences when he appeared at a forum in
Rochester two days later. (Each of the candidates appeared alone
at a forum in the state before all seven appeared together in New
York City.) Mondale set himself apart from Glenn by saying that
he had supported the SALT II Treaty, which Glenn had opposed,
and that he had opposed Reagan's economic program, which
Glenn had supported. The theory was that these are "voting issues" among Democrats, and that Glenn should be put on the
defensive. Mondale then took to saying that he was the "real Democrat." Glenn came back at Mondale at the all-candidate forum by
suggesting, in his closing statement, that the Democrats would lose
if they "offer a Party that can't say no to any group with a letterhead and a mailing list . . . is against any weapons system . . .
wants to replace the Reagan program of the twenties with programs of the sixties." Mondale took the next opportunity to fire
back, at the Jefferson-Jackson Day dinner in Des Moines, on October 8th, when he delivered a blistering attack on Glenn's support of "Reaganomics" and his opposition to SALT II. Mondale
called the Reagan economic program "perhaps the most radical
measure of our time" and the most "comprehensive onslaught
against social justice in modern time." He continued, "Of all the
measures in modern political history in which the forces of special
interest clashed with the profound public interest of our nation, I
cannot recall a single instance where the issues were as clear. . . .
That would have been a good time for a Democrat who's against
special interests to stand up and vote no." Glenn's response to

reporters, two days later, went further than his advisers had planned, saying that the Reagan economic program was a necessary antidote to the "disastrous, failed policies" of the Carter Administration. Mondale, scarcely able to disguise his glee, said he was amazed that Glenn would be running as a defender of Reaganomics. Glenn's problem was compounded when he could not tell reporters of any instances in which he had opposed Carter's economic policies—and, subsequently, statements Glenn had made in 1980 that the economy was improving came to light, as did the fact that Glenn had been a strong supporter in the Senate of Carter's programs. In the course of the campaign, Glenn had offered varying rationales for his support of Reagan's tax-cut program: that the economic theories behind it might be correct; that the Democrats could not put through a program of their own and the public had demanded a change in economic policy. Glenn's advisers were distressed that he had got himself tied to Reaganomics and had gone so far in attacking Carter. Carter may not be enormously popular these days, but he does have some support within the Democratic Party, and even Democrats who don't much admire him didn't like to see such an attack on him from within their own party. Glenn also complained to reporters that "some of our specific votes were . . . brought up for specific comment or ridicule or criticism." He was correct in pointing out that only seven Democratic senators had voted against the final form of the Reagan tax-cut bill.

This whole business overtook a substantive speech Glenn gave at the National Press Club, on October 12th, about arms control—but it may have been just as well, from his point of view. In an attempt to show that he favored certain new arms-control initiatives, he proposed a moratorium on the stationing of ground-launched cruise missiles in Europe, scheduled for this fall. Such a move would undermine those Western European nations that had already taken the politically difficult step of agreeing to accept the cruise missiles. It would also exacerbate the problem facing West Germany, which was being asked to accept Pershing missiles, which can reach the Soviet Union in a few minutes, and which are the sorest subject in the whole controversy about the intermediate-nuclear-force deployment; Germany has insisted that it would not accept the Pershings unless the other Western European nations accepted the cruise missiles. And the most serious arms-control problem in connection with cruise missiles involves sea-launched cruise missiles, which are scheduled to be deployed soon and whose location cannot be detected, and which might be armed with either conventional or nuclear weapons. Last summer, Glenn opposed proposals in the Senate for a moratorium on the deployment of sea-launched cruise missiles subject to reaching a verifiable agreement on them with the Soviet Union. Glenn argued that the Soviet Union already had sea-launched cruise missiles; Charles McC. Mathias, who proposed the moratorium, argued that the Soviet sea-launched missiles are inferior but that the United States would not be able to maintain its technological advantage. Glenn's opposition to the SALT II Treaty, in 1979, on the ground that it could not be adequately verified—in the face of assurances by the Joint Chiefs of Staff and the intelligence agencies that the monitoring stations in Iran, which had been lost, would be replaced in time through arrangements that were then being made with China—was seen by many of his colleagues as an example of his stubbornness. Intelligence experts say that the loss of the monitoring stations in Iran did not mean that, as Glenn has said, we were "blind."

Not long ago, I had a conversation with Glenn. I wanted to explore his thinking about some of the issues that had come up. Last March, Glenn moved into the new Hart Senate Office Building, and as we sat in his large office, with its eighteen-foot-high ceiling, Glenn looked small. As always, his demeanor was unaffected and pleasant.

I asked Glenn what he had in mind when he said, as he had been doing lately, that "we have to bite the bullet and raise taxes."

He said that he would repeal the third year of the three-year tax cut (this cut went into effect on July 1st of this year) and would repeal that section of the 1981 tax-cut bill which indexed taxes to inflation from January 1, 1985, on. Beyond that, he said, he might impose a surtax, and he went back and forth on the question of whether he would favor a value-added tax. He said nothing about revoking some of the large tax breaks for business which were enacted in 1981, or about closing loopholes, but he did say that the tax code should be "simplified."

When I asked Glenn which of the nineteen-sixties programs he thought had gone wrong, he said that the problem had been "our zeal to try and sort of do everything for everybody." When I asked him what he would not have done during that period, he replied that he had some problems with CETA (the Comprehensive Employment and Training Act). CETA, which grew out of nineteen-sixties job-training programs, was in fact enacted in 1973. Glenn said that the program had got out of hand—that city governments had used funds that were supposed to go for hiring unemployed poor people to rehire laid-off municipal employees. A number of people had agreed that this was a problem, and, in fact, the program was amended a couple of years later to prohibit this. Glenn also said that "food-stamp programs got expanded far beyond anything we foresaw at the outset," but he added, "I'm not saying that I would reduce food stamps now—probably would not—but programs like that got all carried away." The major expansion of the food-stamp program occurred during the Nixon Administration, under the prodding of the Democratic Congress. Glenn also mentioned a higher-education program that allowed parents who were not in financial need to borrow from the government. This came about in 1978, in part because it was argued that loans were preferable to grants in the face of rising tuition costs. Glenn's complaint was widely concurred in, however, and the program was changed in 1981, to make families earning incomes above a certain level ineligible. Glenn also said he felt that welfare programs could have been streamlined, especially in the costs of administration.

Later in the conversation, I asked Glenn what his concept of a special interest is.

He replied that he believes this country has a "constituency of the whole." He continued, "Now, within that, you have an awful lot of special-interest people who want you to promise a lot of things to them, whether it be a certain minimum wage or a certain health benefit or a certain something else. You have only so much money and you only have certain things you can promise up to a certain level before you start then having the constituency of the whole have to take more from *that* to support the special interest with whatever it is they want. Now, that's where you have to draw the line, it seems to me, and what I try to do is think whether it's going to be in the best interest of all the people in the country. If you get beyond that and then start—I guess the current word would be 'pandering'—start promising beyond what is going to be best for most of the people in the country, then I think that gets into special interests."

When I asked him what role he saw for the interest groups in this country, Glenn said that he recognized that these groups often had items on their agenda that were for the good of the greatest number of people in this country, and that those were matters everyone could agree on. "But then you get to where—are you being asked to promise too high a minimum wage? Are you being asked to guarantee too high a corporate profit, on the other hand? And so you have a balance that has to be set between all these different groups, and that's the role of leadership—not just to advocate a new program but to say no." He continued, "That's most evident between business and labor, where government's role is to set the proper balance. It's obvious that if we enforced every single environmental law right to the hilt immediately, now, we put millions of people out of work, probably. So it's a balance there, how fast you put these things in and what it's going to do in destroying jobs. So there are balances across the board in our society, and that's the balance you have to hit. And if you go over-board on one side, then is it in the long-term best interests of our nation or is it not? I don't think it is. I think you have to be careful to continually set that balance. Now, that means everybody is going to be a little bit unhappy with you a lot of the time, probably, but I think that's in the best long-term interest of the country."

When I asked Glenn how he would, as President, work with the constituency groups of the Democratic Party, he talked about the need to work with all the elements of the Party and all the ele-ments of our society. When I asked him whether he saw a distinc-tion between broad-based interest groups, such as the A.F.L.-C.I.O., the Wilderness Society, the N.A.A.C.P., and the National Council of Senior Citizens, and the interests that line up outside the Senate Finance Committee when it is writing a tax bill, seeking some change in the tax code, he responded, "If you have some-thing that is going to be a drastic change in income-tax policy for everybody in this country, obviously that's more important and should take priority over the Wilderness group wanting two square acres to be added to a park someplace." And he continued, "Do I see them any differently? No, I see them all as having a particular view on whatever the legislation is. I have found their efforts useful, as a matter of fact; sometimes you have things brought up that are of particular interest to their particular group that have not been brought out adequately until they come before a committee or come for an office visit here and we're able to explore some of these things." But, he said, "the more narrowly focussed the group's interest is, the less impact it normally has—not always, but normally has—on all the people of the country. But do I look at the groups as having less credibility because they represent a more narrow field, a more narrow view on a particular interest area? No, I certainly don't. They're all very valid—it's people getting together and expressing their view on things by joining an organization or supporting an effort, and that's something I would not try and alter at all."

One issue that Glenn had raised against Mondale was Mondale's acknowledging his own disagreement with various decisions taken during the Carter Administration—many of them decisions Mondale had defended publicly at the time. I asked Glenn what his concept of the role of the Vice-Presidency was. He replied at first by saying that he was against the idea of selecting a Vice-President in order to provide an ideological balance to the ticket. (Glenn, by the way, was one of five candidates whom Carter had considered as a running mate, and was said to have been very disappointed that he was not chosen.) I then asked Glenn if he would expect his Vice-President to agree with him on all questions. He replied that not only would he "absolutely not" expect such a thing but "if it was something he felt so strongly about, that he thought was really an error—why, I would assume he would feel free to speak out if it was that important."

When I suggested to Glenn that having a Vice-President speak out in disagreement with his President would cause quite a furor, he replied that "the option would be to keep quiet if you really had a serious disagreement." He continued, referring to his argument with Mondale, "What I disagree with strongly is saying one thing publicly, and working very hard to do something and being a front person for it, and then coming back later and saying that privately you were against it all the time. Somewhere you have the courage of your convictions. If you really are against something, and it's something important, it seems to me that you don't build up much trust in public office—which is the only thing we really have going for us in public office—if you do one thing in private and another thing in public."

Glenn and Mondale had different reactions both to the events in Lebanon and to those in Grenada. On the Sunday of the attack on the Marines' headquarters in Beirut, which killed, by current count, two hundred and thirty-three American servicemen, Mondale said that it was a day of mourning; after conferring with advisers on Monday, he said the following day that the Administration should clarify the role of our forces in Lebanon, and raised the question of whether they had been adequately protected. He said that his policy would be to present the Gemayel government with a timetable for Lebanese takeover of primary responsibility for the security of the Beirut airport, which the Marines had been protecting, and to work to get the United Nations forces (UNIFIL) now in southern Lebanon transferred to the Beirut airport, and he would rely more on sea and air power than on "small contingents of ground forces that can neither fight nor keep the peace." He criticized the Administration for not having had a high-level negotiator at work on the problem of Lebanon, and listed specific steps he would take to put pressure on the Syrians to withdraw from Lebanon. He added that he would forge a greater strategic cooperation with Israel in Lebanon. This is a subject of deep controversy: whether the United States should join with Israel to bring pressure on Syria (and whether both countries have the will and the resources to do so), or whether the United States should be a more neutral force in trying to negotiate a settlement in Lebanon. Glenn, on the day of the attack said that the President should make clearer what the role of the Marines is, and in a conversation we had some time after the attack he, too, said that the UNIFIL forces should be moved from southern Lebanon to Beirut, but he warned against taking steps that might lead to a growing confrontation between the United States and Syria. Rather than work more closely with Israel, Glenn said, "we should do whatever we're doing on an international basis."

As for the invasion of Grenada, on the day after it occurred Mondale raised questions about whether American citizens had really been in danger there—saying the evidence was "unpersuasive"—and about whether all diplomatic remedies had been exhausted. (The five hundred and fifty medical students who were eventually evacuated from Grenada were recently brought to the White House, where, before the television cameras, they waved little American flags and praised the President. There has been an argument in Washington over the value and purpose of the Soviet and Cuban weapons found on the island, and the estimate of the number of actual Cuban combatants on the island has been lowered again, from about seven hundred and fifty to roughly one hundred. And the governor-general of Grenada, Paul Scoon, has asked that the airport—which Reagan has said was being built for military purposes—be completed, as it is needed for tourism. This is what the late Prime Minister of Grenada, Maurice Bishop, had said the airport was to be for. However, most of the House Democrats who recently toured Grenada said they had concluded that the invasion was necessary—that Americans there had indeed been in jeopardy. And House Speaker Thomas P. O'Neill, reversing course, said that the invasion was "justified." Polls were showing strong public support of the President's action. Meanwhile, Administration officials said they could not predict when American troops would leave the island.) Just after the invasion, Mondale said that it did not appear that the President had adequately consulted with the Congress or with our allies before the invasion, and he asked how, if American citizens were not in danger, the invasion could be justified under international law. He suggested that the United States would pay a heavy price for the action, saying it had undermined "the high ground this nation needs as a leader in the world." When I talked to Mondale about this a few days later, he said that the evidence was building that the Americans had not been in danger and that there had been no real diplomatic effort to get them out. He also raised the question of whether the Organization of Eastern Caribbean States, whose request for help had been one of Reagan's rationales for invading Grenada, had been requested to make the request. Mondale also said that he was not drawing final conclusions about Grenada, because the severely restricted press coverage during the invasion limited his access to the facts. Glenn, by contrast, said in a phone conversation at the same time that "the more that's come out, the more it indicates that the rescue was warranted." He also said that the rescue issue should be a separate one from the issue of invading and occupying the island, and that the Administration would have to provide evidence of the Soviet-Cuban threat it said it had found. He added, "I hope the invasion won't be used, except for rescue, as a precedent."

The Mondale people, for all their confidence, which is considerable, know that one important thing that remains to be done is to define Mondale more clearly in the public mind. Mondale has stressed and, according to the polls, got across that he is experienced—Mondale argues that he is the most qualified of the Democratic candidates to be President—but there are other impressions about him that his people feel they have yet to get across. They want to show him as a man who has a core of beliefs and has fought important fights in the past—for social justice and for arms control—and then project the kind of leader he would be. They want to show him as an activist leader—in implicit contrast with Glenn. Part of the problem is that the acceleration of the campaign has left the establishment of the candidates' themes behind—but the Mondale people say that there is still time. And part of the problem is that Mondale is long on specifics about what he wants to do, and he understands the complexity of the issues, but he hasn't established overarching themes. Mondale is not a simplifier, and he is not theatrical. He can talk knowledgeably about issues and raise the roof in partisan assemblages, and he can impress people in small groups, but he does have the problem with television. The Mondale people recognize that his opponents' attempt to paint him as an old pol, a captive of special interests, a figure of the past, a man somewhat lacking in strength, could cause trouble. But this is where the strength of the organization that the Mondale people have built is expected to come in; as one Mondale adviser put it, "As attacks are increasingly focussed on issues and character, the campaign is there to support us." Of course, if Mondale continues his tough political fight, and starts actually winning, then he could acquire in the public eye the attribute of "winnerness," which will affect the over-all impression of him. So will the extent to which he can show an ability to maintain his equilibrium and roll with events. The big question about Mondale is whether, if he does succeed in putting the pieces together to win the nomination, and perhaps the election, he will also establish the chemical relationship with the American public that will enable him to lead.

When Mondale appears on interview programs, he is earnest and responsive but does not appear in command. He looks worried and wary. Mondale is a funny man, but he keeps this trait well hidden in his television appearances. He has his moods, and when he is fatigued he can come across as flat—as he did at the forum in New York City. He does fatigue at times—so, as a matter of fact, does Glenn—and sometimes forgets that that one appearance may be the only time some interested voters will see him in person. Roy Spence, a thirty-five-year-old Texan, has been hired to work with Mondale on his media appearances, and Mondale is said to be more willing than before to take advice. Spence is an advertising man who in 1982 worked in Texas on the successful gubernatorial campaign of Mark White, who defeated a well-financed Republican incumbent. Spence says that Mondale's themes will stress that he would be a President who starts from strength and not from scratch, and who has fought important fights—fights that should tell people what kind of person he is and what he cares about. Another focus will be on the "three 'E's" (the economy, education, and the environment)—stressing Mondale's plans for the future. And another will be on arms control and weaponry—stressing the need to be prudent in arms expenditures. The Glenn people feel that Mondale can be depicted as having opposed too many weapons systems, while the Mondale people feel that they can show that Mondale has supported a number of new systems but that he would not go as far as Reagan, or Glenn. The Mondale people say that the danger of Mondale's being painted as a figure of the past will be overcome by his emphasis on what he will do in the future. The Mondale people also feel that the arguments between Mondale and Glenn have redounded to Mondale's benefit: that they have shown a clear differentiation between the two men, and have highlighted what the Mondale people believe to be "voting issues" among Democrats—Reaganomics and SALT II. They believe that the recent polls showing Mondale increasing his lead over Glenn bear this out, and validate their strategy of getting attention focussed on Glenn. Mondale's people insist that the special-interests issue is not a "voting issue"—they cite polls taken for them in Iowa, New Hampshire, and Georgia which indicate that the endorsement of Mondale by these groups is of no great concern to Democrats.

The Mondale people are confident that they have accomplished the goals they set for themselves this year: accelerating the process (which included pushing Glenn out of his orbit as a hero and forcing him into political combat); nationalizing the campaign; defining the size of the job of being President; emphasizing the consensus within the Party and showing that Mondale is most in tune with that consensus; and keeping the focus on the future—

making sure, as a defensive measure, that there is no "new ideas" gap. James Johnson, Mondale's acting campaign chairman, lists seven other objectives for 1983 which, he says, have been met (Johnson has a very systematic mind): to raise substantially more money than anybody else; to get the A.F.L.-C.I.O. endorsement; to get the N.E.A. endorsement; to lead in Iowa both organizationally and in popular support; to lead in New Hampshire both organizationally and in popular support; to pay enough political attention to Georgia, Florida, and Alabama to be seen as competitive with Glenn there; and to have substantially more black support than any other candidate with the possible exception of Jesse Jackson. By nationalizing the campaign, the Mondale people have prevented a third strong candidate from emerging thus far; first they concentrated on diminishing Hart's and then Cranston's standing. They have wanted a two-way race all along, on the theory that Mondale would be stronger than any other single candidate (including Kennedy). Hart had begun the year by organizing well in Iowa and hoping to make a splash there. Johnson says, "Gary Hart lost out in Iowa because he lost in Massachusetts and then failed to save himself in Wisconsin. There was no event in Iowa that hurt him in Iowa."

The Mondale people would love to coax Glenn into an ideological fight, figuring that there is no way Glenn can win such a fight within the Democratic Party. Similarly, they are convinced not only that rounding up the support of the most important constituency groups within the Party is the way to win the nomination but that the intense support of these groups can be of great value in a general election. (Some people within the Reagan camp think the same thing.) And the Mondale people argue that, as opposed to what some people have said, the A.F.L.-C.I.O. endorsement is not a burden in the South. They point out that several Democratic governors in the South were elected with labor and black support. The importance of the A.F.L.-C.I.O. endorsement is that there are about fourteen million members, and the federation has committed itself to doing everything in its power to persuade them to vote for Mondale: through mailings, phoning, organizing. This relieves the Mondale organization of having to make that effort. (The Glenn people say that such help is worth about twenty million dollars; the Mondale people refuse to put a figure on it, saying that it would be impossible to come up with one.) The extent to which the unions' help will materialize into actual votes will depend on the effectiveness of the campaign run by Mondale. The N.E.A. has a million seven hundred thousand members and is a highly active group politically. Mondale has long been popular with it because of his many years of championing the cause of education, and because he fought hard as Vice-President for the establishment of a Department of Education—an idea of questionable merit. Mondale also has the support of the American Federation of Teachers, which has five hundred and eighty thousand members, many of them highly activist (and many of them black).

If Mondale does have a political problem as a result of these endorsements, it would be because he would be seen as a bit too eager to have them, and as perhaps too grateful to deal with the groups from strength. This will be tied up, then, with the total impression that Mondale makes as the campaign proceeds. The impression that Mondale may be too eager to please may be reinforced by the particular issues that he has said that he disagreed with Carter on: a number of them—such as the imposition of a grain embargo on the Soviet Union after the invasion of Afghanistan and the sale of F-15 planes to Saudi Arabia— are issues of interest to important voting blocs. (Other differences he has cited—in response to a question put to him by Glenn at the Harvard forum on arms control—were over the decisions to deploy the MX missile and to sell nuclear fuel to India. He had told me in the summer of 1979 that he felt that the diagnosis of the nation as suffering from a "malaise"—which led to Carter's famous speech in July of that year about the country's "crisis of spirit"—was "crazy.") Mondale's critics have challenged him to cite differences with the groups that support him, or to go before one of the groups and challenge it on an issue; but, of course, even if Mondale were of a disposition to do that, it would now be written off as a stagy bit of business to show how independent he was. Mondale does have some differences with these groups: he is readier to endorse a form of merit pay for teachers than the N.E.A. is, and he and labor differ on certain defense issues, such as the B-1 bomber and the MX, which labor has supported. But Mondale has no interest in dampening the enthusiasm of his supporters, and it is part of the catechism of the Mondale campaign that "we do not emphasize differences with our friends." The Mondale people also complain that Reagan and Glenn aren't urged to go before groups and cite their differences with them.

The endorsements of Mondale by various politicians have been well timed and carry with them more than a pat on the head. The simultaneous endorsement of Mondale by Governor Cuomo, a liberal, and New York Senator Daniel Patrick Moynihan, a centrist, took place on October 13th, during the week that *The Right Stuff* had its première amidst much hoopla. This was followed by the endorsement of Michael Dukakis, the governor of Massachusetts, who has a powerful organization and access to political funding (Glenn had been endorsed by Massachusetts Senator Paul Tsongas), and by that of Leo McCarthy, the lieutenant-governor of California, who is, after Cranston, the highest-ranking Democrat in the state. Several House members have already endorsed Mondale as well (and some have endorsed Glenn). The endorsements of Mondale carry with them pledges to put organizations to work for him and, in many cases, to help raise money.

Since the Mondale organization is so highly praised, I asked Johnson what having a good organization actually meant. Johnson, who is thirty-nine, has a long history in politics: he worked for the McCarthy campaign in 1968 and the Muskie and then the McGovern campaign in 1972, and he worked on and off for Mondale from 1972 until 1976, when he joined his Vice-Presidential campaign and, after Mondale went to the White House, became his executive assistant. (Johnson, by the way, has taken the title of acting chairman to save the slot of chairman in case the campaign wants to fill it with some prominent figure whose chairmanship could be of political importance.) Johnson said, "The most important factor in being organized is understanding in a public dimension and a political dimension what's going to happen. A good organization anticipates. It's understanding what the game is. After our defeat in Wisconsin, I said it would never happen again; being good organizationally means that you learn as you go along. The Wisconsin straw poll, four months afterward, is a very minor matter for Cranston, and a very minor matter for Mondale, and when we went to Maine we took every word of what we'd learned in Wisconsin and we killed the competition. The biggest strength of our organization is the number of things we can do at once, because we have a depth of political pros that goes way beyond our payroll—people around the country Mondale met ten, fifteen, twenty years ago, able people we've worked with for years. That's what's deep about our organization. Walter Mondale can go into Rock Island, Illinois, and not only do the best and the smartest political people know him but he knows them. So it's feel, history, anticipation, flexibility, organizational vitality, and the ability to change and move. The idea of organization is to be appropriate to the challenge. Resources in Presidential campaigns are severely limited. Allocating them effectively is a significant part of the organizational challenge, and effective allocation means using not one dollar more, or one person more, than is needed to accomplish the task." For example, Johnson said, the Mondale people knew that Askew would win the straw poll at the Florida state convention, so they put in enough resources to meet their objective of coming in a strong second. And he continued, "In Michigan, where we have very substantial organizational and political allies—the A.F.L.-C.I.O., the U.A.W., the teachers, the governor, the mayor of Detroit, and a number of county chairmen and legislative leaders—we will expect to spend fewer resources and put in fewer outside campaign people than in other states, because of the strength of what's there."

In a conversation I had with Mondale recently, he said he thought that the arguments between him and Glenn were useful. "I thought it was inevitable that we would all be required to define our differences—on issues, not on personalities," he said. "I think the American people have a right to know our differences. I didn't want it to happen too soon, but I think the American people were getting irritated that we weren't doing that." Mondale's opening up of the differences between him and Glenn may have had as much to do with what Mondale saw as the political advantages of doing so as with any sense of civic duty, of course. And the three issues that Mondale stressed when we talked—Reaganomics, SALT II, and what Mondale calls "poison nerve gas"—are all, as he sees it, good political issues for him. The nerve-gas issue stems from a vote that Glenn cast last summer to end the moratorium— which had existed since the Nixon Administration—on development of new nerve gas. The argument in favor of developing the new form of the gas was that it would be safer to store; the Senate approved authorizing funds for it when Vice-President George Bush broke a tie. The Senate has just voted to appropriate funds for the nerve gas—again with Bush breaking a tie and again with

Glenn voting in favor. Mondale also said that a point he stressed in Rochester about "the commitment to social justice" was "a personal question of where one's spirit and drive will be found in the Presidency"—and, obviously, a difference from Glenn he wants to emphasize. And he said he felt that the controversy "has had an effect." He added, "I know it has; it gives Democrats a view of us on things about which they feel deeply."

A couple of days before my talk with Mondale, Glenn had given a speech at the Florida state convention in which he attacked the notion that Democrats should be subjected to "litmus tests" and questions of "ideological purity." I asked Mondale about that.

He replied, "It doesn't bother me a bit. It's a straw man. I'm not talking about driving anybody out of the Party. I've always had an ecumenical approach. But I think people should see where we stand on our future." One would have thought that Mondale was raising questions about the past, but he turned these into questions about the future: "Reaganomics bears on the future of our economy; failure to ratify SALT II has undermined arms control; on the question of nerve gas, are we going to escalate where every President since Nixon has held back? Glenn started with the special-interest salvo—asking if we were able to say no to any group with a letterhead and a mailing list. I said that's right: Let's talk about Reaganomics; that was full of special interests."

I asked Mondale what the biggest challenge to his candidacy was now.

He replied, "There are several. Some are organizational and some have to do with policy. Organizationally, we're ahead of the others, but we have to raise money and handle a million local problems. It's hard to explain how many things you have to do. On policy, we have to get the debate focussed on the future, so that Americans are looking at me as President. I think we've made the issues with Glenn clear, and we may have to do it again, but I have to get across what I would do as President, and I have to get back to that as the focus of the campaign."

I asked Mondale what his themes would be.

"I think I've got the experience theme across," he replied. "I've talked about getting America's edge back. Making America work again—things like that. I haven't settled on three or four words that will be my theme—it's a little early yet—but I'm hopeful I will at some point."

I asked Mondale what he felt was the greatest danger to his campaign.

He paused and then he said, "That circumstances will prevent me from doing what we just talked about. The day-to-day pressures to do the minor things, and the need to raise all that money—there's a dinner coming up in New Hampshire, a fund-raising event in Chicago; it's limitless. You have to find a way to get up through all that and make that speech."

I asked Mondale if he was trying to have it both ways on the matter of the Vice-Presidency: asking people to support him because he had had such an important job, and separating himself from the Carter Presidency where it was politically convenient to do so.

He replied, "I believe that as Americans focus on that they will think that my position is exactly correct. I would expect my Vice-President to be the same way. In exchange for unlimited access, I would expect loyalty—you can't have any other guidelines. Then, should the Vice-President run for President, I don't think it would be acceptable for him to claim that the record of his Vice-Presidency was off limits. We had issues that are now relevant; I believe that I should answer questions about them. There are some instances where confidentiality must be protected. Otherwise, I think I should answer questions."

I asked Mondale if it might have been more advisable for him simply to say that his relationship with the President had been one of confidentiality, and let it go at that.

"I don't think that would have been acceptable," he replied. "First, some of it comes out. Second, charges are made. Third, if the issues are deep enough the public has a right to know."

I asked him about the distinction that Glenn made in my conversation with him between simply disagreeing internally and disagreeing and then going out and lobbying hard in public for something one has disagreed with.

"I think he's dead wrong," Mondale said. "If I were the principal in my own right, he'd have a point. But I occupied a different constitutional position. I was Vice-President; I was speaking for the Administration, and I tried to do it honorably and effectively. I can't believe he wouldn't want his Vice-President to behave in the same way."

I reminded Mondale that in a conversation we had had earlier in the year he had said that if he was elected he would want to be elected with a mandate, and that he could then go to the interest groups that supported him and say, "This is what I was elected to do." I suggested that there was no evidence that Mondale was asking for a mandate to do anything different from what the groups supporting him wanted.

He replied, "I said in my speech before the A.F.L.-C.I.O. what I expected everyone to do. I didn't dwell on it, but it wasn't a litany of what they wanted." (In the speech, he said that, as President, "to workers I will say, 'Let's put quality and productivity first.'") He continued, "I said to the N.E.A. that we had to have higher standards—we've all got to do better." (He told the N.E.A., "I will ask our teachers to insist on higher standards for your students and yourselves.") Mondale said, "I told a group of my business supporters that we all got more tax relief than we deserved. Lane Kirkland"—the president of the A.F.L.-C.I.O—"never asked me for one thing. They know what I'm saying about getting deficits down and about macro-economic policy. I think the strongest case I can make is getting these parties to the table and being able to get all of them to make concessions for the national interest—in a respectful environment. That's very important: at different times in this country, labor is up and management is down, or management is up and labor is down. I want to get past that, to long-term strategies to get this country's edge back. I think I'm winning this argument."

I asked Mondale why his campaign was so insistent on not talking about differences with friends.

"Let's be frank," he replied. "I want to win this campaign and I want to unite people and I want to be positive. Plus, I don't apologize for a moment for having the support of labor and senior citizens and teachers and women and farmers. These are groups that have been pounded by this Administration. I'm proud to have their support, and I've gained it by legitimate and honorable means. There hasn't been one deal made, and no one has charged that there has." Of course, deals are not necessary; these groups know where Mondale stands on questions of importance to them. He continued, "And we're working against what I think is one of the most special-interest Administrations in modern times."

I asked Mondale about Glenn's charge that if the Democrats offered the public a party that represented the policies of the sixties, it would lose.

"He's absolutely right," he replied. "And that's why I've spoken of the future. We have to get ready for the eighties. We can't do it with a trillion-dollar debt, and we have to be specific about how we bring that deficit down." (Mondale has proposed scaling back the tax cuts for both individuals and businesses; imposing cost containment on medical care; saving money by changing the management of agriculture programs and improving international trade in farm products; and cancelling the Clinch River breeder reactor. These actions, he says, would lead to lower interest on the debt and would justify a more relaxed monetary policy, which would, in turn, cause a drop in unemployment. He would not ask for any across-the-board tax increases at this point, "because I'm so offended by the lack of progressivity in the tax code.") Mondale said that the difference between the sixties and now is that the priorities are different: that now, unlike then, we have an energy problem; a problem of losing our competitive edge, and a need to save our industrial base; problems of international trade and currency misalignment; a need for renaissance in education and science; a need to face a new generation of complicated environmental issues. "It's not that civil rights and social justice aren't important—they're very important—but we also have a new agenda," Mondale said, and he continued, "We have to be specific about how to restore our edge in science and technology; how to restore a sense of fairness in American life; how to reassert American leadership internationally, in a way that shows understanding of the complexities of the world. It's a homily to say that we should prepare for the future. The question is how do you see the future, what are your qualifications, and what does your record instruct about your qualifications and capacities?"

Before long, the candidates will hear what the voters have to say.

IX

This year simply refused to end tidily. The closing weeks felt more like an overture than the conclusion of much of anything. Most years close out, just as this one is doing, amid talk here—often for lack of other things to talk about—of Administration deliberations on the next year's budget. But this year ended with the sense— even leaving aside, if possible, the fact that next year is an election year—of a large number of big questions pending, and of a great deal going on. There are the questions of whether the Administration will find a way to extricate itself from Lebanon anytime soon and whether it will have any more success on arms control than it has had so far, and there are also a number of vexing domestic questions facing the Administration. The President's job-approval ratings as measured in the polls have risen to the highest point since the early months of his Presidency, but—assuming that Reagan will run again—his most thoughtful advisers are taking nothing for granted.

Ever since Reagan's triumph, in his first months in office, in getting Congress to pass a bill cutting taxes by an estimated total of seven hundred and fifty billion dollars, it has become a year-end ritual to have a public airing of the debate within the Administration over whether taxes should be raised. This year's round simply became more unseemly, and even White House aides—in particular, James Baker, the chief of staff—who had led earlier fights to get the President to raise taxes felt that things had got out of hand. Martin Feldstein, the chairman of the Council of Economic Advisers and a traditional conservative economist, and Donald Regan, the Secretary of the Treasury, whose views have proved more adaptable, had been arguing for months over how serious the projected deficits are. Feldstein's sin was that he talked so much out loud about the need to increase taxes (the White House aides, in previous years, had been more circumspect) and also that he said recently that the projected deficits—about two hundred billion dollars a year, indefinitely—were the result not of increases in domestic spending but of the tax cut and increases in defense spending. Feldstein did speak out more than usual for an Administration member. (He went as far as to point out that domestic spending had been dropping as a percentage of the gross national product.) Even some of the President's Republican allies on Capitol Hill had long been arguing—since the fall of 1981, actually— that domestic-spending cuts had gone about as far as they could until some political accommodation was worked out to do something about such middle-class entitlement programs as Social Security and Medicare, and that the increases in defense spending should be curbed. (An accommodation was worked out on Social Security earlier this year, as the result of work done by a bipartisan commission.) And this year congressional Republicans took the lead in reducing the President's requested increase in defense spending from ten per cent to five after inflation. (One problem is that many of the things being added to the defense arsenal cost less in the early years than they will later on, so a built-in increase has been enacted.) The President was successful in getting Congress to approve the MX. Now Defense Secretary Caspar Weinberger is back arguing for another large increase—at first, it was twenty-two per cent, and the Administration is said to have agreed to ask for an amount ranging from ten to fourteen per cent more.

Reagan, according to his closest aides, does not accept the judgment that cuts in domestic spending have reached the permissible political limits. Still, the Administration will make some proposal to raise revenues, if for no other reason than to produce a lower deficit figure in its proposed budget. How realistic its proposal will be—various ones are under consideration—and how hard it will push for it are in question. (It did not push for this year's proposal of a "contingency" tax—contingent on budget cuts Congress did not want to make.) Some members of both parties on Capitol Hill believe that if the President would stay out of the matter—that is, not actively oppose a tax increase—Congress might do something serious about the deficit next year, election or not. If economic conditions got worrisome enough, the President could accept a tax increase that had been worked up by Congress, as he did in 1982. Reagan is often more flexible than he sounds. That way, he gets credit both for "leadership" and for being pragmatic. This year, some incipient efforts were made in Congress to raise taxes, but they fell through. The feeling on Capitol Hill that something should be done about the deficits has, as usual, a variety of motivations, and the question of what is to be done about them naturally elicits a variety of responses, but there is an unusual consensus on the nature of the problem: that the deficits are keeping interest rates too high; that the high interest rates threaten the recovery, discourage investment, hurt exports, and exacerbate the debt problems of Third World nations; and that the obligations for future government interest payments on the debt are simply too great. (It is estimated that by fiscal 1988 it will take eighty billion dollars just to pay the interest on the national debt.) Everyone is agreed that the economy is recovering strongly from the worst recession since the Great Depression—the third-quarter growth was 7.7 per cent, for a recovery rate of 6.6 per cent so far this year—and unemployment in the month of November stood at 8.4 per cent, the lowest figure in two years. The rate of inflation is now about 5 per cent. Actually, what worries some members of the Administration—and also some officials at the Federal Reserve—is that the recovery may be too quick and, given the size of the deficits, require a further tightening of credit, and thus still higher interest rates, perhaps at a politically inopportune time next year. Real interest rates (that is, after inflation) are more than double what they were in 1980, and the rate of business investment in plant and equipment is lower than it was in the 1979–81 period. However, Reagan is a man of formidable skill at defining things his way.

There was near-apoplexy among some of the President's advisers when Edwin Meese, counsellor to the President, said in an interview with some wire-service reporters a couple of weeks before Christmas, "I don't know of any authoritative figures that there are hungry children. I've heard a lot of anecdotal stuff, but I haven't heard any authoritative figures." And he went on to say that "people go to soup kitchens because the food is free and that's easier than paying for it." Then, a few days later, he gave what he presumably thought was an amusing speech at the National Press Club, in which he said that he, like Scrooge, was the victim of a bad press and that Bob Cratchit wasn't so badly off. The "fairness issue" is one of the tenderest ones for the Reagan Administration: for some time now, there has been evidence—and several authoritative reports—that the number of people in this country who are without sufficient food has been growing, and we have been seeing on our television screens pictures of people lining up at soup kitchens. This week, Senator Edward Kennedy, who has held five regional hearings on the subject, will issue a report saying (with statistical backing) that the need for more nutritional help "is not anecdotal, but overwhelming," and that hunger is on the increase in America for the first time since the nineteen-sixties, and possibly since the Great Depression. The Kennedy report places the blame on the recession and the Reagan Administration's budget cuts. Other reports by outside groups are in the works. The recession and cuts in various domestic programs produced a larger number of needy people, and at the same time the Administration cut food programs—food stamps and children's nutrition programs—by several billion dollars, and would have cut them by about twice as much if Congress had not objected. The President's attempt to quiet the controversy stirred by Meese's remarks was not entirely successful. He said that "as long as there is one person in this country who is hungry, that's one person too many," but he also backed Meese up by saying that it was "logical" that, just as there were welfare cheats, there were people going to soup kitchens who didn't really need to. Reagan may have a small point, but it misses the much larger point, and his selective indignation keeps causing him trouble—aimed, as it is, at the poor. And he seems to be frequently explaining things that Presidents shouldn't have to explain: just as this time he had to say he was against hunger, in November, following the showing on ABC of the film *The Day After*, about a fictional nuclear attack on Kansas City, he had to explain that he was against nuclear war. Now the Administration is in a bit of a trap on the hunger issue, because last August, in the face of increasing criticism of its policies, the President appointed a commission that, as he put it, was to find out why federal food programs were not taking care of the hunger problem. The commission's report is due in January. It has been assumed within the Administration as well as outside that the commission was safely stocked with members who would not cause the Administration embarrassment, but the problem is that the Administration will be caused embarrassment no matter what the commission says in its report.

Meese, an affable man of ruddy complexion and conservative

beliefs, presides over the most ideological shop at the White House—one that is often at war with the "pragmatists," headed by James Baker—and he often reflects and reinforces Reagan's own instincts. Moreover, Meese has served Reagan for a long time— since Reagan was elected governor of California, in 1966. Meese was the architect of the recent triumph—or fiasco, depending on one's point of view—of reconstructing the Civil Rights Commission. The commission, which was established in 1957, has often been a nuisance to Administrations, since it has issued reports critical of their enforcement of the civil-rights laws. But only the Reagan Administration has gone as far as to try to fire members of the supposedly independent commission in order to gain control of it—an action that is legally questionable. The argument over this became entangled with the issue of extending the life of the commission, which was due to expire at the end of November. In the end, a bipartisan group on Capitol Hill struck a deal with the White House—or thought it had done so—to reconstitute the commission, so that it would be composed of eight, rather than six, members, four of them to be chosen by Congress and four by the Administration, and to arrange for the reappointment of certain former commission members. But two reappointments— those of Jill Ruckelshaus and Mary Louise Smith, both prominent moderate Republicans—were not made. This guaranteed the Administration control over the commission, but to several of the President's advisers the victory wasn't worth it. (Congress's action reestablishing the commission mooted a court case regarding the firings.) At the end of the year, the Administration and Congress were still at loggerheads over the Legal Services Corporation, which the Administration has tried to kill—Reagan and Meese had found this program bothersome ever since their California days—and, while Congress has balked, the Administration has repeatedly submitted nominees to the Legal Services Corporation's board whom the Senate, although it is controlled by Republicans, has found unsuitable. None of the Administration's nominees to the Legal Services board—several sets have been proposed—have been confirmed.

Jill Ruckelshaus's husband, William, who was brought in in May to head the Environmental Protection Agency after Anne Gorsuch Burford was forced to resign, and whose appointment was supposed to help Reagan with the environmentalists, has been blocked by the Administration from presenting a plan to control acid rain. The E.P.A. has, however, just recently come up with a policy to deal with dioxin, one of the most dangerous chemicals. In December, Rita Lavelle, who had headed the E.P.A.'s hazardous-waste-cleanup program, returned to our consciousness when she was convicted of obstructing a congressional inquiry into the program, and of perjury before Congress about when she learned that her former employer, Aerojet-General, had dumped wastes at the Stringfellow Acid Pits, in California. James Watt, the former Secretary of the Interior, was at year's end happily making a fortune on the speaking circuit—at fifteen thousand dollars a lecture. The President, not content to let the situation alone, devoted one of his Saturday radio talks recently to a defense of Watt's record.

Several foreign-policy matters were refusing to yield to the Administration's desires by the year's end, and this situation has been making a number of the President's advisers nervous. Now that the Administration has its second Secretary of State and third national-security adviser in three years, controversy over the conduct of foreign policy has calmed down a bit, but deep divisions over policy remain within the Administration. The Pentagon, headed by Weinberger, and the State Department, headed by George Shultz, do not see eye to eye on many questions, and it is reliably said that the National Security Council, headed by Robert McFarlane, has been more interested than either of the two departments in aggressive action in Lebanon. The Pentagon was unhappy from the outset about its role in Lebanon, figuring—rightly, as things turned out—that it was being put in an impossible position. Grenada was, of course, a political triumph for the Reagan Administration, and the American combat troops were removed by December 15th—thus meeting the deadline voted by both the House and the Senate under the War Powers Act—but three hundred military people are to remain indefinitely. (At last report, eighteen American servicemen died in the invasion, and a hundred and sixteen were wounded; and, according to a Washington *Post* report, at least a hundred and sixty Grenadians and seventy-one Cubans were killed. The State Department puts the number of Grenadians and Cubans killed much lower. A mental hospital was accidentally bombed. Because of the tight restrictions on press coverage of the invasion, Americans saw little of the carnage.) Grenada provided the American people with a "victory," and even a number of Democrats were reluctant to be critical of the invasion, not simply because of the popular reaction but also because they thought maybe it wasn't a bad idea to remove a Cuban beachhead. (Few bought Reagan's argument that the American medical students on the island were in danger of being taken hostage.) While the Grenada adventure is usually cited as the reason for the rise this autumn in the President's job-approval ratings, Richard Wirthlin, Reagan's pollster, suggests that the underlying reason for that rise was the improvement in the economy—that that gave people more confidence in Reagan and made them more willing to support him on other issues. Grenada, Wirthlin says, seemed to validate Reagan's "get tough" policy, and did so at a time when people were very emotional and wanted a success. The Grenada invasion, after all, followed the tragedy of the truck-bomb attack on the Marine headquarters in Beirut that killed two hundred and forty-one Marines, according to the latest official count—an event that could have been quite a political liability for Reagan. Wirthlin says that the speech Reagan gave the following Thursday, on the subjects of Lebanon and Grenada, changed public attitudes more than any other speech of his Presidency, and had a more lasting effect than such events usually have.

Still, many of the President's political advisers have been quite worried about the potential impact of Lebanon and other foreign-policy developments on Reagan's standing. A total of two hundred and fifty-seven Marines have lost their lives in Lebanon. (Moreover, the question of how it was that the Marines were left in such a vulnerable position is not closed. A recent House subcommittee report was quite critical of the security arrangements and criticized the entire military chain of command; and a Pentagon report, which is due to be made public shortly, is also said to be very critical.) Eventually, the question gets to not just the precise security arrangements but also the civilian decisions that determined the nature of the Marines' mission, and how they were to operate. The fiction that the Marines are in Lebanon as a "peacekeeping" force has just about disappeared. Lately, the Administration has been searching for a way to maintain them there as a "presence"—to give the Lebanese government time to strengthen its hold and its army while negotiating with rival factions—without being so vulnerable. There is talk now of removing the Marines from the airport, where they can be shot at from the surrounding hills, but there is the problem of how they can maintain a "presence" and be invulnerable. In any event, it is widely agreed that if the President really means what he has been saying—that the Marines will not be removed until stability is restored to Lebanon and all foreign forces (meaning Israeli and Syrian) are withdrawn—the Marines will be in Lebanon for some time. The President recently added the possibility that the Marines would return home if there was "a complete collapse" in Lebanon, but this was simply stating the obvious. Still, he was constrained to say at his recent press conference that maybe this had been "a bad choice of words" and that he "wasn't trying to send anyone a message or anything." (There had been some concern that the President's earlier remark would be interpreted as pressure on Amin Gemayel, the President of Lebanon, and would encourage the Syrians to hold out.) There is almost no support, even within the President's own party, for the increased military action against Syrian-held areas of Lebanon—a bombing raid in retaliation for Syrian attacks on American reconnaissance planes, and shelling from warships stationed offshore, including the New Jersey, which has the largest guns of any naval vessel afloat. In the bombing raid, on December 4th, two American planes were shot down; one airman was killed and another was captured. (The New Jersey's sixteen-inch guns weren't used at first, Administration officials explained at the time, because their shells were so large and their aim was so imprecise that they might cause civilian casualties and excessive damage.) It is a fact that the Administration (or part of it, at least) had been looking for a way to make a military point to Syria, which it holds responsible for the attack—and which it believes was carried out by Shiite Muslims with connections to Iran—on the Marine headquarters, and also for a way to persuade Syria to withdraw from Lebanon. Within the Administration, there is much disagreement over the substance as well as the politics of the Lebanon "policy." Several officials want the Administration to reduce its goals in Lebanon and slip away soon. Actually, it is clear from conversations with Administration foreign-policy officials that much of the policy is travelling on hope and crossed fingers. One hope is that Israel, with which the Administration has had a somewhat turbulent relationship—it encouraged Israel's advance into Lebanon last year, then encouraged Israel to withdraw, and then was unhappy that Israel withdrew so far so fast, leaving the area around Beirut open to new strife—will once again play a more active role in Lebanon, and will bring its influence to bear upon those Lebanese factions with which it has influence. Another hope is that Amin Gemayel will share power with the Muslim majority—this means give up power—sufficiently to calm things down. One very high Administration official offered the thought recently that one reason things might calm down in Lebanon is that "the glue that held that place together for a long time was that everybody made money," and that this couldn't happen under current conditions. (The Shiite Muslims, now the largest group in Lebanon, were not sharing in the money-making.)

The extent to which the Administration is prepared to accept some Syrian sway over Lebanon—Syria was invited into Lebanon in 1976 to protect the Christian government, and the United States approved the move—is one question. Whether the Administration understands Syria, or Lebanon, is another. Some Middle East experts here say that the Administration committed a major blunder in negotiating a withdrawal agreement between Israel and Lebanon last May and in assuming that this would induce Syria to withdraw. Syria objects to both the terms and the fact of the agreement. Yet a high Administration official said the other day that he couldn't for the life of him understand why Syria objected to the Israel-Lebanon agreement, and that he assumed that Syria's position was a bluff. The President did say toward the end of his press conference (remarking, in an indication that he had forgotten part of the rehearsal, that he should have mentioned it earlier) that the Administration has believed all along that the settlement in Lebanon "must be political," that the situation "can't be settled by force."

There is some evidence that the Administration underestimated the reaction of other Arab countries to the new (albeit somewhat vague) security arrangements with Israel, and perhaps even underestimated the degree of reluctance within Israel to have much to do with Lebanon anymore. And the Administration, like other parts of the world, is grappling with the resurgence of Islamic fundamentalism, now in part taking the form of suicide-attack terrorism—such as that carried out against the American Embassy and the Marine headquarters in Beirut and, more recently, against the American Embassy, the French Embassy, and four other sites in Kuwait. (Washington itself has taken on something of the aspect of a protected camp. Security on Capitol Hill has become much tighter since a bomb exploded in the Capitol in early November. The bombing occurred late at night, and so there were no injuries, but there was damage to part of the Senate wing. And there are now security barricades at the White House and the State Department. These new arrangements are generally accepted as an unhappy necessity. Longstanding assumptions about security are gone. And recently we learned that surface-to-air missiles have been placed around the White House.) Though Congress is out of session, several members, including some—such as House Speaker Thomas P. O'Neill and Senate Majority Leader Howard Baker—who supported the move earlier this fall to approve an eighteen-month extension of the Marines' tour in Lebanon under the War Powers Act, are publicly and privately expressing grave doubts about what is going on. Some are threatening to propose shortening the time period. Members of Congress are in a bit of a trap of their own, however: they do not want to appear to be responsible for the Administration's policy in Lebanon, yet they will also be reluctant, as they were this fall, to take responsibility for ending the Marines' tour there. Most people here think now that Congress will make a lot of noise about Lebanon but won't actually do anything—though the noise level might affect the Administration's thinking. One Presidential aide says he thinks it important to have the Marines out by the time the Democrats have a nominee; and it is widely assumed here that the Administration will somehow find a way out of Lebanon before the election. At his press conference, the President insisted that such a decision would never "be made by me for a political reason." Yet there are all sorts of ways to define the mission as accomplished. Some Administration officials say vigorously that they will work with all their might to keep Congress from cutting short the Marines' stay in Lebanon; a few say regretfully that the Administration will not be so fortunate as to be obliged by Congress to cut short the Marines' stay.

Some Administration officials portray the deployment of cruise missiles and Pershing 2s in Great Britain and West Germany this fall as a political triumph over the Soviet Union, and say that now the Soviet Union will be ready to bargain in earnest over intermediate-range nuclear missiles, despite its breaking off of the talks in late November. However, some important officials are pessimistic about the chances that these talks will resume. Moreover, it is said by many observers that our relations with our European allies have deteriorated considerably as a result of this and other foreign-policy matters. The Administration got off to a bit of a bad start on the subject of arms control because of officials' statements about limited nuclear war and nuclear "demonstration" shots in Europe, and it was slow to get around to dealing with arms control at all. Some officials believe that arms control, at least on any basis that is acceptable to the Soviet Union, is not in the United States' interest. Last year, in the Secretary of Defense's annual statement on our "military posture," Weinberger called arms control "a melancholy chapter in the troubled history of the last decade or two."

The Administration's arms-control policy has been marked by fierce internal battles, and those who have sought to put sand in the gears have been successful. Administration critics argue that opportunities were missed at the intermediate-range nuclear force talks. One very high Administration official said to me not long ago, talking about relations with the Soviet Union in general, that he wished the Administration had taken more of a problem-solving approach to the Soviet Union, instead of constantly questioning its morality, and even its legitimacy. Now the Pentagon opponents of arms control are working to block what many have seen as the one way to get an I.N.F. agreement: merging the talks on intermediate-range weapons with those on strategic weapons, so that more items will be on the table for trading. Some Administration officials are more optimistic that the Strategic Arms Reduction Talks, or START, which have recessed without a date for resumption, will in fact resume, but not a great deal of hope is expressed that they will be successful.

There is a fair amount of alarm within the Administration that the government forces in El Salvador, backed by the United States, will collapse before long. This seems to be one reason that Administration officials have been publicly outspoken about the increasing activity of the "death squads" in El Savador, saying that they operate with the government's approval. Both Reagan and Vice-President George Bush have made strong representations to the El Salvadoran government. One concern is that unless the death-squad activity is reduced Congress will cut off military aid to El Salvador; another is that neither a military victory nor a negotiated settlement is possible as long as the death-squad activity continues. Yet on the same day that Kenneth Dam, the Deputy Secretary of State, made a strong speech on the subject, Reagan remarked in a television appearance that he suspected that some of the death-squad activities were committed by left-wing guerrillas, in order to halt United States aid to El Salvador. It was because the death-squad activity was so out of hand, people here believe, that Reagan vetoed a bill extending the law calling for him to certify that progress was being made on human rights in El Salvador in order that military assistance could be continued. Reagan signed such statements in the past, but this time it would be too much. There is a division of views within the Administration on how seriously to regard feelers that have been coming from Nicaragua on the possibility of the Sandinista government's reaching an accommodation with the United States, which is backing efforts to overthrow it.

Meanwhile, the President's aides and other political advisers have been gearing up for some time for a presumed Reagan reelection bid. Although there remain a few reservoirs of doubt here, the President's men say they would be astonished if he did not run. The President and Mrs. Reagan went through the pre-Christmas round of White House celebrations in good cheer, and the President looks remarkably well. He does not seem to worry—that is part of his public appeal. And recently we were treated to a picture of him, on the cover of *Parade,* pumping iron. Still, the White House is not a particularly happy place these days. A number of people there are worn down by the nearly constant ideological fights, and a few are leaving. James Baker, having lost out on a bid to become national-security adviser, is staying, but he has made it clear he wants to move on after the election. (Four years as chief of staff is a long haul for anyone, even in a more harmonious Administration.) There was also the matter of the Justice Department investigation of senior White House aides with regard to a leak about Lebanon policy earlier this fall—a leak that the White House was at no pains to deny at the time. The investigation, which was instigated by William Clark, the former national-security adviser, and by Meese, was another chapter in the ongoing saga of the hard-liners versus the moderates. (The Justice Department ended the investigation without identifying the source of the leak or finding that it had caused any serious problem.) And there remains the cloud of the briefing-book question—whether sensitive documents, including the briefing book prepared for Jimmy Carter for the debate with Reagan in 1980, were stolen from the White House and used by the Reagan campaign. The contradictory statements of James Baker and William Casey, the director of the Central Intelligence Agency, have not been reconciled, and a House subcommittee will hold hearings on the matter early in the year. While the polls are comforting to the President's advisers, they are far from conclusive. According to the latest Gallup poll, Reagan's approval rating is fifty-three per cent (Wirthlin puts the number at sixty-two)—the first time it has been over fifty per cent in two years. And Reagan has consistently run close to either Walter Mondale or John Glenn—and sometimes behind them. A recent Washington *Post*/ABC poll had him running behind Mondale. Several of the President's political advisers have come around to the view that Mondale would be the strongest opponent for Reagan, and they say that they believe it will be a tough, close election. They say this in part because they want to prevent complacency among their own troops, but also because they believe it to be true.

1984

X

JANUARY 3

WASHINGTON. Today, another round of the 1984 Presidential campaign begins. Last year, there were the preliminaries—which might turn out to have been more than preliminaries—and now the candidates are facing the real contests, and will be subjected to greater scrutiny as the press coverage increases and the public tunes in. An unusual mystery hangs over the Democratic contest at this point: one candidate, Walter Mondale, is, by just about every measurable standard, so far ahead of his rivals that there is a large body of opinion that the race is, in effect, over. By these measures—polls, money, endorsements, organizational strength—Mondale may, in fact, be farther ahead of his rivals than a front-runner has been in any really contested race in memory. Analogies with previous front-runners fail. However, the public is just beginning to pay attention; the kinds of events that can sway opinion, such as televised debates, have yet to occur; and unexpected developments, by definition, have not yet happened. So the mystery is whether a race that so many people assume is over is really over. An important question, even if Mondale does stumble, is who would be in a position to pick up the pieces and win. John Glenn, presumably the next-strongest candidate, has not had a particularly good last few months. In December, the Gallup poll had him twenty-eight points behind Mondale (in the previous poll, he had been eleven points behind); his campaign has seemed to lack definition; and he is running into money problems. The costs of maintaining a campaign staff and sending the candidate out on the road, not to mention the buying of advertising time, which has barely begun, are so great as to squeeze the resources of all the candidates. Other candidates—Reubin Askew, Alan Cranston, Gary Hart, Fritz Hollings, and George McGovern—have not broken through yet, and not because the press hasn't paid them attention: they have received more attention than back-

221

of-the-pack candidates ordinarily do in a preelection year. And they have had several opportunities to break through—straw polls, joint appearances of candidates, and so on. And if one of them should break through in an early contest there is some question of how—given the clustering of the contests this year, and the tremendous amount of money and, presumably, organization required—he could capitalize on that sufficiently. But part of the charm of politics is its mysteriousness and capacity for surprise. Jesse Jackson, who entered the race November 3rd, keeps scrambling the picture and the calculations by virtue of his nerve and his highly developed sense of theatre. Jackson has always known how to get attention, often at the expense of others (which is one reason he has many antagonists in the black community). Now he has scored a spectacular by going to Syria and obtaining this morning the release of Navy Lieutenant Robert Goodman, the airman who was shot down during a bombing raid over Syrian-held Lebanese territory on December 4th. Among other things, Jackson's feat will interfere with, if not ruin, Mondale's day. Today, Tuesday, the first day after the New Year's weekend, Mondale is to open his 1984 campaign with a speech on foreign policy to the National Press Club—a speech long in the planning and considered important to the campaign—and then go on the road for a trip that his staff considers to be of much significance: to the South where he will compete with Glenn, and where the share of the black vote that Jackson gets could be decisive.

But beyond the question of where each of the candidates stands in the ranking at this point are the questions about what the candidates are saying and, related to that, about the nature of the race that is shaping up among the Democrats against the Republicans. While Democrats are fighting each other in the next few months, the themes that the nominee will use against his Republican opponent will be developing. There can be no question that this will be an important election—especially if Reagan runs. Reagan has brought about probably the most dramatic change in the nature and the direction of government since the New Deal; he has a view of the world and of the conduct of foreign policy which represents a break with his Republican, not to mention his Democratic, predecessors. Whoever is elected in 1984 could well have an opportunity to make a number of Supreme Court appointments, and perhaps determine the Court's direction for decades. Moreover, it is an article of faith among many Democrats that America is in the midst of a changing economy and that Americans are looking for someone who can guide them into the future. This assumption has its tactical basis, of course, and may involve some wishful thinking: that Reagan, whatever his strengths, does not come across as someone who can guide the country into the future. One important thing that Reagan has done for politics is make it clear that—whatever one's point of view—it does matter who is President. This has already led to more intensity about the 1984 election than any in a long time—more involvement by more groups, a more widespread sense that there are stakes.

Today, with his speech and his trip, Mondale is raising the curtain on the next round. Glenn's campaign will effectively begin in a few days. Now the candidates will have to clarify their messages and have little time to do so, and will be under pressure from the others and not left alone to do so. I have decided to spend some time on the road with Mondale and Glenn, and talk with their aides and advisers, to see how each is handling the situation now and what they are saying.

The Capital Hilton Hotel. Noon. A large crowd has turned out for Mondale's speech, to be given here in the Presidential Ballroom, a big room, decorated in gold, that is the site of the annual Gridiron Dinner. (The National Press Club's building is being refurbished, so the luncheon address is being staged here.) A large segment of the crowd consists of Mondale supporters, and many others are here because this is the first political event of the new year, after a relatively peaceful holiday lull. With Congress gone since November 18th and the President out of town for a week, until yesterday, it has been fairly quiet, even though there were events to react to. Washington needed a break, and took one. But a lot of people are here because of the drama of Mondale's situation right now. The mechanics of his campaign thus far have been impressive—even, in the minds of some, brilliant. Mondale himself has been deft. Still—and not entirely through fault of his own—his voice has not yet come through. He has said no memorable thing. Strong position though he may be in, this is the period of maximum peril for Mondale. He will be receiving closer scrutiny than ever before and, as the front-runner, than any of his rivals. And all his rivals will be taking aim at him. Because of his position, more will be demanded of him. When a front-runner stumbles, the pouncing on him is relentless, if sometimes disproportionate. No politician wants to be, or is at his best, on the defensive. The Mondale group has felt that a lot is riding on this speech: on the quality of his performance, and on the political effectiveness of the substance. He must look like a leader—and a winner.

The speech has gone through something like nine drafts (at one point, thanks to all the experts who had a hand in it, it resembled a musty government policy paper), but the central theme was settled on weeks ago: creating a safer world. Dealing with such a theme enables Mondale to do three things at once: to display his experience with and grasp of foreign policy (with the implicit contrast with Reagan and Glenn) and present himself as capable of being a world leader; to deal with a subject on which Reagan is quite vulnerable; and to take some swipes at Glenn. As Mondale and his advisers see it, Mondale has the good, and unusual, fortune to be able to run a campaign simultaneously against both his chief opponent for the nomination and his presumed opponent for the general election. Often, a candidate for the Democratic nomination has to do battle on his left and then reach for the centrist vote in the general election, but the Mondale people see no serious, or unmanageable, threat on the left just now, and Mondale has been able to occupy a broad spectrum of the Party. The two most important issues that Mondale has against Reagan he also has, in a form, against Glenn: Reagan's economic program, which Glenn voted for in 1981; and arms control, since Glenn's opposition to the SALT II treaty was a major factor in its death in the Senate. By making a strong case against Reagan, as Mondale will do in this speech and during the rest of the nomination contest, he not only gets in position for the fall but implicitly makes the case that he can wage a tough campaign against Reagan—one of Glenn's principal arguments having been that he would be the stronger candidate against Reagan. For this speech, and for the rest of the campaign, Mondale has settled on three themes: "a more competitive economy, a more just society, and a safer world."

Mondale, arriving at the head table, looks ruddy and healthy. He took a week's skiing vacation in Vail, Colorado, over Christmas, and then returned for a week of intense meetings with his staff and outside advisers on a wide range of subjects. This was probably the last chance for sustained attention to these things until the nomination fight is settled. What much of the press here wants to know is how Mondale will respond to the story of the day—Jackson's successful mission to Syria. Reagan, who had kept his distance from the venture, has now embraced it, which is the only sensible thing to do politically. It's a bit embarrassing that Jackson succeeded where the Administration had not, and even more so since Reagan's special Mideast envoy, Donald Rumsfeld, failed to bring up the question of Goodman's release when he talked with Syrian officials recently. But, despite his associating himself with the airman's release, Reagan is still saddled with a Lebanon policy that is fast losing political support. The report, released last week, of a Pentagon-appointed commission headed by retired Admiral Robert L. J. Long not only was a devastating indictment of the security arrangements that led to the death of two hundred and forty-one Marines as a result of the truck-bomb attack in October but called into question the President's entire Lebanon policy. (It had become known by then that the Joint Chiefs of Staff had unanimously opposed sending the Marines into Lebanon.) Reagan, in an attempt to minimize the damage to himself and pre-empt debate on the report, said last week that he took responsibility for the lack of security measures, and that local commanders on the ground should not be punished—that they had "suffered enough." But this theatrical and somewhat belated gesture did not allay the questions about a policy that had, among other things, caused the death of over two hundred and sixty Marines and led the United States into confrontation on yet another front.

On Saturday, Mondale, breaking with his previous position, called for withdrawal of the Marines from Lebanon within forty-five days. Before that, he had had a five-point program of steps for the Administration to take. His aides explained that the change of position came as a result of his reading the Long Commission report and an earlier one, by the House Armed Services Committee, and of the failure of the Lebanese government to take effective steps that might lead to a settlement. But there were, obviously, other imperatives as well: If Mondale did not move, he risked being left behind by both Democrats and Republicans who were talking about withdrawing their support of the Administration's policy, and it was not inconceivable that the President would find a way to extricate himself before long. And if Mondale was to move, the sooner the better. His announcement was deliberately made three days before the Press Club speech, so that it would not take the headlines from other things he wanted to say in the speech, and had he not got the subject out of the way he would have had to spend some time during the question period at the Press Club defending a policy on which time was running out. Other candidates had already called for withdrawal of the Marines—leaving only Mondale and Glenn in support of the Marines' presence. (Glenn's aides had hoped that he would change his policy in recent weeks, but he balked.) Mondale's statement, when one gets to the fine print, is not so radical as it first appears: he calls for maintaining the United States naval forces off the Lebanese shore—a concession to supporters of Israel who support the Lebanon policy—and he makes other bows in the direction of Israel.

Today, at the Press Club luncheon, Mondale begins by praising Jackson's feat; there is nothing else he can do. One of the curiosities of the hullabaloo over Jackson's exploit is the amount of comment suggesting that it shows how much more verve Jackson has than his rivals; yet if any of Jackson's rivals had tried a similar thing they'd have been subjected to merciless criticism for involving themselves in foreign affairs for their own political gain. Jackson has got away with it to the extent he has because he is extra-political—and provides wonderful theatre. Politics is much more of an entertainment business than we care to admit. The one theatrical line in a debate gets far more attention than all the rest of what happens. The more contention there is in a debate, the more it is valued—never mind substance, or what all this has to do with the capacity for being President. (Who remembers what happened in the Republican debate in Nashua, New Hampshire, in 1980 except that Reagan said, "I am paying for this microphone, Mr. Green"?) The Mondale people are concerned not just about how many black votes Jackson will take from Mondale but also about Jackson's capacity for roiling the waters over the next several months. He has already challenged the rules under which the nominating contest is being fought, arguing that they discriminate against minority candidates as well as candidates who are not front-runners. In fact, the rules were approved by a number of black officials, including some who are supporting Jackson (and the Party has strong affirmative-action rules), and what they were designed to do was produce consensus and a winner. Whatever way the rules are written works to the advantage of someone: this time, the Party's interest was in preventing a long-shot candidacy and in getting the thing over with. The more graciously the Mondale people and Party officials treat Jackson, the thinking is, the more reasonable he might be, and the less likely it is that blacks sympathetic to Jackson will be alienated.

In his speech, Mondale begins by arguing that "this election in my opinion is a turning point for America, for we must decide many things," and he raises the questions that must be answered, under the headings of his themes. These themes will, to the extent Mondale can control the debate, constitute his case for himself, and against Reagan. "First," he says, "we'll be deciding what kind of economy we'll have. Will America get its competitive edge back and lead the world economy again? Or will we saddle our kids with debt, second-rate jobs, impossible interest rates, and a falling standard of living?" With the economy improving (if it continues to improve), the Democrats will have to make their case against the immediate and long-run effects of one result of Reagan's program—the staggering budget deficits—and also against the program's "unfairness." "Second," Mondale says, "we must decide what kind of people we are. Will we restore a sense of fairness and decency in American life? Or will it be the rich against the rest?" He continues, "Third, we must decide what kind of future we will have—if any," and he talks about the danger of nuclear weapons. Mondale goes after Glenn and Reagan simultaneously when he talks about the need to make "tough choices" on defense; and when he talks about "compassion" he is taking direct aim at Reagan but indirect aim at Glenn, who has chosen to run a relatively conservative campaign. This speech, Mondale explains, will be focussed on the third theme, and he turns back on Reagan the famous question Reagan asked in his debate with Carter in 1980. (The memorable line from that debate: "Are you better off than you were four years ago?") "Do we live in a safer world than we did three years ago?" Mondale asks. "Are we further from nuclear war? After a thousand days of Mr. Reagan, is the world anywhere less tense, anywhere closer to peace?" Then he cites the wars in the Middle East and Central America, the low state of United States-Soviet relations, the collapse of all arms talks between the United States and the Soviet Union, the escalation of the arms race. And then he hits at what he believes to be a Reagan vulnerability—the impression that Reagan isn't very well informed, or in command: "When the globe is a tinderbox, we need a President who knows what he's doing." Continuing to make the case against Reagan, and attempting to draw an implicit contrast with himself, Mondale says, "We need a President who sees the world as it is, in all of its subtleties, its complexities, its dangers, and its potential; who's been tested by experience; who's read and remembers history; who will reduce the risk of nuclear war; who sees force as a last and not a first resort; who will speak up for American values; and who knows that it's the President himself who must command and drive American policy." To protect himself from a charge of being "soft," Mondale cites the record of Soviet actions that cannot be approved of. Actually, Mondale's political roots are in the wing of the Democratic Party which was highly anti-Communist in the forties and fifties, and this still affects his thinking. But he goes on to make the case for a more sophisticated way of dealing with the Soviet Union than the Reagan Administration has followed: "The job of a President is both to check the Soviets through means short of war and to meet them on the common ground of survival." He talks of the need to keep up communications, on several levels ("The superpowers cannot communicate only by growling through megaphones"), and repeats a proposal he has made before—for annual summit conferences. He calls for a "strong defense" but says, "I refuse to support Mr. Reagan's incoherent program or sign Mr. Weinberger's"—Defense Secretary Caspar Weinberger—"blank check," and he attacks in specific terms the Reagan defense program: he says that the Navy's new mission, of stationing ships off the Soviet Union, to be in a position to attack the Soviet land mass, "is irrational," and he says that "where a President must make choices, Mr. Reagan can't say no." Running through this are implicit attacks on Glenn as well—raising the question of whether Glenn is sufficiently experienced for the job, and whether Glenn would be sufficiently rigorous about defense spending. And when Mondale now criticizes Reagan for opposing "every effort of every President of both parties to control nuclear weapons," and attacks him for the lack of any progress on arms control, he also gets in a dig at Glenn, by saying that the SALT II agreement "should have been approved, and I wish every senator had voted for it."

Mondale's delivery is strong but not theatrical; he simply isn't a theatrical man. "Flair" is not a word one would apply to him. But he does speak as if from conviction and thought, and this is what he is trying to get across: that he has thought about the important questions (Mondale actually enjoys getting deeply involved in sub- stance, and he is an avid reader of history); that he cares about important things; that he is the most knowledgeable and experi- enced of the candidates. He talks about a deterioration in relations with our allies, and about the importance of stressing human rights ("America must not only stand tall, it must stand for some- thing"). And then he goes at Reagan's management of foreign policy, citing the turnover in top foreign-policy officials and the zigs and zags on Middle East policy. He cites the contrast with the achievement of the Camp David agreement between Egypt and Israel, which President Carter brought about through his per- sonal attention, and which was to be an ongoing process, but which the Reagan Administration let lapse. "A President cannot ad-lib foreign policy," Mondale says. "He cannot delegate war and peace." Mondale clearly feels that this is a good issue against Reagan. He cites a number of things he would do, including up- date SALT II and resubmit it, and seek deeper cuts within the SALT II framework; repropose the agreement that was tentatively reached between American and Soviet negotiators on intermedi- ate-range nuclear forces during their famous "walk in the woods" (an agreement that was turned down by both governments but apparently by the American government first); kill the MX missile and proceed with the smaller Midgetman (here Glenn agrees); kill the B-1 bomber (here Glenn disagrees); renew the fight against nuclear proliferation (Glenn has sponsored legislation on this); push for a mutual, verifiable freeze on nuclear weapons (all the candidates except Askew favor this, despite its many complica- tions); block production of what Mondale chooses to refer to as "poison nerve gas" (Glenn voted last year to renew production of it); reaffirm America's commitment to the anti-ballistic-missile treaty, which Reagan's "Star Wars" program of developing defen- sive weapons systems in outer space would destroy; and a number of other steps. Under the "walk in the woods" agreement, the United States and the Soviet Union would have been limited to seventy-five cruise-missile launchers and seventy-five SS-20s re- spectively, and the United States would not have installed Pershing 2 missiles. Again making his case against both Reagan and Glenn,

Mondale says, "The 1984 election will pose sharp tests for all candidates. Americans will be asking, Who will lead us toward a safer world? Who has the best record of support of arms control? Who has made the tough choices in weapons systems? Who has the depth of understanding in national security and diplomacy? Who has been the most outspoken advocate of American values in the world? Who is the most ready to run an organization as complex as our government?" One of Mondale's major refrains last year was "I'm ready." Mondale has given an effective speech, and one that is important to his campaign—but television coverage of it will be essentially blanked out by Jesse Jackson.

During the question period, Mondale is asked whether there is any special-interest group that he has not sought the support of or made promises to. Mondale is clearly prepared for this sort of question, and he gives his best-developed response thus far. Looking as if he isn't the least fazed, he smiles broadly and says, "This issue is going to be the most fun in 1984. Let me tell you where I stand: I think there are millions of unemployed who ought to have jobs, and I am very interested in putting them back to work. I think there are millions of children, young people, who need good educations and are being denied it by this Reagan Administration, and I'm going to make certain that this next generation is the best educated in American history. I think that in this country discrimination based on race or sex is inexcusable and intolerable. And I think this Administration has a shameful record of nonenforcement and I intend to turn that around. I think our children are entitled to have those environmental laws protected—our air, our water, our land, our public health—and I intend to, as I said, fire everybody they hired and hire everybody they fired and get on with enforcing the law."

Mondale continues, "I believe this country is not a selfish nation. Matter of fact, I know it isn't. And when people are suffering from hunger, at a time when we can deduct three-hundred-dollar business lunches without a whimper, at a time when under the mismanagement of this agriculture policy they're spending something like twenty-one billion or thirty-one billion dollars to reduce food production—I would much prefer to be on the side of using American agricultural funds to feed the hungry here and to help people around the world who are starving and will not have a chance without our help. I think it's long overdue that the Equal Rights Amendment be ratified, and that we have an all-out attack against the cruellest thing going on in our country—the feminization of poverty. And, finally, in international affairs, as I've spelled out today, I'm for a strong defense, but I want that defense used in peace, and I want our strength used to reduce the risk of nuclear war. If those are special interests, count me in. I'm proud of every one of them."

Then he is asked another question that comes at him with some frequency, in various forms: "How do you plan to address the perception by some that you are an uninspiring candidate?"

Mondale replies, "I know only one way to work in public life, and that is to first of all believe in what I'm trying to do, be personally persuaded that it's essential, and then to go on out and on the basis of that conviction try to persuade the American people to come along with me. It's going very well. We have, I think, in this past year made more progress than anybody expected." He refers to house parties held on Saturday, December 10th, which were attended by over a hundred thousand people and raised $1.4 million dollars in small amounts. "You can't order people to do that," Mondale says. "They wanted to do it." (On that same Saturday, Mondale received the endorsements of the National Organization of Women and the Alabama Democratic Conference—the black wing of the state Democratic Party. Jackson contested Mondale for the latter endorsement, and a compromise was worked out whereby the organization endorsed Mondale for President and Jackson for Vice-President. Mondale had, of course, already received the endorsements of the A.F.L.-C.I.O., the National Education Association, and the American Federation of Teachers, and on December 14th he was endorsed by the United Mine Workers.) Under questioning, he makes a strong indictment of the Administration's conduct of foreign policy in Central America (it "Americanized the dispute, widened it, and militarized it"), and he tempers his acceptance of the invasion of Grenada—he says that if he thought American lives were at risk he would use force, and that he was impressed by the support of the action by some Democratic congressmen who visited the area—by adding that the Administration is now, in effect, seeking "to dominate the transitional life of that island" and "we should have gotten out."

After his Press Club appearance, I speak with Mondale for a few minutes. I want to try to assess his state of mind at this point.

"I feel good," Mondale says. "As a matter of fact, I think the issues that are developing in 1984 are developing in a way that enhances our chances. I don't say that loosely. I think people are increasingly concerned about the safety of the world; and are jumpy about Reagan's instincts and feel he's not in charge. I think that will be big in '84. I think the fairness issue is building, as well as where is America going in terms of its competitive edge. I think the issues are building as well as you can hope."

.I ask him what he thinks his biggest challenge is right now.

Referring to a conversation we had last fall, he says, "It's the same as it was when we talked the last time: to make the case, and to be seen and understood as a President, with the abilities and experience and all that goes into that job. That's what I tried to do today—not just give a speech but show how my mind works, where I'm coming from."

I ask Mondale if it isn't the case that since last fall he has got further along in developing his themes.

He replies that he has, and cites his three themes, but, he adds, "I still have to end up with some overarching something. We still don't have that yet—it'll come." He continues, "You notice that I talked more than I have before about a President who is in charge. I think that question worries Americans. I didn't give a stump speech. I gave a twenty-five-minute, serious speech about how I view the Presidency, and I spelled out the contrasts in Reagan's and my views of the alliance, arms-control strategy, and so on."

I ask him how he feels about being questioned, as he was today, about his ability to light a fire.

He replies, "I can't stand up and say I do light fires. That's not an answer. But I think things are going fine—I get a good response. I answer by showing what's happening: the polls, the ability to raise money. I think that talk is just rumble. Things are happening."

I ask him what he thinks is his greatest peril now.

He replies, "The reverse of what we've been talking about. If people are not reassured in their answer to the question of what kind of President I would be, I'm in trouble."

JACKSON, MISSISSIPPI. On this, the first stop of his Southern swing, Mondale is attending a reception of "Mississippians for Mondale," his state campaign steering committee—a biracial group of more than two hundred and fifty members, representing all the state's eighty-two counties. This trip, which is to cover Mississippi, Arkansas, Alabama, Georgia, and Florida, was thought up six weeks ago by James Johnson, Mondale's campaign chairman (the word "acting" has been dropped from his title), and has several concurrent purposes, among them to get the jump on Glenn, who is counting on a strong showing in the South, and to show that Mondale has strong Southern support. (The Mondale organization has taken its own polls in Georgia, Alabama, and Florida, and, according to Johnson, Mondale is ahead of Glenn and Jackson in all three states—and Mondale is very far ahead of Glenn, with Jackson trailing far behind, in Georgia and Alabama. The Glenn people dispute the Alabama finding. The Florida poll also indicated that if Askew, who is running a conservative campaign, pulled out, his support would be divided evenly between Mondale and Glenn.) Another reason for this trip is to show that Mondale is solidifying his Southern base. It is the Mondale camp's belief, based on its polling, that Glenn's principal problem is that people do not see him as a future President—that he has failed to establish himself in the voters' minds as being in the Presidential league. One important Republican strategist in Washington says he believes that Glenn may have made a fatal mistake in attacking Mondale last fall, before he had established his own credentials as Presidential material.

There has been a widespread assumption that Glenn would be stronger in the South, because it is considered more pro-defense and more conservative than other areas, and because Glenn has been saying that he would be strong in the South, but the politics of several Southern states (and also Texas) might belie this, since they have progressive Democratic governors who were elected by coalitions that included labor and blacks (and, in the case of Texas, Hispanics), and also farmers. Mondale is trying to put together this sort of coalition for himself in the Southern states. Alabama, Florida, and Georgia will hold their nomination contests on March 13th and Mississippi and Arkansas on March 17th—a crucial period in the Democratic calendar. Mississippi and Arkansas will select their Convention delegates by caucus, a process that is even more dependent on good organization than a primary is. The idea, Johnson says, is that "in the caucus states we would focus on building our organization, motivating our supporters, and putting them in a position to sustain organizing activities through a long absence on our part, while we campaign in Iowa and New Hampshire and the Southern primary states." He continues, "We have believed all along that we could be competitive in the South, and have tried at every juncture to make symbolic gestures so that everyone who followed politics in the South would see how serious we were." Moreover, the Democrats are not prepared to concede these, or a number of other Southern states, to the Republicans in 1984. Reagan carried several of them narrowly in 1980.

To Johnson, it is important to be putting the pressure on Glenn, rather than have it the other way around. Later this week, Bob Beckel, the campaign manager, will go to Cleveland and announce that Mondale will be campaigning actively for the Ohio primary, which takes place on May 8th; this, too, was a Johnson idea—he figures that the very thought that Mondale will challenge Glenn in his own territory will throw Glenn off, and might even lead him to spend additional time shoring up his base in Ohio. Also, working through an ally in Cleveland, Tim Hagan, who was formerly the Democratic chairman of Cuyahoga County and is now a county commissioner, the Mondale people succeeded in seeing to it that the rules by which Ohio selects its delegates will not be as favorable to Glenn as they might have been. And the Ohio primary was moved up in the schedule, as the Glenn people sought, but not by nearly as much as they wanted.

And so Mondale came to Jackson on his first trip after he announced for the Presidency last February, and he is making his first campaign stop of 1984 here this afternoon. Arrayed behind Mondale on the stage is his Mississippi steering committee. And symbolic of what has happened to Mississippi in the last twenty years is that Mondale's co-chairmen are Unita Blackwell, a black woman who was a member of the Mississippi Freedom Democratic Party at the 1964 Convention and is now vice-chairman of the state party and mayor of Mayersville, and Carroll Ingram, a white former state senator. The audience, of about five hundred, is also biracial and is made up largely of union members and teachers. The incumbent governor, William Winter, a progressive, is here, as is his successor-elect, William Allain. Neither man has endorsed a candidate, but Winter, who is considering running for the Senate, gives Mondale a warm introduction—one that indicates the benefits of Mondale's many years in political life. "He comes to Mississippi as no stranger," Winter says of Mondale. "He won

many friends here as Vice-President—coming here and demonstrating his understanding of the problems we have here." Expressing his gratitude to Mondale for coming to Mississippi at the
beginning of his campaign last year and this, Winter says, "I'm
glad that we are finding ourselves now in the mainstream of the
political process."

Mondale, familiar with Mississippi's political landscape, makes
some jokes about local politics. And then he goes into his new
stump speech, honed from the speeches he gave last year, and
made to fit more tightly around the three themes of his campaign.
He says he has travelled this country in the past three years more
than any other living American, and that Americans "are asking
for a new President who will take charge and do three things:
One, lead this nation and lead this world toward a safer world,
where peace is more possible. The second is to restore the competitive posture of the American economy so we can grow and grow
and put our people back to work. And the third is to restore a
sense of fairness in American life again"—he is applauded—"so
that when we look to the White House and listen to the President
we hear words that tell us that we're not in this world just by
ourselves and for ourselves but we're in it to be kind and caring
toward one another as Americans and human beings." Mondale
speaks without notes and with feeling. He goes on, "We need a
President who will take charge, we need a President who will keep
us strong, and we need to use that strength to keep the peace. We
need to reach agreements to control those god-awful nuclear
weapons."

Then Mondale launches into an attack on the Reagan economic
program, bringing it to the local level. Unemployment is very high
in Mississippi—over ten per cent—and the state is very dependent
on agricultural exports. "Reaganomics has attacked the state of
Mississippi in ways that have given you inordinately high unemployment and personal suffering," he says. "The bottom fell out of
the nation's economy and the economy here in Mississippi as a
result of Reaganomics." Then he explains in simple terms what the
theory of Reaganomics was, and says that the result was "to create
deficits of two hundred billion dollars a year as far as the eye can
see." He continues, "Just as soon as that program went in place,
real interest rates doubled, the housing and the other industries of
this country stopped, we were driven into the deepest recession

since the Great Depression. The effect of this economic policy has been to push us off the field in terms of international play—not only in terms of industrial products, but in this great state of Mississippi, where you have all this agriculture, it has pushed agriculture exports back, the worst they have ever been in over four years. And the result is high unemployment in Mississippi, the worst suffering in rural Mississippi in recent times, deep deficits here at home, and next year could well be worse than this year under the policies of this Administration." He speaks slowly and with assurance; this is the case he will be making against the Reagan economic program. "I'm going to turn that around," he says. "I'm going to bring those deficits down. I'm going to cut Reagan's deficits by more than half." This, he says, will lower interest rates, restore competitiveness in international markets, restore jobs, and "add wealth and add strength to this country, including the state of Mississippi."

Turning to another of his major subjects, Mondale says that "the next thing we've got to do to be competitive is to make sure that these young people here that are coming along, this next generation, is the best educated in the history of our country," and he praises Winter for progress that has been made in Mississippi. Mondale now fits education, which used to be a separate topic, under the theme of a more competitive America: that we need better education so that our country can be more competitive with the rest of the world.

Mondale's delivery is polished. He is not an especially handsome man—he has a slightly beaked nose (the result of football injuries) and prominent blue eyes—but when he is rested he gives off an aura of fitness and well-being. His straight, dark-blond hair has more gray in it these days, giving it a silvery tone. Mondale's public persona is an odd combination of the gregarious politician and the contained private man. He has been in public life for a long, long time, and he shakes hands and makes small talk with the best of them, and his public smile is a wide, openmouthed grin. Mondale is an undemonstrative man, publicly and privately—a trait that is often attributed to his Norwegian heritage and his childhood as a minister's son. People who know him well know that there are both private matters and public issues that he cares very much about, and have seen him moved to joy and grief, but he is generally uncomfortable about showing his emotions. When he relaxes among friends and close associates, he can be witty, and even uproarious, but, despite the urging of his advisers, he is still reluctant to let much of his humor show in public.

"Finally," Mondale says, "we need a President to restore a sense of fairness in American life—and that's what I rejoice about in Mississippi. You are starting to give an example to the rest of the nation of how things can change, how progress can be made, how people can work together when they put their differences behind them." And then he says, "Someone once said ours is a government of the people, by the people, for the people; but what we've got today is government of the rich, by the rich, for the rich." He says, "We're becoming two Americas—one for that thin veneer of the wealthiest who are doing better and better, and the other for the rest of America who are doing less and less well. Whether it's utility bills or telephone bills or taxes or health costs or heating costs, it seems that the cost of the average family raising their family is going up and up and up and increasingly beyond the reach of decent, hardworking Americans. And they're trying to solve that by cutting back on Social Security, cutting back on Medicare, cutting back on student loans, cutting back on the very things that people of modest incomes cannot do without if they are going to have a decent life." And then, in a revealing line, Mondale declares, "I am a people's Democrat." He is running as a populist, setting himself as the defender of the middle class and the poor against a government that he characterizes as being for the rich. He explains how the Reagan tax cut helped the rich at the expense of the middle class and the poor. "If you make two hundred thousand dollars a year, you get sixty thousand in tax relief from the federal government. But if you make thirty thousand a year, or less, all taxes considered, your taxes went up." In part, this populism stems from his Midwestern progressive Democratic-Farmer-Labor Party background, and in part it is a way of attempting to collect a majority against Reagan. (And his aides believe that this is not an approach Glenn can follow, on the basis of his record or his instincts.) Mondale is presenting himself as a friend of the poor but is also saying that middle-income people have been hurt by the Reagan policies. And he has a list of examples that he draws upon in various appearances: the deductibility of three-hundred-dollar lunches; tax shelters; low corporate taxes; the rise in phone bills as a result of the recent breakup of

A.T. & T. (which someone I know refers to as the Vietnam of deregulation); utility rates; the tax cut; and so on. "A people's Democrat" is redolent of Harry Truman, summoning up the image of a scrapper against the big guys, but whether Mondale has the inner assurance, the decisiveness, of Truman is not clear. "I want a nation in which the White House fights to prohibit discrimination," Mondale tells this racially mixed Mississippi audience. Referring to, and somewhat exaggerating, White House Counsellor Edwin Meese's famous pre-Christmas remarks, he says, "A few weeks ago, we were told everyone in America who's hungry is a hustler. They never raise a whimper when somebody deducts a three-hundred-dollar business lunch. But if you want to feed a hungry child in this country there's supposed to be something wrong with you. That's why I want to be President. To get on with the blessed work of our marvellous nation. To restore our competition, so we can grow and prosper and have the jobs and the wealth coming to our country for our people. To restore a sense of fairness, so that everyone has an equal chance for the fullness of American life. And to keep us strong but to use that strength to keep the peace and to reflect American values. If you'll help me here in Mississippi to be nominated, if you'll help me here in Mississippi to be elected, I'll be that kind of President, and Mississippi will have a good friend."

LITTLE ROCK, ARKANSAS. The chartered DC-9 in which we have been travelling—carrying thirteen Mondale staff members as well as the candidate, thirty-three reporters, and eleven still photographers, members of television crews, and television producers—arrived here early this evening. Mondale also has Zell Miller, the Lieutenant Governor of Georgia, and Ned McWherter, the Speaker of the House of Tennessee, travelling with him, and he introduces them at his various stops. Mondale was met here this evening by Arkansas's Governor Bill Clinton, who has not endorsed a candidate but is an old friend of Mondale's. (Like Winter, Clinton, who is thirty-seven, has his own political exigencies. He must seek reelection this year, and was once turned out of the governorship. Neither man, therefore, wants to split his state party. This is the meaning of the expression "All politics is local.") Now, at shortly after eight, Mondale is holding a news conference at the Excelsior Hotel and announcing another steering commit-

tee. Bill Alexander, a forty-nine-year-old congressman from Os-
ceola, and Chief Deputy Majority Whip, who endorsed Mondale
some time ago, tells the audience (made up of the press and some
Mondale supporters) that Mondale "can embrace a wide range of
interests of the Democratic Party under one banner," and that he
"knows what to do when he becomes President of the United
States." Mondale has begun to look tired; it's been a long day
(we're on Central Time here, so it's an hour later in Washington,
where he started out), and he's put a lot into it. When Mondale
becomes tired, pouches grow under his eyes. In a quieter voice
than before, he states his rationale for seeking the Presidency
("The only justification for seeking the Presidency is that a person
has a vision of the future") and summarizes briefly his three
themes. He points out that Arkansas is a farm state, dependent on
exports. When he gets to fairness, he says, "We are not a jungle
where just the fittest and the richest survive in our country."

When Mondale takes questions, he is asked what effect he
thinks the release of Lieutenant Goodman will have on Jackson's
candidacy. Jackson has been hovering over this trip all day—and
he dominated the news tonight. Only NBC even mentioned the
substance of Mondale's Press Club speech. In response to the
question, Mondale repeats the praise he gave Jackson at the Press
Club, and adds, "I am, however, confident that I will be nominated. I've got to earn it, but I feel good about it."

He is asked how he plans to cut the budget deficit by more than
half, and he replies that he will be making a series of recommendations in the course of the campaign. The plan is that he will spell
out his deficit-cutting proposals incrementally. One component,
cutting the costs of health care by means of a health-care-cost-
containment program, will be spelled out in Florida on Friday. He
also says that he can cut the cost of farm programs substantially
without hurting farmers, and he has said that he favors increasing
the defense budget by four or five per cent after inflation. His
savings, he argues, will lead to reduced interest costs to the government through both a lower deficit and lower interest rates.

Mondale's aides say that the point of not laying out all his deficit-
reduction proposals in one speech is to have each component get
separate attention. They add that he cannot offer specific tax-
increase plans until Reagan's own budget is announced, and ana-
lyzed independently, so that it can be seen how much revenue

must be raised. Mondale has made some proposals for raising revenues: putting a cap on the third year of Reagan's tax cut, and thus reducing the benefits to the very rich; repealing the provision of the 1981 tax-cut law which will index taxes for inflation as of January 1, 1985 (the repeal could actually hurt low- and middle-income people); increasing some business taxes; and closing some loopholes. He has preferred not to get more specific, but he is considering a list of loophole-closing, revenue-raising proposals. He is said to understand that he will be under pressure for specificity (Reagan did not spell out his economic proposals until September of 1980, in his so-called "mirrors speech"), and Mondale's advisers say that he will offer more detailed proposals later and that the only question is one of timing. Offering a detailed tax program at this point in a campaign is a bit unusual, even absurd—and it would serve to stir up opponents of reform. Mondale will try to deny Reagan credibility on the subject of the deficit, and show that the way he would cut the deficit is fairer than the way either Reagan or Glenn would do it. Glenn has proposed what he describes as a ten-per-cent "progressive" surtax on personal income; Mondale says that Glenn's proposal compounds the inequities of the tax code. (Glenn also proposed raising corporate taxes through a ten-per-cent surtax, but after it was pointed out that corporate taxes are already so low that this would make little difference he modified his proposal somewhat. A recent congressional study indicates that corporations in 1982 paid taxes on only sixteen per cent of their income, and therefore a ten-per-cent increase would raise this to 17.6 per cent. When Glenn was asked about this on *Meet the Press* in December, he replied that since corporate taxes were so low, little revenue could be raised even from doubling them. Two days later, he proposed a modest additional corporate tax.)

Still, perhaps because of his fatigue, Mondale seems on uncertain ground tonight when he is faced with more questions about his deficit-cutting plan. On being asked how soon he would cut the deficit in half, he responds, "We want to do it as quickly as possible, but by the end of the first term." Then he perks up and says, "I see the outsized size of the Reagan deficit as being one of the incredible problems of our time," and he cites the effects of the deficit. He adds, "There's a dirty little secret about this Reagan Administration, and that is that they haven't cut spending. They are perhaps, as a percentage of national wealth, the biggest peacetime spenders in the nation's history. They are spending a much higher percentage of the nation's wealth than we did, but it's not going for people or for jobs or for our future—it's going for defense costs, it's going for a soaring interest bill, it's going for the cost of paying for unemployment."

A reporter asks him, "Can you really overcome the perception that you are a tired old liberal with tired old coalitions and tired old answers?"

Now he gets worked up, and says, "My only reason for seeking the Presidency is to deal with our future. In order to have a sound economic policy, you can't borrow massively to deal with that future; you've got to bring those deficits down, and our generation has to pay its own way—to prune budgetary policies. In order to deal with that future, we've got to educate this next generation as the best educated in American history. We have to reinvest in science and technology and training so that they are prepared for the knowledge-intensive life that they will undoubtedly lead. I don't know whether it's old or new, but the idea of being fair, of prohibiting discrimination, of making it possible for senior citizens to retire on Social Security and to have their Medicare and to have a little decency in this country—if that's old, count me in."

The Bethel Baptist Church, Little Rock. About three hundred people, almost all of them black, are gathered in this small, simple building at shortly before 9 P.M. About a dozen Jackson supporters outside the church are noisily chanting "We want Jackson!" and some are holding up large posters with a photograph of Jackson and Goodman. Word has come that tomorrow Reagan will greet Goodman and Jackson at the White House, and the event will undoubtedly once again have Jackson dominating the news and increase his standing among blacks, but no one—not even in the Mondale group, which has followed the signs of Jackson's standing among blacks closely, and nervously—can judge what all this will mean in terms of Jackson's ability to win votes, or delegates. The Mondale people stress that Jackson has little organization or money, and that in caucus states, like Arkansas and Mississippi, he will need strong organization to get results. Another view might be that Jackson's campaign, being extra-political and extraordinarily successful at getting press coverage, is less dependent on mechanics than other campaigns, such as Mondale's. Johnson's view is that Jackson's achievement will have an effect on the campaign, but that it will not be a substantial electoral effect. He argues that while people are saying that Jackson has taken the limelight from Mondale, Mondale, being the front-runner, is in the limelight, and the effect is far worse for the other candidates, who are more in need of attention at this point.

At the Bethel church tonight, the invocation is given by the minister, who is, as it happens, a Jackson supporter, and there are a number of people in the audience wearing Jackson buttons. A Mondale aide said that the Mondale group was aware that there was substantial support for Jackson in this area. The man who introduces Mondale tonight says, "This is the first time a person who is running for President of the United States has taken the time to come into our community."

Mondale, who seems to have revived, begins with some friendly jokes about members of the audience he knows. And then he goes into a talk in which he makes his case to these people. Again, he speaks slowly and clearly, and draws on the things in his own experience, and the issues he has been talking about, which he hopes will convince these people. He's no match for Jimmy Carter in black churches, for Carter had grown up among them and could speak with their language and rhythms, but Mondale knows how to talk to these audiences, and he has a long record of commitment to civil rights to draw upon. He often tells audiences, as he does this one, that he grew up poor. "I wanted to be with you tonight because we've got a lot of work to do," he begins. "You know it, and I know it. This government of ours is supposed to be of the people, by the people, and for the people; what we've got is government of the rich, and by the rich, and for the rich." He tells them, "I am a people's Democrat," and he tells them, "I was trained by the best—Hubert Humphrey." He continues, "This government, this nation of ours, is not what it should be unless we have a President in that White House who is working for all of us." And the audience is still as he says, "America is not a jungle for just the richest or the fittest to survive and prosper. America is a community, a family, a nation for all of us. We are all children of God. We are all Americans, and we're entitled to a President that pursues that fundamental, basic philosophy that makes us one nation." He tells them, "We need a President that knows how it hurts to be without a job, what it's like to go home and to be unable to care for your family. We need a President who understands what it's like to be young and to believe every minute of your life that you've failed, that you're not learning, that you can't make it, that you can't find a job, that you're a failure. We can't tolerate that. We need a President who understands the sting and the curse of discrimination. We can't permit that in this country."

When Mondale speaks to these audiences, he conveys that he cares about what he is saying, that he is indignant about the inequities he is describing. The indignation is authentic—it is a characteristic he has shown over the years. It fits in with the populism. Much is made of Mondale's "caution," especially in this campaign, but what comes across as caution has several origins. One is his personal inhibition, his lack of theatricality and flair. Another is the way his mind works: Mondale knows that things are complicated and is not given to simplification—and this can be a political drawback. He has taken on some issues of importance in his political career, but his political style in general is to work with the givens. He is often hesitant to move until he is certain what all the givens are. He is a coalition-builder. The whole question of caution and daring in politics is often mixed up with style: Some politicians seem more daring because of the style with which they make an argument. And some, of course, are temperamentally more willing to go against the grain than Mondale typically is. He supported the Johnson Administration on the Vietnam War until September of 1968—a position he later described to me as "the biggest mistake of my public career." But it seemed at the time that he was trapped in part at least by his loyalty to Hubert Humphrey, Lyndon Johnson's Vice-President, who was running for President in 1968 (Mondale was his co-campaign manager), and who himself could not break free of Johnson's policy. Mondale had, in fact, urged Humphrey to give a speech breaking with the Johnson policy, but Humphrey had declined. So what comes across as caution in Mondale's current campaign is a product of certain personality traits and also of the position he's in. Front-runners tend not to take chances; it's for those who have less, or nothing, to lose to roll the dice. Daring in a President is not necessarily a good thing. The heart of the question about Mondale's caution is whether it represents a combination of good sense and recognition of the political position he's in or whether it represents a certain weakness—a tendency to follow rather than lead, an indecisiveness. If it's the latter, he would have difficulty governing.

Now, at the black church, Mondale refers to the Administration's recent reconstruction of the Civil Rights Commission to make it more to its liking. He says, "Does this President and that Administration know what it feels like to read that the Civil Rights Commission has been trashed? Do they know what that signal is? For twenty-five years, every President, including Mr. Nixon—and he was not my favorite President—not even he trashed that Civil Rights Commission." Sometimes Mondale tells black audiences that if Reagan is reelected he might be able to shape a majority on the Supreme Court. Tonight, Mondale talks about the need for better education, saying. "We've got to build again on the strength of those black colleges," and the audience applauds. "For a hundred years, those colleges were the only avenue for generation after generation—many of you are in this room, aren't you?" Mondale says. "There weren't many black middle class in this country at all or black trained professionals—and just as then, those colleges are reaching out and extending help and education to thousands and thousands and thousands of young Americans who wouldn't have a chance." (Reagan cutbacks in student aid have hit black colleges especially hard.) Mondale tells the audience, "As President, I promise to build again from that White House the strength of those black colleges—to pass a special title that goes directly to those schools." Mondale has an ineluctably programmatic mind. Jesse Jackson can't promise these people more money for black colleges. Mondale talks about how the Carter Administration had begun to build minority entrepreneurship. He says, "Reagan says he has a perception problem when it comes to you. And he does. He can't see you at all. But you can see right through him." The audience laughs and applauds. He says that the Carter Administration enforced the civil-rights laws and appointed many blacks to federal judgeships. "You know me," Mondale tells the audience. "I haven't just been right, I've been there."

It's now 11 P.M. Washington time, and Mondale has agreed to stop by two more gatherings: one of state legislators and one of black businessmen who have raised money for him. He can't not stop by: they know he's here, and he may not be back in Arkansas for a long time, if ever, during the nomination contest. What he does here has to last while he seeks votes in other states.

JANUARY 4

Mondale has had a fund-raising breakfast, and now, at shortly before nine, he is meeting with a large group of farmers and

people in farm-related businesses who have been having a breakfast in a showroom at the Arkansas State Fairgrounds. The farmers are wearing blue-and-white farm caps with Mondale's name
printed over an outline of the state of Arkansas. When Mondale
arrives, the television lights go on, and, as a blue-grass group
plays, Mondale spends quite a bit of time shaking hands with
people, smiling and talking with them. One reason he fits in with
all these groups is that he has been there: he has been involved in
civil-rights fights; he comes from a rural background and has
been involved in farm policy; he has worked on issues that concern the elderly; and he has been an ally of labor for all his
political life. He knows what is on these groups' minds and how to
talk to them. One question about Mondale is the ratio between his
ability to relate to these groups and his ability to be independent
of them.

Representative Alexander gives Mondale an enthusiastic introduction. Mondale begins by establishing his familiarity with several of the people here, and talking about the number of times he
has been in the area. "This could well be the worst farm year in
American history," he tells the audience, and he adds, "Unless we
change economic policy in a few years, something that's indispensable, if not sacred, to American life will be gone—this thing called
the family farmer." And he tells the group, "Americans must understand again what farmers have meant to this nation and what a
farm recession means to non-farmers." He talks of the importance
of farm products as an export commodity, and says, "What's the
biggest business in America today? Agriculture." He explains,
"When farmers are doing well and they can buy a tractor and that
equipment and the things they need for modern farming, the rest
of the economy does well." He says, "It's been a long time since a
candidate for President has talked directly and specifically to
farmers. I am the only farm kid running for President." He tells
them that the first major speech he gave after he announced for
the Presidency was on the subject of agriculture, to a farm co-op.
And then he goes into a clear, careful explanation of the relationship of the deficits to the agricultural economy. The deficits
"caused a gross distortion in the value of international currencies," he explains. "And the value of the dollar has shot up in a
distorted way, and the value of the currencies of our major trading
partners—Japan, Western Europe, name it, all the agricultural

producing areas, Brazil, Argentina, Australia, name it—went straight downhill. And the result is that every time something you produce competes in international markets with another source, their stuff is cheaper than yours even though you're the most efficient, competitive farmers on earth. What happened two years ago? Did you suddenly become inefficient? Did you forget how to farm?"

It is a part of Mondale's strategy to explain to farmers, and to other groups as well, how the deficit is affecting them adversely. Mondale is quite interested in the subject of the misalignment of currencies—to the consternation of some of his advisers, who fear that he will get into an abstruse-seeming subject in his campaign appearances. In his talk here, he is trying to explain the subject in simple terms—and the words "misalignment of currencies" do not cross his lips. A number of people have advised Mondale to drop the subject from his speeches, but he refuses to do so. This issue and the connected issue of trade are very important in Mondale's mind. He believes that the trade issue includes jobs, the economy, the Third World debt, how Americans feel about themselves vis-à-vis the rest of the world, and so on. And trade is a classic upper-Midwest theme, so this, too, comes right out of Mondale's roots. Moreover, a big part of Mondale's case is that he is the person best prepared to be President, and the assumption is that when the contrast is drawn between him and Glenn he will win.

In his speech, Mondale says that agricultural exports went up for twelve consecutive years, but since 1981 they have dropped by more than twenty per cent. He says, "And they're going to be worse next year than this year, and it's like a dagger in the heart of the farmers of Arkansas." He says, "We need a President who makes sense." He tells them, "I believe in free international competition, but increasingly two or three things are happening that are robbing you of your competitive posture. I don't say this to flatter you, but there's no agriculture on earth that produces like American agriculture." He tells the audience, "And if you can play on a level table, if the rules are fair, you'll beat them all." He mentions other nations "lowballing credit terms"—in effect, supporting agricultural exports with a public bank that extends credit terms. Then he refers to the European Common Market, which subsidizes European products. "You must be expected to compete with the foreign farmer—that's your business," Mondale says.

"But you cannot be asked to compete against a foreign government." He continues, "And what I want to do as President of the United States is tell our friends, 'That's enough of that.' I'm going to be the President of the United States that stands up for American workers and American businesses and American farmers again and insists on a fair deal in international competition that protects your rights in international competition."

Last year, Mondale received criticism for using strident rhetoric on the subject of trade and for seeming to want to introduce protectionist policies. (He and Glenn both back the "domestic content" legislation, supported by the United Auto Workers, which would require that all cars sold in the United States contain a certain percentage of American parts and labor.) Mondale has since calmed the rhetoric, and says that what he wants to do is strengthen America's trade-negotiating position by threatening to retaliate. Glenn, in attacking Mondale for "overpromising," cites Mondale's telling the A.F.L.-C.I.O. last October, when he accepted its endorsement, that he would "match other countries' export subsidies product for product and dollar for dollar." Glenn points out that Reubin Askew, who was formerly the Special Trade Representative, has said that this would cost a hundred and thirty billion dollars. Maxine Isaacs, Mondale's press secretary, says that Mondale was simply saying that he would threaten to do these things, for negotiating purposes.

Mondale points out to the farm community gathered here that Jimmy Carter wrote in his book that Mondale opposed the grain embargo imposed after the Soviet Union invaded Afghanistan. Mondale says he didn't think the embargo would work—he thought that other countries would pick up our markets, and that is what happened. And he says, "As President of the United States, I'm not going to embargo the export of American goods." And then he says something else that is important to the rationale of his campaign: to try to get across that by winning the endorsement and trust of various groups in American society he can work with them and bring them together. He now stresses this in another attempt to take the edge off the "special interests" argument: "Rural America must stand together. In fact, America must stand together. We've got to quit snarling at each other. We've got to start working together—labor and management have to sit down together and work these problems out." And then he lambastes the

Reagan Administration's handling of farm policy, which led to great surpluses in 1981 and 1982, thus reducing farm income, and points out that this was followed by a hugely expensive one-year program—the Payment-in-Kind program, or PIK—to reduce those surpluses. Mondale says, "I think they're trying to destroy public respect for those basic commodity programs." The cost of all farm programs came to twenty-one billion dollars in the last fiscal year, and PIK cost another ten to twelve billion dollars. Mondale points out that before the Reagan Administration took office farm programs had not cost more than five billion dollars, and he argues that he can save a great deal of money through better management of those programs. Mondale's talking about the Administration's farm policy, then, is meant to do two other things: to stir farmers' concern that another Republican Administration would be detrimental to their interests (Harry Truman's successful stirring of farmers' fears was an important ingredient of his 1948 victory), and to offer another example of where he would cut the deficit. Johnson says that the fact that Mondale has credibility on rural issues will be a major advantage both in the primaries and in the general election in the South.

Mondale links the issue of agricultural policy to the fairness issue—one of his three themes—to show that he is stressing the same themes everywhere. "I would like to see some of those resources used to pay farmers to produce," Mondale says. "That's what you're good at—not reducing production but producing, to feed hungry people. Look, it isn't a child's fault when they're hungry." Mondale is speaking with feeling, as he has done throughout this speech, and he has the close attention of the audience. He says, "We ought to be ashamed of ourselves that we can't match agricultural abundance with nutritional needs in our own country." He adds, "We're peddling arms all over the world, and I'd like to see us come to some of those countries in the form of food." He recalls the Food for Peace program, and he talks about the Sahel, in Africa: "There are millions of fellow human beings without enough to get them through the next day." He says, "We can't afford a lot of new money, we know that. But can't we shape our policies so that America again is seen as a nation that uses its resources, its people, its genius, its spirit to reach out and touch in a good and a decent way the lives of other human beings on earth?" And he finishes by saying, with some passion, "I see

American family farmers and American agriculture as one of the greatest assets and marvels of America. And I don't want to see it ended. I want to strengthen rural America. I want to be your President and I want to work for you to get it done."

Following Mondale's presentation, Alexander asks the audience whether it can imagine John Glenn or Ronald Reagan making such a clear explanation of farm policy. The Mondale staff is delighted.

On one level, the Mondale campaign is quite confident—and also wants to get across the impression that it is a winner. On another level, the chief Mondale strategists do not want to appear overconfident—and, in fact, being experienced in politics, they know that there is room for doubt. In talking about this dilemma, Johnson says, "One concept of confidence has to do with how you stand with those things that are predictable and measurable; the other is confidence that you're going to win. There are so many uncertainties, unexplainable variables, possible turns in the road, that if you're confident you're going to win at this stage you don't understand Presidential politics. I am very confident that we are doing very well in working toward all the objectives we can clearly perceive; I am very confident we perceive many of the critical elements; I'm not the least bit confident that we have perceived all the critical elements, and there will be a number of developments, thoroughly unexpected, that will test us." Johnson, who recently turned forty, is a tall man who dresses conservatively and wears round tortoiseshell glasses. He is probably Mondale's closest political confidant, and in some ways the two men are alike. Johnson, like Mondale, is a Minnesotan of Norwegian extraction, somewhat inhibited and outwardly contained. But he has a fine sense of humor, a big laugh, and enjoys the teasing of his friends about his Norwegian roots and his methodical approach to life. (One of Johnson's friends once joked, "Jim lays out his sentences in the morning.") Johnson grew up in politics; his father was Speaker of the Minnesota House. The other member of the Mondale entourage who is quite close to the candidate is John Reilly, a fifty-five-year-old lawyer who entered politics with the Kennedys, and who brought Mondale into his law firm after the 1980 election, giving him a base from which to earn money and travel and speak. (Johnson, who is a close friend of Reilly's, had a hand in this arrangement, and set up his own business consulting firm just down the hall from the Reilly law offices.) Reilly is the closest thing to a peer that Mondale has in this campaign—the one who can tell him flat out that he's wrong.

Much is being made of the Mondale organization these days— largely because of what it has been able to accomplish thus far. Should Mondale lose, some will say that this occurred despite his organization, and some revisionism will go on about just how good the organization was. Its apparent strength is not only in its numbers but in its number of experienced people, in the number of things it is able to do at once, and in the number of people who are not officially part of the Mondale organization but are helping out. Mondale and Johnson, drawing on their years of political experience and wide range of contacts, started putting this organization together early, which gave them a head start on their rivals. They began their planning very shortly after the 1980 election, and, actually, the election campaign is eighteen months old; its real debut was at the Democratic Party's midterm conference, in Philadelphia, in June of 1982. Except for McGovern and Jackson, all the candidates made an appearance (including Edward Kennedy, who had not yet pulled out of the race), and the Mondale people even then put on a great show of strength.

All has not been entirely smooth within the Mondale organization, however. As of the first of this year, it was on its third field director and its fourth head of scheduling. It recently had to make a change in the management of its Iowa campaign. "We're not born ready," Johnson says. "You have to test and retest and adjust." Two striking things about Johnson are his capacity for long-sightedness and the number of things he can deal with—calmly— at once. He is along on this trip because of its particular importance. (He will not have the time to travel with Mondale often.) Among the things on his mind during this period are the television commercials that will be cut next week, and involve a number of important strategic decisions; seeing to it that Mondale is properly prepared for the three-hour debate among all the candidates that is to take place on January 15th, in New Hampshire (this involves a number of meetings about format, trying to anticipate the questions, and so on); the way the exchange with Glenn goes; the dialogue with Reagan; the meeting of the Democratic National Committee Executive Committee, on

January 20th, to deal with Jackson's complaints; preparing for how to react to Reagan's State of the Union address and budget recommendations. Through Johnson, the campaign as a whole is working on: seeking the endorsements of about a dozen major Democratic leaders, each one involving delicate diplomacy and politics; the Democratic Convention—the politics involved in the choices of the key figures; the campaign budget. Johnson says, "For the next seventy days, we will spend at a rate of around seven hundred thousand dollars a week, so there are a lot of budget, staffing, polling, media choices that flow from that." Mondale's schedule for the last two weeks of January is now being made final, so Johnson, in the course of this trip, has been on the telephone with Washington about that; he has also been on the phone with headquarters about the Convention decisions, the endorsements, the January 15th debate, and developments in Iowa and New Hampshire. "They're not sitting still," Johnson says.

As is the case in all election campaigns, a number of political figures try to calculate when it makes sense to cast their lot with whom. People want to have been with the winner at the right time. This year, because of the presumed acceleration of the entire process, these decisions are being forced on people earlier than usual. Recently, word began to get around that Robert Strauss, the former chairman of the Democratic National Committee, who is still a major figure around Washington, was giving strong consideration to throwing his weight behind Mondale soon. This would be significant—at least to people who think these things are significant—because Strauss has been carefully straddling the race, and because throwing in with Mondale would be a clear sign that a political pro, and a man with a lot of contacts, had made a conclusive judgment about the race. Strauss is a political barometer, as he knows. A number of important political figures have told Mondale that they will be with him "at the right time"—reserving to themselves the right to determine when the right time is.

Among the other things that Johnson has been dealing with in recent days: Yesterday, Glenn's first radio commercial ran in New Hampshire, and a decision had to be made whether to respond to it (Glenn argued that he had more experience for the Presidency than Mondale); the decision was not to do so. Michael Ford, a deputy campaign manager and the field director, is in Minnesota to organize Minnesotans to travel to Iowa to help him in the campaign. There was what seemed to be a very credible rumor that Joseph Biden, a Democratic senator from Delaware, would file in the New Hampshire primary (the final filing day was yesterday), and the Mondale organization was busy tracking down the rumor and trying to figure out how to respond. (The Biden filing did not occur.) Johnson says, "The point about running a campaign of this size is that there are hundreds of seemingly routine decisions that, given this period of increased scrutiny, have the potential to affect the campaign, including Mondale."

According to Johnson, all the major political planning had been completed before Christmas: major scheduling choices had been made for January, and the outlines of a schedule for February and March had been drawn up. In fact, the Mondale organization spent almost two months—November and December—focussing on 1984, while Mondale was out on the road and getting the endorsements of NOW, the Alabama Democratic Conference, and the United Mine Workers, and building support for the house parties. Johnson says, "By the time we got to Christmas, we had really finished our political, logistical, scheduling, non-substantive, non-Mondale strategic decisions. Then the week between Christmas and New Year's was devoted, with Mondale, to substance and important political strategy." The Mondale management style is to hire good people—or people they hope are good—and delegate to them. Thus, while Mondale obviously keeps abreast of what is going on in the campaign, and steeps himself in the issues and is involved in the large strategic questions, there are all sorts of questions he doesn't get involved with. Last week, between Christmas and New Year's, he and his aides, together with outside advisers, had all-day meetings on a variety of subjects: macroeconomic policy, tax and budget policy, natural-gas prices, acid rain and the environment, industrial policy, health-care-cost containment, foreign and defense issues. Often, Mondale would send his advisers off to do more work on questions he'd raised. Also, the Mondale people spent a substantial amount of time last week trying to anticipate Glenn's moves in the coming weeks.

It is the belief of the Mondale organization that even if things do not go well in the early contests it has, as Johnson puts it, "substantially more recovery potential than anybody else." (For instance, there is always the danger that the mathematics of the way the vote is divided in a many-candidate contest—such as the one in New Hampshire, a relatively conservative state—will hurt Mondale.) First, there is the simple matter of money. On January 3rd, the candidates received their first matching money from the federal government. Last year, Mondale raised $9.6 million and Glenn raised $5.7 million. Mondale received $3.1 million from the Federal Election Commission, while Glenn, having raised more of his money in larger amounts, received $1.6 million. (The government matches contributions of up to two hundred and fifty dollars; in order to qualify for federal funds a candidate has to raise five thousand dollars in contributions from individuals in twenty different states.) All the other candidates except McGovern and Jackson received funds, but only Cranston, who received $1.1 million, came near Mondale or Glenn—a reflection of the various candidates' relative ability to raise money last year. Making a good showing (or appearing to make a good showing) and raising money are inextricably related. The candidates will continue to try to raise money this year, but it will be even more difficult for those who are not doing well. Their most enthusiastic supporters will have already given, and most of the Democratic pools will have been drained. Only the winners will have much chance of raising more, as people hedge their bets or try to win gratitude in time. Even the Mondale people expect to run low on money by mid-March, since they expect to spend between seven and eight million dollars in the first three months of the year. How much can be spent on each contest is governed by federal regulation, but the money will go fast, because this year the limits are fairly high and the contests are close together. Furthermore, the ceilings have a certain flexibility in them. For example, only about fourteen per cent of the money spent on advertising on television in Boston, which reaches most of the state of New Hampshire, is charged against the budget for New Hampshire. And, of course, Mondale has, in addition to superior financial resources, the help that the organizations that endorsed him can provide—through mailings and phone banks and the like. So not only does Mondale start out with a financial edge but the changes in the schedule of the primary contests—the so-called front-loading—is presumed to work in his favor. There will be seven more contests by March 30th than there were in 1980. And there are other important differences: there is much less time between the Iowa and New Hampshire contests and those that follow, so an unexpected victor would have less opportunity to take advantage of his victory; the fact that the Michigan caucus was moved up to an earlier date this year (March 17th, as opposed to April 26th—Mondale should do very well in Michigan, and his forces worked to bring about this change of dates); and the fact that this year more of the contests will be caucuses rather than primaries. The Mondale organization encouraged some of the states to change their contests from primaries to caucuses.

Nevertheless, despite all Mondale's advantages and potential for recovery, there is a point at which political vulnerability is beyond organizational strength to recover. Johnson says, "There have been some situations in the past where when a candidate was politically dead he was dead, even though there was still some good organization behind him." The Muskie campaign of 1972 is an example. Johnson says, "There can come a point when you are losing and appear to be flawed to such a degree that no organization can recover. But there are a lot of other situations in which people have sustained losses and recovered, and I believe, given the current system and the finances and our institutional support, and the depth of Mondale's support, we will have more impressive recovery ability than anyone—probably ever."

GREENBRIER, ALABAMA. Mondale has had a barbecue lunch with some farmers and some important Party members in this tiny crossroads in the north-central part of the state, near Huntsville, and now he is standing in the Elliott & Son cotton gin. (Following the lunch, Mondale received the endorsement of Tom Drake, the Speaker of the House of Alabama.) The gin is not in operation—it's not the ginning season. The point of this stop is to reinforce his farm message in another part of the South, and also to make use of new technology on this trip. Mondale's chat in this gin with some cotton farmers is being videotaped by the campaign and offered by satellite around the country, with special efforts being made to interest stations in farm areas of states that hold early contests: Iowa, southern Illinois, Mississippi, Florida, Georgia, Arkansas, and Washington. The use of this technology is intended to serve several purposes: to indicate that Mondale is not saying one thing in one place and something else in another; to get his message to as many key areas as possible; and to indicate that Mondale is with it when it comes to the new technology. (When

Gary Hart announced his entry into the race last February, the speech was beamed around the country by satellite.) Mondale talks to the group here in a casual, conversational tone about the effect of the high dollar on agricultural exports, and so on. When it comes to performance on this new technology, however, Mondale has a way to go. He is simply not comfortable with television—which could be a serious liability for him as the campaign proceeds—and resists direction. As he goes through this procedure here, one aide moves the microphone closer to him, so that his voice can be picked up better. At another point, an aide tries to get Mondale to turn more toward the cameras and Mondale waves him away. Mondale is a natural performer before political audiences but still not before the television cameras—which is, of course, where most voters will see him. More than once on this trip, I have heard people who were in the audience observe afterward that Mondale came across much better in person—"warmer" was a word sometimes used—than he did on TV. But most voters won't see him in person.

JANUARY 5

BIRMINGHAM, ALABAMA. Now Mondale is focussing on industrial Alabama: Alabama is in fact the most heavily industrialized of the Southern states, and it has been hit very hard in the past couple of years. Moreover, the politics of Alabama has been changing: George Wallace is governor once again, having won in 1982 with black support. Last evening Mondale made a stop in Muscle Shoals, in the northwest part of Alabama, a relatively conservative area. Unemployment in the area is about fifteen per cent. The Mondale people had faced some obstacles in getting out a crowd for his appearance there—at the University of Northern Alabama—and how they got one out shows the value of the Mondale support system. The university is out of session now and Wednesday night is Bible Class night for the community. Working over the New Year's weekend and the next two days, the Mondale people got out a crowd by calling on their friends, the teachers, Party officials, and labor (the building-trades and aluminum workers). At his appearance last night, Mondale stressed his three themes and then attacked the Reagan economic program, once again bringing it home. "Alabama knows what Reaganomics has cost this country. More than almost any other state, with the possible exception of one or two, Alabama has paid a dreadful price," he told his audience. And then he carefully went through the premise and the results of the Reagan program, explaining how the deficits have caused a rise in interest rates ("Real interest rates—the spread between what you pay and underlying inflation—doubled"), which led to a recession, a decline in the value of the dollar, and a drop in exports. And he cited the Alabama export industries that had been hurt. "The result is that it was almost a dagger in the heart of the economy of this state," he told them, and then, perhaps remembering that this was the second dagger of the day, added, "And to many other states in the union." He was making the strongest case he could against the Reagan program, and for his own values, to a heavily blue-collar audience. "We must invest in research across the board, and we must invest in training again," he said. He stressed the importance of developing vocational skills and of doing more for education. "This Administration may be the most anti-education Administration in modern American history, and we cannot tolerate that kind of backward approach to our future," he said.

One of the reasons some key Reagan advisers have concluded that Mondale would be Reagan's strongest opponent is that they feel that, unlike Glenn, he would have the intense support of Democratic constituency groups. (They have also concluded that he is a better politician than Glenn.) In his talk last night, Mondale showed how he made the case to those groups, and to the blue-collar workers who may be up for grabs. And, as he does in some appearances, he talked about his own background, trying to draw a contrast between his political ethic and Reagan's—to stress that Reagan is the rich person's President: "Here's where you ought to know a little bit about where I'm coming from. I believe that ours should be a government of the people and by the people and for the people. I grew up in several small towns in southern Minnesota. My dad was a minister, my mother was a music teacher. And we went from community to community serving those communities. My dad and mom didn't worry about money. They didn't have any. It wasn't important. But I don't think that diminished the importance of their lives at all. They were good parents. We had a strong family. They served their faith. They served their neighbors. They were good citizens. And they served our country. It wasn't that they were on the make. They weren't. They were just fine, decent Americans doing what millions of Americans do throughout their lives. I don't want a nation just for those on the make. I want a nation that's for everybody, where we respect and honor and help all Americans who are decent and kind and deserve that kindness and thoughtfulness." And he talked about how much more the rich got from the Reagan tax cut than those who make thirty thousand dollars a year or less. "I stand for sensible economics and for growth," Mondale said, "but I'm also going to stand for fairness and decency and compassion in this country." He said, "We are not a jungle. We are a community, a family, a nation, and a President has a duty to pull us together and to make us feel as one people with justice and decency in our land and fairness for all Americans."

Mondale talked about arms control, saying that the danger of nuclear weapons "is not just another problem, it is *the* problem," and he attacked Reagan's arms-control policy. And he said that Reagan had criticized every arms-control effort as "a sign of weakness." It was Mondale's strongest delivery yet, the most thorough tour of his themes. He also drew on the theme he had used in his announcement of his candidacy: "I am ready and I know what I'm doing." He said, "We don't and cannot afford the luxury of an on-the-job-training educational program in the toughest job on earth. Isn't it time that we tried somebody in that office who just might happen to know what he's doing?'

At a news conference this morning in Birmingham, Mondale is endorsed by Mayor Richard Arrington, a black, who is very popular in this area. And standing behind Arrington and a beaming Mondale as Arrington makes his announcement is a group of thirty people, blacks and whites, men and women, also lending their support to Mondale. Among them are Tom Drake, the Speaker of the Alabama House, who endorsed Mondale yesterday in Greenbrier and who is very close to Wallace, and Jim Folsom, Jr., a state public-services commissioner and the son of a former governor. The timing could hardly be better from Mondale's point of view. The Mondale people feel that Alabama is potentially Jackson's strongest state, and this week's events make the endorsement especially fortunate. Arrington had helped work out the compromise whereby the Alabama Democratic Conference endorsed Mondale for President and Jackson for Vice-President.

After Arrington reads his statement endorsing Mondale, and Mondale makes a brief statement, the first question is directed at Arrington: "Mayor, I wonder if you could tell us why you're supporting Mr. Mondale rather than Jesse Jackson."

Arrington replies with a little lesson in realpolitik. "Both Mr. Mondale and Mr. Jackson are good friends of mine—outstanding Americans. My major concern is that we win the White House and that we have someone there whose views are compatible with those views which I believe are held by a majority of Americans and those views which I hold—someone who is indeed a proven friend, and someone who stands a good chance of winning. And I think Mr. Mondale stands an excellent chance of winning." He says that Jackson will raise some important issues, "but at this time the priority is to win the White House." On being asked another question about Jackson, Arrington says he believes that Jackson has some support in the black community, but adds, "Walter Mondale is no newcomer to the black community. He's a national leader who has also paid his dues." These press conferences, like other things Mondale does on his stops, are designed to get him local news coverage. Sometimes he is shown in the presence of important dignitaries, and usually there has been a substantial greeting committee at each airport stop. To the extent that there are questions at the press conferences about any of Mondale's rivals, they are about Jackson—not Glenn.

TUSCALOOSA. This afternoon, Mondale is in a studio at the University of Alabama conducting a panel discussion, via satellite hookup, with Governor Michael Dukakis, of Massachusetts. (Dukakis has endorsed Mondale.) The points of this exercise are to once again show Mondale in touch with modern technology; have him discuss a problem of interest to both Alabama and New England (the program will reach the New Hampshire media market); and show him dealing with an issue that is an important part of the Democratic agenda—industrial policy. Actually, Mondale does not use the term "industrial policy"—his advisers think it is less than enticing; moreover, the term has come to embrace so many concepts that it is just about meaningless. According to Martin Kaplan, deputy campaign manager and an adviser on issues, and the person who writes most of Mondale's speeches (he was Mondale's chief speechwriter when Mondale was in the White House), Mondale supports the idea of a national strategy for economic growth—involving trade, dealing with the deficit, capital investment, and so on—but is not ready to write a specific industrial-policy bill. Mondale's emphasis here is on cooperation among business, labor, the local community, and the universities to deal with local economic problems. This is an approach Mondale has said he would use in the White House. Taking on this question here also gets at the special-interest question in two ways: it suggests, as Mondale has suggested in the past, that he would try to use his entrée with various groups to bring them together to cooperate in dealing with economic problems; and it shows, with the question being talked about in two regions and broadcast by satellite (the program will be offered to television stations throughout the country), that he is a national candidate, not saying different things in different parts of the country. Mondale has not signed on to industrial-policy schemes to encourage the development of certain new industries, or to help declining industries. Such schemes are full of pitfalls: Who would make the choices, and how would they be made? Could such schemes possibly escape being shaped by the politically strongest economic forces? By emphasizing cooperation, he has chosen the least controversial and, in many ways, most attractive part of the question, because it deals with how various segments of our society might work together (as they have when certain companies were in peril). Moreover, a political campaign isn't the place for deciding just how such a policy would work; it's for a President to get in good people and take some time thinking it through and working it out. The example Mondale is talking about on this program is a carburetor plant in Tuscaloosa, which General Motors nearly closed, and which was saved through cooperation, including several cost-cutting measures. The television program is not the smoothest one that has ever been produced, and Mondale does not seem entirely comfortable, but he comes across as earnest and truly interested. And he concludes by making his point here: We need "a President who leads our nation toward a cooperative spirit." He says, "What we've seen in Tuscaloosa, what we've seen in Washington, we see in every community in this nation. After all, we're all in this together. We're all Americans. And if we cooperate, if we work together, we can retain—we can restore our edge and restore the competitive values of America in the world."

On the charter plane en route to St. Petersburg. Mondale's last stop of the day was at Columbus, Georgia—a conservative, pro-defense area. This fits with the week's strategy of going into areas where others are supposedly strong—in this case, Glenn. More-over, Glenn has accused Mondale of being weak on defense. So Mondale went to Columbus, where Fort Benning is the principal industry, and conducted a panel discussion before a local audience on the subject of conventional forces. Among those on the panel were retired General David Jones, the former chairman of the Joint Chiefs of Staff, and James Schlesinger, the former, among other things, Secretary of Defense. The event was designed to show that Mondale is informed about defense questions, con-cerned about the strength of conventional forces (which keep los-ing out to big weapons systems in the competition for defense dollars), and able to talk about these things with some dis-tinguished experts. Following the event, Mondale met privately with some local black leaders. Tomorrow, during stops in Florida, he will talk about his plan for reducing the cost of health care under Medicare. This, too, is a "fairness" issue, a budget-reduc-tion issue, and a populist issue. (The two ways to cut Medicare costs are to hold down the cost of the services and to cut back on the benefits. Mondale has chosen the former—proposing that the program be run by the states. There is, however, a question of why some benefits should not be reduced for those who can afford to pay for them.) Following his appearances in Florida, he will go to Savannah, a conservative area of Georgia, and to Atlanta, and then to New Hampshire.

Today is Mondale's fifty-sixth birthday, and tonight, on the plane, he is in a very good mood. He feels that he has had a good week and that the Jackson cloud is lifting. And today a story broke that the Glenn campaign was in financial trouble. Mondale is en-joying the feeling, however temporary, that the competition is fading. He is an experienced enough politician to know that the pressure will return soon enough. When he is presented with a birthday cake by his staff, he happily joins in the celebration.

JANUARY 8

DUBUQUE. On this Sunday afternoon, John Glenn set off from Washington for a campaign swing through Iowa. It is a critical period for the Glenn campaign: his advisers recognize that he has little time to catch Mondale, and that his campaign needs improvement and his candidacy definition. The biggest problem, according to his advisers, is that their polls indicate that people do not know much about him other than that he was an astronaut, and do not see him as Presidential. (That the Mondale polling turned up the same thing is not coincidental; professional pollsters working for different camps most often do turn up similar information.) David Sawyer, Glenn's media adviser, said to me recently, "The problem is identification. We have to fill in the information about John Glenn." Sawyer, in fact, had argued all along that the film *The Right Stuff* would be harmful to the Glenn campaign, because it would reinforce the impression that Glenn was running on his fame as an astronaut. (Ironically, the connection of the movie to Glenn led to a disappointing box-office, apparently because so many people thought that it was about a politician.) The Glenn campaign's earliest radio and television ads stress that there are other aspects to his career (though they start out identifying him as an astronaut)—that he has been a businessman and has been in the Senate for ten years. Using some exaggeration, they list some of his Senate accomplishments. Glenn's radio ad, which has run in New Hampshire, concludes, "Walter Mondale says experience is the most important thing in this election, and when you look at John Glenn's experience, don't you agree?" The Glenn people take some comfort from a Gallup poll published today that shows Mondale leading Glenn forty per cent to twenty-four per cent (Jackson was third, with ten per cent), only because the previous Gallup poll had Mondale leading Glenn by twenty-eight percentage points. The Mondale people had mixed feelings about the previous poll: they were delighted by the gap between Mondale and Glenn, but assumed that it would narrow, and had some concern that much would be made of this. The new Gallup poll shows Reagan leading both Mondale and Glenn—Glenn by four points (which is within the statistical margin of difference) and Mondale by seven points. In the November Gallup poll, Glenn was tied with Reagan, and Mondale was one point ahead. According to one Glenn adviser, in the states where the Glenn organization has polled—Iowa, New Hampshire, Georgia, Florida, and Alabama—Glenn's biggest negative is the sense that he lacks experience. Greg Schneiders, Glenn's director of communications and chief aide-de-camp, said to me on the plane on the way out here, "Experience, according to recent evidence of Presidential campaigns, is a threshold issue. If you don't meet the threshold, you're out of contention—no matter what the voters like about you or their closeness to you on the issues. Once you reach that threshold, then it becomes a test of character—honesty, integrity, leadership—and closeness on the issues." Schneiders says that once Glenn has established that his experience qualifies him for the Presidency he can then move on to the next two things he needs to do: show that his views are closer to those of the Democratic electorate than Mondale's are, and demonstrate his "character of leadership." The Glenn people say that Mondale has serious negatives—mainly that he is seen as a politician and as a figure of the past—and they believe that Glenn comes across as more likable and as closer to the voters on the issues.

One way the Glenn people tried to gauge Democratic voters' attitudes was through a survey done by their pollster, William Hamilton, in which descriptions of two different types of Democrats were offered and the respondents were asked which type they would prefer. One description read:

He is a moderate-to-liberal Democrat, someone who has the support of and will look out for groups like labor, teachers, blacks, and the poor; someone who will do everything possible to gain an arms control treaty with the Soviet Union as soon as possible; someone who will undo Reagan's economic programs and spend less on the military defense and more on domestic social programs.

The other description was:

He is a moderate-to-conservative Democrat who will repair the worst of Reaganomics but not go back to the usual big spending policies; someone who will push for a treaty with the Soviets but who will be tough with them and will support a strong military defense; someone who will set goals and challenge the country working for the national interest even if that means not always going along with the programs supported by traditional Democratic groups.

Not very amazingly, the survey turned up what Glenn people say was substantially more support for the "new" politician than for the "old" one, especially in New Hampshire and the South (but not in Iowa). One Glenn adviser said he realized that the descriptions were a bit loaded, but said that they were a fair representation of the case the Glenn campaign would be making. What disturbs the Glenn campaign is the number of people who describe themselves as moderate-to-conservative Democrats and support Mondale. Hamilton says, "Mondale's holding some people we think we can get—people in almost every state whom, if we could get out the information about Glenn, we could get. That's what we're trying to do with our paid media."

The Glenn people are also vexed by Mondale's successes in 1983. One says (despite the fact that the Glenn campaign plans to continue to attack Mondale as the creature of the "special interests") that Mondale was helped in the polls by coming across as being able to pull people together, and also as experienced—in contrast to Glenn the astronaut. Another Glenn adviser says, "I have to admit that Mondale did better at his game plan than I expected, and it hurt us." Among other things, Mondale's large lead in the polls toward the end of the year hurt Glenn's ability to raise money. The Glenn people maintain that Mondale's support is "soft"—meaning that it is subject to change—but they also say that the support for their own candidate is "soft." (The Mondale people say that support for Glenn is softer than support for Mondale.) If both candidates' support actually is soft, what probably has as much to do with this as anything else—including the widely assumed inability of the candidates to stir excitement—is the fact that for most of the voters it's still early in the game.

Glenn's people say that their candidate's performance has to improve. Sawyer says, "What he has to do now is ignite a spark. Even though we're right on things, we have to find ways to communicate them with energy and conviction, have to communicate issues with some passion. It's important to be able to galvanize people; we haven't yet done it as a campaign." Glenn's advisers have been urging him to give more focus to what he is saying, and shorten his answers—but he resists direction. Sawyer says, "We have to be able to seize aggressively some issues." There is some concern within the Glenn camp about Glenn's ability to seize issues and react quickly. For example, his advisers had hoped that he would seize on the Lebanon issue, but he has declined, even though he opposed the sending of the Marines to Lebanon in the first place. Glenn's hesitance may stem from his reluctance to rile Jewish voters (who have been suspicious of him in the past), or from his sense of responsibility, or from his own natural caution. Glenn is inherently slow to take positions, and once he takes them he is hard to move. Glenn now tells people that the Marines cannot be taken out of Lebanon precipitately because we have made "a commitment."

Another thing that vexes the Glenn people is the Mondale people's skill in handling Glenn's attacks. One Glenn adviser says, "The Mondale people have been very skillful at avoiding the attacks." (Some Reagan advisers were impressed, too. "They're better counterpunchers than I'd thought," one said to me recently.) Following the round last October in which Mondale responded to Glenn's charges that he was a candidate of the special interests by throwing back at Glenn his vote for Reagan's economic program, Glenn opened another barrage. On two successive days in mid-November, Glenn attacked Mondale—first for being weak on defense (he listed a number of weapons systems Mondale had opposed when he served in the Senate) and then for being a big spender. Mondale responded to the first speech by saying that "there's a big difference between a sensible, balanced defense and a blank-check approach," which he accused Glenn of seeking. Mondale did not even respond to the second speech but left it to his aides to reply. Johnson put out a statement that Glenn's accounting of how much Mondale's proposals might cost amounted to "voodoo arithmetic," and that Glenn was "trying to shift the spotlight from his support of two-hundred-billion-dollar deficits." (Glenn did stretch things a bit. For example, he took a Mondale pledge to "put millions of people back to work" to be an endorsement of a federally subsidized jobs program, which, he said, would cost twenty billion dollars. Mondale has expressed approval of some job-creating program, but he has said that most of the increase in employment he seeks would be achieved through macroeconomic policy.) This exchange, as has been noted, was widely considered to have damaged Glenn, because he engaged in the attacks before he had established his own credentials as a possible President. However, the Glenn people felt that they had to go after Mondale, because he was pulling away in the polls.

There were other problems with the attacks: Coming as they did on two days in succession, they lost some of their potential impact. Moreover, in his speech attacking Mondale as a big spender Glenn attempted to show that he favors some progressive things—more funding for education and nutrition, a program of voluntary service whereby people would earn tuition grants, and restoring cuts in Medicaid—but since this was combined with his attack on Mondale all that got press attention, predictably, was the attack. (Actually, Glenn's programs would end up costing more than he suggested.) A Glenn aide said to me recently that one problem with Glenn's attacks on Mondale was that "people misunderstood them in the sense that they took them literally." Nevertheless, this aide said, the attacks will continue, because they are essential to an important theme of the Glenn campaign: character. The object is to show that Glenn has the character to be President, and that Mondale, as an overpromiser, an all-things-to-all-people, a captive of the special interests, does not. The Glenn people have made some ads to this effect, but have not yet run them. The Glenn people say they think that the attacks will not backfire as long as they are not too frequent and are "strictly factual." Some Glenn advisers had worried all along that for Glenn to go on the attack would detract from his hero image. The essential theme of the Glenn campaign, according to Sawyer, is leadership—the character to lead the country into a future that is uncertain. Glenn's campaign slogan is "Believe in the future again." Even Glenn's opposition to the SALT II treaty, Sawyer suggests, can be portrayed as illustrative of Glenn's character, because it was an example of his standing up under tremendous pressure. Schneiders says that the four terms that are to be associated with Glenn are honesty, courage, independence, and common sense. (Schneiders refers to the negative side of Glenn's campaign as "differentiation.")

The Glenn campaign is still shaking itself out from the staff upheaval that went on in the closing months of the year; new field workers are being sent to various states, and a number of key decisions are yet to be made. The question arises of how a group seeking the Presidency could have allowed its campaign to fall into such disarray. There are a number of small answers—this man wasn't right for the job, that man is inexperienced—but they don't answer the larger question, about competence. Over the holiday period, Glenn skied in Vail from December 23rd until New Year's Eve, and after that Schneiders and Sawyer spent two days with him in Washington, taping television ads and talking about various aspects of the campaign—reviewing its basic themes and how they were being incorporated in Glenn's stump speech and media presentations. The difference between how Mondale and Glenn used the lull—even though they both went skiing in Vail—is striking. Several of the questions now facing the Glenn campaign revolve around the allocation of scarce—at least, relative to Mondale's—resources. In the past few days, stories broke in the papers about the Glenn campaign's financial problems: fund-raising in the last quarter fell two hundred thousand dollars short, and, beyond that, Glenn received far less in matching money than Mondale did. Nearly a fourth of the staff members at the Washington headquarters will be laid off. Moreover, Glenn's financial problems are likely to be self-compounding: not only are people less likely to contribute when they see a campaign getting in trouble, but it was easier for candidates to borrow money last year— using as collateral the federal matching money they would receive this year. Now that the matching money is being handed out, few of the candidates can offer any assurance that they will be in a position to receive more of it. The Glenn people are publicly trying to put the best face on the situation—saying that they are simply allocating more of their resources to the field than to their Washington headquarters, and that by the end of January they will have more staff than they do now. But some Glenn advisers I spoke with over the past couple of weeks were very fretful about the money situation. It has inevitably forced some hard decisions about allocation of resources, and up until recently there was some question about this trip to Iowa.

There has been considerable argument within the Glenn organization over how much of an effort to make in Iowa, where Mondale is expected to win handily, as opposed to New Hampshire and elsewhere. Whatever time and money Glenn spends in Iowa will perforce come out of the budget for efforts in other states, and Glenn could be in some danger of coming in third in the state. A poll published by the Des Moines *Register* last month gave Mondale forty-two per cent of the Democratic vote, Glenn sixteen per cent, and Cranston twelve per cent, with the others trailing behind, and Cranston, who has made the nuclear-freeze issue the focal point of his campaign, is said to be organizing well in the state. Hart, meanwhile, is working hard in Iowa and, especially, New Hampshire. Mondale has several advantages in Iowa: it borders on Minnesota, and he has spent a lot of time in Iowa over the years; it is a caucus state, where organization counts for much; and labor, particularly the United Automobile Workers, the United Food and Commercial Workers, and the teachers, can be a potent force within the caucus process. But the deciding factors for Glenn in the state were the concern that if Glenn skipped the first contest he would take a drubbing from the press, because his, like Mondale's, is supposed to be a big-time, national campaign; an assumption that Glenn's participation in the Iowa contest would yield him some useful media exposure elsewhere; and a fear that if Glenn skipped Iowa Reubin Askew, who is running a conservative, anti-abortion campaign, might do well in Iowa and be in a stronger position than otherwise in his home state of Florida, where Glenn must challenge him. Glenn is now committed to spending six days in Iowa in January and six in February, and to running a media campaign there, but he will devote more time to New Hampshire. He will go to the South next week. The Glenn campaign is operating on the premise that it must expand the Democratic electorate, especially in a state like Iowa, where Democratic politics is dominated by activists who tend to be liberal. Schneiders says that among the ways it hopes to do this is to have Glenn appear before organizations that aren't particularly ideological or politically oriented but might be very friendly toward Glenn, such as the Knights of Columbus, the Elks, the Masons, and certain civic groups. Schneiders says, "If we can't expand the electorate in Iowa, we have a very tough row to hoe."

Over the weekend, Mondale and Glenn got into a new contretemps, this one over acid rain and environmental policy in general. Most of the Democratic candidates appeared at a forum on acid rain in New Hampshire which was sponsored by a coalition of environmental groups. Glenn has had a problem with the environmentalists on the subject of acid rain, because Ohio, his home state, is a major source of sulfur-dioxide emissions, which produce acid rain, and it is feared that if strict cleanup proposals were adopted many of the state's miners, who dig high-sulfur coal, would lose their jobs. On Saturday, Glenn offered a proposal for cleaning up acid rain and also said that Mondale was offering the voters "secret plans" on the economy and the environment. Mondale, campaigning in Georgia, shot back that Glenn had "one of the worst environmental records" among Democratic senators. On Sunday, when Mondale appeared before the conference, he offered his own acid-rain proposal and, following the strategy of last week, attacked the environmental records of both Glenn and Reagan. He criticized Glenn for voting for the confirmation of James Watt as Secretary of the Interior—but in fact only twelve

Democratic senators voted against Watt. Mondale also criticized Glenn for voting against a move to restore some of Reagan's budget cuts for the Environmental Protection Agency—a position that was shared by only fourteen Democrats in all. He attacked Glenn for having in the past been critical of proposals to reduce acid rain. He also criticized Glenn for having said, on *Meet the Press* in December, "We could enforce every environmental law and put ten million people out of work, perhaps." Glenn had said something similar to me in an interview earlier last fall. (Mondale's and Glenn's acid-rain proposals differ in scope—Mondale pledges to cut acid rain by more than Glenn does—and in how they would assess charges for the cleanup. Mondale said that he would put more of the burden on the heavier polluters, and that the polluters could not pass on all these costs to consumers, and he criticized Glenn's plan for putting "the same burden on polluters and non-polluters alike." But Mondale did not spell out precisely how the charges on utilities would be assessed.)

Today, at the airport in Washington, Schneiders handed out to reporters a statement that in 1982 Glenn had a seventy-one-percent approval rating from the League of Conservation Voters, which tied him with Cranston and made them the highest-rated of all the senators running for President. In previous years, Glenn had ratings that placed him, on average, next to last among the Democratic candidates. In New Hampshire, Mondale had used these earlier figures and had also pointed out that "the League of Conservation Voters said that Mr. Glenn has a 'very poor voting record on clean-air issues.' " The League also said that Glenn had a good environmental record in some other areas, such as clean water and toxic-waste cleanup. The term "secret plan" is, of course, evocative of Richard Nixon's "secret plan," during the 1968 Presidential campaign, to end the Vietnam War. Asked about this, Glenn said that he was "not drawing any personal characterizations." According to Curtis Wilkie, of the Boston *Globe*, Glenn had made a couple of stabs at the "secret plans" line, but had failed to do it in a way that attracted attention. Then Schneiders typed out a statement for him, and Glenn delivered the "secret plans" attack in a way that got it across. (According to Wilkie, Glenn had just told some reporters that he felt free to criticize Mondale on spending, defense, and promises, but "do I have a 1-2-3-4 list that I'm going to bang him on? No." Then

Schneiders gave him the memo with the list of "secret plans," and Glenn, at his next stop, used it.) Schneiders' relationship with Glenn is unusual, as Glenn is not one for taking much staff advice and the two men have not known each other long; but Schneiders, who is thirty-six, is inventive and combative, and has had a large impact on the campaign. He started out as a restaurant owner in Washington, became interested in the Carter campaign, and joined it in January, 1976, and ended up as a travelling companion and confidant of Carter's. He served in the Carter White House for a while and then held various jobs around Washington, and he joined Glenn in January, 1983, as his press secretary. Now Schneiders provides much of the conceptual thinking, as well as the toe-to-toe tactics, for the Glenn campaign. He is easygoing and amusing—and skilled at working with the press and popular with it.

Glenn is making this swing around Iowa in a chartered forty-eight-seat Convair 580. His press entourage is smaller than Mondale's was last week, and besides his wife, Annie, he is accompanied by a very few staff members. The comparison is not quite valid, however; not only can Glenn not afford to take along so much staff but the Mondale people were making a deliberate display of strength last week. The Glenns sit together toward the back of the plane, and Glenn is unfailingly pleasant, and the atmosphere aboard the plane is relaxed. The Glenns are almost inseparable—Annie Glenn will go off and campaign on her own for a while tomorrow, but this is unusual—and their closeness is affecting. Annie Glenn is a warm, outgoing woman with large, dark, luminous eyes, and she is beloved by the press corps, and by a large number of people in Washington. She has recently conquered her severe stuttering problem, and a very appealing thing about Glenn is the obvious sensitivity he has shown toward her problem over the years. The Glenns grew up in the same town— New Concord, Ohio—and have been a pair since he was three and she was four.

Tonight in Dubuque, Glenn's first stop is at his local campaign headquarters, which is just being opened. It has no telephone yet. About a hundred people are here. Glenn stands before them and tells them that tomorrow his wife will be campaigning elsewhere and that their son, David, is campaigning in the state and their daughter, Lyn, has been in the state several times. "So we're making an all-out effort during this time here, New Hampshire, and on into those early primaries and caucuses." He adds, "How things start out here may determine a lot of what happens later on, so it's real important we get things going here in Iowa." Then he goes into his stump speech: "Now, this is a critical year, there isn't any doubt about it. The choices we'll make this year are going to bend this country in the way it's going to go in the future." He speaks with some vigor, especially for Glenn, who often speaks in flat tones. He continues, "I think one thing that we know right now and that is Ronald Reagan has got to go." He receives applause, and continues, "We can't go on into the future building up two-hundred-billion-a-year deficits. You can't spend a dollar when you're taking in seventy-five cents." He says, "We don't like to see some of the commitments we're making in foreign policy, with our military establishment—Marines in Lebanon, for instance, and things like that. We want to see more education, more research, those things that are going to build the future of this country. We don't want to see cutbacks in civil rights. We thought we were about to be the first country to get racism and bigotry behind us once and for all. Now we see that area cut back in enforcement— we're regressing, we're not making progress in those areas. In other words, we're cutting back on opportunity in this United States of America of ours. Many areas we need to make changes in policy in, and if we're going to make policy changes I don't want to see us just replace those Reagan policies with policies that just repeat the nineteen-sixties or early seventies."

Glenn continues, "I want to see us go forward with honesty, not overpromising. I want to see us have courage enough to tell people the very strong medicine we're going to have to prescribe to deal with the economy. Well, so be it, but let's be honest enough about those things during the campaign—let's not wait and say we're going to have big secret plans on how we're going to do this with the economy, big secret plans for foreign policy, big secret plans for acid rain, big secret plans for everything. I want to see these things brought out, so that we are not once again in a position of having an Administration in Washington that's over-promised and then finds it impossible to perform enough to come up to people's expectations." He says, "That's the reason why I've proposed very honest, straightforward plans: a five-point plan for arms control, very specific plans for how we're going to get control of the economy, very specific plans about education—a number of different areas, research. I mention education and research: I can't think of any two things that are going to be more important for the long-term future in this country. What we do with regard to education, research—those things that have been the hallmark of our American scene—create jobs and employment and industry throughout our country. We've let the rest of the world follow on in our wake, and we're every bit as much capable of doing that today as we've ever been in the past—in fact, it's more necessary today, because we're finding ourselves under enormous competition from abroad. If we're going to create the jobs and create the employment and make certain that this nation sets goals and moves ahead, now is the time to set those goals and change the policies of this Administration, and that's what we want to do." Setting goals for the future is a major Glenn theme. Glenn often talks about the need for "basic, fundamental, breakthrough, seminal, Nobel-laureate research." Now he tells the audience that he needs its help. "Annie and I and our family, we can run all over—we can run ourselves into exhaustion and it won't do much good, because we need your help in those caucuses." He explains that it takes more time to participate in caucuses than to simply cast a ballot in a primary, and he says, "I wish I had one of those World War One recruiting posters dropped down behind me, with Uncle Sam in a top hat with his finger pointing at you. I need one that says, 'John Glenn needs you.' I really do. Because, working together, we can change the future of this country. Working together—that means leadership of this country that is the world's greatest—I think we can outinvent, outresearch, outcompete any nation on the face of this earth if we just do it. We're not going to do it with the policies of this Administration. We're not going to do it if we replace those policies with the old-fashioned policies of the sixties or seventies. We can set goals and objectives."

And then Glenn summons up his experience as an astronaut. The Glenn people may feel that the identification of Glenn as an astronaut is a problem, but they clearly also think it's an asset, and Glenn is understandably proud of the defining moment of his life. "I've been privileged to look back at this country and to see this world from a little different vantage point—a space capsule. Most people haven't had the opportunity to do it. You look down and wonder why our man-made, people-made problems, our home-made problems, can't be solved." Then he evokes, as he likes to do, his association with John F. Kennedy. "I think back to those days of the space program when John Kennedy was setting the nation on a course that was proud of academic excellence, setting goals. Once again, we can do that with pride, with confidence, as we did back in those days—setting objectives, setting goals." And then he paraphrases George Bernard Shaw (as Robert Kennedy did in his campaign for the Presidency, in 1968): "Some men see things as they are and say why; I dream of things that never were and say why not." He concludes, "This has been a why-not nation. We have set goals; we have tried to reach those objectives; we've been successful at that, and that's the kind of attitude we have to have to build this nation in the future. With your help, we can set goals; with your help we can achieve them. And it all starts right here in Iowa. With your help, we can change the future of this country."

The audience is friendly but not especially enthusiastic. Afterward, Glenn mingles with the group, shakes hands, and signs a few autographs.

Following the reception at the headquarters, Glenn attends the championship game of the National Catholic Basketball Tournament, in Dubuque. Basketball is big in Iowa, and Dubuque is a heavily Catholic area. Although this game is being televised only on a local cable channel, and neither of the finalist teams is from Dubuque, Glenn's staff believes that his being here will get excellent newspaper coverage, and he takes time out for a television interview. This game is taking a lot of Glenn's time. First, he makes a brief appearance on court at halftime, and gives a little talk about competition and fair play representing "the spirit of this country," and then he sits through the second half of the game in order to participate, along with several others, in handing out the awards. When Glenn is introduced at halftime, he receives polite applause. For this crowd, the serious business is basketball, not politics. After a lengthy process of shaking hands with winners and runners-up and members of the third-place team and the fourth-place team and the All-American team, Glenn attends a reception upstairs in the basketball stadium, and then leaves to fly to Moline, Illinois—one of the Quad Cities, on the Mississippi

River. We arrive at the Holiday Inn in Moline—which has a startling huge stuffed polar bear in the lobby (I remember that bear from the Edward Kennedy campaign, in 1980)—shortly before midnight, or nearly 1 A.M. in Washington, where we started out.

JANUARY 9

WILTON, IOWA. Just before 8 A.M., Glenn is standing outside the security office of the North Star Steel plant. The Quad Cities area has been beset by job layoffs, and the Glenn people say that their polling and field work suggest that a large number of the rank-and-file workers are not satisfied with Mondale or with their union leaders. Shaking hands at plant gates is a campaign staple, but Glenn appears to be still getting the hang of it. (Last week, in New Hampshire, he arrived at a plant after the change of shifts had occurred.) He is pleasant and friendly with the workers as they come out of the security office, where they sign in, but he often fails to introduce himself, and several workers just go on by him. Rex McCreight, a maintenance worker in the plant, stands in a cowboy hat and a brown suit and tries to get the workers to stop and meet Glenn. It's very cold out this morning. Sometimes Glenn says, "Hi, I'm John Glenn and I need your help in all this effort," but only a few of the workers stop to talk or to ask him questions. One worker asks him why he came to this plant, and he replies that this sort of steel plant (known as a mini-mill) has taken over fifteen per cent of the steel processing in this country, and then he takes the opportunity to get in a lick at Mondale and his endorsements. A Glenn adviser had told me that the campaign planned to challenge the legitimacy of the A.F.L.-C.I.O. endorsement—to suggest that Mondale may have been the choice of "the bosses" but not of the workingmen. The Glenn people base their argument on a New York *Times*/CBS News poll published last October which indicated that rank-and-file union members were about evenly divided in their support for Mondale and Glenn. The *Times* story about the poll also said that seventy per cent of the union members polled said their views on the nomination had not been sought by the union leadership. The *Times*/CBS poll did not separate Democratic from Republican union members (Reagan received about forty-four per cent of the labor vote in 1980)—and the Mondale people were quick to point this out. (The A.F.L.-

C.I.O. says that the process was lengthy and wide open, and that
Mondale emerged as the clear favorite of its members; it also says
that the *Times*/CBS poll confirms that between twenty-five and
thirty per cent of its members were contacted, and that this is a far
higher percentage than is reached by professional polls.) Actually,
Glenn made an effort to get the A.F.L.-C.I.O. endorsement—or, at
least, to try to block Mondale from getting it—and tried for other
groups' endorsements as well. This morning, Glenn tells the steel-
worker who asks him why he has come to this plant, "I'm taking
my campaign to labor as much as anyone else in this country. I
thought it was wrong for organized labor to endorse as early as
they did, and put all that effort in—only a fourth of the workers
had been polled, and they came out even between Mondale and
me. So, just as I do in Ohio, I'm taking my campaign to the
workers themselves." Crews from local television stations are here,
so Glenn is getting a chance to make his case on the free media.
This trip is designed to reach all the major media markets in Iowa.
To a worker who has asked him about the possibility of achieving a
balanced budget, Glenn replies that he has proposed the most
thorough plan for reducing the deficit, including a ten-per-cent
surcharge on both corporate and personal income (he appears to
have forgotten about his amended version of the corporate tax),
and repeal of the section of the 1981 tax-cut act that provided for
the indexing of taxes. Glenn says that this would raise eighty billion dollars in fiscal 1988. Mr. McCreight tells reporters that he
and some others are "beating the bushes" to get people to attend
the caucuses who never have before—sending them information
kits, telling them which of their neighbors are going. He is asked
how much of an effort the local union has made for Mondale. He
replies, "None. They're more disorganized than we are."

At the Copper Kettle II Cafe, in Wilton, Glenn sits at a rectangular table with some local citizens, drinking coffee and eating
coffee cake. Several of the seats at the table are not filled for some
time. A woman at the table asks Glenn if he thinks there will be a
nuclear war. Glenn says he knows that "that's the overriding concern that people have," and he says that as a result of having
served in two wars he started working in that area when he got to
the Senate. He cites his authorship of the Nuclear Nonproliferation Act of 1978, and cites his five-point program for
arms control: seeking a freeze on nuclear weapons, if it can be

mutual and verifiable; pushing for reduction talks, using the best negotiators and seeking incremental reductions, as was done in SALT II (he does not mention that he opposed the SALT II treaty), instead of making sweeping proposals that the Soviets cannot accept, as the Reagan Administration has done; getting other nations with nuclear weapons involved in the talks as soon as possible; reducing the spread of nuclear weapons; and reducing conventional arms. Then Glenn says again that he has been through two wars and adds, as he often does, that he has "had to sit down and write those next-of-kin letters." (David Sawyer, Glenn's media adviser, says that a good thing about Glenn's talking about the next-of-kin letters is that it conveys passion on a subject of deep concern to people.) Glenn says, "That sears your soul. Nobody is going to work harder than I will for peace."

In answer to another question, Glenn goes after Mondale for "overpromising," and talks about the cost of Mondale's proposals, citing the figures he used in his speech last November. "I will not overpromise," Glenn says. "I think we have to have the courage to tell people some of the tough things that have to be done." It is noticeable that Glenn applies to himself some of the words— "courage," "honesty"—that his advisers want the public to apply to him. He tells this group that the deficits are causing lower exports, but, unlike Mondale, he doesn't go into an explanation, and he says that he voted for the Reagan tax-cut program—after trying to change it—because economic conditions under Carter had been so bad, and "I think that's why we lost the election." He explains that his surtax would be used "solely for deficit reduction," and that any new programs would have to be offset by budget cuts. "Some people aren't aware of my experience," he tells them, and he recites his career. He comes across in this setting as sincere, straight, and attentive. When he is asked about the military budget, he says that he would not give the Pentagon a blank check, and cites the weapons systems he opposes—the MX, the Bradley Fighting Vehicle—and says that he would save money on the Rapid Deployment Force (he has long said that "it's not rapid, it's not deployable, and it's not a force") and on the Division Air Defense System (a mechanized ground-to-air weapon). But he does say that "the Soviets have outbuilt us and outspent us thirty to fifty per cent in the last fifteen years." (This figure is in much dispute.) And he goes on, "Unless we do some modernizing now we're not going to have the capability. I see a crossover point where the Soviets would have superior military power by 1988–1990." (This prediction, too, is very much in dispute.) When he is asked what he would do to help the steel industry compete for exports, Glenn, like Mondale, says that he is a free trader but thinks certain actions have to be taken to make sure that the competition is fair. He points out that he supports the local-content legislation. He says that "if we just hang back and try to go back to those Reagan policies of the twenties and thirties or to the programs we had in the sixties or seventies, if we come before the people of this country as the party of overspending, weak on defense, I think we'll go down to defeat." Now Glenn goes into a little summary of his stump speech.

DES MOINES. Glenn holds a brief press conference at his headquarters here. The local press asks him questions about the status of the race, and Glenn shrugs off, as he must, its supposed problems. He says, as his advisers do, that "people are just beginning to focus" on the race, that the financial shortfall is no big thing, and that, as for the polls, "polls go up, polls go down."

COUNCIL BLUFFS. The Glenn campaign has chosen this Western city, situated just across the Missouri River from Omaha, the site of the Strategic Air Command, to give a speech on nuclear nonproliferation. The people here are understood to be especially sensitive to the danger of a nuclear outbreak, knowing that they live in an area likely to be an early, and perhaps the first, target of an enemy attack. Schneiders has told me that the Glenn campaign intends to have the candidate give one substantive speech a week. And for Glenn to talk about nuclear nonproliferation in Iowa, where pro-freeze sentiment is very strong, was seen as a good move. Glenn gives the speech in a new auditorium at Iowa Western Community College. The audience consists of students, some adults, and some deaf children (for whom a sign linguist has been provided). Glenn reads a long speech about a critical subject, interpolating from time to time. He cites in his speech the nations "that may have nuclear weapons within the decade"—Iraq, Libya, Brazil, Argentina, Israel, India, Pakistan, South Africa, South Korea, Taiwan, and Egypt—and he says that "others are not far behind." He asks the audience to "imagine a world in which a Qaddafi of Libya or the Ayatollah Khomeini of Iran has nuclear weapons," and he says he believes that that is the intent of those countries. He interpolates that there have been rumors that Qaddafi tried to purchase nuclear material from China and was refused, and that Qaddafi also wanted to work with Pakistan on an "Islamic bomb." He says that when he entered the Senate, in 1975, India had already carried out a nuclear explosion, and other countries, including Pakistan, were reported to be working on building a nuclear capability. "It seemed to me that the world was in imminent danger of becoming a nuclear-armed camp, and I resolved to do all I could from the United States Senate to stop it." He says he successfully co-sponsored an amendment requiring the termination of economic and military aid to any country that received or transferred certain sensitive nuclear materials or technology (the amendment was later applied to Pakistan), and he cites his work on the Nuclear Nonproliferation Act of 1978. He says that the Carter Administration tried to weaken his bill. The 1978 law established controls on nuclear exports, sanctions to be applied to violators, and a policy of nuclear assistance to countries that agreed to forgo developing nuclear weapons. And he says that the law was then undermined by the Carter Administration's decision to supply nuclear fuel to India in 1980, despite the fact that India had refused to apply certain safeguards and to sign the nuclear-nonproliferation treaty, which provides for inspection of nuclear facilities. At an arms-control forum at Harvard last October, Glenn asked Mondale where, as Vice-President, he had stood on, among other things, the sale of nuclear fuel to India. Mondale replied, "I was the strongest advocate of the imposition of restraints on the distribution of weapons material." Now, in his speech, Glenn attacks the Reagan Administration for a "laissez-faire" attitude toward nonproliferation, saying that it has allowed South Africa to "escape a five-year U.S. nuclear-fuel embargo;" has provided previously restricted economic and military aid to Pakistan without assurances that Pakistan will stop its nuclear-weapons program; has approved the transfer of nuclear-related material and equipment to Argentina, despite Argentina's refusal to accept comprehensive safeguards; and has promised to send nuclear components to India. Some of the language in Glenn's speech is strong, and the subject is one that can arouse passions, and he clearly cares about it—but he does not deliver the speech with any passion. This is a subject that should have people out of their chairs. The audience seems unmoved. Glenn mentions a number of things he would do as President to tighten controls on nuclear proliferation, and says that in order to "overcome the bureaucratic tendency to subordinate nonproliferation to other foreign-policy concerns" he would name a special White House assistant for nonproliferation. He closes by referring to his combat experience in two wars—and interpolates a sentence about the next-of-kin letters—and says that he has "stood on the site of the Nagasaki nuclear explosion" and thought about what an all-out exchange of nuclear weapons would mean. And then he refers to his earth-orbiting flight: "I saw this fragile craft we call earth in a way few human beings have been privileged to see it." He says, "As one of my fellow-astronauts put it, we have solved the problems of leaving this earth. Now it's up to you and me to solve the problems of living on it. That's what I want to do." When he finishes, the audience applauds politely.

As Glenn leaves the auditorium, he stops and talks, through the sign linguist, to the deaf children. He tells them he is sorry that his wife, Annie, is not here, because she has a great interest in their problem. He says that if she were here she would tell them—and then he makes a sign that means "I love you."

I have an interview with Glenn in the car that takes him back to the airport. Along the way, he notices a windmill, and talks briefly about how useful it would be if we could learn to store electrical energy. He is to appear at a forum on uses of alternative energy tonight in Sioux City, and the subject seems to be on his mind.

I begin by asking Glenn where he thinks his campaign stands, in terms of what he needs to do.

"I started a year and a half, at least, after Mondale," Glenn replies, and he says that his campaign had to decide whether to pour money into organization or "were we going to have a reasonable organization and have money available to expand in the time period leading up to when people really make up their minds on voting—and that's what we decided to do, and that's what we're doing right now."

I ask Glenn what his biggest challenge is, and he replies, "I suppose we always wish we had more money—then you can do a lot of things." But he also says what he said in Des Moines—that the financial shortfall is no big thing.

But, I ask him, what is it that he feels he has to do at this stage in terms of issues and impressions he has to get across?

"Experience—I think that's a major one," he replies. "I've had a background, of course, that people go back with almost twenty-two years, and most people think about me in that vein—as an astronaut, I guess. And so our job is to flesh it out—that there are lots of other experiences and accomplishments that have something to do with the Presidency of the United States." Then he says a line he has been using on this trip: "Mondale has said that he felt the nomination should go to the person with the greatest experience, and I agree with that"—and he recites his experience, in just the same terms as he had on stops along this trip, and, in fact, in interviews over the past year. ("I went through two wars. As I say, I've had to write too many of those next-of-kin letters, so nobody's going to work harder for peace out of that experience than I will.") He adds, "If we get this idea of experience across, I think that could make a big difference—I think that's one of our biggest jobs."

I ask if the fact that he talks frequently about his experience as an astronaut reinforces the problem he has just described.

Glenn replies, "Oh, I don't know. I only mention it usually in the light I just did just now—that it's experience in research that I think is valuable—and I certainly don't try and downplay it, I just try to add on to it. Most people, when they think back to those days, are proud of those days," and then he talks, as he has in his appearances all along the way, of the spirit evoked by John F. Kennedy. It is unclear whether Glenn is aware that anyone who has observed him over the past year, and has been along on this trip, has heard these things many times, verbatim.

I ask Glenn what he thinks is the biggest peril to his campaign.

He replies, "I suppose the biggest peril once again would be that we need more money than we would have. But I don't think that's unique in this campaign. I think that most campaigns suffer from lack of all the money they'd like to have."

I ask him what else he thinks he himself has to get across, and he talks again about the need to get across his experience.

Glenn replies, "Once again, getting that message across isn't just me talking about it—it's what we do on TV and radio." And then he goes into a mini-version of his stump speech—about the choice that the Democratic Party has to make, and that if it is perceived as weak on defense and as the party of big spending and overpromising, "then we'll be setting the stage for defeat." He says, "I think most Democrats—in fact, most Americans, most people of either party—just want responsible leadership that's going to tell it like it is," and then he talks about the special interests. "So I think we have a real choice this time as to what the future of the Party is going to be and whether it's going to be those mainstream Democrats who are going to really come out and vote and say where the Party is going, or is it going to be those who claim Party leadership of the special interests and are trying to bring their blocs of people in and lead them around by the nose. And I don't think people want that to happen. I think most Democrats are fully capable of making up their own minds on the basis of what they see on TV and read in the magazines and the newspapers and hear on the radio; they don't need to be led around by the nose. That was more customary back several decades ago, but I think over the last twenty years or so Americans have been more making up their own minds. I just hope we can convince them to do exactly that in this election. Lane Kirkland says that forty per cent of his membership went over against the exhortations of all the leaders and voted for Ronald Reagan last time around, which shows that these people are not just being led around by the nose. They're thinking for themselves. And those are the people I hope to get out and vote and take part in the caucuses and primaries."

I ask Glenn whether he feels that he has developed some overarching themes for his campaign, or whether he thinks it matters.

He replies that he thinks it does matter, and he refers to a speech he is planning to give on Wednesday at Faneuil Hall, in Boston. Schneiders told me about this speech on the plane coming out to Iowa. He described it as "the longest and hopefully most eloquent articulation of the themes of the campaign, an attempt to say in a general way what kind of President he would be," and added, "It does not attempt to be programmatic; it's a serious attempt to give people a pretty clear idea of what they could expect from him."

I tell Glenn that I will not be able to be in Boston for the speech and will read the text later, but that I would like to hear from him what he thinks are the important things he will be saying in the speech.

He replies that the point of the speech is to get beyond the "day-in, day-out" controversies on acid rain, and things like that, and get to "what the big picture is for the country." He describes it as "a philosophical speech on values and types of programs and commitments and things like that."

I ask Glenn what he thinks is most important about what he is going to be saying in his speech.

Glenn asks Schneiders, who is riding in the front of the car, whether he has a copy of it. Schneiders says that he doesn't have one with him.

I tell Glenn that I don't need to see a copy of the speech now—I just wondered what he thinks is important in it.

Glenn says, "Well, it's much more of a general statement of things and—I don't know, I could get the briefcase and go through the general ideas of it."

Schneiders tells me that the speech is very much along the lines he described to me on the plane, and then Glenn asks, "The swing of the Party interests back and forth, Greg, is that what we're talking about—the left-right—"

Schneiders tells Glenn, "Yes, the left-right, and character of leadership."

I ask Glenn what he was referring to last night when, in the course of talking about "secret plans," he mentioned a secret plan on foreign policy. I say that I wonder what he meant by that, particularly in light of Mondale's Press Club speech last week.

Glenn refers to a speech Mondale gave in Sacramento last January, to the state Democratic convention, in which he said that as soon as he became President "I'd get on that hot line . . . and I'd say this: 'Dear Mr. Andropov, please meet me in Geneva this afternoon, and let's sit down and do some work to bring some easing of tensions.'" It was a bit of rhetorical excess before a partisan crowd—and suggested an obliviousness of travel times—but Mondale also said other things about arms control and foreign policy in that speech (and pledged to resubmit the SALT II treaty to the Senate for ratification), and has said many other things about arms control and foreign policy since then.

Glenn says, of Mondale's line about calling Andropov on the hot line, "That's not a policy. I mean, that's not a program of how you accomplish that. This five-point thing [of mine] that you've heard ad nauseam"—so Glenn is aware that observers have been hearing these things—"I think it's very valid and I think it's still the best program that anybody has put forward. And just to lead people into thinking that you're going to have arms control, and no plan really to do it except a phone call, isn't realistic." And then Glenn says again that Mondale has "no specifics" for his "secret plan" for the economy.

I ask Glenn if he is aware of what Mondale said in his Press Club speech.

Glenn replies that he is aware of it, "but I don't think it's still anyway near as specific as what I've proposed." And then he goes into his stump criticisms of Mondale's plans for dealing with the budget and acid rain, and his stump statements about the need for education and basic research.

I ask him if he feels he is getting somewhere on the question of his experience.

"Oh yes, very much so," he replies. "I think people have to have a feeling: Hey, this person is really capable of being President of the United States." And then he says what he has been saying on this trip about some people just getting their experience through politics. He says, "Once you get beyond that point, which I think is an important one, then I think all these other things I say on specific issues perhaps are more likely to be accepted—will be accepted more fully. Not that people don't believe me when I say something, but I'll be more fully believed. I think we've come a long ways on that, too." He continues, "In fact, wherever I go now I have people bringing up my background and experience and talking to me about it—that they hadn't thought about it that way. They think that's a very forceful argument. I just remember that people volunteer that. So I think we're making excellent headway with that." He adds, "It's that I'm not limited to just being a professional politician—that's a better way to put it."

SIOUX CITY. Tonight, at the energy forum—there are about eighty people in the audience—Glenn reads a short speech warning that the oil glut won't last and talking about Iranian threats to close the Strait of Hormuz, which he calls the "jugular" of the Persian Gulf oil outlet. He criticizes the Administration for selling coal off Western lands "at fire-sale prices"—this was one of James Watt's most controversial actions—and for cutting funds for energy research. Glenn looks very tired tonight. These have been long days, and his schedules have provided him little respite.

(Mondale is more carefully scheduled: he is given time to make calls, talk with his staff, and get the kind of rest that any human being going through this kind of thing needs.) Glenn is not a man of superhuman energy—some politicians seem to have more adrenaline to draw on—and when he is fatigued his eyes seem to recede into his head, and become slits. As before, as he reads his speech it doesn't come across as his—as coming from him. But when he goes into the question period an unusual thing happens. Glenn, who does not show much depth on many issues, has clearly steeped himself in the technical question of energy sources and is very interested in it, and he gives long, long technical answers. This is the one time on this trip when he has seemed to be deviating from a script. At one point, Glenn refers to having seen a windmill this afternoon in—and goes blank on where he saw it. Anyone who has taken these sorts of trips knows that eventually the stops become indistinguishable; and, in one's fatigue, one doesn't remember where one has been. Glenn does not try to hide this fact, and looks over in my direction for help. I summon up Council Bluffs and call it out to him, and he smiles and says, "Council Bluffs." It is a guileless, human moment.

In the course of the answer to one question, Glenn tells the audience, "If you had one energy wish you could have tonight before you went to bed, what would it be? I'm sure half the audience would wish for an oil well in their back yard, number one. But you know what I would wish for if I wanted energy independence for this country? It would be better electrical-energy storage. If we could put better-concentrated amounts of electrical energy in storage, then the electric automobile becomes practical. Well, we've tried electrical cars in the past and it didn't work. But they didn't work because we didn't have the range of current batteries. And before this Administration chopped off some of that research we had some extremely promising things going in electrical-energy storage. And the reason I say that's so important is if you get better electrical-energy storage you can take the output of a number of different sources, whether it's photovoltaic, or it's hydropower where the water just runs over the dam in non-peak-load periods and just runs down the river someplace, whether it's solar changeover, whether it's running plants at a constant level all day—in non-peak periods—and run them at a steady load just as though they're on during the peak-loads periods in the evening, but let them store energy during that time period. They can be much more efficient." Then he refers to going through the Lawrence Livermore Laboratory, in California, and says, "I was out there and went through the lab with them and looked at this thing—it was an aluminum air battery, they called it. I won't go into details of it, but it was decomposition of aluminum with an electric release and with a bunch of trays here"—Glenn gestures—"and by this process you released enough energy off of this tray of aluminum plates to drive a car, they estimated, fifteen hundred miles, and they thought once they had this process perfected it would probably take a car three thousand miles on one load of these plates, pull into a station, slide a new bunch of plates in, another three thousand miles. And this looked like it was becoming promising and *they cancelled the thing—cancelled the project.*" Continuing with the same answer, he talks about visiting a NASA lab in Cleveland, describes in detail how a Chinese gas vat works. In answer to another question, he describes in detail how an automobile acceleration system works, and its effect on gasoline consumption, and he talks about the need for "regenerative braking."

At the end of his appearance here, Glenn gives his stump speech, and talks about his experience. "I want to use the background I have had, and I think it is a unique background no other candidate has had," he says, and "Our leading competition for this nomination has said that he thinks the nomination should go to the person with the greatest experience." He says, "But to me the greatest experience is not just having spent all your life in professional political life and not have experience in anything else." He continues, "I've had ten years in Washington. I know how the political system works there. I'm not that slow a learner that I haven't learned how it works in ten years. And so I'm proud of that. And so, as far as being that much of a professional politician, I'm there. But along with that I've run an international corporation for several years—travelled all over this world." After Glenn left NASA, he joined Royal Crown Cola as a corporate vice-president, and then became the president of Royal Crown International. He spent much of his time travelling around the world promoting Royal Crown. He continues, "I've started four small businesses—they were successful." This is odd; one of his businesses, he told me in an interview last year, went bankrupt ("So I know both sides of the business world"). Glenn's small businesses consisted of Holiday Inn franchises, which he got involved with through friends. These franchises, including a lucrative one near Disney World, made Glenn a wealthy man. "I was in the research business," he says, referring to his experience with NASA. "I don't think there's any better background anybody has for making these basic, fundamental research decisions on where this country is going to go and how we're going to be competitive with Japan and Germany and France and other nations. I was in the Marine Corps. I spent a career there. I don't see how there can be a better background for making defense decisions on what we need." And then he talks about having been in combat in two wars and written the next-of-kin letters—"That sears your soul"—and then he stresses again his ten years in Washington. He clearly wants to get across that he's been there, but not too much. And he talks about setting goals and about his orbital flight, and then he tells the audience that February 20th—the day of the Iowa caucuses—"also happens to be the anniversary of my orbital flight."

JANUARY 10

MASON CITY. This town, in the northern part of the state, close to the Minnesota border, is supposed to be good territory for Mondale, and Cranston has been working hard here, but Glenn has come here nevertheless, to open another headquarters and to meet with the local press. Today, the weather is six below zero, with a wind-chill factor of thirty below. A layer of crusty snow has covered the entire state.

There are no phones in this headquarters, either. About forty people are gathered here to see Glenn, and there is no particular excitement. He goes through his stump speech again. Most politicians repeat their good lines, and even paragraphs, but the word-for-word sameness of what Glenn says in his speeches and in his answers to questions is unusual. Inescapably, it has a programmed effect. Glenn seldom seems spontaneous. He is good-humored but not particularly funny. His audiences may well like him and admire him, but he seems not to get much out of them, because he doesn't give them much. He is agreeable but remote, automatic. He makes no personal connection with his audiences. Skilled politicians establish a connection with their audiences, joke with them, give them some emotion and get some back. An appearance by a skilled politician turns into a chemical experience. Glenn offers no emotion; there is nothing personal in these appearances. It is as if all the audiences were the same for him. Most skilled politicians

take the measure of a crowd and find ways to relate to it specifically. It is as if Glenn were doing a walk-through. Undoubtedly, he
comes across as nice and sincere—and as John Glenn—and as a
man of common sense and plain American values. But little seems
to happen. And even the celebrity value doesn't seem as great as
might have been expected; certainly, some people come to see the
famous astronaut, and some ask for his autograph, but these
things don't seem to happen in any substantial numbers. A striking thing about this trip, in fact, is that there have been no events
at which a large crowd was gathered to hear Glenn—no rallies.

WATERLOO. At lunchtime, Glenn gives a speech on farm policy before the Kiwanis Club, meeting at the Elks Lodge. An Iowa journalist says that this audience—of about two hundred white
males—is probably heavily Republican. The Glenn entourage is
supposed to fly to Boston tonight, so that Glenn can give his
speech there tomorrow, but a snowstorm is predicted for Boston
this evening, and there is some question whether they will be able
to get there. (As things turn out, they cannot, and the speech is
postponed.) Following this event in Waterloo, Glenn is to fly to
Ottumwa, in the southeast corner of the state. Mondale is said to
have a strong grip on the Democratic activists in the area. But it
has been badly hit by the economy, and the Glenn people want
their candidate to show up there. So this afternoon Glenn will go
to Ottumwa to shake hands with workers at the John Deere plant.

XI

Few Presidents in history have known how to set, and hold, the stage as well as Ronald Reagan does, and thus he entered the political year—via his State of the Union Message and his opening of his reelection campaign—with a great splash. Reagan's sense of theatre is unmatched in politics, his use of language unique, and his capacity for arrogating unto himself the symbols and values Americans hold dear—flag, family, God, patriotism, national strength—awesome. He is the master weaver of the national myths. All this was on display as he gave his State of the Union speech, on January 25th, and then, four days later, at ten-fifty-five on a Sunday evening, announced on all three television networks his decision to seek reelection. But when the President's advisers say, as they have done publicly, that they expect the election to be a tight one they are saying what the wisest among them truly believe. All sorts of things that cannot be predicted can affect the outcome: events; the kind of campaign each candidate runs; the nature of the race itself—its own dynamics. Reagan, we know, is a tested national campaigner of superb political instincts and skills. The skills of his opponent, who the Reagan people assume will be Walter Mondale, are only beginning to come into national view. For what it's worth, the Reagan people are impressed; but the chemistry the Democratic nominee establishes with the voters cannot yet be seen. These factors aside, two things are agreed on by both sides, and seem unarguable at this point: the election is up for grabs as of now; and, because it will offer a clear choice and will be very hard-fought, it will be a big election. Moreover, no sooner had the applause for the President's opening performance died than there were new shocks to his economic and foreign policies: the collapse of his Lebanon policy and what was shaping up as a crisis over his economic policy. Some developments, on close examination, showed important things about the unusual nature of the Reagan Presidency.

The first factor that suggests that it could be a close election and, contrary to the general assumption now, winnable by the Democrats, is the math. The nature of Reagan's landslide in 1980 is much misunderstood: Reagan did win a landslide in the electoral college, but he won only fifty-one per cent of the popular vote, and he carried many states narrowly. This time, the Reagan people, anticipating a race between Reagan and Mondale, see the possibility of a close race; in fact, they and the Mondale people see many states in the same light. Both sides see a possibility that the Democrats could carry Washington and Oregon, both of which Reagan carried in 1980. Both sides agree that the Democrats could carry Texas, which Reagan carried handily in 1980. (Black and Hispanic voting went up there substantially in 1982, and the Democrats took over the governorship.) There is some question within the Reagan camp whether the Southern states will fall as plentifully to Reagan this time. (He carried all but Georgia in 1980, and the Mondale people believe they can win several Southern states, perhaps including Florida, which Reagan carried easily in 1980, and which the Reagan people assume they will carry again.) And both sides agree that the outcome in the industrial Midwestern states is uncertain: in 1980 Reagan carried Illinois, Michigan, Ohio, and Pennsylvania, but all these states are in question now. New York, which Reagan carried in 1980, is in doubt now. One Reagan adviser and a key Mondale strategist think there is even a chance Mondale could carry California. Other states that Reagan carried in 1980 are not considered automatically his this time. A critical question is whether Reagan can again win the forty to forty-five per cent of the blue-collar votes that he received in 1980. (Reagan received about eight per cent more of these votes than Ford did in 1976.) "We're facing a much bigger battleground this time," a key Reagan adviser said to me recently. "That's why I'm nervous."

The second factor that suggests it could be a close election is the size and the state of the Democratic base. The Reagan people start with the assumption that fifty-three per cent of the people identify themselves with the Democrats and thirty-five per cent with the Republicans. Richard Wirthlin, Reagan's pollster, says, "Even though the parties are weak, a person's declaring himself a Democrat or Republican is still the best predictor of how he is going to vote. There's much talk about independents. We find that when people say they are independent, and then we ask them which party they lean toward, they are stronger partisans than many of those who declare a party. We get the fifty-three-to-thirty-five split by asking the second question." Moreover, the Reagan people believe that the Democrats have been registering many more new voters than the Republicans have since 1980, and this increases their fear that they could be overwhelmed by sheer numbers in several states. And so both the Reagan-Bush '84 Committee (the President's official reelection committee) and the Republican National Committee are now mounting substantial registration drives. (The Republican Party plans to spend an unprecedented amount on the election.) A large increase in black voting has already affected a number of elections since 1980, and is a threat to Reagan. Republicans also feel that they have to increase their registration in order to offset strenuous efforts this year by labor, women, environmentalists, and black and Hispanic groups and others to get out the vote—against Reagan. Among the groups the Reagan people have targeted for registration are fundamentalist Christians, Asians, and suburban Republicans. But the Republicans concede that their potential voters are more scattered, and harder to find, than those the Democrats are signing up. Moreover, in 1980 twenty-eight per cent of those who had voted for Carter in 1976 stayed home. Wirthlin says, "Mondale's task is to solidify the natural proclivities of Americans to vote Democratic—and that's why it's going to be a close race." The Democratic candidate could be helped by the fact that Reagan is an energizer of the Democrats. So two forces would be converging: if Mondale is nominated, it would be, as Wirthlin himself has said, with the intense support of the Democratic constituencies, which would expend a lot of energy in the general election; at the same time, Reagan will be stirring up that energy. Mondale's Democratic rivals have, of course, been making the sorts of criticisms of him that the Republicans will cheerfully exploit, if he is the nominee, and Mondale has certain vulnerabilities—of the sort that Reagan would relish going after. But at the end of the day the most astute Republican strategists are taking nothing for granted.

The Reagan strategists' plan is to have the President be "Presidential" as long as possible, taking few political—or ostensibly political—trips, but enough to keep his campaign legs in shape. The case against the Democrats is to be carried by Vice-President

George Bush and Cabinet officials and others, but, of course, little that Reagan does will be absent political considerations. Even appearing to be nonpolitical is a political act. The intention is to put Reagan on display as a strong leader—"leadership" being considered a key issue by the Reagan people. In 1980, Wirthlin says, the issue was Carter's "failed leadership." This year, he says, it will be whether people want to continue under Reagan's leadership. The Reagan campaign strategists have mapped out the year, and planned a number of steps to be taken with a view to, among other things, having Reagan dominate the agenda and the news, rather than allow the Democrats or the media to do so. Their plan also deals with the attacks that can be expected from the opposition and outlines the constituencies that have to be reached. The Reagan strategists divided their planning for the election into six stages: the period from mid-October of 1983, when the Reagan-Bush Committee was formed, through the State of the Union Message and the formal beginning of the campaign; the period of the Democratic primaries until about April 1st, when they expect it to be clear who the Democratic opponent will be; the period leading up to the Democratic Convention, in July (the President's political advisers expect his trip to China, in April, to be a very big event); the "doldrums" period between the two party conventions (when they consider it most important that the media not be allowed to set the agenda); the Republican Convention, in August, and the "afterglow" from that; and the period from Labor Day until the election, on November 6th. But they know that, for all their tidy plans, events will occur and mistakes will be made for which there is no plan. One of the most important tests of a campaign is its ability to recover from mistakes.

Reagan, for all his strengths, has vulnerabilities of his own. One thing that has struck a number of people here is that while his approval ratings have gone up this does not necessarily translate into people's saying they would vote for his reelection. Politicians, especially those who are behind in the polls, like to say that "the only poll that matters is the one on Election Day," but there is great truth to the point: Reagan was farther behind Carter at this point in 1980 than Mondale is behind Reagan; Wirthlin says that had the 1980 election occurred on October 1st, in all probability Carter would have won. The possibility of the Reagan electoral-college landslide did not appear until, at most, five days before the election—and there is debate over whether it appeared that soon.

Reagan's State of the Union Message was a revealing road map of the President's political exigencies. There were a number of things for the blue-collar workers. First, there was talk about the economic recovery. Unemployment is higher than when Reagan took office, and real interest rates (after inflation) are higher, but inflation is down—as a result of the recession—and unemployment is dropping. (Economic growth slowed in the last quarter of 1983, which was actually good news for the Administration, since the speed of the recovery increased the danger of higher interest rates.) Wirthlin says that blue-collar voters don't blame Reagan for the recession and give him credit for the recovery. He and other Reagan advisers say that blue-collar voters applaud Reagan's building up of America's defense, that they like his appeal to traditional values and his opposition to affirmative action and quotas—and that they simply like Reagan. Reagan's sheer lack of pomposity, Wirthlin says, is a definite political plus. Reagan has in fact created an almost mythic figure: the regular guy who has "had it up to my keister" with all the perfidies of Washington— leaks, big spending, big government. Reagan, like George Wallace before him, reaches these people through his indignation at "those bureaucrats in Washington" and his talk of the need to cut the size of government. He is seen, his advisers say, as a friendly fellow who is non-elitist, the product of a lower-middle-class Irish home. He may prefer the company of the rich (and may have received the generous backing of a number of them), but his political base has always been among the middle class and the lower middle class, whose angers and resentments, as well as patriotic and religious inclinations, he appeals to expertly. Reagan's amiability, which is genuine, is a powerful weapon. His invoking of moral values in his State of the Union speech (just as he had done in his acceptance speech in Detroit in 1980)—his citing the values of faith, family, work, neighborhood, peace, and freedom—was essentially aimed (as it was in his acceptance speech) at the blue-collar voter. His calls for certain "social" legislation—constitutional amendments to allow prayer in the schools and to prohibit most abortions—were aimed beyond his natural base, at the blue-collar voter as well. This social agenda has got nowhere since Reagan came into office, to the disappointment of some of his original followers. Now Reagan is making new efforts to reaffirm that base. The President's political advisers are concerned that the fundamentalist Christians, who gave Reagan important support in 1980, and whose voting strength can make a difference, particularly in the Southern states, may not support Reagan with sufficient intensity this year. In his brief announcement of his candidacy, he spoke of "seeing if we can't find room in our schools for God." And Reagan's first public appearance on the day after his announcement was before a convention of the National Religious Broadcasters, in Washington, in which he invoked God and the Bible numerous times. Of the Bible he said, "Within the covers of that single Book are all the answers to all the problems that face us today." He likened the issue of prohibiting abortion to the Civil War struggle to end slavery, and he said that "medical-science doctors confirm that when the lives of the unborn are snuffed out they often feel pain, pain that is long and agonizing." (The American College of Obstetricians and Gynecologists, representing twenty-four thousand doctors, disputes this.) He called again for prayer in the schools, and he came out against child pornography and the American Civil Liberties Union. Besides the President's own actions, another step the Reagan campaign will take to reinsure the support of the evangelical Christians is to have James Watt, the former Secretary of the Interior, make a number of appearances before them. Senator Paul Laxalt, Republican of Nevada, the President's close friend and the general chairman of the Reagan reelection campaign, told me, "I don't know of a politician in this country more respected by the fundamentalists than Jim." (However, a poll taken for a conservative group last fall found that there is a "gender gap"—a tendency of men to support Reagan to a greater degree than women do—among fundamentalists, and that either Mondale or John Glenn would receive more support among this group than Carter did in 1980.) Watt will also be raising money for Reagan. Reagan's call in his State of the Union address for tuition tax credits was also aimed at blue-collar voters (and Hispanic voters as well), as was his call for tougher action against crime. (Edwin Meese, whom Reagan has designated as his new Attorney General, can be expected to be quite vociferous on that subject.)

One of the biggest potential problems facing the President is, of course, the enormous budget deficits. There has been disagreement among his advisers as to how much of a political problem the deficits pose, but not much disagreement over what the political effect would be if the deficits led to higher interest rates, a stall in the economy, or an increase in the inflation rate before the election. The President's political advisers took comfort in two aspects of the politics of the deficit issue: first, according to their polls, most people blame Congress for the size of the deficit, even though it is essentially Reagan's tax cuts and increases in defense spending that have caused the deficit to more than triple since he took office, and even though Congress has been holding down spending on "controllable" domestic programs (that is, non-entitlements); second, they figure that Reagan's opponent will be on the "wrong" side of the deficit issue—will call for more taxes. One Reagan campaign aide says, "Give me a choice between a big deficit or taxes, I'll take a deficit." But another campaign official, talking about the politics of the deficit, says, "It's not that easy. If the economy goes flat or interest rates go up, it's the deficit that could destroy our house." In the State of the Union speech, the President made a number of passes at the deficit without actually confronting it. He shook his rhetoric at it. ("We might well begin with common sense in federal budgeting: Government spending no more than government takes in." "We can begin by limiting the size and scope of government." "A pattern of overspending has been in place for half a century.") He ruled out raising taxes. One of Reagan's most impressive skills is his ability to cast an issue his way—stating a proposition that seems unarguable, or posing a question to which there seems only one obvious answer. In his speech, he said, "Whether government borrows or increases taxes, it will be taking the same amount of money from the private sector." As a statement of fact, this is correct. (It is a simplification of something the economist Milton Friedman has been saying.) But Reagan's implication is that it does not matter whether the deficit is paid for by taxes or by borrowing. This raises the question of why there should be any taxes at all, and overlooks the matter of the interest that must be paid on the debt, and the many consequences of the high interest rates that result from running such a large deficit. But Reagan's line may have been more than just a rhetorical turn. In White House meetings, he says that paying interest on the deficit doesn't matter, since we pay it to ourselves. (In fact, his own Economic Report of this year points out that forty per cent of the interest goes to foreigners who have invested in this country because of the strong dollar and the high interest rates. Moreover, the debt diminishes private investment, thus shrinking the economy over the long term; it hurts exports—the United States is now running the highest trade deficit in history; it leads to the risk of inflation or an overly restrictive monetary policy; and it could, of course, cause a crisis of confidence in the financial markets.) That crisis may have already begun. The Dow Jones industrial average has dropped ninety-four points in the three weeks since Congress returned; the reason most often cited has been fear that the deficit would not be substantially reduced. Why this possibility was news to the stock market is a mystery.

There is actually a large question of how much Reagan understands about economic policy, as there is about his understanding of other areas, such as arms control and foreign policy. According to people within the Administration who have reason to know how the President thinks, he does not understand or accept the figures that his economic advisers present to him. It is not, according to these sources, that Reagan is wrestling with competing goods; he isn't wrestling at all—he dismisses the idea that there is a problem. He often asserts that the deficit was there when he came to office, and refuses to recognize that there is a significant difference between a sixty-billion-dollar deficit (the size of Carter's last deficit) and a hundred-and-eighty-billion-dollar deficit (which the Reagan Administration projects for the next several fiscal years)—a difference that most of his economic advisers, and a great many other people, do recognize. Even the hundred-and-eighty-billion figure is optimistic; the Congressional Budget Office, which is politically independent, says that the deficits for this year and future years are a good bit higher than the Reagan Administration predicts, and will reach over three hundred billion by fiscal 1989. Among other things, the Reagan budget is based on optimistic, not to say unrealistic, assumptions: about strong, sustained economic growth over the next four years, and about interest rates and inflation. At that, the interest on the debt for fiscal 1985 is estimated by the Administration at a hundred and sixteen billion. The President is wont to say to his advisers that the Democrats created the deficit, we hoped it would go away, and it didn't—and leave it at that. When Reagan's economic advisers show him the charts indicating how the deficits have grown during his Presidency, it does no good. He believes that the size of the deficit is being exaggerated, because he assumes that economic growth will continue; he does not appear to absorb the fact that the calculation of the size of the deficit already assumes strong economic growth—though this has been explained to him many times. Thus, there is a certain routine to White House conversations on this subject. Reagan assumes that since some economic projections have been wrong—the strength of the recovery was generally underestimated—all economic predictions are probably wrong, and he is not interested in hearing uncongenial news. Moreover, he does have his own ideas, gleaned from his reading and stories he has heard, about the nature of the problem. The anecdotes for which he is famous are not arguing points; they represent his thinking. For example, the President apparently picked up somewhere that if one added up the cost of all federal programs to help people and divided it by the number of poor people it would come to each person's getting well over thirty thousand dollars. The problem is that of the programs that go into the total that is divided up only a small portion actually goes to poor people. (The figure includes Social Security, unemployment insurance, Medicare, and federal retirement benefits.) But the President cannot be dissuaded of his thought. And, it seems, as long as he has his own idea of what the problem is and the way to solve it—his own explanation of the problem—he can dismiss the solutions that his advisers suggest. But then, apparently, he doesn't press his aides to come up with a program that fits his idea of the problem—he just goes on to the next subject. So the President's approach to the economy has not just proceeded from his well-known aversion to taxes; it is that he thinks there is another solution. More than one observer has noted that the President proceeds with an extraordinary detachment from his institutional role and the authority he has; he will rule out what advisers suggest that he do if he finds it unpleasant, but then does not use his office to get them to do something else—or even to carry out what he thinks, on whatever basis, can be done. A responsible foreign-policy figure has told me that when he meets with Reagan he finds him disconcertingly disengaged. I have heard more than one government official use the word "notion" to describe the President's thoughts: he has a notion about this, a notion about that—the clear implication being that these thoughts are not firmly based on fact but are firmly fixed in the President's mind.

Thus, the Administration came up with a budget that is wildly, perhaps dangerously, out of balance not because the President has a canny long-range strategy but because he does not accept that there is a real problem. (When Reagan ran for office, he pledged a balanced budget by fiscal 1983, and when he came to office and presented his supply-side tax-cut plan he said that the budget would be balanced by fiscal 1984.) He is said to assume that the deficit can be dealt with in the future by further attacks on "waste" and "overhead." David Stockman, the director of the Office of Management and Budget, and Martin Feldstein, the chairman of the Council of Economic Advisers, proposed for this year a seven-and-a-half-per-cent surtax on individuals and corporations. But James Baker, the White House Chief of Staff, and Richard Darman, deputy to the Chief of Staff, who had earlier backed moves to get the President to raise taxes, knew that he would not agree, and did not fight for the proposition. A contingency tax—contingent on Congress's making certain budget cuts—was considered but was not agreed to, either. (Last year, the Administration proposed such a tax but did not push it, and Congress did not approve it.) Some thought was given to having the President offer a sweeping tax reform, coupled with some sort of flat tax, or a consumption tax, but this, too, would have dodged the question, for such a sweeping change would take a long time to pass and implement. (When, in his State of the Union speech, the President said that he had asked for a study to be made of a simplified tax code and a broader-based tax, and that it be presented to him in December—after the election—Democrats laughed.)

Despite the President's belief that the deficit problem was being overblown, he did agree, on the morning he was to give his speech, to a proposition that he ask Congress to join him in negotiations to find a way to reduce the deficit by a hundred billion dollars over the next three years, as a "down payment." The idea had been floating around the White House for about ten days, and by all reports came to fruition because Donald Regan, the Treasury Secretary, who had been standing with the President in his refusal to make any serious move to raise taxes, became worried that the Administration would go before the country in an implausible position. (The idea of a bipartisan commission to deal with the budget had been floated by the White House, to predictable catcalls. The commission idea had been used up, and to pro-

pose one would be an obvious dodge.) The President apparently
finally accepted the idea of the negotiation for a "down payment"
because he felt that even though the Democrats had started the
deficit the press and others might blame him for it and he had
better make some move. The move he did make was a deft one. In
one stroke, he diminished his own vulnerability on the deficit issue
and increased that of the Democrats. If they didn't cooperate, or if
the negotiations fell through, they would be blamed. The Democrats, having been through a similar, unsuccessful exercise in
1982, were, to say the least, wary—and were also resentful that the
President, with this one maneuver, had made their position so
awkward. So when the President talks in honeyed tones about
bipartisanship, as he did in his State of the Union speech, the
Democrats are, from experience, on guard. They know that Reagan is preparing the way to turn around and zap them. Reagan is
a maestro of the politics of blame.

Reagan's aides have been quite forthright about the fact that the
Administration has little interest in offering politically controversial proposals to cut spending in an election year. Thus, the budget, which the President submitted to Congress a week after his
State of the Union Message, proposed fewer cuts in domestic programs than in the past, but, once again, many of them involved
programs for the poor, and several of them had been rejected by
Congress in the past; and it suggested some changes in the tax
code that would amount to $7.9 billion in new revenues. Several of
the more controversial proposals for domestic cuts the Administration had been considering were toned down or withdrawn. (A
proposal to reduce Medicare benefits for most recipients, which
was leaked to the press earlier this year, to poor reviews from
members of both parties, was considerably moderated.) The politics of the situation had taken over the budget process. Most of
the "easy" (politically easy) cuts had been made—in programs
affecting the poor. Neither Republicans nor Democrats had the
heart to go much farther there. This left programs for the middle
class, defense, and taxes as areas for reducing the deficit. An
Administration official said to me after the budget was submitted,
"It's the classic embodiment of the free lunch. We can have our tax
cut; we can have our defense spending; we can avoid inflicting
pain on the electorate. We can blame the past and say that everything will be better after the election. It's pretty irresponsible."

The Administration's budget proposed a growth in defense
spending of thirteen per cent after inflation. If Reagan's new defense budget is approved, the growth in defense spending will
total sixty per cent, after inflation, since the Reagan Administration took office. (About ten to fifteen billion dollars of the three
hundred and five billion now being asked for defense is pad-
ding—put in in the knowledge that Congress will make cuts. This
is a tradition.) Moreover, most of the things that are now driving
up the costs of defense—new weapons systems, a vastly enlarged
Navy—have already been approved. The defense budget, then, is
on automatic pilot within the Administration. Stockman, who
used to fight to reduce it, has largely given up. There has, in fact,
not been a serious discussion of the defense budget within the
Administration since the summer of 1981 (following passage of
the large tax-cut bill), when Stockman argued that if the defense
budget wasn't reduced and other things weren't done the deficit
would reach the awful level of eighty-five billion dollars.

The hundred-billion-dollar "down payment" over three years
which the President called for does not seriously address the deficit problem: assuming that the Congressional Budget Office's prediction that the deficit will be over three hundred billion by fiscal
1989 is correct, reasonable people believe that the deficit needs to
be reduced by a hundred billion to a hundred and fifty billion
dollars *per year*. Some of the savings, the President and his aides
said, could be found in the "less contentious spending cuts" that
the President had proposed in the past but Congress had not
approved; but this is a contradiction in terms. And some savings,
they said, could be found in minor changes in the tax law; many of
these proposals, too, have been beaten back before by the interested parties. The Administration's ideas of how to save a hundred
billion dollars involve some mirrors: some of the savings are already included in the budget, and are therefore being counted
twice. The Administration has been ambiguous about from what
baseline the saving of a hundred billion dollars begins, and there
are different ideas about this within the Administration. And part
of the saving, the President and his aides said, could be made by
enacting some of the proposals made by a commission headed by
J. Peter Grace, the businessman. The Grace Commission report—
actually a series of forty-seven reports, containing nearly twenty-
five hundred recommendations—cites a number of savings that in

a nonpolitical world might make sense. (Some of the potential savings here, according to a number of authorities, are inflated.) But the Grace Commission report was quite unwelcome in Washington. A Senate Republican leadership aide described it to me as "a bunch of hooey," and Stockman is known to view it dubiously. Still, the Grace Commission provides the President with more artillery for his rhetorical battle against government spending.

The Democrats, predictably, huffed and puffed after the President made his proposal for a negotiation on a "down payment," and they were seriously divided about what to do. But that they would have to cooperate was never really in question. A number of Republicans—especially senators up for reelection this year—were relieved at the President's proposal. They want to appear "responsible" about the deficit but don't want to take any action that might not sit well with the voters. Many Republicans feel that the deficit is more of a current political issue than the President's advisers do; they see farmers, exporters, and businesses that compete with imports all being hurt, and say that bankers and realtors are becoming alarmed. There was, however, one big political flaw in the President's budget moves: Reagan left himself open to all manner of charges by Democrats about the terrible things he will do to reduce the budget if he is reelected.

In the days immediately following the issuing of the budget, Administration officials provided some nice comedy: Stockman told a congressional committee that the government was "in the same position of many companies on the eve of chapter eleven;" Feldstein told reporters that "the budget is not what we want to see happen in [fiscal] 1985;" and Regan told a congressional committee that Congress might as well "throw away" the economic report prepared by Feldstein's advisers and issued on February 2nd, which, reflecting Feldstein's more orthodox conservative economic views, took a more dire view of the effect of the high deficits than did Regan, whose department houses the last of the supply-siders in the government, and who prefers to ally himself with the President. The argument between Regan and Feldstein was a continuation of one that had been going on for months, now intensified by the embarrassing budget. A political adviser to the President fretted to me that the row might not reflect well on the President's "leadership." Then Paul Volcker, the chairman of the Federal Reserve Board, told Congress that the deficits were threatening economic growth and the stability of domestic and international financial markets, and even Regan said that the deficits could bring on another recession. Volcker was both stating a truth and somewhat reacting to the slide in the stock market, and Regan was reacting to Wall Street. And, in the way these things seem to work, Wall Street, in turn, reacted to what Volcker and Regan said, and slid further.

In his State of the Union speech, the President, without any apparent embarrassment, renewed his call, first made in 1982, for a constitutional amendment "mandating a balanced federal budget." He also asked for a constitutional amendment that would permit him to veto a single item in an appropriation bill (the "line-item veto"), rather than have to veto the entire bill if some part of it displeased him. This, too, was a symbolic proposal, since the great proportion of the budget—defense, entitlements (Social Security, Medicare, pensions, and other programs for which payments are mandated by law), and interest on the debt—would be off-limits. Moreover, it would bring about a change in the institutional balance of power which gives members of both parties pause. (It is interesting that Reagan, a conservative, has endorsed four amendments to the Constitution: on abortion, school prayer, the balanced budget, and the line-item veto.)

Reagan's other great political vulnerability is, of course, his conduct of foreign policy. As of late, it has been the one that has worried his advisers most. Their cluster of concerns has included the low state of affairs between the United States and the Soviet Union, and the lack of any progress—and, at this point, even negotiations—on arms control; Lebanon; and Central America. Beyond all this, the President's advisers are aware that his handling of foreign affairs has hurt him politically, and that the Democrats will try to make the case that he prefers the use of force to negotiation, and will question his competence in managing foreign policy. So in his State of the Union speech the President laid great stress on his quest for peace, just as nine days earlier he had made a televised address in which he struck a more conciliatory tone toward the Soviet Union than he had used in the past. Many people around the President do not believe that an arms-control agreement will be reached this year (if one were, his political advisers believe, he would be nearly impossible to beat), in large part because some important people in the President's bureaucracy don't want an agreement. Some Administration members who do favor arms control worked very hard to play down the Administration's report, issued in mid-January, of alleged Soviet violations of arms-control agreements. They saw the report as an effort by some members of the bureaucracy to wreck arms control. Some of the alleged violations are ambiguous, and there is a strong difference of opinion within the Administration about their seriousness; in previous Administrations, complaints about violations were dealt with quietly, through an established international mechanism. Moreover, the subject of compliance is a highly technical one, understood by few within the government. I am told that Caspar Weinberger, the Secretary of Defense, frequently tells the President that "the Soviets are cheating on the treaties we have with them, as you know." This is something that the President is quite inclined to believe. Some of the President's advisers, and particularly his political advisers, now say that if an arms-control agreement is not reached this year it will be because the Soviets want to see Reagan defeated. The death of Soviet leader Yuri Andropov, on February 9th, added a new element to the speculation, but in fact Andropov had been quite ill for months, and it is generally believed that others had been making policy decisions; a lot of history has already gone into the United States-Soviet relationship, but perhaps Reagan can now attribute any lack of progress to the changes in Soviet leadership. One political adviser said to me recently that the Soviet Union undoubtedly assumes that it can get a better deal from Mondale; when I asked him if this argument would be used in the campaign, he just smiled. Another adviser said simply, "The President will blame everything on the Russians and the Democrats."

The President was apparently of the view that the less said about Lebanon in his State of the Union speech the better, so he gave it brief mention. He did say that "there is hope for a free, independent and sovereign Lebanon," and that "we must not be driven from our objectives for peace in Lebanon by state-sponsored terrorism." But even as he spoke, support for the President's policy was diminishing among both parties and within his own Administration, and the situation in Lebanon was deteriorating. As it turns out, planning for withdrawal of the Marines to ships offshore Lebanon was already going on within the Administration, but this did not prevent the President from continuing to set forth high stakes for keeping the Marines in Lebanon, or from bashing House Democrats, who were working up a resolution calling for "prompt and orderly withdrawal" of the Marines. In an interview given to the *Wall Street Journal* on Thursday, February 2nd, Reagan said, referring to House Speaker Thomas P. O'Neill, "He may be ready to surrender, but I'm not." In his radio address on Saturday, he said that though the situation in Lebanon "is difficult, frustrating and dangerous . . . that is no reason to turn our backs on friends and to cut and run." On Sunday, the Cabinet of President Amin Gemayel resigned—in a move led by its Muslim faction— and the Army disintegrated, and the civil war reached a new intensity. (On that same day, National Security Adviser Robert McFarlane, in an article in the Boston *Globe*, stated that among the reasons "we must not leave Lebanon now" is that "the presence of the Multinational Force provides needed stability during the negotiating and reconciliation process.") On Tuesday, Reagan issued a statement that the Marines would be withdrawn to the ships offshore, and that the ships could use their guns to fire on Syrian-held territory, regardless of whether the Marines were under attack. The President, who was en route to his ranch from Las Vegas, where he had made a couple of appearances (the day before, he had picturesquely celebrated his seventy-third birthday in Dixon, Illinois, his home town), did not read the statement for the television cameras. He was not to be associated with bad news. To the consternation of some of his political advisers, he then disappeared to his ranch. On the following day, Administration officials explained that the planning for the change in policy had been approved on February 1st. Weinberger and the Joint Chiefs of Staff had wanted to get the Marines out of their untenable position, but the President and Secretary of State George Shultz had been opposed—arguing that the removal of the Marines, even to an offshore position, would amount to a withdrawal that would give pause to all of our friends in the Middle East, and encourage our adversaries. They were assuaged, according to officials, by those parts of the withdrawal plan which changed the rules of engagement for the ships offshore and put in more training forces to work with what was left of the Lebanese Army. One official told me, "In the President's mind, if you just pull the Marines out and compensate for that in other ways you don't pull the rug out from Gemayel." The President, by a number of accounts, was fairly uninvolved in the planning process. (There are also questions about how carefully the decision to send the Marines in in the first place was considered.) Administration officials insisted that the announcement of the decision to withdraw the Marines was to have been made in any event the day after it was made, irrespective of what was happening in Lebanon, and that it was moved up one day because it began to leak to the press. They said that what the President did was different from what the House Democrats were considering (they had put off consideration after Gemayel's government came apart), because the Democrats wanted simply to pull the Marines out; in fact the draft House resolution would not have removed the offshore presence of the ships. I asked one official what use the Marines would be on the ships. He replied, "I can't explain that." (While all this was going on, Shultz was on a tour of Central and South America and, on the day of the President's announcement, arrived in Grenada, landing on the Cuban-built runway that the Administration had said was being built for military purposes; the former government of Grenada had said that it was intended for tourism. Shultz said, "Now the regime here is different. The airport is needed to carry planes . . . for tourists.") Washington, stunned by the swift series of events, is still sorting them out. The Marines are not out of Lebanon yet, and there is some worry that it may have been dangerous to announce their withdrawal before it was a fact. Within days, there was much confusion over just when the Marines would be withdrawn: Administration officials were saying the Marines might be in Lebanon for another four months, but when members of both parties hit the roof an official suggested the withdrawal might take one month. Weinberger said, "We are not leaving Lebanon. The Marines are being redeployed two or three miles to the west." The President remained secluded through all this. There were widespread concerns about the heavy firing from the ships—including extensive use of the sixteen-inch shells of the battleship *New Jersey*—and the implications of this for reaching a settlement in Lebanon, which some Middle East experts still do not rule out. When members of Congress objected that, under the War Powers Act, the Administration had been authorized only to fire to protect the Marines, the Administration, changing course, announced that that was now its policy. Inevitably, the political implications of the events were weighed: many people believe that Reagan was, once again, lucky—that these events had happened early enough in the year that they would be largely forgotten by the time of the election. But this was not the only foreign-policy matter that the Democrats would raise, nor was the matter closed. Whatever the politics of the situation, the facts were unpleasant. Two hundred and sixty-three servicemen had died in a futile cause. And the Administration, like Administrations before it, had undertaken a feckless military mission and by saying that United States prestige was involved in its success had made that so.

On Central America, the President, in his State of the Union speech, simply called on Congress to implement the report of the commission headed by Henry Kissinger, which was transformed in the speech into "the Henry Jackson Plan." Kissinger's name was not mentioned. This solves two problems: Kissinger, despite his own efforts, is still not beloved by all of the President's followers; and by naming the commission's report after the late Senator Jackson, a Democrat, the President reaches for bipartisan support. (Jackson had suggested that the commission be established, and he was a "counsellor" to it.) The commission, though bipartisan, was dominated by foreign-policy conservatives, and its report, issued January 11th, reflected the view that the problem in Central America is an East-West struggle, though it did also say that the problems there had local origins as well. It called for large increases in economic and military aid to Central America. At the insistence of some of its members, it recommended tying aid to El Salvador to progress in human rights—a policy that the President, through a veto, had rejected last year, and continues to resist. Now the Administration has extended indefinitely the military presence in Honduras, so the military "exercises" there have just officially ended.

In another part of his speech, the President dealt with what both parties think is an issue in 1984: which candidate is equipped to lead us into the future. Pollsters offer a number of explanations of why this question of leadership for the future arises. (It could be because the pollsters ask about it.) It is suggested that Reagan has provided such a dramatic break with the past that now the question is where we go from here; that people sense that the economy is undergoing a profound change and are uneasy; that people sense that the economic future is indeed cloudy. In any event, the President proposed, for "our next frontier," a permanently manned space station. The President's advisers explained that this would offer all manner of opportunities for commercial enterprise in space, for developing medicines, and so on. Echoing John F. Kennedy's call in 1961 for putting a man on the moon within the decade, Reagan said, "Tonight, I am directing NASA to develop a permanently manned space station, and to do it within a decade." The funding for the space station would come to a hundred million dollars in fiscal year 1985, and its total cost is officially estimated at eight billion dollars. But it is widely understood that the total cost of the project would be more on the order of twenty or thirty billion dollars. The space lab is a big new mission that NASA has been seeking for some time (the aerospace industry has been championing it as well), and for two years Stockman managed to keep it out of the budget. The President didn't say anything in his speech about his famous "Star Wars" proposal of last year, for an anti-missile system in space, which had become quite controversial. Yet funding for it continues, though not on as grand a scale as sought by the Pentagon; the scientific community is quite divided on it on both doctrinal and technical grounds.

One of the groups that the President's political advisers worry most about is women. The "gender gap" turned up in the 1980 election, and is believed to have grown since then. Women are affected by "the peace issue" but also by the Administration's apparent insensitivity to their concerns, which include economic questions as well as what are called "women's issues." (This is not true of all women, of course, and the President's political advisers have now developed a method of subdividing women into roughly sixty-four categories—among some of which the President gets a very high rating, and among some a very low one.) So there was a little bit for women in the State of the Union address: a statement that "in 1983, women filled seventy-three per cent of all new jobs in managerial, professional, and technical fields." This statistic was one of a number that the President used rather loosely: it included clerical jobs in these "fields." He also made a passing reference to "women's rights," and mentioned some other matters of concern to women: equal treatment in pension rights; day care; and enforcement of child-support payments. Despite all the fuss stirred up about hunger by Meese in the period just before Christmas, and the President's solemn vow then that he would not be satisfied "as long as there is one person in this country who is hungry," Reagan gave the subject only a glancing mention in his speech. In early January, the commission he had appointed to look into the matter reported—as had been expected, given its composition— that the problem was not very serious.

And there was in the speech a little bit for environmentalists, whose opposition to Reagan Administration policies has been made into a politically dangerous force. (And many environmentalists are independent voters, whose support Reagan needs in order to win.) William Clark, since he took over as Secretary of the Interior last November, has succeeded in defanging the movement somewhat by reversing a number of Watt's policies and getting rid of some of his most controversial appointees. In his speech, Reagan said that he would request for the Environmental Protection Agency "one of the largest percentage budget increases of any agency;" in fact, the E.P.A. budget would still be ten per cent less than it was before Reagan took office. The President also proposed doubling funds for the research program for acid rain—which still leaves the Administration without a program to deal with acid rain. William Ruckelshaus, the head of the E.P.A., and a progressive Republican whose appointment to the agency last March was intended to help Reagan politically, had sought a funding increase of twice the size that the President proposed, and had lost a fight with the Office of Management and Budget to proceed with a program to deal with acid rain. (When Reagan named Ruckelshaus to the job, he said that controlling acid rain should be of high priority.) Nevertheless, the President made it appear that he was doing more for the E.P.A. than he was, and, for good measure, Ruckelshaus was invited to observe the State of the Union speech from the gallery where the First Lady sits—even though in meetings the President gets Ruckelshaus confused with Donald Rumsfeld, the special Middle East envoy.

The most striking thing about the President's speech, beyond its politics, was its pyrotechnical display of Reagan's rhetorical devices and skills. It's not simply the husky voice speaking practicedly into the microphone—making a much greater impression on the viewer at home, at whom it is aimed, than on the people in the House chamber, who are props. It's more Reagan's unique use of language and his patented uplift tone. He is George M. Cohan

and Gary Cooper: "America is back—standing tall." Reagan's
stories have happy endings; no problems are daunting. The analogy with the movies he used to play in is irresistible. He tells a
story that people want to hear. Reagan's is a melodramatic, heroic
prose that other politicians would blush to use, but he gets away
with it, because in his case it is authentic. He is a throwback figure
out of the fifties, a time when problems seemed simpler and
America's military might was unchallenged. He invokes God and
the flag again and again, and he aligns himself foursquare with
the family. He shamelessly appropriates heroes, but there is no
reason to doubt that he relishes the heroic tales he tells so often.
For the State of the Union speech, there was Sergeant Stephen
Trujillo, a Ranger medic, who was seated in the front row of the
First Lady's gallery, next to Reagan's daughter Maureen, and
whose heroism in the invasion of Grenada Reagan described. (For-
tunately, the hero had a Hispanic surname, and the deed was
done in Grenada, which has been a political plus for Reagan, and
not in Lebanon. There were no parents of the Marines who died
in Lebanon in the gallery.) Two years ago, Reagan had sitting in
the gallery, and paid homage to, Lenny Skutnik, a young government worker who had dived into an icy Potomac River to help
rescue a victim of an airplane crash.

Presidents, as a breed, are wont to boast of their achievements
and give themselves good grades and, from time to time, stretch
the facts; but Reagan throws around questionable numbers to a
degree that may be unprecedented. He dazzles with his statistics,
and he grins and glides away from problems with more agility
than any other President in memory. Reagan understands the
importance of having a vision and stating it forcefully, and knows
that this can be far more powerful than the facts. People who
intrude with the facts are "doomsayers" and "handwringers," who
must be ignored. Now it is clear that this is what the President
really believes. The fascinating thing about Reagan is that he
seems at once to have a very shrewd understanding of what he is
doing with his rhetoric and to deeply believe what he is saying;
there is no disconnection, and therefore he comes off as without
artifice. (We knew when Johnson and Nixon and Carter were
faking it.) Reagan's acting skills are of great value to him in his
Presidency, but much of what he does is beyond acting: he is
speaking from conviction, not simply from a script. This is part of
his power. He also understands the importance of repetition, of

stating a case over and over until it becomes a "fact." He has painted such a dark picture so often of the national situation before he took office that it has become a received truth. (He makes the economic situation worse than it was, and, to hear him tell it, the United States was unilaterally disarming, when in fact every leg of the defense triad—land, sea, and air—was being strengthened.) But this is shrewd, too. How many politicians want to stand up and defend Jimmy Carter? Reagan will run against Carter, big spending, and government. He will have no hesitation in running against government, even though he will have been heading it for nearly four years; he did the same thing in 1970, when he ran for reelection as governor of California, successfully.

XII

FEBRUARY 13

MANCHESTER, NEW HAMPSHIRE. Once again, in defiance of all logic or proportion, the New Hampshire primary has assumed a position of great importance in the Democratic contest for the Presidential nomination. The Democratic Party tried to push New Hampshire back and make it take its place among other contests, where it would matter less, but the state, protective of its momentary prominence and mindful of the lucrativeness of holding a contest to which so much attention is paid, resisted. And so, two weeks from tomorrow, on February 28th, the state will hold the second contest for the nomination, following the Iowa precinct caucuses by eight days. At long last, the voters will be heard from. Walter Mondale and his campaign aides will find out whether, after more than three years of planning, thousands of meetings, uncounted phone calls and miles on the road, they have been right. As of now, Mondale is comfortably ahead of his opponents in the polls, and his people are expecting a very large victory in Iowa, and a victory here—but they are tense. Part of it is simply the fact that reality is upon them; part of it is the skittishness that comes from knowing that, no matter how many things they have thought of, how many eventualities they have anticipated, how many resources they have thrown into assuring the first two victories, something could go wrong. The attacks on Mondale by the other candidates, which have increased in frequency and stridency and have been directed at his character rather than at differences on the issues; the possibility of something going off the rails in the debates; the approaching "expectations" game, in which the results are judged not as facts in themselves but in terms of the expectations, mysteriously arrived at, of how the candidates should have done—all these are beyond the Mondale people's control and could waylay their plans.

New Hampshire is the kind of state that makes people—especially front-runners—nervous. In 1952, when New Hampshire

first put the candidates' names on the ballot and thrust itself into
the big time (this was also the first year of television coverage of
political campaigns), Estes Kefauver upset President Truman
here. In 1968, Lyndon Johnson won the New Hampshire primary—with a write-in vote, at that—yet Eugene McCarthy, who
received forty-two per cent of the vote, was deemed the "winner."
In 1972, Edmund Muskie won it, with forty-six per cent of the
vote, yet George McGovern, who received thirty-seven per cent of
the vote, was deemed the winner. New Hampshire is the pro-
genitor of what might be known as the "B.T.E. factor"—a candidate's doing "better than expected." A kind of circular process
goes on here: the results of the New Hampshire contest receive
disproportionate attention because of where it comes in the calendar, and, because of that attention, the candidates put a disproportionate amount of their energy and resources into the contest.
New Hampshire sends only twenty-two delegates to the Democratic Convention, or about one-half of one per cent of the total,
and has a tiny Democratic Party (there are about a hundred and
thirty-four thousand registered Democrats), which is unrepresen-
tative of the Democratic Party as a whole—it has a higher income
and far fewer minorities and is more conservative. (An unpredictable number of independents also vote in the Democratic primary.) Moreover, New Hampshire has the lowest unemployment
rate in the country. Many of the people in the more populous
southern part of the state work in the high-tech companies in
Boston but live in New Hampshire, because it has no state income
or sales taxes. High-tech industry is also growing in the southern
part of the state itself. New Hampshire's place in the calendar and
the attention given it are presumed to have an overflow effect on
subsequent contests. Whether the presumption is parent to, or
coincidental with, the reality that since 1952 no one has become
President who did not win the New Hampshire primary, no one
can be sure. In 1976, Jimmy Carter won the primary here (barely)
and was propelled to the nomination because twenty-three thousand people voted for him. New Hampshire is a difficult state to
campaign in: Its voters have come to take it for granted that they
will be wooed on a virtual one-to-one basis by the candidates and
tend to be diffident; they hold back on their commitments, producing a large, and nerve-racking, undecided vote until very late
in the game. The voters are scattered in a number of medium-

sized and small towns throughout the state—places that are often not easily accessible in the winter. The state is so conservative and Republican that the Democratic nominee, who probably spends more time here than anywhere else during the fight for the nomination, doesn't bother to come back for the general election.

The Mondale people are leaving as little to chance here (and in Iowa) as possible. Every night, the campaign makes about fifteen thousand telephone calls in the two states combined, to see how its candidate is doing, how the other candidates are doing, what sorts of changes in the candidates' relative support are occurring. From the phone calls, it is determined where foot canvassers should be sent. While Mondale is doing well in the phone canvassing (and did well in the Mondale campaign's recent poll in New Hampshire), one thing the campaign finds perturbing is that the number of people who say they are undecided or refuse to cite a preference is very high. The most recent Boston *Globe* poll of New Hampshire had Mondale at forty-two per cent, John Glenn at nineteen, Jesse Jackson at ten, Gary Hart at eight, and the rest— Alan Cranston, Fritz Hollings, George McGovern, and Reubin Askew—behind them. The Mondale campaign's most recent private poll has Mondale at thirty-seven, Glenn at eighteen, Jackson at eight, and Hart at four. Still, in Iowa the campaign believes it has identified about sixty thousand people who are definitely for Mondale and plan to go to the caucuses. So the Mondale people believe that they are approaching a very big victory there, and their only concern is that the turnout will be low and the press will discount the victory as having taken place amid apathy. The campaign is planning a new ad, stressing the importance of attending the caucuses. The plain fact is that there are no searing issues within the Democratic Party this year; the policy disagreements are marginal. This year is not like 1968 or 1972, when the Vietnam War divided the Party; it is not like 1980, when Edward Kennedy, a major force within the Party, tried to unseat Carter. Even in 1976, a relatively peaceful year, there were stronger divisions within the Party than there are now. Part of Mondale's strength thus far is that there is more consensus within the Party than in a very long time and that he appears to represent that consensus. (It had been one of the assumptions of his strategists all along that this consensus would exist.) The other candidates' failure to find a big issue, or to catch on as yet, has driven most of them to go after Mondale in a personal way that seems without precedent. Glenn, who has been running second to Mondale but whose position in the race has been slipping and whose campaign has been floundering, has led the attack, but some of the others—in particular, Hart and Cranston—have recently joined in. Hollings and Askew have taken their whacks at Mondale as well. Jackson has been off in his own universe, but in attacking as he has the rules of the nomination contest he is challenging the legitimacy of the process by which Mondale is leading. Only McGovern has tried to play the role of pacifier. "Sometimes front-runners get nominated," he cautioned his colleagues during the debate at Dartmouth on January 15th.

The gist of the collective criticism is that Mondale is the tool of the "special interests," and has made more promises than he can keep. Hart gave a speech in Council Bluffs, Iowa, last week in which there were a number of targets—Reagan, the press, the Democrats in Congress, the "political establishment"—but the biggest blows were aimed at Mondale. Attacking Mondale, though not by name, for offering "a leadership based on calculation and caution," he criticized him for caution on Lebanon, on Grenada, and on the Vietnam War: "The pattern is always there, caution until consensus forms." And he criticized him for citing disagreements with Jimmy Carter only on unpopular policies. He also attacked the Party "establishment" for "dictating" rules that favored Mondale (they would also have favored Kennedy or any other strong contender, and the Hart people have a theory on how they could actually help Hart); the "special interests" for throwing resources behind Mondale; and all those who say the race is already over. Today, in Atlanta, Glenn, referring to the president of the A.F.L.-C.I.O., said, "What does Lane Kirkland think he's buying with his twenty million dollars—a President who will never disagree with the A.F.L.-C.I.O.?" (The twenty-million-dollar figure is one that the Glenn people have put out; the A.F.L.-C.I.O. isn't saying how much it is spending on the Mondale campaign, and neither are the Mondale people.) Glenn was shown saying this on television tonight, and two networks ran stories about Mondale's continuing to "duck" the question, posed by Hart in Saturday's debate, sponsored by the Des Moines *Register*, about when he had ever disagreed with the A.F.L.-C.I.O., or organized labor, on an issue. Mondale's response then was not particularly deft (he said, "As a matter of fact, they came to me in support of my proposals . . . This was not the case of a deal, of my agreeing to do something for them"), and his evasion of the question was noticeable. Last fall, in an interview with me, he cited his opposition to the B-1 bomber and the MX missile, both of which labor supported, but he has taken the general position that he is not going to go around pointing out his differences with the groups supporting him. The "promises" issue is not so clear-cut—his opponents don't actually cite many specifics, and most of them have pledged to do good things, too—nor is the "special interests" issue. Many of his opponents sought the same endorsements that they now criticize.

Yet Mondale has invited some of the problems. He *is* cautious, which has its advantages and disadvantages; he is disinclined to take a step until he is certain he knows the terrain very well, and has had the advice of experts. Mondale is a great admirer of expertise, which can cause him to be knowledgeable, make sound proposals, and all that, but which can also suffocate instincts and blur the focus. He hasn't seemed to give people enough to hang on to; he seems at times to be coasting through because the polls indicate that he can. Perhaps if he had shown more edge on something, he wouldn't be under attack on so many other things. His ads have no bite; they are designed to assure that Mondale is experienced. The special-interests/promises criticism might have been tempered not by any great strategic change (or by, as some urged, a stagy going before a group that supported him and saying he disagreed with it) but by subtle shadings of style. Mondale's natural, long-honed political style is to persuade people to believe that he agrees with them, and he may now be paying a price for that. He has responses to the criticisms, but he hasn't got them across. He has, as he has said, told some of his supporters things they didn't necessarily want to hear, but it has been sotto-voce, and so surrounded by agreeable things that the point of difference hasn't come through. He is proposing to raise taxes, but, rather than make a virtue of this facing up to reality, he has approached the campaign thus far as if he were not going to do anything that would be difficult on anyone—except the rich. (In fact, his tax program would affect everyone with an income over twenty-five thousand dollars.) Mondale's approach is to build the support now—get a "mandate"—and, using the support he has built, conduct the hard transactions later. And, unlike most people who run for President, he has a theory about carrying the campaign into governing. The question is whether it is in him to conduct those hard transactions; he firmly believes that it is, and he has been too close to a paralyzed President to want to have a similar experience. But gathering the support of groups on the ground that you will protect their interests can make you a hostage to their next demands. Mondale has understood all along that the special-interests issue is really a question about his strength.

Mondale's campaign strategists have been preoccupied with a large number of matters, in addition to deciding how, or whether, to respond to the attacks. When I visited James Johnson, Mondale's campaign chairman, in his Washington office last week, one of the decisions that had just been made was to ignore Hart's Council Bluffs speech, so as not to build him up. Last year, before the shape of the campaign became at all clear, the Mondale people were somewhat concerned about Hart—worried that he could make his "old generation-new generation" and "old ideas-new ideas" argument stick, and could build strong grass-roots organizations for the early contests. But the Mondale people believe that they succeeded in forcing Hart into a national contest, in which he seemed to be going nowhere, and only lately has there been a bit of a flurry in the press suggesting that he was on the move in New Hampshire. (The recent poll taken by the Mondale people in New Hampshire indicated that this was not the case.) For a number of reasons, the Mondale people prefer Glenn as a target: Glenn has not proved himself a very adroit combatant, and in taking him on one is not taking on any of the activist segments of the Party; going against Glenn is best suited to the appeal that Mondale is trying to make, and, moreover, the Mondale people value the fact that in many instances they can take on Glenn and Reagan at the same time. Besides, all the polls have Glenn in second place.

Characteristically, Johnson was thinking about a great many short-range and long-range strategic questions at once: how to assure a sufficient turnout in Iowa, and how to build the impact of the expected victory there; how to refine Mondale's message for New Hampshire—to make it clear he will stand up for the average family, and protect it on taxes, the environment, and retirement, and to attack Glenn's tax program on the ground that it would cost middle-income people more than Mondale's would, and that it was not as progressive as Mondale's, and would not take as much from corporations or the wealthy. I asked Johnson, an unusually calm person, whether there was anything in particular he was worried about. He replied, "Sure, I worry about everything. But I can't say how I think it can go wrong. In Iowa, we look stronger and stronger. New Hampshire looks stable, but I don't rule out a loss there; you can't rule it out."

The strategy of seeking endorsements is still proceeding. Mondale recently received the endorsement of Robert Strauss and of House Speaker Thomas P. O'Neill, who departed from his prior practice in making the endorsement. These endorsements were taken as a sign that major Party figures thought the race was over—which was the intended effect. Mondale was also endorsed by Wilson Goode, the mayor of Philadelphia, and a black; Mondale is trying to gather all the black support he can, to counteract Jesse Jackson. Mondale had helped Goode raise funds for his mayoralty race, last November. He was recently endorsed by Joseph Brennan, the governor of Maine, and by George Mitchell, Maine's Democratic senator. The Maine caucuses will occur on March 4th, and these endorsements were intended to solidify the lead the Mondale people assume that they have, as a result of their successful efforts in a straw poll there last fall. Mondale was also endorsed recently by Governor William O'Neill, of Connecticut, which holds its primary on March 27th. And in late January Mondale won public commitments from seventy-three of the hundred and sixty-four House Democrats who were selected as delegates to the Convention, in July. (The Mondale people say they have private commitments from twenty-seven other members.) Many of these endorsements were made on the grounds that Mondale is the best candidate and a winner, of course, but it is also true that Mondale's years of travel on behalf of other politicians, and raising money for them, are paying off. From February, 1981, until November of 1982, he maintained his own political-action committee, which financed his travel and enabled him to make contributions to others—and win gratitude. Johnson spends a great deal of time studying the other candidates' schedules, which he keeps on his desk, to see what they can tell him about the others' strategies, and to counteract where he can, by placement of ads and reconsidering Mondale's schedule. Johnson says, "I spend most of my day thinking, I wonder why they did that, why they said that, why they were in Cedar Rapids instead of Ottumwa."

Long range, the Mondale campaign is focussing on what it assumes will be its eventual race against Reagan, and is consciously developing issues now that it thinks will help it in the fall. A lot of thought has also gone into the Convention, which the Mondale people feel must present a harmonious picture to the public: the 1972 Convention, where the forces backing Hubert Humphrey were still fighting George McGovern, offered a disastrous picture; the harmonious 1976 Convention gave a real boost to Jimmy Carter's campaign; the 1980 Convention, where Edward Kennedy and Carter were still fighting, was one of the many things that did not help Carter in the fall. According to Johnson, Mondale is trying to keep relations with the other candidates as pleasant as possible under the circumstances. (Mondale passed up a planned trip into Ohio, which had been designed to shake up Glenn.) The Mondale people keep in touch with a lot of supporters of the other candidates—people who went along with those candidates for home-state reasons but might come over when the others drop out—and have maintained contact with Jackson on the questions of the Party rules and voter registration, among other things, in order to keep a line open to him in the hope of making peace later. And, of course, they are thinking about who should be on the ticket with Mondale as the Vice-Presidential nominee. As for the criticism that the other candidates are levelling at Mondale, Johnson says that if the Democrats hold a harmonious Convention, then, once the fall campaign begins and "we get down to whether Mondale or Reagan is elected, all this will seem as from the nineteenth century." The Mondale people are also encouraged by the fact that the criticisms have caused no perceptible drop in Mondale's standing in the polls. But first the Mondale people have New Hampshire to worry about.

Charles Campion, an engaging twenty-eight-year-old Bostonian from a political family, has been living in New Hampshire since December 15, 1982, running the Mondale effort here. Campion worked for Mondale when Mondale was Vice-President. He was the first to set up shop here for a Democratic candidate. He says, "Jim Johnson knew from Day One that New Hampshire would be important in the end—even before we knew that New Hampshire would still be early. He recognized it's come down to New Hampshire many times, and the press is used to coming here." Campion continues, "To do well in New Hampshire, you have to be a presence here, become part of it. I've probably been out of the state ten days since I came here. And there hasn't been a month since the campaign began that Mr. Mondale wasn't here at least one day. And his wife, Joan, was here often, too." Joan Mondale has become an accomplished campaigner, and has been making a major effort. Campion says, "The other political point about New Hampshire is that its historic role has given people here a sophistication about the political process and the personalities of the people around the candidates, and they're very, very wary of outsiders. People think I'm from New Hampshire now." (Campion's deputy, Kathi Rogers, is an experienced New Hampshire political organizer.) Campion explains that New Hampshire has its own set of unwritten rules governing what one does and does not do when campaigning here—having to do with the way one talks to people, the amount of time one must spend listening, places one must go. One must start out in the right living rooms, with the right people gathered, or all can be lost. Campion says, "You have to let people know you're going to take them seriously and participate fully here."

Most Democratic campaigns start off with all the candidates running around the state talking to the same three hundred-some activists, signing them up. Which prominent activists have signed up with whom is very big news in New Hampshire. The fact that Hart signed up Jeanne Shaheen, a respected political organizer, who ran the Carter effort here in 1980, is one of the reasons he is believed to have a good organization here. (Mondale got some of the people who might have been for Alan Cranston by promising to help them with future fund-raising efforts.) Campion says that the Mondale campaign has reached ninety-two thousand five hundred homes by phone. Campion, coining a new term, says, "We household it. We're literally finding out how everyone in the house feels; it often takes several calls." It is now a standard campaign technique to identify voters by degree of support. The ranking goes: 1, absolutely committed; 2, committed but shaky; 3, undecided; 4, committed to another candidate. Campion says, "Now we're trying to make 2s and 3s into 1s, and we're even going after the 4s; usually you forget the 4s. It's said that our support is soft.

Our opponents' support is much softer than ours—so, basically, we're out there talking to everybody."

Labor, though it is not a large force in the state, is helping Mondale here—making calls and sending mailings to its members and trying to get out its voters. For its national effort, labor has also made films about Mondale, which have been shown at meetings. Lane Kirkland has made appearances with Mondale at regional labor meetings. Labor is helpful in other ways: it leases its phone banks to the Mondale organization, thus saving the Mondale group the cost of setting them up, and, in some places, leases its office space. There have been charges, particularly by the Glenn campaign, that the Mondale camp is being charged less than fair market value for the use of the phones and the headquarters, and that therefore the election laws are being violated, but so far nothing has come of this. The labor efforts are a new factor in the nomination contest. Individual unions backed one candidate or another in the past, but this time Kirkland took a gamble that he could unite the A.F.L.-C.I.O. behind one candidate, and assure a nominee who would be sympathetic to labor—as he felt that George McGovern and Jimmy Carter were not. (What the A.F.L.-C.I.O. would have done if Edward Kennedy, who has also been close to labor, had run is a puzzle.) Labor is throwing its resources into the early contests in the hope of getting the nomination over with soon.

FEBRUARY 14

The Westside Community Center. At one-thirty, about sixty elderly people are here, playing bingo. Antoinette McNally, who is in charge of this city-run program, wishes them a Happy Valentine's Day. Fritz Hollings is expected shortly. I ask one of the women whether any of the other candidates have been here, and, eliding a few elections, she says that Hart and Barry Goldwater have. A Hollings aide arrives with a huge blue-and-white Hollings poster, some red-white-and-blue bunting, and some carnations. In a few minutes, Hollings arrives, accompanied only by an aide and the Secret Service and a couple of reporters. Hollings has been concentrating his efforts on New Hampshire, to try to show that he has Northern support, and appears to be waging a rather lonely campaign; his candidacy has been generally written off. Hollings' problem goes beyond the fact that he has a deep Southern accent and a voice that seems to go down rather than out and sometimes is difficult to understand, or that he has a mean streak that he seems unable to contain. (In the Dartmouth debate, irritated with Askew at one point, he said to Askew, who has a facial tic, "You've got a tic in your ear, too.") His problem seems to be that he has no political base and no particular strategy for establishing one. Hollings is not alone among politicians in having a high estimation of himself, or in taking a look at others who have run for, or been, President and figuring that he is at least as well qualified. He is a smart man, with a quick mind and a sharp wit, but there is a certain lack of discipline to him; one can never be sure what is going to come out of his mouth when he is riled—and he easily is. He is capable of personal kindness and thoughtfulness, and is an interesting man to talk to, but his great pride and good opinion of himself and the mean streak do not make for a warm public persona. Moreover, one cannot simply decide that one is smart and go out and run for President and get very far; one has to build a base, have a long-sighted strategy. Jimmy Carter decided he was as smart as or smarter than the rest of them, but he and his advisers had a very long-sighted strategy, which included the building of a coalition to win the nomination.

Hollings, arriving at the community center, looks ruddy and well. He has, as usual, ramrod bearing (he attended the Citadel), and his distinguished white hair is a bit in need of a cut. I ask him why he doesn't look tired. He replies, "There's some hope. People are beginning to focus in on the campaign. They're listening about the budget and the economy." Hollings has been preaching fiscal prudence, and arguing that the Democrats have lost a number of elections because they didn't convince people that they could handle the economy. Hollings' main proposal is for a freeze on all federal spending. He tells the bingo group, "I came to wish you a Happy Valentine's Day. All the candidates love you now, and we'll promise you anything." But, he continues, "we're not paying our bills." He says, "I'm the candidate who comes around and not only talks of a nuclear freeze—because we're all fearful of a nuclear holocaust—but I'm the candidate who talks about a budget freeze also." He says that his proposal would save a hundred billion dollars. He tells the group, "If we'd sacrifice a little today, we can have a much brighter tomorrow. Unfortunately, we're all coming around and talking to you, but we're not ready to do that." He tells the people here he hopes they'll be for him on the twenty-eighth, and concludes, "Happy Valentine's Day. We love you all." The audience seems pleased with this courtly-seeming, handsome man.

As Hollings starts to go around the room to greet people, Mrs. McNally asks him to call a bingo game, and declares that this is to be a "shotgun" game, meaning that all the numbers on a card must be covered. Hollings has no choice but to go along, and—interminably, it seems—he spins the wire cage again and again, pulling out the balls with the numbers on them. He does it sportingly, joking about his accent—"n" comes out as a two-syllable word ("ayun")—until at last someone gets bingo. Then Hollings, released at last from his unexpected duty, circles the room and hands out carnations.

DERRY. Gary Hart is addressing a group of about a hundred people, most of them young, at the Westside Community Center, in this town southeast of Manchester. Hart now has a substantial entourage. The singer Carole King is campaigning with him here. (Paul Newman campaigned with Mondale in New Hampshire last week.) Hart, a slim, youthful-looking man with chiselled features, a full head of brown hair, and hazel eyes, stands before the group, one hand in a pocket, John F. Kennedy–like. "This is a crucial election for this country's future," he says. On foreign policy, he says, "It is about whether this country will stand for a foreign policy that gives us as Americans something to be proud of other than just our invasions." He talks of the importance of cleaning up acid rain, of protecting the environment, of "putting millions of Americans back to work." He talks of the importance of "open and aggressive trade policies, and not protectionism." Unlike Mondale and Glenn, he opposes "domestic content" legislation, backed by labor, which would require that all cars sold in the United States contain a certain percentage of United States parts and labor. He talks about "the increasingly scandalous and corrupt tax code," and about arms control. He speaks crisply and rather quietly, making no attempt to arouse emotion. He talks about the necessity "of caring for our elderly, of caring for our young, of providing decent housing, decent education, job training, the kind of modern and growing economy that this nation desperately needs in the nineteen-eighties." He says that "we cannot balance the disastrous Reagan deficits so long as we're pouring tens of billions of dollars unnecessarily into MX missiles and B-1 bombers and nuclear weapons." Thus far, his ideas and his goals are not unlike Mondale's. But then he says, "This election is not just between the Democrats and the Republicans. It's not just between liberals and conservatives. It's between the future and the past." He is staking out a nonideological position, but this also reflects his politics. He says, "You can send a signal to the rest of this country that suggests we are tired of the politics of the past, we are tired of the politics of special arrangements and old arrangements and old deals, of special-interest groups and political-action-committee money." (Both Hart and Mondale have rejected PAC contributions to their campaigns.) He says, "We want reforms of our military institutions. We want a strong defense, but one that is effective, and not just expensive." Hart has taken as his own the idea of "military reform," which means finding ways to get more value for military expenditures, and getting more maneuverability through simpler weapons; he did not invent the idea, but he has spent a lot of time on it. "We want to take our tax dollars away from nuclear weapons systems," he says. "It is vitally important that we elect a candidate who is not beholden to a collection of special interests."

In the debates, in which Hart has done well, and in his campaign, Hart has been asserting that he is the candidate of "new ideas," but his ideas are not always particularly novel or striking. He does back an American Defense Education Act, which would provide funds to improve the teaching of math, science, languages, and technology. The proposed program was in fact drafted by the National Education Association. Mondale, who has been endorsed by the N.E.A., declined to back the program, and proposed a broader one of his own. Hart has also proposed what he calls individual training accounts, which would have workers and employers make tax-deductible contributions to a fund to provide retraining and relocation. (He has not made much of this proposal until lately, and it is not the subject of any of his many position papers.) The difference between Hart and the other candidates is less substantive than stylistic. Hart is forty-seven; Mondale is fifty-six. (Hart's official biography said he was a year younger, and when questions arose about this Hart said, "It's whatever the records say. It's no big deal.") However, Hart and Mondale are from different political generations, and different political

traditions. Mondale comes from Minnesota progressive liberalism; Hart's is a more rootless heritage—he moved to Colorado
shortly before he entered politics, and his political style was
formed in the seventies, when the winds were shifting. He talks
favorably about the liberal agenda, but it never seems to be at the
core of his concerns; he is cool and deliberately modern. Hart is
actually hard to locate; he seems to be inventing himself. A couple
of years ago, he identified himself with a group known as "neo-
liberals" (Hart told me that he disliked the term), which was
searching for various ways to break with the Party's past. He has
been part of the group of "Atari Democrats," fascinated, perhaps
excessively, with the potential of high tech for restoring the economy. (One of Hart's television ads even has digital-looking print.)
Yet he cannot run for the nomination of the Democratic Party
disavowing all the Party's traditions; digital politics is not enough.
The questions raised by Mondale's relationship with the Democratic interest groups have been explored, but there are also questions about Hart's—and Glenn's—lack of relationship with them,
and their expressed hostility to the role of those groups in the
campaign. Jimmy Carter ran saying (not quite accurately), "I owe
the special interests nothing," and his inability to deal with these
groups was one of the reasons he couldn't govern effectively.
Hart's campaign appears to be aimed at the young and the upper
middle class: trendy. (Hart did have labor support in his Senate
campaigns.) But these groups don't encompass the base of the
Democratic Party. So his candidacy raises two questions: Can a
Democrat win the election without the support of blue-collar
voters, and could a Democratic President who did not have a
working relationship with the Party's interest groups govern? The
Democratic Party has been through class warfare before, to no
good end. (In an interview I had with Hart last year, he tried to
make a distinction between "special interests" and "narrow interests," and said that "the danger isn't women or labor." But he
seems to have dropped the distinction.)

Hart is not in the habit of working in concert with others; like
Glenn, he is pretty much of a loner in the Senate. Even those who
know him best say that they do not know him well. He is a man of
some charm, but not warmth. (Hart grew up poor in Kansas, in
the strict discipline of the Church of the Nazarene—no movies, no
dancing, a rigid dress code. His name used to be Hartpence, but

he changed it in 1961, when he changed his career goals—leaving the Yale Divinity School and entering Yale Law School, headed for politics.) All politicians are driven, but some soften their edges more than others; Hart's edges show. Last year, he tried to run his campaign essentially by himself. He wavered in his themes: at one point his focus was on appealing to the women's vote. Now he is said to be more amenable to advice. A key adviser of late is Patrick Caddell, the pollster, who worked with Hart when Hart managed the McGovern Presidential campaign in 1972, but had had a somewhat strained relationship with him in recent times. (McGovern and Hart have a very strained relationship; McGovern resents the distance that Hart has put between himself and McGovern when this has seemed politically exigent—as do others who were involved in the 1972 campaign.) Caddell, who is thirty-three, has a brilliant, imaginative mind, and has his own theory, which he has tested by some polling, of what the electorate is seeking: someone not identified with the past; someone who comes across as new, with bold and innovative ideas, who will, as it happens, call for a new generation of leadership and for sacrifice, and who will run an anti-establishment campaign. And Caddell has a strong dislike for Mondale. In a long paper Caddell wrote last fall (when he was still hoping a new candidate would enter the race), he set forth a case that the Party is essentially liberal to moderate, and populist, pro-"new ideas," and anti-establishment—and that no candidate had positioned himself to take advantage of this. He also said that there is a "fault line" between the Party establishment and everyone else in the Party. And he said that the possibility that the "baby boom" generation, which has tended to stay away from the polls, would begin to vote in large numbers made it the potentially decisive voting group.

One of the reasons for Caddell's feelings about Mondale was Mondale's telling me in 1979, after Carter's famous retreat to Camp David to reexamine his Presidency, that he thought Caddell's diagnosis that the country was suffering from a "malaise," which led to Carter's "crisis of the spirit" speech, was "crazy." Mondale's repetition, last fall, of that point of disagreement with Carter did not help matters. (Nor did the Mondale campaign's saying it had not offered Caddell a job as its pollster.) Beyond that, Caddell is unsympathetic, to say the least, toward Mondale's political style—and was when Mondale was Vice-President and Caddell was Carter's pollster. Caddell's and Mondale's temperaments are utterly different. Mondale is linear, programmatic; Caddell is non-linear, thematic. Mondale is contained, inward; Caddell is emotional, even explosive. Caddell shopped around for an alternative candidate to Mondale—he hoped that Senator Dale Bumpers, of Arkansas, would enter, and advised him for a while, and he was involved in the near-entry, early this year, in the New Hampshire primary of Senator Joseph Biden, of Delaware—and when no one else entered the race he decided to help Hart, who had turned to him for advice at the end of the year. At that point, Hart seemed to be going nowhere. Hart read Caddell's paper, and Caddell began to help him sharpen his themes, make new ads, and prepare for the Dartmouth debate.

During the question period that follows Hart's talk here, Hart says that he favors proposals to simplify the tax code, including one along the lines of a proposal made by Senator Bill Bradley, Democrat of New Jersey, and Representative Richard Gephardt, Democrat of Missouri, but says that his proposal would have more tax brackets, to make it more progressive. (Under the Bradley-Gephardt proposal, all but a few deductions would be eliminated, and people would pay according to three brackets. The plan would not increase revenues.) Hart tells the audience that under his proposal from eighty to eighty-five per cent of the people would pay no more taxes than they do now. He also mentions a form of a consumption tax, which would tax spending and reward savings and investment. (Critics say that this would put the greater burden on those who are not in a position to save.) The Bradley-Gephardt proposal and the consumption tax are utterly different approaches; Hart has wavered between them for some time. Hart speaks with clarity and intelligence, but he does not get applause unless he encourages it.

I have an interview with Hart as he is driven from Derry to Concord, his next stop. I begin by asking him how he assesses his own situation as of now.

He replies, "There is clearly a movement of some substantial proportions in our direction—not only here but in Iowa and around the country." He continues, "One thing leads to another. It's kind of a never-ending cycle. The better you do, the better the press; the better the press, the better you do."

I ask Hart why he thinks that that is happening now, and he says that this is the time when people look at the candidates intensively, and that he had always thought that it would happen at this point, and that "people began to analyze the race the way I've always felt they would—that is, between the Party's future and its past, not between its left and its right." He points out that the debates are "levelling events," putting the front-runners on the same footing as the others, and says, "I, as I felt that I would, did well in those." He continues, "The front-runners don't look extraordinarily better than anyone else, and in the case of Senator Glenn probably worse. And in the case of Vice-President Mondale—he consistently gets by by just not making a mistake."

I ask Hart if there have been any changes in his approach.

He replies, "Yes, but it was all conscious, purposeful, and planned. I set out, when I announced, to lay an issues base—spend as much time as it took across the country and in the early primary and caucus states to lay out my economics, lay out my defense and military-reform policies, arms-control and foreign policies, issues on education, and the rest. That takes a long time. It's done in the living rooms in Iowa and New Hampshire. It's done in apartments in New York and back yards in Beverly Hills. It's letting people know who you are, but, first of all, in my case, laying out what I think. And as a result of that I got dubbed the candidate of issues or ideas and dismissed, almost. That's exactly what I wanted to be known as." In a dig at McGovern, he says that in 1972 the Party had a candidate "against the war in Vietnam who then tried to put the economics and other foreign policy and military policy together, to some grief." Hart says, "But I had always planned by some time toward the end of '83 and in the early part of '84 to shift to a kind of thematic summary of those ideas—having recruited what activists I could on the ideas and the issues—and then to begin to condense and consolidate the message into a set of themes having to do with the past and the future, the old politics and the new politics, the generational change, the period of transition that we're in, and how, essentially, the politics of the past of both parties is increasingly irrelevant to the problems of our time. People sort of wandered into that transition cold—a lot of observers—and, ironically, all of a sudden I began to read stories about 'Hart's only talking in generalities. He has no new ideas.' So I finally struck a balance about four weeks ago in which I delivered the thematic speech and punctuated it with specific ideas, like the individual training account or, for example, a freeze on plutonium." He continues, "The other rap on me was that I was cold and aloof, and not a good campaigner. And I kept telling people I don't know how they thought I got elected twice in Colorado if I was so cold and aloof. I meet and greet people as well as any other candidate in this race. Better than most. And I think reporters see that and they say, 'Well, this guy's not cold and aloof. He's changed.' They could not have been wrong, so they say I've changed." And he says, "And then, finally, I see Glenn and Cranston declining very quickly. That caused the vacuum to be formed among those who are looking for an alternative to Fritz Mondale, and I think that clearly I'm the best qualified to fill that. I think that's happening. I said over a year ago that this would become a contest between Fritz and myself. And I'm more convinced than ever that that's going to be the case."

I ask Hart if he is concerned that the intra-Party debate might damage Mondale in the general election if Mondale is the nominee.

He replies, "I can only account for myself. What I've tried to do is establish a contrast more of political style than of character. When I criticize Fritz's caution on Lebanon and Grenada or Vietnam, it's really to contrast approach to public policy—in this case, mostly in the foreign-policy area, but that's increasingly important. To suggest that some in this society and in politics—in public office—learned the lessons of Vietnam, others didn't." Hart expresses some anger that the A.F.L.-C.I.O. is pouring such large resources into the attempt to elect Mondale, and his annoyance is understandable. He says he did not realize that labor's endorsement would carry with it such a commitment of resources. He says, "I have an Oriental view of politics: everyone's strength is also a weakness. In this case, with labor endorsing Mondale, then turning out the troops, making phone calls for him, bending arms, it seems to me a legitimate question to ask him whether there is one area where he's disagreed with labor." It is the case that Hart, while he might not have the base that Mondale does, also does not have the negatives attached to him that Mondale does (Carter, "special interests," "old liberal"). Hart also expresses annoyance that so many people are saying that the race is in effect over and that Mondale's rivals should not criticize him. This is a hard thing for Mondale's rivals to accept before there has been any voting. He also expresses anger ("I'm sore") at suggestions on the part of Mondale's people that it would be impossible for any other candidate to overtake Mondale after New Hampshire. He says, "Mondale and his people played a critical role in stacking the deck purely for the purpose of making it in their judgment impossible—in my judgment, difficult—for a dark horse to win. And then they come back two years later, not having said so at the time, and say, 'Well, look, even if a lot of Democrats in this party want somebody else they can't have somebody else, because of the rules.' I think it's wrong. Look, I wouldn't be wasting my time if I thought it was impossible. I could spell out a scenario where Mondale could be defeated by these very rules."

What Hart and Caddell have in mind is that Hart could come out of New Hampshire with a great wave of publicity, if he does well enough here, and the subsequent bunched contests, which were designed to keep a long shot from having time to suddenly build an organization, could, in effect, turn into a national primary in which Hart, riding the publicity, could win. Caddell has believed ever since the nomination rules were established that this is how a dark horse could pull off a "jujitsu of the rules." Caddell's theory, as he explained it to me recently, is that Glenn was an excellent foil for Mondale, and the contest between them offered people a real choice, but that if Glenn's candidacy continued to collapse Mondale would be more damaged than any of the others, because this would open the way for another candidate to pick up the support of a great many of those who do not support Mondale. Caddell, who did some polling in Iowa in late November to test the theories in his paper, said, "I have thought since I looked at my Iowa poll that if no one else got in the race, Gary's the alternative to Mondale." He said, "If Glenn collapses, a lot of people will be loose, with only one candidacy to support. They'll see, if Gary's doing well, that there's no reason to support any of the lesser candidacies. If Gary comes in second in New Hampshire, then he has eliminated the rest of the field except Mondale, and then there will be some people who won't want the race to be shut down. Gary will get money and workers and free media—the media can't take a no-campaign campaign year."

Caddell has advised Hart, who has been spending most of his time in New Hampshire, to spend more time in Iowa, saying that if he comes in at least third there he will do well in New

Hampshire. Caddell said to me that he could understand that the Mondale people would prefer a one-on-one with Glenn rather than with Hart, because, he says, his own polling indicates that most of the voters want a candidate who represents a new generation of politics. He said, "Gary and Mondale are yin and yang. That's why the Mondale people were worrying about him last year." Caddell said, "The Mondale people's argument now is that they'll get the delegates out of the early caucuses, which require organization. But if they lose race after race, they're dead. Gary won't necessarily be stopped by the structure of the nomination contest. There are enough delegates elected after mid-March to win this thing, and some of the delegates chosen earlier could switch. If Gary emerges and starts to win the primaries, it's all over." The "realists" say that Hart is simply not equipped, monetarily or organizationally, to fight in the Southern primaries and caucuses that will occur on March 13th, and does not have the full number of delegates filed in Florida (March 13th), Illinois (March 20th), and Pennsylvania (April 10th). By March 20th, almost half the delegates will have been chosen. (However, several contests involving large numbers of delegates will occur after that.) Moreover, Hart's campaign is in debt. Should Hart do well in New Hampshire, he would have to pick off some small victories here and there and then beat Mondale somewhere where it counts. Along the way, he would be raising, and building, a question of Mondale's legitimacy as the Party's candidate, even though Mondale may have more delegates. (Toward the end of the 1976 nomination campaign, Carter lost contests in several states as a similar question arose.) Now, in my interview with him, Hart says, "We have some major fund-raisers planned for after New Hampshire. There are a lot of phone calls going on. A lot of things are going to happen in a two-week period. I think, as I always have, that the showdown will come in the California primary, in June, and that whoever wins that will win the nomination."

In Concord, Hart addresses a large upper-middle-class group in a redeveloped shopping mall. With eloquence, he recalls John F. Kennedy as "a President who said we ought to ask ourselves what we can do for our country . . . that government service and public service was as honorable a thing as any American could engage in . . . [who] challenged this country to move into the future." (It may be remembered that Kennedy's campaign, in 1960, was pretty nonideological, too.) He says, "That President offered this country hope. He stood, in my judgment, for what is best in this country. He was not perfect—he, like the rest of us, had his weaknesses and failings. But he challenged a generation." Hart's voice is ringing out now. "He challenged us to get involved in the government and the control of our lives." Now Hart associates himself with John Kennedy and Robert Kennedy and he praises George McGovern's courage in taking on the Vietnam War in 1972. (Hart's ads also identify him with the Kennedys.) He says, "We believe the only success and the only chance for success in 1984—perhaps the only chance for this country and the world—is to have the kind of bold leadership that those individuals represented." He sets forth an idealistic view of what this nation should be, and asks for the people's help "not just for a candidate or not just for a campaign but for a cause. The cause is the redemption of this land."

FEBRUARY 15

Sheraton Wayfarer Inn, just outside Manchester. This is the hangout for reporters covering the New Hampshire primary (the waterfall in front of which television reporters often do their stand-ups is on the grounds here), so from time to time candidates drop by for press conferences. This morning, Alan Cranston is holding one here. He was supposed to hold it yesterday afternoon but was unable to get here, because of fog. The fog that is covering much of the state, like the one that has been covering Iowa in recent days, has thrown off many plans. Cranston, as always, looks cheerful, grinning his big, toothy grin. His appearance is startling; he has dyed his fringes of hair orange and applied tanning lotion to his face, in order to look healthier. (He is a jogger, and has a stringy appearance.) Cranston, a distinguished, respected senator, has come to this. He is of a cheerful nature, and has great determination, and so, despite the odds against his success, he is pressing on. There is some speculation that he could come in second or third in Iowa, but it is hard to see where that would take him. His making the nuclear-freeze movement the focus of his campaign did give him a base, but not a very broad one; moreover, all the other candidates, except Reubin Askew, support a nuclear freeze. And his support of the B-1 bomber has made him suspect among some arms-controllers. Today, Cranston announces a new jobs program. Cranston tells reporters, who are more interested in

how he assesses his chances than in his jobs program, that his
objective in Iowa and New Hampshire is "to emerge as the alternative to Walter Mondale and John Glenn," and says, "That means
I have to be victorious in the so-called second tier." With Mondale
considered so far in the lead and Glenn presumed to be second,
leadership of the "second tier" has, for whatever reason, become
the prize that a number of the other candidates are seeking. This
is new. Cranston is asked what will happen if he does well in Iowa
but not in New Hampshire. He replies, "I can't conceive of circumstances developing in Iowa and New Hampshire that would
cause me to drop out of the race."

Two of the other contenders for the second tier—George
McGovern and Reubin Askew—will not be in New Hampshire this
week, because they are concentrating on Iowa. McGovern has won
an affectionate following in this campaign, based in part on nostalgia but also in part on the way he has handled himself. He comes
across as dignified, relaxed, well spoken, and, thus far, realistic
about the race—and therefore philosophical. In the debate in Des
Moines, he won a large response by saying that many people
thought that to vote for him would be to "throw away" their vote,
but voting for him, he said, would be sending a message to the
nominee, so "don't throw away your conscience." What doesn't
seem to have been widely realized was that this, too, intentionally
or not, was a way of helping Mondale, who is a good friend of
McGovern's. For one thing, McGovern, in the course of his statement, good-humoredly suggested that the nominee was likely to
be Mondale; more important, McGovern's presence in the race
helps Mondale, because McGovern is presumed to take votes that
might otherwise go to Cranston or Hart. Askew, who is running as
"the different Democrat"—he opposes a nuclear freeze and wants
to restrict abortions—is counting on anti-abortionists and a network of Amway distributors to help him in Iowa.

NORTH SUTTON. This afternoon, Jesse Jackson is to appear before
a mock convention at Kearsarge Regional High School, in this
hamlet in the central part of the state. Jackson has been stirring an
unexpected amount of excitement in New Hampshire, and has
spent a lot of time here. Navy Lieutenant Robert Goodman, the
airman whom Jackson rescued from Syria, is from the state, but

the interest in Jackson seems to go beyond that here—as it does elsewhere. Jackson has more flair than the other candidates, and, being extra-political, he isn't held to the same standards. If his facts aren't quite right, so be it—he's interesting, fun. But there is something else about Jackson's campaign: he can, on the basis of his special talents and his long experience, make a compelling moral case. He may be, as some think, on an extravagant exercise in self-promotion, or, as some think, a bit of a charlatan, or, as New York Governor Mario Cuomo has said, "cunning," but he does know how to get people's attention. Jackson has turned into more of a force than many people expected, including the Mondale people. He hasn't had to do what others have had to do to get himself across; his ability to command free television time has taken many people aback. Jackson's effectiveness thus far has given pause to some black leaders who had indicated that they would support Mondale—not so much because now they support Jackson but because they don't want to get wrong with a big proportion of their own political base. Andrew Young, the mayor of Atlanta, still shows up at the airport when Mondale arrives in his city, and says nice things about him, and is known to favor him, but he has declined to endorse him. (The Mondale people are continuing to work on this, and hope to have Young and other black leaders campaigning for Mondale by the time of the Southern contests on March 13th.) Harold Washington, the mayor of Chicago, who had been letting it be known that he would support Mondale, has now expressed a "preference" for Jackson. This had to do, it is said, with the fact that if Washington had not endorsed Jackson at least tacitly, Jackson would have backed delegates in Chicago who could have embarrassed Washington by defeating his delegates. The question that remains about Jackson is to what end he will put all this. He has said that he does not want to help reelect Reagan, and he is a subtle man, but it will take a lot of subtle moves, and discipline, on Jackson's part for his candidacy not to end up dividing the Democratic Party. He is a beguiling figure in person, but he sometimes comes across on television as threatening, especially when he's shown shouting; and there are segments of the Democratic Party—especially blue-collar workers, who are essential to victory—who will not welcome the sight of Jackson getting too much attention at the Convention. There are also tensions between Jackson and some Jewish groups, as a result of what is widely seen as Jackson's pro-Arab policy and of statements Jackson has made in the past.

Just before his appearance here, Jackson spoke to an audience of comfortable white college women, plus several adults, at a college nearby, and had their total attention and, in the end, enthusiasm. Jackson does make a strong moral case, and he puts on a great show. Now seven hundred-odd high-school students who have come from around the Northeast for this mock convention are excitedly awaiting Jackson's arrival. He is chronically late for his appearances. The hall is decorated in red-white-and-blue bunting, and the "convention" attendants are arranged by state, as if it were a National Convention. As Jackson arrives onstage, he is greeted with cries of enthusiasm and tremendous applause; he holds up his hands in V signs, pleased with his effect. Jackson is dressed in a smart brown suit and vest. He is a largish, handsome man, and there is something physical in his effect on audiences. He begins his talk quietly, saying, "This is perhaps the most politically sensitive generation in the history of our nation." He tells these students, as he has told other audiences, "Our nation is great not because it is always right but because we have the right to protest for the right," and he says, "Democracy is the greatest political system the world has ever known." He starts out positive, a unifier, uncontroversial. "Every generation has the challenge to speak to its day," he says. "All of us cannot be famous, because all of us cannot be well known. All of us can be great, because all of us can serve." Jackson speaks in measured, clear sentences, and as he goes on his voice grows stronger and he falls into the cadences of a preacher. (He is, after all, an ordained Baptist minister.) But what Jackson does is beyond preaching. A man I know who has observed Jackson for many years says that he is the shrewdest reader of audiences he has ever seen. Jackson sweeps the audience into what he is saying. He pauses for effect at just the right moments. His eyes flick over the audience, taking it all in. Now he talks about having grown up black. Jackson had a hard childhood—he was an illegitimate child in a small South Carolina town—and one senses in him a great desire to get even with the world, and no small amount of anger. (At his appearance prior to this one, Jackson said, "One thing I learned about being poor as a child was that you could believe in everything, and wish for it, too, but if you don't have the power to fight you can't get it.") He talks now about

Martin Luther King, Jr.,'s struggle (in which he played an important part): "A non-violent movement moved this nation to a higher level of consciousness." Now, becoming still more the preacher, he says, "Every generation must dream. You must reserve the right to dream; the genius of dreaming is that you can stand an abysmal and ugly reality and dream beyond your situation of what ought to be." He says, "This generation must speak to its present day." The audience is dead silent, listening to him with total attention. He spells out some of the issues of the day: the limits on women's rights, the limits on the rights of blacks and Hispanics, and peace. One of Jackson's talents is to make an argument in an original, interesting way. He says, "We could have war based upon a margin of human error, computer malfunction," and adds, "We cannot just relate to the Soviet Union on the basis of a nuclear standoff—where we will not sell them first-rate computers—and political gimmicks." He asks, "Why allow them to have first-class weapons and third-class computers when a computer error could wipe us out and wipe them out?"

On occasion, Jackson is a bit loose with the facts. For example, in arguing, in his earlier appearance today, that the United States should not be so concerned about revolutionary regimes he seemed to imply that America had been ruled for some time by a military dictatorship. He said, "America was formed, you know, on the Revolution, headed by General George Washington, who later became President George Washington. And then a century later a civil war—and so our own democracy did not take place overnight." Then he goes through a litany of things that he says are "morally wrong," repeating the phrase several times, with emphasis: "When our nation uses resources to overthrow the government of Nicaragua, it's *morally wrong*; when we would question educational aid in our nation and increase military aid to El Salvador, we are *morally wrong*." He points out that "America is about six per cent of the world," that "most people in the world are black or brown or yellow or red, non-Christian, poor, don't speak English." Jackson says, "This generation must learn to live with the people of the world. We must make the adjustment, the post-World War II adjustment, of not living over the world but living with the world and sometimes depending upon the world." Jackson is the only candidate who deals to any real extent with the question of the Third World. One need not do this out of romanticism or good will. Somehow, the long-range strategic importance of dealing with the Third World doesn't come into our political dialogue—it's too remote, it seems, from our everyday concerns. Now, his voice rising to a shout, Jackson indicts the Reagan Administration's domestic policy: "There are five million more poor people since Mr. Reagan; three million more children poor since Mr. Reagan; mothers without prenatal care since Mr. Reagan." He criticizes cuts in education. Some of Jackson's talk here sounds like what he has told black students for years, as part of his PUSH-Excel program to improve inner-city schools. The program was funded by the Carter Administration, at the behest of Hubert Humphrey. (The use of the funds for the program is now being audited by the federal government.) He lectures the students here on the importance of showing up for class, and of not watching too much television. "People are good at what they work at," he says. "Those who practice basketball four or five hours a day without a radio or a television or a telephone or social visitation—you are good at what you work at. If you spent four or five hours a night reading, writing, counting, and thinking, you could slam-dunk a thought just like you slam-dunk a basketball." He gets laughter and applause for this. Jackson lectures and motivates—but he does it entertainingly.

Jackson says that this nation's character will be judged "by how we treat the least of these," and he goes on, "We shall measure character by how we treat children in the dawn of life—that's real leadership—how we treat poor folks in the pit of life. It's the measurement of our character and our values." (In his earlier appearance, he told the young women, "I've travelled to too many hospitals around the nation and watched people downstairs too poor to go upstairs to get a bed and too sick to go back home. And there were rooms and beds upstairs empty, waiting for somebody to get sick who was rich.") Now he says, "If a President says, 'I want children protected; I want poor folks given a chance and trained to develop, our old folk to have a sense that our nation appreciates them,' then the technicians will devise budgets to meet the President's values." Jackson continues, "If a President says, 'I want a man on the moon to bring back *moon-dust rocks*' "—here he extends the words and says them sarcastically, and the audience laughs—"then seventy-five per cent of all of our scientists will figure out a way to get to the moon and bring back *moon-dust rocks*.

Because our values cause our budget." His style here is the demagogic Southern political style, a style that uses humor and sarcasm
and exaggeration; one thinks of the Longs, or of George Wallace.
Then he goes into a lecture on the importance of voting, recalling
for the audience that the elections of John Kennedy in 1960 and
Richard Nixon in 1968 and Jimmy Carter in 1976 were very close.
"Can a handicapped person be President?" he asks. And then he
says that Franklin Roosevelt lifted the nation out of the Depression, adding, "It was Roosevelt, *in a wheelchair*; Presidents don't
have to ride horses and eat peanuts and carry their own baggage."
Then he says, as he said earlier today, "If poor folks can survive
three years of Reagan, surely a woman can guide this nation." The
sentence doesn't make much sense, but it gets laughter and applause. And he delivers, preacherlike, some thumping exhortations: "Choose the human race over the nuclear race—*stand together, pull together*." Taking a swipe at Mondale, he says, "I stand
before you today prepared as a leader to face the head wind. I do
not come before you to follow opinion polls, being driven by a tail
wind." His solution to the budget deficit doesn't add up, but it
doesn't seem to matter to this or any other audience. He uses vivid
imagery, explaining that the "hot line" is not a telephone but "an
old teletype system," and, to the amusement of the audience, he
acts out the creaky mechanics involved and says, "And Reagan
would read it when he wakes up." Jackson has a comedian's lines
and sense of timing. He says, "We keep the process going of
threats, as if the Russian people are not people," and he continues, "Can you trust the Russians? Well, you woke up this morning—that's one evidence you can trust them at that level. Can you
trust Andropov? He's dead and didn't kill you and he could have.
He could have decided in his waning hours, 'Well, I'm going and I
need some company.'"

Jackson, as he finishes, gets a standing ovation. Then, as he
frequently does in his appearances, he instructs the people in the
audience to sit down and then asks all those to stand who are
eighteen and over and are not registered to vote. As usual, it takes
a while before a few people muster the courage to stand. Jackson
is at once firm and gentle with them, asking the audience to applaud them for their courage. Then, bit by bit, he gets more
people to stand. Then he instructs them, "Come on down," beck-
oning them to the front of the audience, where they are to be

signed up to register to vote. "Come on down," he exhorts, again and again, smiling and cajoling. "We need you," he says. This has now turned into a religious meeting, and he has done it in an unthreatening way, and has people laughing with him.

FEBRUARY 16

MANCHESTER. The campaign of John Glenn has continued to slide in the polls and to be marked by a certain organizational and substantive confusion. The campaign organization was shaken up once again in late January, and it is now completely dominated by political professionals with no long-standing ties to Glenn. Still, Glenn is expected to do relatively well here as of now, because of the conservative nature of the state. One Glenn adviser said to me recently that the campaign's hope was that now the voters who had decided not to vote for Mondale would give Glenn another look. This man said, "If people don't like what they see, Hart is the most likely recipient of their support." Glenn's schedule has been the subject of confusion, too: at first, he was to spend the entire week in the South; then this was changed so that he would come into Manchester for a couple of days this week; then this was changed to have him attend some events in Nashua and Salem yesterday and today and ski in Waterville Valley, to the north, tomorrow. A number of experts on New Hampshire, as well as members of Glenn's own staff, thought the skiing trip a rather poor idea. (Among other things, it would take important time from campaigning, and have him skiing where well-to-do out-of-staters tend to go.) Then, yesterday, the visits to New Hampshire were cancelled, because, Glenn's staff said, he has the flu. Still, Glenn held a press conference in Washington today, in which he made yet another attack on Mondale.

Late last month, Glenn did eventually give a speech at Faneuil Hall, in Boston—which had been scheduled for a couple of weeks earlier but had been cancelled because of bad weather—in which he laid out his political philosophy, saying that he would be a President of the "sensible center." The idea was to contrast him with the more liberal Mondale, and there were a number of other implicit criticisms of Mondale in the speech. Glenn said, "I think it's time we set a reasonable, middle course in this country, and I think it's time we elected a President who cares a little less about ideology—and a little more about results." But the Glenn cam-

paign still isn't getting a clear message across, and his aides say
that their polling shows that people still have questions about his
qualifications for the Presidency. They have attempted to improve
his campaign performance by scheduling fewer events and trying
to have Glenn show more animation, and they are continuing
their losing battle to have him give a crisper stump speech and
sharpen his replies to questions. When I recently asked William
Hamilton, Glenn's pollster, what he wanted to see Glenn do in the
coming weeks, he replied, "Show energy and lay out in a focussed
way what he sees leadership for the future to be." Robert Keefe, a
Washington lobbyist and consultant, who is the Glenn campaign's
senior political adviser, said to me not long ago, "There's always
the constant effort to get the right words together for him."

The Glenn people feel that their attacks on Mondale are taking
hold, and are the only way to catch up to him. David Sawyer,
Glenn's media adviser, said to me today, "The focus is coming to
where we have wanted it to be—on Mondale's character, on character of leadership." Also today, I asked Jerry Vento, who is now
Glenn's campaign manager, why Glenn was attacking Mondale
even more, and he replied, "It's worked, for one reason." Glenn is
running a number of negative ads here. Vento said, "Our phone
canvassing tells us that a number of people feel that Mondale has
made too many promises, so the question is: Can we catch up in
time?" (Glenn's staff, in a change of policy, and in contrast to the
policy of other campaigns, will not release cassettes of the ads to
the press. The reason appears to be that the ads are quite controversial. Even inquiries about when the ads might be seen on New
Hampshire television are not replied to.)

Glenn made a fairly unimpressive showing in the Iowa debate.
(He skipped an earlier debate there, on farm policy.) He started
off with a strong statement about Lebanon, but then sounded
more than ever as if he were talking by rote, at times rushing his
responses so that he sounded as if he were on fast-forward.
Glenn's campaign is now in debt, and recently borrowed two and a
half million dollars from Ohio banks. (Some questions have been
raised about the collateral for these loans.) Still, Glenn's aides say
that he will come in second in Iowa, and that he must do so, and
that he will come in second in New Hampshire, and then will take
on Mondale in the South, where, they say, he should be strong—
especially in Alabama. (The Mondale people continue to dispute

this.) But, as Keefe says, "at some point we have to start winning."

A nationwide Gallup poll released today gave Mondale forty-nine per cent, Jackson fourteen per cent, and Glenn thirteen per cent, with everyone else at three per cent or less.

FEBRUARY 17

On this Friday afternoon, Walter Mondale is standing in the equipment barn of the Manchester Highway Department, talking to a group of about a hundred and fifty city sanitation and street-maintenance workers—all members of the American Federation of State, County, and Municipal Employees (AFSCME), which has endorsed him. Behind him are large orange sanding and salting trucks. Mondale, who is wearing a gray suit, cheerfully greets the workers individually, but he looks, and is, very tired. He has just flown in from Iowa, and has been following a gruelling schedule for a long time now. In keeping with his running a national campaign, and trying to firm up his support in a large number of states early, he has, since earlier this year, been in—besides Iowa and New Hampshire—the South, Massachusetts, Indiana, Washington, California, Kentucky, Puerto Rico (which holds its primary on March 18th), Minnesota, Pennsylvania, Illinois, and Wisconsin. His fatigue was also quite apparent in the recent debate in Des Moines, but other factors were at work there, too. Mondale has survived the debates—even been deemed a winner, by appearing not to lose ground while other candidates were ganging up on him—but he has done few memorable things in them and, with a few exceptions, has been less effective than he is when he campaigns. Part of it seems to be Mondale's innate disinclination to be theatrical; part of it is his own lack of enthusiasm for these forums, which provide a cacophony of voices vying to be heard and little opportunity to develop a thought; and part of it is his own disinclination to get into more of a fight than necessary with his competitors, whose support he assumes he will be seeking down the road. But Mondale did very well in his debate against Robert Dole, in 1976, when the two men were running for Vice-President, and Mondale's aides insist that when the pressure is on him in the fall—assuming he gets the nomination—he will do fine. Moreover, the degree to which Mondale is holding up or moving ahead in the polls indicates to him and some of his advisers that he is doing well enough in these performances.

Despite his fatigue, Mondale is in good spirits: the latest telephone canvassing indicates that he will have a very big win in Iowa three days from now, and that thus far his lead in New Hampshire is holding. The Mondale surveys also indicate that Glenn's support is continuing to drop in Iowa, and that there is now a real question about who will come in second. The cumulative negative advertising and campaigning by the other candidates appears to be taking something of a toll on Mondale here, however, and his campaign's own canvassing and polling indicates that the "promises" charge is beginning to stick. To deal with the "promises" question, Mondale, in late January, released his proposed budget, which he said would carry out his pledge to reduce the Reagan deficit by more than half in four years. He said he would increase revenues by at least sixty billion dollars (by putting a lid on the third year of the Reagan tax cut for those who have taxable incomes of sixty thousand dollars or more; deferring indexing of taxes to inflation, due to take effect in January, 1985, for those earning over twenty-five thousand dollars; putting a ten-per-cent surtax on incomes over a hundred thousand dollars; raising taxes on corporations; closing various loopholes; and expanding the enforcement of tax collection). Mondale also said that he would reduce spending by at least seventy billion dollars (through cuts in defense spending; reductions in the costs of medical-care and farm programs; and savings in interest on the debt as the deficit goes down). And he said that he would add new spending of about thirty billion dollars. Mondale's program is far more specific than any other candidate's at such an early point, but it still carries assumptions—about economic eventualities, about congressional cooperation—that may or may not pan out. Whether he or anyone can actually reduce the deficit significantly without cutting middle-class entitlement programs is questionable.

Johnson, with whom I spoke by phone yesterday, still maintains that the criticism is not hurting Mondale in any important way now, and that it will not hurt him in the fall. As for now, he points to the polls. As for the fall, he says, "The general election will be about who's the best man for the next four years; who stands up for the things people want stood up for; who's going to do the most for peace." He said, "Mondale is sufficiently well established and trusted that efforts to paint him as a tool of labor unions and others are simply not credible. Further, Ronald Reagan has no credibility in trying to cast Mondale as a special-interest candidate when the American people overwhelmingly believe that Ronald Reagan cares more about rich people than about other people. In my mind, there's no chance that Reagan could ever win an argument about special interests." He added, "I think the Republicans' case will change, as ours will, based on the realities of the post-Convention period."

On Tuesday, Mondale, who had been saying, "I'm not going to spend my time finding ways to offend people whose help I'm going to need to govern," switched tactics and, in an attempt to put the issue behind him, cited some differences he had with the A.F.L.-C.I.O.: on the B-1 bomber, on the Clinch River breeder reactor (which labor had supported, and which may now be dead), and on clean-air standards. On the same day, Mondale, dealing with the new political reality in the Administration's relationship with the Soviet Union—the death of Andropov and the talk coming out of the Administration of the possibility of a summit meeting this year—made some new proposals. Saying that the selection of Konstantin Chernenko as the new Soviet leader offered "a window in U.S.-Soviet relations," Mondale proposed that the United States declare a six-month suspension of underground testing of nuclear weapons and challenge the Soviets to respond in kind, adding that any sizable tests can be detected; and he called for a temporary moratorium on the testing of anti-satellite weapons, and for a challenge to the Soviets to follow suit—leading to a treaty to ban such weapons.

"February twenty-eighth is the day when the whole world will look at New Hampshire," Mondale now tells the Manchester city workers. He cites, as he has for some time in his campaign, Abraham Lincoln's saying that this should be a government "of the people, by the people, and for the people," and says that what we have now is a government "of the rich, and by the rich, and for the rich." And he points out that the wealthy benefitted most from the Reagan Administration's 1981 tax cut. Now, taking advantage of the opening the Reagan Administration has provided him by declining to say what it will do about the large budget deficit until after the election, Mondale says, "What are they planning for you next?" Referring to Reagan's State of the Union address, he says, "If you heard the President the other night, he said we're going to study more taxes and we're going to get a report right after the election on what to do. Now, why do you suppose that they want to tell you after the election, and not before the election, who is going to pay the higher taxes? Because you're going to pay those higher taxes." He says, "Across the board, this Administration is putting the cost on the average American. And look where they cut the budget. They cut the budget for your kids so they can't go on to college. They cut the budget on Social Security and Medicare." Then, striking a theme he has been using for some time, Mondale says, "I'm a people's Democrat." This is at the heart of Mondale's election strategy; he plans to run a populist campaign against Reagan, and feels that he will have a majority behind him. He also expects to have the support of various businessmen, who will say that the economy will be better off under Mondale than under Reagan; moreover, it is Mondale's belief that a large number of wealthy people accept his argument that there should be more equity in the arrangement of government benefits and relief. Mondale talks in a low voice to the people in Manchester— perhaps because it is a small group, perhaps because he is tired. (After a while, it is not easy to arrange appearances in New Hampshire; places get used up. The Mondale people had tried to hold this afternoon's event in a certain plant in Manchester, but the manager had politely asked if they could please hold it somewhere else—he had a client coming in, and business to do. Some companies have taken to asking candidates if they could come during the lunch hour or a coffee break, so as to reduce the interruption to their business. The AFSCME workers provided Mondale with an audience this afternoon—just as unions have been doing throughout this campaign.) "You will go out and beat Mr. Reagan, and I'll be your friend," Mondale tells the workers. "I'm going to be the friend of working Americans, the way I've been all my life." This is his classic style. He adds, "I know how to run that office. I've been there. And I can be tough and I will be tough." Mondale has taken to saying this kind of thing lately. ("There is no problem with my backbone; I've got a good one.") He is said to be annoyed that this question has been raised about him.

At a news conference in the equipment barn after his appearance before the workers, Mondale reads a statement attacking the National Conservative Political Action Committee (NCPAC), which has just announced that it will spend two million dollars "to expose the regular and completely liberal record" of Mondale. NCPAC, which, since it was founded, in 1975, has made a career of going after liberal senators with negative advertising, much of it quite distorted, spent 1.9 million dollars in "independent expenditures" for Reagan in 1980—and is actually a lovely target for Mondale. NCPAC is something that all Democrats can agree on, and it was much less effective in Senate races in 1982 than in 1980, as more candidates figured out how to combat it. Asked about the candidates' attacks on each other, and a letter to the candidates from Charles Manatt, the Party chairman, calling for a stop to this, Mondale, at whom the letter was not aimed, says, "I agree with that. We can't forget that what we're doing is fighting for the nomination in order to defeat Mr. Reagan." He cites his campaign themes—fairness, regaining America's competitive edge, and seeking a safer world—and says, "Let's keep within limits so that once this nomination is over the person who is nominated—and I hope and believe I will be that person—will be able to unite the Party and win the election." He adds, "Frankly, I think that's almost a certainty. This is trash time." He adds, "Once the nominating process is over we will be back together—a good and solid and unified Party."

Asked whether he believes people think that because he has been endorsed by labor he would be beholden to it, Mondale shows how he now deals with this question. "I don't believe that people believe that at all," he says. "I've got a record of public leadership which stands there for all to see, and it's been a record of public leadership demonstrating independence and a backbone. There are times when I've disagreed with the labor movement. I spelled out some of that. But I don't intend to spend my time trying to offend people who are trying to help me. What we need now is the support of everybody. And no one needs a President more than working men and women. The average family has been singled out by this Administration in every conceivable way: by high unemployment, by the highest real interest-rate charges in American history, by a grossly unfair tax program that puts the burden on that average family, by cuts in federal budgets that go directly to families of average income—whether it's student loans or Social Security or Medicare. The average American does not have a friend in the White House today. And the reason that they are so involved in this campaign to remove Mr. Reagan and the reason that many of them have come to my support is that they want a change, and my record over a lifetime of public service—I call myself a people's Democrat—is one that commends itself to working men and women, and I'm proud of that support."

Dartmouth College, Hanover. Mondale has arrived late for an appearance this evening before a group that includes students and also adults from the community. He had a brief rest this afternoon but still seems tired, and he speaks slowly and quietly. The audience is attentive but not particularly responsive. Mondale uses the occasion to give a little talk about foreign policy. The case he makes against Reagan goes beyond any particular event.

"This President and those around him do not understand that if you are to become involved in the affairs of another nation it's absolutely indispensable that you understand that nation—its history, its culture, its religion, its political compulsions," Mondale says. "It's only by understanding and respecting others when you seek to deal with another nation that your foreign policy can succeed, or have an authority, or be credible, or be sustainable, or be explainable." He is applauded. "This is the lesson of history," he says. "So many times, it's our tendency, and the tendency of other powerful Western societies, to believe that by the use of Western power, defined by us, we can somehow involve ourselves in another nation, regardless of their feelings and regardless of the situation and their history and all the rest. It's remarkable that that attitude still exists, because all history collides so powerfully and so tragically with that theory." He goes into brief histories of the war in Vietnam and the experience of the French in Algeria (he urges them to read a book, called *A Savage War of Peace*, about this), and he says, "The Russians have made the same mistake in Afghanistan." He says, "The most powerful religion on earth, the religion that people will die for, is the compulsion for national independence and national dignity. And it's more powerful than any military force that's ever been applied." This, he says, is "the lesson in Nicaragua today." He says that the same lesson applies to El Salvador, and he criticizes the Reagan Administration's policy there. He talks about America's backing of the "covert" war in Nicaragua—"to boot, we are participating with former Somoza supporters." This isn't a stump speech or a crowd-rouser; he's just talking about something that interests him. The Reagan Administration "announced that the fight in El Salvador was East against West, that we were going to beat the Russians in San Salvador, we're going to draw a line and we're going to use that old muscle and we're going to win," he says. "But what happened, of course, was just the reverse. The situation is deteriorating, we've become identified with right-wing extremists, we've looked the other way when these death squads have visited murder upon their own people, and we've been embarrassed, we've been undermined."

Then Mondale talks about Lebanon, and (though he didn't call for a troop withdrawal until the very end of last year) criticizes the Administration for failing to understand the factional nature of the struggle there. He goes into great detail. He criticizes the Administration for the manner in which it handled the withdrawal of the Marines: "They told us then that our troops couldn't leave, because to leave would be surrender. And then, three days later, they said we better leave as fast as we can. They said our troops are leaving, and then, two days later, they said, Slowly. They said the artillery would do it, and take their place. Now we know all that's left from that is holes and death, and now they say that the artillery won't do. A few days ago, the President said that America is back and standing tall. I'll tell you this: America should stand tall. But that's not what's happening. When you deal around this world without knowing what you do, when you think that ignorance is adequate in dealing with these tough problems, when you try to apply force without understanding the underlying circumstances in the society in which you are operating, you are heading for real trouble for our country, real devastation in that society, and humiliation for our nation." One of Mondale's themes is that we need "a President who knows what he's doing." He continues, "That is the kind of leadership that this country needs: with values, with understanding, with respect, and to use strength to keep the peace. Every time we do that, we will gain strength. Every time we remain true to our values, our moral authority grows. Every time we demonstrate that peace and arms control is something that we're proud of, and not an expression of weakness, we will grow stronger." He concludes with an attack on Reagan's record on arms control, and asks why Reagan didn't go to Andropov's funeral, and adds, "Why don't they have a summit? If Mr. Reagan isn't ready now, he never will be." He renews his own proposal for annual summits, and he says, "Stop this 'Star Wars' thing—leave the heavens alone." He is applauded.

In the course of an answer to a question about Hubert Humphrey, Mondale speaks, with feeling, about Humphrey's "compassion," as contrasted, he says, with that of the Administration: "The idea that Reagan's trying to sell us, to become some kind of social-Darwinist society, where it's just the survival of the fittest, or the richest, whatever that means; that if you're black or you're brown you're on your own, if you're hungry you're a hustler, if you're homeless you like it that way"—here he is referring to a comment made by Reagan in late January that some people sleeping on the streets were "homeless, you might say, by choice"—"if you have a kid that wants to go on to college and you can't get a loan that's too bad, if you're unemployed you go out and read the help-wanted ads, if you're old you should have thought about it first and not got into that predicament." He continues, "This kind of icy indifference that they're trying to teach the American people goes to the very basis of the American society. We are a generous people. We are not a selfish people. And justice and compassion, the sense of community and family, is indispensable to all of us. And I want to see that spirit restored in American life here." Mondale receives applause, but he hasn't roused this audience, as he has audiences elsewhere. Perhaps it is that these aren't his people; for whatever reason, this event is flat.

Lebanon, a working-class town not far from Hanover. The Mondale people consider it important to stop here whenever they stop in Hanover, to prevent any resentment. So now Mondale is sitting with a small group of people in a small room in the Grand Army of the Republic Building, a red brick building honoring New Hampshirites who died in the Civil War. This is not exactly a crowd-drawing event; in fact, there have been none thus far on this trip. The roughly sixty people here are all committed Mondale supporters, and had an organizational meeting prior to his arrival. Someone had the idea that Mondale should sit at a rectangular table with twenty-five people (three of them small children), while most of the people around the table, from various walks of life, make little speeches about why they are for him. Mondale manages to look interested as each person talks; sometimes he props his head in his hands to keep the fatigue from showing. Then, quietly but intently, he addresses the concerns they have raised—about hospital costs, Social Security, education, women's rights, and so on. "Reagan seems to be saying that education is for the purpose of making a buck," he says. "That's part of it, but what we need is a far broader concept than that." He refers again to the need to understand history in order to conduct foreign policy, and he says, "We have to see learning for the sake of not just foreign policy or national security or money but literature and poetry and art and enjoyment, and of the human spirit. That's what education is. This President will never, never understand that."

A man at the table with Mondale complains about the special-interest charge, and says that he is a workingman and "if a workingman is a special interest, so be it." This is what Mondale wants to hear. His theory is that what are being condemned as "special interests" are actually large aggregates of people who in combination will help him defeat Reagan.

Mondale replies, "Reagan wants to put us on a guilt trip because working men and women want change." He says, "He's on the side of the polluters; I'm on the side of the environment." Smiling, Mondale says, "We're going to have a lot of fun with that in this campaign." Then he says quietly, "I call myself a people's Democrat—nothing fancy. But when people are hurting, you want a President who can feel that, sense that. When people are out of work, I know what that means. I know it destroys families—it's so basic. I know what it's like to be a senior citizen and worry about that major illness destroying everything. I know what it's like to be a parent and not be able to send your youngsters on to college." Referring to the Reagan Administration, he says, "That's why they're scared. I'm onto them. And a lot of people in this country are onto them."

FEBRUARY 18

BERLIN. This morning, Saturday, Mondale and his entourage left the town of Lebanon in rainy, cloudy weather and flew in three small planes over the White Mountains to this small industrial town in the northern part of New Hampshire. Berlin (pronounced *Burr*-lin) is essentially a paper-mill town (the smell of the chemicals used in the mills permeates it), and produces three and a half percent of the state's Democratic vote. Now, with the mayor of Berlin, Joseph Ottolini, at his side, Mondale is marching in a parade to celebrate Berlin's Winterfest Festival. A fairly large number of people line the streets, many of them holding balloons, and most of them, it seems, wearing Mondale stickers. Hollings is riding in a car a few blocks behind Mondale, who seems to have taken over this event. Mondale, apparently in very good humor, walks and waves and goes from one side of the street to the other shaking hands, chatting, and inspecting babies. Word reaches the press corps that tomorrow's Boston *Globe* will publish a poll of New Hampshire Democrats showing Mondale at thirty-nine per cent, Glenn at eighteen per cent, Jackson at eleven per cent, and Hart at ten per cent, with Hollings and McGovern each having five per cent, Cranston three per cent, and Askew two per cent. The Mondale entourage is already aware of these results, and is pleased.

BOSTON. Mondale has just held a press conference, at which he was endorsed by some leaders of the arms-control and nuclear-freeze movements. Another set of endorsements. Among the new initiatives that Mondale has pledged himself to—in addition to the ones he announced earlier this week—is a temporary moratorium on the testing and deployment of nuclear weapons under development, while freeze negotiations proceed; a moratorium on the deployment of sea-launched nuclear-armed cruise missiles; and moving battlefield nuclear weapons back from the front lines. In his comments, Mondale emphasized that these steps must be verifiable and, within a set period of time, mutual. (The verifiability of whether submarine-based missiles are nuclear is in dispute within the arms-control community.) Mondale cites the example of John Kennedy's temporary ban, in June, 1963, on the atmospheric testing of nuclear weapons, which led, in August, to a joint test-ban treaty. Mondale, trying to emphasize that he is being careful, says, "We cannot rely on trust and we cannot disarm unilaterally." Mondale is going on to Florida today, and then back to Iowa. Before he leaves Boston, I have an interview with him in a room at the airport.

I begin by asking Mondale how he plans to deal with what is bound to be a changing foreign-policy picture, with the Administration doing its best to dominate the agenda.

He replies, "You know, it's hard to know what the changes will be, but I think one of my strengths in this campaign is I've had enough experience that I think I can handle change. And so when something happens it's not new, in the sense that I know how to approach it." And he says he will stress his themes in any event:

"Nuclear-arms control—that's the issue of our time. Two, knowing what you're doing, and reading and remembering history—Nicaragua, Central America, Lebanon are all classic examples of the fact that this Administration simply hasn't bothered to understand or respect the traditions of others. That's why last night I was talking about Algeria, Vietnam, and these others as examples of what happens when a country doesn't. The third is an emphasis on human rights—not in a preachy, pious way but because a foreign policy devoid of values is neither credible nor coherent nor sustainable. And, finally, seasoned, tough management of foreign policy, so that it's coherent again, unified, and has a strategy and a toughness to it that make it sustainable."

Then I ask him about his theory of bringing together a coalition that can win in November.

Mondale says, "And beyond. I see it as important to a strong Presidency. What I'm trying to do is to build a new, strong Democratic Party which runs across this country and reflects a strong majority—some of that coalition is traditional, some of it is new—and hold it together and reduce tensions that have caused a split Party in the past. And I think I'm doing that. And I believe this is what's scared the Republicans. Because, really, since '64 the Democratic Party has been a series of separate pieces floating in the ocean."

I ask Mondale what he means by a new Democratic Party.

He replies, "It's based on this country as we see it today—for example, the women's movement, the environmental movement, the arms-control and foreign-policy people around the country. It's also based on intensity; that's another part of it. A part of it is who is for you, and part of it, to a degree, is participation. I believe that the '84 campaign is going to involve more basics than any campaign we've seen since perhaps '28 or '32. And, because of that, if I handle it right I think we're going to have a very heavy turnout."

I bring up something that Mondale and I have talked about in each of our interviews during the campaign—his getting across his idea of leadership.

"I think it's coming," Mondale says. "You know, I don't have a four-word slogan, or whatever it is, a summary—'Let's get the country moving again'—but I do have the three central objectives: a fairer society, restoring America's competitive edge, and seeking a safer

world. I've now been using this for some months, and it works.
And it summarizes a whole complex of issues. And so we're getting closer. I also think the success I'm having tells people there's a
leader. I think all these debates, which have been risky—I've managed it, and handled it, and that builds confidence that I can lead."

I ask Mondale what damage he thinks all the criticism from his
competitors, repeatedly over a period of several months, is doing
to him for the long run, if not for the nomination.

"I assume it's something," he replies. "But also my personal
hunch is that it's minimal. I remember a year ago *The Right Stuff*
was going to do me in: I never thought it would make any bit of
difference, and it didn't. I think this is the normal, expected pat-
ter at trash time. The fact that the polls show that I've gained with
every attack shows that the public does not buy it and they do not
want this kind of trashing going on, and I believe that their judgment is correct, and I don't see it as a big problem."

I ask Mondale if he thinks there is a problem in the "promises"
issue.

He replies, "I think I'm moving rather successfully in meeting
that. In other words, the fact that I came up with a very specific
budget gives the answer. The attempt to give me programs that I
haven't supported won't last long. If the issue with Reagan is who
will get the deficit down, the longer that debate goes on the more
I'm going to pick up support. If the issue is fairness, I've got all
the votes."

But, I ask Mondale, wouldn't the Republicans try to portray him
as a big spender?

Mondale replies, "They'll try that, and I'll have to win that fight.
And I believe I can. The campaign hasn't started. I think when it
starts and—if I'm nominated—when I'm the only candidate, I
would have a chance to make my case with the public listening.
And I believe I can persuade the public that I am responsible, that
I'm not overpromising, and that the attack on promises is code for
trying to retain an unfair America. And that the promises I've
made I'm proud of, and are essential to the three objectives."

I ask Mondale how, after all the years of effort, he feels now—
since he faces what he knows will be a big victory in Iowa, and New
Hampshire looks pretty good.

Mondale indicates that he is still uneasy about New Hampshire.
"New Hampshire is a tough state," he says. "You never know

what's going to happen there." But then he says, "I feel good. I'm content. I think we've done everything possible. And we're ahead of where I had any reason to believe we would be. These polls could mean anything—you know that. But there is just a general feeling that we're doing well, and I feel that we are. It could all be knocked into a cocked hat, of course, but all my political career I've said, 'Once you've done your best, that's it. Forget about it. Just get a good night's sleep.' And I've done my very best. And everybody around me has."

FEBRUARY 21

WASHINGTON. Last night, Mondale won the Iowa precinct caucuses overwhelmingly, with forty-nine per cent of the vote—a higher percentage than that of all his rivals combined. With seventy-five per cent of the vote now counted, Mondale has won nearly three times as many votes as the next in line, who was, as it turned out, Hart, with 16.4 per cent of the vote. Glenn, who his aides had said would, and had to, come in second, came in sixth, with 3.5 per cent of the vote—after Mondale, Hart, McGovern (10.3), uncommitted (9.4), and Cranston (7.4). Askew got 2.5 per cent of the vote; Jackson, who barely campaigned in Iowa, got 1.5 per cent, and Hollings, who also bypassed the state, less than one per cent. (About eighty-five thousand people turned out—some fifteen thousand fewer than in 1980, which featured the tough Kennedy-Carter fight.) Mondale, looking understandably happy, said on television last night, "I am confident that when this race is over we're going to have a unified Party." Glenn appeared on the three networks trying to look cheerful and making a few points over and over again: "On to New Hampshire;" Iowa elects "only one and a half per cent of the delegates;" New Hampshire has a primary, which has "a secret ballot," instead of a caucus, and "I don't think the people of New Hampshire are going to be led around by the nose;" caucuses are subject to "outside influences." Glenn said, "I'm very up right now. ... We're on to New Hampshire—let's go." Hart, whose second-place showing brought him much attention (even though he was more than thirty points behind Mondale), declared that now it is a two-man race. Hart said, "All I know is that I'll be the nominee of this Party."

FEBRUARY 29

Gary Hart's decisive victory over Walter Mondale in New Hampshire last night has dramatically rearranged the race, and though people are still sorting out what happened—and will be doing so for some time—changed most of the calculations. The count, as of now, gives Hart forty-one per cent of the vote and Mondale twenty-nine per cent, McGovern five, Hollings four, Cranston two, and Askew one. Cranston dropped out of the race this morning, and Hollings and Askew are expected to do so soon. Hart's victory was the result—as is usually the case in politics—of a combination of his own accomplishments and of others' failures and of a mood that can suddenly come over the electorate. By the time of the primary, Hart had sharply honed his themes—that he was the candidate of the "new generation," with the "new ideas"—and he campaigned vigorously and well, with close-in personal campaigning, right up to the end, just as he had done in Iowa. Hart had a clear, simple, and unexceptionable theme—"the future"—while Mondale's was more complicated. Hart, who had in fact been diffident when he first began to campaign, had loosened up. His relative success in Iowa helped that process along. Hart managed to come out of Iowa as the fresh face. Here is where the Mondale people may have made a couple of miscalculations. In focussing so much on Glenn, they let Hart go relatively unexamined—even though one of their original strategies had been to expose all the candidates to scrutiny early, so that there would be no fresh face. When it appeared for so long that Hart wasn't getting anywhere, they let him out of their sights. The other miscalculation may have been the assumption that the bunching of the contests would work in Mondale's favor; the short time between the Iowa and New Hampshire contests turned out to work in Hart's favor. Hart skillfully parlayed his Iowa showing into a good week in New Hampshire; he was the beneficiary of a great deal of free media coverage, and exploited the opportunity well. On Sunday, we saw him on television participating in an axe-hurling contest, wearing a plaid shirt and red suspenders, chewing on something or other, and looking relaxed and terrific. (He even hurled the axe well—hitting his mark.) This picture was shown on television often. And Hart was the beneficiary of that unfortunate cliché of a political phenomenon—"momentum."

But his success was also brought about by other things. It now seems clear that Mondale did suffer both from the cumulative attacks on him by others and from the deficiencies of his own campaign. The attacks on him as an "overpromiser" and as being too close to labor did take their toll—this showed up in the exit polls conducted by the networks. Mondale never got across an answer to these charges, though he felt he had one, and he didn't manage to offset them. After Iowa, the Mondale people spread the word that the other candidates' attacks on him had backfired, but in fact they had no statistical evidence for this; they did know, however, that the attacks were hurting him in New Hampshire. The Glenn campaign, for one, accepted the diagnosis that the negative campaigning had hurt Glenn—and there is reason to think that this is true—and changed course in New Hampshire. Glenn's negative ads were taken off the air, and Glenn campaigned pleasantly and positively—but he still seemed to have little to say. The Hart campaign did not accept the diagnosis, and kept up the attack on Mondale as representing the old ways and being the prisoner of "the establishment." Hart (and Caddell) turned Mondale's experience and endorsements back on him. The diagnosis they were following was the one laid out in Caddell's paper last year. Hart identified himself with the group on one side of the "fault line": anti-Vietnam, anti–Party establishment, post–Great Society, young, affluent. He drew on Mondale's liabilities, and magnified them. In the February 23rd debate in New Hampshire, sponsored by the League of Women Voters, Hart, in his closing remarks, said, "If we want a representative of the Party and its past, we should nominate Vice-President Mondale. If we want new leadership and new ideas and new proposals, then I ask for the help of the people of New Hampshire." Hart also said, in a shrewd appeal to a New Hampshire tradition, "The issue in New Hampshire is whether the debate will end here or whether, as it has in the past, it will only begin." Mondale may have suffered from his own "front-runnerness"—in some respects his own doing, in others beyond his control. His campaign stressed the inevitability of his nomination. He played it safe to the end. His strategy in the League debate seemed to be the same as before: get by. The fact that Mondale can give a passionate speech, stir an audience, seems known only to those who have been in the audience. He still doesn't get himself across on television. In the final days, he deliberately gave the impression of having great confidence in the outcome (though by the weekend he knew there was some cause for alarm): acting as if it were over, he turned to attacking Reagan (whom he charged with "leadership by amnesia"). On the Sunday before the voting, after attending church in New Hampshire, he left the state to campaign in Maine and Vermont. He returned to New Hampshire that night, did an event there Monday morning, and then went to Boston and then to Washington. Mondale later said that leaving New Hampshire may have been a mistake—but it could not explain a loss of this size, as Mondale and his people knew. (Moreover, while in Boston, Mondale was endorsed by Mayor Raymond Flynn—this was deliberately timed for Boston television, and thus for New Hampshire, on Monday night.) Still, it's preferable to lay a loss to a tactical error than to the fact that the people may not have liked you enough.

The Mondale people had known all along that they would face a "new ideas–old ideas" challenge, and were determined that there would be no "new-ideas gap," as Johnson once put it, but they didn't effectively counter it. This gets back to Mondale's caution and his political style: like anyone who has read the current literature and talked to the idea-brokers, he is familiar with the new ideas that are around, and subscribes to some of them, but he doesn't talk much about them. He also is seasoned enough to reject some as gimmicks. Others he has rejected as politically risky: he was doing well in the polls, so why take a chance? But Hart and Caddell had made the "new ideas" theme into a metaphor for something larger.

Hart may have benefitted not only from New Hampshirites' traditional desire to dust up a front-runner but also from, in this case, a resentment of the idea that the nomination contest was over. This may be the price that the Mondale people paid for their efforts to accelerate the race. It is quite possible that Mondale was the target of a protest vote of the sort that is often cast against front-runners but, under more conventional circumstances, later in the race.

Hart certainly did benefit, as both Caddell and the Glenn people had predicted, from the drop in the support for others. (According to a New York *Times*/CBS News exit poll, he also received more than forty per cent—by far the largest number—of the independent vote, which accounted for nearly forty per cent of the Democratic primary vote.) Not only was he running a good campaign but he was the candidate with a sufficiently broad appeal—identifiable as neither left nor right—to pick up the votes of those who did not want to vote for Mondale and to whom the other candidates seemed less attractive or viable. He drew votes from liberals, moderates, and conservatives, and, according to exit polls, was actually stronger among independents than among Democrats. Hart was very strong with the younger voters, while Mondale was stronger with the elderly, the poor, and the less educated. The "baby boom" vote did turn out in unprecedented numbers, and cast about forty per cent of the vote—overwhelmingly for Hart. Hart even split the labor vote with Mondale.

Jackson's drop in support may have been caused in part by a desire of some voters, in the end, as had been widely expected, to cast a "realistic" vote. And it was undoubtedly affected by the controversy that developed over his relationship with Jews. At the heart of the matter was a report in the Washington *Post* on February 13th that Jackson, in conversations with reporters, had referred to Jews as "Hymies" and to New York as "Hymietown." For days, Jackson did not flatly deny the allegation; he said that he had "no recollection" of making the remarks, and he refused to apologize. He also refused to make a distinction between one extremist group—something called Jews Against Jackson, an offshoot of the Jewish Defense League—which was harassing his campaign, and other Jewish groups, which had denounced its tactics. The matter was reaching an ugly pitch when, on the Sunday night before the primary, Jackson went to a Manchester synagogue, admitted making the remarks, and more or less apologized for them. But during this time it was clear from watching Jackson on television that the controversy was taking its toll on him: he looked subdued, as if something had gone out of him, and according to his friends, he really felt that, as he was saying publicly, he was being "hounded" by Jews.

The Mondale people began to sense on the weekend before the primary that things might break badly for them—which at that point meant that Hart would come in second and within ten points of Mondale. (Just after Iowa, they moved seventy-five more campaign workers into New Hampshire.) Hart had said that after New Hampshire he expected to do well in the next three contests: Maine (the following Sunday, March 4th); Vermont (March 6th); and Wyoming (March 10th). So on Friday the Mondale people sent thirty-one people into Vermont (where in fact no delegates are at stake) and about fifteen people into Wyoming, which borders on Hart's home state of Colorado. The Mondale campaign already had an organization in place in Maine, and had decided that the better Hart did in New Hampshire the more it would emphasize the importance of Maine. In the March 13th contests, the Hart campaign is now stressing Massachusetts, which it thinks might be inhospitable to Mondale, and is considering how extensive an effort to make in the South, and where the effort will be focussed. Even before the Mondale people knew that they were going to lose in New Hampshire, they were determined to try to defeat Hart everywhere, soon. They continued to take comfort from the fact that he had little organization in the South.

By Monday, the Mondale people realized that they might be in even more serious trouble in New Hampshire. An ABC News/ Washington *Post* poll published that day put Mondale at thirty-two per cent and Hart at twenty-five per cent. The most ominous thing was that Mondale's support was dropping and Hart's was rising— the sort of trend that is hard to turn around on the eve of an election. The Mondale people did take some consolation from a New York *Times*/CBS News poll to be published in the *Times* on Tuesday which said that among Democrats nationwide Mondale was supported by fifty-seven per cent, Jackson by eight per cent, and Hart and Glenn by seven per cent each. Actually, by Sunday night the ABC/*Post* sampling indicated that Hart had pulled ahead in New Hampshire, but this was thought to be an aberration, and was not made public. On Monday, the sampling continued to indicate a Hart victory, but this, too, was not made public, out of concern that it could be wrong. (On the previous Monday, the day of the Iowa caucuses, Mondale was far ahead of both Glenn and Hart—he had forty-two per cent to Glenn's twenty-six per cent and Hart's six per cent. By Wednesday, Hart had pulled ahead of Glenn, and Mondale was dropping.) To make matters worse for the Mondale people, a blizzard was forecast for New Hampshire on Tuesday; they weren't sure what this would do to their turnout, or even whether they could get back to New Hampshire for Election Night. (They did.) By Tuesday noon, as Mondale was leaving Washington for the Boston airport, the networks' exit polls, which were not yet publicly known, were beginning to indicate a Hart victory, and the Mondale people knew this—but generally exit polls aren't considered conclusive until about two-thirty in the afternoon. When Mondale's plane landed in Boston, at three-twenty-five, the network correspondents in the entourage phoned their offices, learned what the polls were saying, and relayed the news to the Mondale camp.

Last night, after the results of the New Hampshire primary were announced, Mondale, looking neither beaten nor falsely cheerful, said, steadily, "I have won one, I have lost one. This is two states. We've got twenty-five coming up in just three weeks and I'm going to be in all of them; we're going to win this campaign." He also gave what was at least a useful analysis, from his point of view, and perhaps even an at least partially valid one. He said, "I think what happened was that here in New Hampshire the voters decided they didn't want the debate to end." Glenn, who had come in third, looked jubilant, and said, "I'm one of the happiest people in New Hampshire tonight." The source of Glenn's joy was, as he put it, that the results had put an end to "this idea of the inevitability of the Mondale juggernaut." Glenn would head south, where he, Jackson, Mondale—and now Hart—would meet. Hart, looking very happy, said that he would compete with Mondale in the South as well as elsewhere. Mondale had committed himself to every contest; Hart could, for a while, pick his spots. The prospect now is for a bloody fight. Hart said, "This is a very decisive defeat, if I may say so, for Vice-President Mondale. What is different about my candidacy is that I don't just debate the issues of the past; what I try to do is lay out an agenda for the future, and if that confuses the Mondale campaign, that's their problem." He also said that some people who were characterizing his campaign incorrectly had not read his book, *A New Democracy*, or his position papers, and said, "It's easy to characterize people if you're ill-informed or uninformed, and I think a lot of people are. What I've done is debate the issues of the future, not the past." Hart also said, "I'm not prepared—at this moment, at least—to claim the title front-runner. But I know one thing: tonight in New Hampshire we buried the label dark horse."

XIII

MONTGOMERY, ALABAMA. At nine-forty-five this morning, Gary
Hart is standing on the steps of the Alabama statehouse, a large
white building with six big columns. Behind him is a large American flag, and in front of the lectern are two of his campaign
posters—large photographs of Hart, chin on hand, looking
thoughtful, with his name in digital-style print. (Hart's campaign
buttons are in the same print.) Hart is standing on the spot where
Jefferson Davis took the oath of office as President of the Confeder-
acy. Atop the building flies the Confederate flag, along with the
flags of the United States and the State of Alabama. This is the first
of two stops on a pilgrimage Democratic candidates make in Montgomery: a speech to the legislature, and a call on George Wallace,
once again Alabama's governor. Walter Mondale, John Glenn, and
Jesse Jackson have all spoken to the legislature and met with Wallace. Hart is no longer simply a candidate for the Democratic
nomination; he is a political phenomenon—in part a craze, but also
something beyond that. Nothing like what has happened in the past
week has ever happened before in American politics. No other
candidate has been so quickly transformed into such a political
force—"velocity" is the new buzzword—or become the subject of so
much excitement. No one can be sure right now how long all this
will last or just where it is headed, even if Hart should make it to the
White House. For some time to come, there will be analyses of what
this is, and was, all about, and attempts to apply a grand theory,
even though the truth is usually more complicated. There will also
be analyses of why this turn of events was unpredicted, but in fact
that is not difficult to explain. The unpredictability of it is connected with some of the elements of what this is all about.

The liabilities and vulnerabilities of Mondale, who had been
considered a front-runner further along than any front-runner
had ever been before, were known. What those who understood

that Mondale had liabilities and vulnerabilities could not figure
out was who would be in a position to pick up the pieces, or
whether anyone would, if he stumbled. It isn't just that Hart was
not registering in the polls, which can only be a snapshot of the
moment; it is that in fact his campaign was not getting anywhere
until sometime toward mid-January, when he participated in the
debate at Dartmouth, and offered his theme of "a new generation
of leadership" with crispness, if little explanation. But Hart came
over well. Even after that, there were only glimmerings that he
might be doing better than he had been, which did not mean that
he was doing terribly well. When Hart appeared at an all-candidate forum in New York City last October, he turned in an un-
memorable performance. His own aides say that his speeches on
"issues" last year put his audiences to sleep. He had set forth his
theme some time ago that it was time for a new generation of
politicians (it suited his purposes, since he could with some justification describe himself as representing a younger generation of
politicians), but he wavered from that theme: late last year, when
other things didn't seem to be working, his emphasis was on appealing for the women's vote. (The "new generation" theme is not
a new one for Hart. He used it when he first ran for the Senate, in
1974: "They've had their turn; now it's our turn.") It was because
Hart sensed he wasn't getting anywhere that at the end of the year
he turned for help to the pollster Patrick Caddell, with whom he
had worked when he managed the McGovern campaign, but
whose advice, like that of others, he had been resisting. And the
whole point of a long paper that Caddell wrote last fall, defining
the possibilities for some new candidate who might enter the race,
was that no one currently in the race, including Hart, had positioned himself to take advantage of the opening that Caddell believed he saw—an opening for a candidate who would run an anti-
establishment campaign, offering new ideas, and appealing to
younger voters who were not participating in the political process.
Hart's approach included some pieces of what Caddell was talking
about, and once they got together Caddell helped him flesh out
the picture and sharpen his themes. How far Hart would have got
without this help the world will never know (and is the subject of
some tension between Hart and Caddell and between Hart's campaign staff and Caddell). The world will also never know what
would have happened if the first contest had taken place in a state

that is larger and more representative of the Democratic Party than New Hampshire, and less subject to the influence of independents, and also to grass-roots organization. This is not to say that Mondale's vulnerabilities were not there (and the collective criticism of his rivals helped drive them home); and it is now clear that the support for him was not as intense as his campaign had supposed, or hoped. But it is also possible that had the Democratic race begun somewhere else it would have had a different dynamic. It is also true that James Johnson, Mondale's campaign chairman, recognized all along that some combination of forces could come together and undo the Mondale campaign's best-laid plans. Mondale himself was always wary of New Hampshire. And Caddell says that the Mondale campaign strategy nearly worked. Referring to Johnson, Caddell says, "I think Jim understood that Mondale couldn't win if he started to die, so they tried to get everyone to appoint a President before a vote. In that sense, it was a brilliant strategy, and it came within an eyelash of working."

The Hart victory in New Hampshire washed over into Maine, which held its precinct caucuses last Sunday, and into Vermont, which held a popularity contest, with no delegates at stake (that comes later), on Tuesday. That this effect was occurring was apparent to both the Hart and the Mondale camps within two days of the New Hampshire contest, as was the fact that the chemistry of the contests that will take place here in the South and elsewhere on March 13th had changed. (On the thirteenth, five states will hold primaries and four will hold caucuses.) Two days after New Hampshire, the Mondale people found, to their horror, that Hart had gained some twenty points in the South. Something big had been set loose, and what that something is is what people are trying to figure out now. Hart won the Maine caucuses fifty-one per cent to forty-four per cent. (For what it's worth, the difference in the two candidates' actual votes was eleven hundred and ninety-three.) In Vermont, where the Mondale campaign effectively pulled out when it saw what was coming, Hart won by seventy per cent to twenty per cent for Mondale. (Vermont is typically heavily affected by what happens in New Hampshire, and is a state where a large number of independents and Republicans vote in the Democratic contest. Moreover, a high percentage of the Vermont Democrats are professionals, to whom Hart appeals, and Hart also received a heavy proportion of "John Anderson Republicans.")

Though both Hart and Caddell had seen the possibility of parlay-
ing a successful showing in New Hampshire (even a second-place
victory) into a publicity wave that could carry Hart further, neither
of them, by their own testimony, had foreseen anything like this.

What "this" is is some combination of an unlocking of certain
pent-up political desires, an extraordinary carry by the media,
sheer excitement, and a certain thrill-seeking. These elements
cannot be separated out. The very fact that numerous people now
tell reporters that they favor Hart even though they don't know
much, or anything, about him is part of the phenomenon. He is
young, good-looking, and fresh, and offers himself as someone
who will change the "old ways." His approach is sufficiently
nonideological—deliberately so—that people can impute to him
what they want. Hart is, as of now, the inkblot candidate. The fact
that the voters have seen little of him until now and know little
about him is an advantage. He's not old hat, like Mondale, or even
Glenn. It is clear that there were a lot of unrealized hopes, anx-
ieties, dissatisfactions, and rejections of the overly familiar floating
around out there, and Hart became the beneficiary of them. He
does not have Mondale's liabilities (Carter, interest-group support,
the aura of "old liberal"). His adaptation of the mannerisms of
John F. Kennedy goes over well. It may be remembered that just
last fall we went through an extended media commemoration of
the twentieth anniversary of Kennedy's death—a repeated re-
minder of what had been lost. Now along comes someone who has
not only adopted Kennedy's mannerisms but whose speeches are
fashioned in part by Theodore Sorensen, who was Kennedy's
speechwriter and is co-chairman of Hart's campaign. An associate
of Hart's says of the Kennedy mannerisms, "Gary's studied that a
bit. It's not natural." Before the Dartmouth debate, Hart reviewed
tapes of the Kennedy-Nixon debates of 1960.

This week, as a result of his New Hampshire victory, Hart is on
the covers of *Newsweek*, *Time* (sharing this one with Mondale), *U.S.
News & World Report*, *New York*, and *The Economist*. Not only has he
been the recipient of a great deal of television coverage but the
sort of coverage he has received—compared to Mondale's—has
been striking. The Maine and Vermont contests, which are, in the
context of the Democratic race as a whole, minor events, were
made into very big events. Hart has been depicted night after
night as on the move, the one stirring all the excitement; Mondale

has been depicted as reeling, "desperate," "fighting for his political life." (We were even shown a scene of the Secret Service's letting a door slam in Mondale's face—the scene being presented as a metaphor for Mondale's political situation.) Harold Himmelman, a Washington attorney who has been an adviser to the Hart campaign for some time, says, "We felt at the end of last year that the Glenn campaign was failing, and that presented us with a vacuum; but we felt we needed more time to fill it. But the Glenn drop in Iowa gave us the chance. When we got that fifteen percent in Iowa that Monday night, the media, which had written us off as a loser, overnight made us a challenger. Now there's this huge wave, and it's media-created. You can't control it; you just ride it." Moreover, Hart is a good television candidate, while Mondale is not. Hart looks good on television: his high cheekbones and lean face are just right for the cameras, and his cool demeanor is just right for the medium. Mondale's is not a good television face (or voice), and he has not adapted himself to the medium. Americans love something new, and Hart is presenting himself as something new. An attractive and articulate something new. Americans are given to crazes, which television and the news magazines speed along, and Hart is currently a craze. Crazes and fads are not new to this country, of course, but the extent and speed of the magnification of them are, and we are more at the mercy of faddishness. A fad gets to the farthest corner of Bozeman, Montana, half an hour after it starts. But fads, by definition, fade. Hart will have to ground his political effort in something that is real, and sustainable, or he will be in trouble at some point. And he will have to be able to withstand glare and pressure he has never experienced before. At times, it seems as if we were living through a movie. But there are some deeper reasons this is happening—reasons that present Hart with both opportunities and dangers.

Part of the phenomenon is that Hart is raising hopes—this is the opportunity and the danger. John Kennedy raised hopes—and Jimmy Carter did so briefly. The hope is that things will be "better;" Americans are addicted to the idea that things can be better, and the successful politician speaks to that. It has become a commonplace to say that since Kennedy's death America has gone through twenty years of disappointments and tragedies—assassinations, Vietnam, Watergate—and, according to the analysts of the American psyche, this has led to alienation and cynicism, and also to hope for something better. Hart believes that he has touched those people who are looking for a renewal of faith. By condemning the "old ways" and "old arrangements" by which government has functioned, by running against "the establishment," he is suggesting that there is a rather clear, and simple, reason things have not gone better, and that he can change that. Running against "the establishment" is, of course, an old political device, which serves the politician, and his followers, well, because it suggests that there is some "they" at whose feet all grievances can be laid. George Wallace did it, and so did Jimmy Carter and Ronald Reagan. It served Hart well that Mondale, with his endorsements and his emphasis on his experience, could be portrayed as quintessentially a creature of "the establishment" and a practitioner of the "old ways." When I asked Caddell, who served as pollster and strategist for both the McGovern 1972 Presidential campaign and Carter's 1976 campaign, how he explained the "velocity," he said, "I never saw this in 1972 or 1976. There's something deep out there; it's been repressed all these months. People were told they had to accept the bland compromise, the choice of the power groups. Gary's theme appeals not just to people's intellect but to their emotions, and there's been an explosion. What I don't know yet is: Are we seeing an explosion, a movement, or a political phenomenon that may have other ramifications—that could bring real change in the political system?" When I asked Caddell if he thoroughly understood the phenomenon, he said that he did not, even though, because of the paper he wrote last fall, he believed he had as much right to argue that he did understand it as anyone. "But I don't completely know what's happened yet," he said. "Something embryonic has burst out. The important thing is its growth. Is it a flash in the pan, a fad, a Cabbage Patch doll? Is it a political movement? Or is it a political revolution? That's all to be decided." If Hart could bring about fundamental changes in the way government works, that could be a salutary thing. But the danger for Hart—and for the country—is that he may be raising hopes he cannot fulfill.

Hart's strategy now is to pursue Mondale in the three Southern states that vote next Tuesday—Alabama, Florida, and Georgia—as well as elsewhere. As Caddell predicted could happen when the new Democratic-nomination-contest calendar was adopted, in

1982, the bunching of the primaries and caucuses has as of now turned the contest into in effect a national primary, working to the benefit of the lesser-known challenger rather than the front-runner. Now it is the Mondale people who would like to slow the whole thing down, in the hope that greater scrutiny of Hart would raise more questions about him in the public mind. Mondale has tried, in recent days, to raise questions about him. He has criticized him for voting against a windfall-profit tax on oil (Hart's real opposition was to imposing the tax on newly discovered oil; this would be of interest to, among others, the oil producers of Hart's home state of Colorado) and against a Carter Administration-backed plan to control hospital costs (Hart voted for a less restrictive version, which carried), and for proposing a ten-dollar-a-barrel fee on imported oil (this, too, would benefit domestic oil producers; Hart says the purpose is to promote energy conservation). Mondale has also criticized Hart for being slow to back the nuclear freeze. And Mondale has criticized Hart for backing the idea of a nuclear "build-down," whereby two warheads would be removed for every new one deployed. Mondale argues that this is antithetical to the idea of a freeze, because it would allow for modernization, and that it was backed by the Reagan Administration in order to kill the freeze. In fact, the build-down idea, which originated in Congress with bipartisan sponsorship, was an alternative to the freeze and was picked up by the Reagan Administration to get the MX through. (At that point, Hart, who opposes the MX, voted against the build-down.) Its real danger is that it could be destabilizing, by leaving each side with fewer weapons, and perhaps more dangerous ones, for the other to target; and it is antithetical to the idea of deploying many single-warhead Midgetman missiles, so as to make the land-based force less vulnerable. Hart, like Mondale, supports the Midgetman concept—but he is not alone among members of Congress in backing contradictory arms-control proposals.

Hart's Senate record is not marked by a great deal of success, and is marked by a certain caution—despite his calls now for "bold leadership." (His position on Lebanon has been more hedged than he suggests.) His lack of achievement in the Senate stems in large part from his by now much discussed disinclination to work in concert with colleagues, to form coalitions. Hart has often seemed more interested in making a point—his amendment was better than somebody else's amendment—than in getting something done. This is one of the characteristics that have made him less than popular with his colleagues—even the best of them. Another is his loner style. Hart has strikingly few friends in the Senate. He is an intelligent man, and a serious one, but even those colleagues most favorably disposed toward him raise a question about his depth. One of these said to me recently, "I find him a bit"—and he paused—"thin." Another said, "Gary's intelligent, but he's no genius." Someone who has served in the Senate with Hart says that he finds him "opportunistic" about issues. The criticism of Hart by his colleagues is often written off as so much jealousy, or as the talk of Washington mediocrities. But these people I have referred to are all serious, able men, capable of generous comments about their colleagues. Peer judgment does count for something. (It may be remembered that Jimmy Carter was unpopular among his fellow-governors.) Hart represents some contradictions: he is a remote personality who, not unlike other politicians, wants to be loved by the crowds. He is a man who is quite loath to talk about himself but who wants to lead a movement. He talks in a way that suggests he has a sense of Destiny about himself, has enormous self-confidence, but even some of those who know him best aren't sure whether this is real. (During his 1976 campaign, Carter displayed a similar confidence, but it soon faded.) But that Hart is capable of tough-minded pursuit of a goal is in little doubt. In his professional dealings, Hart trusts almost nobody. One man who knows him perhaps as well as anyone says that Hart has a deeply suspicious nature. All these things raise questions about how he would be at governing; but those questions are irrelevant to the whirlwind that is sweeping him along now, as are Mondale's criticisms of this vote or that.

The Mondale campaign has already virtually given up on Massachusetts and Rhode Island, which hold their primaries next Tuesday, as well as on Wyoming, which holds its caucuses on Saturday, and where the Mondale people had for a brief time hoped to checkmate Hart. (Mondale has the endorsement of the governor of Massachusetts and the mayor of Boston, but this is no longer relevant.) Mondale had planned to campaign in the West this week as well as in the South, but he is now spending the entire week in the South, knowing that his hopes of surviving beyond next Tuesday (which has come to be known as Super Tuesday) depend on the outcome in the three big Southern states—states that not very long ago his campaign was confident of winning. Now Hart, who had made no effort here before, is closing in fast in all of them. The surveys taken by his campaign in the days after the New Hampshire primary indicated that all three Southern states were winnable, and, besides, Caddell, a devotee of military strategy, says, "It's a classic military doctrine that when you've got someone on the retreat go the maximum; you don't let up and let them regroup. We won't let them gather their resources and focus on one state." Among the many ironies of this campaign is that the theory of not letting an opponent concentrate on one state is what the Mondale people were applying to Hart, or thought they were, in the early contests. Caddell says, "The money is pouring in, we've got the resources to go everywhere, so my instinct is go everywhere." One liberal activist has arranged a loan of one and a half million dollars for the Hart campaign.

The Hart campaign is feeling the pressures of going from a small effort to the one it is conducting now. In December, it had only a handful of people working in its headquarters, and was broke. One Hart adviser says, "The campaign was near an end organizationally." Now it is showing the strains of its sudden success, and is more than chaotic. The decision-making is not exactly orderly. Telephone lines are busy; events are being slapped together; the travel arrangements are often in a state of disorder. Hart's campaign manager, Oliver Henkel, who is a classmate from Yale Law School, has never been involved in a national campaign before. And Hart himself has made a somewhat shaky transition from a campaign that did not receive major attention, and was not under much pressure, to the national campaign he is now in. His tendency to jab competitors was shown on the national stage on Saturday when, at a joint appearance with Mondale at a dinner in Atlanta, he handed Mondale a shower head and—in a reference to a remark by Mondale on the night of the New Hampshire primary that "sometimes a cold shower is good for you"—said, "I think you're going to have a chance to use it on many Tuesdays to come." Then, on Sunday, during another joint appearance, this one in Boston, Hart said, "I bet Fritz is not going to claim the title of front-runner again. He's a very humble man. Instead, I think Fritz still would rather be considered a little-known dark horse struggling to get by on twelve million dollars and an A.F.L.-C.I.O.

endorsement." For this, Hart was booed by some members of the audience, which included politicians with ties to labor. Hart's campaign advisers were troubled by these remarks, and told him so.

After making a short stump speech on the steps of the Capitol, Hart addresses the Alabama state legislature, developing the themes in his stump speech further. A trim figure, he is dressed in a navy suit, a white shirt, a navy tie with a crest, and is wearing Western boots. "Occasionally, there are historic watershed periods where this nation has to decide not whether to move left or right, or even whether to become Democratic or Republican, but must decide whether to move to the future or the past," Hart says. This is a clever message, in which Hart paints himself as non-ideological—or beyond ideology. But does he really mean to suggest that it does not matter whether the country votes for a Democratic or a Republican President? He says that the choice before the nation "is a choice of new leadership for the nineteen-eighties and nineteen-nineties: a new leadership that will move this nation beyond the irrelevant debate between the two parties and between outworn agendas; a new leadership that will open up the White House to all in this nation on equal terms, and to none on the basis of special favors; a new leadership that will ask everyone in this nation to share the burdens of putting our country back on the track . . . a new leadership that will be a partner of the people of this country, and not a servant of the selfish or the greedy or the left or the right; a new leadership faithful to the traditional values of America and demanding something more than politics as usual." This sounds appealing, but what does it mean, and how would it work? Placing himself in the lineage of some of the great men of the Democratic Party, Hart says, "The oldest ideal of the party to which I and many of you belong is to stand for new ideas, from the New Freedom of Woodrow Wilson to the New Deal of Franklin Roosevelt to the New Frontier of John Kennedy, and I believe to a New Democracy for this country in the nineteen-eighties."

A New Democracy is the title of a book Hart published last year, as part of his preparation for this year. It is a compendium of ideas gathered from many sources, some of the ideas contradictory, some of them based on anecdotal experience—one company tried this or that and it worked—and some of them not exactly original. Hart's proposal that industry be revived through collective decisions taken by labor, management, and government is now received wisdom among Democrats, including Mondale, and was, in fact, tried by the Carter Administration. Another proposal put forth by the Carter Administration and now offered by Hart is a tax-based incomes policy, or TIP—a cumbersome plan for holding down inflation which sank of its own weight not long after Carter proposed it. Later, even Carter Administration officials said it was unworkable. Several of the other ideas Hart advertises as new have been around for some time. The idea of jointly banning the manufacturing of plutonium was proposed to the Soviet Union by the Eisenhower, Kennedy, Johnson, Nixon, and Carter Administrations. (The proposal was actually a broader one, covering all fissionable materials.) The idea of individual training accounts, to set aside tax-deductible contributions for retraining workers, has been in circulation for years. (This proposal is at odds with one of the tax-reform plans Hart backs, which would virtually eliminate tax deductions. Critics also say that it does not come to grips with the retraining problem, and that the tax deduction is of little help to low-income workers.) Politicians can play a useful role in moving ideas onto the national agenda. To offer them indiscriminately and uncritically can devalue the exercise. Several of the ideas in the book are interesting, and potentially useful, but the book conveys a certain lack of discrimination, an infatuation with ideas for their own sake, a tendency to be impressed by the idea brokers, whatever the relative merits of their ideas. In the book, Hart proposes a Council on Emerging Issues, a concept with a certain surface appeal but one that could lead the government into looking for trends, and overinterpreting the evidence—taking us the way of "Megatrends." There are plenty of instruments within government for tracking "emerging issues," and plenty of pollsters to add their advice.

Hart now tells the Alabama legislators that the economy has been transformed from a manufacturing base into one that employs two-thirds of the work force in service industries, which he defines as information, communications, and high technology. (He appears to be lumping those who work in such service industries as hamburger chains with those who work in high tech. This is a confusion shared by some of his fellow Atari Democrats. The new service industries Hart mentions can be added to a manufacturing base but are unlikely to provide an equivalent number of jobs. And, in any case, the making of Atari video games and Atari home-computer products has moved from Silicon Valley to Hong Kong and Taiwan. In part, the great interest of some members of Congress in high tech was inspired by the semiconductor industry, which was seeking certain trade policies and tax breaks.) Hart talks about the importance of "a new economic agenda that offers to rebuild and restructure the very foundation of this nation's economy," including government loan guarantees for the modernization of basic manufacturing plants. (It is not clear what sort of plan Hart is advocating here.) Hart also proposes "a fifteen-to-twenty-year jobs program" that will put people to work rebuilding the nation's infrastructure. (He has been unclear on how this would be paid for.) Hart pulls together the two themes by saying, "I believe only by restructuring the very foundation of this nation's economy will we meet our obligations of economic opportunity for all Americans, and, more importantly, raise the resources necessary to address the human needs of those who cannot look after themselves: those who are out of work, the poor, the children, and the elderly in this society." Hart is sensitive to Mondale's charge that he does not show sufficient concern for these groups. In fact, Hart has an acceptable Democratic voting record on issues of concern to these groups; but his real interest seems to be elsewhere. The emphasis is on the digital politics. Moreover, Hart is from an affluent Western state where the ethos has more to do with growth than with the left-out and minorities, and the following he is attracting includes few blacks.

Hart talks about his involvement in "the military-reform movement," which he calls "one of the most important political movements in this country today." He explains its point: that the real tests of what is to be spent on defense should be the effectivenesss of the weapons—whether the weapons are adaptable to and maintainable under combat conditions, and affordable in sufficient numbers. He also stresses the importance of paying military personnel better. Hart has in fact been working on these questions for some time, and the political appeal of approaching defense questions this way is clear. By framing the issue in these terms, he has removed himself from the ideology of the defense debate: to defense conservatives he sounds like an advocate of a strong defense (they are probably not aware that Hart's budget calls for only a three-per-cent growth in defense), and to defense liberals it sounds as if he were cutting the size of defense. By talking about increasing military pay, Hart keeps the military from getting too upset with him over his other proposals. Moreover, the military-reform movement, while it deals with such things as the maneuverability of surface ships, does not take on the big questions of redundancy, such as why each military branch has its own air force. Now Hart talks about the need to curb the arms race, and about the importance of "civil rights for all our citizens."

Interestingly, Hart says, "I believe the only solution for this country's challenges in the nineteen-eighties is a government of national unity . . . rising above partisanship and ideology." It is not clear what he means, but the inspiration for this may come from a recent book by Sorensen, called *A Different Kind of Presidency*, in which he calls for a "temporary bipartisan 'grand coalition' of national unity." Under Sorensen's plan, there would be a President and a Vice-President from different parties; a Cabinet and a Sub-cabinet equally divided between the two parties; an "experienced bipartisan White House staff;" and "a Presidential advisory council of elder statesmen." Aside from the implausibility and probable unworkability of such a scheme, the idea of a council of wise men is inconsonant with Hart's central theme: that he would open up government to fresh ideas. Hart has begun to modify his claim to being the candidate of "new ideas" by saying that what he means is that he would open up the corridors of government to fresh ideas. He speaks now about the need to "free" the political process from "the grasp of the special interests." He talks more than the other candidates of the need to curb the power of political-action committees. Echoing John Kennedy, he says now, as he often does, "We must once again have Presidents and political leaders who ask us what we can do for our country, and not what our country can do for us." Hart, speaking clearly and crisply, pushes his voice to full volume, adding a sense of intensity and urgency, and a touch of eloquence, and the timbre of Kennedy. On occasion, his voice can't make it, and squeaks. Hart laughs and pushes on. Hart does, in fact, have a good sense of humor, a strong streak of fun in him; he enjoys story swapping and laughing. Now he concludes, "We must do what this nation has done in its greatest periods, and that is leave past programs and past policies behind and launch this country into the future. We have the power, literally, to change the course of American history. With the help of the people of this state, with the help of the people across the South and the North and the West, I believe we will in this decade create a New Democracy." This is a sweeping vision.

Hart's is a thematic speech that touches a lot of buttons. A couple of themes he uses before other audiences he left out in speaking to the Alabama legislature. Before other audiences, he says that he wants a foreign policy "that does not send our sons to die without cause in Lebanon or to serve as bodyguards for dictators in Central America." He also says that "the real enemy in the Third World . . . is poverty, and not Communism." These statements appeal to the young voters Hart is trying to attract and to the anti-Vietnam sentiment he is drawing upon, and deal with real foreign-policy issues. But he picks his spots for saying them. The major point that Hart is making, in a variety of ways, is that he is going to rearrange, fundamentally, the way things are done in Washington. Hart is very good at what he is doing now. His speaking style has improved markedly, which has something to do with confidence. He seems convincing, and offers people something to put their faith in—but it is faith.

Hart's commercials in the South are aimed at the region's anti-establishment streak, and also at what Caddell sees as its desire for change. Caddell, who is from Jacksonville, Florida, says that people underestimate the South's desire for change and its pride in the changes that have occurred here. One Hart ad says, in part, "I'm a Democrat and proud of it. But I'm also a Westerner and fiercely independent. The Washington insiders and special interests have handpicked their candidate for President. But I offer our Party and our country a choice. This election is about the failure of the past and the promise of the future. . . . Make your vote Tuesday a declaration of independence." Another has Hart saying, "I believe the South, more than any other section of the nation, understands breaking the chains of the past and moving into the future," and the announcer saying, "Hope for America's future," and then Hart saying, "The South can once more change the course of history by voting for new leadership, new ideas, and a fresh start for America."

Hart's Kennedy mannerisms go beyond the hand in the pocket or the hand chopping the air: he tugs at a jacket lapel, fiddles with a jacket button, smooths his tie, races up a plane ramp. The adoption of the mannerisms, like his changing of his name, from Hart-pence, and his age (making himself a year younger), suggests a man who is constantly inventing himself. (The changes in name and age would be raising fewer questions if Hart had not dissembled about both matters. On the matter of the name, he said that both parents, particularly his mother, wanted the change, and had made the change, when the court records show that it was Hart himself who made the main presentation. When questions about his age continued, he said, "I can't account for every piece of paper that's been written by my campaign or anyone else," and it then emerged that Hart himself on various occasions had made the change.) A close colleague of Hart's, speaking about the way Hart is presenting himself in this campaign, said to me recently, "What I don't know is whether Gary will shed this skin, too."

THE ORLANDO AIRPORT. Late afternoon. Despite the glow and the excitement that surround the Hart campaign now, it is facing some down-to-earth realities. The thing that concerns the Hart people is that the support for him in some areas is "soft," and needs to be firmed up through people's having a stronger sense of why they are for Hart. Kathy Bushkin, Hart's press secretary, says that the sudden rush of interest in Hart has put a lot of pressure on his campaign to get across who he is. "The hardest part is getting the information out there, and, frankly, we have to rely on the evening news, and we're trying to supplement that with substantive speeches," she says. "Mondale is trying to portray Gary as a media candidate." She adds, "There is enormous interest in who is Gary Hart. We need to get that question answered our way. Mondale is trying to answer it his way." She says that the debate to take place this Sunday night in Atlanta "is a very important event for us—to harden the support that's now based on momentum and excitement, which, frankly, help us." Ray Strother, who handles Hart's media, says that the daily tracking polls show dramatic movement in Hart's direction from the time before the evening news programs to after the evening news programs.

Another reality is that the Hart campaign has a somewhat contradictory approach on the matter of its anti-establishment theme. It wants an aura of legitimacy, and is seeking endorsements from other politicians. This morning, it announced that three California congressmen who had supported Cranston, who has dropped out of the race, now support Hart. The endorsement of others is being actively pursued. Senator Christopher Dodd, of Connecticut, a close friend of Caddell's, will endorse Hart on Saturday. When Hart goes to Oklahoma tomorrow, he will be endorsed by former House Speaker Carl Albert. Here at the Orlando airport, Hart announced that he had the support of Congressman Kenneth MacKay, who represents a district in central Florida. Hart is also gathering what Florida state officials he can to help him here next week. At his last stop, in Pensacola, he was endorsed by W. D. Childers, a state senator and conservative leader in that most conservative part of the state, who announced that some local candidates to be Convention delegates for Reubin Askew, who has dropped out, would support Hart. Hart is trying to make up for the failure to have filed complete delegate slates by winning over Askew delegates, with some success. (He also tried, but failed, to get Askew's endorsement; Askew has endorsed no one.) The larger contradiction is that Hart is running an anti-establishment campaign that he and his people do not want to be viewed hostilely, or with fright, by what passes for the Washington establishment. There is, after all, a nomination to be sewed up and an election to be won. Caddell says, "One of the things we have to do is diffuse the sense that this is an insurgency movement, and enforce the sense that this is a transition movement." Some of Hart's associates in Washington are deliberately reaching out to people there and reassuring them that the attitude of the Hart entourage will be one of forgiveness toward those who were not with Hart earlier—and this is a message that many Washingtonians are, of course, relieved to hear. The positioners—those many people in Washington who expend their efforts, make their moves, to get in position for good jobs in a future Administration—have suddenly found themselves in a most uncomfortable position. With Mondale's nomination appearing so likely, and with so many of them having had previous associations with Mondale, many positioners were already trying on their jobs in the Mondale Administration. Conversations about who would have which job were not uncommon. Now people are quickly discovering their ties to Hart and his entourage, and Washingtonians are just beginning to adjust to the fact that there might be a whole new pecking order. New Hampshire not only scrambled the nomination contest; it made and unmade would-be hostesses. The hairdresser to

Hart's wife, Lee, is ecstatic—Washington hairdressers being a particularly competitive lot.

Most of Hart's stops today are at airports—an efficient way to get him on local television. Hart did address an enthusiastic rally in Pensacola, and attended a fund-raiser there. Now, in his remarks at the Orlando airport—in a state with a considerable percentage of retired people—Hart puts more emphasis than he did earlier in the day on the impact of the budget deficits on the elderly, and mentions some of his other themes. During a press conference that follows, he is asked about his having sought and received, through a special waiver, a commission in the Navy in 1980. Hart sought the commission before the 1980 election, in which he ran for reelection to the Senate, but the Navy Department put the matter off until after the election. Hart had no previous military experience. During the 1980 campaign, he made an ad in which he drove a tank. Hart won reelection very narrowly, by about one per cent, even though his opponent was not nominated until September and was not prepared to run a Senate campaign, and did not have the support of the Colorado Republican Party. The narrowness of his escape was said to have left Hart shaken, but his victory, in a year when a number of Senate Democrats lost, enhanced his national reputation, and set him on the road to the Presidency. Hart now explains that he sought the commission "primarily because I was concerned, as others were in the nineteen-seventies, about the very likely possibility that this nation would become involved in a military action in the Persian Gulf," and he says, "I had a teen-age son who was beginning to approach draft age and I made a personal decision at that time that if this country were to become involved in that war that I could not stay in the Senate"—that he would have resigned his Senate seat and entered active duty. (Hart's son, John, was fourteen at the time.) In an answer to a question about his prospects in Florida, Hart complains about the primary schedule (which at the moment is helping him), and he praises Askew, who, he says, "made a tremendous contribution to the substantive debate in 1983 and 1984." Askew was not actually one of the more memorable participants in the debate. He did, as a former Special Trade Representative, help Hart make the case against some of Mondale's protectionist positions, but his other principal themes were anti-abortion and against the nuclear freeze. In answer to a question about whether he would end military aid to El Salvador even if that assured a victory of the leftists, Hart says that he doesn't think that that would happen, and that El Salvador might do something more about the death squads there if it knew an Administration was serious about shutting off funds if it did not. He adds that even if the hypothesis of the question were true the answer to it would be yes. Asked whether he has ever supported Reagan budget cuts or tax cuts, Hart says, "No, I don't think so." (Actually, Hart, like most Senate Democrats, did support the Reagan budget cuts at one point in 1981.)

MIAMI. Hart has arrived at the Miami airport in time to do live interviews on each of the three main local television stations' evening news programs. The state of electronics now enables candidates to do this without going to the stations, and his being on live enables him to make his case without editorial comment, and to make more of a splash. ("Senator Gary Hart has just arrived in Miami and here he is, live!") By now, Hart is bone tired and his face is pale, but he pulls himself up and stands looking into the camera—seeming to be aware of which angle is best for him—and talks clearly. "I think our campaign just happened to represent what people were looking for," he tells one interviewer. Asked about charisma, Hart replies, "I said throughout 1983 that charisma came when you started winning primaries, and I think that's what happened." It is true that in 1983, when Hart's campaign associates urged him to liven up his style, and despaired of the speeches he was giving then, he told them that he would have charisma after he won his first primary. Hart, being shrewd, understands how this works. He has the makings of charisma—the looks, the now polished style—but charisma is something that is usually acquired after a candidate starts to look successful. (John Kennedy did not start out charismatic, and it is probably forgotten that there was a time when Jimmy Carter was charismatic.) Charisma involves an interchange between the candidate and the public, in which the public begins to sense something exciting about the candidate, and the candidate, buoyed by that, gets better at projecting himself. Charisma is a chemical reaction between a candidate and the people: if the crowds went away, the charisma would be gone. One does not walk down the street, or go out to get the morning papers, being charismatic. Charisma probably also involves an ingredient of hope; the charismatic candidate is one who is raising hopes. (Ray Strother, Hart's media manager, says, "We're advertising hope.") Now, at the Miami airport, Hart tells another interviewer of the important role he believes Askew has played, and adds, "I think he has a role to play in the Hart Administration." This is pretty conventional politics. In one of the interviews, he is asked about a recent column in the Washington *Post* referring to an earlier interview he gave the *Post*, in which he said that Cuba was not a totalitarian state. He replies that that is not what happened. (It is.)

Tomorrow, Hart will go to Oklahoma, which is to hold caucuses on the thirteenth, and then to Illinois, to plant the flag for the primary that will occur there a week later. Mondale should be in good shape in Illinois, where his campaign has made a large effort, and where James Johnson ran a very successful primary campaign for Carter, over Kennedy, in 1980. But Caddell is in Chicago today, seeing Mayor Harold Washington, and trying to stir up trouble for Mondale, who campaigned for one of Washington's opponents—Richard M. Daley, son of the late mayor—in the fight for the mayoralty nomination last year, and who has been endorsed by Edward Vrdolyak, the chairman of the Cook County Democratic Central Committee (the remains of the Daley machine) and a bitter foe of Washington. (Daley had helped the Carter-Mondale ticket in 1980, and his chief opponent last year was presumed to be Mayor Jane Byrne, who had backed Kennedy. Mondale made his commitment to Daley before Washington got into the race.) Mondale has tried, without success, to make peace with the various factions in Chicago. Washington is for the moment allied with Jackson, whose base is Chicago, but this is an alliance of convenience, not affection.

Following a press conference, I have an interview with Hart in a small room at the Miami airport. He has just spoken by phone with his son, who is in Ireland for a while. (Hart's wife, Lee, often campaigns with him, but today she is campaigning elsewhere. The Harts have been separated twice in recent years, and reconciled shortly before Hart entered the Presidential race. Lee Hart is an attractive, spunky, direct woman.)

The thing that interests me most about Hart at this point is what he means by the "new ways" he says must be brought to government, since he is holding out the hope that under him the way that government works would profoundly change. I ask him what he means by this.

Hart begins by responding that he wants to "reinvolve talented and creative people in this country." He says, "I think one thing that has not happened under previous Administrations—this one and previous ones—is the kind of opening up of the process to the best minds and the best leaders of our society."

But, I suggest to Hart, he seems to be saying in his speeches that under him there would be structural changes in the way that government works. I tell him that what I think I hear him saying is that he would try to rearrange the arrangements.

"Not really, no," Hart replies. He continues, "I think the arrangements are frankly rearranging themselves with the kind of people who are getting elected to Congress. One of the accusations about me is that I'm not a good vote trader, I'm not a good manipulator of the process. But what most people don't realize is most of the newer members of Congress aren't, either." (Not everyone would agree with this assessment.) He goes on, "Take the military-reform movement: that really is a cross-ideological movement, and it's composed primarily of newer members of Congress who are fed up with the old ideological left-right debate on defense. I think that same kind of thing can be done on the economy: it's not pro-business or pro-labor to want to restructure a manufacturing base, and you can engage Republicans who are pro-business in that effort and you can engage liberal Democrats who want jobs for labor in that effort. And that's the kind of bipartisan coalition-building, or nonpartisan coalition-building, that I think needs to be done. And what I'm saying is that newer members of Congress, I think, are more amenable to that than older people, who may be more rigid ideologically or may be more partisan."

Hart is describing a style difference between some of the more senior members of Congress and some of the younger ones—a newer, cooler generation, particularly of Democrats, who are less influenced by party traditions and ideology than their seniors. But there is also a large number of younger members, of both parties, who are scrappy partisans, and believers in their parties' traditions. Caddell has told me that Hart's message is "supra-ideological" and, as Caddell sees it, involves moving politics "beyond the old definitions."

I ask Hart if he has in mind any new approaches for working with Congress.

He replies: "Yes—well, I certainly am thinking about that. I haven't come up with any novel proposals yet, but certainly the impact of the political-action committees has to be curbed. What kind of results that will have, I'm not sure. I'm thinking; I'm giving a lot of thought to it."

I ask Hart what his picture is of how Gary Hart governs along with the powerful interests in Washington, some of which are a part of the Democratic constituency.

"Offer them a deal," he replies. "Collectively. Take the indus-trial-modernization approach: that's essentially give-and-take for all parties—management, labor, private capital. You get this but you have to give up that—make it a package. Obviously, there is arbitration and negotiation of that package, but essentially it gets down at the final analysis to take it or leave it, and if it's a balanced and workable package there's going to be a tremendous incentive on the part of all those participants to go along. Now, in the final analysis, it's a voluntary system, and you can't mandate anything. But then I think the power of the Presidency in educating the American people and bringing the force of public opinion to bear on management or workers or investors is a very potent one— particularly early in the Administration."

I ask Hart what he thinks the popular response to him now suggests he has unlocked.

He replies, "Too early to say. Desire for change, desire for hope, a break with the past—with the failed past, not with values or principles but with a failed governing past. A desire to move for- ward, to let newer people try, to break out of a kind of stagnant nation and world. I don't know. I haven't quite defined it yet, and I think we're still in the middle of it, frankly—whatever it is."

I ask Hart if it ever worries him that he might let all those excited people down.

He replies. "Yeah, oh, absolutely. Worries me a lot. It's a tremen- dous burden. But I think, with the help of others, I'm up to it."

This evening, Hart goes to a condominium complex in North Miami Beach. This audience, of a couple of hundred elderly Jew- ish people, should be Mondale's constituency, if anyone is. But Hart is having a go at it. He is introduced to the audience by Mike Abrams, a young state representative from this area, who backed

Edward Kennedy's nomination effort in 1980. Mike Abrams, of North Miami Beach, and W. D. Childers, of Pensacola, represent different philosophies and different worlds, but Hart has brought them together. Hart removes the microphone from its stand and talks earnestly to this audience. He makes an argument to it that is similar to one he makes to others—that "this election is critical to this nation's future"—but with this audience the emphasis changes. He says, as he has before, "The decision we make as Americans about who will lead this country in the nineteen-eighties not only will decide whether the Democrats or the Republicans will be in the White House—" but now he adds, "I hope the Democrats will," and the audience laughs and applauds. He continues, saying that the election is about "not simply whether this country will move left or right but whether we as Americans and human beings will meet the challenges of the nineteen-eighties—not only for our generation but for generations to come." Hart says, "Some of you here, I know, remember Franklin Roosevelt," and he is applauded. He continues, "My generation remembers President John Kennedy." He is applauded again. He goes on, "The reason we remember those two Presidents particularly today is because they both shared the values of the Democratic Party of America. Values of a country dedicated to total equality for all of our citizens: the opportunity for every citizen, regardless of economic background or ethnic or national origin, and social justice for the people of this country—for the elderly, for the retired, for the poor, for the children, for the disadvantaged, the disabled, for those who needed the help of their society. That is why I'm a Democrat." This is the first time he's talked this way today. He adds, "But those two Presidents stood for something else. They stood for a government which was willing to meet the challenges of its own time and move this country into the future. They did that by their willingness to be bold, to break with the past, to try new methods and new solutions, to meet the problems of this country. I think that is the kind of leadership this country must have in the nineteen-eighties if we are to continue our promise and our ideal and our dream." Hart says, "This election could well determine whether those who are retired, those who are elderly, have the support of their government in time of need." And, sounding now like Mondale, he says, "This Administration has cut social programs in health and nutrition. It has sought to reduce

benefits in Social Security and Medicare and Medicaid. And if you
know that's what this Administration has done in its first term ask
yourself what will happen in the second term, when the President
and his Administration does not have to concern itself with reelection." He adds, "It means that there will be enormous burdens on
all of you and others like you across this country in terms of
Medicare, Medicaid, Social Security, health and nutrition programs necessary to meet just a basic standard of living for the
millions and millions of retired Americans." And he continues,
"Now, I think this election is critical to the future of our senior
citizens and our retired people in this country, and on that issue
alone Ronald Reagan should be dismissed from office." And he is
applauded again. He is much more the partisan Democrat here,
and the people in the audience seem to like this attractive young
man who reminds them, undoubtedly, of John Kennedy. He talks
at some length about the need to control the costs of medical care.
(Earlier this year, Mondale launched his own plan to deal with
this, but not much has been heard about it since then.) And then
Hart makes an interesting appeal to this audience. "People who
have lived their adult lives and gone into retirement and into their
mature years are quite often the most hopeful and the most optimistic citizens in our society. And I think that is true for one
reason. I think the people of judgment and experience and
wisdom know the strength and the character of the American
people—strength and character that too many politicians don't
admit or don't understand. I'll tell you what concerns me about
our country today—it's the loss of hope among our young people
and our children." He continues, "I believe this election must
restore hope and promise to our young people, the people who
have not voted, the people who have dropped out of the system,
the people who have abandoned the political process and the
hope that their government can turn this country and the world
around." He talks about the importance of protecting the environment and reducing the nuclear risk, and of America's alliance with
Israel. "We must once again tell our children that they can live in a
safe world, a world with hope and promise," he says.

In response to some questions, Hart says that Israel should not
negotiate with the Palestine Liberation Organization "until all the
states and interests in the Middle East" are willing to accept the
security of Israel's borders; that Israel should give up its settle-

ments on the West Bank "only as part of an overall bargaining process that guarantees Israel's borders;" and that he would favor moving the American Embassy from Tel Aviv to Jerusalem as "something the United States can commit as part of its contribution to the bargaining process, and as that bargaining goes forward and is successful." The audience seems to be pleased with his answers, as it seems to be with him. Hart, unlike Mondale, does not go in and tell an audience what he has done—in part because he doesn't have a record of much accomplishment. But Hart offers an attractive vision—of possibilities, of promise. Mondale, by arguing about where he has been, reinforces that he is of the "past." Hart is dewy, new, freshly minted. He has minted himself. And something in people wants to take a chance. Moreover, Hart's insight that the Democratic Party needs to offer something fresh is well founded. Mondale understood this, too, but failed to act on it. Now Mondale has the aura of a loser and Hart not only of a winner but, according to the calculations of the moment, of the man more likely to defeat Reagan. Mondale talks about where he has been. Hart talks, in a general way, about where he is going.

MARCH 12

TAMPA. Tomorrow, the large set of contests will take place, and today Mondale is making the most extensive one-day swing of his campaign—eight cities in three states (Florida, Georgia, and Alabama), beginning early this morning and ending at midnight. Mondale's main effort now is to raise questions in the voters' minds about Hart, to try to slow the rush to him. This has caused Mondale to go on the attack—an approach that does not present him at his most attractive, but one that, the consensus in his camp holds, must be pursued. Johnson said to me shortly after New Hampshire, "If we're running against a movie star, we have to make this into a serious race." The theory is that things have been moving too fast to wait for the press to give Hart critical attention, and that the positive things Mondale does say don't get much, or any, coverage. In the first aftershock following New Hampshire, the Mondale campaign made certain adjustments, most of them cosmetic, as a way of saying it had got the message. Mondale announced that he had told his staff that the front-runner talk was to end, saying to reporters, "There seeped into my campaign, and maybe in my own mind, a front-runner, inevitability psychology that people smelled." He later made jokes about this, saying he had deliberately tried to shed the front-runner image by losing New Hampshire, then Maine, and then Vermont. He also took to saying that his greatest mistake had been not to respond to Hart's attacks earlier. This was a deliberate strategy decision his campaign had made, so as not to build Hart up. His campaign people also say they concluded that Mondale had been doing too many "institutional" events, and was not seen among "the people" enough, so they have been having him turn up at carryouts and barbecue places, and now, here in Tampa this morning, he is at the Village Inn Pancake House, circulating among the breakfasters and flipping pancakes. None of the reasons that the Mondale people cite publicly for the New Hampshire outcome completely explain it, of course, but, like Mondale's having said right after New Hampshire that he shouldn't have left the state just before the voting, they offer some reasons for public consumption that avoid the probable deeper reason: that the support for Mondale simply wasn't strong enough.

The Mondale people still aren't entirely clear about what hit them—although Johnson and Mondale, at some level, knew all along that New Hampshire could trip them up, as it usually does front-runners. What no one seemed prepared for, understandably, was the magnitude of the aftereffects of New Hampshire. Even Hart and Caddell weren't prepared for it. Inevitably, the Mondale people have engaged in some "what-iffing." What if George McGovern had received his federal matching money in time for the Iowa contest, in which he received about fourteen hundred fewer votes than Hart (he qualified for it three days later), and the Mondale people had taken some steps to help McGovern? What if Glenn's slide (which the Mondale people had done their best to help along) had not been so sudden and so steep? These questions are interesting historically but not of much help to the Mondale campaign now. A key Mondale adviser says, "People make a mistake trying to pick one or two or five factors to explain what happened to us. A large number of factors came together at the same time in a manner that caused an explosion." There have been some divisions within the Mondale camp over the strategy of seeking the endorsements of the interest groups, but his chief strategists believed, and still believe, that it was the right strategy. Mondale, being who he is and given his political

history, could hardly run as an outsider. To have tried to change
Mondale himself radically would not have worked. But there are
some second thoughts about the handling of the issue of the endorsements, and there is some wish that the problem it was causing Mondale had been recognized earlier, or anticipated. The
Mondale people simply did not believe that the special interests/
promises charge was sinking in to the extent that it was. They
believed that they had a rational answer to it (that the other candidates had sought the endorsements, that Mondale had not made
many more promises than anyone else), and that that would be
accepted. They knew that organized labor had a negative image,
but they did not believe that that would become attached to Mondale. The Mondale people are rationalists, but things did not follow a rational course. This is not unusual in politics.

Since New Hampshire, Mondale has tried a variety of approaches. Caddell is correct in saying that the Mondale campaign
was premised on the quick kill, in part to get the thing over with
and unite the Party, in part because, as Caddell says, there was
concern that Mondale's candidacy could not sustain a long struggle. In the days following New Hampshire, the Mondale campaign has been trying to adjust to the new reality. Since it is such a
big campaign, involving so many people, this took some doing.
"We had become the battleship Missouri," says one Mondale adviser. Size was no longer such an asset. In a speech at Faneuil Hall
last Monday, Mondale said, "The message-sending is over. The
posturing is over. Now we're coming down to picking a real, live
person," and he attacked specific Hart votes and proposals. Some
of the attacks (on the windfall-profit tax, a tax on imported oil,
and hospital-cost containment) have been designed to bolster a
populist appeal that Mondale has tried to make in the South. He
has attacked Hart for a lack of commitment to traditional Democratic values. "Listen to his speeches," Mondale said last week.
"You don't hear him talking about restoring the sense of social
justice, reaching out and helping the vulnerable, the emphasis as I
do on Social Security and Medicare." He ridiculed Hart's book:
"He wrote a book about his vision of America. You need an F.B.I.
investigator to find one word in there expressing concern about
people in trouble." And he has offered himself to the public as a
straightforward man in political trouble. After months of avoiding
the television interview programs—his staff felt (correctly) that

these were not his forte, and, moreover, he did not need to appear on them—Mondale was suddenly available. When David Hartman asked Mondale about this when he appeared last Monday on *Good Morning America*, Mondale said, matter-of-factly, and smiling, that he was there because "I'm in trouble, I need help." Mondale has also taken to saying, "I am who I am. What you see is what you get." In doing this, Mondale is both saying that he is a natural, if not a compelling, television personality, and suggesting that there is a bit of pretense in what Hart is offering the public. He has said that Hart is a candidate of "tinsel." He asks, "Where's the heart? Where's the soul?" He says, "No one can teach you to have guts, no one can teach you to care." And, "What you see is what you get. No new hair spray. No new perfume. No new slogans. I am who I am: the product of my history, my values, my experience, my commitment." Throughout what has to be the biggest crisis of his public life, Mondale has kept his dignity and his sense of humor, but he seems to be almost offended at the idea that he might be rejected in favor of someone he sees as tailoring himself to fit the current mood and running on empty slogans, and whose commitment to certain values he doubts.

Last Tuesday, in Tampa, Mondale made a speech in which he defined what he believed the race was all about. (The speech received scant coverage.) He said that the campaign was "not just a horse race" but a battle for the soul of the Democratic Party and the future of our country. Mondale said, "We're about to decide whether we'll be a generous Party and a caring nation or whether we won't. Then, after making a strong populist attack on the Reagan Administration (which carried an implicit attack on Hart), Mondale said, "Mark me well, because today there's a new argument in this land—a new idea about the Democratic Party and where it should go. This new idea is the essence of the battle that we're in. The idea is this: If you fight for the values that the Democratic Party has always believed in, you're supposed to go on a guilt trip. But if you fight against them you're supposed to be applauded. If you fight for better schools, you're old. But if you fight for big oil you're new. . . . If a worker wants a raise, that's greedy. But if a plant closes down that's trendy. If you want big corporations to pay their share of taxes, you're old hat. But if you want working families to pay more taxes you're high tech." Mondale said, "I don't accept it. And I won't cut my values to fit this year's fashion." He added, "It's not a campaign for new ideas against old ideas. It's a fight between what's right and what's wrong. That is the issue in this campaign." Mondale distorted Hart's positions a bit, but he was making his case for what this fight is about, as he sees it: a fight between those to whom the traditional values of the Democratic Party are paramount and those who are seeking to redefine the Party, giving it a cooler, more pragmatic, technocratic look. Unfortunately for Mondale, however important his case may be, the more he makes it the more he may play into Hart's hands—portraying himself as representing "the past." Mondale is probably as knowledgeable and sophisticated in his thinking as anyone in politics, but, through a mixture of natural instincts, old habits, deep belief, and a desire to draw the line between himself and Hart and to fire up his own core constituency, he is increasingly letting this side of him fade from view.

On Friday, at Emory University, in Atlanta, Mondale, speaking to an audience of college students, took on Hart from another avenue. Citing analyses of the formative political experiences of the generation he was speaking to—Vietnam and Watergate—and the economic "roller coaster of booms and busts" that is said to make them anxious about their future, he said, "Culturally, you've lived in an earthquake zone. Other generations have known stability and tradition. But you've known turmoil and hype." He said, "In an age of Cabbage Patch dolls, no wonder you are suspected of being addicted to novelty." Then, in an unmistakable reference to Hart, Mondale said, "If a Presidential candidate wanted to capitalize on these things that are said about you, imagine how he might try to win your vote. To appeal to supposed cynicism, he would market himself as an outsider, gunning for the establishment. To play toward your alleged insecurity, he would build a platform with plenty of room for self-interest and little space for generosity. And to exploit your rumored taste for tinsel, he would drape himself in newness." Pointing out that he has three children, all in their twenties, Mondale said he thought that the above analysis of their generation was wrong, and then he listed some of the questions—about civil rights, about the use of power, about arms control, and so on—that he said he knew were on their minds. "These are good questions," Mondale said. "They deserve good answers, and not loose slogans. What counts is not whether an idea is new or old. What counts is whether it's right or wrong, whether it will work or won't work." Mondale also said, "I believe unashamedly in the core commitments of the Democratic Party." He attacked Hart, saying that his "record gives few clues to his basic values." He said that Hart had said that Reaganomics was a good idea and then said that it was a bad idea. He also said that Hart had supported Reagan budget cuts and then opposed them, that he had supported the Reagan defense budget and then opposed it. (These things are true.) Mondale added, "He has attacked labor unions for supporting me, but only after his own attempts to win their endorsement had failed." (Last year, Hart said that he would like the endorsement of each of the Democratic Party's interest groups, and in filling out a questionnaire submitted by the National Education Association he made the same promises to the organization that Mondale did.) Mondale cited his own record of fighting for civil rights, for children ("And when I ask you to join me in the battle against hunger, disease, and ignorance, I know the meaning of compassion"), his involvement in every fight for arms control. He cited some of the advice he has been receiving lately (and Mondale is receiving a lot of advice): "I'm being advised to adopt what is called a 'shtick'—a gimmick, a catch phrase like 'supply side' or 'new ideas'—and I've said no. Some people are urging me to be more dovish, even though I know the Soviets to be ruthless, dangerous adversaries. I'm being counselled to be more hawkish, even though I know that military force must be the last, and not the first, resort. . . . I am being advised to offend my supporters for the sake of political theatre. . . . I'm being exhorted to go after the upscale, upper-income sway vote, and forget about the average American who has been at the center of my campaigns, whom I've always sought to protect." To all these things, Mondale reiterated, "I say no." He added, "Instead, I'm campaigning on my record, my values, and my vision for the future. I am making promises. I am saying what I will do as President. There may not be enough slogans, but I don't think it lacks in substance." And then Mondale talked in the Emory speech about the things he wanted to do as President, and about the importance of picking a President who's experienced, "who knows what he's doing." This speech, too, received little attention.

Mondale's failure to find a clear theme or slogan has, in fact, been a subject of controversy and anxiety within his campaign. Some of his advisers argued that Mondale should find a clear theme to campaign on, but this never occurred, mainly because Mondale didn't think it was necessary. Several of his advisers were concerned that unless Mondale set forth a theme that overarched his politics he would be defined by his politics—an affinity for programs, alliances with interest groups, and so on. At one point early last year, Mondale toyed with a proposal that he set forth the theme of excellence—of improving schools, productivity—as a way of suggesting he would prod the nation (and his backers) to something better, and he talked about this briefly, and then dropped it. In the summer of last year, when the campaign's polling in New Hampshire turned up some negative attitudes toward Mondale, a go was made at getting him to run a strong populist campaign. But while some of the populism survived, the picture was muddied by Mondale's running around receiving the endorsements. Mondale's speech accepting the A.F.L.-C.I.O. endorsement, on October 6th, was the subject of a row within the Mondale camp, with some aides urging Mondale to put his alliance with the labor federation in a larger context of what everyone had to do, including some sacrificing, to make America a better place. Mondale rejected this and made only a fleeting reference to the point. Mondale has simply never accepted the importance of an overarching theme or slogan. His interests are programmatic and alliance-oriented. He likes to talk about a lot of things, and in detail. Getting him to condense his message into three themes at the start of this year—a fairer society, a more competitive America, a safer world—was quite an achievement. He mentioned the lack of a slogan in interviews we had as the campaign proceeded, saying he thought one would come along, but he seemed ambivalent, saying also that he felt that the three themes were working. Because Mondale did not define himself with a clear message, he permitted himself to be defined by others. His main theme, that he was experienced, not only was not enough but backfired.

Yesterday, in Atlanta, in the debate sponsored by the League of Women Voters, Mondale and the other remaining candidates— Glenn, McGovern, and Jackson—all went after Hart, who did not quite do what it seemed that he needed to do: demonstrate that there is substance behind his themes. He passed up some opportunities to do so. In response to a criticism of Hart's theme of "the past versus the future" by McGovern, who said he didn't know what that meant, Hart said that he had sent McGovern his book and his position papers. In the hall, Hart looked pale and somewhat tense, but he came over well on television. Glenn, who has been campaigning in the South on his record as an astronaut and a fighter pilot, attacked Hart's military-reform program, as he has been doing in other appearances, saying that it would deprive the military of the best technology. Glenn also attacked Hart for having said he would use federal projects to bring pressure for approval of the Equal Rights Amendment—a charge that Hart denied. (Hart had actually made the pledge last summer, to the National Women's Political Caucus.) Oddly, Hart chose to refute a charge he said Mondale had made against him (having to do with a vote on the Occupational Safety and Health Administration) that Mondale hadn't made. The "refutation" did enable Hart to assert that he is against excessive government regulation. When Hart suggested that one of the differences between him and Mondale was that "I think we can meet the basic human needs and commitments of the people of this country by restoring entrepreneurship," Mondale, smiling broadly, said, "What's new about becoming entrepreneurs?" And, in a line he had clearly prepared, Mondale said, borrowing from a television commercial, "When I hear your new ideas, I'm reminded of that ad, 'Where's the beef?'" Hart also said that "ninety per cent of the new jobs in this society have come from small businesses." (This is a highly exaggerated figure, put out by representatives of small-business organizations and also by some of the idea brokers.) But Mondale's attacking of Hart had a slightly frantic touch to it, including the closing statement, in which Mondale attacked three Hart positions, rather than make the case for himself.

When Mondale arrived in Tampa last night, he repeated those attacks, and plans to throughout the day today. The first charge was that Hart (in the Washington *Post* interview) had said that Castro was not a dictator, and that on being asked what he was Hart said, "I don't know." (This is what Hart said.) The second was that Hart, in a recent interview, had said that in case of a war in the Persian Gulf, threatening oil supplies, our allies would be "on their own." The reference is to a recent interview Hart gave to *New York*, and what Hart actually said was "We have to first strive for our own independence from Middle East oil, and then tell our allies, who will always need it, that they can't rely on us when things explode there. There'll be no 82nd Airborne, no American invasion force. We can help with supply, but if they want intervention, this time they're the ones who are going to have to do it." In other statements, Hart has said that he would make a plan with our allies to keep open the Strait of Hormuz, through which the oil is shipped, and that the United States should offer the allies air and sea support if they choose to intervene—but that American lives should not be involved. Mondale, reducing what Hart said to "They're on their own," called this "naive." Mondale's third charge was against Hart's varying positions on the freeze and the build-down. "On seven different occasions, my opponent took inconsistent, uncertain positions," Mondale said. He says that Hart's record on arms control is "weak." (Hart has been inconsistent on the freeze and the build-down, but he was a strong supporter of the SALT II agreement, and worked hard to try to get it through the Senate.) The point of all this, Mondale said, was that "we need a President who knows what he's doing, who's surefooted and experienced—a President who will enhance our national security and increase the chances for peace." He asked "the voters of Florida" to "pause when you go into the voting booth on Tuesday and ask who is the best qualified person to be the next President." He added, "We've heard so much about new ideas, and finally tonight I said, 'Where are those ideas? Where's the beef?' " He said, as he had said in the debate, "We are not electing momentum." And last night he added, "We're not electing a can of hair spray." Mondale is doing what he can to slow Hart down, and has come back to the theme with which he began his campaign: "I'm ready." It hasn't turned out to be a very exciting theme, but it's the one his people obviously now feel places Mondale in the best contrast with Hart. And they say that the one negative about Hart that they are picking up in their polling and phone canvassing is doubt whether he is experienced enough to be President.

The Mondale people have been on an emotional roller coaster of their own of late. They had to absorb the shock of the idea that they might in fact lose. They hit bottom in the middle of last week, when it appeared from the polls that Hart was pulling even with Mondale, or ahead of him, in all three of the big Southern states. In the last couple of days, Mondale has been seen to be pulling ahead in Alabama and catching up with Hart in Florida, and now the race in Georgia looks neck and neck. All things being relative, the Mondale people have taken these latest entrails as a good sign—that perhaps Hart is indeed being slowed. Mondale's schedule for the past week has gone through several changes. He did get Coretta King and the Reverend Martin Luther King, Sr., to endorse him last week, but Andrew Young, though known to be sympathetic to Mondale, remained technically neutral. On Saturday, Mondale joined Jimmy Carter at a fund-raising picnic in Plains, and there has been much to-do over whether or not this was a good idea. But the event had been scheduled some time ago, and it would have been graceless to cancel it, as some urged; besides, the prevailing view in the Mondale camp is that Mondale's tie to Carter is helpful in Georgia. Mondale has told his staff to level with him about what the figures show. Maxine Isaacs, Mondale's press secretary, says, "This has been a very frank period."

MIAMI BEACH. Mondale is addressing a fairly large crowd, made up of elderly people and union members, at an outdoor rally in the southern end of Miami Beach. It is a warm, sunny day, and the crowd is seated on chairs facing a bandstand. A band and balloons are here, to put some festiveness into the occasion, but there is something sad about it. Mondale has been introduced, at some length, by Claude Pepper, an eighty-three-year-old Florida congressman who is known as a champion of the elderly. Mondale is exhausted, and has pouches beneath his eyes, and a sunburn from his many outdoor appearances in the past days. But, despite his fatigue, he manages to stand there and talk vigorously—about the importance of the issue of war and peace in the election, and of values. "You've been around a long time," Mondale says. "You've seen this country in good times and in bad times. You've seen us at war and you've seen us at peace. You've seen us when we've been generous and kind and caring and you've seen us when we've been selfish and hateful. And you know what a President means. He can lead us to our best, he can lead us toward the future, he can lead us toward peace, he can lead us toward generosity and caring, or he can lead us in the direction of our lesser angels. A President is so important to all of us. And I seek the Presidency because I want to lead us toward those broader purposes again." He says, "There are no statues to Harding or Hoover, but there are to the Lincolns, the Roosevelts, and to the Kennedys, who have asked us to be generous and caring." He quotes, as he has throughout the campaign, Lincoln's saying we should have a government of the people, by the people, and for the people, and says, "I am the candidate talking again about a generous America, and I'm not just talking—I mean it." And, as is his wont, he says, "Give me your help and you'll have a friend in that White House." The contrast between the presentations made by Mondale here in south Miami Beach today and Hart in the more affluent North Beach last week is interesting. They struck many of the same notes, but differently: Mondale is passionate, indignant, reminding these people of his years at their side, throwing himself on their mercy; Hart was collected, stylish, introducing himself to those people and making a case for letting the younger generation take charge. Now Mondale talks about the importance of having "a President who measures up to the awesome responsibility of that job" and who "will insure our national security," and "a President who knows what he's doing," and he makes the three attacks on Hart. During his talk, Mondale's voice gives out on him temporarily, and he seems to cut his remarks short. At a brief press conference afterward, he is asked if he is saying that Gary Hart is insensitive. He replies, "I'm talking about my policies, the key points of difference; it's a matter of emphasis." He says, "Claude Pepper knows there's a difference between people who just vote right and those who are heavily, deeply, and emotionally involved in the great issues of our times. These big issues, like Social Security, civil rights, women's rights, the other great questions of justice in our country—they're not won just by people who appear on the right side as the battle ends. They're won by people who were there at the beginning of the battle and fight all the way through and make the difference."

I have an interview with Mondale as he rides back to the Miami airport. He says that he feels "liberated, in the sense that I got that front-runner thing off my shoulders," which may or may not be the case. I ask him to explain further, and he says, "Well, I didn't realize it at the time, but there's a funny psychology to being the alleged front-runner." Then, waving back to a group of people who have waved to him, he says, "You see, people are pulling for me now. They know I need their help. It feels a lot better than when people are just asked to approve, approve. So I like that. I find I hit the issues harder, too. It loosens you up." He continues, "The worst mistake we made was letting Hart have a month or more of making those criticisms without answering. That was a bad mistake. But, I thought, I didn't want to fight with yet another person if I could help it, so that we could put the Party together. It didn't work out that way. We did what we thought was right at the time. Hindsight is a great thing. We thought it through. But it's clear that, while the polls were slow to respond, those unanswered charges came to be believed by too many people, and it was that perception that then began cutting against me."

I ask Mondale if it bothers him that the kind of approach Hart is using might be working.

"Yes," he replies. "See, if you look at Gary's pitch, it's all shaped by pollsters, not by substance. 'We need new ideas, not old, not the past.' What's that got to do with anything? It's all posturing. It tends to be a generational argument when in fact the key issues I'm talking about deal with the problems of all generations. And I believe that it has little to do with the problems of the Presidency. What I've got to do is get the issue back. In the debate last night, I kept trying to pull him down from this posturing to reality, where real issues are decided." Referring to his speech at Emory University, Mondale talks now about "what you would do if you looked on this younger generation as cynical—you'd probably talk about new versus old, and you'd probably make an appeal based on a generous amount of self-interest and a modest amount of generosity. If you look at the appeal, that's what it is." Mondale is disturbed at what he sees as basically an isolationist approach to foreign policy by Hart, and by his calling for, among his tax proposals, a consumption tax, which critics say would be harder on the average earners, who must spend a higher percentage of their income, than on those better off. Mondale continues, "I believe that the Democratic Party is the trustee of justice in this country. I believe there's a lot of fights to be won and a lot of progress to be preserved. That will only occur with a strong President who believes as I do. I want to hear, and haven't heard, Senator Hart speak to those questions that I find persuasive. I haven't heard it. And that's sacred to me."

I suggest to Mondale that his saying "I am who I am" seems to be a way of trying to get at Hart on a couple of levels.

"That's right," he replies. "It's a contrast argument. It's also my way of saying that I'll do what I'm saying. Look, to be what I call 'a people's Democrat' is almost a cultural decision. It's considered out of style by many. The easiest thing to do in public life is to ignore these vulnerable folks. I don't say that to be noble. It's really trendy to ignore them today. There's also the question of realism about the world in which we live. Presidents don't get to eat off a clean plate. You've got to be tough, you've got to see the world as it really is; from time to time, force must be used. You've got to work with your allies, which means you give as well as take. You have to be able to manage several miserable problems simultaneously and keep a theme and a purpose apparent to the public. And that gets to the question of being ready for the job."

I ask Mondale if he is surprised by what has been happening.

"Yes," he replies. "What I was surprised at was the way in which one victory just seemed to sweep the country, unattended by substance. You can read the papers any day: Man in the street: 'I'm for Hart.' 'Why?' 'I don't know. I'm for his new ideas.' 'What are they?' 'Can't think of any.' But I think that's changing now."

It is clearly important to Mondale that, whatever happens, he'll end up with people thinking that he gave it a good fight—that he was a scrapper, and not a quitter. (His having got out of the 1976 Presidential race in 1974, saying, "I don't think anyone should be President who is not willing to go through fire," and the questions this raised about whether he had "fire in the belly" seem to be something he now wants to live down.) Mondale talks often about not wanting to disappoint his children, and this seems to be a truly important thing to him. His dignity is obviously very important to him, and he clearly wants to be seen as having fought for the things he believes in.

Gingerly, I bring up with Mondale ("That's O.K., go ahead," he says) the question of when the time comes to recognize that a campaign might be, as Johnson put it in a conversation we had at the outset of the year, politically dead, even though the race is not technically over. I ask Mondale how he thinks about that.

He replies, "Look, my career has been one, I believe, of recognizing reality. But reality now is that we've got a big fight here, with some important questions, and I believe it's starting to resonate. I think we're coming back. The debate has begun. And I believe that my people are working harder, are more energized, and I think we're starting to make the case. And I'm confident I'm going to be nominated. But it's going to be a lot tougher than I had originally assumed."

MUSCLE SHOALS, ALABAMA. Mondale has made three more airport stops—in Orlando, Jacksonville, and Atlanta—and now, this evening, has come back to this industrial area in the northwestern part of Alabama, a relatively conservative area, where he was on his Southern swing at the outset of the year. That seems like a year ago now. At each of the airports, Mondale was met by a cluster of people sent out by the unions and the teachers' organizations. His constituency seems circumscribed now; no one else seems to come to see him. One wonders whether he could ever attract the constituency Hart is attracting. It is a cultural clash that is going on in the Democratic Party now, and the chasm, once opened, may be hard to bridge. At each stop, Mondale made the same attacks on Hart (and included Hart's proposal for a ten-dollar-a-barrel tax on imported oil). Often, Mondale said he didn't think that Hart had thought through something he had said. At each stop, the press tried to get him to go further: Are you saying that Senator Hart is naive? How would you characterize what you are saying about him? And each time Mondale resisted. He is trying to walk a very delicate line. For all his brave talk, he is not unconscious of the fact that it is possible that Hart will be the Party's nominee and that he will be campaigning for Hart. Throughout the day, Mondale has shown remarkable resilience—though at times, because of the fatigue, he slurred his words—and has kept his sense of humor. Still, there was something unnoble about what Mondale was doing, and something frantic about it. Sadly, it evoked Hubert Humphrey toward the end of his 1972 nomination fight against McGovern. The show that Mondale has put on today may have been necessary, as some members of his staff believe, but it was not Mondale at his best—the decent, passionate, committed, funny man that people who know him see but that he has not got across in this campaign. The campaign's predominant theory now is that there is little incremental value, or potential coverage, in Mondale's talking about the positive things he talked about earlier. But what if he talked about what he stood for in some arresting way? Moreover, the message he does have is cluttered. It is not necessarily an encouraging thing that the importance and power of television put a premium on the punchy, memorable slogan, but that is the given with which Mondale must operate, and he knows it, even if he does not accept it. The theory behind what Mondale has been doing today is, as Johnson puts it, to "raise the stakes"—to set forth three areas involving national security in which Hart, as Mondale sees it, has fallen short, and to raise the question in the voters' minds of whether Hart is ready to be President.

On the plane from Atlanta to Muscle Shoals, Johnson told me, "The challenge in the eight days we've had since Maine has been to find some way to bring Hart out of the stratosphere, where he's sailing along with little resistance, with little substance, and without much focus on whether he'd be a good President. We've done that in two ways: consistently talking about how important the decision the voters will make is; and, through a wide variety of issues, to raise the question of who he is and what he really stands for—to raise enough questions to create a sense that people should pause." Johnson drew an analogy with the situation that the Mondale people felt they faced last fall in regard to Glenn. He said, "If we're going to face Glenn as a hero, a nonpolitician, an astronaut, that's dangerous business. The same thing is true with Gary Hart. If we're going to face Gary Hart as a movie star, the next generation, that's tough to win. If we face Gary Hart on who's better prepared, who has better values, who's better on key issues, that's winnable." Johnson continued, "It's clear to me that Hart's greatest area of vulnerability right now is people's feeling he has not crossed the threshold of being a President. What we're doing today is identifying national security as the preeminent responsibility of the President, showing three statements or positions that are not thought through, and suggesting that that's indicative of somebody who's not surefooted. That helps us draw a contrast and make a point. It's clear to me that if Hart continues to fly on his own without serious questions being asked about who he is or what his values are or whether he's sufficiently sophisticated and thoughtful to be the next President, then he's not likely to be stopped. It's a fairly straightforward theory."

Johnson is a great one for planning ahead, and, while there are some plans he has made, and a lot of planning has gone into the forthcoming efforts in Michigan and Illinois, the circumstances are such that, as Johnson puts it, "so much strategy flows from the weekly results now." With the exception of Alabama, about which the Mondale people are nervously confident, they simply don't know what will happen in the two other states in the South tomorrow. Massachusetts and Rhode Island and the Western states aren't even mentioned anymore.

I asked Johnson whether Illinois would be affected by what happened in the South tomorrow.

"Of course," he replied. "Everything affects everything now."

At a press conference at the Atlanta airport, Mondale challenged Hart to a debate before each of the major contests remaining—"up to California, if necessary." He added, under questioning, that it would be fine if the other remaining candidates participated. Mondale and his aides feel that they did make headway against Hart in the debate yesterday, but the challenge was laid down at the Atlanta airport also to keep the story of the debate alive in the Atlanta media market, and to let the Mondale people know that Mondale intends to fight on. Also, it was another move in the strategy of, as Johnson puts it, "getting Hart into the game."

At a spirited rally at a Holiday Inn in Muscle Shoals—a rock band, balloons, confetti—Mondale strikes another theme that he suggested earlier in the day. "The South has not yet been given a chance to speak," he says. This is an ironic echo of Hart's appeal to the voters of New Hampshire to speak for themselves, and not accept the dictates of the Party "establishment." Mondale points out that unemployment in the area is nearly twenty per cent, and he says, "I'm a people's Democrat. And I'm for jobs and employment and giving people a chance to care for themselves with dignity and pride." He makes the same arguments he has been making against Hart all day, but then he returns to the Mondale that appeared here earlier this year—even talking, as he did then, about the overvalued dollar, and its effect on exports. Talking to this predominantly labor audience, he says, "I've been kicked around a little bit for fighting for American workers. They say that's a special interest. It's an interest that's special to me and I'm proud of it. What's wrong with that?" He continues, "In this country of ours, working men and women are American citizens entitled to the dignity and all the rights that the law gives to workers." As he has done before, he tells of his own background, and then he says, "You should be entitled to decent Social Security. You should be entitled to a safe job. Your kids should have a chance to go on to college or vocational school. When you retire, you ought to be certain that that Social Security and that Medicare are there. If you're black or if you're brown or if you're a woman, never should it be possible to discriminate against you. You are an American in the fullest sense of the word, and those laws ought to be enforced. When you're handicapped, retarded, or whatever, you've got some rights, too, in this country. You should have some opportunity for the fullness of life. And when you're hungry in this great country of ours it ought to be possible to eat. And when you're homeless it ought to be possible to find some shelter." Mondale is speaking with feeling now. Then he says quietly, "I'm not a fancy candidate. I'm down-home." He asks, "When you pick your President, pick someone who shares your views. Pick someone who cares about you. Pick someone who hurts when you hurt. Pick someone with some guts." He says, "All my life I've fought for the people—that's where I'm coming from, that's what I believe in, it's what America is all about. If you'll fight for me tomorrow, when I get in that White House I'll fight for you." Mondale pumps as much energy into his speech as an exhausted man can, and it goes over well with this audience, but it is old-fashioned talk, not cut out for television; he's correct that it isn't stylish. In the course of his talk, Mondale says, "Roosevelt in the darkest days of the Depression said something I often quote. I don't know if I can get the words right, but it's what I think is the issue in 1984." Then, paraphrasing Roosevelt, he says, "He said, 'Governments can err, Presidents do make mistakes. But the Divine Judge tells us that he measures the sins of the coldhearted and the mistakes of the warm-blooded on different scales. Better the occasional faults,' he said, 'of a government operating in the spirit of charity than the sins of omission of government frozen in the ice of its own indifference.' "

THE BIRMINGHAM AIRPORT. Another statement, another press conference. More union and teachers'-organization representatives on hand to meet Mondale, as is Richard Arrington, the black mayor of Birmingham, who endorsed Mondale during his swing through here at the first of the year. (There seem to be no young faces around Mondale at these stops.) Arrington's support and the relatively strong power of the unions in Alabama are what make the Mondale people hopeful about carrying the state tomorrow. Moreover, Alabama has higher unemployment than the two other states, and is poorer than they are. Mondale beams, just as he did a little over two months ago, as Arrington makes a spirited case for him. Then, after raising the questions about Hart he has raised all day, Mondale says, "Compare our records on people's issues. All my life, I've fought for people. I've got the guts to stand up to the special interests and for the people's interests."

THE MOBILE AIRPORT. It is now 9:40 P.M. Eastern time (an hour earlier here), and this is the last stop of the day before flying on to Atlanta for the night. Tomorrow, before flying back to Washington, Mondale will greet people at a subway stop in Atlanta. No leaving the state before election day this time, whether it makes that much difference or not. Now, on a dark, rainy night, about four hundred people—who seem, once again, to have been organized by the unions and the teachers—are gathered inside a hangar for a rally for Mondale. The sound of their cheers resonates in the hangar. This probably makes Mondale feel as good as he can, under the circumstances. He makes his points against Hart, and he says, "We need a President concerned with fairness," and goes through some of the things he said earlier in Muscle Shoals: "I'm a people's Democrat. Nothing fancy. Down-home. What you see is what you get."

MARCH 14

WASHINGTON. Last night, Hart won Florida (thirty-nine per cent to thirty-three per cent for Mondale, with Jackson getting twelve per cent and Glenn eleven); Mondale won Alabama easily, with Glenn and Hart virtually tied for second; and Mondale squeaked out a victory in Georgia (thirty per cent to twenty-seven per cent, with Jackson getting twenty-one and Glenn coming in fourth). Glenn, for whom this was to have been a big day, won nowhere, and is expected to drop out soon. His campaign is in debt. Hart won Massachusetts (McGovern, who came in third, will drop out) and Rhode Island. He also won in Nevada and Oklahoma and the state of Washington, where Mondale had the support of a number of political leaders and had once expected to do well. Mondale won thirty-two per cent of the vote in Hawaii, but sixty-three per cent supported uncommitted delegates. So Mondale got a breather. (He also got most of the delegates out of the contests, but there are twenty-two delegates in Florida whose allegiance is unknown.) It is clear that if Jackson had not been in the race, competing for black votes, Mondale would have done better. As in the earlier contests, Mondale's support consisted of blacks, the elderly, the poor, and union families, while Hart did best among the younger and more affluent, and independents. (However, Hart got most of the labor vote in Massachusetts.) On television last night, Hart, with justification, said that the results showed that he was a national candidate. Hart said, "The voters of Massachusetts, of Florida and Rhode Island, indeed of Georgia and Alabama—I hope some of the Western caucus states—have joined the ranks of those in New England and in Wyoming who have said that the politics of the past will not address the challenges of the nineteen-eighties." The Mondale people were encouraged by the fact that exit polls indicated that those who made up their minds shortly before the vote went more for Mondale than for Hart. Mondale, on television, tried to set the stage for a long fight. He said, "What looked like it might be a hundred-yard dash, first for me, then for Senator Hart, is now going to be a marathon—maybe right into the San Francisco Convention."

MARCH 21

Walter Mondale's victory in the Illinois primary last night gave the campaign a new, if uncertain, shape. Mondale's victory was decisive, especially given the circumstances he was up against. He won forty-one per cent of the vote to Hart's thirty-five per cent and Jackson's twenty-one per cent, with Jackson winning about four-fifths of the black vote, much of which would otherwise presumably have gone to Mondale. Mondale also won a large majority of the hundred and seventy-one delegates at stake in Illinois, giving him, at this point, six hundred and forty in all; Hart, three hundred and fifty-eight; and Jackson, seventy-two. Glenn and McGovern dropped out of the race last week. According to the exit polls, Mondale won a higher percentage of the labor vote than he had in some of the earlier contests, and, as usual, he did better than Hart among the elderly and the poorer voters; but, for the first time, he held his own with Hart among suburban voters. And he won more of the younger voters than he had before. Also, as was to be expected, Mondale did well in the caucuses in his home state of Minnesota last night.

Mondale's victories in yesterday's contests followed successes on Saturday in Michigan and Arkansas and, on Sunday, in Puerto Rico. He was expected to win in Michigan, which conducted hard-to-get-to caucuses in which the United Auto Workers played a strong hand. Mondale was also supported in Michigan by James Blanchard, the governor, and Coleman Young, the mayor of Detroit and a black. Moreover, in Michigan Mondale stood to benefit from his favoring "domestic content" legislation, which would require that all cars sold in the United States contain a certain percentage of United States parts and labor (Hart is opposed), and from his attack on Hart's having opposed legislation to provide a federal financial "bailout" of the Chrysler Corporation. (The Chrysler bailout was successful.) The Michigan contest was one of those that were moved up earlier in the calendar, at the behest of Mondale people, who had thought that they might need Michigan at that point to slow down Glenn if he did well in the South on the thirteenth. Had Mondale lost Michigan, it would have been a very bad sign for him.

The turnout in Michigan was higher than expected, and Mondale won with forty-nine per cent of the vote, to Hart's thirty-one per cent and Jackson's sixteen per cent. In Mississippi, which also held caucuses on Saturday, and where Mondale had been expected to win, he received thirty per cent of the vote, and Uncommitted received thirty per cent of the vote, while Jackson received twenty-eight per cent and Hart twelve per cent. In Arkansas, Mondale received thirty-six per cent, Jackson thirty-four per cent, Hart twenty-four per cent. In South Carolina, which also held caucuses Saturday, over fifty per cent of the votes went to Uncommitted, twenty-five per cent to Jackson, twelve per cent to Hart, and ten per cent to Mondale. Fritz Hollings, who is a South Carolina senator, endorsed Hart after he himself dropped out of the race. South Carolina has a tradition of voting for Uncommitted. The allocation of the delegates in the Southern contests may be a point of dispute at the Convention, because in some areas Jackson did not receive delegates in proportion to his votes. But in some places the rules worked to his advantage. (The rules actually worked to Mondale's disadvantage in Mississippi.) The meaning of the outcome in Puerto Rico, where Mondale received ninety-nine per cent of the vote, is not clear, since the Hart camp did not participate in the primary and conducted its own set of caucuses.

The real questions about what happened in Illinois have to do with what it means in terms of the dynamic of the race from now on, and also its content. Once again, the "late deciders," according to the exit polls, broke for Mondale. This led to some belief that Hart, who had gone roaring into Illinois on the same wave that carried him out of New Hampshire, may have had his "momentum" broken. Perhaps the voters were asking more questions about him, or perhaps it was simply that Illinois is a very different kind of state from those that Hart has been winning in so far. (And, like Alabama, it has above-average unemployment.) A poll taken by the Mondale campaign showed Hart thirteen points ahead of Mondale on the Thursday before the primary, and as late as Saturday Hart was leading Mondale by eight points in the Washington *Post*/ABC News poll. Mondale slugged away at Hart and may have succeeded in getting him "into the game," in Johnson's term, and in getting the argument onto the ground he wants—which man is best suited to be President. At the same time, Hart became the subject of much tougher examination by the media—with continuing questions being raised about his name and age changes, and also about contradictory positions Hart had been taking. And Hart himself made some mistakes, which reflected the fact that his campaign organization is stretched very thin and is not deep in experience, and the mistakes played into Mondale's hands. Hart criticized Mondale for allegedly having run an ad raising questions about his name and age changes, and when the Mondale camp said that no such ad existed Hart had to retract and apologize. Then Hart ran an ad specifically criticizing Mondale for his tie to Vrdolyak, and then he said he hadn't approved the ad and had ordered it taken off the air, but in fact it remained on the air for another two days. Mondale, leaping on this, said, "Here's a person who says he wants to be the President of the United States and he says he can run the federal government, and he can't get an ad off TV—that he pays for—in forty-eight hours." So Hart, in trying to make Mondale's involvement in Chicago's factional politics costly to Mondale, got dragged in himself. Mondale remained on the attack throughout, charging, in his appearances and in his ads, that Hart was "naive" and "unsure, unsteady, and untested." The Hart people feel that Hart has been hurt in recent days, and slowed down, by the increasing number of questions being raised about him. As a matter of fact, for all their discounting of the Michigan caucuses, there was a time when the Hart people had a glimmer of hope that they could win them, then win in Illinois, and have a quick victory. Some of his advisers also feel that Hart went off the beam in the last few days, and erred in making the case more against Reagan than against Mondale, and that the differences between Hart and Mondale, such as they are, have to be drawn more sharply. In addition, it was believed within the Hart camp that Hart had to show what his approaches to government would actually be. The slogan, it was feared, might be wearing thin.

The nature of the attacks Mondale made, and Hart's eventual response, may have opened up a wound in the Democratic Party that will be difficult to reheal in time. Of all things, the two major candidates were refighting the Party's battle over Vietnam. Mondale kept up the attack on Hart for seeming to place a lower priority on "compassion," and criticized him for not having been as involved in civil-rights fights as he himself had been. But the real fissure came on foreign policy. In a speech before the Chicago Council on Foreign Relations last Wednesday, Mondale attacked Hart for embracing what Mondale portrayed as an isolationist approach. He criticized Hart again on the subjects of Castro, the Persian Gulf, and arms control. He also set forth some of the arms-control proposals he had made earlier in the campaign. The arms-control point was to place Mondale on the liberal side of the foreign-policy argument, but the rest of his case placed him elsewhere, and this was the emphasis that came across. "I offer a strong, experienced, and mature internationalism that would strengthen us by strengthening our alliances," Mondale said. "Mr. Hart has introduced a strange new vision of our role in the world that threatens to weaken our crucial alliances, and either ignores or underestimates what I think history teaches us." He said that what Hart says about the real enemy in the Third World being hunger, poverty, and disease is "partly true . . . but it's only part of the truth." He said, "The people of Afghanistan and Cambodia could tell Gary Hart about the other part," and he also mentioned Poland. Mondale criticized Hart for calling for "unilateral withdrawal of American forces in Central America," saying that he didn't think that had been thought through. And, while criticizing the Administration's policy and saying he would work with the Contadora group—Mexico, Panama, Venezuela, and Colombia—

Mondale also said that he would withdraw only part of the American forces stationed in Honduras until Nicaragua agreed to certain conditions. "We *have* made mistakes in the past in the use of American strength," Mondale said, adding, "Guilt is not a foreign policy." Again, in the final days, there was a certain frantic appearance to Mondale's attacks, and he again evoked the picture of Humphrey in 1972, or of a man more in tune with the foreign-policy views of the late Henry Jackson than had been generally understood. (But it worked, just as Mondale's attacks in the final days before March 13th seemed to work.) In fact, Mondale's roots are in the internationalism of old liberalism, and he came of political age during the Cold War. But in opening up this fight Mondale was opening up a big one—one that presented certain dangers to him. Yet when one is fighting for political survival, as Mondale has been, one uses what one can, since there may be no tomorrow to worry about. The Mondale people also made the political calculations that the approach Mondale was taking would keep some ethnic, blue-collar voters from defecting from him, and also that those voters who are attracted to the kinds of foreign-policy statements Hart has been making would not support Mondale anyway. They also felt that should Mondale get the nomination this foreign-policy approach would put him in a less vulnerable position against Reagan. But until then there were no deep divisions over issues among the Democrats. Inevitably, Hart came back at Mondale for having supported the Vietnam War for so long—a criticism he had made in a speech in Council Bluffs in January. Hart said, "A reading of Mr. Mondale's comments about Central America last week . . . suggests he has not learned the lesson of Vietnam." Hart also said, "On the greatest foreign issue of our time, Walter Mondale did not question our policy until the rest of the Democratic Party was already in dissent." Mondale replied, "Vietnam was a mistake, and I was part of that mistake in the early years. . . . But the lesson from Vietnam is not that we should forgo power everywhere at all times."

The two men also started an argument that will carry over into the next big contest, in New York, on April 3rd. This was over whether Hart had "flip-flopped" on the question of moving the American Embassy in Israel from Tel Aviv to Jerusalem. In a debate held in Chicago on Sunday night, Hart said that he favored moving the Embassy, without qualification. His press secretary,

Kathy Bushkin, said this was a new position, but his Washington office claimed that he had taken it for some time, as did Hart—when there was ample evidence that he had not. (When I saw him at his Miami Beach appearance a couple of weeks ago, he was conditional on this matter.) Now the fight will go to Connecticut, which holds its primary on March 27th, and which, since Connecticut is a heavily suburban and an affluent state, Hart is expected to win, and to the big states of New York and Pennsylvania. (The Mondale campaign, as a result of having spent a large amount of money early, in an attempt to get the nomination contest over quickly, is now nearing the legal spending ceiling, and it has had to cut salaries and let people go. The Mondale people had assumed that all the other candidates would be running out of money at this point.) Jackson, as a result of his ability to win black votes (if not much else), will remain a presence and, as was prefigured at the outset, will make certain demands at the Convention—demands that if met would not please all segments of the Party. Given the divisions in the Party that have been demonstrated, and are growing, even if Mondale should manage to get the nomination it would not be a nomination of the sort he and his people had hoped for at the outset—one that was settled on early and without rancor, or damage to him. There is a view that this fight has toughened Mondale and brought him into sharper focus—but the result of the trade-off can't be known until later. Hart is now facing a rougher time than he had been until quite recently; last night, on television, he seemed shaken and defensive. The Democrats could still get lucky, of course, and perhaps could close the divisions that have been opened, but as of right now—right now being all one can safely consider, the way things have been going—there is a growing question as to whether the Democratic nomination will be much worth having.

XIV

The best thing about the political season just ended is that the cherry blossoms came out in time for a beautiful Sunday—the Sunday between the New York and Pennsylvania primaries, and as the news was breaking that the C.I.A. was participating in the mining of Nicaraguan harbors, and a bitter controversy was developing over a speech by President Reagan criticizing Congress for interfering in foreign policy. At such a time, the cherry blossoms were particularly needed, as was the beautiful Sunday. (The cherry blossoms sometimes come out in cold weather and quickly die, leaving us with a feeling of being robbed.) The political season had been such an intense one that even its observers were left feeling exhausted. The candidates themselves were beyond exhaustion: when I last saw them, not long ago, Gary Hart seemed pale and drawn, Walter Mondale looked as if he had reached the bottom of his reservoir of energy, and Jesse Jackson, who has a great deal of energy, was weary and complaining about the demands of the campaign. While it is not uncommon for nomination contests to go on for several months, or through the entire calendar of primaries and caucuses, the intensity of the period just ended, and the fact that there had been widespread expectations that the contest would end early—first with a Mondale victory and then with a Hart victory—left the sense of a campaign that just wouldn't behave. (The Mondale and Hart camps had shared these respective expectations.) The fact that there would be only minor contests for almost a month after the Pennsylvania primary led to talk about a "lull"—as if everyone could go to the beach for six weeks. In fact, there would be no real lull—and the campaign may be headed for the most interesting period yet. Meanwhile, President Reagan, who, to the relief of his key aides, had been essentially out of sight, and out of the reach of controversy, while the Democrats battled, reentered the picture in a big way.

Even before Hart's substantial defeats in New York on April 3rd and in Pennsylvania on April 10th, he and his aides were talking about carrying the battle to the end no matter what happened, and there was a certain logic to that. There is, after all, a history of the voters in the later primaries registering their dissatisfaction with the apparent nominee: this happened to Carter in 1976 and, to a lesser extent, in 1980; and it happened to Reagan in 1980. Hart's aides were also talking about retuning the candidate and his campaign after Pennsylvania even before the vote there. And the Mondale people were concerned about the "lull," and what might follow, even if they were successful in Pennsylvania.

Hart seemed to enter the New York primary off stride, following his large defeat in Illinois on March 20th, and never regained his footing. And as he began his New York campaign he made what both his own associates and the Mondale people believe was a very big mistake. This was when, in speaking before a Jewish organization on March 22nd, he said, as he had in Illinois, that he favored moving the American Embassy from Tel Aviv to Jerusalem, and said that this had been his position all along, even though it was a recorded fact that he had previously said that this question should be the subject of negotiations. Then, to make matters worse, he blamed his staff for a letter that had gone out in his name saying that the move should be the subject of negotiations. Both James Johnson, Mondale's campaign chairman, and Oliver Henkel, Hart's campaign manager, say that by making the speech Hart appeared to be "pandering," thus neutralizing an issue that he had tried to use against Mondale. The Mondale people were delighted with Hart's statements about the embassy, because it gave them more ammunition with which to attack Hart's "character." What become issues in a campaign often—perhaps usually—have little to do with their intrinsic importance or the merits of the arguments. They are fanned by one camp or another for tactical advantage. No one was pretending that the question of moving the embassy had much to do with the large questions of the Middle East; nor, according to several accounts, is it, compared with other matters, of great importance within the Jewish community. But the subject was on the agenda because Senator Daniel Patrick Moynihan, Democrat of New York, had introduced a bill calling for the embassy to be moved, Mondale endorsed it, Hart did his about-face, and Mondale pounced. The key to the

Mondale strategy has been to use issues against Hart which the Mondale people think could help them portray Hart as "naive," "unsure," "inconsistent," "unprepared to be President." Thus, Mondale made a big thing about Hart's positions on the Persian Gulf and Castro and the windfall-profit tax and the Chrysler bailout not because his campaign believed that this would gain Mondale two per cent here and three per cent there but because they fit the case Mondale was trying to make. Johnson says, "We have endless issues we could use. The question is which ones cut the most. Our theory is that those that cut the most are those that show Hart to be weak and unsteady on foreign policy, and not on the side of the average family." Some issues were rejected by the Mondale people as too complex, requiring too much explanation, and not as strong as others. For example, though they felt there was a case to make against Hart's idea for individual training accounts—tax-deductible contributions by workers and employers for retraining workers—they did not do so, for these reasons. Moreover, they did not particularly want to showcase a Hart idea at all, and make it seem important. Shortly before the New York primary, Johnson told me he believed that if Mondale won the nomination it would be because, following Hart's victories in New Hampshire, Maine, and Vermont, the Mondale campaign was able to get Hart "out of the stratosphere"—something it was not sure for a while that it would be able to do—and onto political ground. Johnson added that the four days before the large number of March 13th contests, and then the four days before the Illinois primary—days when, as Johnson sees it, Mondale succeeded in raising questions in the voters' minds about Hart—will have been the critical ones.

The Mondale campaign itself had a few bad days early in the New York contest. Hart, inevitably, seized on the foreign-policy speech that Mondale had made in Chicago in which, among other things, Mondale said that he would withdraw only part of the American forces stationed in Honduras until Nicaragua agreed to certain conditions. Hart said that "if the Mondale or Reagan policies" were followed in Central America, "not only will this country light a fuse leading toward an explosion . . . but I am absolutely convinced this decade will see a rather large loss of American lives." To underscore the point, Hart ran an ad with a picture of a lighted fuse, and a voice saying, "When President Reagan sent our troops to Central America, he called them advisers. Remember Vietnam? Our troops now serve as bodyguards to dictators—and are a slow-burning fuse to war. Vice-President Mondale agrees with President Reagan and said he, too, would leave some of the troops there—as bargaining chips with Nicaragua. . . . Our sons as bargaining chips—will we never learn?" (Some members of the Hart camp thought this ad went too far, and Hart was never able to explain where American troops are serving as "bodyguards to dictators.") On Monday, March 26th, Mondale was seen on the television news programs unable to explain under what circumstances he would keep troops in Honduras. It was apparent that Mondale, in another attempt to suggest that Hart hadn't thought things through, had opened up this issue without himself thinking it through. Hart continued to say, as he had begun to in Chicago, that Mondale had not learned the lesson of Vietnam, and Mondale continued to say that Hart had learned the wrong lesson from Vietnam. This argument was one that some young liberal Democrats in Congress, among others, who support Mondale, wished hadn't been started, and so informed the Mondale people. Mondale's camp was divided over the political wisdom of having got into the whole thing, but the prevailing view was that it was useful to paint Hart as to the left of Mondale. The Mondale campaign was proceeding on the basis of poll data indicating that forty per cent of the Democrats in New York describe themselves as liberals, and a large proportion of those are blacks, many of whom would be attracted to Jackson. So the strategy was to try to appeal to blacks, hold the Jewish vote, and defeat Hart among moderates and conservatives. It was assumed, as it had been in Illinois, that certain elements of the foreign-policy-liberal vote would never be Mondale's anyway. The Central American strategy fit here. According to the exit polls in Illinois, Mondale did better than Hart among moderates and conservatives, and the Mondale people were pleased, for both the near and the long term, with the idea that Hart seemed to be on the way to becoming a candidate to the left of Mondale—thus limiting his appeal within the Party and putting Mondale in a stronger position for the general election. With Glenn out of the race, Mondale, beginning in Illinois, was for the first time in a situation where there was no candidate to the right of him—and this called for some delicate calibration, which sometimes missed. Hart also ran an ad in New York stressing

Mondale's ties to the Carter Administration's liabilities—the high inflation, and the high interest rates that occurred toward the end of Carter's term. Mondale's campaign ran an ad it had run in Illinois and, before that, in the South, which showed a red phone with a large red light blinking and had a voice saying, "The most awesome, powerful responsibility in the world lies in the hand that picks up this phone. The idea of an unsure, unsteady, untested hand is something to really think about."

On Tuesday, the result of the primary in Connecticut—which Mondale, foreseeing a loss in such a highly suburban and affluent state, did not really contest—was a larger victory for Hart than had been expected, and this was played as big news. (Hart won fifty-three per cent of the vote, Mondale twenty-nine per cent, and Jackson twelve per cent.) By Wednesday, Hart, who had been running behind Mondale in New York, pulled slightly ahead in the Washington *Post*/ABC News daily sampling. The Mondale people had decided that in the debate sponsored and broadcast by CBS that night Mondale should try to turn the Central America issue back on Hart as a character issue, and thus Mondale challenged Hart: "Why do you run those ads that suggest that I'm out trying to kill kids, when you know better?" A decision had been made within the Mondale camp that Mondale should be aggressive in the debate, challenging Hart on this position and that, but the degree of Mondale's aggressiveness startled even his own people—and worried some of his supporters, who felt that he was beginning to look like a heavy. The lasting memory of the debate is one of the three candidates cheek by jowl around a table— Mondale carrying on, Hart glowering angrily, and Jackson playing the situation to his best advantage by placing himself above such goings-on. Mondale, dominating the agenda, wrangled with Hart about this vote and that ("No, I didn't," "Oh, yes," "No, I didn't"), and, as is his wont, talked Washington talk—about tabling motions, and so on, often about obscure points.

Still, the poll figures began to get better for Mondale after the debate, and Hart did a few other things that played into Mondale's hands. He said that he opposed gun control, and then tried to fuzz his position. He said that the tax code was "encouraging people to have disrespect for the government and in the process, I think, Europeanizing this country," and added that Richard Nixon was "the first European President we ever had, in the sense of introducing a basic cynicism into public life." (Mondale said, "If a President had said what Mr. Hart said yesterday about Europe, he would have to spend weeks explaining what he meant.") And Hart managed to end up in the same place as Mondale on the question of troops in Honduras. (In the CBS debate, Mondale had explained that he opposed the presence of combat forces in Honduras but would continue "a modest military-assistance program" there, and later in the week Hart said that he would continue military assistance to Honduras.) Mondale's strategy worked, but perhaps at a price. He made the case against Hart, but he was still not offering something that people could be for. Most of his advisers felt, as they had since the New England shock, that there was little to be gained from positive speeches. Mondale did, as he has done throughout his campaign, say some positive things from time to time, but he did not take an opportunity to do more—to give people a reason to want to follow him. Mondale is not drawn to inspirational talk, to offering a vision—he refers to this as "words." In this respect, he is the antithesis of Reagan.

Hart was described to me by his advisers as tired and on edge as he went into New York, some of the weariness stemming from his receiving so much conflicting advice. Hart had, after all, come under enormous pressure quickly—going from being one of several back-runners to an overnight phenomenon to a national candidate under intense scrutiny from the press and faced with a battering by his opponent. No other candidate had come from relative obscurity into so much pressure so quickly: in 1976, Jimmy Carter had much more time to establish himself, and also had weaker, and divided, opposition. And the Hart camp had become a conflict-ridden place. The people who had been with Hart during the bleak months—more than a year, actually—resented the fact that a few seasoned political advisers were brought in. Other experienced political people were ready to join the Hart campaign but, seeing the divisions and tensions, stayed away. The strains between Hart and Patrick Caddell, the pollster, who had begun to help Hart early this year, and between Caddell and Hart's original campaign aides continued. Warren Beatty, the actor and Hart's good friend, went to New York to try to calm things down—with little apparent success. (Caddell was involved in the campaign and then on the sidelines several times within a brief period; now he is quite involved again.) And Hart, according to

several accounts, sought to be his own campaign manager, resisting advice. The larger point is that Hart, who had been brilliant in
his political tactics in New Hampshire, and who is longsighted and
emotionally tough, was not prepared for the rough political struggle and the increasingly close and questioning attention from the
media which followed. His message had worn thin, and his major
effort to bolster it—through a half-hour address on CBS—did not
come off. (Up to the last moments, Hart's aides were arguing over
what should be in the address, and Hart hardly saw it before he
gave it.) Hart entered New York, according to his own polling,
eighteen points behind Mondale, and this is where he ended up.
Also, Mondale had some advantages going in: New York is the
most heavily unionized state; in contrast with most of the previous
states, New York (like Pennsylvania) allows only Democrats to vote
in the primary—and Hart had been drawing considerable support
from independents; and Mondale had the active support of Governor Mario Cuomo and Mayor Edward Koch, who agree on little
else, as well as of Senator Moynihan and other political figures in
New York. The reserved Minnesotan, already more at home with
ethnic politics than Hart, fit into the New York landscape more
easily than did the more distant and less politically experienced
Coloradan.

A number of Hart advisers say that what went wrong for Hart in
New York is that he got away from his basic themes—that he was
offering a new leadership and had a better vision of the future
and offered change—and remained on the defensive. Some
thought he should be more aggressive against Mondale; some
thought that by being as aggressive, and negative, as he was he
blotted his image as a fresh, nonpolitical candidate. Mondale,
some realized, was turning the New York contest into a referendum on Hart. On occasion, Hart said that there were no real
differences of belief between himself and Mondale, which further
blurred the image. One Hart adviser told me that he felt that Hart
had succumbed to the pressures of being on the road, where the
mood of the immediate entourage tends to be excitable and reac-
tive to each volley from the opponent—and that all this was exacerbated by fatigue and the speed with which the contests confronted him. One adviser told me, "A lot of our problem is that
Gary still tends to feel that he can do it all." This adviser added,
"Gary will never be a convincing conventional politician, and
when he gets into conventional politics, as he did on the embassy

question, he loses his basic message, which is, Let's look at these problems in a new way."

Over lunch in Washington on the day before the Pennsylvania primary, Henkel told me that Hart's own polls showed him one point behind Mondale on the Friday before the New York primary, five points behind on Saturday, and eighteen points behind on Sunday. "There was no particular thing that occurred on Sunday," Henkel said. "We think what happened in the minds of the voters in New York at the last minute was that they were getting concerned with the 'flakiness' of the new and the fresh, so they opted for experience." He added, "New York was like a reverse New Hampshire. There was no reason for it to go that strongly at the end." Henkel and Caddell don't agree on much, but they do agree that there was no defining event that made New York turn out so badly for Hart. Caddell told me, "The focus came back to Gary Hart. There was no one big thing. Nobody's negatives or positives moved." Caddell was referring to the polls' indications of voters' attitudes toward the candidates. He continued, "People got up to the water's edge and said no." Mondale's victory—forty-five per cent to Hart's twenty-seven per cent and Jackson's twenty-six per cent—was across the board. He defeated Hart among the younger, more affluent voters, who had been giving Hart major support in earlier contests, and handily defeated him among union households. Jackson received the support of nearly nine out of ten black voters—and black turnout was substantially increased over 1980—but few votes from whites. (After Illinois, Jackson took to blaming whites for not voting for him, saying, "Whites have developed over their history a lack of regard for the intelligence and hard work of black people.") Hart, in his television appearances after the New York vote was in, attributed his loss to Mondale's negative campaigning (though Hart had engaged in a bit of this himself) and to Mondale's support from the political "establishment." In New Hampshire, Hart had been able to turn Mondale's "establishment" support back on him. In New York, Mondale's important backers made a point of not simply saying that they endorsed him but giving reasons, thus helping to make the case for Mondale and against Hart. "Steadiness" and "experience" were major themes of their campaign.

The big question going into Pennsylvania—or so many people thought at the time—was whether the Pennsylvania voters would be positively impressed by Mondale's showing in New York or would wish to vote against the reestablished front-runner. (Mondale has avoided the term assiduously.) One theory that enjoys some fashion is that the voters reject whoever is ahead. This is the theory that lies behind much of Hart's strategy for the next round. Whatever its validity, it turned out not to apply to Pennsylvania this year.

The Hart people felt that, as Henkel told me, Hart's campaign had lost its coherence in New York—a process that, he said, began in Illinois. "We got thrown off our rhythm," Henkel said. "It's important that we stay with our message." Henkel also said that the Mondale campaign had had some success in raising the questions "Do you really know who Gary Hart is? Do you know what kind of leader he will be?" and with suggesting that, as Henkel put it, "he is the candidate of media hype and lacks substance." Henkel finds it irritating that Hart, who was criticized last year for going around giving "issue" speeches, is now criticized for lacking substance. He said, "He became a national candidate overnight, and of necessity got into the airport-stop mode, with glitz and glitter and not a lot of substance. There wasn't time then for substantive speeches." Because of Mondale's success, Hart's advisers felt that, as Henkel put it, "we had been slow to fill out ourselves the definition of who Gary Hart is." So Hart, against his own inclinations, in this instance bent to the wishes of his advisers and, in Pennsylvania, started talking about his origins. In the debate that took place in Pittsburgh, on April 5th, Hart, in his closing remarks, stressed his modest, working-class background, and said, "I helped earn my way through school working on the railroads of Kansas and Colorado." The Hart campaign also ran a biographical ad in Pennsylvania, saying that Hart's was "an American story—raised in the heart of the nation—Kansas—by farming and laboring parents," and that "as a young man he worked on railroad crews." It gave his educational background and then talked about his having been attracted to politics by John Kennedy. Henkel said that it was hoped that showing Hart's working-class background would help him gain rapport with blue-collar workers, and offset the impression that he was the candidate of the upscale voters.

In planning the debate, for which I was the moderator, I deliberately set out to give these events more dignity and structure (this decision was made before the New York debates, one sponsored by CBS and the other by WNBC), on the theory that, now that the field had thinned, having the candidates sitting around in chairs competing for time and outshouting each other was avoidable and undesirable, because it was demeaning both to them and to politics. The theory was to try to get back to what debates are supposed to be—with the time allocated equally and controlled, and the candiates behind podiums, and competing on their ideas and wit, with whatever degree of combativeness they chose. As it turned out, the Mondale people had decided to lower the temperature of his debate performance—and in the course of the debate Mondale himself lowered it by more than the plan had called for. This caused the others to lower their thermostats as well. (Inevitably, a few people who had enjoyed the wrestling-match nature of the earlier debates, even while critical of it, were disappointed. But soundings taken by the candidates' camps—and by the Reagan campaign—had indicated that the public was becoming increasingly bothered by the rancorousness of the earlier encounters, and disgusted with the candidates themselves and with politics in general.) Still, the candidates did compete on a number of substantive issues, including taxes, industrial policy, and how they would try to change the way the government works, and there was a fair amount of argument, if with a different tone. None of the candidates, however, was willing to say he would, as most observers think is necessary, raise taxes on the middle class or cut middle-class entitlement programs in order to get a significant reduction in the budget deficit.

In the course of the Pennsylvania campaign, Mondale continued to attack Hart—for having opposed the Chrysler bailout and also for having opposed a Carter Administration plan for a federal loan to the Wheeling-Pittsburgh Steel Corporation to build a new plant that added four hundred jobs to its payroll. In a jab at Hart's book *A New Democracy*, in which Hart lays out his "new ideas," and trying to portray Hart as cold, Mondale said, "My nose is not buried in a textbook. I see the world as it really is. When you hurt, the President should hurt." Both Hart and Mondale stressed that they would help the steel industry, but both kept their pledges fairly general—avoiding specific commitments and also some of the more far-reaching, and politically risky, industrial-policy schemes. By the time both eventually spelled out their industrial policies, they were actually not far apart. Hart continued to argue, as he had in defense of his opposition to the Chrysler bailout, that plans to help failing businesses should not be "case-by-case bailouts" but should be industry-wide. He declined to say how he would decide which industries should be helped, but said that he would help such "keystone industries" as the steel, auto, and machine-tool industries—all of them major industries in Pennsylvania. Hart said that only companies that modernized their plants should be given tax breaks (this is already government policy), and proposed a law requiring companies that are about to close plants to notify the public and give the workers and communities time to come up with financing to keep the plants open. Hart talked about getting steel executives, labor leaders, and "private capital" into the Oval Office and seeking mutual concessions that would lead to government-guaranteed loans. Mondale offered his plans for the steel industry in a macro-economic context—getting the deficit and interest rates down. He also talked about establishing a Council on Economic Competitiveness, with labor, management, and government representatives, to analyze the effects of government policies on long-term competitiveness and to make recommendations for revitalizing "economic sectors" along the line of the Chrysler plan—including concesssions by labor and management, and government loans and guarantees and changes in trade policies—and said that the steel industry would have the first priority. (Actually, the Carter Administration had begun to work on an industry-wide steel agreement, but it did not press for concessions.) But the real problems of the steel industry have to do with above-average salaries, overcapacity, and obsolete equipment. Neither candidate embraced the idea, which has been floating around, of a new Reconstruction Finance Corporation, which would lend money to revitalize industries and explicitly get into the controversial business of "picking winners;" and both, of course, avoided schemes, which have been in vogue among younger Democrats (the "Atari Democrats"), to give more emphasis to the development of high-tech and other sunrise industries than to basic industries. Hart had to overcome the impression that his real interest is in high-tech, and, despite all his reported study of industrial policy, he apparently did not make a convincing case. The New York and Pennsylvania outcomes continued a pattern of Mondale victories in states with high unemployment.

In Pennsylvania, Hart attacked Mondale, through an ad, as too obligated to the special interests—a theme he had used to good effect earlier in the campaign. Hart was also critical of the fact that in Pennsylvania, as in New York and earlier contests, the Mondale campaign was using "delegate committees" to raise and spend money that would not be counted against the total amount that could be spent by the campaign in a given state. The campaign-finance law allows committees to be formed to raise and spend money on behalf of individuals running as delegates to the national convention, but these committees are not to be part of the candidate's national campaign. Through this device, the Mondale campaign could raise, indirectly, money from political-action committees—which it had forsworn in the campaign itself—and from individuals who had given the maximum allowed under law to the Mondale campaign itself. (Mondale eventually asked the delegate committees to stop taking PAC money.) The raising and spending of funds by delegate committees is legal under the federal election laws, but if done extensively it becomes a violation of the spirit, if not the letter, of the law. In Pennsylvania, Mondale delegate committees hired laid-off Mondale campaign workers, and were more active than they had been in the earlier states. (The Hart campaign has filed a complaint with the Federal Election Commission about the Mondale campaign's use of delegate committees, but, as the Mondale people know, the F.E.C. is very slow to rule on such complaints. Not until May, 1983, did it penalize the Reagan campaign for overspending in the New Hampshire primary in 1980, and only recently did it settle another complaint about the 1980 Reagan campaign.) The Mondale campaign is edging closer toward the ceiling that it can spend overall in the nomination contest—$20.2 million, plus another four million that can be spent on fund-raising. However, in New York and Pennsylvania the unions and teachers' organizations backing Mondale provided valuable help. Moreover, both Johnson and Henkel agree that as the campaign goes on, and receives increasing attention in the "free media," paid advertising is of decreasing marginal value. (In New York and Pennsylvania, Hart outspent Mondale on advertising by more than two to one.) The outcome in Pennsylvania was worse for Hart than his people had expected: Mondale won with forty-seven per cent of the vote; Hart received thirty-five per cent; and Jackson received seventeen per cent. Jackson carried the city of Philadelphia, even though its mayor, Wilson Goode, a black, had endorsed Mondale. Again, Mondale carried union households, and he split the young professionals' vote with Hart.

While Jackson was clearly stirring excitement among blacks, an unpleasant, and sad, aspect of his campaign took on larger proportions. It grew out of Jackson's remarks, published earlier this year in the Washington *Post*, referring to Jews as "Hymies." Shortly before the New York voting, it became known that in a radio broadcast Louis Farrakhan, the leader of a Black Muslim group, had threatened the life of Milton Coleman, the black *Post* reporter who told his paper of Jackson's remarks, and that Farrakhan had also threatened to punish Coleman's wife. Farrakhan said that "no physical harm" would come to Coleman now but "one day soon we will punish you with death." Farrakhan later said that his remarks about Coleman had been misinterpreted. (The *Post* took the threat seriously enough to remove Coleman from his reporting role for a while.) Jackson at first refused to disavow Farrakhan's remarks. Later, he did so, but he refused to dissociate himself from Farrakhan, who has provided him with important backing. (Among other things, Farrakhan provided bodyguards for Jackson before Jackson received Secret Service protection, and he addresses Jackson rallies.) During the earlier controversy over Jackson's remarks, Farrakhan, speaking in Jackson's presence at a rally, made a threat against Jews, saying, "If you harm this brother, I warn you in the name of Allah, this is the last one you harm." Jackson refused to disavow this remark as well. Throughout this latest episode, Jackson conveyed the same attitude he had in the course of the earlier one—that he felt he was being put upon, that unfair demands were being made of him. (On the day before the Pennsylvania primary, it was announced that PUSH-EXCEL, an organization founded by Jackson, had been asked by the Department of Education to return some seven hundred thousand dollars that the department said had been misspent.) The whole business raised some ugly, and unnecessary, issues, and, as if things weren't bad enough, Vice-President George Bush tried to exploit them by going before a Jewish organization on April 9th and attacking Hart and Mondale for not having been more critical of Jackson for Farrakhan's remarks. Bush said that Reagan and his Administration "denounce the intrusion of anti-Semitism into the American political process." Both Hart and Mondale had in fact been critical of Farrakhan's remarks, but they had not confronted Jackson directly on the matter; Jackson, after all, has a following that the

Democratic nominee will need. (After Bush's remarks, Hart did say he thought that a candidate for President should dissociate himself from anyone making the kinds of remarks Farrakhan had.)

The end of the first round of primaries and caucuses left Mondale with over a thousand delegates (nineteen hundred and sixty-seven are needed for the nomination), Hart with over five hundred and fifty, Jackson with about a hundred and fifty. (Delegate counts are imprecise because in several states—including Iowa, where the first precinct caucuses were held—the process of delegate selection is still going on. What is shown on television on primary and caucus nights is an estimate of how many delegates the candidates will have.) The end of the first round also left all three camps regrouping, and political observers speculating about what would happen next. After the Pennsylvania vote, Mondale still shunned the title of front-runner, but he did allow that it was possible that he might end up having enough delegates for the nomination before the Convention. Hart, more gracious than he had been on earlier election nights, was seen cheering on his supporters, and arguing that a number of the upcoming contests would be in the West, and therefore in states more hospitable to him. Hart, who had a bad cold, returned to Denver for a brief rest, and Mondale went off to raise more funds and planned to take a few days off in Washington. When Henkel and I had lunch on the day before the Pennsylvania primary, he said that if Hart lost Pennsylvania it would be very important for him to win somewhere soon, and that the Hart campaign had stepped up its efforts in Arizona, which was holding caucuses on Saturday, April 14th. (Hart won, with forty-five per cent of the vote, to Mondale's forty per cent and Jackson's thirteen.) The Hart camp plans to try to make Mondale's accusations that Hart is a servant of the oil interests (for opposing a windfall-profit tax and for supporting an oil-import fee) an advantage in Texas, which holds caucuses on May 5th. While some of the upcoming contests are in the West, others are in Southern and border states, and on May 8th there will be contests in Ohio and Indiana (as well as North Carolina and Maryland). If Hart has not built up steam by then, his chances of reviving his candidacy will be seriously diminished. (As of May 9th, eighty-three per cent of the delegates will have been chosen.) After the Pennsylvania primary, Hart would have to win almost eighty per cent of all the remaining delegates at stake in order to have enough for the nomination going into the Convention. (Mondale would have to win slightly more than half.) The Hart camp's idea is to have Hart defeat Mondale in a number of the final contests, and continue to show up in the polls as the strongest candidate against Reagan, and create a stampede in his direction toward the end and impress the Party leaders with Hart's "electability." (Under the new Party rules, no delegates are bound.) The Mondale camp's idea is, of course, to prevent such a thing from happening. Henkel said, "Though the Democratic Party is more comfortable with Walter Mondale, we think it will go with the more electable rather than the more comfortable."

Mondale, despite his lead, has been talking about the importance of the contests to come, aware of the danger of losing popularity contests toward the end even if he continues to gain in the delegate count. Both candidates' campaigns have been engaged for some time in keeping track of their own delegates and those who are uncommitted, or committed to a candidate who has dropped out. Should neither candidate have enough delegates before the Convention, delegates up for grabs will have no peace in the weeks leading up to it. (Those who want something from the candidates will have a fine time.) There is, of course, a great deal of speculation about what role Jackson will play, and what his demands will be. The strength of his role will be determined to some extent by the relative number of delegates the candidates have; if Jackson's delegates make the difference, his role will, of course, be greater, but in any case his black following will still be seen as essential for the election. But, much as he enjoys the speculation, Jackson will be under pressure from other black leaders (whom he may or may not choose to listen to), and at some point will have to decide, if he has not done so already, whether he wants to be the black who contributed to Reagan's reelection, and what actions risk bringing that about. A few people here have considered the possibility of a truly brokered Convention, with neither Hart nor Mondale being viable candidates by then, and some political figures have enjoyed the thought that they would be the brokers. Most people, however, dismiss the idea. There has been some talk of a new candidate's entering the late contests, but, because of filing deadlines, this would be possible in only a very few states. In 1976, Jerry Brown and Frank Church entered late and won their first contests in May.

Both the Hart and Mondale camps have been considering how to use the "lull" to advantage. Henkel says that Hart will stress more than before that Mondale has made a lot of promises, some of which may have to be broken, whereas he himself is independent and knows how to say no. There will be an attempt to turn his opposition to the Chrysler bailout into a plus. Hart, Henkel says, will stress that having experience doesn't mean that one can provide leadership, and will cite instances Mondale has given of having opposed certain Carter policies as indications that Mondale wasn't much of a leader when he was Vice-President. Caddell, who is, as of now, again a major strategist, says that Hart has to deepen his message—to explain why he is campaigning and what is at stake in this election, to infuse his candidacy with some urgency. Caddell says that Hart "has to make his campaign a movement, a cause—he has to be an advocate for certain things rather than for himself." He also says he believes that if Hart does this he will be a better candidate, more comfortable with promoting a cause than with promoting himself. In the recent contests, he says, Hart didn't appear to be fighting for anything, and his recitation of the phrases "new ideas" and "new leadership" had no force. Caddell has advised Hart that it will not be enough for him to say "Vote for me, I can beat Reagan"—that he must, as Caddell puts it, "convince people emotionally, morally, and substantively that he can beat Reagan." Caddell says that Hart has to put some passion into his campaign—"be more Robert Kennedy than John Kennedy"—and explain why it is vital to change direction now, to give his case some imperatives. The Mondale people were concerned even before the Pennsylvania vote that a victory there would put Mondale back in the position he was in before all these contests began—in Iowa—of being the front-runner and presumed nominee, against whom a reaction sets in. They have been concerned that the very strategy the Hart people have been planning might work out— that Mondale would win delegates while Hart won popularity contests. But Johnson says the Mondale campaign will continue with what it believes is a "winning strategy": put the focus on the questions of who would be the best President and who cares more about the average family, and draw the contrast with Hart on certain issues. And both camps are also thinking about the post-nomination period, in case their candidate wins. The Mondale people are back to thinking about who their Vice-Presidential selection might be—the sort of thinking that they were doing earlier this year but that circumstances then made luxurious. The Hart campaign is doing more research to prepare Hart for a race against Reagan, and is developing more detailed information about the states as they relate to the general election, and is thinking about how to use Hart's time if he is the nominee. And Henkel also told me that one goal during the post-Pennsylvania period was to make people "more comfortable with Gary." He added, "It's one of my responsibilities to figure out how to do that." Henkel said that these efforts are geared to the general election as well as to the nomination contest. Hart would run against Reagan, Henkel says, in much the same way he has run against Mondale—stressing that it is time for new leadership and fresh ideas. But the Hart people are aware that one of Reagan's assets is that people tend to feel comfortable with him. Henkel says, "We can't reach the Ronald Reagan level, but we can narrow the gap."

For what it's worth, Reagan's aides are largely back to thinking that Mondale will be Reagan's opponent, but they are, as before, divided over how great a challenge Mondale will present, and some still think that Hart would be the stronger opponent. Richard Wirthlin, Reagan's pollster, believes, as he did before, that Mondale will be quite a strong challenger—all the stronger for the fight he has been through. A number of people think that Mondale is tougher as a result of the fight, but some people close to Mondale say that he hasn't really changed. He has always been a very scrappy partisan, they point out, but—with the exception, to some degree, of the fight against Kennedy four years ago—he has not trained his energies on intraparty fights. He coasted early this year because he thought he could afford to and because he wanted to open as few intraparty wounds as possible (though he did not hesitate to tear into John Glenn when that seemed necessary). But the thinking that Mondale has changed, whatever its validity, is helpful to Mondale. It is no longer said that Mondale lacks "fire in the belly," and the argument that he has always advanced in politics through the patronage of others has been mooted. There can be little question that Mondale, faced with political humiliation, and even extinction, reached for reserves in himself that he had not been required to call on before. He pulled himself out of a crisis, when a large number of people, including some of those around him, doubted whether it was possible. This has to have given him confidence. And because his strategy has worked thus far, one of his aides says, he probably has more confidence in his instincts. (Mondale was the recipient of a great deal of advice following his early defeats.) And the fact that people are saying that Mondale is a tougher, better candidate, one of Mondale's associates points out, helps to make him so, impressions counting for as much as they do in politics.

A couple of weeks ago, one of Reagan's top advisers said to me, "There are a lot of negatives for us out there, but all the attention is on the Democrats." He added, of course, that that was just as well. For a while, it seemed that Reagan didn't exist. It is a cliché that Reagan is lucky, but even those who are cliché-resistant began to succumb to the idea this spring. Just before the New Hampshire primary, after all, the question of whether Reagan was on top of his job was dominating the agenda, and the President's costly Lebanon policy collapsed. Then Hart upset Mondale, and everyone seemed to forget about Reagan. The press and the public can't focus on many things at once, and subjects, like fashions, change. By "negatives," Reagan's adviser meant, among other things, the controversy over the Administration's policy in Central America, and over Edwin Meese, the President's counsellor and nominee for Attorney General, who, it emerged in the course of his confirmation hearings, had received financial assistance from a number of people who received federal jobs. Many Republican senators who were disturbed by the revelations about Meese were reluctant to face up to the question they raised of whether he should be confirmed, for a couple of reasons: Meese is close to the President and, perhaps more important, is a favorite of the Republican right wing, which many Republicans (especially those preparing to run for President someday) are loath to offend. So, focussing as they often do on the wrong question, and seeking as they often do something that would make their decision easier for them, the politicians turned the question about Meese into whether he had committed a crime. (He had failed to list one loan on a federal disclosure form.) An investigation by a special prosecutor is now under way. The Democrats have sought to exploit what has come to be called the "sleaze" issue—the rather large number of Administration officials who have been found to have behaved unethically, at the least, and many of whom have had to leave office. But the Democrats have done so in a rather ham-handed way—the Democratic Congressional Campaign Committee has produced a television ad that overpoliticizes the issue. Reagan, as is his wont, brushes the whole thing off, but some of his advisers see it as potentially damaging in the fall, when it could become part of the "fairness" issue—when the Democrats will no doubt try to paint the Reagan Administration as one that is of, by, and for the rich. (Both Mondale and Hart have made this general case, and have also raised the "sleaze" issue.) It is to be remembered that the blue-collar voters will be the ones most fought over this fall, and a picture of an Administration that looks out for the rich and feathers its own nest could have a powerful effect. That's what has some of the President's advisers worried.

But it is on foreign policy that the Administration has managed to explode all over itself in recent days. First, on April 6th the President gave a speech in which he was ostensibly calling for bipartisanship in the conduct of foreign policy and then blamed Congress for "second-guessing" his policy in Lebanon, saying that this "severely undermined our policy," and for "wavering" in its support for his Central American policy, saying that such wavering "can only encourage the enemies of democracy who are determined to wear us down." Presidents and Secretaries of State generally find congressional "meddling" in foreign policy irritating—this is an institutional question, not a partisan one. But it is a fact that the framers of the Constitution deliberately divided authority over foreign policy—making the President the Commander-in-Chief but reserving to Congress the power to declare war—so that Presidents could not take the country into war without the consent of the people's representatives. This arrangement seldom works tidily. And it is also a fact that Congress is usually complaisant toward Presidents' conduct of foreign policy unless mightily provoked—not wishing to be accused of the very things that Reagan accused the current one of. And this Congress has been especially complaisant toward the Reagan Administration—in the case of Lebanon and, thus far, in the case of Central America, despite changed rationales and lack of real consultation. (The strongest and most effective opposition to the Lebanon policy came from within the executive branch, including the Pentagon.) Reagan's latest exercise in the politics of blame appears to have backfired, at least in Washington—even the Republican leaders on Capitol Hill openly expressed their unhappiness. And there was some consternation among the President's advisers—a feeling that, rather than open a discussion of Congress's proper role in foreign policy, the President had managed to reopen a discussion of his Lebanon policy, which had been nearly forgotten. The warships containing the American Marines were ordered elsewhere, and hardly anyone noticed—the Administration had nearly succeeded in silently slipping away. Now the issue was back.

The news that the C.I.A. was participating in the mining of Nicaraguan ports broke on the weekend between the New York and Pennsylvania primaries, and set off a predictable storm. Even the Democratic fight could not drown this one out. And the news about the mining was surrounded by reports that the Administration was planning a wider role in Central America after the election. Administrations usually have contingency plans for all sorts of things, but in this case Secretary of Defense Caspar Weinberger denied that there were any such plans and then one of his aides said that there were. (Weinberger also said, "The United States is not mining the harbors of Nicaragua.") The mining—which damaged several ships of various nations—had been the subject of some controversy within the Administration but, apparently, little serious examination, and was said to have been presented to the President as "part of a package" of actions to harass the Sandinista regime. The point that such mining risked incurring the displeasure of our allies—including Britain and France, who were engaged in shipping to Nicaragua—was raised by Secretary of State George Shultz but never seriously considered. The controversy over the mining was exacerbated by the Administration's announcement on Sunday, in the face of a plan by the Nicaraguan government to take the issue of the mining to the World Court, that for the next two years it would not abide by decisions of the Court concerning Central America. Although State Department lawyers came up with a rationale for the decision, some high officials in the State Department and the White House were appalled by it. One State Department official told me that the matter of the Nicaraguan complaint could have been dealt with by having the governments of El Salvador and Honduras file counter-complaints about Nicaraguan activities in the region. The immediate outburst in Congress, which passed a nonbinding resolution condemning the mining operation—the resolution was nonbinding even in this instance—was prompted by a combination of anger and embarrassment. (The vote in the Senate for the resolution, on Tuesday, was by a large, bipartisan majority, but by the time the House voted two days later the President at least had the support

of the Republican leaders.) The reasons for the anger are clear
enough. The reasons for the embarrassment have to do with the
fact that Congress has been approving the funding of the "covert"
war and either knew or should have known about the mining.
Senator Barry Goldwater, Republican of Arizona, the chairman of
the Senate Intelligence Committee, said that he had not been
informed, and the Administration said that he had been. The
House Intelligence Committee was apparently more thoroughly
briefed on the matter than the Senate committee was, though
some senators later said that they did know about the mining. The
point may be that the C.I.A. has a way of running some information by the congressional committees so that the committees
hardly notice (the "information" provided to the Senate committee in this case was one vague sentence)—and realize later that
they should have raised more questions. The vote on the mining,
just before the Easter recess, gave Congress a vehicle for expressing indignation without really doing anything. (The Administration says that the mining has stopped.) But some Administration
officials are concerned that the mining put in jeopardy the whole
program of aiding the "contras" fighting the Nicaraguan regime—aid that, depending on which rationale the Administration
offers, has been provided to "interdict" weapons going from Nicaragua to the rebels in El Salvador, to "harass" the Nicaraguan
regime into stopping aid to rebels in El Salvador, to change the
Nicaraguan form of government. (This last rationale was suggested by the President in an interview with the New York *Times*
recently, and was quickly corrected by his aides.)

Despite their divided opinion over whether Mondale or Hart
would be the stronger opponent against Reagan, and the President's good standing in the polls, Reagan's political advisers are
not complacent—largely because of the number of things that are
beyond their control. They recognize that unpleasant foreign-policy developments can occur at any time. They see that interest
rates have been going up—and the President is among the few
people who don't think that this has anything to do with the
deficit. In any event, all the talk and speculation about how whoever would do against Reagan is meaningless at this point: that
contest doesn't really begin until the Democrats have picked a
nominee.

XV

The continuing refusal of the Democratic nomination race to settle down and get itself over with—though these races usually go to the end—has tended to distract people from other matters of consequence here, and set the town off on a whole new round of speculation. Those who had been longing for a brokered Convention—some for the sheer sport of it, some for less impersonal reasons—took new hope. New imagined sequences of events were spelled out. Once again, just when another consensus had formed—this time, that with victories in Ohio, Indiana, Maryland, and North Carolina on May 8th Walter Mondale would have the nomination all but in hand—the voters in Ohio and Indiana rose up and smote that consensus. Gary Hart's victories in Ohio and Indiana by narrow margins—while he lost North Carolina and Maryland—changed the chemistry and substance of the campaign period ahead, whether or not they changed its outcome. Yesterday, Hart, as expected, won primaries in Oregon and Nebraska, by large margins; Mondale, knowing that both states would be inclined toward Hart, did not really contest Oregon and put a minimal effort into Nebraska. Meanwhile, some big questions have been before the politicians and policymakers here—questions that are bound to play a role in the fall election: how to come to grips with the deficit; how to deal with Central America; whether the arms race, which is proceeding and is about to enter new phases, will be slowed at all. This period may be looked back upon as one in which, in all these areas, the country got itself into a substantially larger bind, and historians may well ask why more wasn't done about it.

Before the contests on May 8th, when one talked to the Hart people and to everybody else one had two very different conversations. Everybody else knew that the nomination contest was just

425

about over. Mondale had, after all, defeated Hart in every important contest since Mondale won Pennsylvania, on April 10th, and
had defeated him in all the major industrial states, through Pennsylvania. Hart, therefore, had been a temporary phenomenon.
His campaign seemed to lack focus. Mondale defeated him by a
wide margin in the Missouri caucuses, on April 18th; in the Tennessee primary, on May 1st; and in the Texas caucuses, on May
5th. The loss in Tennessee was a particularly big blow, as the Hart
people had hoped to win there; Hart lost to Mondale by twelve
points. The Mondale people set out to make sure, by putting
more resources and more of the candidate's time into the state,
that Tennessee did not provide Hart with a "second New
Hampshire." (For all of both candidates' efforts, only sixteen per
cent of the eligible voters turned out.) This loss may, as one of
Hart's closest advisers thinks, have accounted for Hart's drawn,
almost distracted look in a debate in Dallas the following night.
After Hart's substantial defeat in Texas—Mondale beat him by
twenty-three points, aided by the fact that the contest was by caucus, which requires organization, and by his support from labor
and the large Hispanic population—Mondale became "inevitable"
once more. The expectation grew that Mondale would win all four
states on the eighth—the Mondale people shared this expectation,
and helped spread it—and the interest was in whether Hart would
have the good grace to step aside, and in how the issues among
Mondale, Hart, and Jesse Jackson might be worked out in advance
of the Convention.

Conversations with the Hart people were of a different nature.
Hart's advisers did say that if Hart failed to win any important
victories on the eighth he would be facing some hard questions
about whether to continue his campaign and, if so, with what
degree of intensity. (Among other things, his campaign is heavily
in debt, and the less you win, the less the money comes in. Contributors are realists. Mondale's campaign is in debt as well. Both
campaigns have long since tapped the readily willing donors. The
Mondale campaign let more people go after the eighth, and Hart's
is deferring its workers' pay. Working for a Presidential campaign
is perilous. Both candidates will be trying to raise more money
while they fight to the end for the nomination.) But a couple of
Hart advisers told me they thought that Hart had a good chance
of carrying Ohio and Indiana: their polling in Ohio showed that

Hart started off close to Mondale, albeit behind, and that there was a lot of discontent with Mondale in the state and, when the subject was raised, with what had happened to the state economically during the Carter Administration—or what Hart calls "the Carter-Mondale Administration." (Ohio fared less well economically during that period than other industrial states did.) The Hart surveys also found a lot of interest in "new ideas." Five important newspapers endorsed Hart. And Ohio, unlike New York and Pennsylvania, allowed independents and Republicans to vote in the primary. (Maryland and North Carolina allowed only Democrats to vote.) The Hart people also felt that if Hart won Ohio the victory would have more impact if it came as a surprise, so they did not talk publicly about their optimistic expectations.

In the course of the week before the Texas caucuses, which took place on a Saturday, and the Ohio primary, the following Tuesday, Patrick Caddell, the pollster, told me, "Since no one expects Hart to win Ohio and Indiana, his doing so would be a shock to the system." He thought then that there was a good chance that Hart would win both. Caddell said that surveys done for the Hart campaign in the North and the South in mid-April, preparatory to the latest round of contests, showed that "we were in deep trouble in the South—they didn't know Gary." Oliver Henkel, Hart's campaign manager, said to me before the Ohio primary that a victory in Ohio, which he, too, thought was possible, would show that Hart had broad popular support—"in the face of Mondale's being backed by the unions and by a popular governor." Governor Richard Celeste had supported Ohio's Senator John Glenn until Glenn dropped out of the race, and then, having had close ties to Mondale over the years, endorsed him in late April. Henkel, who is from Cleveland, was encouraged not only by the poll data and the newspaper endorsements but by "the independent-mindedness of Ohio voters, including in union households." Henkel also said that the Hart campaign had organized early and quietly in both Ohio and Indiana, and he believes that "organization may be the most important factor in this election—for both candidates." He said, "We were able to do well in New Hampshire not because Gary finished second in Iowa but because when he took off and started to get media attention he had a very strong organization in place." Caddell now says that another factor in Hart's victory was that he made the case against the economic effects of the Carter

Administration in Ohio—and by implication showed the effect of Reagan's making such a case. Hart made several appearances with Ohio workers, and his ads had blue-collar workers complaining about the Carter Administration. ("What we're all saying is that Mondale had his chance and he did nothing. Why take him again?") Hart, his campaign having recognized the opportunity, spent more time in the state, and more money on media there, than Mondale did. (Though there is a school of thought that political advertising may not count for much, especially at this point in the campaign, nobody really knows.) Henkel believes that the key thing Hart was able to do in Ohio, as opposed to New York and Pennsylvania, was to "neutralize the jobs issue and get us out from under, to a very large degree, the effect of the discussion of the Chrysler bailout"—which Hart had opposed. Hart argued, in a speech in Cleveland early in the Ohio contest, "The Chrysler example does not show the success of the bailout strategy; it shows what happens, bailout or not, when there is no strategy for the industry as a whole." Hart and Mondale have had a running argument over how many jobs the Chrysler bailout saved—each proceeding from a different base.

Meanwhile, the Mondale people believed that they would win Ohio: their polling indicated a ten-point lead on the Wednesday before the primary; and on the Saturday before it their tracking poll (a daily sampling of a small number of people to indicate shifts in opinion) indicated that they still led, but more narrowly. Their tracking poll on Monday night had them ahead by thirteen points in Ohio and by nine points in Indiana. In conversations before the Ohio primary, they suggested that Ohio resembled western Pennsylvania, where Mondale had run strong. They saw nothing particularly favorable happening to Hart that would lead to a sudden change in his fortunes after he'd lost a series of contests by rather substantial margins. They said that Hart could have opened up some differences with Mondale if he had concentrated on Ohio more but that he had failed to do so. They had settled on a strategy of trying to make sure that Hart didn't win Tennessee, and to win Texas big and then win all four contests on May 8th, and had allocated the campaign's resources and Mondale's time accordingly. Ohio didn't seem to demand any unusual effort. In other words, they misread the situation.

On the day before the Ohio primary, a senior Mondale cam-

paign official said to me, "Hart has opened no line of attack that
stuck." He said he had been worried that Hart's attacks on unemployment during the Carter Administration would stick, but believed they hadn't. The polling, he said, indicated that Mondale
got higher marks than Hart on the subject of jobs. Hart in fact
carried the industrial areas of Youngstown and the Akron as well
as Dayton and Columbus, and came close to Mondale in
Cuyahoga County (Cleveland). Mondale officials say that they have
checked throughout the campaign to see if Mondale's ties to labor
were hurting him with the voters, and kept finding that they were
not. The Mondale people have also maintained that Mondale's
opponents have little to gain by trying to hang Carter around his
neck. (That Carter is so discredited these days is a curious phenomenon, explained by a number of factors. He was sincere, tried
hard, and had many important accomplishments—but he could
not connect with the public, and failed as a leader. Moreover, as a
loner, he had few allies and, having lost, has few defenders. There
is little political mileage in defending Jimmy Carter. Losers do not
enjoy much stature unless theirs was a noble loss, and Carter
doesn't have the characteristics of nobility; he is easily car-
icatured—the voice, the diminutive stature, the lack of confidence
he conveyed. And he was, and remains, up against skilled detrac-
tors. His record is painted as worse than it was, but few people
want to invest very much in defending him. So he is shunned.) As
for Mondale's association with Carter, James Johnson, Mondale's
campaign chairman, said to me a couple of weeks ago, "There's a
very limited appeal to trying to beat Mondale over the head with
Carter." Johnson has held this belief since 1981, when he and
Mondale's pollster, Peter Hart, conducted a "focus-group interview" (in which a free-flowing conversation is held with a small
group of voters) and found that people didn't consider a Vice-
President a sufficiently important figure to be tied to the policies
of a President. The Hart campaign has been arguing in recent
weeks that if Mondale wants to take credit for his "experience" as
Vice-President he can justifiably be criticized for the policies he
had some experience with—that he can't have it both ways.
Johnson said to me, "The lesson of the last two years is that Mondale *can* have it both ways."

The Hart people argue that tying Mondale to Carter is both
valid in itself and also part of the larger point about "electability"

which Hart is trying to make. Having failed to make a substantial gain on Mondale, or to run much better against Reagan than Mondale does in the polls, Hart talked less explicitly about electability. ("That doesn't sell," an adviser told me.) He turned to trying to show the Party that he is more electable than Mondale because he does not have Mondale's presumed vulnerabilities—the ties to the "special interests," the association with Carter, the identification with "the past"—which Reagan was bound to exploit. One of Hart's most controversial moves—his attack, in Texas, on Mondale for having been part of an Administration that brought the nation "days of shame" during the hostage crisis in Iran—was defended by some of Hart's advisers on this ground. One of them said to me, "That was a terrible period for this country. There *was* the perception that America was weak in the world. Reagan beat the Carter-Mondale Administration in large part on that issue and on the economic issue, and he will call those issues to mind again. The Democrats have to remember that they're selecting a nominee to run against Reagan. Next fall, we'll see ads of our people in pajamas, blindfolded, being paraded around Teheran; we'll hear about interest rates and inflation during the Carter-Mondale Administration. I think we'd better recall those days or we'll nominate a very nice fellow who will be crucified in 1984 as much as in 1980." In the Iran speech, Hart also accused the Carter Administration of letting the state of military readiness slip to the point where the attempted rescue mission failed, and said, "Carter-Mondale actually gave us an America held hostage to the Ayatollahs of the world." The speech re-raised a painful problem for which there were no good answers, and was strongly criticized, outside the Mondale camp, as going over a line, and became the subject of controversy within the Hart camp; and Hart himself was plainly, and oddly, ambivalent about it. When the subject came up in the Dallas debate, Hart said that he had only been referring to the issue of military readiness. Then, in Ohio, he briefly revived the matter.

Inevitably, there were a hundred explanations for the outcomes in Ohio and Indiana, and, given the closeness of those outcomes— Hart won Ohio with forty-two per cent of the vote, compared with Mondale's forty and Jesse Jackson's sixteen, and he carried Indiana by forty-two per cent, compared with Mondale's forty-one and

Jackson's thirteen—any number, or all, of the explanations would do. It was overinterpretation time. Probably no one explanation would serve: voters usually have a variety of things on their minds. A friend of mine who is involved in politics says, "I have concluded that nobody ever knows why anything happens." A shift of about thirteen thousand votes in Ohio—out of nearly one and a half million—would have produced analyses of why Hart failed. The exit polls can be helpful but they are not definitive. One theory is that the voters had once again turned against the front-runner—a phenomenon that had occurred in previous nomination campaigns, and had bedevilled Mondale in New Hampshire. Thus, Mondale was taking pains not to appear too confident, while Hart, when all seemed lost, kept insisting, almost eerily, "I will be the nominee." Yet Mondale did begin to suggest that he thought he would have the nomination in hand before the Convention. Apparently, it's all right to express confidence if you're behind but not if you're ahead. The fact that independents and Republicans could vote in Ohio and Indiana, while they had not been able to participate in New York and Pennsylvania, was said to make a difference, and it unquestionably did. About a fourth of the voters in Ohio were independents, whom Hart carried five to three. (Independents could also vote in Tennessee—which was one reason the Hart people had been hopeful about the state.) According to exit polls, independents had provided Hart's margin of victory in New Hampshire and Florida—two of the most important contests of his candidacy. Independents will be much fought over in November, and Hart makes the argument that he has shown that he can attract them. John Anderson's announcement, in late April, that he will not run for President again this year was taken as good news by the Democrats, who believe he cost them several states in 1980. It was said that the result in Ohio showed that Mondale's candidacy has vulnerabilities—potentially serious ones—and that is true. So does Hart's—but they are different vulnerabilities. The Reagan people disagree among themselves over which man would be the stronger—or weaker—candidate. After the Ohio primary, Johnson said he still believed that "Carter-bashing" and "labor-bashing" had not helped Hart—that what had helped Hart was "Mondale-bashing": in particular, his ad stressing that Mondale had not been able to deliver on jobs in Ohio. Johnson said that this was a tactic peculiarly suited to Ohio.

It was explained that Ohio and Indiana are more conservative than the industrial states that voted earlier, and there is truth to that. Indiana regularly goes Republican in November, and Ohio usually does. The New York *Times*/CBS News exit polling suggested that Glenn's having been a candidate helped Hart in Ohio. This figures: Hart, like Glenn, appealed to those who are not hard-core Democrats; and the tough combat between Glenn and Mondale earlier in the campaign would not have been likely to leave Glenn supporters with warm feelings toward Mondale. It was said that Hart successfully played on anti-union sentiment in these states—something he had been trying, somewhat tentatively, to do before. (The exit polls found more anti-union feeling in these two states than they had in other industrial states.) In this case, Hart did not attack unions as such—they are, after all, strong in Ohio and Indiana—but went after Mondale's ties to them and the acceptance of political-action-committee funds by delegate committees working on Mondale's behalf.

One of the interesting, and mysterious, things about politics is the way a campaign can do well in one state and misfire in another. There was every reason to expect Hart to do well in North Carolina—Jackson would take a high percentage of the black vote, and Hart would appeal to the university and research communities. But Hart apparently mishandled his campaign there. He had never been expected to do very well in Maryland, where Mondale had the strong support of strong political leaders as well as of labor and of the large number of government workers who live there, just outside Washington. It was said that Mondale should have spent less time in the other states, and the Mondale people say that, knowing what they know now, they would have spent less time in Tennessee and Texas and more in Ohio. Mondale had been very hopeful of winning all four states on the eighth, and his campaign did not give up on Ohio until late that night; when the results were clear, Mondale was very disheartened.

There was, of course, a lot of speculation in political circles about what it all meant. There is a kind of mass psychology among political practitioners which sets them to reacting feverishly, if most often uselessly, to important political events. There is an increase in huddled conversations off the Senate and House floors; reporters call state chairmen and state chairmen call each other; governors, Party officials, former Party officials, former Administration officials—all are on the phone. Rumors are even more abundant than usual. (The four most used words are "What do you hear?") "Opinion"—the sum total of a lot of instincts and conversations—shifts. Now X is in trouble, now Y is in trouble. In this case, as on earlier occasions this year, names of those the Party might turn to—however that might happen—resurfaced: New York Governor Mario Cuomo, Arkansas Senator Dale Bumpers, and, inevitably, Edward Kennedy. The possibilities of such a thing happening are solemnly weighed. Following Ohio, there was talk that it meant that the voters really didn't want Mondale but that they didn't seem keen on Hart, either. There was a widespread, and certainly valid, view that if Mondale still succeeded in getting the nomination it would be under more difficult circumstances. Some thought that May 8th was the day that Mondale lost the general election.

For the Party to turn to someone else, a major rebellion would have to occur, a great many commitments would have to be broken, and there would have to be more upset within the Party than there is—at least, as yet. A mixture of motives drives the various Party figures: some would simply want to stick with their commitments, or at least be seen as sticking with their commitments, to Mondale; some would not want to anger labor by jumping ship; some, while newly concerned about Mondale's electoral prospects, do not regard Hart as someone they want to see as President; some, truth be told, considering their own Presidential ambitions for 1988, would, for all their real concern about Reagan, have mixed feelings about another Democrat gaining the White House in 1984. House members, many of whom have committed to Mondale, tend to feel that they have established strong relationships with their districts, and feel autonomous—less threatened than senators tend to by what happens to the top of the ticket. It's fun to think about the drama of the Party turning to someone else, but far more damage would have to be inflicted on the candidates for that to happen—yet it goes without question that more damage will be inflicted.

After an important turn of political events, the campaigns compete to establish, in journalists' and the public's minds, their version of what happened. After the contests in Ohio, Indiana, North

Carolina, and Maryland, the Mondale camp described the story as one of an inexorable march toward enough delegates for the nomination; the Hart people described it as one that showed that Mondale's candidacy is too flawed for him to defeat Reagan—the electability argument. Politics is so much a game of "perceptions" that a great deal of effort goes into affecting what those perceptions will be. Sometimes, though, sheer luck is involved. When Mondale squeaked by in two out of five primaries on March 13th, this was portrayed by the networks that night as a victory. On May 9th, both camps held briefings for reporters. Johnson said that Mondale would have between 1,750 and 1,800 delegates by June 4th, and that after the final primaries, on June 5th, he would have the 1,967 required for the nomination.

In fact, Mondale won more delegates on May 8th than Hart did, and as of today, according to the delegate count by United Press International, Mondale has 1,564 delegates, Hart has 941, and Jackson 291. Yet Hart's victories in Ohio and Indiana, though narrow, altered both the perception and the actuality of the race. Hart, had he lost, would have been under pressure to get out, or be a good soldier (the odds are he wouldn't have got out), and there would have ensued a period of consolidation around Mondale, and of peacemaking. Now there would be at least a month more of the candidates' bashing each other.

Johnson's prediction that Mondale would still pick up enough delegates was based on delegates Johnson believed Mondale would win in the forthcoming contests (even though most of them would be difficult for Mondale to win, he could still pick up delegates); on delegates to be selected as the caucus states completed their processes; on uncommitted delegates already chosen; and on "unpledged" delegates—Party leaders who are automatically delegates, and delegates chosen by state committees or state conventions, and members of Congress already selected as delegates who have not yet publicly announced their preference. There are 568 "unpledged" delegates in all. (The delegate-selection process will not be completed until June 23rd.) The Mondale campaign had privately said that it had had a large number of "unpledged" delegates—at least a couple of hundred of them—ready to be announced for some time, but had held off, because it did not want to be seen as trying to win the nomination through a mechanical delegate count, and with Party officials, as opposed to winning primaries and caucuses. Now the Mondale campaign has decided that the time has come to win the delegate fight, and it began announcing some of its other delegates shortly after Ohio. Both campaigns are now engaged in the unglamorous but crucial business of delegate persuasion, with an eye to what those totals will be after the voting on June 5th. The reasons behind the Mondale campaign's announcement that Mondale would have nearly enough delegates before June 5th and enough after June 5th were twofold, and perhaps at odds. The Mondale people wanted to show confidence after Ohio, and indicate that they were close to having the nomination, so as to discourage mischief at a moment when people might be hesitating, and when many states were making their final delegate decisions; they also wanted voters on June 5th to feel that they have an opportunity to put Mondale over the top. (The danger, of course, is that voters in these states will react against the Mondale campaign's having said that it will win no matter what they do, and it is perhaps for this reason that Mondale has now backed off saying that he will have enough delegates as of June 5th.) Mondale may well be facing a situation his campaign had feared: that though he wins delegates, he loses a string of contests, thus raising questions about his popular appeal.

Hart, who cannot win enough delegates for the nomination in the remaining contests, is, of course, hoping for a string of victories, to further raise the electability issue. There would be eight contests in the period between the May 8th primaries and June 5th, many or most of them in states favorable to Hart. Now the preponderance of the contests would be in the West—as Hart had said, somewhat inaccurately, would be the case after Pennsylvania. These last states were not supposed to be important, according to the Mondale campaign's Plan A (Mondale sews up the nomination early) or its Plan B (the contest is effectively over as of May 8th). Henkel says, "If we are able to sweep, or nearly sweep, the remaining primaries, that, combined with Ohio and Indiana, makes a very persuasive case for uncommitted and unpledged delegates to vote for Hart. That's our 'backloaded' strategy." Henkel adds, "The Mondale campaign seems to have gone to the technical argument rather than the political argument, but we're in a political process. If Gary wins most of the remaining contests, he'll have the momentum and be in a position of real strength at the Convention. That's political, and it doesn't intimidate us if we're behind in the delegate count." Henkel says, "There's a whole lot to happen between now and the Convention, and that's where the fun lies." Both camps will be concentrating on New Jersey and California, which have primaries on June 5th and will produce a large number of delegates—especially California, where both campaigns say the candidates will spend the most time, while campaign officials work hard on New Jersey. Johnson does not accept the prevailing idea that Mondale is bound to lose badly to Hart in California, or agree that he will necessarily lose at all. (New Jersey is no safe bet for Mondale.) A few days after the Ohio primary, Johnson said to me, "I think our chances of winning California increased on Wednesday morning—because once again it's viewed as a contest, as opposed to asking California to ratify what everyone has done."

The Mondale campaign's explanation for what had gone wrong in Ohio was that Hart had spent time and money in the state, and that Mondale had failed to take on Hart sufficiently there. In the period leading up to the May 8th contests, Mondale had not actually let up on Hart, but neither had he waged the relentless attack on him that he had after the losses in New England. Mondale did continue to suggest, in a variety of ways, that Hart had not fought for things as hard as he had, that Hart has been inconsistent, that he is naive and not surefooted—not the person the nation would want to have pick up that emergency red phone. He continued to criticize Hart for having opposed the Chrysler bailout and the federal loan guarantees to the Wheeling-Pittsburgh Steel Corporation, which has plants in Ohio. But during the period that began after the Pennsylvania primary Mondale also gave a series of "issues" speeches—on the future, on education, on arms control, on observance of the law, and on high technology—which were designed to do two things at once: to reach out to the Hart constituency, and to begin the argument over whether the future would be better under Mondale or Reagan. That Mondale was more willing to give such speeches during this period was an indication that he no longer felt that he was fighting for his political life, and that now that his candidacy had been revived he had the standing and the credibility to have such speeches listened to. The Mondale campaign concluded after Ohio that Mondale would have to go at Hart harder.

Thus, in his first campaign stop after Ohio—in Omaha,

Nebraska—Mondale piled on Hart as never before. He combined most of the charges he had made earlier in the campaign—about Hart's statements on Castro and on the Persian Gulf, about Hart's having said, in New York, that the United States had become "corrupt like Europe" and that Richard Nixon was our "first European President," about Hart's "flip-flops" on arms control (his having belatedly supported the freeze and then a "build-down")—and also took on Hart's statement about the hostage crisis. Mondale said that while Hart had recently been critical of the Carter Administration's handling of the crisis, Hart's own record during the period showed that he initially supported the Administration's handling of the problem, then "did an about-face" and suggested that the United States mine Iran's harbors and bomb Teheran's generating plant, and then, after the hostages returned home, co-sponsored a resolution commending Carter's handling of the crisis. Mondale often asks what would have happened if a President had said some of the things that Hart has said. This is the strategy of "raising the stakes" which Mondale has been following, with varying degrees of intensity, since March, and which his campaign believes saved him in the South on March 13th, and in Illinois, New York, and Pennsylvania. Whether or not it did is not the point, nor is whether anything else would have been effective. The disappointed and edgy Mondale people instinctively reached for what they believed was a tested strategy and what they knew how to do.

Hart, for his part, gave a series of interviews in the wake of his Ohio and Indiana victories in which he spilled out his anger and resentment at Mondale for the attacks on his record, and said that Mondale was risking his own integrity and might end up destroying himself "in almost a Biblical or Greek way." (This may also be a tactical move to try to make Mondale's attacks more costly to Mondale.) In some instances, Hart had a point: while he may have wavered recently on arms-control questions, he was one of the leaders in the fight for the SALT II treaty; Mondale has attacked Hart for not being strong enough on women's issues, but Hart has a perfectly good record on those issues. Mondale sometimes makes a small point into a big point, but that is not unusual in campaigning. The main thing Mondale is doing that clearly annoys Hart is using a number of votes, issues, statements to attempt to question some fundamental things about Hart's record and character. But Hart, though his style is cooler, has been trying to raise some fundamental questions about Mondale as well. Even when Hart is being "positive," and says that this is a contest "between the future and the past," he is dismissing Mondale as simply the past, and, despite his occasional denials, he seems to be dismissing the Party's traditions.

The magnitude of the miscalculation that the Mondale campaign made in its handling of the delegate committees is difficult to gauge at this point, but there is no question that it was damaging. While the campaign-finance law allows committees to be formed to raise and spend money on behalf of individuals running as delegates to the Convention, the intent of the law was to allow delegate committees to make certain "grass roots" expenditures on the delegates' behalf but not to supplement the Presidential candidate's campaign. This is not the only example where provisions put in the law in the name of encouraging "grass roots" activity produce weeds. The law is murky, and the regulations put out by the Federal Election Commission do not make it clear what kind of coordination between the delegate committees and the candidate's campaign may take place. The only thing that is expressly forbidden is the use of delegate-committee funds for promoting the candidate through any mass media, such as advertising or direct mail. But the law does say that if the delegate committees are "established or financed or maintained or controlled" by the same person or group of persons, they are to be considered affiliated. The question then becomes whether the facts of each instance that came to light suggested that this legal line had been breached, or whether the pattern of activity could lead to that conclusion. For example, delegate committees can take money from individuals and groups who have given the maximum allowed by law to the candidate's campaign (one thousand and five thousand dollars, respectively). If, as emerged in the case of the Mondale delegate committees, a major Mondale fund raiser made contributions to a number of delegate committees, it would matter, according to election-law lawyers, at whose suggestion he did this. It emerged that delegate committees had hired laid-off campaign workers, had hired campaign workers who moved from state to state, and that they had forwarded surplus funds to delegate committees in other states. If all of this was coordinated by the Mondale campaign, the law may have been violated. Even where the law isn't, strictly speaking, broken, it can be stretched to the point where it becomes meaningless. Sometimes the delegate committees went beyond "grass roots" efforts on their own behalf, and distributed Mondale campaign literature. All such activities would, of course, free Mondale campaign funds for media expenditures. The delegate committees can become a vehicle for getting around the limits on how much an individual or group may contribute and how much may be spent in a given state. (In New Hampshire, delegate committees spent over a hundred thousand dollars, while the Mondale campaign itself spent nearly the full four hundred thousand dollars permitted under the law.) If this was intentionally coordinated by the Mondale campaign, it was a violation of the law.

There was a second issue about these committees which Hart raised: the fact that Mondale delegate committees were accepting political-action-committee (PAC) contributions. The announcements by Hart and Mondale last year that they would not accept political-action-committee funds for their campaigns (Hart beat Mondale to the announcement by only hours) represented a bit of piety on both their parts. Yet both men do believe in reform of the campaign-finance laws, and at some points in their campaigns have argued for it. Political-action committees traditionally don't get much involved in nomination contests, not wishing to choose sides, and Hart was not likely to receive much political-action-committee money in any event. Mondale, on the other hand, was hoping for the endorsements of several interest groups, which would spend money on his behalf separately from his campaign. (The Mondale people hoped that the renunciation of PAC money would remove some of the possible criticism of Mondale's interest-group backing.) The Mondale people in effect accepted PAC money through the back door: they encouraged the establishment of delegate committees and at least winked at the committees' acceptance of PAC money. And it was found that political-action committees, mainly of labor, gave totals of tens of thousands of dollars to delegate committees. If these contributions were coordinated by the campaign, legal experts say, the election-finance laws may have been violated. When Hart first raised the issue, during the New York primary, Mondale, after some hesitation, asked the delegate committees to stop accepting PAC money. Some newspapers had begun to investigate the delegate committees, however, and Hart, who had filed a complaint with the Federal Election Commission on April 6th, kept at it. Mondale became increasingly disturbed by this, and by the fact that the subject was coming to dominate his press conferences—especially one he held on April 24th, after he had given a strong speech, in Cleveland, criticizing Reagan for proceeding with the development of anti-satellite weapons and of the missile-defense system in outer space ("Star Wars"), and calling for a moratorium on deploying weapons in space, and negotiations to prevent them. (The Administration has said that it would not negotiate on anti-satellite weapons, and recent testimony on Capitol Hill about the "Star Wars" plan raised questions about both its feasibility and the danger it posed of a new escalation of the arms race.)

On Wednesday, April 25th, in Chattanooga, Mondale announced that he had asked that the delegate committees be disbanded, saying that the controversy over them was "undermining my capacity to carry on a campaign on matters that count." On the same day, after Mondale made his announcement, Hart gave a speech in Nashville criticizing the growing influence of political-action committees on the political process and criticizing Mondale for his handling of the delegate-committee matter. And, in a line that was a bit strange but effective, Hart said, "Give the money back, Walter." (It was strange because Hart refers to Mondale by his nickname, Fritz, and Hart looked awkward as he delivered the line.) By this time, Johnson and other members of the Mondale high command were reviewing in detail exactly what had gone on with the delegate committees, and press stories about them continued that day and the next. On Thursday, Johnson convened a meeting at Mondale's law offices—a meeting that lasted many hours. While the Mondale campaign lawyers had assured campaign officials that the activities of the delegate committees were legal, it was clear by now that the campaign had gone into some areas that were at least gray. And press stories were likely to continue. Mondale was by this time, according to several accounts, quite upset over the matter. He had earned a reputation for integrity, and this had always been very important to him, and he was quite disturbed that now it might be questioned. Moreover, he wanted to make a case in the fall against ethically questionable actions of members of the Reagan Administration.

So the Mondale campaign decided to try to put an end to the

matter, and head off further press interest in it, by taking further steps. On Friday, Mondale announced that he would treat the committees as if they had been part of his campaign, and count their expenditures against his own spending ceiling, and that he would return money that would not have been accepted by his campaign (PAC money, and contributions from individuals that exceeded the maximum allowed under the law). The Mondale people were aware that this action would cause them to have exceeded the spending limit in New Hampshire—for which they would be penalized by the F.E.C. Absorbing the delegate-committee spending put more pressure on the Mondale campaign, and returning money would be a headache in a couple of respects: the records kept by such committees are less than orderly (no one is even sure how many committees there were), and the Mondale campaign doesn't have the money. (It could borrow the funds.) The Mondale people are currently involved in negotiations with the F.E.C. over when the money has to be returned and how it is to be returned (without F.E.C. approval, the campaign can't write a check for, say, forty thousand dollars to a union PAC), and they hope that the F.E.C. will find that the campaign's having absorbed the committees and agreed to return the money will moot the question of the legality of their activities. The total amount involved is reported to be about five hundred thousand dollars— perhaps more. Certainly, whatever the amount, it wasn't worth it. Not only did it risk blemishing Mondale's reputation for integrity but it compounded the problem of his appearing to have too many entanglements with the "special interests." His aides believed that they should take the maximum advantage of the law. The Mondale people knew that the committees' accepting PAC money would come to light, because the committees would have to file reports with the F.E.C. However, the reports would not be filed until April 15th, and the Mondale people figured that by then the nomination would be sewed up and, anyway, people probably wouldn't care very much. The use of delegate committees was not new, nor was the use of them to receive contributions that could not be made to the campaign, nor was the tactic of stretching the campaign-finance laws. But delegate committees had never been used to such an extent. The Mondale people miscalculated, and did not anticipate having an opponent who would make the matter an issue, and only gradually came to see the political impact.

The Reagan people were no slouches at finding ways to get

extra money into the 1980 Presidential campaign, and Reagan's nomination campaign has been found by the F.E.C. to have violated the campaign-finance laws in two instances. It, too, went over the ceiling in New Hampshire, for which it was penalized; and it was fined for having Reagan's own political-action committee, Citizens for the Republic, pick up some of the Reagan campaign's expenses. Citizens for the Republic still exists, with Reagan's name on the letterhead as chairman emeritus. Reagan's PAC can take money from individuals who have contributed the maximum to his campaign and from other political-action committees. Having a PAC with a sitting President's name on its letterhead is unusual. The Supreme Court's recent refusal to expedite the hearing of a case involving the legality of unlimited spending by "independent" committees on behalf of a candidate means that the issue will probably not be settled before the election, and the Presidential campaign will again be awash in money beyond what the candidates are allowed to spend. (In 1980, independent committees spent twelve million dollars for Reagan's election, and they are reported to be gearing up to spend more than twenty million dollars this year. Both parties are planning to raise "soft" money—money that cannot legally be spent in federal elections but can go into what are ostensibly state activities.) Nevertheless, if Mondale is the nominee Reagan is very likely to summon up the Mondale delegate committees' acceptance of PAC funds as he paints Mondale as a creature of the "special interests." Hart, meanwhile, has kept the issue going by charging that well over five hundred delegates elected by such committees are "tainted," and warning that they will be challenged at the Convention.

The Mondale camp made a brief run at trying to resolve some of the issues among Mondale, Hart, and Jackson before the Convention—on the theory that the sooner the peace talks began, the better. Mondale aides have actually been in contact with Jackson all along, and it was Jackson who had been raising issues that he said would have to be settled at the Convention—issues concerning the Party's nominating rules, and runoff primaries in Southern states. Following the Pennsylvania primary, the Mondale people began discussions among themselves and with Party leaders to try to find a mechanism for resolving the issues. The idea emerged of having Robert Strauss, the former Party chairman and

Special Trade Representative during the Carter Administration, try to work things out. Strauss is a skilled negotiator and has worked with Jackson in the past; as a Texan and former Party chairman, he has strong ties to key Southerners; as a Jew, he might be able to mollify Jewish leaders who are upset by the tensions between blacks and Jews which have occurred as a result of the Jackson campaign. The prospect of Strauss's role surfaced when Strauss met with Mondale and Jackson on the night of the Dallas debate—Jackson having signalled a willingness to try to work things out. But within a few days Jackson, under pressure from people who argued that such negotiations were premature and would reduce his leverage with the Party, began to back off. The Hart campaign, sensing that the peace initiative was a move to shut down the campaign early, or stack the results in Mondale's favor—Strauss had, after all, endorsed Mondale—balked. So the whole effort got caught in a political whirlpool even before the May 8th contests.

When Hart was resisting the effort, it seemed to many that he was simply being graceless—refusing to bow to the inevitable. Yet not only did Hart have different thoughts about what was inevitable but also, even if he were to lose the next contests and, in effect, the nomination fight, the losing candidate is often reluctant, in apparent defiance of common sense and Party unity, to give up the fight. Among other things, it is physically and psychologically easier to keep going: the adrenaline is still flowing, and the cessation of activity becomes something to be dreaded. Moreover, one is convinced that one is engaged in leading an important cause—one has to be convinced of that to keep up the effort—and that the cause must not be let down, so the fight must be taken to the Convention. And one is egged on by aides and supporters who don't want to let go, either. Two other factors that come into play are anger and hope (which sometimes takes the form of fantasy). Despite all the smiling tableaux at the end of conventions, and the talk of politics' being a sport, in which it's understood that there will be combat, political campaigns often produce anger in the chief protagonists and, perhaps more important, in their entourages. The attacks do get under the candidates' skin, seem unfair—and the candidates' aides and advisers are often enraged. A fair amount of that has developed in this campaign. The hope is that something might still happen: the apparent nominee might still get tripped up; the delegates might change their minds. The more one is convinced of the rightness of one's cause, the more likely one is to entertain these ideas. By carrying the fight, or some fight, to the Convention—if not for the nomination, then for a platform plank, a change in the rules, or, better yet, by making a dramatic speech there—one keeps the constituency energized, and primed for the next fight (Reagan at the 1976 Convention; Kennedy at the 1980 Convention). There is every reason to assume that Hart, if he does not win the nomination this year, will conduct himself with an eye to 1988. Moreover, Hart, at least at this point, appears to feel more bitterness toward Mondale than candidates usually have felt toward opponents. One of Hart's closest associates says that Hart, given his independent, loner streak, is temperamentally unsuited to running for, or serving in, the secondary position of Vice-President. The Mondale people have no great affection for Hart anyway; the staff seems angrier at Hart than Mondale does.

Jackson is in, if anything, a more complicated situation than Hart is. While there has never been any chance of his getting the nomination, he has been more successful than almost everyone, including those who supported his entering the race, expected. Jackson won the primary in the District of Columbia, on May 1st, where seventy per cent of the population is black. He also won the primary in Louisiana, on May 5th; the state Party had wanted to hold caucuses, and after the courts upheld a Jackson complaint that a switch from a primary to caucuses would result in a dilution of black voting strength the governor, Edwin Edwards, urged people to boycott the primary. This had the effect of inspiring even more black participation. Jackson is, in fact, in the front of a movement. This somewhat constricts his freedom of action, and explains his recent switching of signals on whether he was ready to enter into pre-Convention negotiations. Jackson is said by his friends to understand that he cannot act in a way that divides the Party to the point where he could be held responsible for the reelection of Reagan. Yet the whole notion of a black candidacy, as it was discussed by a group of black leaders some time ago, was that it would push the Party into taking a more affirmative position on some issues of importance to blacks. Therefore, Jackson has to be seen to have exacted something from the Party or its nominee—and he is subject to conflicting advice on what that needs to be, and under what circumstances.

Jackson has complained that the Party nomination rules are unfair, since the number of delegates he has received is not commensurate with his popular vote. The new Party rules were designed deliberately not to produce proportional representation but to give an advantage to the stronger candidates, in the interests of producing a consensus, and to discourage splinter candidates. Jackson has particularly objected to the rule requiring that a candidate reach a "threshold" of a certain percentage of the votes in a district or a state (usually twenty per cent) before he can receive any delegates. Earlier this year, the Mondale camp was willing to modify that rule, but Democratic National Committee Chairman Charles Manatt failed to get the committee to agree to the change. (The Mondale campaign was not pleased.) The issue of the runoff primary—a requirement by ten Southern states that if a candidate does not win a majority of the votes a runoff must be held—divides black leaders, some of whom came to office under such a system. They, along with some whites, argue that the system is a moderating force, since it prevents a fringe candidate in a multi-candidate field from winning by gaining a plurality and it encourages runoff candidates to seek a wide base of support. Most Southern white leaders oppose a change, for whatever reason, and some of Jackson's advisers were reluctant to have him out on a limb on this issue. (In any event, the question is a matter of state law, and there is little the national Party can do about it, beyond being hortatory.) So Jackson, who had for a time said that he could not support any candidate who did not favor abolishing the runoff primary, then modified his position, leaving open the possibility of compromise, and then seemed to toughen it again.

Jackson's backers expect him to have some demonstrable effect on the platform. Carl Holman, the president of the Urban Coalition, who has supported the idea of Jackson's candidacy, told me over lunch recently, "Jesse has to be able to go out and say, 'Here's what we're running on'—and it can't be a dishwater platform. That's what his running means to people. They have to see the Party move on things it might not have moved on, and the nominee has to go out and talk about it. So this has to be worked out." Holman and other blacks, including some, such as Vernon Jordan, the former president of the Urban League, who did not favor Jackson's running, say that Jackson has brought more blacks into the political process than anybody expected—that although black participation had been increasing, Jackson's candidacy has made a substantial difference. And Holman maintains that now these blacks will stay in the process. The Mondale people, knowing that Jackson would draw votes from Mondale, had tried to persuade Jackson to head a registration drive rather than run. (If Jackson were not in the race, Mondale in all probability would have the nomination by now.) Holman said that that idea was "ridiculous," because "the power to stir people to register and vote comes not from a functionary but from a candidate being out there." He added, "Young people are saying, 'Jesse Jackson is running; I'll back him, not because I think he'll be President but because I or some other black could someday.' " Holman also said that Jackson's candidacy has encouraged blacks to run for other offices. "For some of us, the most important thing was, Who is going to take the issues to the group that has been the most loyal to the Party? It seemed that blacks were not going to be carried by the liberals who were running," he said, and he added, "Some of the quarrel Jesse has with labor all blacks have with labor, and without Jesse in the race liberals would use an eyedropper approach." He was referring to, in particular, Jackson's argument that labor should open up its apprentice programs to more blacks. Holman said, "What we're saying is 'Let's arrive at a set of basic things on which blacks would perhaps like to go further than the rest of the Party but which the Party could embrace.' " He said that a number of blacks feared that once Mondale had received the required number of delegates "the status-quo-ante people will be back in the saddle, and they will say, 'Concede as little as possible to Jackson.' " He said that he hoped the Mondale people realized what Jackson could deliver and that they would deal with "people who can read their own people." By this he meant Jackson, as distinguished from blacks who failed to back Jackson.

I asked Holman about the more troubling aspects of the Jackson candidacy—his failure, or inability, to attract whites, and the exacerbated tensions with Jews. Jackson's prediction that he would attract a "rainbow coalition"—of blacks, Hispanics, women, American Indians, peace advocates, and others—has not come to pass. Yet other black politicians—elected officials—have succeeded in winning white votes. Jackson has essentially run his campaign as a black campaign, and his style strikes many whites as confrontational. His rhetoric is hot—especially as it comes across on television—and he often appears to be appealing to blacks to gain power at the expense of whites. Whatever the merits of this approach, it is not likely to make many whites comfortable.

Holman is a wise and gentle man who has practiced coalition politics throughout his career. When I asked him about Jackson's failure to achieve coalition politics, he replied, "We wrestled with the question of a black candidacy for months, and nobody else got out there. It takes an audacity to do it; and it's life-threatening. The terrible dilemma that black political leaders face in this period is: When you move from city to statewide and national elections, how do you reach out to enough whites to get elected when they're not going to elect a black they consider too abrasive, too aggressive, and you have to be aggressive enough to take blacks along. I'm pretty certain that on the state and national level you're going to have to get someone who will hold the home base and reach out to others. The problem is that the first time out we have the national problem that blacks haven't been registering and voting, and to get them back into politics you have to have someone who is a lightning rod. Now that Jesse has done it, and broken the sound barrier, what he's done begins to be something that is thinkable. The trailblazers are not always the ones who can capitalize on the trailblazing." As for the increased tensions between blacks and Jews—brought about by Jackson's having referred to Jews as "Hymies" and his refusal to dissociate himself from Louis Farrakhan, the leader of a Black Muslim group, who has said, among other things, that Hitler was "a very great man," though "wickedly great"—Holman does not deny that Jackson's candidacy has exacerbated a problem, and says that Jackson could have handled the situation better. He says, "What worries me now is that it has become a topic of very angry discussion among black people." Many blacks, he says, feel that the criticism of Jackson in this area has been disproportionate. "It is more difficult now to get certain blacks to agree, Let's take this away from Jesse, and sit down and resume some contacts. They say that that is likely to be interpreted as reaching out to Jesse's enemies and those who are trying to destroy him." Holman added, "What I'm worried about is that we still have that day-in-and-day-out cooperative action going on between blacks and Jews, but there's a problem with the notion, which has been considered, of having some kind of joint statement come out. The question was: What could you say that would not reawaken the whole thing? Was it not better to try to renormalize the relationship and deal with some of the myths? What some of us have decided is that we'll keep our lines open and keep trying." As for Jackson's handling of the Farrakhan issue, Holman says that ministers—Jackson is a minister—"make a big thing of saving people," and that Jackson and Farrakhan have been helping each other, and that while Jackson and Farrakhan have agreed to play down the relationship (a scheduled appearance by Farrakhan at a recent Washington rally for Jackson was cancelled), Jackson still refuses to renounce Farrakhan. Holman said, "Jesse keeps pointing out, 'What I'm doing I've done all the time—ask what is the redemptive way. It's the way I deal with companies—I leave them a way out.' " Holman said, "Jesse has taken a position that comes out of a religious past. It isn't good politics, it isn't good logic, but it's where Jesse stands on that."

The Tuesday of the Ohio and Indiana contests was an unusual one in Washington, and was symptomatic of both the information vacuum and the overload of events in the recent period. People who had access to what the networks' exit polls were showing knew by early afternoon that Hart had pulled even with Mondale in Ohio and was slightly ahead in Indiana. That moment symbolized the mystery of elections—the time when the voters take the decision into their own hands, leaving the experts suspended, unable to offer an analysis until they know which outcome they should be analyzing—but it was clear that afternoon that what the voters did could produce two very different kinds of stories, and interpretations.

As for the overload, among the other events of that day, the Soviet Union announced that it would not participate in the Olympics, to be held this summer in Los Angeles. (This had been prefigured when Jimmy Carter had the United States boycott the 1980 Olympics in reaction to the Soviet invasion of Afghanistan, and was made still more likely by the current state of relations between the United States and the Soviet Union.) In fact, relations with the Soviet Union are at the lowest state since the end of the Cold War, as a result of the Reagan Administration's highly ideological approach to the Soviet Union, and the Soviet Union's unwillingness to give Reagan anything that might help him politically. Nuclear-arms-control negotiations are nonexistent, those Administration officials who don't really want to negotiate with the Soviets having prevailed. Also on that Tuesday, there were reports of an assassination plot against the Libyan leader Colonel Muammar Quaddafi (it failed); a man sprayed the Quebec National Assembly with submachine-gun fire; a terrible thunderstorm ripped through Washington, blackening the late afternoon. A pleasanter aspect of the day was the commemoration, in events in Congress and at the White House, of the hundredth anniversary of the birth of Harry S Truman, whose leadership qualities and unaffected style have gained him a degree of admiration he never had during his Presidency. (Later in the week, Richard Nixon, who is enjoying his own form of rehabilitation, spoke before, of all things, the American Society of Newspaper Editors, which responded to him warmly. Memories fade, and, besides, Nixon displayed a grasp of foreign policy that is not matched by the current President, and a certain humor. That Nixon remains bitter, and still doesn't understand why he had to leave office, is clear from interviews he gives, but Nixon is never not interesting.) And, in what may have been another political event of great significance on Tuesday, the prime interest rate rose, from twelve to twelve and a half per cent. This was the third rise since mid-March, when the prime rate was eleven per cent. The rise in interest rates makes the President's advisers nervous, and the Administration immediately blamed the Federal Reserve Board. The Fed and the Administration have had a tentative relationship at best all along: in 1981, in order to keep the Administration's loose fiscal policies (the large tax cut and the increase in defense spending) from leading to inflation, the Fed tightened credit and thus contributed to the recession; from mid-1982 through the spring of 1983, it loosened credit and helped spur the recovery; now, in the face of the extraordinary deficits, it is tightening credit again. Long-term interest rates, which are not under the control of the Fed but are determined by people's expectations about inflation, deficits, and other economic factors, have gone up even more sharply than the short-term rates directly influenced by the Fed. The rise in the prime rate treated us to another round in the battle between Donald Regan, the Treasury Secretary, and Martin Feldstein, the chairman of the Council of Economic Advisers. Regan criticized the Fed for the rise in interest rates and said that its policy could have a worrisome effect on the economy by the time of the election. (A number of economists think that

Regan's criticizing the Fed set off fears of an inflationary policy and caused long-term rates to go up again.) Feldstein said, "The Fed is pursuing the right kind of policies." Feldstein added that the deficit should be cut by twice as much as the Administration was asking. And on Wednesday he resigned, effective this summer; he said that he had always planned to return to Harvard in the fall. The President made no effort to encourage Feldstein to stay.

On Wednesday night, the President went on television to ask that Congress approve his request for more military aid to El Salvador. The House was to vote on the matter the next day. The President's political advisers saw that there was some risk in having the President, by making a television address, become even more identified with another policy that could go bad, but they concluded that it was, as one put it, "worth the candle," because the President's speech came far enough away from the election, and because if things did go bad in Central America the President would be in a better position to blame Congress. The President's speech portrayed the Central American problem as simply an East-West struggle, and dramatically cited the dangers the President saw if his request wasn't approved. Reagan also termed critics of his policy "new isolationists," who "would yield to the temptation to do nothing" in the face of Cuban-Soviet aggression. Though his recounting of events overlooked some facts, and gave his own version of some others, he seemed utterly convinced of what he was saying, and his case was, on the face of it, convincing. There are many people, and not just Democrats, who have a different, and more complex, view of what is happening in Central America, but the President does not seem to recognize complexity. (From what is known of his work habits, it is hard to imagine him calling in a number of experts and questioning them about the complexities of the matter.) This makes it easier for him to make his case—in this area as in others. The Democrats are in the opposite situation. Because they see the problem, and the solutions, as more complex, they have a harder time explaining themselves. Senator Joseph Biden, Democrat of Delaware, who is a member of the Senate Foreign Relations Committee and of the Intelligence Committee, said, "We have to say 'Give aid, but—' That's harder to explain." Biden says that another problem facing the Democrats is that "this Administration has, as a consequence of making many, and wrong, judgments along the way, narrowed the range of options that are available—to everyone. To them, to us." He was referring to the militarization of the region, the lack of pressure on the El Salvador government for reform, the assumption that the only way to influence the Sandinista regime in Nicaragua is through military action. (The Administration has not only expanded the United States' military presence in El Salvador, and funded and directed the contras fighting the Nicaraguan government, but has stationed three thousand troops in Honduras and has drawn Honduras and Costa Rica—the contras operate from both countries—closer to the conflict.) An action-reaction cycle is under way, and no one knows where it will lead.

In addition, Congress remains reluctant to challenge the President on foreign policy—especially in an election year. Moreover, the election, on May 6th, of José Napoleón Duarte, a reformer who seeks political accommodation, as President of El Salvador made Congress more willing to approve the aid. The only issue was on what terms. The day after the speech, the House narrowly agreed to authorize the funds, essentially without conditions about dealing with the death squads and seeking political accommodation. Most Democrats had argued that the aid should be tied to economic and social reforms. (On the same day, the World Court held, in a preliminary ruling, that the United States should halt any attempts to mine or blockade Nicaraguan ports. The State Department said there was nothing in the decision that it could not accept; officials had said that the mining stopped in late March.) But the argument over the terms of aid, while not unimportant, was not about what really concerns people—of both parties—here. The real question about El Salvador is whether the situation is salvageable, and how, and at what cost. The real fear is that the military situation in Central America has not only grown but become open-ended. No one is certain that the negotiating path will work either within El Salvador or with Nicaragua through the Contadora nations—Mexico, Panama, Venezuela, and Colombia—but very few people, including people within the government, believe that the military approach will be ultimately successful. Another question is whether our political system and our temperament allow for the patience that a problem like Central America requires.

Today, the House narrowly voted to continue production of the

MX missile. In a compromise arrived at with the White House by Representative Les Aspin, Democrat of Wisconsin, fewer additional missiles would be built than the President sought, and the money would not be spent if the Soviet Union returned to the strategic-arms talks. The rationale for proceeding with the missile was stood on its head: last year, the argument was that giving the President the MX would make him more forthcoming on arms control; now that there are no talks, the argument was that proceeding with the MX would give the Soviets an incentive to negotiate. In the debate, Representative Les AuCoin, Democrat of Oregon, said, "If we can't kill the MX missile when there are negotiations, and we can't kill the MX missile when there are no negotiations, when can we kill a missile that everyone agrees makes no intrinsic military sense?"

In his Central America speech, the President made only a brief reference to his recent trip to China, which produced lovely pictures of him at banquets, at the Great Wall, looking at excavations. On his trip, Reagan, who was widely given great credit for recognizing the importance of dealing with China (Nixon had started that), pushed things a bit in some of his appearances by criticizing the Soviet Union and talking about religious freedom and democratic values—only to have his comments censored by Chinese television. And his major tangible achievement, an agreement to sell nuclear equipment and technology to China, turns out to have relied for its safeguards against China's exporting the technology on an ambiguous dinner toast delivered by Chinese Premier Zhao Ziyang. Congress is now looking into the matter.

XVI

BELMAR, NEW JERSEY. At nine-thirty on this cold and rainy morning, Gary Hart, wearing a dark-blue parka, is standing under an awning on a dock, denouncing sludge. He has just returned from a boat trip, which he took to inspect—or, more to the point, to have the cameras record him as inspecting—the largest ocean dump site off the coast of New Jersey. But the driving rain and choppy water caused his expedition to turn back, and now, surrounded by some environmentalists, the mayor of Belmar, and some of his delegates for next Tuesday's primary, Hart says, "I have throughout this campaign called for a new environmental decade," and says that he will not only reverse the Reagan Administration policies but offer new approaches. "Acid rain must end and will end under a Hart Administration in the nineteen-eighties," he says, with apparent conviction. He also says that he will end federal subsidies for nuclear power plants. Walter Mondale has gone further, calling, in Pennsylvania, for the closing down of the Three Mile Island nuclear plant and, in California, for the closing of the Diablo Canyon nuclear plant, which, among other things, sits atop an earthquake fault line. When Mondale called for the closing of the Diablo Canyon plant, he was booed by union members fearful of losing their jobs—which, from his campaign's point of view, was all to the good, since it demonstrated that Mondale and labor are not always in accord. Now Hart pledges to "abolish ocean dumping as soon as it feasibly can be done," and says he supports tighter federal restrictions on ocean dumping. He refers often to "the Hart Administration." He says, "This is a tragedy we're seeing here," referring to a species of fish that has been driven from this commercial-fishing area, and he denounces "the callous, indifferent dumping of toxic materials." Perhaps because of the terrible weather, Hart cuts his remarks short. He was supposed to call for the taxing of polluters—one of

453

his "new ideas," and a controversial one—but, according to an aide, he forgot. Earlier this morning, he was to stop at a diner en route here—a stop that was laid on by his advance people late last night—but when the entourage arrived at the diner no one was there, so it went on.

Once again, and now for the last time this year, the voters have it within their power to send this nomination contest in one direction or the other, and by now we have learned that the outcomes are usually determined by swings of opinion at the end. So no one can be sure what will happen next Tuesday, June 5th, when the final round of primaries is held—here in New Jersey, and in California, West Virginia, New Mexico, and South Dakota, with a total of 486 delegates at stake. New Jersey and California count for the most not simply because they have the largest pools of delegates but also because the end of this struggle is both a numerical and a pyschological contest. Numerically, Mondale is well ahead in the delegate count—as of yesterday morning, he had 1,644, Hart had 964, and Jesse Jackson had 308—and Mondale's campaign has been working feverishly, almost frantically, to reach its stated goal of at least 1,750 delegates by next Monday, thus putting Mondale in a position to obtain the 1,967 necessary for the nomination as a result of Tuesday's contests. But the Mondale people, while confident that they will win the necessary number of delegates next week, both from Tuesday's voting and from getting the support of other delegates who will be selected in the course of the week, or from those who have already been selected, know that they need to win the psychological battle as well as the numerical one. They are confident of winning the nomination, but they know that if Mondale should lose both New Jersey and California next week he would, even with a sufficient number of delegates, be in for a turbulent pre-Convention period and a turbulent Convention. If Mondale should win both states, both the Mondale and the Hart people agree, Hart will not have much of a case. The Hart people say that if Mondale wins New Jersey and Hart wins California Hart will press on. In the eventuality of either Mondale losses in both states or a split decision, the Hart people, as of now, plan to argue that Mondale has lost the majority of the contests since April 10th, when he won Pennsylvania (Hart won the Idaho caucuses last week), and that Hart has won more contests over all, and, if the numbers bear them out, that Hart has won more of the popular votes than Mondale has. The number-of-states argument is somewhat misleading, because Mondale did not contest several states, particularly Western ones with small numbers of delegates, and many of the states Hart won go Republican in November.

A Hart adviser said to me yesterday, "To imagine the Party nominating Mondale under those circumstances is, if not unimaginable, unthinkable." He added, "If we win California and come respectably close in New Jersey, where we started off behind, then everything we set out to achieve will be done, and it's a question of whether we can take the nomination away." The Mondale people are convinced not only that Hart will not succeed in winning the nomination but also that the Convention will not turn to someone else. While the delegates this year are not bound to support the candidate in whose name they were selected, they are not the equivalent of free-floating voters: they have been chosen by the campaigns, especially the Mondale campaign, with care. Their allegiances are not easily transferrable. The Mondale people and others believe that if there were an anti-Mondale revolt within the Party it will have been set off by a collective decision by Party leaders—House Speaker Thomas P. O'Neill, A.F.L.-C.I.O. President Lane Kirkland, and others—that Mondale was not only not electable but that his candidacy would do untold damage to the Party in November. It is also assumed by the Mondale people, and others, that such is the dislike of Hart within the Party, or so great are the doubts about him, that he would not be seen as a suitable alternative, and that trying to nominate someone who has not run would be seen as inviting great disruption. So, this thinking goes, if Mondale does less than very well on Tuesday there may be a period of flurry, and even chaos, but in the end the Party will settle on Mondale. The Hart people, of course, do not accept this logic.

As of now, the polls show Mondale to be ahead in New Jersey, but not beyond reach. Hart has several factors working in his favor in this state: independents can vote in the primary (only Democrats can vote in California); the state prides itself on its new high-tech industries; New Jersey is highly suburban, relatively affluent, and has low unemployment; Hart has more of the Party structure (including the state chairman) in his favor here than he has had in other important states; and New Jersey voted Republican in 1976 and 1980, and voted against the Democratic front-runner, Jimmy Carter, in the last two nomination contests. Jackson, as he has done all along, is likely to take a substantial proportion of the black vote that would have otherwise gone to Mondale. Since Mondale, despite all this, has been "expected" to win New Jersey, his defeat here would be very damaging. Mondale is expected to do well in West Virginia, and recently won the endorsement of its governor, Jay Rockefeller, but has essentially skipped South Dakota and New Mexico.

In California, the polls show Mondale and Hart to be about dead even at the moment, but because of the way that primary was set up—in order to help Alan Cranston, who has long since dropped out of the race—the contest is more complicated than in the other states. The voting will be simply for delegate slates in the state's forty-five congressional districts, and the candidate with a plurality in a given district is likely to win all its delegates, since people aren't expected to split their votes. Victories in some of the districts are more valuable than in others, because they have more delegates; delegates are apportioned according to the Democratic turnout in the last two elections. The general assumption is that Hart is strong in the high-tech area of Silicon Valley, south of San Francisco, and in some parts of San Francisco; that Mondale is strong in areas dominated by Hispanics and by traditional Democrats (eighteen congressional districts have a Hispanic population of twenty per cent or more); that Jackson will carry the four districts whose populations are more than twenty per cent black; and that many districts are up for grabs. There are four congressional districts in the Los Angeles area with a heavily Jewish population, which might be expected to go for Mondale, but the congressmen from three of them endorsed Hart in early March, at the height of his post-New Hampshire crest, and have the makings of the only political machine in the state. However, according to several reports, these congressmen have been disappointed in Hart's performance since their endorsement of him—in particular his failure to attract Jewish support in New York and, more recently, his suggestion that he might accept Jackson as his running mate. Hart, who made the statement during a television interview in Los Angeles, hedged his reply by saying that Jackson would have to change his views on the Middle East "substantially," but such are the tensions between many blacks and Jews as a result of Jackson's campaign that Hart's amendment was of little help. (New Jersey has a substantial Jewish population as well.)

Hart has been generally expected to win California (an expectation that Hart shares), but the Mondale people say that he will not necessarily do so, and that even if he does Mondale will extract a large number of delegates from the state. The most recent poll published by the California pollster Mervin Field indicated that Mondale was leading Hart by two points, and a poll taken by the Mondale campaign over the weekend of May 19th–20th indicated that Mondale was one point behind. These numbers are so close as to be within the statistical margin of error. Moreover, the poll numbers give no indication of how the delegates will be allocated. While California is often considered the land of hot tubs and high tech, the Mondale people say that labor, along with ethnic groups and other minorities, has a strong presence in the state. Mickey Kantor, a Los Angeles lawyer who has been a major figure in the California Democratic Party and is running Mondale's campaign there, says, "If you did a poll in the cocktail lounge of the Beverly Wilshire Hotel, we'd lose, but there are over a million members of the A.F.L.-C.I.O. in the state, and while labor may not be as strong as it is in some other states it is working hard for Mondale." He adds that senior citizens' groups, teachers' organizations, and women's groups are working for Mondale. Hart has a large group of volunteers working for him. Moreover, there is a view, shared by even some Mondale supporters, that California is simply not Mondale's natural habitat. It is a cliché but true that the state is accustomed to media politics rather than organizational politics, and Mondale is still not an accomplished media politician. Hart, who is hip and can be loose, seems more suited to the California style than Mondale, whose public persona is more buttoned up than he is—but the public persona is what the voters see. California tends to go for politicians with flair—Jerry Brown, Ronald Reagan—and "flair" is not a word one associates with Mondale. (Hart has the support of a number of movie stars.) There are exceptions to these generalizations, of course, but it is also a fact that California, like New Jersey, has been contrary in its Democratic primary politics. It voted for insurgency candidates in 1968 and 1972 (Robert Kennedy and George McGovern), and since 1972 it has not voted for the person who became the nominee of the Party. Hart has always assumed that California would be hospitable to his candidacy, and when I interviewed him in New Hampshire in mid-February, before Iowa or New Hampshire voted, he said he was certain that he would meet Mondale in the California primary.

Because of the importance of New Jersey, both candidates have placed their top organizers here (Mondale even has his campaign manager and his political director here), and both have added to the time they originally planned to spend here. Mondale, having extended his latest visit, left yesterday (his campaign didn't want to leave Hart alone in the state too much), and Hart will be flying to California this afternoon. Hart's campaign manager in the state, Paul Bograd (he organized Connecticut and Ohio for Hart), said to me this morning that Hart had been doing nicely here until Friday, when he joked at a fund-raiser in California that "the good news" for his wife, Lee, "is she campaigns in California and I campaign in New Jersey," and went on to say, after Lee Hart said that she had held a koala bear, "I won't tell you what I got to hold—samples from a toxic-waste dump." The joking may seem like a small matter in the great scheme of things, but it offended New Jerseyans, who don't find New Jersey jokes amusing; it raised another question about Hart's judgment; and it dominated the news about Hart's campaign in New Jersey for several days. One of the puzzling aspects of the episode is why Hart did not apologize and get it over with; instead, he said that the remarks had been misrepresented, and that Mondale and the Republican governor of the state, Thomas Kean, were trying to exploit the matter. Of course they were—inevitably. Hart's errors in this campaign—and there have been several damaging ones—seem to stem from both faulty judgment and inexperience. Mondale has, after all, been around the track several times. He was something of a national figure when Carter chose him as Vice-President in 1976, and this is his third national campaign. For Hart, it's the first time out; still, he has been in politics in some form since 1972, and must know some basics—such as what you say about New Jersey in California is likely to be reported in New Jersey.

Hart's ads for New Jersey, shot at the Meadowlands sports complex, stress his identification with New Jersey's progress. He tells a group of citizens in one of the ads: "You have built the bridge between the past and the future. . . . Now this country has to get busy and do the same thing that you've done here in New Jersey." In another, he says, "New Jersey's on the cutting edge of change. . . . It's not like New York. It's not like Pennsylvania. This state really *is* moving forward." (Bograd tells me that it is significant that the ads show the New York skyline in the background, to symbolize the distance, and difference, between New York and New Jersey.) Another ad, reminiscent of one that Hart ran in Ohio, has a woman saying, "We've done it ourselves. We had to overcome Carter/Mondale high interest rates and Carter/Mondale inflation," and a man saying, "Walter Mondale had his chance, and because of his inability and Jimmy Carter's inability to lead this country, we've winded up with Ronald Reagan. It's time for a change." Over the weekend, Hart posed for an ad walking along a California beach, evoking memories of Robert Kennedy. One of Hart's California ads will show the beach scene and Hart talking to a crowd, with the sound of a heartbeat in the background—to demonstrate excitement, momentum. Another ad the Hart campaign is running in California, which it calls its "inoculation" ad, shows the text of Mondale's lavish praise of Hart when he was helping Hart in his 1980 reelection effort.

The Mondale campaign is acting on the conclusions it drew from Mondale's loss to Hart in Ohio: that Mondale must take Hart on directly and consistently, and must try to dominate the agenda with his issues. While Hart has been trying to get the debate onto the question of whether he or Mondale has a better vision for the future, Mondale, in both New Jersey and California, has attacked Hart for missing hearings on, not participating in the drafting of, and not voting on the question of passage of the bill, passed in 1980, to establish a "superfund" to clean up toxic-waste sites. Most of the money for the fund was to come from taxes on companies that produce or import petroleum-based chemicals, thus making the legislation highly controversial among oil and chemical companies, which are heavily represented in Colorado, and which contributed large sums of money to defeat the bill's main supporters in the 1980 elections, when Hart was up for reelection. (Hart's aides have pointed out that the bill passed the Senate overwhelmingly, and Hart's vote was not needed, and that Hart was present in the Senate for critical votes on the subject. The Hart campaign has also said that Mondale was simply being negative.) Mondale's attack followed a claim by Hart that he had been a major initiator of legislation in this area and Mondale had not. The toxic-waste issue is also important in California, and in recent weeks toxic-waste dumps have been a major feature of this campaign. The other issue Mondale has stressed is Hart's support of the nuclear build-down, saying, as he has since the attacks on Hart began after New Hampshire, that Hart has been inconsistent—supporting the freeze late, and supporting the build-down, which had been offered as an alternative to the freeze and which could lead to a qualitative arms race. Why Hart, who has been a strong supporter of arms control, supported the build-down has never been clear. In both of these instances, Mondale's attacks had several concurrent purposes: to raise doubts about Hart on these issues in the minds of important activist groups (which would include both Democrats and independents); to raise a broader question about Hart's consistency and steadiness, his readiness to be President; to throw Hart off stride and on the defensive. That Hart is irritated by the attacks, and displays his irritation, does not displease the Mondale people.

Now, at twelve-forty, Hart is marching arm in arm with leaders of a nuclear-freeze voter-registration drive down two blocks of Raritan Avenue, in Highland Park, New Jersey. (A solar eclipse is taking place, but the sky has been so gray all morning that it's hard to tell the difference.) This mini-march will provide more good material for television. A little earlier, Hart made a brief arms-control talk in the auditorium of St. Paul's School here. Hart has become quite accomplished in his public appearances: he projects his voice well, and speaks with strength, clarity, and apparent conviction. Though tired, he looks good; and in his ads he looks very good—Hart's cheekbones are an excellent television asset. In his talk, Hart endorsed the freeze, and said, "As President of the United States I intend to negotiate that agreement." He was applauded enthusiastically; the assurance with which he stated his case seemed to reduce Mondale's argument about the build-down to a quibble. Then Hart restated a proposal he had offered earlier in the year, calling for a freeze on the production of plutonium. He also said that his arms-control agenda "as senator and as the next President" included a moratorium on the testing of nuclear weapons; the negotiation of a test-ban treaty; a moratorium on the testing of anti-satellite weapons; and negotiation of a treaty banning weapons in space. (He and Mondale are agreed on these things.) Hart also cited his proposal for establishing a crisis-monitoring center with the Soviet Union, "so that neither side accidentally starts World War III." He said that he would seek a reduction of fifty per cent or more in multiple-warhead land-based missiles, and he pledged "a unilateral step by myself as the next President to cancel the MX missile and the B-1 bomber." With each of his pledges, he was applauded strongly. (Hart has repeated his support for the build-down, saying that for every new weapons system that was deployed two weapons systems would have to be removed. This is incorrect: two warheads would have to be removed for every new warhead deployed.) Hart didn't go on with his statement very much, and seemed to cut it short abruptly. Hart has talked, with varying degrees of specificity and vagueness, about what he is for at the same time that he has campaigned against "the old ways." He has not been very clear about which old ways he is rejecting, nor has Mondale done much to challenge Hart—except episodically—on the "new-old" issue. Hart has taken some rough shots at Mondale on other subjects—Lebanon, Iran, Central America, "special interests," and, of course, delegate committees—but has managed to come across as sounding other notes as well. Mondale has talked about things other than Hart's record, but not in a way that has got through. He made some substantive and "theme" speeches in the period leading up to the Ohio primary, but the result of that primary suggested to his advisers that another course was required. The Mondale campaign, not unlike other campaigns (especially those with a crisis on their hands), tends to think tactically, in terms of the immediate payoff, of what will work for next Tuesday. This has paid off many times, but at a price to Mondale.

On the Hart plane, en route to California. This is the third coast-to-coast trip for Hart within the last six days. The flight, on a crowded DC-9, is to take about seven hours, including a refuelling stop in St. Louis. Much of Hart's campaign entourage is on the plane. His campaign organization is more than a little chaotic: a number of people, almost all of them from the McGovern campaign of 1972, joined it after Hart's success in New Hampshire—having until then been sitting on the sidelines, assuming Hart would go nowhere, or frying other fish. The newcomers fight with those who were there before New Hampshire, and sometimes with each other. Hart's law-school friend Oliver Henkel took on the job of manager of the Hart campaign last year when no one else would, giving up his law practice in Cleveland and living in a basement apartment on Capitol Hill, away from his family. Henkel is a decent man but politically inexperienced, and the newcomers' warfare with him has been played out in the press, often in a way humiliating to Henkel. This has been going on for months now, but Hart has neither faced it nor dealt with it. So the Hart campaign is a hydra-headed thing, with many voices, and decisions are arrived at only with difficulty. Another striking thing about the Hart campaign is that there are people associated with it who speak about Hart disparagingly or talk about him in troubled, and troubling, terms. This is the worry, and the dilemma, about Hart. He is a man of some charm and of intelligence, but it is, with a few exceptions, the people who know the most about him who raise the most serious questions about his candidacy; they are the ones who question whether Hart is mature enough, settled enough, and open enough with other people to be President. This is unusual. There are, to be sure, people around Hart who are devoted to him, but the number of detached outriders, and of previous and current doubters, is noticeable.

On the plane, Hart wears a blue boating cap with gold braid and "Captain" printed on it in gold, which he received on the boat trip this morning; during the flight he confers with his advisers, reads a biography of Andrew Jackson, and kids around with the television technicians in the back of the plane. He looks better than he did in mid-campaign: there is more color in his face, and he seems more relaxed. At times, it seems almost as if he were in a state of exhilaration despite the terrible wearingness of this campaign. He has come further than just about anyone—except, according to Hart, himself—expected, and, no matter what happens from here on, he has done very well. For all the drain and strain, there is considerable satisfaction in being the object of so much attention and applause; it undoubtedly beats sitting in subcommittee meetings and going to the Senate floor to vote; there is undoubtedly satisfaction in standing out from one's peers. Others who might have run, or might run in the future, are sitting in subcommittee meetings and going to the Senate floor to vote—and wondering whether Hart has preempted them for some time to come. Hart has become something of a conspicuous cutup in recent weeks: insisting on going dancing at Gilley's, a famous bar outside Houston (his aides dissuaded him from riding a mechanical bull); shooting the rapids in Oregon, à la Robert Kennedy, and having to be dissuaded from attempting the most dangerous waters (he remarked to a reporter, "I love danger"), and, on plane trips, engaging in pillow fights and "sky-surfing"—putting his feet on plastic emergency-information cards and, as the plane takes off, sliding down the aisle. Mark Hogan, a friend of Hart's from Colorado, who has been lieutenant governor of the state and chairman of the state Democratic Party, and who has been travelling with Hart since mid-March to lend a sort of gray-haired presence, says that this behavior is both a release from the discipline and strain of campaigning and a political tactic. Hogan says, "I think it bothered Gary that he was considered cold and aloof, so he was willing to go a bit further to show that he's not cold and aloof—putting on a mustache, and so on. It's hard for the press, if they've been on the plane, to write about him as a stuffed shirt."

Conversations with the Hart entourage on the plane make it clear that, as of now, unless Hart does badly next Tuesday, and even if Mondale has enough delegates for the nomination as of then, they will persevere. Hogan says, "If we win both California and New Jersey, it's really not going to matter how many delegates Mondale claims. At that point, we'll be dealing with a relatively small number of politically savvy people, and Mondale is not going to be able to hold them. All we have to do is legitimately deny Mondale a first-ballot victory, and he begins immediately to lose ground and we begin immediately to gain ground. Mondale knows that; it's the reason he's scrambling as frantically as he is. Mondale now has to win New Jersey, and if it comes out anything close to a tie that's as good as a win for us—it's easier for us to explain than for Mondale." Hogan says that if Hart wins California but not New Jersey "then we go out and make an absolutely brilliant case on what we have done and, more important, what Mondale hasn't been able to do and how Mondale can't win the election." He says, "Our argument is the same either way: the Mondale people have to realize that the nomination toward which he is scraping and struggling is not worth as much to him, because he has not been able to win it with the juggernaut, as advertised. Yet if Gary wins it he's Gary the Giant-Killer. If Gary gets the nomination, the Republicans really have got a problem. I think our bigger problem is the nomination, not the election in the fall."

I ask Hogan what happens if Hart loses both big states on Tuesday.

He replies, "Then we have a very difficult case to make, because we don't have the momentum. We will want to analyze what we lost, how we lost, did we really lose. It's a crazy enough year that I wouldn't rule anything out, but it would be hard to know what our selling points would be in that situation." He adds, "If we get hit between the eyes on June 5th, then it will be a question of what the political reaction is, and we'd think about how to affect the platform and the rules and to have a major impact on the Convention—and start planning for 1988."

John McEvoy, a Washington attorney who had been an adviser to Hart for some time and took on a major role after the Pennsylvania primary, says, "If there is a split on the fifth, it's the same as winning both." When I asked him why, he replied, "Why not? Campaigns go on until there's no hope or no money." (Hart's campaign is in fact somewhere between four and five million dollars in debt, and at the same time that Hart is trying to raise the money to pay it off he will have to begin raising money for his Senate-reelection race in 1986. Mondale has a debt of about two and a half million dollars and, when the costs of going to the Convention—staff members have been asked to pay their own way—and of the activities required to raise money for paying off the debt are taken into account, is nearing the legal spending ceiling. One reason Mondale is in this situation is that his campaign spent so much money last year—about ten million dollars, or nearly half the full amount allowed—on the assumption that this year's struggle would not take long.) In response to a question about whether Hart might run the risk of being seen as a Party-wrecker, McEvoy says, "There's a real problem of the guy who is declared to be ahead—it's the fourth time this year the press will have claimed him the winner—saying the other guy should quit. Walter Mondale will have won fewer states, probably fewer popular votes, and is under the shadow of a Federal Election Commission ruling on the delegate committees. There's another problem, in terms of what this campaign is all about—new leadership, advancing new ideas. At what point do you give that up? The campaign has gone too far and too long to stop." He adds, "To quit on the basis of a less than conclusive outcome is to say that everything we've been building in the last two years should be abandoned." Hart's advisers are now drawing up plans for the period between June 5th and the Convention: plans for Hart to call on members of Congress to seek their support; to call unpledged "superdelegates"—

elected and Party officials who will attend the Convention and who may or may not have made a commitment to a candidate (Mondale has by far the most commitments from this group); to attend state conventions where the final stages of the delegate-selection process will be carried out; to make a lot of telephone calls.

From the way the Hart people describe the struggle that is going on, it becomes clear that two things are taking place at once. One is the contest for who will be the Democratic nominee; the other is a struggle for a new order as opposed to the old order. Labor's angry attacks on Hart (for having criticized Mondale's backing by labor) reinforce this view. As the Hart people see it, it is a contest of who will establish the national agenda, and they say that Hart is not going to give up that role lightly. One of Hart's advisers says, "It's not just a contest between two constituencies; it's about the future agenda. It's not a question of which side wins; it's whether the Party goes with what hasn't worked before." The fact that some key Hart people see things this way suggests the nature of the struggle that lies ahead no matter what happens on the fifth. Also, in fighting to change the rules, as they may well do, Hart and Jackson will be fighting to break the power of those who set those rules—the Party establishment. The fight, then, is over power within the Party from here out. There is also something of a cultural war going on: Mondale and Hart do represent two different political styles and bases; their followings are essentially different. The parallels between the contest in California this year and the one that took place there in 1972 are almost eerie. Then it was McGovern, supported by peace activists and other insurgency forces, against Humphrey, backed by the Party establishment, including labor. Now it is Hart, McGovern's campaign manager, surrounded by a number of McGovernites and backed by a number of insurgents, against Mondale, Humphrey's protege, backed by labor and the Party establishment. (The California contest, which McGovern won, was followed by a challenge at the Convention of the rules for the contest—but that time the Humphrey forces challenged the rules, and the McGovern forces, led by Hart, successfully defended the status quo.)

Hart has continued to attack Mondale on the use of delegate committees, raising the stakes. He has asked that Mondale have the proceedings before the F.E.C. opened, and expedited. (According to lawyers familiar with the federal election-spending laws, it is not within Mondale's power to expedite the proceedings; and while the statute says that the proceedings are to be closed unless the respondent asks that they be opened, no respondent has ever done so, and none is likely to.) He has asked why Mondale has not yet returned the money to political-action committees that contributed to the delegate committees, as Mondale has said he would—perhaps unaware that Mondale cannot legally do this without clearance by the F.E.C. (When I asked one of Hart's advisers whether he was aware that Mondale could not return the money without F.E.C. clearance, he said that he was not—but suggested that this would not deter the campaign from pressing the point.) Mondale has placed four hundred thousand dollars in escrow, to be repaid when the arrangements have been worked out with the F.E.C. Hart has also suggested that the Justice Department might launch an investigation of the matter if Mondale is nominated and thus create a serious problem for the Party in the fall. This is considered highly unlikely, unless the Reagan Administration, which has assiduously avoided an investigation of how campaign documents got from the Carter camp to the Reagan camp in 1980, wants to open a proceeding that would be obviously political and could backfire. Hart has an issue, and he is pushing it for all it's worth; he is going overboard, but at times like this campaigns don't always recognize limits. Recently, Henkel told me that the campaign's count of what it terms "tainted delegates"—delegates elected with the help of delegate-committee funds—is 669. It is counting any delegate elected in a district where there was a delegate committee, no matter how it was formed or managed. Even calling the delegates "tainted" is pressing the point a bit far; it suggests that the Mondale delegates helped by delegate committees would not otherwise have been elected, a conclusion that election-law experts think is way out of proportion to the facts. The Hart campaign has hinted broadly that these delegates may be challenged in the Credentials Committee or at the Convention. Delegate committees have been used before and are not illegal per se, of course—though the Hart campaign has by now spread the impression that they are—and while the Mondale campaign undoubtedly stretched, and perhaps broke, the law, this does not mean that delegates selected thereby were illegally selected. Moreover, the Hart campaign has already missed the deadline for filing complaints against most of these delegates—though it will probably protest the deadline rule as well. On one occasion, Hart suggested that he might not challenge the "tainted" delegates but that "someone" would. One Hart adviser has said to me, knowingly, that Jackson was getting "some very good legal advice" for making a number of challenges on rules and delegate selection. He added, "It seems there are areas of community of interests on procedural questions, where events link the courses of those two candidates"—Hart and Jackson. "As we move to the Convention, a lot of things may happen that haven't occurred to people yet."

Miles Rubin, a wealthy businessman who worked in the McGovern campaign, has been helping Hart raise money and is working on plans for the post-primary period, including plans to try to wrest the nomination from Mondale. Through a combination of disorganization and circumstance, the Hart campaign has done little to try to add to Hart's delegate total by obtaining the support of unpledged or uncommitted delegates. The circumstance is that it doesn't have a very strong case to make as yet, but hopes to have one after June 5th. The Hart campaign has compiled lists of potential endorsers (even if they have endorsed Mondale), and is making calls. Fritz Hollings, who endorsed Hart after he dropped out of the race, is said to be helpful. Senators and congressmen who have endorsed Hart, and Democratic financial contributors, have been asked to make calls. A memo was prepared, to go out over the names of Senator Christopher Dodd, of Connecticut, and Representative Timothy Wirth, of Colorado, both of whom support Hart, to Senate and House members, saying that Hart will want to see them after the fifth, and citing selected poll data from some states indicating that Hart is stronger in them than Mondale. (One of the states is Iowa, which Mondale, of course, won in February.) Governors' past advisers or financial contributors have been asked to call governors. Hart himself has made calls while he has been on the road. The recipients of the calls usually want to know the delegate tally, and Hart usually replies that he is convinced that he will win California and New Jersey and that as a result Mondale will not be able to win the nomination. Hart has picked up only a few delegates through this procedure; political figures, being realists, are looking at the delegate tallies and waiting to see what happens on June 5th. The

Hart people say that there are a number of people committed to Mondale who are now uncomfortable with their commitment and may move after the fifth.

Kathy Bushkin, Hart's press secretary, divides what Hart has been through into four phases: "Everything up to New Hampshire, which was a struggle—a struggle for money, name recognition, endorsements, everything." She continues, "Then there was the tidal-wave period after New Hampshire, when everything came almost too easily—name recognition, attention, new support." And, she agreed, new friends. "Then came a rocky period, as we settled in. I think it was inevitable: you couldn't stay on the wave forever, and Mondale realized that the only way to stop our nomination was to be as negative as he was, and when Gary was unknown the negative had an effect. Now we're in the post-Ohio period, in which we've regained our message, our footing, and our ability to shape the news, and we're back on the offensive." Mrs. Bushkin says that Hart "is a much better candidate today— he looks better, he sounds better." She adds, "The process caused that."

The nominating process is much maligned, and for good reasons: it is too long, too expensive, and rewards some of the wrong qualities. But it does have its plusses: we learn things about the candidates that under much more protected circumstances we might not find out in time; the candidates learn more about the country, and are tested in some useful ways. All three of the candidates now remaining seem to have grown in the course of the year. All the proposals for change have their drawbacks, too, and every adjustment leads to readjustments. The British system, in which the leaders, who are chosen by their parties, emerge from Parliamentary and Cabinet experience, and elections take about three weeks, might be nice, but it is out of the question. Party activists in both parties wouldn't stand for it—and even in Britain there is growing pressure by party activists for more power. The oft-proposed idea of grouping the contests by regions and having four major contests would give even more reward to the candidate who can make a media splash. One big problem is that the system tends to reward those who have the time (years) to prepare the ground for running, yet it is hard to think of a law that would prevent a would-be candidate from traipsing around Iowa a year or more before the caucuses. Former President Gerald Ford has made the interesting proposal that candidates be prohibited from raising money before the election year. There may be technical, and even constitutional, problems with this, but Ford is getting at an important point. The truth is that there is no perfect system, and that the democratic impulses that have spawned our system aren't going to go away. It is also true, for all the deriding of candidates, that the process demands certain real skills—whether they are Ronald Reagan's skills or Walter Mondale's skills or Gary Hart's skills. It is not a sport for amateurs.

Kathy Bushkin says that Hart is genuinely angry at Mondale for two reasons: he thinks that Mondale doesn't really believe the things he is saying about Hart, and he objects to the kinds of issues Mondale has chosen to attack on. She says, "It hasn't been Mondale saying he doesn't like Gary's proposal for individual training accounts. It's Mondale saying Gary doesn't believe in civil rights or arms control; that cuts Gary deep. It created that look on his face in the New York debate"—a look of cold anger. She says, "Those things rile him. He risked a lot in fighting for SALT II—it wasn't popular in Colorado. He has a good record on civil rights. To Gary, what Mondale has done goes pretty far in personal attacks."

To Mondale, such criticisms of Hart are valid, and part of the political rough-and-tumble; to Hart, they are invalid and unacceptable. And by criticizing Mondale's "negativism" the Hart campaign is trying to turn Mondale's attacks back on him, and make the attacking itself an issue.

In the early evening, after the refuelling stop, I have an interview with Hart on the plane. I ask him why he seems more relaxed now than he was earlier in the campaign.

"I think there's a little different rhythm to it now," he replies. "We've gotten some control of the schedule and I've gotten adjusted psychologically to my opponent's style."

I ask him if he is angry at Mondale.

" 'Disappointed' is, I think, the better word," Hart says. "Part of it is, I think, the fact that we know each other. Had we not known each other— Or maybe what has happened here is that I presumed a friendship that never existed. Either I presumed a friendship that never was or he is behaving in a way that is not consistent with a friendship. I make that statement discounting for politics—this is not politics as usual. And I discount for generational politics. I may have just misunderstood who Fritz Mondale was. I've given him every benefit of the doubt. It wasn't until a couple of weeks ago that I concluded he was consciously misstating facts."

I ask Hart why he has always believed he would get the nomination.

He replies, "I don't know—probably for the same reason I thought George McGovern would get the nomination in 1972; the same reason I thought I'd win the Senate campaign. It's intuitive. I thought McGovern would inherit Eugene McCarthy's and Robert Kennedy's constituencies. I travelled across the country in 1981 and 1982 and knew that we couldn't go back—that the Party couldn't proceed with Edward Kennedy and Walter Mondale. I knew there were enough people out there in the Party who were looking for something new, and if no one else in the nineteen-seventies class got into the race I would inherit that. I thought that Mondale would be the established leader, and I would be the new approach. I thought that from 1983."

I ask Hart if he has given any thought to being in the position, or being seen to be in the position, of hurting the Party.

He replies, "I can't hypothesize anything but that the contest will go to the Convention and I'll win on the first ballot. I can't mentally put myself in any other frame of mind. Maybe I could on June 6th, but I expect to be strengthened on June 6th. Clearly, something is going on in the Party. There was a lot of evidence in February-March and in May-June that people don't want Mondale, that this candidacy offers something in terms of electability and governance."

Hart says he doesn't think a protracted fight will necessarily be damaging, "because this is not an ideological fight." He adds, "It's between two types of candidates—the more beholden versus the less beholden. The constituency groups can't be unhappy with me at the top of the ticket. We don't disagree on the merits of most of the issues. I don't have the disagreements with labor that George McGovern did. I'm not concerned about dividing the Party. If anyone has divided the Party, it's Walter Mondale. He started attacking me February 29th"—the day after the New Hampshire primary—"and after Super Tuesday, March 13th, he became Fighting Fritz—good old Fighting Fritz. My candidacy represents

half or nearly half of the Party, or maybe more than half of the
Party. Why aren't *his* attacks dividing the Party? Party people are
supporting me, too."

In reply to a question about how he sees the year thus far, Hart
says, "We've done, if I may say so, extraordinary things in three
months. We've turned the Democratic Party around. I don't think
it will be the same again."

Even if, I ask, Mondale gets the nomination by what Hart sees as
the old ways, and with the backing of the Party establishment?

He replies, "A lot of people are empowered now who weren't
interested—who thought it would be a Mondale-Glenn race. Lots
and lots of people have said they have got involved for the first
time, or for the first time since Bobby Kennedy was killed. I've
won at least half the states. The base has been broadened, geo-
graphically and economically. We've brought in independent people and people who might have joined a third party. The leadership of the Party will change, either in 1988 or in 1984—I think
1984, because that's the only way we can win the election. The
issue of electability—of how to beat Reagan—will dominate the
next six weeks. I think that after June 5th I'm going to run
stronger in the polls than Mondale against Reagan, and the uncommitted delegates are going to have to face that fact."

FRESNO, CALIFORNIA. We arrived here at 6:30 P.M. Pacific Daylight
Time, or 9:30 P.M. Eastern Time—about a half hour late. It's a
hundred and three degrees here—a sharp change from the
weather in New Jersey. This agricultural center, midway between
San Francisco and Los Angeles, is considered a tossup area. Toward the end of the flight, Hart rebelled against his heavy schedule in the next few days, and his attendance at some fund-raisers
has been cancelled. At a rally of about seven hundred people,
Hart, looking remarkably refreshed, gives his stump speech. Flirting a bit with danger, it seems, under the circumstances, he refers
to having been in New Jersey this morning and says, "Coming
from that cold climate to this warm reception, we appreciate it
very much." Then he tells the audience, "The Democratic Party in
1984 must offer this country new leadership and a new vision for
the nineteen-eighties to win this election and to send Ronald Reagan back to his ranch for good." He receives enthusiastic applause.
His voice rings out. He has become a much better speaker since

the early days in New Hampshire. An adviser says that Hart is very tired and not as good as he can be at these events, but he seems to be quite effective. He says, to frequent cheers, "We must not give this President four more years to turn back on civil rights for all minority citizens and on equal rights for the women of this country. We must not let this President have four more years to sell off this nation's environment to the highest bidder. We must not let this President have four more years to wreck the agricultural economy of this county and this state. Most of all, we cannot let this President have four more years of control over the issues of war and peace." Then he says, "We must not send our sons to die without cause in Lebanon, or serve as bodyguards for dictators in Central America." He has been saying this for some time, even though the question has arisen of what Central American countries he is referring to. "This nation is too young to turn back and fail," he says. "We must resist the old policies that have failed us in the past; resist the temptation of protectionist trade legislation." He calls for more spending for education and training and for "school lunches for poor children and guaranteed student loans for students going to college." He goes on, "And when I debate Mr. Reagan next fall"—to laughter and cheers from the audience—"and he says 'Senator Hart, how do you intend to pay for these education programs and these farm programs?' I intend to say 'Mr. Reagan, by cancelling the MX missile and the B-1 bomber.' " Hart has proposed a number of other things as well, and cancelling those weapons won't pay for them. Hart's pledges outrun his revenues, but no one seems to care about this sort of question anymore. Now he calls for a nuclear freeze and an end to the arms race. "Let's have a foreign policy in the nineteen-eighties that makes sense," he says. "This country has an interest in Central America and the Third World, but we will not achieve those interests or support the goals and values of this nation and the wishes of those people by deploying Marines and combat forces. Let's send to Central America doctors and nurses." He concludes, "I am here this afternoon to ask for your help, not just for a candidate, not just for a candidacy or a campaign, but for this community and for this state and for this nation and for the future of mankind in the nineteen-eighties and beyond." Hart is now following advice that Patrick Caddell, the pollster, gave him after he lost the Pennsylvania primary—to make his candidacy into a cause. "This campaign is about the future of America," Hart tells the crowd.

Hart then takes questions from the audience, and the questions come from people who represent constituency groups—the elderly, veterans, Indians, Hispanics, women. Perhaps this is no accident. In each case, Hart says he is for what the questioner is seeking, just as this morning he told environmentalists and peace activists what they wanted to hear. Hart, because of his style, and because he has asserted that he does not represent "the old ways," can get away with this; Mondale can't.

Back on the plane, Hart's advisers have been handed a copy of today's Los Angeles *Times*, in which the lead story carries the headline "HART, JACKSON CAMPS JOIN TO STOP MONDALE" and goes on to describe, with quotes from Henkel, how Hart and Jackson forces have cooperated in various states as they complete their delegate-selection process. The reaction of the advisers is a clap of hands to foreheads.

LOS ANGELES. The Biltmore Hotel. Hart is at a fund-raiser attended mainly by young entrepreneurs and people who work in high-tech industries, with about eight tables taken by the gay community, where Hart has strong support, and with a sprinkling of show-business people. Hart's good friend Warren Beatty is here, and so are Debra Winger and Marsha Mason. Among the entertainers performing at the fund-raiser are Ronee Blakley and Burt Bacharach and Carole Bayer Sager. (Among other stars who support Hart are Robert Redford, Jack Nicholson, and Goldie Hawn.) Finally, shortly before eleven, Hart is introduced. Lee Hart and their daughter, Andrea, are on the stage with him. Hart says, "I want to begin this evening by saying I love New Jersey"—he is flirting with danger again—"and I love California." When Hart says these things, he punctuates them with a short, gigglelike laugh that sometimes comes out when he tries to be funny. Hart, giggling again, says that his son, John, is attending a prom in Oklahoma—"He loves Oklahoma." Then he gives a few lines from his stump speech, describing the race as between the future and the past, saying that he has a vision for the future that is very different from Ronald Reagan's: "It is my vision that has propelled me and many of you to support candidates like John Kennedy in 1960, Robert Kennedy in 1968, George McGovern in

1972, and other candidates throughout our adult lives that we felt offered the best hope and promise for this nation's future." He talks about cleaning up toxic waste and cancelling the MX and achieving true equality for women, and says that he wants a foreign policy that "instead of sending Marines and combat forces into Central America sends doctors and nurses and teachers and agricultural experts." He speaks slowly and is obviously very tired, and he keeps his remarks brief. He doesn't particularly invigorate this audience; perhaps he's simply too worn out. He concludes, talking more about his vision, "No single individual can do that, no single political party can do that. But the American people can do that and we will do it. And we'll start by winning this nomination in San Francisco and winning this election next fall, for all the people of this country once again to have confidence in their government and participate in the issues that affect their lives. That's what this election is about. It's about our future and we are going to win."

MAY 31

LOS ANGELES. Early this morning, Walter Mondale took the ferry from Tiburon, in Marin County, across the bay to San Francisco (a good photo opportunity); then he campaigned in Fresno, where Hart was yesterday; and now he is appearing at a labor rally here. His first stop in Los Angeles this afternoon was at the Martin Luther King, Jr., Hospital, in Watts. Mickey Kantor says that though the district is one-third black, it has a large Hispanic population, and that Mondale's support by Los Angeles Mayor Tom Bradley, a black, and Kenneth Hahn, the Los Angeles County Supervisor from the Watts area and a popular white, gives him a chance there. (Mondale is also supported by Dianne Feinstein, the mayor of San Francisco.) Mondale is far beyond exhaustion now, and, like Hart, is rebelling at the heaviness of his schedule. Mondale has shown more stamina and resilience than anyone, perhaps including Mondale himself, thought he had, but he seems now to be near the end of his rope. He and Hart are in different situations, professionally and emotionally, which may be why, though both are worn out, the toll seems greater on Mondale at the moment. Mondale has been at it longer than Hart, has had a different experience this year, and has more at stake. For Mondale, who expected to win, and thought he had the nomination wrapped up a couple of times, the defeats were a blow. He kept coming back, but it took a tremendous effort. As he told me in an interview in March, his dignity and self-respect and future peace of mind required that he put everything he had into the fight, not be seen as a quitter. He felt strongly about emerging from the contest with a reputation his children would be proud of. The label "quitter" had been applied to him, and he was determined to peel it off. There was a time, after New Hampshire, when his advisers were gloomier about his prospects than he allowed himself to be. If he does not win the nomination, which he has been aiming for, in various forms, for ten years, this will be the end of his political career. For Hart, who has done better than had been expected, this race has to be a satisfying one no matter how it turns out. And Hart can look at this as the beginning of big things, not the end. Mondale, despite his fatigue, pulled himself together for the event at the Martin Luther King, Jr., Hospital, speaking with feeling about his commitment to civil rights, and attacking Reagan's record. The fact that Jackson is in the race, winning black votes that Mondale had expected to win, and denying him the decisive victory margins he would have otherwise had, must bother Mondale, but, if so, this is something he can't mention.

Now, at shortly after six, at a union hall in the garment district, in the south-central part of Los Angeles, as Mondale waits off-stage, Lane Kirkland fires up a crowd of several hundred union members, excoriating both Reagan and Hart. Kirkland is an unusual man: he is sophisticated, an intellectual, and he and his wife, Irena, travel in Washington's most fashionable social circles. In conversation, Kirkland talks quietly, with a soft South Carolina accent. But he didn't get to the top of the labor movement without being tough or knowing how to talk to his people, and now he is laying it on hard. (He started out in the merchant marine, and is a member of the Masters, Mates, and Pilots union.) Kirkland has a problem: in lining up the A.F.L.-C.I.O. behind Mondale, for the federation's first pre-Convention endorsement of a Presidential candidate, he took a big risk—though the move perhaps seemed less risky at the time than it did at various points this year. The theory was to consolidate labor's strength within the Democratic Party, to try to get a nominee it liked (it hasn't had one since Hubert Humphrey) and who would, if he won, give it, at the least, a voice (labor had a rocky relationship with Carter). The risk, of course, was that if Mondale lost, labor would be shown to be powerless. A secondary risk, which was probably not foreseen, involved the fact that organized labor has a negative image, and its endorsement could be viewed as a liability. That Kirkland is angry that some of Mondale's opponents tried to turn the labor endorsement—which they, too, sought—into a liability for Mondale, and that he is very angry at Hart in particular, cannot be in question from the way he talks here today. (This makes Hart's suggestion to me that he could receive labor's support as the nominee seem a bit unrealistic.)

"None of us thought it would be easy," Kirkland tells the workers. "The attacks on Fritz Mondale have become attacks on the American trade-union movement—on you and the members you represent. That means that more than ever Fritz's fight is our fight, a fight for our legitimate place in this nation's political life." Kirkland says, "Now, we always knew that if Fritz Mondale won the Democratic nomination with our support Ronald Reagan would assail him as the tool of the labor bosses—that is a sure and certain crowd-pleaser." He continues, his big voice filling the hall, "But who would have thought that labor-baiting would become a major theme of another Democratic candidate, Gary Hart—the man who has himself supped most generously in the past at labor's table?" He says, "Now we have a candidate for President named Gary Hart who can't tell the difference between the friends of the Party that he wants to lead and its enemies. . . . His only new idea as far as I've been able to see is his novel doctrine of anti-labor liberalism." He says that Hart is "faithless to the constituencies he has offered himself to in the past," that Hart had come before the A.F.L.-C.I.O.'s executive council and "praised us for our forward-looking policies and asked for our support." Rhetorically, he asks Hart, "When you sought and accepted over a hundred and thirty-five thousand dollars in labor contributions to your last Senate campaign, did you become an indentured servant to labor?" And he continues, "Mr. Hart should promptly return all the money we gave him in 1980." Mondale, says Kirkland, "is not contrived of silicon and microchips." He says, "The question has been raised during the course of this campaign in snide and accusing tones as to what price labor shall put on its support," and he says, "The only price is that the President"—and he paraphrases the oath of office.

Mondale comes on to big cheers. Tom Bradley and various California labor leaders are with him, and a band plays "Happy Days Are Here Again." This is good, old-fashioned Democratic politics, and Mondale is clearly at home. Whether these will have been happy days or the last hurrah won't be known for months. Mondale has for some time been suggesting an analogy between his candidacy and that of Harry Truman, and now someone in the crowd calls out "Give 'em hell, Fritz," and Mondale, evoking Truman, responds, "No, I will tell them the truth and they will think it's hell." Mondale tells the labor crowd, "I am proud to have your support. I'm proud to carry your endorsement into this nomination campaign, into the Democratic Convention, and into the White House." He receives big cheers from the labor people. "I need your help," he tells them, appearing very much to mean it, and, of course, he does. "This is your country as much as it is anybody else's," he tells them. "We've got a President who doesn't think you count," he says. Blue-collar workers will be a much fought-over group in the fall election. But first, the nomination. "One of my opponents says you're a special interest," Mondale says, and, like Kirkland, he points out that Hart was willing to take labor's money for his 1980 Senate race, and sought the A.F.L.-C.I.O. endorsement for the Presidential campaign. Then Mondale, jacket off, voice at full throttle, goes through a litany of things he stands for, preceding each one with "I'm a person who believes," and he talks about jobs, health and safety in the workplace, the right to strike, "and the right to be received with dignity and respect—" Here he is interrupted by loud applause and cheers. The list goes on: Social Security, civil rights, the Equal Rights Amendment. Mondale's programmatic mind is at work. He knows what the constituency groups want, and he shares most of their goals. The question remains of how Mondale would handle the hard trade-offs that have to be made. He insists that having these groups' support will enable him to deal with them. And the big question about labor is whether, if Mondale is elected, it will overreach. It is not only some of the people around Hart who are concerned that labor is seeking too large a role in the Party.

Mondale continues his litany: "I'm a person who believes that our future is to be found in our children and that a mind is a terrible thing to waste. . . . I'm a person who believes in protecting the beauty of our land and the purity of our air and water." Now he says, face red from the effort, "Those are my special interests, and if they are special interests count me in." Mondale has been developing this line of argument all year, and if he is nominated we can expect to hear more of it. Some of his own supporters, somewhat disappointed with his campaign, say that Mondale need never have got on the defensive on this question, that the campaign has been conducted in a way that accentuated his vulnerabilities: his at least perceived oversolicitousness toward the interest groups; his being seen as an old-style pol; his perceived inability to reach out to certain constituencies; his not being seen as very interesting or up-to-date. The irony is that Mondale has come across as a known quantity, old hat, in large part because, through a combination of his own inhibitions and his campaign's sense of the short-term tactical requirements, certain aspects of him have remained largely out of view. He has shown endurance, but people seem yet to be convinced that he has strength. He does fine in this kind of setting, but he has yet to get across to the general audience what he is for. He has yet to crystallize and communicate his themes. The short-term tactics have got him through a crisis, but they haven't laid the groundwork for the longer run. He has yet to project that elusive quality, leadership—presenting yourself in such a way that people want to follow you.

Now Mondale does something he's good at—expresses indignation. He says, "In Reagan's America, if you're rich they give you tax cuts, if you're poor they give you cheese. If you're sick, they make you pay more. If you're old, they call a fixed income a fortune. If you're a woman, they blame you for unemployment. If you're Hispanic, they say you enjoy overcrowded housing." This is a new one on his list: he is referring to a recent statement by the Under-Secretary of the Department of Housing and Urban Development that Hispanic families live in overcrowded housing because that is "a cultural preference." Mondale continues his list: "If you're hungry, they call you a hustler, and if you're homeless they say you want it that way." He says, "Mr. Reagan, you don't understand what's going on in this country with people of average income. This country is not some kind of jungle where just the richest and the fittest, whatever that means, prosper; this is the United States of America, and this nation is a community, a family, in which we care for one another." He says that he wants to get the deficits down and help the economy grow, to rectify the trade deficit. He mentions, as he did earlier this year, that currencies are out of line. "We need a President willing to stand up for American workers and American—" Once again the crowd drowns him out with its cheers. He urges the crowd, as he has done with other labor audiences, to "elect someone who will remember who put him there." He says, "Elect someone who realizes that a President is not an elected king of America. He's elected a public servant who works for the people of this country. Elect someone who understands not just what Lincoln said, but believes it," and he quotes, as he has all year, Lincoln's saying this is a government of, by, and for the people. His voice reaching full volume, a shout, he says, "You're looking at the person who *his whole life* has fought on behalf of working people in this country." Then he makes the audience laugh as he goes through a description of the cushioned life at the White House, and he says, his voice rising with indignation again, that Presidents can forget that there are people who are unemployed, that there are children who aren't getting an education, that there are people being discriminated against, that there are people who are ill and can't get medical care, that there are toxic-waste dumps. He says—no, shouts—"There are problems in this country that require a President's leadership, but Presidents cannot lead if they don't know what's going on in the life of the average American."

The Mondale campaign is on a two-track course now: while Mondale is out on the road trying to win delegates through the primary contests that remain, his top aides are back in Washington working almost around the clock to obtain the support of still more of the "superdelegates"—five hundred and sixty-eight members of Congress and other Party officials, from whom Mondale already has sizable support—and of delegates who were elected uncommitted or on behalf of a candidate who has dropped out of the race. The campaign has also been working to win the support of delegates in the states still completing their delegate-selection process. The effort has been a frenzied one, and was set off by Mondale's loss in Ohio, on May 8th, which came as a surprise to the Mondale camp. At that point, in an effort to make Mondale's nomination "inevitable" once again, his campaign chairman, James Johnson, announced that Mondale would have from 1,750 to 1,800 delegates by June 4th, and would receive enough from the balloting on the fifth to have the 1,967 needed for the nomination. This was something of a gamble. From that moment on, Johnson and Tom Donilon, a deputy campaign manager, aided by eight campaign workers (more were added later) pulled in from the road in the course of the campaign and set to the task of tracking the delegates, have been giving their all to making the prediction come true—an exercise that has not been easy. Donilon, who is twenty-nine, was the boy-wonder chief delegate-counter for the Carter campaign in 1980. He had been working on, among other things, making sure that Mondale's delegates would be in line at the Convention, but after Ohio the effort backed up to one of making sure there would be enough Mondale delegates at the Convention. Since May 8th, Mondale has picked up a hundred and fifty delegates, only thirty of them in the three contests that have been held since then (Oregon, Nebraska, and Idaho), which Mondale did not contend in and lost. Some of the delegates Mondale has picked up were in caucus states, such as Virginia and Alaska, which were finishing their delegate-selection process. Others came from the superdelegates chosen in such states as New York and Ohio. (The Hart forces were irritated that though Hart won the Ohio primary—by two points—Mondale received nine of the ten superdelegates available in the state.)

But the most wearing exercise for the Mondale people has been the phoning and cajoling to get a delegate here, a congressman there, a bloc of uncommitted delegates in one state or a group of, say, Glenn delegates somewhere else. Johnson makes calls, Mondale makes calls, allies make calls. Johnson and Donilon met with the political directors of the unions and made assignments. When I visited Johnson in his office last week, he ticked off various states where he hoped to pick up specific numbers of votes: in Alabama, seven Glenn delegates, plus some unpledged delegates; in South Carolina, a potential twelve uncommitted delegates; in Georgia, a potential twelve unpledged superdelegates. In Kentucky, Governor Martha Layne Collins was holding a block of fifteen uncommitted delegates. Mrs. Collins will chair the Democratic Convention, so she is neutral, and apparently believes that taking uncommitted delegates to the Convention will enhance her influence, but Robert Strauss and Senator Wendell Ford, of Kentucky, are trying to persuade Mrs. Collins to release her delegates. Grant Sawyer, a former governor of Nevada, was sought out by a Democratic senator, by Strauss, and by an official of the A.F.L.-C.I.O., to see if he could persuade the current governor of Nevada, Richard Bryan, to endorse Mondale and deliver three delegates. Senators Thomas Eagleton, of Missouri, and Paul Sarbanes, of Maryland, have made calls on Mondale's behalf, and so have leaders of various labor organizations and of women's groups. Donna Small, a delegate from Montana who is uncommitted, has been called on Mondale's behalf by the lieutenant governor of the state and, after the Mondale people learned that she was a nurse, by Judy Goldsmith, the president of the National Organization for Women. Labor leaders have called a certain senator who would not commit to Mondale, and after this Johnson met with him several times. The senator eventually committed. A certain congressman who is holding out—says he likes Mondale and voted for him in his state but won't commit—has been called on by Johnson and has been reached by one of his major contributors. He continues to hold out. Some senators don't want to choose sides when they are up for reelection. Some politicians are simply concerned that by choosing sides they might jeopardize their political future. Some white elected officials tell the Mondale people they will support Mondale at the Convention but cannot announce this publicly, because they need black support. A major Mondale fund raiser who is a friend of a former governor of Wyoming is helping to get the support of that state's Party chair and vice-chair. Jane Paxton, a delegate in Maine who is a teacher, has been called by George Mitchell, a Maine senator; by Judy Goldsmith; and by Mary Futrell, the president of the National Education Association. Johnson said, "We've just got every angle going on every person we can, and we're going full tilt." Strauss, who was Special Trade Representative in the Carter Administration, called a delegate concerned about Mondale's support of domestic-content legislation. Eagleton, a Catholic, called two uncommitted delegates in North Dakota who support right-to-life legislation. Hubert Humphrey's son Skip, who is now the attorney general of Minnesota, was to go to Fargo to meet with five uncommitted North Dakota delegates. Johnson has gone to Texas to see Governor Mark White, who is uncommitted, and is planning to go to Florida to see Governor Bob Graham, who is holding about seven delegates (it is unclear how many he can bring with his endorsement)—unpledged, uncommitted, or pledged to John Glenn or Reubin Askew. Johnson, usually a very low-key man, said, "Christ,

I'd go anywhere for two delegates at this point." Roland Burris, who is the state comptroller of Illinois and whom the Carter forces had to spend some time placating during the Carter-Kennedy fight in 1980, is holding out for what he considers a satisfactory role in the general-election campaign. Another Illinois state official felt that he had been left out of an important meeting, so Mondale had to call him, and he came around. Brad Dye, the lieutenant governor of Mississippi, has come in for a lot of attention. Mississippi has twelve uncommitted delegates. Johnson spoke with Dye about a dozen times in the last week, and Mondale spoke with him twice. Dye has pledged to support Mondale, and is now working to obtain the support of the other delegates. At Dye's suggestion, Mondale called the state auditor of Mississippi. Dye also called Johnson and said he would need to characterize Mondale's health and education positions to a certain delegate, and Johnson told him what he could say. Dye called Johnson on another occasion and said that one delegate wanted to pass along his opinion about who should be selected as Vice-President. At Dye's suggestion, Mondale called another Mississippi delegate. To obtain as many of the seven Glenn delegates in Alabama as possible, the Mondale campaign is working through Bill Baxley, the lieutenant governor, who headed the Glenn campaign in the state. Baxley had told Mondale that he would be for him if his candidacy looked strong. If a Mondale state leader suggested putting someone on the delegation who would support Mondale at the Convention but not before, the Mondale people told the leader to find someone else. This past Tuesday, Johnson, who had worked throughout the Memorial Day weekend with Donilon and other delegate searchers, said that Mondale had just received a commitment from Mark White, and that Brad Dye would be announcing his support that day, carrying with him eight other delegates from Mississippi. "I got six delegates last night," he said, sounding triumphant—a governor, a state chair, a state vice-chair, and some uncommitteds.

There was a bit of confusion in the Mondale camp over when, exactly, it hoped to have enough delegates for the nomination. While Johnson said as of the voting on the fifth, Mondale on a couple of occasions said as of the Convention. Mondale's aides say that there was no great significance to this—that it was simply a result of Mondale's fatigue—and finally Mondale settled the mat-

ter by saying he would announce that he had enough delegates at
11:59 A.M., Central Daylight Time, on June 6th. (The results from
California would come in late.) Donilon spends hours with the
delegate-counters from the wire services, the New York *Times*, and
the networks, because the Mondale campaign obviously doesn't
want to be in the position of announcing that it has a sufficient
number of delegates only to have the news services disagree.
(U.P.I. has been more conservative than other delegate-counters,
and does not agree with, among other things, the Mondale campaign's estimates of how many delegates it will get out of Texas
and a few other caucus states.) Each time a delegate is obtained,
the name is given to the news services, who call the delegate to
check out the commitment. In some instances, an official will
make a private commitment—allowing his or her name to be
given to the news services, and agreeing to confirm it, but not to
make it public. Mondale also took to saying that he would win New
Jersey and California—a shift in the policy of not appearing overconfident, inspired by the need to shake loose the non-elected
delegates. This was also the purpose of Johnson's announcing the
goal: the campaign was telling the non-elected delegates and uncommitted leaders all over the country that it was time to get
aboard. Announcing the goal also had the purpose of creating a
sense of urgency within the Mondale organization—and of dis-
pelling the idea, which was turning up in the press, that Mondale
was anxious about whether he would receive the nomination.

Now, at shortly before nine, Mondale and Hart are standing beside a platform in the sculpture garden of the home of Stanley and
Betty Sheinbaum, in Brentwood. Sheinbaum, a liberal activist, is
holding a fund-raiser to help George McGovern pay off his campaign debt. (Before Mondale came here, he went to a fund-raiser
in the Pacific Palisades, forty-five minutes and many cultural miles
from the union hall, attended by members of the gay community.
Not many people were there, and, because of his fatigue, Mondale
had wanted to skip the event, but was told that this could cost him
support in the gay community. So Mondale went through with it,
and reaffirmed his support of homosexuals' rights, but he seemed
somewhat unhappy and ill at ease.) This event at the Sheinbaums'
home was billed as a "unity" party, but it hasn't quite turned out
that way. Jackson declined to come, saying in an angry letter to

McGovern that it was "too premature a celebration of party unity," and that McGovern had been "unprincipled and unfair," and had forfeited the role as "the conscience of the Party," by having recently endorsed the idea of a Mondale-Hart ticket. Jackson once again protested the nomination rules, which have prevented him from getting the number of delegates commensurate with his popular vote. Moreover, none of the candidates—and especially not Hart or Jackson—are ready for unity just yet. The brief attempt to achieve unity made by the Mondale forces, with Strauss at the forefront, before the Ohio primary was aborted even before that contest was held.

Now Hart stands on the platform to make some remarks. "In pursuit of unity," he jokes, once again breaking into his gigglelike laugh, "which is a word we heard a lot more of before the Ohio primary, I am prepared to suggest to my friend Walter Mondale a deal, and that is that whoever turns out to be the winner offers the loser visitation rights on the weekend." Hart laughs, and the audience laughs politely. He says, "I know Fritz was pretty pleased when George, a couple of weeks ago, announced that he was in favor of a Mondale-Hart ticket. What Fritz probably didn't hear was George's statement that he was behind that ticket a thousand per cent." Again Hart giggles, but the audience seems uncomfortable; Hart is referring to McGovern's embarrassing mistake, in 1972, of saying that he was behind his Vice-Presidential choice, Thomas Eagleton, "a thousand per cent" when stories broke that Eagleton had suffered from mental illness, and then dropping Eagleton from the ticket. Now Hart jokes about how much he did for McGovern in 1972 ("I helped push the campaign uphill"). He laughs again. He concludes his remarks by praising McGovern as "the most honest and decent individual that I have ever met in American politics."

Mondale, in his remarks, makes a couple of light comments and goes on to criticize Reagan, saying, "Whatever may trouble us as Democrats—one against the other—we cannot permit the President to remain in office." He talks about the arms race, about human rights and civil rights and the environment. This is not Mondale's crowd; these are people who in another day would have supported McGovern, and, between Mondale and Hart, favor Hart. One liberal activist here tonight tells me that while he thinks it is desperately important that Reagan not be reelected he can't get excited about any of the Democratic candidates. There seems to be a lot of that this year. The requirement that political candidates excite may not be new, but it seems to be more prevalent, and it is risky. Harry Truman was not exciting; Hitler was exciting.

Then McGovern makes a few remarks. He has had a good year, and seems to feel redeemed for the first time since 1972. His calm, lucid, and gentle candidacy won him a following anew, and his calling for peace among the candidates early in the campaign made him something of a hero. So now McGovern, despite the fact that he had to drop out of the race in March, is frequently interviewed on television and has somewhat mysteriously acquired the mantle of "the conscience of the Party"—which he clearly enjoys. Tonight, he jokes about his new position: "We lost to Nixon and for the next ten years I was known as the big loser in American politics. And then I came in third in Iowa and people said, 'Isn't George wonderful?' We have a tie for fourth in New Hampshire and they say, 'You know, he's really a great statesman, he's really performing brilliantly.' " And then, addressing himself to the two candidates present, McGovern says that the issues they have raised against each other—Mondale's delegate committees, Hart's support for the build-down—aren't the real issues; the real issues are Reagan's policies. "Go as gently as you can with each other," McGovern says. But the candidates don't seem particularly pleased by his message: they are using what issues they can against each other in a tough fight with high stakes. This is a very tense situation.

JUNE 1

This morning, Mondale has talked to the editorial board of the Los Angeles *Herald-Examiner* and toured a Hispanic market, and now, as he rides toward his next appointment, an appearance on the Michael Jackson show, a popular radio program (Hart appeared on it earlier this morning), I have an interview with him. Mondale is, by his own admission, exhausted, and tired of campaigning. "This has been an interminable process," he says. The pockets of fatigue under his eyes now seem as if they are permanent. He says that the other thing that bothers him about the campaign is that it doesn't have enough substance to it. "There's some substance to it, but not what it should be," he says, and he continues, "I don't know. Yesterday, I opened the issue on trade, which I think is a disaster—these new trade-deficit figures are a disaster, and the agreement that Reagan just made with the Japanese to increase the value of the yen against the dollar will actually reduce the value of the yen—and I might as well have spit in San Francisco Bay. And now we have this peculiar thing where we're tilting to Iraq."

This morning's Los Angeles *Times* headline is "REAGAN TILTS TOWARD IRAQ," and the story quotes from an interview Reagan gave in which he criticized Iran, Iraq's enemy in the three-and-a-half-year-old war, for attacking trading ships of neutral countries in the Persian Gulf. Reagan also said that Iraq (which started the war) was justified in hitting ships trading with Iran. Until the President's statement, the Administration had taken pains to appear neutral. The Administration has been in a quandary about the war since the firing on the ships by Iraq and Iran escalated three weeks ago. The President had vowed to keep open the Strait of Hormuz, through which ships pass from the Persian Gulf, and now there is some dispute within the Administration over whether this meant, or implied, that he would also protect shipping in the Gulf. Some members of the Administration—in particular Secretary of State George Shultz, who still thinks the United States pulled out of Lebanon precipitately—think that the United States should take a more active role in the Persian Gulf dispute; so far, the prevailing view is that it should not.

Referring to Reagan's comments, Mondale says, "What is that about? I can't see any justification; I see a lot of risks. Maybe they know something I don't know, but I try to make an issue about that—and see if that goes anywhere. Anyway, I'm tired." Mondale says that the difference between other long campaigns and this one is that the others "had an explanation, like the Vietnam War, or had enormous emotion, like the Kennedy-Carter fight." He adds, "This doesn't seem to have those elements." He continues, "As long as it's going to be this long, the one redeeming element could be that we'd have a good debate about issues; in the last three weeks or so, my impression is that there's little or nothing happening on the issue side. If when you're going through this you could see that it had a redeeming virtue to it that would enhance the process and make us better candidates, or something, I'd feel better about it; but I don't. You know, this international thing is terrible. These countries are going bankrupt; these democracies are being destabilized; the trade balances are horrible; we're sucking the capital out of those countries; they can't pay their bills. We've got the economic summit conference coming up where these things are supposed to be worked on and the President's in the morning papers saying it'll be mostly ceremony this time. Jesus, this ought to be an issue. But, alas."

I ask Mondale what he now thinks about the prospects, if he wins the nomination, of uniting the Party.

He sighs heavily, and says, "It's unknown at this point." Mondale clearly believes that the loss of Ohio was a real setback in terms of the time lost to unite the Party, the continued combat and growing bitterness, the compounding of the fatigue. He expects to win, but the delay has been costly. But, of course, he can't complain publicly; he just has to push on, summoning whatever reserves he has left, which don't appear to be very many. He was knocked on the mat once this year, got up and fought back, and, just when he thought the fight would be over, found that he had to continue fighting. Now, sounding a bit more hopeful about unity, he says, "My hope is that it will prove to be much more doable than you might believe from the rhetoric. And I think there's a real chance of that. There's a lot of virtue in two good nights' sleep, which no one has had. There's the fact that none of us want Reagan, and, whatever our differences, they are less than those that divide us from Reagan. I think the public feels that way and will press in that direction." Then he says, "But right now I would say that tensions are rising." Mondale is concerned not only about the nature of his debates with Hart but also about the tone of Jackson's letter to McGovern. Even if Mondale gets the requisite number of delegates soon, there will be little peace. He is planning to get some rest, but knows that he has his work cut out for him in unifying the Party; that he is facing challenges over the rules, credentials, and platform; that the Vice-Presidential selection must be carefully considered; that there will be hundreds of little decisions to make about the Convention—who gets to speak when, and so on.

I ask Mondale his reaction to Hart's saying to me that he is personally disappointed in Mondale, that Mondale is distorting his record.

"He has no right to say that," Mondale replies. "He keeps complaining that way, but he doesn't answer what I'm saying. I have not been personal once; I am talking about real issues. Why is he for the build-down? He keeps talking about how the build-down eliminates two weapons systems when it's two warheads. He can just say he's for it if he wants to, but he shouldn't distort it." He goes on to criticize Hart's position on the Diablo Canyon nuclear plant and his record on toxic waste. ("He's the one that raised the question of leadership over toxic waste.") He says, "I've been very careful to stay on the merits, and instead of answering the merits he goes off on this personal stuff. It's a matter of record, of course, that for a year he was saying every conceivable thing about me and I wasn't responding."

I point out to Mondale that it isn't just Hart who says that his campaigning has been too negative.

"Yes," he replies. "I don't know how to handle that. I'm talking about the issues that I think are right. I'm shaping the issues that I deem to be correct. I am challenging Gary Hart to speak out on those issues—that's what I'm doing."

The conversation turns to the prospect that even if Mondale wins the delegates needed for the nomination Hart will challenge the legitimacy of his candidacy. "There's nothing new about that," Mondale says. "They've been doing that for a hundred years. As I say, it goes something like this: 'I know I lost New York, but I'd rather have the delegates.' Won't sell."

I ask Mondale what happened to his effort to find a theme, or phrase—four or five words to sum up his candidacy—which he had said last year he needed to do.

"I'm still working on it," he replies. "You see, what I tried to do was to in effect campaign for the Democratic Party against Mr. Reagan. And I spent a year doing that and Hart spent that year campaigning against me. Nearly knocked me out. So I had to then back up and start debating Gary Hart, and that's what I've done, and every time I've debated him I've won and every time I haven't I've lost. So that's what we've had to do now."

Mondale says that he is hopeful about the fall election. The widely held view at the moment is that there isn't much reason for him to be hopeful: his Party is divided; he is running behind Reagan in the polls (but not by as much as might be expected, given the months of open warfare among the Democrats and the President's picturesque trip to China and his victories in the Congress). Mondale says, "See, I think there's a perception that Reagan's flying high, with a Teflon coat around him, but the fact of it is that that campaign hasn't started yet." (Representative Patricia Schroeder, Democrat of Colorado, originated the phrase that Reagan's is a "Teflon-coated Presidency.") Mondale continues, "I haven't seen a single poll that says he's beyond striking range. Most of them show it's close. And, second, I've travelled this country and I know what's going on, and the American people do not agree fundamentally with what he's doing—for example, arms control, these deficits, unfairness, the environment, and so on— and when that issue is joined I think he's in for a big surprise."

JUNE 4

WASHINGTON. This afternoon, I spoke with one of the members of the House who have endorsed Mondale but whom the Hart forces hope to persuade to change their minds. The man is a young, modern politician. When I asked him what the possibility was that he would switch, as the Hart forces hope, he replied as follows: "They are pipe-dreaming. I would think the reason they think I might be switchable is that I came to Congress around the same time that Hart did, and have been among those in the House and Senate who have been staking out somewhat different positions from the traditional Democrats: huge amounts of government borrowing bothers me; protectionism bothers me; I feel strongly about research-and-development efforts through tax incentives as well as through government grants. So along comes Hart and probably thinks, That group is ripe for the picking. The trouble is, we're not choosing a bunch of position papers; we're choosing a candidate, and the one that we think is best prepared to lead the Party and the country. Jimmy Carter had a nice resume but couldn't lead the country. Also, there is a factor about Hart that leaves a lot of us unsettled. Mondale is closer to Tip O'Neill and traditional politics than some of us are, so if he's elected we'll fight the good fight and be independent of him where necessary. We'd rather go with someone we know. I like Hart's position papers, but he's a mystery to me."

I asked him what he meant by that.

"I've watched Gary in meetings we've attended—in the White House during the Carter years, and on the Hill," he said. "He always seemed an aloof, remote person. I've never had a feeling about where his passion was. And there's something about the whole Kennedyesque 'We need new ideas' thing without a lot of substance that leaves me uneasy. Third, his being unable to say how old he is or what his name is—those may seem to idle observers to be grains of sand, but they raise questions for those of us who are in the business: Who is this guy? Or, more to the point, who does *he* think he is?"

As for the possibility of trying to deny the nomination to Mondale, the congressman said, "There is not disaffection with Mondale to the point where people would be willing to get behind anybody else. People know what the problems are, but if we have problems now because of division within the Party those problems would be minute compared with taking the nomination away from someone who has the requisite number of delegates at the end of the nomination process. While Mondale doesn't command wild-eyed enthusiasm, there are people deeply committed to him and loyal to him who would be bitter at any attempt to take the nomination away from him. That would be a greater problem than the ones we have now."

Early this evening, I spoke with Tom Donilon, to see how the Mondale delegate hunt was coming. He said that the number of delegates obtained was now 1,762 "and still adding." Donilon said that shortly U.P.I. would say that Mondale has 1,732 delegates. He said, "We had a very good weekend and a very good day today." The Mondale camp added eighteen delegates from Pennsylvania over the weekend, and today got thirteen from Hawaii. Hawaii was polished off after a conversation over the weekend between Mondale, in Los Angeles, and Hawaii's Governor George Ariyoshi, who had initially turned Mondale down. Two congressmen and one senator came aboard today, and, also today, Bill Baxley, in Alabama, announced that four of the seven Glenn delegates in the state would be for Mondale. The Mondale camp picked up four uncommitted delegates in South Carolina today—giving it seven previously uncommitted delegates from there. Governor Graham of Florida still hasn't moved, but Johnson and Mondale will try to reach him within the next twenty-four hours. (Mondale flew all night from California to New Jersey last night and then, after a very brief rest, began campaigning in New Jersey at seven-thirty, then flew on to West Virginia, New Mexico, and back to California. After staying in San Francisco tonight, he will go to St. Paul,

Minnesota, to await the returns tomorrow night. Hart flew to Washington for his son's graduation today and then went on to New Jersey, and he will return to Los Angeles tomorrow. Jackson campaigned in California today.) On Saturday night, Mondale also called Norman Fletcher, the only Glenn delegate from Georgia, whom the Mondale campaign tracked down in a hotel in Arizona. Fletcher is now a Mondale delegate. Governor Collins of Kentucky is still holding out, as are Donna Small, the nurse from Montana, and Jane Paxton, the teacher in Maine. As Donilon talked, a cheer went up in the background: a Hart supporter who had been elected uncommitted in South Carolina had been won over.

Today, the Field poll in California said that Mondale leads Hart by seven points.

JUNE 5

Tonight, Mondale won New Jersey strongly, with forty-five per cent to Hart's thirty per cent and Jackson's twenty-three per cent, and he also carried West Virginia; Hart has won New Mexico and South Dakota. The word is that the exit polls in California indicate that the voting for Mondale and Hart is close, but the returns are incomplete, and no one knows how the voting will break out in terms of delegates. This morning, there was a story in the Washington *Post* saying that the Hart people are hoping that Representatives Gillis Long, of Louisiana, the chairman of the House Democratic Caucus, and Morris Udall, of Arizona, will lead a revolt of House members in Hart's direction. There appears to be more to the Long rumor than to the one about Udall; and in any event the panzer divisions went forth from the Mondale headquarters to Capitol Hill this morning. Calls and visits from the Mondale camp and its allies—in Congress, around Washington—ensued. In Minnesota, Mondale, joined by Donilon and Johnson, was making phone calls to line up still more delegates. In Washington, Richard Moe, an attorney and a longtime associate of Mondale's, who has been in charge of the effort to obtain the support of members of Congress, made a flurry of phone calls, and also saw Long and Udall. Moe told the people he called about the delegate count, saying that Mondale was in a position to "go over the top" as a result of today's voting. As of this morning, CBS gave Mondale 1,741 delegates, and U.P.I. gave him 1,732. The Mondale people have decided not to claim victory until the delegates from California are in hand—and to have Mondale make his announcement, as promised, at 11:59 A.M. tomorrow. Tonight, on television, Mondale, looking happy and relaxed, told his supporters in Minnesota, "Two months ago, I said this race would be a marathon." (Mondale had said this on the night of March 13th.) He continued, smiling broadly, "Now, marathons are long and hard. But every one of them has a finish line and a winner. Well, this is it, and here I am." But this was as far as he went in claiming victory. CBS now gives him 1,867 delegates. Jackson, on television, says that he will ask the Party for certain commitments. Jackson will now have to work out what he is going to ask for, and the Mondale people will have to work out what they are prepared to give. There is only so far that they can go without riling certain constituencies—particularly Southerners and Jews, but also blue-collar workers. It is also the case that Jackson cannot let himself be seen as the black who, through his actions from here out, helped bring about Reagan's reelection. Hart appears on television telling his supporters that he has won in California—"the last, the largest, and, I believe, the most important state in the Democratic process"—and that the list of states he has won "reads like an honor roll for victory in 1984." He concludes with a rallying cry: "On to San Francisco and on to the White House."

JUNE 6

The Mondale campaign's long struggle encountered one last glitch. Though the number of people who voted for Hart and Mondale in California was close—Hart led by three points—Hart trounced Mondale in the delegate race, winning more than two hundred delegates, to about seventy for Mondale. The Mondale people went to sleep not knowing how badly things would go in California, but Donilon was told in the middle of the night, and the other campaign leaders learned early this morning and, joined by Mondale, went to work. Two out of the three networks gave Mondale enough delegates for the nomination this morning, but U.P.I. did not. (Also on the morning news programs was live coverage of Reagan arriving in Normandy for the commemoration of the fortieth anniversary of D Day. The beach where the Americans landed and the sheer cliffs they climbed were in the background. The timing was exquisite.) Now, at noon, after an-

other furious round of calls, Mondale is on television claiming he
has the delegates for the nomination. He says he has 2,008; U.P.I.
gives him 1,969—two more than necessary. Had Johnson not
taken his gamble after the Ohio defeat, Mondale could well be
going into the Convention without enough delegates; at that, he
had a narrow escape. Hart and Jackson are also holding press
conferences, in which they decline to concede victory to Mondale.
Jackson, of course, could never get the delegates for the nomination, and now his delegates aren't needed at the Convention by the
front-runner—this was always a long shot—but he can still cause
problems. Hart's chances of getting the nomination seem virtually
nil now. He has about 1,200 delegates, roughly 700 fewer than
Mondale. The earthquake that might have shaken the nomination
loose from Mondale's grip has not occurred. Hart is to meet the
Democratic leaders, including O'Neill, on Capitol Hill tomorrow,
and will undoubtedly be told the realities. It is not uncommon for
the losing candidate to take his campaign to the Convention, and
sometimes this has been done benignly; the worry among many
Democrats is that Hart will keep the fight going in one form or
another, delay the healing, and diminish the Party's chances of
winning in November. Reagan's Presidency has made Democrats
feel a great deal of urgency about healing the Party, and this will
put pressure on Hart. For the moment, though, he seems angry,
and to be resisting the idea of giving up at all. But, for his own
future, he, too, can't be seen as having helped to cause Reagan to
win in November. He, too, will have to calibrate his actions carefully in the coming weeks. Hart's people have been talking a lot
about Hart's making another try for the Presidency in 1988, and a
real question is whether, way in there, Hart wants Mondale to win
in November.

On television, Mondale looks very happy and remarkably well;
victory has at least temporarily brushed aside the signs of fatigue.
This victory is something he has sought for a very long time, and
though winning it took a bit longer than he expected it to, it seems
no less sweet for being tardy. Perhaps sweeter, because in winning
it this way Mondale has vindicated himself and proved something
both to himself and to others. Now he congratulates Hart and
Jackson, and says, "Today, I am pleased to claim victory, and I will
be the nominee of the Democratic Party." He continues, "The time
has now come to plan a unified Convention. Our Democratic

Party is a family, and as families sometimes do, we squabble. But our bonds are stronger than our battles." He goes on, "We have a powerful case to make to our country." He points out that in an interview with Walter Cronkite in Normandy this morning Reagan, on being asked how he will deal with the Democrats, replied, "I'll pretend they're not there." Mondale says, "Well, he's done a lot of pretending," and goes on to say, "For nearly four years, he's pretended that the nuclear-arms race isn't there. He's pretended that unemployment and huge deficits and mounting trade imbalances and rising interest rates aren't there. He's pretended that pollution and toxic-waste dumps aren't there. He's pretended that women, seniors, and minorities aren't there." This is the case that Mondale will make against Reagan. He continues, "We Democrats see a different America and a better future. Next month, the Democratic Party will select me as its fortieth nominee. I will make the general election a contest between two visions of America, of our future." This would be a new theme. He adds, "Today, I'm the underdog in that race, but come November I predict victory for our Party, change for America, and hope for our future."

JUNE 13

A week after Mondale declared he had the nomination, the reality seems to be settling in that he does have it—but neither Hart nor Jackson accepts this yet. Both are still contesting his nomination and talking about the fights they will make over the platform and the nomination rules. Hart was told the blunt truth about his chances when he made the rounds on Capitol Hill last Thursday, and members of Congress gratefully accepted Hart's assurances that he would be "positive" from then on. In fact, Hart had no choice, as his own advisers admit; the only good politics was for him to cease criticism of Mondale. But he couldn't quite do that. It is clear from talking to the people around Hart that he is motivated by the theory that lightning might still strike, by continuing anger at Mondale, and by the simple, and understandable, difficulty with ceasing activity. The Hart people tell each other, and Hart, that the polls might start showing Hart running better against Reagan than Mondale, that the F.E.C. might come down with a ruling damaging to Mondale, that the delegates might start changing their minds. They argue that Hart won more states and perhaps more of the popular vote (actually, Mondale appears to have won more of the popular vote)—a tactic New York Governor Mario Cuomo likens to saying "I won more innings than you did. I should have won the game." One of Hart's key advisers said to me earlier this week that the time between June 5th and the Convention is the equivalent of one third of the time between New Hampshire and the Convention: "A lot can happen in that time," he said. The plain truth is that a number of the people who are advising Hart do not care whether Mondale is elected or not—they say they assume he cannot be—and are themselves reluctant to give up the fight, which is probably more interesting than whatever they were doing before. They also want Hart to fight for changes in the rules so that he might be better served by them in 1988. Hart's newer advisers are urging a more aggressive approach than many of the people who have been with him longer, who think his interests are better served by being a "good Democrat" in the weeks ahead. (The newer advisers are also still preoccupied with ousting Henkel.) Almost no one is urging Hart to take his name out of the race so that he cannot be nominated at the Convention. One concern on the part of a number of Hart's advisers is that he improve his relations with labor—both for his Senate race in 1986 and for his next Presidential run. They think that the best way for him to do this, and also to improve his standing in the Party, is to accept the Vice-Presidential nomination. (Doing that would also keep another Democrat from preempting Hart for 1988.) Hart himself is said to be ambivalent on this point; among other things, he recognizes that being in a secondary position is not very compatible with his temperament. He has continued to portray himself as the candidate with the best vision of the future, and to draw the contrast between himself and Mondale, while not naming Mondale. In his testimony before the Platform Committee on Monday, he urged the Party to be "daring and bold once again, not cautious or calculating," to reject "the traditional approach of some in our Party who promise everything to everyone." In case reporters didn't get it, Hart aides pointed out that Hart was referring to Mondale. The Hart people are still threatening to challenge the "tainted" delegates—a threat one Hart adviser told me was being held out to give Hart leverage. Moreover, the Hart campaign's general counsel, Jack Quinn, argued before the Credentials Committee last Friday on Jackson's behalf that the Party should adopt a system of proportional representation of delegates, beginning with this year's contest. (This is probably what the Hart adviser was referring to when he said that Jackson was getting good legal help.) Jackson, like Hart, is said to be angry—the anger seemed to grow toward the end of the campaign, and surfaced in Jackson's letter to McGovern. Jackson, too, has around him some people who do not much care whether Mondale is elected, and who want to make last-ditch fights, regardless of the consequences. These people are reacting to a host of real and imagined grievances, and have fed Jackson's anger and resentment. Jackson talks often now of wanting "respect." Another group of Jackson's advisers is more concerned with getting some things in the platform that could be helpful to blacks—on, for example, jobs—and with defeating Reagan in November.

Mondale's aides have been busy on a number of fronts. They have been getting more delegates—they now claim 2,025, and, as of today, U.P.I. gives them 1,993. McGovern endorsed Mondale today, and the Mondale people hope that most of his twenty-three delegates will support Mondale, as McGovern urged. They also expect to win several uncommitted delegates in Kentucky soon, and some from Virginia after a little longer. Governor Graham continues to resist, but Andrew Young and Gillis Long were among those who came through on the sixth. Senator James Sasser, of Tennessee, who had backed Glenn, was met at the Washington airport by a labor leader that morning, and phoned Mondale from the airport and signed on. Roland Burris came around later. The Vice-Presidential selection process has been set in motion: Mondale is reliably said to be of an open mind about the question now. Neither he nor his aides have had a lot of time to think about it before this. Mondale will spend much of the period leading up to the Convention in his home just outside St. Paul—away from the noise and demands of Washington—and the Vice-Presidential prospects will begin making visits there next week. (Not everyone who is being considered—Hart, for instance—will be required to go to Minnesota.) The Mondale people are also working on, and worrying about, the Convention. They are preparing for both a fractious Convention and a smooth one. Their operating theory now about Hart and Jackson is that both need more time to cool off and face the realities, and that though there are contacts with both camps, there is not much point in getting into serious dealing for a while. Mondale has called Hart and

Jackson, but the Mondale people aren't keen on having Mondale meet them if they are going to use the opportunity to tell the waiting press that they are still challenging Mondale for the nomination or that they are making demands that can't be met. Mondale is winding up a vacation in Southampton, and this weekend will make some appearances in which he will develop further the case he will make against Reagan. A general election campaign is a very different thing from a campaign for the nomination—it is far less tactical and more national—and in the coming weeks it will be seen how well the Mondale campaign makes the transition.

XVII

Sunday. Tomorrow, Walter Mondale and his designated Vice-Presidential candidate, Geraldine Ferraro, will arrive here, and the Democratic Convention will begin. Mondale's selection of Ferraro, which he announced on Thursday, came as a lightning bolt across the political landscape, and has changed, if not transformed, the atmosphere surrounding the Mondale campaign. The excitement set off by the choice, while not unalloyed, or without some misgivings, has given a lift to the Convention even before it begins, and the excitement is felt by far more than the women activists who had been agitating for the selection of a woman. It had come to be accepted wisdom that Mondale would never do anything "bold"—President Reagan's political advisers shared this view—and Mondale's Vice-Presidential selection process, in which he openly interviewed a number of minority candidates, had been widely written off as a sham. Yet there had been strong advocates for some time within the Mondale campaign for Mondale's choosing a woman, a black, or a Hispanic. This school, which included, among others, John Reilly, Mondale's law partner and close adviser, who headed the Vice-Presidential selection process, was operating on two not necessarily contradictory principles: that Mondale's best, and perhaps only, hope of winning the election was to do something dramatic, something that changed the equation (this was the "roll the dice" theory); and that the time had come to break down another barrier, that doing something new would be both good politics and right. A corollary of the latter theory was that by choosing a woman or member of a minority as his running mate Mondale could increase the participation of an important part of the base of the Democratic Party—and perhaps also attract some of Gary Hart's constituency, and independents.

Mondale has had a bad few weeks—some of it his own and his campaign's doing and some of it inflicted on him by others, Jesse

Jackson in particular. A Gallup poll published on July 1st showed Mondale losing to Reagan by nineteen points—a figure that shook and perplexed the Mondale campaign. A New York *Times*/CBS poll published at the same time showed Reagan beating Mondale by fifteen points. Polls published closer to Convention time showed the gap as narrower, but by now Democrats were very discouraged, and had begun to worry about what would happen not just at the top of the ticket but in elections down the line. What should have been a period of consolidation (and rest) for Mondale, after he claimed the nomination, on June 6th, was instead a time of having to deal with one problem after another, and once again he lost one of the most precious commodities in an election: time. Many of the problems were worked out—deals were made with Hart and Jackson on questions about credentials, the delegate-selection rules, and the platform, thus getting out of the way things that could have caused serious problems here this week. But Hart still hasn't given up on the nomination, and Jackson, who has swung from conciliatory to angry moods with, it seems, increasing rapidity, is making new demands. Neither of Mondale's remaining opponents is prepared to go gently. To add to the problems, Mondale and his organization managed to set off a howling uproar this weekend by their now abortive move to replace Charles Manatt as the chairman of the Democratic National Committee with Bert Lance, Jimmy Carter's director of the Office of Management and Budget, who had to leave the government over charges of mismanagement of his two Georgia banks. (He was later indicted on thirty-three counts of bank fraud and conspiracy. The judge dismissed twenty-one of the counts, the jury acquitted Lance of nine of them, and on three counts it deadlocked.) The Manatt-Lance episode was magnified by the fact that the thousands of politicians, journalists, delegates, campaign strategists, lobbyists, and hangers-on gathering here had little else to talk about this weekend—the nomination is settled, whether or not Hart accepts that fact, and the Vice-Presidential nominee has been selected—and because the hotel lobbies and cocktail parties amplify whatever is going on. The episode raised questions about the Mondale campaign organization which many people found disturbing, and put a damper on the excitement over Ferraro. There was a resentment that the Mondale campaign, which had already disappointed many Democrats in the course of the year, wouldn't let them enjoy their newfound happiness for more than a couple of days.

The process that led to Mondale's choosing of Geraldine Ferraro, a three-term member of Congress from Queens, as his running mate was circuitous and controversial, and contained a number of side excursions and dead ends. The exact mix of boldness, narrowed options, political insight, accommodation, and shrewdness that went into the decision can never be known—perhaps even to the key participants. But it is clear that from the beginning there was a strong school of thought within the Mondale camp that something unconventional should be done, and that at the end Ferraro fit more neatly the case Mondale wanted to take to the country than almost anyone understood—except perhaps Mondale himself. Along the way, others were considered—or appeared to be considered—as Mondale conducted a series of interviews at his home in North Oaks, Minnesota, just outside St. Paul. The idea of going to Minnesota was to get Mondale out of his Washington setting and his conservative suits, but the interviewing process was criticized by many as too closely resembling Carter's in 1976, when prospective candidates were invited to Plains, Georgia. Anything that reminds of Carter is, apparently, out. At least one adviser warned that this would happen, and now some Mondale aides say they would have done things somewhat differently. The process did, however, accomplish the purpose of helping Mondale continue to close down the nomination fight.

Lloyd Bentsen, a moderate Texas senator, wanted the Vice-Presidential slot badly, and had lobbied for it, and was seen by his supporters, who were outside the Mondale camp, as providing the best hope of the ticket's carrying Texas, and perhaps some other Southern states. But there were always some strong arguments against Bentsen's selection: it would have been seen as the most conventional of politics; while Bentsen is an able senator, he is not a very compelling speaker, and his appeal outside Texas was questionable—it was not even clear that he could provide the difference in Texas; and Bentsen and Mondale differ on key issues, such as the nuclear freeze, the B-1 bomber, and the MX, which could make things a bit awkward in a general election.

Dale Bumpers, a senator from Arkansas, is an eloquent speaker whose populist politics are more in line with Mondale's, and who had been seen by many as someone who could at once enliven the ticket and attract votes in the south and also gain the support of some of Hart's constituency. But Bumpers had misgivings about running—his family argued that he, too, would seem a conventional choice, and that it would make him an establishment candidate if he wanted to run in 1988. (Bumpers had considered running this year and then pulled back, figuring that Mondale's head start was too formidable.) Such have been the dynamics of this year that Bumpers, whom many people saw earlier in the year as the candidate likely to add the most pizzazz to the Mondale ticket, was now viewed as a "conventional" choice. By now, there was so much outside pressure on Mondale to choose a woman, to do something "bold," that the choice of a white male "ticket balancer" (Bumpers represented a different region, if not a different set of politics), however estimable the person, was taking on the aspect of the sort of old-hat politics Mondale was already identified with. Mondale seemed more interested in Bumpers than did the people around him. The consideration of Bumpers ended on a sour note. Early in the process, Bumpers told Reilly that he did not want to meet with Mondale in North Oaks or, later, in Washington until he had definitely made up his mind that he wanted to be on the ticket. (He was not alone in not wanting to be seen publicly as a supplicant for the job.) Then, in late June, when Reilly called to set up a meeting in Washington, Bumpers told him that he had made his decision and wanted his name removed from the list of those being considered. Reilly, and then Mondale, asked Bumpers that he not let it be known he had done this—it would not look good for Mondale to be seen as being rejected by a number of possible running mates—and Bumpers agreed. Subsequent news reports coming out of North Oaks describing Bumpers, whose prospects were still ostensibly alive, as playing Hamlet irritated Bumpers to the point where, on July 10th, he phoned Mondale and issued a statement saying he had asked that his name be taken out of consideration.

Governor Mario Cuomo, of New York, had taken his name out of consideration at the outset, saying that he had to keep his pledge, made while running for the governorship in 1982, that he would serve out a full four-year term. Not to have done so would have painted Cuomo as just "another politician." There was a school of thought, shared by some who know Cuomo well and also

by some of those high in the Mondale camp, that Cuomo might
have yielded to an argument by Mondale that his presence on the
ticket offered the best possible chance to beat Reagan. (Some of
Reagan's advisers most feared Cuomo's presence on the ticket.)
Mondale invited Cuomo to come to North Oaks to talk about the
Convention keynote speech, which Cuomo was to make, and a trip
was scheduled, but Cuomo decided he didn't want to give any
appearance of undergoing a Vice-Presidential interview, so he and
Mondale agreed to meet in Boston, where Mondale was to attend
a fund-raiser on July 5th. By this time, according to people close
to these events, the Mondale people were taking increasingly seriously the idea that Cuomo would not run for Vice-President,
were having mixed feelings about pursuing him, and were not
eager to give him another opportunity to turn down an invitation,
with the good possibility that his people would let the world know
that this had happened. At the Boston meeting, when Cuomo
made it clear he was still not interested, Mondale did not choose to
press the case.

Then, of course, there was Hart. To have chosen Hart would
have put Mondale in the position of selecting someone with whom
he would not, to say the least, feel compatible—the smiles and
handshakes after the primaries were over notwithstanding. It
seems clear that Mondale had the very misgivings about Hart's
steadiness which he had raised during the nomination contest.
Moreover, even Hart recognized, as he said publicly, that he is "not
particularly good at carrying out other people's policies and orders." To have chosen Hart would also have been conventional
politics: awarding the second slot to whoever came in second. But
Hart had to be considered, and he was considered, because he did
have a constituency, and because while both the public and private
polls available to the Mondale campaign were very inconclusive
about the effect of choosing a woman, they did suggest that Hart
would add strength to the ticket. While "name recognition" undoubtedly had something to do with this, Mondale was receiving
advice from several, and sometimes surprising, political quarters
that Hart would help him most. Hart, though ambivalent, according to the people around him, had concluded that he wanted the
Vice-Presidential nomination, and came to believe that he would
get it. In late June, Reilly met secretly with Hart in Washington to
see if he wanted to be considered, and Hart indicated that he did,

with certain conditions. But, whatever the strength of his case—
and from the way the Mondale people talked privately it was never
overwhelming—his behavior during the period between the primaries and the Convention did not help him. He was still saying
that he would be the nominee; he could not resist taking some
shots at Mondale. (In early July, he said that Mondale's Vice-Presidential selection process had the appearance of "pandering.")
And there were renewed questions about the stability of his private life. (Some Republican strategists were gleeful over the prospect of running against Hart.) Hart's actions during this period
reinforced questions about how steady a candidate he would be,
and how well he would hold up over time. (Republican strategists
did not believe he would wear well.)

Two of the visitors to North Oaks seem to have been invited as a
courtesy. One, Wilson Goode, the mayor of Philadelphia and a
black, had gone on the line for Mondale in the face of a tidal wave
of support for Jackson in his city. But Goode has been mayor of
Philadelphia only since January. Martha Layne Collins, as governor of Kentucky, is the highest Democratic woman officeholder in
the country, and is to serve as chair of the Convention; but, among
other things, she is not particularly popular among feminist
groups, and was not seriously under consideration. Tom Bradley,
the black mayor of Los Angeles, was under serious consideration
for some time; Mondale and his aides like Bradley, who backed
Mondale, very much, and he had some strong support among
Mondale's advisers. But Bradley is sixty-six, and there was a question of how much energy he would add to the ticket; moreover, he
had lost, though narrowly, a race for the governorship of California in 1982. And there was the larger question of whether the
country was ready for a black on the ticket. Ironically, Jesse Jackson's candidacy had complicated this question.

In the end, the four finalists were Dianne Feinstein, the mayor
of San Francisco; Henry Cisneros, the mayor of San Antonio;
Michael Dukakis, the governor of Massachusetts; and Ferraro.
And toward the end Ferraro's prospects were not especially bright.
Feinstein, whom Mondale had known for a long time, made a
strong impression on him during his interview with her in North
Oaks and during her session with the press which followed.
Cisneros, who had backed Mondale, is one of the most attractive
and promising young politicians in the country, and impressed

Reilly and James Johnson, Mondale's campaign chairman, in a secret two-hour session they had with him in Chicago a week before he was to meet with Mondale in Minnesota, and his interview with Mondale was said to have gone quite well. Mondale deliberately interviewed Cisneros on the Fourth of July, as a way of making a statement. But Cisneros, who has two master's degrees, and a doctorate in public administration, and served in Washington as a White House Fellow, and also on the Kissinger Commission on Central America, is only thirty-seven, and has been mayor—albeit an extremely popular one—for only three years. (He won reelection in 1983 with ninety-four per cent of the vote.) One of Mondale's advisers believes that mayors are not yet seen to have the kind of training that fits them for the Presidency or Vice-Presidency. And it would have been hard to argue that Cisneros was any more qualified than Feinstein or Ferraro. Dukakis was on the final list in case the others had to be eliminated, and because Mondale thinks highly of him. Politically, he represents the newer class of modern politician who might appeal to the Hart constituency (he can talk about high tech with the best of them); personally, he had forged the kind of bond with Mondale this year that only politicians understand. Dukakis, who had endorsed Mondale, gave him unstinting moral and political support—at some risk to himself—in the gloom of the post–New Hampshire period, while Maine and Vermont went for Hart as well, and the Mondale campaign seemed on the verge of collapse. During those days, Mondale was finding it harder to get his calls returned. And Dukakis's willingness to stand by as a possible running mate, with the world knowing it, took a certain gallantry.

Meanwhile, as the Vice-Presidential selection process went on, the pressure from women activists for a woman on the ticket was increasing, and this complicated Mondale's situation. The idea got on the national agenda at a convention of the National Organization for Women in October, 1983, at which all the Democratic candidates for the nomination except Reubin Askew appeared and pledged to consider putting a woman on the ticket. At the time, this seemed to be an act more of necessity than of conviction. In the course of the campaign, only Jesse Jackson promised that he would do so. This spring, House Speaker Thomas P. O'Neill, of all people—O'Neill is much put down as a hopelessly old-school pol—publicly endorsed Ferraro. O'Neill had already told Mondale that he thought his only two choices were Hart or a woman, and that, of the women, Ferraro, whom O'Neill had promoted for various Party roles in the House, was the best. O'Neill says that he described Ferraro to Mondale as "spunky and game"; he was impressed that she had defeated the Democratic organization in her district; and he felt she might help bring back blue-collar voters. I asked O'Neill recently what led him to the view that a woman should be chosen. "It was time for an innovative move," he replied.

The idea of a woman on the ticket developed a backing of unexpected breadth—especially in the last few weeks. In part, Mondale allowed this to happen by his protracted search for a running mate, and by his encouraging the idea that he might indeed pick a woman. His aides now say that he was deliberately doing this, because he was serious about the possibility of making an unconventional choice. Mondale was said by several people to have been irritated by the action of NOW on July 1st, when it adopted a resolution saying that if the Democratic nominee did not name a woman to the ticket one would be nominated from the floor. The irritation stemmed mainly from the fact that if Mondale went ahead and selected a woman this would be seen by many as capitulation to pressure. Nearly half the delegates at the Convention would be women, and a women's caucus planned to meet every morning of the Convention. At the time, the Mondale people said privately that they believed they could win such a fight if they selected the right male candidate. They believed that Hart and Cuomo had sufficient support from women for them to prevail, and that it would be difficult for the women to put up a fight against a black or a Hispanic. Then, on July 4th, Mondale met in Minnesota with a group of women activists and elected officials who back him, and got from them an assurance that they would support whomever he selected. However, in the meeting some of the elected officials argued that their own candidacies had attracted votes from beyond the traditional Democratic base. And the feminist writer Betty Friedan, a longtime friend of Mondale's, made an argument that Mondale and his advisers referred to often in subsequent days. During Mondale's entire life in politics, she pointed out, he had been trying to get across with words that he stood for the expanding of opportunities. "Why don't you try showing it in a picture?" Friedan asked. And Mondale's wife, Joan, had been advocating the choice of a woman.

Ferraro's first meeting with Mondale in Minnesota, about the platform, on June 16th, had not gone particularly well, according to several accounts; nor had Mondale's lieutenants been especially impressed with her performance as the chairman of the platform committee. Her interest, they said, was in moving the meeting along, but she showed little interest in or understanding of the substantive nuances of what was going on. Ferraro further irritated Mondale's aides by saying, in an appearance before the National Press Club, in Washington, in late June, that she would be pleased if her name were put in nomination for Vice-President from the Convention floor. (She later backed away from this.) Her press conference after she met with Mondale about the Vice-Presidency, on July 2nd, was not without its problems, either. (When Mondale said that he was looking for "the best possible person" to run with him, Ferraro said, "If it were not done looking at how you get the most electoral votes, I would be not only amazed, I would be nonsupportive.") Some high Mondale aides worried that Ferraro was accident-prone, and were also annoyed by her obvious lobbying for the job. But Mondale apparently did not take these missteps as seriously as his advisers did, and recalled that he'd been rather determined to be selected by Jimmy Carter. Still, by the following weekend, only a few days before he selected Ferraro, Mondale seemed to some of those around him to be most interested in Feinstein. According to all accounts, however, Mondale didn't tip his hand during the course of the considerations. He would talk with his aides for hours about the possibilities of one person, and they would think he was leaning that way, and then in the next session his mind was on someone else. According to Mondale's aides, when Mondale has the time to make a decision he takes the time, floats around in there, makes arguments and counterarguments. Several days before he selected Ferraro, it was clear to some around Mondale that he was leaning in the direction of selecting a woman, and felt that the meeting with his women supporters on July 4th had mitigated the pressure of NOW's action. And some think that he was definitely leaning toward Feinstein on the weekend before Ferraro was chosen. High officials in his campaign were indicating to reporters that Ferraro's chances seemed slight. In the next few days, though, misgivings about Feinstein's presence on the ticket grew, and as Mondale thought more about how the selection of the running mate fit with the campaign he intended to wage, the more Ferraro seemed to be the right choice.

Mondale wanted to stress middle-class values and try to reach blue-collar votes. Feinstein was well-to-do, three times married (one husband had died), Jewish, and from an exotic city. Ferraro, though financially comfortable now, is a Catholic and had shown that she knew how to attract the blue-collar voters. And her story exemplifies things that Mondale wanted to emphasize—she was the child of an immigrant father who had died when she was quite young; she had grown up poor; she had been a housewife, raised three children, been married to the same man, John Zaccaro, for twenty-four years, and worked her way up. Mondale had consulted with others and satisfied himself that Ferraro was smart and could learn quickly, and that she had a grasp of substance once she had been briefed. By this time, through his work on his acceptance speech, Mondale knew that one of his themes was going to be opening doors, expanding opportunity, letting people with merit and discipline rise to the top. As one of his advisers says, "How could he pass up an opportunity to show that philosophy and belief and make a statement about it through his Vice-Presidential choice?" Mondale, being—at least most of the time—an astute politician, may have seen things in Ferraro's personality as well which helped him make the choice. She comes across as warm, direct, real, spunky, and tough, though feminine. Her energy had the possibility of energizing the voters. One interesting point is that Mondale himself looks better when he is standing beside her: this was clear from the moment he announced her selection, before a cheering crowd at the Minnesota State Legislature, in St. Paul, on Thursday. He looks courtly, warmer, more human—and, in fact, more manly. (Early in the selection process, Mondale's press secretary, Maxine Isaacs, pointed out in a staff meeting that in the press conferences following a Vice-Presidential interview Mondale looked his best when he stood next to a woman.) Another consideration was that since Mondale was planning to make the question of who has a better grasp of how to deal with the future an issue against Reagan, his selection of a running mate should reflect a moving into the future, a sense of departure. And the choice of a woman gave him a better chance, it was believed, of reaching younger voters and independents.

Mondale's aides realized that the choice of Ferraro was high risk, but some of them had urged a high-risk strategy all along. For the moment, the choice of Ferraro seems to be paying off.

(The Mondale people had considered all along announcing the choice before the Convention—another break with precedent—so as to keep control of the proceedings here, and not have the Convention dominated by Vice-Presidential speculation, rumors, and still more pressures. The one exception might have been if they had chosen a white male. One of Mondale's highest aides said to me not long ago, "In that case, we'll announce on the last morning of the Convention and hit our whip system like the Normandy beaches.") In a stroke, Mondale reduced, at least, the assumption that he is incapable of bold action—though boldness in a President is not always a good thing; and he reduced interest in Hart and Jackson at this Convention. Nevertheless, even some of Ferraro's strongest supporters here, among people who have served with her in the House, are aware that there is a risk, and worry about Ferraro's tendency to speak too quickly at times. Friday, in Minnesota, she made an ill-advised comment questioning Reagan's Christianity in light of his policies: "The President walks around calling himself a good Christian, but I don't for one minute believe it, because the policies are so terribly unfair." It was clear what she was getting at, but she got at it maladroitly. (The Reagan Administration itself seems a bit thrown by the Ferraro choice. On Friday, Reagan suggested that the selection represented "tokenism" and "cynical symbolism.") A young congressman who likes Ferraro very much and is pleased she was chosen said to me yesterday, "If Gerry flops, we're sunk."

The Lance episode has been settled, at least for now—in a way that is less than wonderful for Mondale. As a result of the furor it touched off, Manatt is to stay on as Party chairman, though Michael Berman, a longtime and close aide to Mondale, who has handled all manner of difficult things for him, will be installed to essentially run the place. Berman has already been installed at the Mondale campaign headquarters to administer the general-election effort. Though the result of the Lance-Manatt business presents a picture of a candidate who can't even get rid of his Party chairman, the Mondale people wanted to recover as quickly as possible from their mistake, and get the matter behind them before the Convention opened. Besides, various groups were laying claim to the job—among them black women, who argued to the Mondale people that white women had received something, and they should, too—and the path of least resistance was simply to leave the job with Manatt. A new role was concocted for Lance— that of a "general chairman," who would coordinate the Mondale campaign with the senatorial, House, and gubernatorial cam- paigns. This improvisation, if it lasts—about which there is some question—will take some working out.

The Mondale campaign's misjudgment seems to have stemmed from the fact that, despite Lance's earlier troubles, he had under- gone a resurrection and is now chairman of the Georgia Party and a major figure in Southern politics. For some time, Lance had been playing a public role in the Mondale effort, and, according to the Mondale people, no one had suggested to them that this was not a good idea. Moreover, Mondale was grateful to Lance: he had helped save his candidacy in the Southern primaries on March 13th, and had been helpful in the negotiations with Jackson. The major champions of replacing Manatt with Lance were Mondale himself and Johnson, and Bob Beckel, the Mondale campaign manager, is said to have favored the move as well. A few other people in the Mondale campaign knew about the possible move, but the matter does not appear to have been the subject of lengthy or widespread discussions within the Mondale camp, and was not discussed outside it at all. (Some key people, such as Lane Kirkland, the president of the A.F.L.-C.I.O., had told Mondale that it was his prerogative to do what he would about the chair- manship of the Party, and the Mondale people took this to mean that they had a free hand.) A couple of people within the Mondale campaign did raise objections to naming Lance, saying that this would cause problems. Mondale and Johnson listened to them and decided that they were wrong. Mondale himself argued that he believed that anyone who had been cleared of charges should be considered cleared. So while these people knew there would be some concern about giving Lance such a prominent role, they grossly underestimated its extent. As it turned out, Lance as chair- man of the Georgia Party is one thing, as chairman of the National Committee is quite another. Jimmy Carter is to speak here tomor- row night, but Carter is still considered "baggage" for Mondale as it is, and no further reminders are wanted; moreover, Lance did have to leave office under a cloud, and the Democrats had wanted to use "the sleaze factor"—the number of Reagan Administration figures who have had to resign for misdeeds or, like Edwin Meese, are under investigation—against the Republicans in the fall. The reaction here is being fed in part by the fact that the management of the Mondale campaign is a very small group, which many people, both inside and outside the campaign, find it hard to get through to, and resentment has been building up over the course of the year. A mistake such as this—and the Mondale people now know it was a mistake—provides an opportunity for the frustration to spill out into the open, with many ready listeners at hand.

Manatt is not a particularly popular figure within the Party—something about his personality irritates many Democrats—and the Mondale people had felt for some time that he had not done a good job. They were annoyed with Manatt for his failure to put through a rules change earlier in the year which would have assuaged one of Jackson's concerns—though there was good reason for not making such a change at that point, and, if it had gone through, Mondale might have had a still harder time sewing up the nomination. Manatt has been widely criticized for failing to raise more money for the Party—a telethon he staged last year against the advice of a number of people, including even Frank Fahrenkopf, the chairman of the Republican National Committee, landed the Party a debt of over three million dollars, and the Party now has a debt of over five million. Manatt did begin to put the D.N.C.'s fund-raising efforts on a broader base—aiming, as the Republicans began to do years ago, at smaller contributions through direct mail. But still the Democrats are far behind the Republicans in fund-raising this year, and the Republicans can be expected, through the various routes available, to put far more money into the election than the $40.4 million each Presidential campaign will receive from the federal government—perhaps twice as much. Even Manatt's defenders say that he has attracted a poor staff (with the major exception of Ann Lewis, the D.N.C.'s political director).

The failure of the Mondale people to foresee the consequences of their action is laid to the fact that the Mondale camp—or some of it—is now sequestered at Lake Tahoe, where Mondale and Ferraro and their entourages are preparing for the coming week, but the decision to name Lance was made before Mondale went to Lake Tahoe. Johnson had flown to Atlanta last Monday for a long talk with Lance about it. Though the final decision about the Vice-Presidency hadn't been made, it was clear that it would not be someone from the Southern states, or Bentsen (whom Lance had championed), and the Mondale people wanted to mollify the South. (Johnson at one point had the idea of installing a woman as chairman of the National Committee if one wasn't chosen as Mondale's running mate.) Among the things they failed to see were that Lance is not looked to as a leader by a number of Southern politicians (Lance appeared to lead the Mondale campaign to believe that his standing among them was higher than it was); that Democrats at large were not as accustomed to Lance as they were; that Manatt, though not widely popular, has a following among the financial people who put up large sums of money to hold the Convention here, where Manatt wanted it (such money does not count as a contribution to the Party or a candidate and therefore is outside the limits on donations), and who have already come to town, prepared to enjoy themselves; that Manatt has been active within the Democratic Party's organization since his college days, and has allies within that group; that a number of people found it rude to oust the chairman of the Party on the eve of the Convention—in his home state, no less. (Manatt is from Los Angeles.)

The communications between the Mondale high command in San Francisco and the one in Lake Tahoe had to do with convincing the group at Tahoe, which included Johnson and Mondale, that the Lance decision simply wouldn't sit with the Party, that another solution had to be found. Yesterday morning, Beckel and Tom Donilon, a deputy campaign manager, who is in charge of the political management of this Convention, informed the campaign high command at Lake Tahoe that the reaction to the proposed Lance move was very bad. In addition, Lane Kirkland and O'Neill telephoned Lake Tahoe to register their unhappiness with the move, as did Representative Tony Coelho, Democrat of California and the chairman of the Democratic Congressional Campaign Committee and a friend of Manatt's. A solution was found, but Johnson, who very rarely admits to being shaken, is, according to his friends, shaken.

The Mondale campaign had put considerable effort into making this a smooth Convention in the past few weeks. Through concurrent negotiations with the Jackson forces and the Hart forces, a number of deals were struck. In the deliberations over the platform, which took place in Washington in late June, the Mondale forces, though they had the votes to dominate the platform proceedings, used the exercise to try to achieve "unity" before the Convention. Whereas the Carter forces in 1980 had turned back just about everything proposed by the forces representing Edward Kennedy, who carried his campaign into the Convention and posed a large number of platform fights there, the Mondale forces this year negotiated on everything possible, with the exception of those proposals so controversial that it was impossible to accept them in any form. Therefore, a good bit of Hart language about "the future" and a number of his "new ideas" were incorporated, but specific Hart proposals and wording were avoided, so as to obviate any win/loss scorecard. Individual training accounts made it into the platform by way of other wording, and Hart's proposal for a freeze on production of plutonium did, too. Mondale's positions were already reflected in the staff draft, which also reflected the Party's wish that this year's platform not contain a "laundry list" of requests, or price tags—so as to make it less vulnerable to Republican charges of "big spending." Such Mondale proposals as favoring "domestic content" in the manufacturing of automobiles are in the platform, but under more generalized terms. The Hart people wanted a denunciation of protectionism—one of Hart's issues against Mondale in the campaign—and after negotiations that lasted until 4 A.M. wording was found that both sides could agree on.

The Jackson forces were accommodated by the inclusion of wording that in effect criticized labor for its record on affirmative action, and by incorporating as often as possible Jackson's draft language that was more descriptive about the need for jobs, justice, aid to cities, and the like. A Jackson proposal favoring an independent state for the Palestinians was, of course, rejected outright. A Hart proposal calling for restrictions on the use of force in the Persian Gulf was rejected by the Mondale camp on the ground that it was code for what had been a major Mondale-Hart argument throughout the primaries, and also on the substantive ground that the platform should not spell out conditions for a President's use of force. The Hart people had sufficient votes to bring a minority report on this to the floor this week. Though the platform says that the United States should "move toward the adoption of" a policy of no first use of nuclear weapons in Europe, in connection with "achieving a balance of conventional forces," Jackson and some peace activists filed a minority report that simply calls for adoption of a no-first-use policy. Mondale argued during the primaries that the government should be ambiguous about this—and a floor fight is to occur. Jackson has also filed a minority report calling for an absolute reduction in military spending; the platform itself is critical of the Reagan management of defense, and calls for a number of changes, but does not advocate the cancellation of specific weapons systems or stipulate an acceptable level of growth in defense spending. And Jackson has filed a minority report that advocates permitting the use of quotas in redressing racial imbalances in employment. The majority report rejects quotas. Jackson won the votes to bring these issues to the floor because a sufficient number of Mondale and Hart platform-committee members agreed with his position on them, and the Mondale aides in charge of the platform proceedings felt they could ask—as they did—their delegates to vote against their own wishes only so many times. Another Jackson minority report calls for an absolute ban on runoff primaries, rather than, as the platform proposes, only those which are found to be discriminatory; as part of the deal that was worked out with Jackson, the Mondale people gave him enough votes to bring the minority report on runoff primaries to the Convention floor. But the Mondale people are now continuing a set of negotiations that began in Washington to try to reduce still further the number of platform fights this week. Beckel, who has maintained contact with Jackson all year, has told the Jackson forces that Mondale cannot compromise on the runoff primaries (to do so would alienate many of his Southern supporters) or the military budget, but the Mondale campaign would like to find a compromise on the no-first-use and quotas issues. The Jackson forces had begun to compromise on these two items, but then demanded that they be coupled with compromises on the other two. "This comes to me as no surprise," Beckel said to me wearily Friday evening. Also as part of the deal struck with Jackson, the Mondale people have allotted him a slot for a prime-time speech on Tuesday night and pledged to have his complaints about the nomination rules taken up by a new "Fairness Commission," to make changes in the Party rules for the future. In exchange for the latter, Jackson agreed not to bring up the question of the rules at the Convention.

The Fairness Commission was also part of a deal with Hart, but Hart and Jackson were after slightly different things, and there was a brief crisis until this was worked out, in the course of a breakfast meeting that Mondale and Hart had in New York on June 26th—their first meeting after the primaries. Among the concessions Mondale made was to agree to urge the commission to lower the "threshold" of the number of votes a candidate would need to receive any delegates (the "threshold" was a major source of Jackson's complaints), and to reduce by about half the number of "superdelegates"—elected and Party officials—who would attend the next Convention. Mondale was reluctant to give on the issue of superdelegates, but finally did so in order to head off other trouble. (Members of Congress, and other elected officials, who had no idea that this change was being discussed, were not happy.) The Hart people, true to form, were undermining each other during these negotiations. There are good arguments for the presence of the superdelegates, who account for fourteen per cent of the delegates this year: it reattaches the elected officials to the Party and its platform; the superdelegates, being professional politicians, know how to negotiate; and they can provide a stabilizing force at the Convention. What irritated the Hart and Jackson forces was that such a large proportion of the superdelegates endorsed Mondale, many of them before the nomination contest had even begun, and some of them, later, even though Hart had carried their state. But one of the points of the superdelegates was to have some professional politicians decide what they thought was best for the Party. (Kennedy, who had flown to Minnesota June 24th to endorse Mondale the following day, got involved in the last-minute negotiations, along with some dissident members of the Hart campaign; and Kennedy's aides, for reasons of their own, exaggerated Kennedy's role in working out the final agreement between Hart and Mondale. In fact, the meeting between Mondale and Hart had been tentatively set long before Kennedy got involved, and some of Kennedy's contribution had to be rescinded when Jackson objected.) What Mondale got from Hart was an agreement not to join Jackson in a challenge of the rules of this year's nomination contest at the Convention—the Hart people had indicated that they might join Jackson in demanding that this year's rules be changed to require proportional representation— and to drop challenges of the seating of what Hart had termed "tainted delegates." (The agreements with Hart and Jackson were both put in writing.) There was always some evidence that Hart, the Hart campaign, or some part of it, was feinting about the superdelegates, for to have challenged them would have caused an unholy mess at the Convention—and perhaps destroyed Hart's future in the Democratic Party. Also, the Hart people knew that they would lose such a challenge. The Hart campaign is still riven, and some of Hart's advisers were urging some drastic moves, but the prevailing view was that the best course for Hart would be to get what he could from Mondale on the platform and on rules governing future nomination contests—and avoid tearing the Party apart at the Convention.

Inevitably, monumental as these strides toward unity were, they were not enough. Now the Jackson people are saying that Jackson needs a "victory" to take out of the Convention, so that he can support the ticket wholeheartedly—though there is little left to give him. The problem is that Jackson—contrary to the advice of some—didn't set aside an issue, such as jobs, on which it would not be difficult to give him a victory here; the Jackson campaign, perhaps understandably, tends to think even less than others in terms of long-range strategy. Jackson, being extra-political, does not think in political terms. A not unfriendly political practitioner here describes the Jackson campaign as "a rolling road show." There have been endless negotiations with the Jackson people about who is to speak when, how many speakers for Jackson's positions there will be, and other demands for a "victory" here. When previous concessions were pointed out to them, they replied that that was then, that the Convention is a thing unto itself. And Hart still can't quite accept the idea that he will not be nominated: he is said to believe firmly that he could defeat Reagan and that Mondale cannot. So his aides are clutching at straws—the Lance matter, for one—and spreading rumors about "erosion" of Mondale delegates. At a reception this evening—there is quite a bit of social activity going on around the Convention (one Democratic official said it reminded her more of the Kentucky Derby than of a political gathering)—Oliver Henkel, Hart's campaign manager, said to me that the Hart campaign was keeping track of three hundred "soft" Mondale delegates. There appear to be few, if any, people around Hart who will tell him that it's over. Some encourage the view that "something" might still happen. Hart, seeming at a loss as to just how to deal with the period between the primaries and the Convention—a period when technically, of course, the nomination contest is not over—made a few forays to speak to supporters, whose enthusiastic response simply reinforced his thinking that he should be the nominee. This morning, at a meeting with his staff members in the Westin St. Francis Hotel, where he is staying, he gave a talk that, though at times it sounded like a valedictory, kept lapsing back into a campaign speech ("I intend to be the nominee of this Party and the next President of the United States")—perhaps in part out of habit, perhaps because, having stayed in the race, Hart at this point can find no graceful way out. Afterward, John McEvoy, a key adviser to Hart, said to me that what this is all about is a carrying out of what he had told me shortly before the final primaries—that campaigns go on until there's no hope or no money. Now McEvoy said, "He's out of money, but he's not out of hope." He also said that one of the things that Hart wants to do here is talk with younger members of the Party about consolidating the gains he has made in opening up the Party, changing its rules. "He wants to keep the sea from closing behind him," McEvoy said. Thus, the struggle over control of the Party will continue throughout and after this Convention.

Mondale gave up a lot in order to buy short-term peace. I asked one of Mondale's aides if he had any concern whether—looking into an admittedly hypothetical future—if Mondale won the Presidency the rules would have been changed so as to make him more vulnerable to a renomination challenge. He shrugged and said, "We're not worrying about that now." The Hart people have redefined the minority platform report about the use of force in the Persian Gulf into one that covers Central America as well—thus attracting more votes for it—and the combined forces of Hart and Jackson, plus some others, threaten to defeat Mondale on this when the platform comes up on Tuesday. Yesterday, Tom Donilon told the press here that in terms of those delegates who had made public commitments Mondale had 2,107.05 delegates; Hart, 1,230.75; Jackson, 386.2; George McGovern, 6; John Glenn, 1; Harold Washington, 36; and Uncommitted, 166. He said that Mondale had private commitments from almost half the uncommitted delegates. (The .05 of a delegate is arrived at when delegations divide up votes to satisfy various factions.) But the Mondale people don't just want to win the nomination; they want a peaceful Convention.

Jackson arrived here yesterday sounding fairly conciliatory, but he has been so mercurial of late that no one knows what to expect from day to day. Some liberal members of Congress already here say that Jackson's campaign has so alienated Jews that the situation is probably beyond repair, and has also begun to alienate white Protestants. There is a distinct worry about this inside the Mondale camp, which has been internally divided over how to deal with Jackson. The dominant opinion is that it must try to deal with him, frustrating and wearing as the exercise has come to be, because of his potential for getting black voters registered and to the polls, particularly in some Deep South states that the Mondale strategists believe they have a chance of winning. The pattern of Jackson's behavior over the past few weeks suggests, among other things, that he dislikes being out of the news, and there is some concern within the Mondale camp that his being upstaged by Ferraro will make him more difficult in the coming days. They are hoping that he will use his moment on Tuesday night, when he makes his speech—one of those moments in politics which can define or redefine things—to try to repair some of the strains.

Jackson's mood swings in recent weeks nearly drove the Mondale camp, and Mondale himself, to distraction. When Louis Farrakhan, the leader of a Black Muslim group, was quoted in the papers in late June as having said in a Sunday speech in Chicago to his Nation of Islam followers that "the presence of a state called Israel is an outlaw act," that its establishment was brought about by "a criminal conspiracy," and that Judaism is a "gutter religion," some Jewish leaders demanded that Mondale dissociate himself from Jackson. (There was later some dispute as to whether Farrakhan had called Judaism a "gutter" religion or a "dirty" religion—not that it made any difference.) Mondale denounced Farrakhan's statement as "venomous, bigoted, and obscene," and said that Jackson should "repudiate" Farrakhan's support, but the first reaction of Jackson, who was in Cuba at the time, was to say, on the CBS Morning News, "I don't understand the context of it. I feel no obligation to respond to it." Mondale also came under pressure from others besides Jewish leaders to openly separate himself from Jackson. Mondale, who had always had support from both blacks and Jews, was described as heartsick over the whole affair. So bad had things become that some white Democrats who have been sensitive to civil-rights issues began to say aloud that Mondale would win more white votes than he would lose black votes if he publicly repudiated Jackson. There was talk by some Jewish leaders that Jackson should be barred from speaking at the Convention unless he repudiated Farrakhan. Reagan's reelection strategists saw an opportunity and put out the word to their spokesmen to tie Mondale to Farrakhan, via Jackson. (One Reagan strategist joked to me a few days later, "I don't know how much we're paying Jackson, but it probably isn't enough.") Vice-President George Bush weighed in and denounced Farrakhan and Jackson. Republican strategists say that their polling indicates an increase in Jewish support of Reagan over 1980—a development that can help in such swing states as New York, New Jersey, and Illinois.

Finally, on Thursday, June 28th, Jackson's campaign put out a statement in Jackson's name (Jackson was still in Cuba) saying that Farrakhan's recent comments were "reprehensible and morally indefensible" and "have no place in my own thinking or in this campaign." A large number of people, including Beckel, had a hand in convincing the Jackson campaign that Jackson had to be convinced that such a statement was essential. Mondale, not wishing to seem too pleased, called Jackson's statement "a hopeful step." Jackson's trip itself—to Panama, Nicaragua, El Salvador, and Cuba—stirred a lot of controversy, because, among other things, it was marked by Jackson statements denouncing American policy, in a breach of the rules of the game, and reflected his radical views about the Third World. (Similarly, on a trip to Mexico in late May Jackson accused the United States government of "arrogance" that has "led to big-stick diplomacy and military intervention.")

Jackson and some of his advisers often complain that he does not get the proper "respect," but the plain truth is he has done things that would have destroyed a white politician, and some of his statements, and his record, have received fairly light treatment—because he is extra-political. Jackson wants to be taken seriously, but doesn't play by the rules, in large part because he is not a politician. His background is as an activist, as a confrontationalist—making demands, sometimes deliberately outrageous, and then bargaining. Moreover, his candidacy inevitably attracted some radicals, who worked to undermine the more conventional people around him. And the more attention Jackson got, the more he seemed to need. His return from Cuba (with twenty-two Americans who had been held in Cuban prisons, some of them on drug-running charges, and twenty-six Cuban political prisoners in tow) was followed by his suggesting that he should have a voice in the selection of Mondale's Secretaries of State and Defense and his running mate—and that perhaps he himself ought to be Secretary of State. (Few things could have more upset Jews.) He has also announced that he plans to visit South Africa and the Soviet Union before November; while in the Soviet Union, he said, he plans to try to free Andrei Sakharov, the physicist and dissident, who had gone on a hunger strike, and whose whereabouts and physical condition are unknown. Then, after a fairly harmonious meeting on July 3rd with Mondale in Kansas City, where the N.A.A.C.P. was meeting, Jackson turned around and said that his followers should await his "signal" after the Convention before supporting the Democratic nominee. (One thing that clearly bothers Jackson is the Mondale campaign's deliberate attempt to build up its own black allies; there will be more black Mondale delegates than black Jackson delegates at the Convention.) Then he said that Mondale had not considered him as his running mate because of pressure from Jews, and attacked the press for displaying "Aryan arrogance." Mondale, deciding the time had come to speak out, said in an interview aired on the CBS Morning News on July 12th that he couldn't choose Jackson as his running mate "because we have too many differences that are— that I think are basic." He cited differences on the Middle East and defense cuts. Referring to Jackson's saying that Jews had blocked him from being considered for Vice-President, Mondale said, "I disagree with his statements; I think they're unacceptable." (Mondale called Jackson to tell him about the interview before it was aired, and Jackson said that he quite understood.)

As these events unfolded, I spoke with someone who has been close to Jackson, to get his explanation of them. "I can't totally explain the behavior," he said. "So much of the growth in Jesse over the past few months seems to be dissipating. He's letting all his feelings about personal slights take over. After he got pushed to issue the Farrakhan statement, some of the others around him said he was being forced to play in others' yard and that Jewish people were trying to make him a pariah. This is the trickiest time, and we're going to have to effect a landing in a lot of crosswinds." This man said that Jackson was also affected by "the absolute, the battered-out fatigue level." Some of Jackson's friends had argued that because of that fatigue he should not have gone to Central America. Jackson, throughout the year, had nothing close to the support system that Mondale and Hart had, and even they ended the campaign thoroughly exhausted. Jackson's campaign ran on wit, nerve, and adrenaline, with some of the people who travelled with him only feeding his anger. This man said, "The style, which has been Jesse's civil-rights style, put in the pressure cooker of the campaign, puts a new kind of pressure on him. In the civil-rights movement, you could make a demand one day and then change your tactics—you could make day-to-day tactical decisions. And you never got this constant attention. You can't operate that way in a campaign. Jesse feels set upon and his ego is bruised, and people are playing to that. It was inevitable that Mondale would call in Tom Bradley and not Jesse, and Jesse in a rational mood would understand that." He said he didn't believe that Jackson was acting out of any calculated plan but more like "a punch-drunk fighter." He said, "Somebody has to remind him that he is a young man and has a lot of time. The problem is that people who are telling him to be reasonable are seen by others as telling him to give up on his principles."

JULY 16

Late Monday afternoon. The Moscone Center, the Convention site. This Convention hall is underground, which is only one of its oddities. It is so difficult to see the podium from so much of the hall that television screens have been hung about. Some corridors are so crowded that trying to get through them is a traumatic experience. This afternoon, Mondale, at a press conference at the Meridien Hotel, a couple of blocks from the Convention center, where he and his entourage are staying, was asked why he had wanted to get rid of Manatt and then reversed himself. With a big smile, Mondale said, "I will concede this was not handled very well, for two reasons: one, it wasn't, and, two, it's obvious it wasn't." Mondale is to meet tonight with Hart and Jackson, after Cuomo gives the keynote address; the negotiations over the platform are still going on, and Mondale is eager to keep his lines to his opponents open. (Mondale had invited Hart to meet him in Tahoe, but Hart, still a candidate, declined, and the two agreed to meet in San Francisco. Hart and Jackson still have some things they want from Mondale regarding the Fairness Commission.) Others are also pressing Mondale. The Hispanics are saying that they might abstain on the first ballot, because they don't feel Mondale has been strong enough in his denunciation of the Simpson-Mazzoli immigration bill, which has been passed by the House and the Senate and is to go to conference. Hispanic leaders oppose the bill because, they argue, its provision for sanctions against employers who hire illegal aliens will lead to discrimination against Hispanics; moreover, the House-passed version reinstitutes the "guest worker," or *bracero*, program, in which foreign workers can be hired on a temporary basis to do farm labor. (Organized labor, which otherwise supports the Simpson-Mazzoli bill, opposes this provision.) Mondale has many times stated his opposition to the bill, but the Convention offers an opportunity to press him and other Democratic leaders further. (The bill passed the House by only five votes.) Henry Cisneros, who opposes the immigration bill, is trying to mediate between the Mondale people and the Hispanics, and as a result of his new prominence the Hispanics expect him to produce something for them. Labor—having been so prominent in the nomination contest—is playing a quiet role here, but other groups are treating the Convention as a sort of bazaar.

Whether the Democratic Party can ever amount to more than a loose and uneasy collection of its interest groups is still in question, as is whether a Democratic President could ever harness the centrifugal force of these groups sufficiently to govern. The Mondale campaign is equipped here as if for war—it had to be, in case war broke out. It has five trailers, three hundred and fifty floor whips, fourteen "cluster leaders" (people in charge of several delegations) on the floor, who are in contact with fourteen delegate-trackers in one of the trailers. Standing within the space enclosed by the circled trailers—which gives one the feeling of being in a Western—Tom Donilon tells me this afternoon that there is "big trouble" on some of the minority reports on the platform. He is concerned that because what is now the "Central American" minority report is supported by both the Hart and Jackson forces, the Mondale forces might lose on it. Donilon has been negotiating with Hart aides on it, and says that Mondale and Hart will talk about it in their meeting tonight. Now the Hart aides, too, are saying that they have to have a victory for their people, and that they have to give their activists something to organize around. The Convention is not only a bazaar, it is a summer camp where pent-up energies must be given a chance to be released, and where the counsellors must soothe psyches. Winning the election does not seem to be foremost on a lot of people's agendas at the moment.

At shortly after six, Jimmy Carter is addressing the Convention. (This will have him be seen in prime time in the East.) Carter was greeted by the Convention warmly, and there seems to be some real affection for him in the hall—perhaps a feeling that he has been judged too harshly. He and his wife, Rosalynn, have been giving a number of television interviews since they got here yesterday, and it is clear that Mrs. Carter still feels that her husband was treated badly by the Party in 1980. Now Carter is cheered when he talks about human rights and arms control. It is not within his power to lift this Convention by his speech, but a reconciliation of sorts is taking place.

Giving the keynote address is a perilous act. A keynoter is expected to put on a performance, inspire the crowd. Some keynoters have bombed (John Glenn in 1976). Though the Democrats assembled here tonight are in a better frame of mind—thanks to the choice of Ferraro—than they might have been, they still have a morale problem. They lost badly four years ago; Reagan, though vulnerable, eludes them; their all-but-official candidate ran a campaign that left him far more scarred than when he started out; and the last few weeks, until the choice of Ferraro, were not encouraging. Few people give the Democrats a chance of winning this year. Though it is still mathematically possible for Mondale to win, what he and the Party went through during the primaries and afterward has raised the odds against its happening. As a party, the Democrats are still searching for how to define themselves—to the extent that the Democratic Party, given its diversity, can be coherent on such a subject—how to explain what they are for. Even those who admire and like Mondale—and many people here do—are aware that he has liabilities as a candidate. Part of the

Democrats' dilemma is that the economy is undergoing a strong recovery—albeit one produced by Keynesian economics of borrowing and spending rather than by the supply-side theory of enhanced investment which was offered as the rationale for the President's 1981 tax cuts. Unemployment is now at 7.1 per cent, or slightly lower than it was when Reagan took office. (However, business investment is down.) If the realpolitik theory—that people vote according to their economic well-being at the moment—is correct, the Democrats have to get around this by summoning up the memory of the 1982 recession and raising fears of the future effects of the deficit. They have to portray themselves as more fiscally responsible than the Republicans, which will take some adjustment of long-held preconceptions. Each danger sign will be pointed to with alarm: rising interest rates, falling housing starts, decreased exports, a poor farm economy. But though almost everyone who has seriously thought about the matter believes that there will be a heavy price to pay for the deficit, no one is sure when that will become due, and few think that it will occur before the election. So the voters will be presented with two realities, the present one and a potential one, and it is hard to know how concerned they can be made to get about the potential one.

Mondale chose Cuomo as the keynoter because he admires his speaking ability—Cuomo's inaugural address, when he became governor of New York, in January, 1983, made a big impression on Mondale—and because Cuomo's politics, an unembarrassed affirmation of the Party's liberal tradition and an ability to talk about middle-class values, fit with what Mondale wants emphasized here this week. Cuomo had somehow allowed himself to get maneuvered into representing Edward Kennedy's interest in being the keynote speaker, but Mondale insisted to Cuomo that he wanted him to give the speech. Now, in his speech, Cuomo gently draws the audience to him, speaking in quiet tones—no bombast here. He makes the moral case: that while Reagan refers to America as "a shining city on a hill . . . there's another city, another part of the city, the part where some people can't pay their mortgages and most young people can't afford one, where students can't afford the education they need and middle-class parents watch the dreams they hold for their children evaporate." He continues, "In this part of the city, there are more poor than ever, more families in trouble," and he graphically, dramatically—even melodramatically, but in this kind of situation it works, as people want to be moved—describes the life of the poor. "There is despair, Mr. President, in the faces that you don't see, in places that you don't visit in your shining city," he says. Cuomo has appropriated one of Reagan's terms and turned it back on him.

Before Cuomo turned to politics, he was a trial attorney, and he has a lawyer's ability to pose an argument, and a certain deftness with a verbal knife. He has come into high political fashion of late, is considered a "hot property"—a development that obviously pleases him. He gives off the impression of a man who never expected to become charismatic—he runs down his looks in private conversation—and quite enjoys the impact he is making. But while Cuomo is not a classically handsome man, his gentle looks and voice draw the audience to him; he establishes an intimacy with the audience. It is something close to what Reagan does, but with more warmth. With Reagan, one is aware of the acting skills; Cuomo seems to know exactly what he is doing, but, perhaps because the skills are less honed, he seems more natural. Tonight, Cuomo is papal, rabbinical—talking to the audience like a stern but loving papa, making it feel better about itself. His hands are used expressively; he times his pauses carefully. He criticizes Reagan for practicing "social Darwinism"—he had talked about this in his inaugural speech, and Mondale also talked about it in the course of his campaign. Cuomo draws a contrast between what he sees as the difference between the inhumane traditions of the Republican Party and the humane traditions of the Democratic Party—thus trying to give the Party its moorings. He praises the diversity of the Democratic "family"—his referring in his inaugural speech to society as a family whose members must care for one another was one of the things that impressed Mondale, and it has been much imitated. Now Cuomo says, "Here we are at this Convention to remind ourselves where we come from and to claim the future for ourselves and for our children." He continues, "Today, our great Democratic Party, which has saved this nation from depression, from Fascism, from racism, from corruption, is called upon to do it again—this time to save the nation from confusion and division, from the threat of eventual fiscal disaster, and most of all from the fear of a nuclear holocaust."

Now Cuomo instructs on how to confront Reagan. He says, "In order to succeed, we must answer our opponent's polished and appealing rhetoric with a more telling reasonableness and rationality. We must win this case on the merits. We must get the American public to look past the glitter, beyond the showmanship—to reality, to the hard substance of things. And we will do that not so much with speeches that sound good as with speeches that are good and sound. Not so much with speeches that will bring people to their feet as with speeches that bring people to their senses." He is trying to appeal to his listeners' intelligence as well as their emotions. He moves them to applause and cheers as his speech builds, and sometimes he gets them to their feet. He is making them feel better, and encouraging them to believe that there is a point to their trying to win the election, and that there is a way to crack Reagan's "Teflon" coating. But he also warns that the Democrats will have "no chance" of convincing the nation of their cause "if what comes out of this Convention is a babel of arguing voices." One wonders whether the audience will really listen to what he is saying. "We Democrats must unite," he says. "Now, we should not be embarrassed, we should not be embarrassed or dismayed or chagrined if the process of unifying is difficult, even wrenching at times." He makes a case against the Reagan record. He says that inflation has been reduced since 1980, but by the worst recession since 1932; that the deficit—"the largest in the history of this universe"—is one "that can be paid only in pain and that could bring this nation to its knees." He asks, "What chance would the Republican candidate have had in 1980 if he had told the American people that he intended to pay for his so-called economic recovery with bankruptcies, unemployment, more homeless, more hungry, and the largest government debt known to humankind?

"That was an election won under false pretenses," Cuomo says. But, of course, it was won for other reasons, too. He says that the Reagan Administration claims it has made the world safer, and adds, "By creating the largest defense budget in history . . . By escalating to a frenzy the nuclear-arms race. By incendiary rhetoric. By refusing to discuss peace with our enemies. By the loss of two hundred and seventy-nine young Americans in Lebanon in pursuit of a plan and a policy that no one can find or describe." Democrats seem to have mixed feelings about attacking the policy in Lebanon (Mondale's problem is that he supported the policy for a long time), but Cuomo believes strongly in doing so. And now he is cheered. It is a kind of release for the Democrats, who are frustrated at Reagan's ability to glide away from the Lebanon collapse. The audience is unusually attentive for a Convention audience. Cuomo has drawn them in and held their interest as well as fed their partisan spirit. His own rhetoric escalating, Cuomo gets a tremendous cheer when, in a reference to El Salvador—and going a bit far, it seems—he says, "We give money to Latin-American governments that murder nuns and then lie about it." He adds, lest anyone conclude otherwise, "Of course, Democrats believe that there are times when we must stand and fight." He refers to the need to protect human rights, whether those of Sakharov or Bishop Tutu in South Africa, thus covering a wide ideological band.

Cuomo says that the American people's lack of full understanding of the Republican record "I can only attribute to the President's amiability and the failure by some to separate the salesman from the product." Cuomo believes that the way for the Democrats to get a handle on Reagan is to say that he seems to be a very pleasant man and then go after his policies. Mondale has taken to saying lately that Reagan offers "salesmanship, not leadership." Now, his voice rising, Cuomo says that the Party must "remind Americans that if they are not happy with all the President has done so far they should consider how much worse it will be if he is left to his radical proclivities for another four years unrestrained. Unrestrained." And the audience cheers. Referring to Reagan's recent appointment to an advisory committee on environmental policy of Anne Gorsuch Burford, the former administrator of the Environmental Protection Agency, who resigned under pressure in March, 1983—an appointment that appalled some of Reagan's own strategists—Cuomo says, "If July brings back Anne Gorsuch Burford, what can we expect of December?" He is cheered and applauded. One of Mondale's devices, which he began to use in the primaries and is expected to use more in the coming months, is to say—in a conscious parody of the Republicans' predictions in 1980 that Carter planned an "October surprise" having to do with the hostages in Iran—that Reagan will spring a "December surprise." In this case, the "surprise" is generic, a code for anything anyone fears that Reagan might do. Some Democrats, in their speeches to constituents, say that Reagan will widen the war in Central America if he is reelected; some warn of dire budget cuts.

"Where would another four years take us?" Cuomo asks. He has the audience totally with him now. The healing has begun to take effect—at least for the moment. He lists some of the fears: "How much larger will the deficit be? How much deeper the cuts in programs for the struggling middle class and the poor to limit that deficit? How high will the interest rates be? How much more acid rain killing our forests and fouling our lakes?" He adds, "And, ladies and gentlemen, the nation must think of this: What kind of Supreme Court will we have?" At this, the people in the audience, who have been cheering each question, cheer, applaud, and stamp their feet. Democratic strategists have been divided over whether much of an issue could be made of the possibility of Reagan's appointing more members of the Supreme Court, but I have heard politicians raise the issue all year, always to applause. And the Court's recent rash of rulings cutting back on individual rights has made the subject more immediate. A senator I am standing near on the Convention floor says he still doesn't think that the Supreme Court issue "cuts" with the electorate. Perhaps not, but it certainly had an impact here.

"The election will measure the record of the past four years," Cuomo says. "But, more than that, it will answer the question of what kind of people we want to be." And then, offering the Democrats a credo, he says, "We believe in only the government we need but we insist on all the government we need." He continues, "We believe in a government that is characterized by fairness and reasonableness." He says, "We believe in a government strong enough to use the words 'love' and 'compassion' and smart enough to convert our noblest aspirations into practical realities." Some of his lines are a bit simplistic: he refers to "the simple truth that peace is better than war because life is better than death." He continues, "For fifty years, we Democrats created a better future for our children, using traditional democratic principles as a fixed beacon, giving us direction and purpose, but constantly innovating, adapting to new realities." He lists the "innovations" of various Democratic Presidents. Democrats have done it before and can do it again, he says; he uses the word "intelligent" often, to indicate that clear thinking can solve problems. He talks of "marrying common sense and compassion." The struggle to live in dignity, he says, "is the real story of the shining city," and he says that he lived the story, and talks, movingly, about the story of his immigrant parents. He calls his own story "an ineffably beautiful tribute to the democratic process." He has managed to work in religion, patriotism, values, family: he is moving onto Reagan's territory but also saying that the Democrats have reason to be proud of their tradition. Some of the newer, cool Democrats are not comfortable talking about that tradition. He has conducted a psychological as well as a spiritual exercise, and one can sense that a change has come over the hall. He concludes, quietly, "I ask you now, ladies and gentlemen, brothers and sisters: for the good of all of us, for the love of this great nation, for the family of America—for the love of God—please make this nation remember how futures are built."

JULY 17

Late Tuesday afternoon. The Moscone Center. The platform issues did come to the floor this afternoon, after virtual around-the-clock negotiations in which deals were made and came unstuck, and some negotiations were going on right up until the time of the voting. In their meeting last night, Mondale, Hart, and Jackson did not negotiate but did talk a bit about what has now become the Central American resolution, and Mondale made the case to Jackson that he very much wanted to avoid a floor fight over the subject of quotas. Hart and Jackson pressed their concerns about the makeup and direction of the Fairness Commission. They're thinking ahead, and raising the price to Mondale for peace at this Convention. (While the three candidates met, their aides, gathered in the next room, started negotiating over who would head the Fairness Commission.) Talking to the press after the meeting, Jackson said that there would be some "creative tension during the next forty-eight hours." Mondale opposes quotas, and his people knew that the issue had the potential of exacerbating further the serious tensions that had grown within the Democratic Party in recent months and of causing an ugly scene at the Convention. The issue of quotas sets blacks against Jews, labor against blacks. Furthermore, overriding all the Mondale people's actions here is a determination to put on a show before the country which says that the Democratic Party, though it may have its differences—it *is* the Democratic Party—can pull itself together, and could govern. An afternoon dominated by the subject of quotas would not be conducive to such a picture. (This part of the Convention was scheduled so that it would not appear on network television.) Moreover, though the Mondale people knew that they had the votes for the nomination, the votes on the platform issues were less certain. And, especially after the Lance-Manatt mess, the Mondale people wanted to show that they were in command. A number of things had "loosened" some of the Mondale votes for the platform, including the Lance-Manatt mess itself and the pressure that Jackson had been putting on black women, saying that white women had got something out of the Convention already (Ferraro), and black women were owed something. Black Mondale supporters were under pressure in general.

The tensions between blacks supporting Jackson and blacks supporting Mondale had been in evidence all year, and came to a head at the Convention, where they all converged for the first time. Many blacks who had supported Mondale, often against great odds, and even tides, in their own areas felt that they weren't being taken sufficiently into account by the Mondale campaign. They noticed that there were few blacks in high positions in the Mondale campaign—a point Jackson and his allies emphasized. They wondered during the primaries if they had gone on the line for Mondale only to have their votes largely written off in light of the likely strong support for Jackson. At the Convention, blacks who had supported Mondale were under pressure to show some solidarity with Jackson's blacks on the platform—especially on the matters of runoff primaries and quotas, which many of them believe in. After the meeting of the three candidates, Mondale, encouraged, phoned Jackson and said he wanted to see if they could reach an agreement on the quotas section, and so Beckel and two associates went to meet at the Hilton with two key figures in the Jackson entourage—Mayor Richard Hatcher, of Gary, Indiana, and Walter Fauntroy, the District of Columbia's delegate to Congress. At the same time, Donilon and Paul Tully, the Mondale campaign's political director, were meeting with Hart advisers at the Meridien. (Hart's aides, still hoping to stop Mondale on the first ballot, wanted to help Jackson on the questions of quotas and runoff primaries, as well as the chairmanship of the Fairness Commission—hoping to crack Mondale's support. They had hoped to meet and plot with the Jackson people after the candidates' meeting, only to find that the Mondale people had sequestered the Jackson people, and were negotiating with them. And some Hart

aides didn't know that other Hart aides were negotiating with the
Mondale people.) In keeping with their penchant for thoroughness, the Mondale people set up a centralized control system
in one of their offices on the third floor of the hotel, so that both
sets of negotiations could be kept track of at once.

Some white liberals who supported Mondale also wanted to
support certain Jackson platform positions—because they believed
in them, because they had a substantial number of blacks in their
districts, or both. Moreover, many of Mondale's delegates are to
the left of him, and could be told to vote against their real views
only so often. Too much discipline presents its own dangers. And,
as the Convention gathered, inevitably some people's minds
turned to who would have what role in the general election, and
this was another source of tension between the Jackson blacks and
the Mondale blacks. A black who had gone on the line for Mondale was not eager to see a high position in the general-election
campaign taken by a prominent Jackson supporter. At the same
time, Jackson and his advisers were arguing for important roles in
the general-election campaign for his supporters, and Jackson was
making certain demands in connection with his leading a voter-
registration drive. So while the Mondale people were trying to
mollify, pacify, keep people at bay, they were also involved in intri-
cate three-way negotiations designed to prevent any major embarrassment to Mondale this afternoon. Through the night, there
was quite a bit of calling back and forth, and of histrionics, but by
the time the negotiators finished, at about four-thirty in the morning, the Mondale people believed they had made a lot of progress.
They had an agreement with the Jackson camp on the quotas
issue, and thought that they had agreements with it on compromises on the no-first-use and defense-cut planks. The negotiators
with the Hart people got an agreement that Mondale would accept the Persian Gulf/Central American minority report with the
proviso that Mondale, who wasn't happy about this, would put out
a statement giving his own interpretation of it; that the Hart people would instruct their delegates to support the Mondale position
on runoff primaries; that the Hart camp would let it be known
that it supported the Mondale positions on no first use and defense cuts. Another part of the agreement was that Mondale and
Hart would come to a meeting of the minds about the Fairness
Commission.

Late this morning, the Mondale camp learned that the Jackson people had decided that all deals were off—some of those around Jackson were unhappy that he had given in on anything—and the Jackson people started talking again about "linkage" of the various platform proposals and about needing some victories. The Mondale people also learned mid-morning that the Hart group had decided their deal was off, that they wanted assurances about the Fairness Commission. Donilon met midmorning at the Meridien with the Hart people—with a good bit of carrying on and walking out of rooms and banging of doors—and then, as the negotiations continued, Johnson met with them in the early afternoon, and agreed to some of their demands. These had to do with a fairly prompt appointment of the commission—while the Mondale people were still around to honor their pledge—and with how the chairman and members would be selected. The Convention had been delayed while all this was going on. At that point, Donilon, who is twenty-nine, shouted to an aide, "Tell them they can start the Convention; I'm on my way." But there was still an important unsettled matter. Around noon, Mondale had made another call to Jackson, in which he spoke in fairly strong terms to the effect that he thought there had been an agreement, and that a floor fight over quotas would do great damage to the Party. Jackson suggested that Beckel come around again and negotiate some more. As the Convention proceeded, the negotiations continued; speakers were scheduled and rescheduled and their speeches rewritten as events kept changing—speeches that had been written for a certain compromise had to be torn up. The order in which the minority planks were to be considered was being changed as the negotiations went on. Finally, the Jackson people came up with a substitute term for quotas: "verifiable measurements." This seemed harmless enough, and no one was clear about what it meant—and ambiguity was just what was needed at that point. The Mondale people checked out the term with their own delegation leaders and other supporters, with Jewish leaders, with trade-union leaders, with teachers' organizations, and on and on—they wanted to be sure they hadn't missed some nuance, that no sudden explosion would ignite on the floor.

Meanwhile, on the Convention floor the minority planks on no first use and defense cuts were overwhelmingly defeated. Though the Mondale people had sought to avoid fights, once fights were at

hand they did not mind having the opportunity to show that they
were in control of the Convention and (after the Lance matter)
competent. The elaborate Mondale floor operation was at work as
if the nomination depended on it. Cluster leaders, in orange vests,
and whips were briskly counting their votes and searching for lost
delegates. (Some had taken the afternoon off to visit the vineyards
in the Napa Valley.) Since superdelegates don't have alternates,
their votes were gone if they were—and several of them were.
When Andrew Young stood up to defend the Mondale position
on runoff primaries, the booing by blacks in the California delegation, where I was standing at the time, was quite loud, and it
continued as Young, in obvious pain, tried to make his speech.
This was the eruption of the tension between the Jackson blacks
and the Mondale blacks. Young is an establishment black who
deals in coalition politics—but who had withheld public support of
Mondale until the end of the primaries because of the obvious
strain of his situation. This manifestation of the deep tensions was
disturbing to many in the hall, and even the cheers for Young,
encouraged by instructions to the floor from the Mondale trailer,
could not overcome the painful moment. The run off-primary
minority report was defeated by more than twelve hundred votes.
As word reached the floor—having been sent out from the Mondale trailer—about the new term "verifiable measurements," the
main reaction was bafflement. When one Mondale aide tried to
explain it to one delegation leader, the delegation leader asked,
only half jokingly, "Do you mean mutually verifiable measurements? Are you sure you don't have this mixed up with a debate
on the nuclear freeze?" But, like all good lieutenants, he spread
the word among his delegation that this new language was acceptable to Mondale and should be accepted on a voice vote. There
was, however, one last wrinkle. Though Barbara Mikulski, a representative from Maryland and a Mondale supporter, told the Convention that the new language did not mean quotas, a Jackson
speaker described it as "a victory for the Rainbow Coalition," and
said that if people wanted blacks to understand the Holocaust and
the importance of the State of Israel, why couldn't they "respect
our need for verifiable measurements," and another talked about
"verifiable measurements, such as quotas, such as goals." Further,
Mondale aides, in order to keep the Jackson camp happy, since it
was losing on everything, pronounced the compromise "a victory
for the Rainbow Coalition." Some Jewish leaders decided that they

had been double-crossed, and sought further assurances from the Mondale camp.

The Hart Persian Gulf/Central American minority report was overwhelmingly accepted.

While all this was going on, Mondale and his speechwriter, Martin Kaplan, continued to work on Mondale's acceptance speech—a process that has been taking place for weeks now. It is Mondale's style to work on a speech up to the end—trying out various themes, seeing how they fit and feel. Mondale has also had to respond to the requests of the politicians who want to see him about one thing or another—including the Lance matter—and the interest groups trying to drain their last from him. And he has had to respond to the pleas of his staff to deal with this and that perceived or real crisis. So while Mondale is trying to redirect his efforts toward the general election, and toward making the case against Reagan about the future, he is still caught up in the last playing out of the nomination effort past. One close observer of all this says he believes that Mondale is more ready to get on with fighting the general election than his campaign organization is.

At shortly before seven, Oliver Henkel, standing near the New Jersey delegation, says to me, "In Florida, we're picking up delegates right and left. Someone in New York switched to us. I think we're going to keep picking them up, and show real movement tomorrow, right up to the roll call. And having Gary speak just before the roll call is so important. The last time a major candidate spoke before the nomination was when William Jennings Bryan did his 'Cross of Gold' speech. There are some prominent public officials ready to go with us, but they don't want to do it alone. We're trying to put together a coalition of them now." Hart, at delegate caucuses today, referring to the Lance matter, warned against "deals and backroom maneuvers and manipulation, and the politics of the past and the old political arrangements." Aides, journalists, are running around this Convention floor and acting as if the nomination were in question, playing out roles that are now irrelevant. A little earlier, a rumor—a false one—went around that NBC had said that Mondale is twenty votes short of the nomination.

No one knows quite what to expect of Jackson's speech tonight, though it has never seemed that he had much choice other than to be conciliatory. Last night, a nervous Beckel, who had spent many, many hours negotiating with Jackson, told him he hoped he'd give a good speech and Jackson teased, "Tomorrow night, you'll either be a chump or a champ." There is so much tension surrounding Jackson that anything could cause further problems. Now, at shortly after seven, Pacific Daylight Time, as Jackson comes to the podium, black delegates cheer him emotionally, some white delegates give him polite applause, and some white delegates simply watch. Jackson, his face looking smoother, younger, and more handsome than in recent weeks, stands there proudly. His very being there is a triumph for him. He likes to point out how many other candidates he outlasted. He begins slowly, and low-key, and reading, which is unusual for him, but then one remembers that it is a Jackson technique to begin on a quiet note, and draw the audience in and build as he goes along. "Tonight, we come together bound by our faith in a mighty God, with genuine respect for our country, and inheriting the legacy of a great party," he begins. One begins to sense relief in the hall. "This is not a perfect party," he says. "Yet we are called to a perfect mission: our mission to feed the hungry, to clothe the naked, to house the homeless, to teach the illiterate, to provide jobs for the jobless, to choose the human race over the nuclear race." All year, he has been saying that he represents "the locked out," and now he says, "My constituency is the damned, disinherited, disrespected, and the despised." He says, "They have voted in record numbers. . . . The Democratic Party must send them a signal that we care." This is somewhat mysterious. When will Jackson decide that that signal has been sent?

Now, his voice rising, Jackson becomes more the preacher, and some of the audience, as if at a church meeting, respond "Yeah" as he says, "Leadership can part the waters and lead our nation in the direction of the Promised Land. Leadership can lift the boats stuck at the bottom." Then, hinting that he recognizes reality, he says, "There is a proper season for everything. There is a time to sow and a time to reap. There is a time to compete and a time to cooperate." And then, to cheers from the black delegates, he says, "I ask for your vote on the first ballot . . . a vote of conviction, a vote of conscience." Jackson has been urging this on caucuses all week, and the Mondale people, loath to have any sign of "erosion," are not pleased. But Jackson goes on to say, to larger cheers, "But I will be proud to support the nominee of this Convention for President of the United States of America." He has wandered, and caused difficulty, but he has come home. At least for now. "If, in my high moments, I have done some good, offered some service, shed some light, healed some wounds, rekindled some hope, or stirred someone from apathy and indifference, or in any way along the way helped somebody, then this campaign has not been in vain," he says. More of the audience is moving toward him. And then he says something surprising, confronting the recent unpleasantness head-on. "If in my low moments, in word, deed, or attitude, through some error of temper, taste, or tone, I have caused anyone discomfort, created pain, or revived someone's fears, that was not my truest self," he says. The hall is dead silent. He continues, "If there were occasions when my grape turned into a raisin and my joy bell lost its resonance, please forgive me." A very large proportion of the audience is visibly moved, and cheers him. One can think of no precedent for this, and part of the mood here is caused by the fact that we are all—Jackson, the delegates, observers—in a new situation. He holds us in suspension, waiting to hear what's next. Jackson's speech is the unfolding of a plot. He continues, "Charge it to my head, and not to my heart. My head is so limited in its finitude; my heart is boundless in its love for the human family." Actually, Jackson has a very smart, perhaps brilliant, if undisciplined, mind. Only a very smart mind would come up with the things he is saying now. The drama builds as Jackson continues, "I am not a perfect servant. I am a public servant. I'm doing my best against the odds. As I develop and serve, be patient." Now his voice is ringing out clearly; his sentences are clipped at the end. He pauses, and then says, "God is not finished with me yet." Only a preacher could get away with such a line. The hall explodes in cheers. He is asking the audience here, and those watching on television, to let him start over; Jackson often says he believes in redemption. The apology is very moving, but will it convince?

Now Jackson talks, as he did early in the campaign, about the American people making up a "quilt." He cites the long civil-rights struggle—from the time that Fannie Lou Hamer and the Mississippi Freedom Democratic Party were given seats at the Convention in Atlantic City in 1964. He talks of the martyrs of the

civil-rights movement and of the three young civil-rights workers
(two of them Jewish) who were murdered in Mississippi in 1964.
He says, "Twenty years ago, tears welled up in our eyes. . . .
Twenty years later, our communities, black and Jewish, are in
anguish, anger, and pain. Feelings have been hurt on both sides.
There is a crisis in communications. Confusion is in the air. We
cannot afford to lose our way. We may agree to agree or agree to
disagree on issues; we must bring back civility to these tensions."
His head-on confrontation with the problem is almost breath-
taking. But does he really understand it now? He talks about the
Judeo-Christian traditions, and also Islam. He says, "We are much
too intelligent; much too bound by our Judeo-Christian heritage;
much too victimized by racism, sexism, militarism, and anti-Semitism; much too threatened as historical scapegoats to go on divided one from another. We must turn from finger-pointing to
clasped hands." Jackson and the audience are responding to each
other now, feeding each other; it seems that as Jackson senses the
impact on the audience of what he is saying, he speaks even more
strongly. All great speakers establish a relationship with the audience, a d Jackson is without question a great speaker. Whatever
happens, this is a very moving moment, and there seems through
much of the hall—on the part of many of those who started out
just watching—a will to believe. A friend of Jackson's has told me
that he believed all along that Jackson is one of the two people in
public life who are best able to make people feel better about
things—the other, he said, is Reagan. Here Jackson is showing the
good he can do—which makes the recent past all the more tragic.

Now Jackson talks about the groups that he says are part of the
Rainbow Coalition—Arab-Americans, American Indians, Asian-
Americans, the disabled. "Don't leave anybody out," he says, and
then, having perfected a line I first heard him use in New
Hampshire, he says, "I would rather have Roosevelt in a wheelchair than Reagan on a horse." This brings the audience to its
feet—laughing, cheering, applauding. Then he goes into a
lengthy and detailed critique of the Reagan record, often using
wit and sarcasm, and then he becomes ever more the preacher.
His voice grows stronger still, until it turns into a shout. One
wonders how this is going over on television. Referring to his
losses on the platform fights this afternoon, he says, "We raised
the right issues." He continues, "Our self-respect and our moral

integrity were at stake. Our heads are perhaps bloodied but not bowed. Our backs are straight. We can go home and face our people." He again makes the case he has been making all along about the lack of black elected officials in the South and the need for ending certain voting practices, including the runoff primaries. Then, in a line that many Southern whites will not particularly like, he says, "We can save the cotton, but we've got to fight the boll weevil. We've got to make a judgment." His face is perspiring and his voice is becoming raspy. "If we lift up a program to feed the hungry, they'll come running," he says. As he goes through a litany along these lines, the audience cheers.

Then, in a dramatic moment, Jackson says, "As I leave you now"—leaving the stage is not easy for Jackson, and he will not really leave it—"I'll try to be faithful to my promise." He talks about the slums and barrios he stayed in in the course of his campaign, and then, his voice becoming even stronger, the perspiration pouring down his face, he says, "I just want young America to do me one favor: exercise the right to dream." This is reminiscent of the late Dr. Martin Luther King, Jr., with whom Jackson worked. But even if Jackson is consciously putting on a performance here, and he is, he is also giving his audience a memorable experience. We become not just listeners but participants in his drama. And Jackson seems to have a special feeling about talking to young people, trying to get them to see that their lives can be better. He continues, "Dream of a new value system: teachers who teach for life and not just for a living, teach because they can't help it. Dream of lawyers more concerned with justice than a judgeship. Dream of doctors more concerned with public health than personal wealth." His hands are waving, and the hall seems almost totally wrapped in what he is saying. Whatever the effect outside the hall, it is extraordinary, and often moving, theatre here. Jackson has always known that he has great speaking ability, and he is obviously determined to show that to the world tonight, to transcend even his own best. And he seems to be quite clear about what he is doing. "Our time has come," he shouts, in a line he has used all year—but now he is giving it new, and perhaps, to some, disturbing, power. His chest heaving as he gasps for air—to great dramatic effect—and with the audience now largely lost in his performance, Jackson does a revivalist peroration. The black delegates, and now many of the white ones, are responding with

"Yeah!" and "That's right!" Jackson cries, "Our time has come. We must leave racial battleground and come to economic common ground and moral higher ground. America, our time has come." He goes on, the emotion he is conveying and that of those in the hall now locked, his face and much of his shirt now totally wet, "We've come from disgrace to Amazing Grace. *Our time has come.* Give me your tired, give me your poor, your huddled masses who yearn to breathe free, and come November there will be a change, because our time has come." And then he closes: "Thank you and God bless you."

Whitney Phipps, a gospel singer, sings, slowly and to a stilled hall, "Ordinary People," and the people in the hall, blacks and whites, stand and join hands and, silently, sway to the music. The soothing music helps calm the emotions that have been set loose in the hall. People need a moment to calm down. What started out as a tense meeting has become a gathering. Cuomo began the healing process last night, and Jackson continued it tonight. The platform fights, such as they were, are over. The people here seem to have wanted to feel better, and now they have begun to do so. Some rock music begins, and the people in the hall clap and move with the music.

JULY 18

Wednesday. The Moscone Center. Late afternoon. Tonight, the balloting for the nomination will take place, preceded by Hart's speech. Last night, some black Mondale supporters met with Mondale and said that they wanted more of a role in his campaign and assurances of jobs in a Mondale Administration. This morning, Mondale met with labor leaders, with the Hispanic caucus, and with the black caucus, and he met with fund raisers about the large registration drive the Party still hopes to put on. The Mondale people figure that even if they hold much of their base and win a large number of independents it may not be enough, so there will be a targeted drive to get more blacks, Hispanics, and women registered. Considerable effort is being spent here, and will be spent in the coming weeks, in raising money for the Party and for nonprofit organizations that run registration programs. (Contributions to such nonprofit groups are tax-deductible, and are not counted against an individual's contribution to the Party.) Also, people will be encouraged to contribute to state Parties, which can accept money that cannot be contributed to federal campaigns—union dues, corporate funds, and individual contributions beyond the federal limit, or "soft money." These state Parties will be conducting registration drives ostensibly for state and local elections. Mondale also has a substantial debt—of about $2.7 million—to be paid off. His campaign spent a great deal of money in 1983—too much, in the view of some Mondale advisers—but it is also the case that the effort made in 1983 is a large part of what saved Mondale in 1984, in addition to his own efforts. A base was laid and commitments were made to him by people who helped pull him through. Hart has a debt of between four and five million dollars, and when Hart and Mondale met in New York they talked briefly about helping each other out, and their aides have been continuing the conversation. (Each can ask his own contributors who have given him the maximum to give to the other.) John Glenn is here, almost unnoticed, trying to raise money to pay off his still substantial debt. This morning, Mondale, referring to his fight for the nomination, said to the Hispanic caucus, which is still considering a boycott of the first ballot (this is mainly at the instigation of Hart Hispanic delegates, but it puts pressure on the others), "As you know, it wasn't easy. And I'm not sure if you hadn't been there I'd be here." He continued, in the Mondale style, "I said then, 'If you remember me, I'll remember you.' And I will. And I will." To the black caucus, he said, "There has not been a fight of any significance over the last twenty years where Walter Mondale wasn't there, fighting." A motion that the Hispanics boycott the first ballot failed today.

At a press briefing in the Meridien this morning, a pale, tired-looking Johnson was asked if labor leaders were complaining "about a lack of consultation with your campaign." Smiling wanly, Johnson replied, "I don't think they're unique in that respect." A number of people said here today that although Jewish leaders put out statements welcoming Jackson's remarks of last night, the tensions are not resolved. The Lance matter is said to be still taking a big toll on the Mondale senior staff. This afternoon, John Reilly went over to the Mondale trailers at the urgent request of Donilon, who wanted someone in the top echelon of the Mondale campaign to work on certain delegates, one by one, who might defect. Jackson is still pressing black delegates to support him on the first ballot, and the Hart people are still trying to figure out something that might prevent a first-ballot nomination. Jackson is said to be let down today after the excitement of last night, and also to be feeling that he has been the target of some new slights. He is pressing anew for a say in the Fairness Commission and in the blacks who will be brought into the Mondale campaign. At the black caucus today, he came under some criticism for not, as his critics saw it, having won anything on the platform. Jackson, instead of talking about what he had won along the way, emphasized the defeat; he apparently wasn't prepared for being accused of having let down the side—so he raised new obstacles to his support for Mondale. The Mondale camp is not seriously worried, but at a staff meeting early this morning Donilon predicted that Mondale would receive two thousand two hundred votes on the first ballot, and he wants every last one of them.

There are a number of striking characteristics about the Democrats at this Convention. One is that they seem more serious than Democrats gathered in the past. There are fewer funny, attention-asking costumes. There are fewer oddball events. And there have been no outbursts of causy demonstrations. There seems to be more of an acceptance that there are limits to what government can do. The Party seems, simply, more mature. This may be attributable to a number of factors: a sobriety brought on by the 1980 election; the fact that Reagan seems to be concentrating the Democrats' minds; the "reform" process of opening up the proceedings having reached a certain maturity—the once outsiders have long since been inside; the large number of labor, regular, delegates; the presence of the superdelegates. (Being Democrats, though, there are the usual number of demands that each group have a certain representation.)

Another noticeable thing is how much young talent there is among the Party's elected officials now—more, it seems, than at any time in memory. There is a strikingly large number of promising young senators, representatives, governors, mayors. (Democrats hold thirty-five of the fifty governorships.) Many of these people are part of the process of redefinition that the Party is going through: for some it is a self-conscious exercise, for some it comes more naturally. Senator Bill Bradley, Democrat of New Jersey, thinks the Democrats should have no problem presenting themselves as seeking a government that nurtures a caring society and believes in social justice and also encourages technological change and a more productive marketplace (bringing along with it more fulfillment for the workers). In a conversation we had here the other day, Bradley told me that he believes the Party could find a way to talk about technological change that does not subvert human needs but in fact meets them. He seemed to be backing away from the cool, technocratic, "Atari Democrat" talk that, along with others, he flirted with a couple of years ago. Some of the Atari Democrats remain on the cool, technocratic side, seeming a little embarrassed about the subject of government except as it can foster technological change. Bradley said, "There is an opening for the Democrats to seize a more value-oriented approach than the Reagan Administration offers, and juxtapose that to the pure materialistic approach of the Administration. The challenge is whether everybody is going to be bought off with the illusion of prosperity or whether they will believe that there is more to life than material enhancement." Cisneros, who has been quite involved in bringing high-tech industry to the San Antonio area, said to me a little while ago, "I think the issue is which party can fairly prepare the country for the transition that's ahead. To me, that's really the guts of it. We're going through a transition from an industrial era to an era of new technology, but we can't leave old industries and cities to die. The Republican strategy would be to say, 'If they don't like it, they should vote with their feet and go elsewhere.' And that's not fair. And in the newer areas of the country it's not fair, either: the new service economies aren't providing enough for the poor. So we're in a transition; that's not in question. The question is which party can handle it so that there's a fairness about it—fairness in the context of change." Cisneros says that he believes that the Democrats ought to talk more, and positively, about free enterprise.

At shortly after six, the Hart people get their moment. Red placards (the red shows up well on television) with Hart's name in white digital print wave throughout the Convention floor. The blue-and-white Mondale placards are out of sight; this next period is to be all Hart's. Hart's appearance on the podium is preceded by a brief film of him, looking very good in an open-necked Western shirt, accompanied by ear-blistering taped electronic music, including "Fanfare for the Common Man" and the

score from *The Magnificent Seven* (also known as the score for
Marlboro ads). Hart's delegates cheer him enthusiastically, but he
doesn't arouse in them the deep emotion that, say, Edward Kennedy did in his followers four years ago. On the podium, Hart
looks handsome, though up close in recent days his face has
looked almost ravaged. I have never known of anyone who has
unsuccessfully run for the Presidency and got over it. Losing candidates seek vindication, explanations, another chance. They entertain fantasies of the Presidency still coming their way. In 1980,
just about everyone who had ever run for the Democratic nomination and was still alive was hovering with aides in New York, plot-
ting and waiting for an "open Convention." Now Hart says that his
was "a quest with many ideas but with one driving theme—that
our Party and our nation need new leadership, new directions,
and new hope." He says, "Together, we stand tonight at the gate of
change." He graciously thanks his supporters and commends his
competitors. One wonders whether he means it when he says, to
Mondale, "You have honored me by being an opponent of unsurpassed grit, perseverance, and determination." And he warns the
Republicans "to take no comfort from this Democratic family tus-
sle." He adds, "Ronald Reagan has provided all the unity we need.
Not one of us is going to sit this campaign out. You have made the
stakes too high." And then Hart carries on his own campaign, as if
not quite ready to let go and not quite sure of the purpose of this
speech. Making, though not quite explicitly, the "electability" argument, he says, "You will decide which candidate has the best
chance to defeat Ronald Reagan and become the next President of
the United States." He does pledge—"whatever the outcome of
your decision"—to "devote every waking hour and every ounce of
energy to the defeat of Ronald Reagan." And he goes on to say
that the country will continue to hear from him. "This is one Hart
you will not leave in San Francisco," he says, and though the line
feels contrived, his delegates cheer enthusiastically.

The conversations among Hart and his advisers these days have
to do with how he can be in the best position to run for the
Presidency again in 1988—the possibility that Mondale might be
elected is not on the table. They saw the Vice-Presidential nomination as one route. Hart is considering not running for the Senate
in 1986, when his term is up: he had a perilously close reelection
in 1980; he would have to raise funds for another Senate race

while he is paying off the debt from the Presidential campaign. He is entertaining the idea of doing what many other Presidential aspirants, including Mondale, have done—find a private means of livelihood and spend the next four years running. Now Hart talks about the stakes in the election and, using a term he has used in recent weeks, the "moral imperative" of defeating Reagan. He poses a series of questions to the delegates, to which they lustily shout no: "Do you want Ronald Reagan to appoint the next Supreme Court? Do you want Ronald Reagan to have four more years to sell off our environment to the highest bidder?" He asks, "Can we allow Ronald Reagan to send our sons to die without cause in another Lebanon"—and then, repeating something he said throughout the primaries, though his meaning was never clear—"or to serve as bodyguards for dictators in Central America?" He asks, "Can we continue to tolerate a President who urges us to love our country but hate our government?" He cites the things he says Democrats are for, including social justice. He talks of his own interest in leading the Party "in recapturing the issue of a sound defense," and he continues, "Mr. Reagan, the American flag does not belong to you and the right wing of the Republican Party. It belongs to all the people." This receives big cheers. Then he repeats some of the gibes at Mondale he made during the primaries. He says, "To achieve our goals, our party and nation must disenthrall themselves from the policies of the comfortable past that do not answer the challenges of tomorrow." He says, "Promises are cheap, rhetoric is hollow, and nostalgia is not a program." And he says, "The Democratic Party must continue to be the party of experimentation, the party of hope, not the party of memory." This all seems off-key for the occasion, but Hart is having trouble leaving the stage and also is planting his own flag for the future. "We need nothing less than a blueprint for the new democracy," he says, in a reference to his own book, "A New Democracy." He talks about the need for an industrial policy, for rebuilding the urban infrastructure, for investment in education and training and scientific research.

The speech is going over well enough, but it is no spellbinder; it does not seem to be moving anyone who was not with him already, and though his own people are obviously with him, he does not seem to be giving them much of a lift, something memorable. The coolness and detachment that are characteristic of Hart prevent

him from engaging his audiences on an emotional level. He holds
something back. And the speech has a cut-and-paste feel to it,
which keeps it from building. He talks about the importance of
arms control and, as he reluctantly began to do during the primaries, about his childhood as a poor boy in Kansas. He talks
about the political generation he claims to represent—the generation that lived through the deaths of John and Robert Kennedy,
that marched in the civil-rights movement, opposed the Vietnam
War, and was dismayed by Watergate. But the generation he appealed to in his campaign was largely a younger one, which now
has another set of concerns. The term "yuppies"—for young, up-
wardly mobile professionals—was popularized by his own campaign, and this group was, broadly speaking, characterized less by
idealism and social activism than by, as the term itself indicates, a
seeking for comfort and economic well-being. It is not clear that
Robert Kennedy and "yuppies" would have understood each
other. This is the paradox of Hart's "generational" appeal. Hart's
followers registered concern about arms control, the environment, and women's issues. The Kennedys may be part of the "yuppie" iconography, for their stylishness, their offering of something
new, and their liberal social values. But Hart may have drawn
young voters less by his summoning up of the social activists than
by his cool, modern, hip demeanor, his non-old-hat-politician
style—and the fact that he was not Mondale. Robert Kennedy had
more in common with Mondale, and was closer to him in age. And
in his campaign Hart consciously modelled himself on the cool,
detached John Kennedy, not the more passionate and engaged
Robert. Now Hart quotes from John Kennedy's inaugural address—"Let the word go forth from this time and place that the
torch has been passed to a new generation of Americans"—and
goes through a rather complicated piece of business about the
torch on the Statue of Liberty and the torch his campaign had
"tried to lift and light." It was, he says, "a torch of hope beyond the
old arrangements and the favored alliances." Then, in Kennedy-
like rhetoric, he says, "I see an America too young to quit, too
courageous to turn back, with a passion for justice and a program
for opportunity, an America with unmet dreams that will never
die." And he concludes, "If not now, someday we will prevail." A
loud, electronic version of the theme from *Chariots of Fire*—a popular theme song this year, along with the theme from *Rocky*

(underdogness and striving are in political vogue)—fills the hall as Hart and his family wave to the delegates.

During the roll call on the balloting for the Democratic Presidential nomination, the Mondale trailer containing the delegate-trackers—each at a telephone—is run with military efficiency. Each time a state is called, Donilon orders a young tracker to check that Mondale got all the votes he was supposed to, and, if not, to find out why. A crisis occurred when Senator Claiborne Pell, a delegate from his home state of Rhode Island, couldn't be found, and a search party was sent for him. The balloting is taking place late, Eastern time, because following Hart's speech there were the nominating speeches for Hart, Jackson, and Mondale, and also for George McGovern, who wanted one more chance to bask, and made a little speech. By this evening, one could feel the morale of the Party rising still more. It is not that many people are predicting victory with any great sense of conviction, but they simply feel better. One experienced politician said to me a few moments ago, "The problem is, we have to leave here and go back to reality. But in 1980 we were not up at all going into the campaign. At least we will leave here more up than we came in. If we weren't up at all, it would be hopeless." A few minutes later, a Southern senator said he saw no way that Mondale would carry his state. Whether Mondale will win, or will lose to another Reagan electoral-college landslide, no one now knows, of course; the odds have changed in the past five months and may do so again. Reagan strategists were thoroughly enjoying Mondale's misery before this Convention began, and assumed, with good reason, that this would be a turbulent one. But by anticipating or dealing with hundreds of small and potentially large problems the Mondale people have thus far pulled off a remarkably smooth Convention. (The Lance matter was, of course, an exception, but it is, at least for the moment, fading from people's minds, though it is not resolved. A little while ago, I saw Lance going onto the Convention floor for the balloting—the large, usually genial and hearty man looking like a sad and wounded hound-dog.)

As the roll call proceeds, Donilon shouts orders to the delegate-trackers: "Henkel was just on the tube saying Gary Hart can't stop Walter Mondale's nomination. *Move it.*" The delegate-trackers, who have been spreading the word and putting out rumors all week, hit the phones and send word to the floor to spread this news. As the count moves along, Donilon, looking like a young, pudgy schoolmaster, paces, and clenches and unclenches his fists. One black delegate from the District of Columbia has switched from Mondale to Jackson, and Donilon swears. There is a temporary worry that some black delegates in North Carolina might switch. Hawaii casts all twenty-seven votes for Mondale; Donilon is pleased—these were delegates he had worked hard to get after the primaries ended. Joy comes with the news that Mondale picked up three delegates in Idaho—as if all this mattered at this point.

What irritates Hart and Jackson about the rules is clear as some of the vote tallies come in: in Maine, Mondale and Hart each get thirteen delegates, even though Hart defeated Mondale in the precinct caucuses there; and in Massachusetts Mondale ends up with ten more delegates than Hart, even though Hart roundly defeated him there. When Mississippi is called, Brad Dye, the lieutenant governor, who after much persuasion backed Mondale and brought along a number of delegates, announces twenty-six votes for Mondale, four for Hart, and thirteen for Jackson. In New Hampshire, the site of Mondale's first humiliation at Hart's hands, Mondale gets two more delegates than Hart. New Jersey passes. Some complicated business is going on: An arrangement has been made for Hart to come to the hall and, as soon as Mondale has the 1,967 votes necessary for the nomination, endorse his nomination. But Hart wants the votes in states where he has substantial numbers of delegates recorded before this occurs, so some Mondale states are getting out of the way—passing—in order to satisfy this arrangement. Others, like New Jersey and Pennsylvania, are passing because they are vying to be the state that puts Mondale over the top, each having been critical to his getting to this point. The Mondale people have promised these two states that they would be the finalists in the little contest, which seems very important at Conventions, to put the nominee over the top. (Campaigns also tend to think that such things can matter in the general election.) A further complication in the arrangements for tonight is that Jackson wants all his delegates counted before the balloting ends, and he has been promised that this will happen. For this reason, Hart will endorse Mondale rather than move that he be nominated by acclamation, and after he makes his statement the other states will be called. A big cheer goes up in the Mondale trailer when New York casts a hundred and fifty-six votes for Mondale—with seventy-five for Hart and fifty-two for Jackson. Donilon calls William Hennessy, the state chairman, on the floor, to congratulate him and thank him. Beckel, who has come into the trailer, sees a picture of Jackson on television watching the results and looking stone-faced. "C'mon, Jesse, smile, *please*," Beckel says to the television screen. At one minute past ten, some Mondale aides bring out bottles of champagne. Hart is in the holding room of the Convention hall, and at the end of the first round of voting, with several states having passed, Mondale has 1,726 votes. Donilon barks, "Florida, Georgia, Alabama—*vote 'em!*" And then, at 10:07, New Jersey—having been given the honor by a grateful Mondale camp (had Mondale lost New Jersey, there's no telling what would be happening tonight)—puts Mondale over the top.

There may not be, as is often said, much enthusiasm for Mondale out in the country, but the Convention floor is a happy place tonight. Now, at ten-thirteen, Hart comes to the podium and says, "There is a time to fight and a time to unite. Our Party has made its choice, and we must now speak with one voice." And he asks "all those in this hall and across this land who fought and bled with me" to support a move to make the nomination unanimous by acclamation. (The signals got confused, and now, after some frantic calls from the Mondale trailer to the podium, in keeping with the pledge to Jackson the roll call is resumed and Pennsylvania, the only remaining state, casts its votes.) Then Jackson appears at the podium and says, "We are now entering the last phase of our struggle," and he recites from the Psalms ("The Lord is my light and salvation; whom shall I fear?"). At the end of the balloting, the delegate count is: Mondale, 2,191; Hart, 1,200.5; and Jackson, 465.5.

Then, suddenly, there is the banging, bonging, bell-ringing music of the "1812 Overture," and fireworks and a red-white-and-blue light show. And then Mondale appears at the podium. His staff had been considering this appearance, and he decided on it this afternoon. Peter Hart, Mondale's pollster, suggested at this morning's staff meeting that Mondale had been long enough in the background of the Convention—that it was time to bring him onstage. Since appearances by a nominee before the acceptance speech are so unusual, the Mondale campaign, with its normal thoroughness (the recent exception notwithstanding), checked for precedents. John Kennedy was the last one to do it at a Democratic Convention; the transcript of what Kennedy had said was obtained. (Reagan appeared at the 1980 Republican Convention on the night he was nominated to put an end to rumors about his Vice-Presidential choice.) Now an obviously and understandably happy Mondale tells the Convention, "Tomorrow, I will accept your nomination," and he says that tonight he and his wife and their children wanted to thank the delegates. He commends his opponents, with a bit of Mondale hyperbole, saying, "Who could be blessed with finer opponents, more decent and honorable human beings than I have?" Then, graciously, he says, "Thank you, Gary, and thank you, Jesse, for what you've done for our nation, for what you've done for all of us." He thanks those who supported him, and says, "Sometimes it doesn't feel very good to lose. I know, because it's happened to me in the past." He adds, "But I've got to have the help of everyone. We're in this together. It's not just my cause, it's our cause." He concludes, "This week, we've made history. Tomorrow, we will make the American future." There was a time when Mondale was worried sick about what might happen at this Convention, when Donilon wasn't sleeping at night because he was so worried about it. All that's hard to remember now, as Mondale and the delegates sing "America the Beautiful" and the delegates sway to the music.

JULY 19

Thursday. This morning, Johnson, drinking a diet cola (his breakfast) as we talk, is, though thoroughly exhausted, feeling good. His mistake over the Lance matter obviously still troubles him, but he is pleased with how the Convention has gone, and with what the Mondale campaign's nightly polling is indicating. Characteristically, Johnson ticks off a list of goals for the Convention. "One, to improve the over-all image of the Party—by showing its diversity, strength, and the attractiveness of its spokespeople, to show that people felt better and better about being Democrats." He adds, "Winning the election depends on the percentage of our base we get; if we get a high percentage, we come close to winning." He continues, "Two, develop the case against Reagan with greater depth and specificity than has been done thus far this year. Three, use the Convention as a platform for Mondale and his ideas for the future." He reads me some of the figures that the polling has been turning up: That when Democrats and independents, who make up nearly seventy per cent of the electorate, were asked who best understands the challenges facing America's future, fifty-one per cent said Mondale and twenty-nine per cent said Reagan; when they were asked who stands up for the average person, seventy-four per cent said Mondale and thirteen per cent said Reagan; when they were asked who will help unify the country and bring all groups together, fifty-seven per cent said Mondale and sixteen per cent said Reagan. When they were asked whether Democrats' criticism that Reagan favors the wealthy is fair or unfair, sixty-eight per cent said it was fair and twenty-nine per cent said it was unfair. And he also reads to me, with obvious satisfaction, a poll result indicating that, as a result of the past few days, forty-four per cent of the people said they had a more favorable view of Mondale and twenty-four per cent said they had a less favorable view, while sixteen per cent said they had a more favorable view of Reagan and forty-six per cent said they had a less favorable view. As for general-election strategy, Johnson says, "There's no great mystery to it. There are about twenty states that you don't fight over, because they are Democratic or Republican, and we have to win most of the rest. And without California there's no way we can have simply a Northern-Midwestern strategy. We have to have some Southern states, and some Western states."

The targeting of the various states will change as the weeks go by and the poll data come in. Bob Beckel says that the reaction to the choice of Ferraro is so great that it can change assumptions about a number of states. One thing that has to be kept in mind when political strategists talk about states they are going after is that a fair amount of feinting takes place—trying to lead the opposition to spend time and money in a state that you don't really intend to fight for. Because of what they have gone through in the past few months, the Mondale people lost precious time in planning for the fall campaign. Following the Convention—and the getting of a little rest—they will have to quickly expand their organization, with little time to work out kinks; raise a lot of money; work out their media strategy. They will have to help Ferraro find a staff (this has already begun) and brief her on Mondale's positions and on foreign policy—fast. The Reagan-Bush campaign has no such pressures on it.

Right now, the Mondale campaign intends to try to get out its own base, increase the turnout, and reach independents, but at some point it will have to face choices of priorities. Most pre-Convention polls indicated that the Mondale campaign was reaching only seventy to eighty per cent of those who called themselves Democrats, and the campaign believes it has to get that number up into the ninety-per-cent range. If, as it assumes, the Democratic Party equals roughly forty-five per cent of the electorate, seventy-five per cent or so of that gives it only thirty-five per cent or so of the electorate. Therefore, it has to find other voters by expanding the base by registering new voters, and, through persuasion, attract "weak Democrats" who supported Reagan in 1980, and also attract independents. In some instances, the interests of weak Democrats and independents converge. Among the target voters—beyond the base—are people who are moderate ideologically: people who are in the middle-income and middle-age categories; some younger voters who were part of the Hart constituency; some blue-collar workers. According to Johnson, some states will be more winnable by registering new voters; some will be more winnable by persuasion, and the persuadables in one part of the country will not be politically like the persuadables somewhere else.

One polling statistic that has received a lot of notice from strategists of both parties is that younger voters—aged forty and under—are inclined to support Reagan. If these "baby-boomers," who could be entering the voting force in large numbers, and constitute half the voting-age population, continue this voting pattern, it would cause a fundamental realignment of party support. Various experts ascribe the Reagan support on the part of voters twenty-five and under to the fact that they have really known only two Presidents—Carter and Reagan. In general, the younger voters are said to be liberal on social matters, but conservative on economic matters. Patrick Caddell, the pollster, says that young males under thirty tend to be very Republican, very pro-military. Stuart Spencer, one of Reagan's most astute political advisers, says that though younger voters tend to be more liberal than Reagan on social matters, they don't expect him to be liberal on them, and they are more in tune with him on economic matters than they are with the Democrats. Moreover, Spencer says, "They like his style—they like a guy who gets Michael Jackson to the White House and can handle it." (Jackson, the most famous enter-

tainer in America at the moment, appeared—sequinned costume
and white glove and all—at the White House on May 14th, to be
praised by Reagan for writing a song that was subsequently used
in a campaign against drunk driving.) Spencer says the younger
voters know things weren't working the other way, and are looking
for a change. In this election, both sides will be going after these
younger voters, many of whom are in their child-rearing years.
Reagan's about-face and sudden support of a federal law raising
the drinking age to twenty-one a few weeks ago was one evidence
of this, as is his talk about concern for missing children. Mondale
will try to reach these people by talking about the future and what
it might hold for their children if he or if Reagan serves for the
next four years. It was no accident that on Tuesday Mondale and
Ferraro went to speak with a group of junior-high-school students
in San Francisco. It is not by accident that the word "family" is so
much in vogue at this Convention. Cuomo was chosen as keynoter
because Mondale likes the way he talks about the nation as a
family and also stresses family values. The choice of Ferraro was
intended, among other things, to reach out to younger voters, and
Ferraro also exemplifies family. Actually, in talking about "family"
the Democrats are talking about different things. Cuomo's metaphor is one of them. According to Martin Kaplan, Mondale's
speechwriter, "family" is a proxy for a whole range of issues, including economic security—a way of talking about the effect of
governmental policy on people's lives without talking about programs and statistics. To describe the effect of unemployment on a
family, as Mondale has been doing, he says, is far more effective
than getting worked up about a number. "Family" also reaches to
parents' concerns about their children's education and future, and
also about their own parents' economic well-being and health care.
In the course of the year, Mondale has talked about policies in
these terms, often drawing on his personal background. (He
seems to have learned something from Reagan.) But the concept
of the impact of policy on "the family" is not new to Mondale; this
is something he talked about in his Senate days, but now he seems
to have given the concept new political flesh. Talk about the family
is also meant to convey a sense of concern about the community,
about safety. Further, it is to suggest that there are other mediating
institutions in our society than government, other vehicles
through which certain values can be encouraged. If the Demo-

cratic Party is to be the majority party, the theory goes, it has to attract people who believe in those things—mainstream Americans. Reagan attracted enough of those people in 1980 to defeat the Democrats, and now the Democrats are fighting to get them back.

This evening, Beckel, now almost ill with fatigue, is still dealing with Jackson over Jackson's demands about the Fairness Commission and his role in the campaign, the people he wants involved in the Mondale campaign, and his role in the voter-registration drive. Beckel has been trying to explain to Jackson that he can't give him answers on everything by tomorrow.

Now, at a few minutes past five-thirty, California time, Geraldine Ferraro is accepting the nomination to run as the Vice-Presidential candidate. The roll call on her nomination was changed to a vote by acclamation midway, because the Convention was running nearly an hour and a half behind schedule and Mondale's managers are determined to get his speech on television in prime time in the East. The emotion in the hall over Ferraro's nomination is a kind of joy I have never seen at a Convention: the fact of it has excited people all week, and the enactment of it this evening took the reaction to a new level. Though Ferraro has been all over town during the week, this is her first appearance before the Convention. There remains, of course, a large reservoir of questions about how she will go over in some parts of the country, how well she will hold up over time, whether she will wear well with the voters, whether many voters will decide that she simply isn't ready to step in as President. On the other side of it, a lot of experienced politicians think that the choice of Ferraro has released energies that will be of enormous help to the ticket, and has transformed Mondale in a lot of people's eyes. But a large part of the impact Ferraro is having right now is beyond politics, or political analysis, and it is, at least for the moment, affecting people who hadn't expected to feel a thing. Her standing up there reaches the experience of women who have been confronted with barriers, inequities, and indignities as they have tried to function in the world— reaches angers long buried and indignities long swallowed—and suggests that maybe now something has changed. (Men who understand what many women have gone through share their reaction now.) It is a feeling much like that which blacks have had about Jackson.

Ferraro tells the Convention, "I stand before you to proclaim tonight: America is the land where dreams can come true for all of us." She looks handsome in a white coat-dress; her blond hair, cut in a neither too soft nor too hard wedge, has already become a trademark. Her voice is clear, if not particularly strong, and tonight, in contrast to some other occasions, she paces herself carefully. She refers to her immigrant father and says, "Our faith that we can shape a better future is what the American dream is all about." This is one of the new ticket's major themes. She continues, "The promise of our country is that the rules are fair. If you work hard and play by the rules, you can earn your share of America's blessings." She works in references to her own life (the Mondale people believe that Ferraro's story is emblematic of the campaign's political message): she was a housewife, raised three children, was a public-school teacher, went to law school at night, became an assistant district attorney—"and I put my share of criminals behind bars." She says that when she first ran for Congress from Queens "the political experts" said that a Democrat could not win. "But I put my faith in the people and the values that we shared." (Her district has gone Republican in the last three Presidential elections.) She talks about the similarity of values held by the people of Queens and those of Elmore, Minnesota, where Mondale grew up, and where she and Mondale visited last week before heading West—the concern that their children have good schools, the "pride in supporting their families through hard work and initiative." She is going at those mainstream values, trying to tug them back from Reagan. She criticizes the Reagan Administration, saying that "it isn't right" that the tax system is as it is, that young people fear they won't get their Social Security (Reagan mentioned this possibility not long ago), that "young couples question whether to bring children into a world of fifty thousand nuclear warheads." She says that "it isn't right that a woman should get paid fifty-nine cents on the dollar for the same work as a man." She receives big cheers.

The writing of Ferraro's speech was coordinated with that of Mondale's, and as Mondale's changed so did Ferraro's. Her delivery is good, and she projects a combination of femininity and toughness—a subliminal message that says, "Don't mess." She gets enormous cheers as she says, "By choosing a woman to run for our nation's second-highest office, you send a powerful signal to all Americans. There are no doors we cannot unlock. We will place no limits on achievement." Unlocking doors was talked about as a theme when Mondale was connecting his Vice-Presidential choice with his campaign message in the discussions at North Oaks, and it was talked about by both Mondale and Ferraro when Mondale introduced Ferraro in St. Paul. She adds, to more cheers, "If we can do this, we can do anything." Something has been unlocked, and Mondale unlocked it—the magnitude of the response seems to be something of a surprise even to the Mondale people. There are certain things that polling and data, and even intuition and instinct, can't tell you—they can only be guessed at until they happen. A phenomenon, by definition, is not subject to prior analysis, and at the moment the reaction to Ferraro is a phenomenon—of what lasting intensity it is impossible to judge now. Right now, the message Mondale is trying to send through his choosing of her is working. This cannot be an easy performance for her—rarely, probably, has anyone been watched more closely. She delivers her speech with assurance, probably born of the same confidence that made her go after the position she now has. Her performance and the reaction of the audience to her seem to legitimize her, make her choice seem neither an accident nor a payoff to pressure—though there will be weeks of seeing her in less glorious circumstances.

Firmly, she says, "To an Administration that would have us debate all over again whether the Voting Rights Act should be renewed and whether segregated schools should be tax-exempt, we say: Mr. President, those debates are over." These references to the Administration's delayed endorsement of an extension of the Voting Rights Act and to its attempting to extend tax-exempt status to Bob Jones University (a move that was rebuffed by the Supreme Court) bring more cheers. She says, "To those concerned about the strength of American family values, as I am, I say: We are going to restore those values—loving, caring, partnership." The Democrats are showing a new appreciation for emblematic talk. "To our students and their parents, we say: We will insist on the highest standards of excellence, because the jobs of the future require skilled minds." This will be another campaign theme. When she mentions the Equal Rights Amendment, there are, of course, enormous cheers. And, as part of the struggle for the votes of the younger generation, she says, "To young Americans who may be called to our country's service, we say: We know your generation of Americans will proudly answer our country's call, as each generation before you." And, moving in on more of Reagan's territory, she cites the recent commemoration of the fortieth anniversary of the invasion of Normandy and the burial at Arlington National Cemetery, on Memorial Day, of an unknown soldier from the Vietnam War—a ceremony in which Reagan, as he did at Normandy, prominently, and effectively, figured. She says, "Let no one doubt we will defend America's security and the freedom around the world. But we want a President who tells us what America is fighting for, not just what we are fighting against." And she calls for the defense of human rights, making, like Cuomo, an embrace of ideologies—"from Chile to Afghanistan, from Poland to South Africa." She closes quietly (she knows how to modulate the voice) by talking, movingly, about using the "gift of life" to help others, by paying tribute to her own family, and by saying, "To all the children of America, I say: The generation before ours kept faith with us, and, like them, we will pass on to you a stronger, more just America." And then, as she stands there with her family, waving to the hall, another set of symbols is on display: we are seeing an amalgam, apparently successful, of the traditional and the quite modern—the family-oriented career woman with the strong, supportive husband. This is both a cultural and a political statement. The orchestra plays the theme from "All in the Family," which was set in a part of Queens—Ferraro lives in a wealthier section—and the Tarantella and then rock music, and a very happy crowd, a joyful one, bounces and sways to the music. I do not recall seeing a Convention so happy.

For all that the Convention has accomplished thus far, there is still much to be accomplished by Mondale's speech tonight. Mondale's own people are aware that he came out of the nomination contest with high "negatives"—the largest problem being that he was not seen as a leader. His fight for the nomination was themeless and lacking focus. A post-primaries poll done for the Mondale campaign showed not only that people thought Mondale lacked leadership but that he hadn't made his case: that people didn't make a connection between the stakes in the election and Mondale. It also indicated that people connected Mondale with "special interests" and "old ways." The data, Mondale and his strategists concluded, called for a bold departure. (One Mondale strategist says, "We spent twenty million dollars in the primaries and hadn't advanced his image very far.") Part of the problem was what Mondale and his campaign staff saw as the exigencies of defeating Hart, part of the problem was the way Mondale's mind works. He sees things on many levels and thinks in terms of lists. Here was a man who wanted to talk to the voters about misalignment of currencies. He is suspicious of themes. The three he started out the year with, in his speech to the Press Club in Washington on January 3rd—arms control, fairness, and restoring America's competitive edge—represented his staff's own best effort to pare the list. There is something to the point that Mondale was appointed to so many of his positions—Attorney General of Minnesota, senator (though he ran successfully for reelection), Vice-President. He had never had to get out there on his own and establish his identity with the voters. He had never been on the line as a leader. This campaign was his first such test, and though he gave some very good speeches on occasion (Mondale's abilities as a speaker are generally underrated), he did not do it often, or with thematic consistency. And there is something ominous about the fact that up until only a few hours ago Mondale's campaign themes were still being worked on, revised. Reagan's themes have been in place for twenty years. (Reagan and Mondale, in fact, entered national politics at about the same time: Reagan as the instantly successful television spokesman for the Goldwater ticket; Mondale as Hubert Humphrey's ally and successor in the Senate.) Reagan's themes are in his bones; that is why he is so convincing. Mondale will have to show that his are not just in his head. And he will have to stay with them with a discipline that he has not yet shown in this regard. Reagan has always offered himself as the champion of a cause; Mondale was a Party man. Mondale did in fact champion causes in the Senate—the cause of civil rights, of migrant workers, of poor children—but this part of his past has receded from view. He still talks with passion, and obvious sincerity, about social justice, but somehow his *politicalness* blurred the picture of him. The "Fighting Fritz" of the nomination contest may have prevailed—and erased doubts about his determination and resilience—but it wasn't his most attractive side.

As for what kind of President he might be, people who have known Mondale over the years believe him to be highly intelligent, sophisticated in his thinking, knowing about government, competent, and decent. He has, for the most part, good taste in people, and admires intelligence and is intellectually curious, and he is probably the best-informed candidate to have run for the office in a long time. There are, however, two big questions about him. One has to do with his personal strength in dealing with others—not with stagy assertiveness that passes for strength but with the ability to say no, to not become paralyzed by conflicting demands. Mondale's campaign thus far has not put this question to rest, though Mondale himself, aware of the question, insists that he will be able to mediate among those demands. The other question has to do with whether, simply, he can establish the kind of relationship with the American people that will enable him to lead. All the good will and intelligence in the world will not suffice if people do not want to follow him. If he cannot establish that kind of relationship, he would be another failed President. The coming campaign should tell us whether he can.

Tonight, Mondale is introduced by Kennedy, who comes to the podium amid big cheers. Kennedy won this spot after failing to be named the keynoter. Kennedy and Mondale have had a sometimes difficult political relationship. In 1980, Mondale was sent out to do the heavy campaigning against Kennedy in his challenge to Carter. This year, Kennedy had told Mondale that he would endorse him when it became necessary, but when, after New Hampshire, Mondale asked Kennedy for his endorsement Kennedy backed off, saying he had meant that he would help Mondale out against Glenn. Mondale was described as crushed (and the decision to write off Massachusetts was made at once), but some of Mondale's advisers think this disappointment was the thing that finally convinced Mondale that if he was to win the nomination he had to do it on his own. But Mondale and Kennedy are political professionals who understand the costs of nursing grievances and the benefits of understanding the other person's position (eventually), and have the ability to put things behind them.

Kennedy's speech is tough, partisan, and funny—the kind of meat-throwing speech that he loves to give. His voice is big and his head bobs in approval of his own effective lines. This is the "hot," partisan Kennedy, employing a style that caused him problems in the 1980 primaries—and that he set aside for his Convention speech then—but that the audience here is eating up. Kennedy, too, helps build the morale of the Party tonight. He says, "In the great struggle of social justice in our century, the Democratic Party has been the tribune of the people, the enemy of the interests. And I do not see how our opponents can ever dare to mention this question in 1984." He is helping Mondale redefine the "special interests" issue. He continues, "For the greatest collection of special interests in all American history has now assembled inside the cold citadel of privilege known as the Republican Party." Kennedy is almost a senior statesman in the Party now; this is the first Democratic Convention since 1968 at which there has not been speculation about him. Inevitably, he turns up on the lists of who will run next time, and clearly he is keeping himself before the Party, but he was rejected last time; it is true that the Carter White House waged a rough campaign against him, but it is also true that Kennedy started out with most people believing that he would prevail. And then the polls indicated that a large number of people still had questions about his character.

Now Kennedy mocks Reagan for calling for a constitutional amendment requiring a balanced budget: "They have had their four years in office—and where, oh where, is their balanced budget?" He refers often to what "President Mondale" will do—trying to help people get used to the idea. He says that all President Reagan's health needs are taken care of, "and if he has to go to the hospital for an X-ray all he has to do to call his helicopter is push a little button," and he adds, "I just hope it's the right button." The Convention hall explodes with cheers and laughter. He criticizes Reagan for his record on arms control and questions the sincerity of the Administration's recent moves to resume talks with the Soviet Union. Kennedy says, "Until now, Ronald Reagan has never met an arms-control agreement he didn't dislike." He says, "In the Cabinet Room in the White House, Mr. Reagan has taken down Harry Truman's picture and put up the portrait of his hero"—and he says, slowly and playfully—"*Calvin Coolidge.*" The audience roars with laughter. Kennedy is giving it a good time. "And how appropriate that is," he adds.

Then Kennedy says something that he talks about in private and that clearly troubles him: "The Reagan advisers now practice polarization politics as a conscious instrument of their campaign." He adds, fitting this speech into one of the themes of the Convention, "We can be proud that our Party has been the political home for generations of immigrants, of every color and from every country and faith." He describes Mondale as "a good man, a strong and caring man, tempered in the Vice-Presidency, tested in a long and hard campaign, a leader of rare gifts and great heart." He closes by saying, "And let me say to any of you who supported someone else: I know you may feel a sense of disappointment. But we have an election to fight and to win and a candidate who unites us in great and common purpose." He adds, "Even when we were on different sides in 1980, I never lost my friendship for Fritz Mondale. I admire his courage and commitment." He says, "The nation does not fully know him yet, but I remember how the best leaders of our time thought of Walter Mondale"—and, his voice breaking for just an instant, he refers to "my brother Robert Kennedy, who was close to him in the Senate." He concludes, with his big voice booming now—Kennedy has done his bit to unify the Party, and done it well—"My fellow-citizens, I present to you our leader, who never gave up in adversity, who came back against the odds, who won at this great Convention, and who will win an even greater victory in November: the nominee of the Democratic Party and the next President of the United States, *Walter Mondale*."

Mondale comes to the podium to great cheers, and the theme from *Rocky* to a rock beat. (Mondale chose the *Rocky* theme for himself earlier this year.) No "Happy Days Are Here Again"— which has been played only a couple of times all week; the Party is doing everything to suggest that it is more modern, with it. The happy crowd shouts, "We want Fritz"—and Mondale beams and seems moved. Lord knows he worked hard for this moment, and at several points it almost eluded him. And even when, in June, he eked out enough delegates there was no reason to expect the mood that is here tonight—nor was there in subsequent weeks. Now the delegates are waving small plastic American flags— twenty thousand of them—in one more move on Reagan's territory, this move a visually striking one. The Democrats surrendered the flag in the nineteen-sixties, when student demonstrators burned it and the followers of Richard Nixon put tiny flag pins in their lapels. Why others didn't put on the flag pin, why they didn't refuse to let the right appropriate the flag, was never clear. As the Republicans became more political about patriotism, the Democrats became vaguely uneasy about it—associating it with militarism and phony bravado. The Democrats haven't known what to do about it—until now. (The idea for the flags tonight was offered by a young Mondale advance man.) The Democrats in the hall seem delighted by the spectacle of themselves waving the flag—they do it cheerfully, without menace. The last time—and the only time in a long time—that the flag was a unifying symbol was on the Fourth of July in 1976, when we celebrated the Bicentennial. The unexpected national happiness on that day was a clue to the desire to stop having patriotism be a divisive question—but then everyone seemed to forget about it.

The hall is utterly still as Mondale begins his speech. He refers to the long contest that led to the nomination: "It was hot—but the heat was passion, and not anger. It was a roller coaster—but it made me a better candidate, and it will make me a stronger President of the United States." One of the purposes of this speech is to introduce Mondale all over again to the American people. Peter Hart, Mondale's pollster, says that Mondale is well known but not known well. In his own celebration of the diversity of the Democratic Party, Mondale says, "I do not envy the drowsy harmony of the Republican Party. They squelch debate, we welcome it." He continues, "Just look at us here tonight: black and white, Asian and Hispanic, native and immigrant, young and old, urban and rural, male and female"—and, in a reach for the coalition he must put together—"from yuppie to lunch pail." He pays tribute to the other speakers and candidates—setting off cheers in each instance. And then, stating his basic theme, the one on which he has decided he wants to fight the election, he mentions his own children and says, "This election is a referendum on their future—and on ours." He is trying to establish the stakes. Then he says simply, "I'm Walter Mondale," and he tells some of the story of his life. It's odd that a political candidate has to do this, but in the course of doing it Mondale shows, as he tried to when he did this in some of his appearances on the campaign trail, something about the values that formed him, and tries to make himself seem more human. Referring to his choice of Ferraro, he says, "Tonight, we open a new door to the future." He continues, "Mr. Reagan calls it 'tokenism.' We call it America." The audience cheers happily. After going on with his biography a bit, he says a surprising thing: "And then in 1980 Ronald Reagan beat the pants off us." This is a disarming thing, and is the beginning of a section in which Mondale, surprising still more, says that he got the message in 1980. Reaching out to the coalition he needs, he says, "So tonight I want to say something to those of you across our country who voted for Mr. Reagan—Republicans, independents, and, yes, some Democrats: I heard you, and your party heard you." Mondale hasn't talked like this before. He talks of his four years of travelling the country and says, "I listened to all of the people of our country," and he makes a little joke about the bags under his eyes that developed in the campaign—this to show his self-deprecating sense of humor, and to indicate, too, that he's not oblivious to the picture people had of him.

He continues, laying out another of his themes, "So tonight we come to you with a new realism: ready for the future and recapturing the best in our tradition." Mondale, the transitional figure, seems to be making the transition before our very eyes. He was not unaware of new realities before this, but during the primaries he fell back on old habits of talking. It disturbed some of his backers that he allowed himself to be seen as old hat when, at least intellectually, he was somewhere else, and that with a little bit of adjustment he could have come across as a more contemporary figure. There was no reason, they thought, for him to concede "the future" to Hart. Now he says, "We know that America must have a strong defense, and a sober view of the Soviets. We know that government must be as well managed as it is well meaning. We know that a healthy, growing private economy is the key to the future." And then, referring to a figure he would like to be likened to, and also trying to deal with a question he and his advisers know is on people's minds, he says, "We know that Harry Truman spoke the truth: A President . . . has to be able to say yes and no, but mostly no." He invites his listeners to "look at our platform," and, once again trying to display a new realism, a pulling back of the Democratic Party from its image as a squanderer—and also anti-business—he says, "There are no defense cuts that weaken our security; no business taxes that weaken our economy; no laundry list that raids our Treasury. We are wiser, stronger, and we are focussed on the future." Then, in a deft move, he says, "If Mr. Reagan wants to rerun the 1980 campaign, fine. Let them fight over the past. We're fighting for the American future." The Reagan campaign does want to rerun the 1980 election, and this may just undercut its efforts. Much of what an election is about is a

competition to control the agenda—to be on the offensive instead
of the defensive. If Mondale can stick with this, can give references to the 1980 election the back of his hand, he will have
accomplished a lot.

Then, in another deft move, Mondale tells those who voted for
Reagan what he believes they did not vote for: a two-hundred-
billion-dollar deficit, an arms race, turning "the heavens into a
battleground." He continues, "You did not vote to destroy family
farming. You did not vote to trash the civil-rights laws. You did not
vote to poison the environment." He is trying to get those who
voted for Reagan out of unhappiness with Carter to stop and
think. Anticipating an argument Reagan is bound to make, Mondale says, "Four years ago, many of you voted for Mr. Reagan
because he promised you'd be better off. And today the rich are
better off. But working Americans are worse off, and the middle
class is standing on a trapdoor." He has to convince the middle
class of that. He repeats something he has said throughout the
primaries, about Lincoln's saying that ours should be a government of, by, and for the people, but now we have a government of,
by, and for the rich. He goes into a populist attack on the Reagan
record. But he will have to keep the populism under control if he
wants to broaden his constituency, and to be able to govern.

"If this Administration has a plan for a better future, they're
keeping it a secret," Mondale says, and he continues, "Here's the
truth about the future: We are living on borrowed money and
borrowed time." He says that by the end of his first term he will
reduce the budget deficit by two-thirds. This ups the ante from
where it was during the campaign, when he said he would reduce
it by half. His people say that they can find the extra thirty billion
dollars or so to meet this goal, that they are working on "alternatives" for fulfilling this pledge and will lay out the plan in due
time. They will be under pressure to do so. And then Mondale
does something very surprising. He says that taxes will have to go
up. He says, "Mr. Reagan will raise taxes, and so will I. He won't
tell you. I just did." This is greeted with great cheers and applause.
It was another bold and clever stroke, accomplishing several
things at once. During the primaries, Mondale had said that taxes
would have to be raised and there was no question that Reagan
would come after him for that, so he has turned a potential liability into a virtue through a bit of preemption. By doing some-

thing bold, he is still changing the picture of him that people have. The theory is that people see strength in a politician who does something that people don't expect politicians to do. (That's why politicians are always prefacing some not particularly controversial proposal with "I shouldn't say this, but . . ." or "My advisers warned me not to do this, but . . .") In this case, Mondale really did something people don't expect politicians to do. Another purpose of the line is to lay in a challenge to Reagan's credibility. As Mondale said the line about taxes, a delegate near where I am standing shouted "Go, Harry!" and said to a fellow-delegate, "It's a new Harry Truman." This whole section of Mondale's speech is part of another theme: that Mondale will speak realistically about the present and the future—leaving people to draw a contrast with Reagan. Now the newly fiscal-conservative Mondale says, "To the Congress, my message is: We must cut spending and pay as we go. If you don't hold the line, I will: that's what the veto is for." Would Mondale really be like that? "Now, that's my plan to cut the deficit," Mondale says. "Mr. Reagan is keeping his plan secret until after the election. That's not leadership; that's salesmanship. And I think the American people know the difference." He challenges Reagan "to put his plan on the table next to mine," and to debate him on it. He is trying to pull Reagan off the plane of symbols and optimism, and down into a sharp debate over what each of them would do. This is probably Mondale's best hope.

Touching on another theme, Mondale says, "It is time for America to have a season of excellence. Parents must turn off that television, students must do their homework, teachers must teach, and America compete." Mondale had toyed with this theme earlier, in part as a response to the charge that he was too tied to the "special interests." He had thought to try to make the point that his connections with teachers, labor, and so on would enable him to encourage them to meet higher standards; while what he says here starts to get at that point, it seems a bit fainthearted. This passage is also a sign of his new interest in symbolic leadership, in what a President can accomplish, beyond programs, by what he says. Whether the interest will last cannot be known now. Mondale returns to the subject of trade, which he talked about during the primaries. At this point, the speech is getting a little listy after all. He talks about human rights, and says, "We know the deep differences with the Soviets." But then he goes on to talk about the importance of arms control, and condemns the Administration's record in this area. "Why has this Administration failed?" he asks, his voice rising. "Why can't they understand the cry of Americans and human beings for sense and sanity in control of these god-awful weapons?" And, to the loud cheers of the audience—the last bit was an interpolation—he says, passionately, "Why? Why?" For the most part, however, his delivery style tonight has been firm and deliberate—no red-faced jowl-shaking tonight. He renews his proposal for annual summit meetings with the Soviet Union. And then he talks about what he wants to see by "the second term of the Mondale-Ferraro Administration" (a deft way of trying to get people to think about what a Reagan Administration might look like four years from now, as well as of laying out the stakes as he sees them): he talks of children no longer having nuclear night-mares, of students saying that they want to be teachers, of there being no hungry children, of America having got its competitive edge back. He says, "By the start of the next decade, I want to point to the Supreme Court and say, 'Justice is in good hands.' " He mentions, of course, the E.R.A. He has won the audience to him with this speech in a way he has never won an audience over before.

The preparation for this moment began Monday, and the Convention proceedings have been a straight line to this—with the Mondale people constantly warding off trouble in the background. The Democrats have been through a sort of therapy session, and they feel far better about themselves than they expected to, or than there was any reason to expect them to. They have their morale back, which is a major achievement. How long they will keep it is a question, but for now it is as if one has witnessed a healing. Challengers have been dispatched with as much grace as was possible. The Party, shattered, demoralized, and confused after 1980, has a new focus. Not a perfect focus—these are Democrats—but more focus than it had a few days ago. Now Mondale, speaking quietly, concludes, returning to two of his basic themes, "My friends, America is a future each generation must enlarge; a door each generation must open; a promise each generation must keep. For the rest of my life, I want to talk to young people about their future." And he says that he wants to hear some of them, "whatever their race, whatever their religion, whatever their sex," say what he is saying tonight "with joy and reverence," and he says, "I want to be the President of the United States."

As more rock music breaks out, a remarkably happy Convention cheers its candidate, then its candidate and his family, then its Presidential and Vice-Presidential candidates. The delegates stomp, rock, and clap to the music. Red, white, and blue balloons drop. Whatever reality waits outside and in the future, there is a reality here that the delegates are consciously treasuring. Not all the followers of Mondale's opponents are overjoyed, of course, but there are fewer stony faces than usual at the end of a contested Convention. Several Hart people say that they give Mondale much credit for what he said tonight. And now people seem to simply want to have a good time. The other candidates appear at the podium, along with a large number of Party notables, and the music turns into a patriotic medley—with the audience happily waving the flags and singing along: "You're a Grand Old Flag," "The Marine Hymn." Then Jennifer Holliday sings a slow, heart-breakingly beautiful version of "The Battle Hymn of the Republic," as the hall is utterly silent. A rabbi asks the people in the hall to join hands while he offers a prayer. And then the Convention ends as thousands of flags wave and the band plays "The Stars and Stripes Forever."

XVIII

Sunday. The Republicans gathering here in this wealthy, swelter-
ing city (108° today) to renominate President Reagan and Vice-
President Bush are confident of victory in November. The polls—
ones taken by their own campaign organization and also the public polls—would seem to justify this confidence. Walter Mondale
did get a big boost out of his Convention—a Gallup poll published
just after the Convention put him two points ahead of Reagan,
and while the Reagan-Bush campaign committee's polls following
the Democratic Convention did not put the election that close,
they did show that Mondale had gained more than the Reagan-
Bush officials had expected, and showed the Reagan ticket leading
by six points. Moreover, at first the Reagan campaign was clearly
at a loss as to how to deal with Geraldine Ferraro as the first
woman Vice-Presidential candidate, and got all tangled up with
itself over how to respond to Mondale's taunt, in his acceptance
speech, that whoever was the next President would have to raise
taxes, and that Mondale was willing to admit it but Reagan wasn't.
There was also a bit of flurry over the fact that during the Reagans'
recent vacation at the ranch Mrs. Reagan was heard muttering, in
response to a question to Reagan about arms control, "Doing
everything we can"—which the President then repeated. Mrs.
Reagan later explained that she was talking to herself and the
President must have overheard her. (However, I saw a similar
thing take place during the 1980 primaries.) The Reagan campaign had in fact had a ragged few weeks: aside from these things,
Reagan, on August 11th, joked into an open microphone as he
was preparing for his Saturday radio address, "My fellow-Amer-
icans, I'm pleased to tell you today that I've signed legislation that
will outlaw Russia forever. We begin bombing in five minutes." His
advisers, who worry about Reagan's being seen by the public as

insufficiently careful and thoughtful in his dealings with the Soviet Union, were dismayed. Then Michael Deaver, the deputy chief of staff and the most loyal of Reagan aides, told Chris Wallace, of NBC News, in an interview broadcast on August 13th, that the President dozes off in cabinet meetings. White House aides tried to mitigate this with explanations that anyone would fall asleep in some of those meetings, or that they had never seen the President fall asleep in a meeting, because the remark went to a larger set of questions about Reagan: how engaged and informed a President he is. Polling done for the campaign has begun to pick up the fact that this is a question on the public's mind. Most of these events took place while the President was on his extended vacation at his ranch—a time when things often seem to go wrong. A close adviser said to me today, with a sigh, "We should learn our lesson; every August when the President goes on vacation, and the staff goes on vacation, we don't prepare ourselves for what might happen."

Nevertheless, despite everything, less than a week after the Democratic Convention the polling done for the Reagan-Bush committee indicated that the Reagan ticket had bounced back and was leading the Mondale ticket by ten points. (A recent poll taken for the campaign in Texas, a key state, showed the Reagan-Bush ticket leading the Mondale-Ferraro ticket by almost two to one.) Then publicly published polls began to show large leads by Reagan: by mid-August, a New York *Times*/CBS poll had Reagan leading by fifteen points; a Louis Harris poll had him ahead by twelve points. And the Reagan campaign's own tracking polls had Reagan ahead by a range of eleven to fourteen points. The electoral-college arithmetic has always been difficult for Mondale, because Reagan starts with a seemingly unshakable base of support in the South and the West (though not necessarily in all states in those regions), and, as things stand now, there are the makings of an electoral-college landslide for Reagan. The counts by both sides early in the year which showed that it was possible for Mondale to win were made before the primaries began, and before anything went wrong for Mondale. Though Reagan's advisers worry about overconfidence and complacency, and raise the usual caveats about what could still go wrong, and assert that the race is bound to narrow, even the most cautious of them find it hard now to see how Reagan could lose.

One theory of what has been happening is that though the public reacted positively to the Democratic Convention—a reaction enlarged in part because the Convention exceeded expectations—it does not react positively to Mondale. Jim Lake, the communications director of the Reagan-Bush campaign, said to me here, "There is no support for Mondale out there; the support he has is anti-Reagan." In fact, something new might have happened this year: it is an axiom of politics that the people do not focus on the Presidential election until after Labor Day, and do not make up their minds until late; but some analysts think that the public has such a strong impression of both Reagan and Mondale by now—Reagan through his forceful and positive presentation of himself as President, Mondale through his scarring, bitter campaign for the nomination (embellished by some fumbles and some bad luck)—that the election may already be settled. One Republican analyst says that at this point four years ago there was a much higher percentage of undecided voters than there is now: twenty per cent as compared with seven per cent. It is clear here not only that there are fractures within the Republican Party but that the Republicans who will begin their Convention tomorrow do not represent a cross-section of the Party—the conservatives and right-wingers far outnumber the moderates. It is also possible that the political picture will change—perhaps several times—before the election. But there is no question that Reagan is a political phenomenon—a man who by force of personality and marvellous stage management superimposes himself over his party, and over his own mistakes and controversial policies. The Democrats find it both a source of frustration and an opportunity that the polls consistently show that Reagan is more popular than his policies are. His over-all job-approval rating (generally in the fifty-five-per-cent range) has been higher than the approval of his handling of the economy, and that has been higher than the approval of his handling of foreign policy. (The foreign-policy rating has been negative for some time.) But it is also a fact that in an apparently strong economy—how healthy it really is is in much dispute—Reagan has still another advantage, for the buoyancy of the economy at the moment (the stock market has recently rallied, presumably in the belief that the Federal Reserve Board will not cause a rise in interest rates before the election) fits right into the politics of optimism and positiveness which is at the heart of the Reagan appeal.

Earlier this summer, the President's political advisers made a point of saying they assumed that the race would tighten in September, perhaps narrowing Reagan's lead to five points. They said this in part because they believed it and in part to prepare the public for such an eventuality. (They said the tendency would be for many Democrats to return to their natural base; a recent poll by Richard Wirthlin, the President's pollster, indicated that fifty-two per cent of the people identify themselves as Democrats and thirty-eight per cent as Republicans.) But while the apparent success of the Democratic Convention and the first polls following it jolted the Reagan people, and while they still say that the margin between Mondale and Reagan will narrow, they are having a harder time looking as if they are seriously worried. In fact, they are now expecting a lead of ten to fifteen points after Labor Day. As of now, they say that they have a lead of about fourteen points—that Reagan leads fifty-three per cent to thirty-nine per cent. Reagan's advisers think that his campaigning right after the Democratic Convention (and sooner than originally planned)—he went to New Jersey, Georgia, and Texas—brought the focus back to the President. Reagan's charge during this trip that the Mondale-Ferraro ticket was "so far left they've left America" was the subject of some dispute among the President's advisers, several of whom thought it was too partisan and "unpresidential." One of Reagan's advisers says, "If the focus is on the President personally, we'll win. If it's on the Party, we'll lose." Even this worry is somewhat ameliorated by the fact that Reagan is now getting a far higher percentage of the Republican vote than Mondale is of the Democratic vote, and Reagan is also getting a majority of independents, plus a fair share of Democrats. Moreover, when Republican pollsters ask people whether they think the country is on the right track or the wrong track, fifty-five per cent say that it is on the right track and forty per cent say that it is on the wrong track. Reagan gets the support of seventy-two per cent of those who think the country is on the right track, while Mondale gets only sixty-four per cent of the vote of those who think the country is on the wrong track. As for the "gender gap," Reagan has a lead of twenty per cent among

males and six per cent among females, and the only subgroup of
women he is not leading among is unmarried females. He has a
strong lead among seventeen-to-twenty-four-year-olds, and leads
in all age groups except that from fifty-five to sixty-four. (He leads
among those over sixty-five.) He has slightly higher support
among Jews than he did in 1980, and about a ten-per-cent lead
among Catholics, and as of now is attracting about half the blue-
collar vote. He is getting about forty per cent of the Hispanic vote
now, a number that his advisers expect to diminish somewhat but
not enough to cause serious trouble.

Therefore, the Reagan people find it hard to see how Mondale
can put together the two hundred and seventy electoral-college
votes necessary for victory. Texas, they believe, is beyond Mondale's reach (they believe that the factors that led to the Democrats'
victory in Texas in 1982 are irrelevant this year—that the main
point was that the incumbent Republican governor was very unpopular), as is California, and, given the states that they believe are
certain to go for Reagan, Mondale must carry either California or
Texas to have a chance. Florida, another state with a large number
of electoral votes, seems well beyond Mondale's reach. The Reagan
people believe that the South crystallized for Reagan in March.
(Ironically, and perhaps uncoincidentally, the Democrats were
fighting in several Southern states in March.) Georgia and Alabama are now considered by the Reagan people beyond Mondale's
reach, and he is given only a slight chance in Louisiana, Mississippi, and some border states. (For all the talk about the Democrats registering blacks in the Southern states, the Republicans,
and their evangelical allies, have been busy registering whites, and
believe that Jesse Jackson has been a net plus for them.) Even in
Arkansas, which was supposed to be Reagan's most vulnerable
Southern state, he now has a lead of thirteen points. Reagan is
seen to be so far ahead in California that his advisers assume that
the Mondale camp's talk about waging a fight there is just feinting.
Reagan's advisers say that Oregon and Washington could present
some difficulties for Reagan. The main point is that Reagan's presumed strength in the Sun Belt states—whose growing population
gives them more electoral votes than in 1980—gives him a major
electoral-vote advantage. Mondale, to win, would have to sweep
the industrial states and carry some New England states, pick up
some Southern and border states, and carry Texas or California—

obviously a daunting challenge. As Reagan's advisers see it, Reagan could do well enough in the South and the West (losing one or two small states in each region) to have, when other states certain to go for him are added, nearly two hundred and seventy electoral votes—without winning any of the industrial states. And, according to the Reagan polls, he is ahead in all the industrial states, by varying margins. Stuart Spencer, one of Reagan's most important political advisers, said to me recently, "This election will be fought from Illinois to New Jersey. In the end, we'll be crossing at airports in those states." As it happens, people in both the Mondale and Reagan campaigns agree that Mondale's task is to virtually redefine the election: to forget the geographics and concentrate on the demographics—to try to move large groups of people all across the country.

The simple fact is, Reagan's advisers believe, that it is difficult to overcome a strong incumbent even when things are going well for the opponent—and, of course, Mondale has had his problems of late. Lee Atwater, the deputy director of the Reagan-Bush campaign, who is a student of political cycles as well as a political practitioner, says that unemployment is the biggest single economic indicator for Republicans, and that unemployment was at an all-time high—since the Great Depression—in 1982. Atwater has a theory that when unemployment goes down by one and a half per cent in the two-year cycle before an election it diffuses itself as an issue, and he points out that unemployment has gone down by three percentage points in the past two years. In other words, the Republicans will benefit more from the recovery from the deep recession than they will be punished for its having happened.

Polls done for the Republicans consistently show that while people are concerned about the deficits, they believe that the Democrats, and not Reagan, are to blame for them. Robert Teeter, who also does polling for the Reagan-Bush campaign, says, "I'm not sure that there is enough time or money in the world for the Democrats to change the perception that Ronald Reagan is for lower taxes, lower spending, and a balanced budget and that Walter Mondale is for higher taxes and more spending." (Polling done for the Republicans has also picked up that people accept the charge that Mondale has made "too many promises.") The Republican pollsters, as well as some independent ones, believe that Reagan even got a political boost out of the Olympics, just ended in Los Angeles. Not only did the Americans win an unprecedented number of gold medals but the whole coverage of the event, and the feel of it, was heavily pro-American, and nationalistic—a feeling encouraged by and associated with Reagan. On the day after the Olympics, Reagan turned up in Los Angeles, donned a red Olympics jacket, and addressed a breakfast honoring the U.S. winners. ("You're living heroes, every one of you—living proof of what happens when America sets its sights high and says, 'Let's create a little excellence.' ")

The Reagan personality is intrinsic to his political appeal. He has a serenity that not only is appealing to the public but gets him by his own problems. Several people who work closely with him describe him as having a fatalistic view that there is a reason for everything. This feeling is said to have intensified after his remarkable recovery from being shot, on March 30, 1981. The serenity reaches into a lot of corners of his Presidency. One longtime aide says, "He doesn't drive himself, and he doesn't worry about little things." Reagan's view of the Presidency, according to several who have been around him, is not of an instrument for his own power but of an opportunity for turning the country in certain directions he has been talking about for years. And this gets to the point of his being "disengaged": he is not an implementer or a forcer of action. He has some directions in mind, and he tends to react to what is put in front of him. Even his much discussed luck, one observer believes, has to do with the fact that Reagan is such a secure person—the serenity, of course, comes from the security—who simply does not get buffeted by things. When something goes wrong, it doesn't ruin his day or, except in extreme circumstances, change his view. All this, plus his ability to forcefully make his case, comes across to the public as "strong leadership"—for which Reagan is very much admired. One of his political advisers says, "Johnson, Nixon, Ford, and Carter all schemed and tried to figure the political angles—and were failed Presidents. Reagan is authentic, and the public recognizes and likes that." Reagan projects the image of a strong leader with a clear plan; his taking a strong stand and appearing to stick to it gives him credit with the public as a strong leader—no matter, it appears, what the stand is. And being for lower taxes and less government spending and a strong America are not unpopular positions. Reagan is superb at making his case in his television speeches; he is a master at asking a rhetorical question that makes it seem that only a fool could disagree with him. People react positively to confidence and serenity and optimism—all marks of the Reagan political personality. We don't particularly enjoy seeing Presidents fret. Though Reagan is often in the end a pragmatist, it does take, by all accounts, a great deal to move him away from his starting position. He is resistant to the little plots hatched by his advisers to get him to change his mind about something—plots that involve getting various people to call him, or going to Mrs. Reagan, who is very influential on certain questions, especially ones having to do with personnel. He is not without his angry moments, and can become quite irritated when the staff starts pulling and hauling in his presence. Sometimes the anger is publicly staged. But Reagan is, by every account, a genuinely courteous and gracious man—also factors in his public appeal. His confident, optimistic nature is both a private and a public asset to him. And though the Democrats try to paint him as a "rich man's President," and the polls indicate people believe this to be the case, Reagan, at least thus far, has managed to get around this—once more, through his personality. Roger Stone, who handles the Northeast for the Reagan-Bush campaign and focusses on the blue-collar vote, says, "Reagan is a cultural Democrat." He continues, "He speaks the language of the common people, forthrightly and instinctively; he talks about growth, jobs, hope, optimism, thrift, neighborhood, patriotism." Reagan is said by a close aide to be conscious of the effect he creates by his confident stride, and to still consciously throw his shoulders back before he makes an entrance.

But despite his vigorous appearance some close observers say that Reagan, now seventy-three, is slowing down. (He has always followed a carefully controlled schedule, fiercely guarded by his wife, and through her, Deaver.) Some who have seen him recently believe that his reaction time has slowed. When he meets with outsiders, he still talks from cue cards and then often wanders off into anecdotes of questionable relevance. (He still enjoys telling Hollywood stories.) Someone who has observed Reagan at close hand says that the one sign of Reagan's advancing age he has noticed is that Reagan is more stubborn. Others say he has his good days and bad days. His press-conference performances are uneven—sometimes he seems up and on, and other times he doesn't seem to be connecting very well. Sometimes his one-liners, which have been part of his political arsenal for a long time, seem spontaneous, sometimes rehearsed. He is described by those who have been around him as shrewd but also intellectually lazy. One does not get much of a picture of Reagan demanding that his staff get to the bottom of something and lay it out before him. It is said that Reagan denies that his policies have benefitted the rich at the expense of the poor—despite numerous studies indicating that this is the case—because he simply does not believe it. Or he will latch onto one statistic that seems to make his case. For example, in a press conference in mid-June he said that people in upper-income brackets are paying a greater percentage of over-all income taxes, and the poor are paying a smaller share, than before his tax-cut program went into effect. However, these statistics are subject to a number of interpretations; one reason for the decline in the tax burden of low-income people was the unemployment caused by the recession.

Reagan is said by his advisers to be at his best when he is acting on his instincts and is on the offensive. It is for this reason, they say, that he muffed his first response to Mondale's tax gambit, in a July 24th press conference. He went through a rather long response that said, in effect, that he wouldn't raise taxes unless revenues fell too short, and it was three weeks before, after more meetings with his top aides, he got the answer to where most of his people were satisfied with it: that he would only raise taxes as "a last resort"— and that even then he would not "consider raising the personal income taxes of working Americans." (There are a number of ways of raising individuals' taxes indirectly, of course—through, for example, a sales tax or a value-added tax.) The President's new position was released in an unusual printed question-and-answer exchange between the President and his press secretary. A week before, Reagan, at his ranch, had said that he had no plans for a tax increase, and Bush, after a lunch with him, said that tax increases were still an "option;" their aides later explained that this occurred because there were no high-level aides around to advise the President and the Vice-President on what to say after they had had lunch together. Reagan's campaign aides blame the whole business of the fumbled responses to Mondale's tax challenge on Reagan's White House staff, whom they see as too "pragmatic," too policy-oriented. The campaign aides are less interested in the fine points of policy. (One told me, "The fight is between those who want the President to 'keep his options open' and those of us who want to win the election. The purpose of all this crap is not to educate the public, it's to win the election.") Eventually, the Reagan campaign not only got a tax response it was content with but believed that it was beginning to turn Mondale's gambit back on him: that it could successfully argue that Mondale would raise taxes as a first resort, while Reagan would raise them only as a last resort, and that Mondale was likely to use the tax revenues for more government spending while Reagan would continue to try to reduce the deficit. An aggressive campaign against Mondale as a taxer and spender is planned.

The to-and-fro within the Reagan campaign on the tax question was symptomatic of the larger points about Reagan as a candidate for reelection. Since it is an article of faith among Reagan's advisers that he is far better on the offensive than on the defensive, they insist that he must be kept in that position. (It can be said that any candidate is better on the offensive than on the defensive, but the difference in Reagan's performances is believed to be considerable.) Though Reagan did win reelection as governor of California, he did it against a not terribly effective opponent, and his reelection margin was much narrower than his first election margin had been. For most of his political career, Reagan has run an insurgency campaign. Running as an incumbent, his aides pointed out to me earlier this summer, has its liabilities: there are controversial policies to defend; there are groups upset by Reagan policies to a greater extent than was the case with more mainstream Republicans (Eisenhower, Nixon, Ford). One of Reagan's long-time advisers says, "Nobody hated Eisenhower. Some people hate Reagan." James Baker, the White House chief of staff, told me earlier this summer, "We have a lightning-rod candidate; he's done things; he stands for things. He generates strong emotions— pro and con." Another disadvantage of incumbency is that it is not as exciting as insurgency. Earlier this summer, Deaver said to me, "The greatest asset the Democrats have is potential complacency on our side. The prairie-fire effect has elected Reagan. It almost got him nominated in '76. He has been able to mobilize the greatest grass-roots organization this country has ever seen. But, because of the nature of the Presidency, you turn Reagan into an

establishment Republican, and that turns a lot of people off. Add
to that the fact that he has made decisions those people don't like,
and the fact that people assume he's going to win. This is the first
election he does not go into as an underdog. The fact that Reagan
has always been underrated was an asset. He'd say, 'There you go
again,' and people were impressed. Now, after four years as a
world leader, as a heroic survivor of the assassination attempt,
people see there's something spectacular there. So he's not underestimated anymore." Deaver also said that the issue of what Reagan would do if reelected would be an easier one for the Democrats than for Reagan. "Every time we say what we'll do, there'll be
a major debate," he said. Reagan raised taxes in his second term as
governor of California, after swearing he wouldn't. It is clear that
whoever is President in the next four years is going to have to do
some politically unpopular things in order to get the deficit down.
There has been an argument within the Administration over
whether to wait to talk about anything specific about taxes until
after the election. As one Reagan adviser told me earlier this
summer, "Popular things cost revenue; unpopular things alienate
people."

While it is commonly assumed that there are enormous advantages to running as the incumbent, and there are, it is also more
complicated. Running as an insurgent, Reagan was a much freer
man: now what he might propose has to be cleared by aides and
bureaucracies. More than one Administration official has complained to me that it is especially difficult to get decisions made
within the Reagan Administration in any event, because Reagan is
such a delegator, and because there are so many checkoff points
within the White House staff; this can keep some unwise things
from happening, of course, but it can also paralyze action. Nonetheless, the appointment of Anne Gorsuch Burford to an advisory
committee having to do with the environment got through; aides
describe this as a matter of "bad timing," since the President was to
meet with some environmentalists for lunch the next day, but Mrs.
Burford was so controversial that no timing would have been pro-
pitious, and some of the President's campaign aides were appalled.
In late July, both the House and the Senate passed non-binding
resolutions calling on the President to withdraw the appointment;
the President said that he would stand by her; and on August 1st
Mrs. Burford withdrew. Meanwhile, she had contributed to the

national vocabulary by describing the advisory committee she was to head as a "nothing-burger."

The tension between insurgency and incumbency is reflected in tensions between the campaign organization at the Reagan-Bush headquarters and the White House staff. There are frequent meetings between the top campaign aides and top White House aides, and everyone is said to agree when it is said that Reagan is better on the offensive and when it is said that Reagan mustn't "sit on his lead." But when it comes to what it means that he should campaign "boldly," that he should propose new initiatives, things begin to break down. A campaign official says, "As an incumbent, you have the Cabinet, the bureaucracy, the White House staff, giving you a million reasons why you can't do something." (I am told there have been, deliberately, no serious discussions, and no proposals committed to paper, within the Administration about how to cut the deficit, out of fear that any such plans would find their way into the press before the election. Similarly, I'm told, the President wasn't shown proposals for his fiscal 1983 budget until Election Day of 1982, so that it could be said of any proposal floating about that the President hadn't seen it.)

The President has, of course, agreed to tax increases, despite his rhetoric. He did so in 1982 and again in 1983, and he recently, quietly, signed into law a fifty-billion-dollar increase in taxes which was part of the "down payment" on the deficit negotiated between him and Congress. Budget cuts of about thirteen billion dollars have been made in entitlement programs, some of them through creative accounting. The argument between the Administration and Congress, in this case including Republicans, over the size of the increase in the defense budget is still under way, but the President long ago agreed with congressional Republicans to cut it, from about thirteen per cent to about eight per cent. (Reagan's original proposal had been padded, in the expectation that Congress would cut it.) The long-run implications of this ostensible paring down may not be so great, however, since most of the new weapons systems the President wants are now on line, and will have to be paid for eventually; stretching out the costs doesn't save money. Several Republicans believe the President pushed the defense increase so far that he broke the consensus within the Party over it. The MX missile is in increasing trouble on Capitol Hill.

The House has again voted to end funding for the "covert" war in Nicaragua, with the support of many Republicans. And the Senate, led by Republicans, has put the question of funding off into the indefinite future. The election of José Napoleón Duarte as President of El Salvador and his successful visits to Washington in May and July helped Reagan recently win seventy million in additional military aid he requested for El Salvador. (The legislators are much taken with Duarte.) For some time, the Administration has been hinting that things might go badly militarily in El Salvador this fall—just in case they do. And if they do the Democratic Congress will be blamed.

Other matters that might have been troublesome for the Administration have more or less gone off the screen. The set of questions surrounding the obtaining of briefing material for Carter for his debate in 1980, and other apparent campaign espionage, evanesced. The House subcommittee looking into the matter could not function on a bipartisan basis, and did not have the support of the House leadership, which was not enthusiastic about dredging up the subject of Carter. So no public hearings were held, and in late May a lengthy report was issued that was inconclusive, for lack of hard evidence. It did say that there was a pattern of "organized efforts" to obtain materials about the Carter campaign, and that it believed that "some crime has occurred" and that any Carter staff member who handed over the Carter material to the Reagan campaign "may have committed embezzlement." But the subcommittee failed to establish how the papers were obtained. In February, the Justice Department closed its investigation into the case, saying it had uncovered "no credible evidence that the transfer violated any criminal law." The department resisted efforts to get it to appoint an independent prosecutor, and in June a Court of Appeals, overruling an order by a lower court that an independent prosecutor be appointed, held that the statute covering the appointment of such a prosecutor did not provide for a court challenge to an Attorney General's refusal to appoint one. As for the agreement to permit the sale of nuclear reactors to China, the high point of Reagan's visit there in April, it has been tucked away as a result of questions about the ambiguous guarantees of nonproliferation the Chinese offered (in a banquet toast).

For all their confidence, the Reagan advisers still offer a list of possible reasons Reagan could lose: interest rates could suddenly shoot up (this would hurt some groups Reagan is most trying to appeal to—young home buyers, farmers, small businessmen); there could be an untoward foreign-policy development. However, it is also the case, as the Reagan people say, that even such a development could play into Reagan's hands, especially if it occurred close to the election. Reagan has not failed yet to make an effective case on television for whatever foreign-policy setback has occurred. There is still some worry that the Democrats could make the "fairness" issue hurt Reagan—could stir up fears that if reelected he will, among other things, make cuts in Medicare and Social Security. (As a precaution, Reagan recently announced that he supported a cost-of-living increase for Social Security recipients next year even if the rate of inflation is so low that the increase is not required by law. This will cost an estimated five billion dollars; but the amount was probably worth the preemption of the Democrats.) However, it is widely believed among the President's advisers that the argument that the Reagan Administration has been unfair to the poor will not hurt, because, as one put it, "those people won't vote for us anyway." What some Reagan people are concerned about is that Mondale will say that, given Reagan's commitment to continue increasing defense spending by substantial amounts and his reluctance to raise taxes, he inevitably will cut Social Security and Medicare. And there is at least a little worry among the people around Reagan that the picture of the Reagan Administration as unfair to the poor is of concern to some independent voters—the same voters who might also be concerned about arms control and the environment. Still, one Reagan adviser pointed out, for Mondale to make such a case "he has to become competitive with us, and right now he's simply not."

When Reagan made his joke about nuclear war, a blip appeared on the Republicans' polling screen, which monitors everything very carefully, showing a drop of five to six points, from a lead of fourteen points, for a few days. Reagan's vulnerability on the subject of nuclear war is something that makes his advisers very nervous. The question has never been, as it is sometimes simplistically put, whether Reagan is a "warmonger": the unease about him has to do with his own seemingly simplistic approach to the Soviet

Union, and his own faith that only the most aggressive of arms buildups will lead to arms control. Reagan's speech in January in which he sounded a conciliatory note toward the Soviet Union was an attempt on the part of his advisers to change the image of him, and when, in June, Reagan was quoted as telling Republican congressional leaders in a White House meeting, "If they want to keep their Mickey Mouse system, that's O.K.," his aides told reporters that this was quite an improvement over Reagan's talk, last year, of the Soviet Union as an "evil empire." Recently, it appeared that there might be talks between the United States and the Soviet Union on anti-satellite weapons—a development that could have been most helpful to Reagan politically. (The Soviet Union has developed and tested a primitive anti-satellite space system, and the United States has developed a more advanced system but has not yet tested it and is planning to do so soon.) In late June, the Soviet Union proposed talks on banning space weapons. In late May and early June, both houses of Congress approved amendments barring the testing of anti-satellite weapons unless the President certified that he was making a good-faith effort to negotiate an agreement on them with the Soviet Union. The necessity and feasibility of such weapons is the subject of some controversy within the Administration—including within the military. However, the civilians in the Pentagon who are in charge of arms-control policy and are opposed to arms control, and who usually win the day, argued that a ban on anti-satellite weapons could not be verified. (This is subject to dispute.) The United States replied to the Soviet suggestion by saying that it "accepted" it but wanted the agenda to include all offensive nuclear weapons—a proposal some Administration officials say they knew the Soviets would refuse. After some extensive, and public, back-and-forth, the exchanges broke down, with each side blaming the other. Some American government officials say they believe that the Soviet government is divided on whether to negotiate with the United States on anything now, and backed off. Some outside experts say they believe that the Soviet Union was serious about trying to stop an arms race in outer space, even if this redounded to the political credit of Reagan. In any event, a number of experts point out that the United States and the Soviet Union are now on the verge of a new qualitative arms race that, like the one that led to both sides having multiple independently targeted reentry vehicles, or

MIRVs, could be impossible to undo. Moreover, in June the Navy quietly deployed the first submarines carrying nuclear-equipped long-range cruise missiles; the deployment had been scheduled, but it came while Congress was considering a moratorium on the weapons. It is now impossible to detect whether a cruise missile is equipped with a nuclear warhead—so yet another qualitative arms race has begun.

The Republicans also realize that they have had an extraordinary piece of good luck in the troubles that are now surrounding Ferraro. The first questions arose, shortly after the Convention, about whether she had validly claimed an exemption from the requirement on a congressional form that a spouse's finances be revealed. The regulations leave very little room for claiming such an exemption. (The members are to have no knowledge of, nor derive any benefit from, such assets, nor expect to derive any.) Ferraro's husband, John Zaccaro, is a real-estate executive. On July 24th, Ferraro defended her action and said in a press release that she would not only disclose her and her husband's holdings in a financial statement that candidates for national office are required by law to file within thirty days of being nominated but would also release his and her tax returns for the past several years. Then, last Sunday, Ferraro brought a heap of trouble on herself by announcing to the press, as she was about to leave for a campaign on the West Coast, that her husband had refused to allow his tax returns to be released. (The law does not require that the candidates, much less their spouses, release their tax returns, but since 1976 some—though not all—candidates have released their returns. Last week, Senator Robert Dole, who ran for Vice-President in 1976, said here that Zaccaro's tax returns should be released, but then it emerged that Dole and his wife, Elizabeth, had not released their returns in 1976.) In early August, the Washington Legal Foundation, a conservative organization, brought a complaint against Ferraro, charging that she had violated the ethics law. A press conference about the complaint was held in a Capitol Hill room that had been arranged for by an organization of conservative Republican congressmen. Another controversy arose over the fact that Zaccaro and the couple's children had lent Ferraro a hundred and thirty thousand dollars for her first race for Congress, in 1978, in violation of the federal election laws. The Federal Election Commission accepted Ferraro's explanation that she had accepted the loans, which she had reported to the F.E.C., because she had been advised by a former F.E.C. attorney that such an action would be legal. Then the lawyer, David Stein, surfaced, and said that this was not the advice he had given Ferraro and her advisers. (Stein, it turns out, had been fired from the commission staff, and William Oldaker, the general counsel of the F.E.C. at the time, said recently that the F.E.C. believed that it was "not improbable" that this was the advice Stein had given the Zaccaros. Oldaker says that using a family member's funds for a campaign is not an unusual mistake, and that if a candidate reported that he or she had done so the agency tended to assume that it was an honest mistake.) It recently emerged that in order to repay the loans Zaccaro sold Ferraro's interest in a building to her partner in the property, who also has other business with Zaccaro, and that Zaccaro himself later bought back his wife's interest from the partner.

Ferraro's statement that her husband's tax returns would not be released inevitably set off a journalistic competition to find out whether she and her husband were hiding something—the assumption was that they must be—and all manner of stories have been printed and allegations and innuendos have been floating about in the past week. (Among the stories that were published was that one of Zaccaro's buildings housed a company that dealt in pornographic materials and allegedly had ties to the Mafia. Zaccaro said that he hadn't been aware of the company's business and would not renew the lease when it expired in January.) At the time that Ferraro made her statement—without any warning to the Mondale people—her husband was resisting the release of his tax returns, but apparently the matter was not closed. But the damage was done, and the Mondale campaign lost time and momentum— Mondale was out campaigning, but little attention was paid to what he said, just as little was paid to what Ferraro said on the West Coast, other than in response to questions about her troubles. (Ferraro's financial statement is to be issued tomorrow, and she is to hold a press conference on Tuesday.) Meanwhile, some Mondale advisers have been helping her deal with these problems, and the Arthur Young accounting firm has been retained by the Zaccaros to go over their affairs.

Time is one of the most precious commodities in politics. And now the Mondale campaign, which had been admired by Reagan's advisers not long ago as one that made few mistakes, was acquiring the dangerous aspect of appearing incompetent. (The Reagan people say this has been turning up in their polls.) Early this month, Bert Lance, as had been inevitable from the time of the Democratic Convention, resigned as general chairman of the Mondale campaign—a job the Mondale people had cobbled together to get past the furor over their attempt, just before the Convention, to replace Charles Manatt, the Democratic National Committee chairman, with Lance. The job was not one that would work, and the controversy over Lance wasn't going to end. And the Mondale people had made no apparent effort to involve Lance in the campaign, and made no effort to deny newspaper reports that he was being elbowed aside. A key Mondale aide had told me toward the end of the Convention that Lance would be gone before long. So Lance left, apparently with hard feelings. (Mondale recently suffered the public embarrassment of having to cancel a scheduled trip to Macon, Georgia, because various Georgia officials, and Lance, said that they couldn't make it that day. Recently, Andrew Young, ostensibly a Mondale ally, told an audience of black journalists that the Mondale campaign was run by a group of "smart-assed white boys who think they know it all.") And now the Ferraro case raised the question of how carefully the Mondale people had looked into the financial affairs of their prospective Vice-Presidential candidates. A form was put together that asked a lot of questions, and lawyers asked questions, and both Ferraro's and Zaccaro's tax returns for the last three years were gone over, but it appears that not a great deal of time was put into the exercise. It was known toward the end of the process that top Mondale aides were flying off to see the finalists and asking them for their financial information, but it seemed inconceivable that more investigative work had not gone on for some time. Now it seems clear that it did not. There was apparently no review of the Zaccaros' financial affairs until Tuesday, July 10th (a Mondale aide who had been seeing Massachusetts Governor Michael Dukakis on Monday was asked that night to go see the Zaccaros the next day); on Wednesday Mondale asked Ferraro to be his running mate, and on Thursday he announced his selection. (There was a certain hurriedness to the final selection, as options narrowed and the pressure on Mondale built to make some announcement. Moreover, Ferraro's chances did not seem high until very shortly before she was chosen.) The Zaccaros did tell the Mondale people about the F.E.C. matter, but they considered it a closed case. The Mondale people knew about Ferraro's having claimed the exemption on the congressional ethics form, and accepted her explanation that she was keeping her and her husband's financial affairs separate. To some extent, the Zaccaros may have downplayed some of their potentially controversial actions for the same reason they took them in the first place: they didn't understand the implications. They clearly underestimated the amount of scrutiny they would inevitably undergo. Also, Ferraro wanted the role very badly.

The effect of the Ferraro problem within the Mondale campaign has been deadly, especially coming, as it has, on top of a very long campaign year in which, it is now clear, a very few people were stretched too thin. John Reilly, Mondale's law partner, who spent much of the campaign on the plane and then headed the Vice-Presidential search, is described by friends as "burned out," and has been taking some time off. Michael Berman, an attorney and a longtime Mondale aide, who was also involved in the Vice-Presidential search and was supposed to be administering both the Mondale campaign and the Democratic National Committee, has been detailed for some time to deal with the Ferraro problem. This cost time in getting the campaign organized, staffed, and budgeted. Fund-raising has been hurt—and continues to be, as the polls show Mondale far behind. Big givers want access to a President. James Johnson, the campaign chairman, was described by a close friend as nearly consumed with the problem—and also shaken by it, and exhausted. This, on top of the Lance matter, was hard for Johnson to take. Another Mondale aide says, "You get a little gun-shy after events like these." One key Mondale adviser has said to me, "We had too rough a year and we're too tired. There are too few of us trying to do it all." A great deal of the strain on the Mondale people about the Ferraro case was that they didn't know where it was headed. Each day brought new wrinkles, new revelations, new allegations, new rumors. They had to sit tight while accountants and lawyers worked on the many threads of the case—and to pray that it didn't end too badly. The morale at North Oaks, Minnesota, where Mondale is based, is said to be not high. Meanwhile, the Republicans, who had been having trouble figuring out how to get at Ferraro before all this started, couldn't be more pleased. There is some division of opinion among them over how much pleasure to show, or how much to say about the matter publicly—privately, they are making their own contribution to the rumor mill—but there is no question that they consider this turn of events a gift.

AUGUST 20

This Convention has a decided right-wing stamp to it, as reflected in the platform that was drafted here last week—a process that even the White House couldn't control. In part, the White House loss of control stems from the fact that the President's "pragmatic" advisers are leery of taking on the right, which has been gunning for them from the outset. In part, the platform committee was dominated by a combination of right-wing activists who had long been Convention agitators and are now in the saddle—Senator Jesse Helms, of North Carolina, and Phyllis Schlafly, the anti-E.R.A. activist. Public hearings on the platform which were to be held around the country were cancelled, so that no dissent could be heard (there was one day of hearings here), and the few moderates around who tried to affect the platform were rolled over. The decline of the moderates as a force in national Republican politics has been long in the making. When Nelson Rockefeller was asked why he had failed to get the nomination in 1968, he replied, "Have you ever seen a Republican Convention?" In 1968, Nixon played to the right, which had no strong candidate—Reagan made an abortive run—sufficiently to win the nomination, and Ford came within an eyelash of losing the nomination to Reagan in 1976. The power of the right forced Ford to drop Rockefeller as his Vice-President, in favor of Robert Dole, who is now seen by what is now the right as too moderate.

The prevailing force here has little to do with the traditional conservatism of a Robert A. Taft, who probably would have been seen by this group as temperamentally and ideologically stodgy. What is in charge here is a combination of old-line conservatives (few of them), old right-wingers, and a new breed of radical populists (the New Right), and the evangelicals. In 1980, the Reverend Jerry Falwell and some other evangelical leaders turned up at the Republican Convention, having been cultivated, and they became an important part of Reagan's base in the 1980 election. This year, they are playing an even more prominent role, both at the Convention and in the election. They will register voters, raise money, and produce anti-Mondale advertising (having to do with, among other things, homosexual rights and abortion). Falwell will deliver the benediction at the Convention on the night Reagan is nominated, and the opening session this morning was blessed by the television evangelist James Robison; the closing benediction for the Convention will be given by Dr. W. A. Criswell, the conservative pastor of the First Baptist Church of Dallas. (The invocations and benedictions will be delivered, as at all conventions, by a smattering of rabbis and priests, but the role of the fundamentalists at this Convention is pronounced.) Such moderate Republicans as Senator Howard Baker, of Tennessee, Dole, and Gerald Ford will address this Convention, but it is doubtful that any one of them could be nominated by this group of people. Richard Nixon will not be at this Convention, for obvious reasons. (As it happens, the tenth anniversary of his leaving office occurred eleven days ago, but, Watergate aside, his domestic and foreign policies would be far too mainstream for the group gathered here.) Even Bush, who received the support of nearly forty-eight per cent of the delegates for the 1988 nomination in a poll conducted by the Dallas *Morning News*, would have a tough go of it. (Twenty-six per cent supported Congressman Jack Kemp, of New York, and sixteen per cent supported Baker.)

Bush was put on the ticket in 1980 despite the Reagans' own misgivings about him (among other things, the Reagan people were unimpressed with his debate performances) in order to unite the Party after negotiations with Gerald Ford over how to give a Vice-President Ford an extra-constitutional role mercifully fell through. (Ford is a nice man and probably would have been an excellent Vice-President, but what both sides were considering was unworkable and probably unconstitutional.) Bush has been a successful Vice-President: he has been loyal, and, if he had misgivings, silent about them; but the right only tolerates Bush, and will fight him in the 1988 primaries with its own candidate or candidates—Kemp, or others. For all his loyalty to Reagan, Bush still represents to the right the "Eastern establishment" that it has worked so hard, and with such success, to overtake. (And his preppy style, which still breaks through, will underscore the cultural difference.) It is a bit absurd to even contemplate the

Republican politics of 1988—the number of candidates and how they divide the vote and accidents will have a great deal to do with what happens then—but much contemplation, and energy, is going into the 1988 race here because, for one thing, there is so little else going on, and, for another, the would-be candidates are taking advantage of this gathering to promote their causes. Nevertheless, as of now the base of the Republican Party—the people who go out and work in the primaries and get involved in the Party machinery—is very conservative.

Another factor in Republican Presidential politics is that the formula for allocating Convention delegates rewards the smaller, and reliably conservative, states in the South and the West. An attempt to change this was offered by some moderate Republicans here yesterday, and of course they were clobbered. The moderates to a large extent brought their demise on themselves, since they believed such activism beneath them, and assumed that they had a permanent hold on the Party. It is the conservatives/right-wingers who have the intensity, and theirs is both a cultural and ideological war against the mainstream—a war against the "Eastern establishment," a war against the moderates (Baker, Dole, and House Minority Leader Robert Michel), who believe in legislative compromise. Baker and Michel have been having an increasingly difficult time controlling their troops, and therefore a deeper implication of what has been going on in the Republican Party, and is being accelerated here, is that the whole idea of governing by compromise, by legislative accommodations and understandings, is coming unravelled—to what end can hardly be imagined. (Baker is retiring from the Senate this year to pursue his Presidential ambitions.)

Reagan presides over a coalition that has a number of internal contradictions. The old-line conservatives and the radical populists are at war; the social conservatism of the fundamentalists is anathema to the old-line conservatives and to younger libertarians and to the moderates who are hanging on, for lack of anywhere else to go. The social conservatism can also present a problem for the "baby boom" generation that both parties are courting. Roger Stone says, "Reagan has become a Chairman Mao-type figure in the Party, because he is so popular. The Party will break into open warfare when Reagan goes." Some think that the warfare will begin even sooner: early in Reagan's term if he is reelected. In fact, it has been going on during his Presidency, but his popularity and force of personality have kept it within bounds.

Several of Reagan's aides and closest allies have been going about the Convention saying that the platform doesn't really matter, and the earnestness with which they press the point suggests that they think it does. And the platform suggests where the energy of the Party is. Activists and ideologues tend to head for platform committees (though it is interesting that the Mondale people were better able to keep their platform committee under control than the Reagan people were theirs). Despite the concern among some Reagan compaign officials about the "gender gap" and the need to win independents, the 1984 platform dropped the Equal Rights Amendment altogether. (The 1980 platform, to the shock of a number of Republican moderates at the time, dropped the Party's endorsement of the E.R.A., but it did "acknowledge the legitimate efforts of those who support or oppose ratification of the Equal Rights Amendment.") This year, the platform committee would not even consider wording, suggested by the President's daughter Maureen (who supports the E.R.A.), that would have acknowledged the sincerity of those who support it. Like the 1980 platform, the 1984 platform called for a constitutional amendment prohibiting abortion and for a denial of federal funds for abortions, and called for appointment to the judiciary of people "who respect traditional family values and the sanctity of innocent human life." (A prior requirement that a member of the judiciary will rule in a certain way is of dubious constitutionality as well as of dubious merit.) Like the 1980 platform, the 1984 platform calls for a constitutional amendment allowing voluntary prayer in schools.

On the subject of taxes, the supply-siders won out over the White House, and wrote a platform statement that simply opposed any tax increases, and in addition they proposed a new set of tax cuts. The platform proposes a doubling of the personal exemption from one thousand to two thousand dollars (this idea had been leaked by the Administration but hadn't been proposed; it would favor the middle class, particularly large families, and would cost over forty billion dollars); it proposes expanding Individual Retirement Accounts to cover homemakers—also a benefit to the middle class. (The White House did manage to keep the

I.R.A. proposal from being even broader.) The platform came out for a "modified flat tax" (the Republican version of the Democratic Bradley-Gephardt "flat tax" bill) sponsored by Kemp and by Senator Robert Kasten, of Wisconsin. The platform and the Kemp-Kasten bill back away from the graduated-tax principle. The main difference between the Kemp-Kasten bill and the Bradley-Gephardt bill is that the Kemp-Kasten bill cuts taxes for people with incomes of over a hundred thousand dollars by about fifteen per cent. (Like the Democratic bill, the Republican one would allow for certain deductions, such as for mortgage interest.) The Republican platform also calls for reducing taxes on interest income, repeal of the windfall-profit tax (the oil lobby struck here), and a number of other tax breaks. Where the money for all this would come from is anyone's guess, but the supply-siders adhere to the theory that lower taxes lead to growth, which leads to more revenue.

The platform calls for cuts in "wasteful and unnecessary government spending" but is not specific, and it endorses Reagan's call for a constitutional amendment requiring a balanced budget. As a matter of fact, if all the budget cuts President Reagan proposed in his latest budget were made, the deficit would be reduced by only about twenty billion dollars. (In its recent midyear budget review, the Administration managed to lop a hundred billion dollars off the deficit, dropping it from two hundred and sixty billion, according to the Congressional Budget Office, to a hundred and sixty billion by fiscal 1989, by assuming that the rate of growth will continue over the next five years at four per cent, and that interest rates will go from their current eleven per cent to five per cent by 1989. Not a lot of people took these estimates seriously.) The platform criticizes the Federal Reserve Board for high interest rates, and suggests a return to the gold standard. This reflects the thinking of Kemp, among others. The Fed gets the blame for high interest rates but not credit for holding down inflation—which was accomplished mainly by the Fed's tightening of money in reaction to the fiscal effects of the Kemp-Roth, supply-side tax cuts put through by Reagan in 1981, to the point where there was a recession. The supply-siders take credit for the current recovery even though it is a demand-side recovery. The Republicans expect a buoyant economy at least through the election—which is the main thing that concerns them at the moment.

In the platform deliberations, the Administration managed to stave off a call for military "superiority" over the Soviet Union, but this was a somewhat limited victory, since the platform does call for "technological" and "qualitative" superiority. It also says, "Our forces must be second to none."

The White House had known for some time that Representative Trent Lott, of Mississippi, the House Minority Whip and chairman of the platform committee, had stacked the committee to the right. Why this was allowed to happen is somewhat mystifying, the most plausible explanation being a President and a White House staff reluctant to take on the right. Lott, a forty-two-year-old conservative who hopes to succeed Michel, is part of a group of young House activists who don't buy the old ways of doing business, substantively or tactically. Among the other members of this group who served on the platform committee are Kemp, Newt Gingrich, of Georgia, and Vin Weber, of Minnesota. Gingrich recently founded something called the Conservative Opportunity Society, the name bespeaking the philosophy that virtually unbridled economic freedom will create opportunity for all. Gingrich is both a serious-minded man and a prankster, and the proportions are hard to sort out. Like other young politicians, he is interested in new ideas but also hooked on the glamour of seeming to be in the new-ideas game. But while this group espouses economic freedom, it is pronouncedly socially conservative: anti-abortion, anti-homosexuality, pro-school prayer, anti-E.R.A. Some Republicans think that this group's linking up with the fundamentalist agenda represents more a political tactic than a philosophical commitment—and some New Right conservatives think that this is a political mistake. Interestingly enough, though there are differences (the social issues being the obvious ones), this group is something of a counterpart to what Gary Hart represented on the Democratic side: a reaction to the "old ways" of doing business, an emphasis on economic growth, and an appeal to the younger generation of voters. Both parties' younger-generation politicians are going after the baby-boom voters (this is why some think the radical conservatives' social agenda is a mistake). The struggle for the future of the Republican Party is not unlike that in the Democratic Party. Both parties are involved in a struggle of generational politics. Essentially, Bush-Baker-Dole are to this group what Mondale was to Hart. The Democrats are in the midst of defining a post-New Deal identity, and the Republicans are in the midst of defining a post-traditional-conservative identity. There is a theory around that the New Deal coalition and philosophy actually came apart during the Johnson Administration, and that only Watergate gave the Democrats a breather. In the Republican Party, the conservative radicals, or New Right, are involved in the struggle for the leadership of a Party that is becoming more democratic (that is, participatory), more Catholic, more lower-middle-class, and less representative of the middle middle and upper middle classes. One New Right activist says, "The country-club group is getting smaller and the doubleknit group is getting larger." The radicals are aggressive, on the theory that this is the way to make themselves heard, and to keep the establishment, as they see it, from smothering ideas. Like their Democratic counterparts, the conservative radicals are reacting to, or playing to, the baby boom and the high degree of cynicism about government among younger voters. They understand that the electorate is changing, becoming younger and better educated and more affluent: they are saying that if the government gets off your back (economically) you can do well. Like their Democratic counterparts, they are entranced with the possibilities of the "information age." (Gingrich is also enthusiastic about the commercial possibilities of the use of outer space.) The House Republican group relies on obstreperous tactics to get attention—and to build a base. It engages in tactical maneuvers to hold up House action and cleverly uses the cable-television coverage of Congress, on C-SPAN, to promote itself—especially through speeches in a special period set aside after regular House business for members to make statements. (This use of C-SPAN caused a tremendous row between this group and Speaker Thomas P. O'Neill earlier in the year—a row in which Michel was caught in the middle and ultimately defeated.)

This evening at the Convention, I had a brief talk with Gingrich, a forty-one-year-old prematurely gray former professor. He has been happily handing out stickers that say, "Honest Money and Honest Disclosures"—a not very subtle reference to Ferraro—and he said that his group would be handing out new stickers each night, as a way of stirring activity and getting attention on the Convention floor. (Some delegates were wearing buttons saying

"Come Clean, Geraldine.") Gingrich told me, "Our strategy is very simple. We're trying to build the consensus that there's an alternative to the welfare state, which we call the Opportunity Society, and keep hammering the idea that the Republican Party is not just talking about budget balancing. Our attitude toward the Convention is that there are people here who want to be interactive, not just listen to speeches. These stickers are a gimmick and also something we thought was cute that people would want to put on. You can see it happening." As we talked, people were continually coming up to Gingrich and asking him for the stickers and putting them on. He continued, "We're also building something for people to do when they get home—a movement, a nationwide university of television politics. People all over the country know about us and watch us on C-SPAN. When I go to a university, kids come up and ask how they can help. What we're engaged in is sloppy, but it has a lot of energy behind it. This nation is much closer to Burt Reynolds or Indiana Jones than to the police. We're trying to give people ways of committing themselves. So while we write books and hold conferences and speak on the floor, our model is the Progressive movement. We're trying to build a more positive and optimistic Republican Party—we're talking about high tech, free enterprise, and traditional values that enable people to lead productive and fulfilling lives, with less centralized government and more take-home pay." Gingrich said that his group consists of about fifteen members of Congress who meet every week, and that another thirty to forty members are very interested, and that a third to a half of the members are for them. He said. "We want the delegates to leave here knowing there's a young, progressive, idea-oriented group in the House and that it's kind of neat." That, he said, would put his group in a stronger position to negotiate with the White House staff, and build for 1988.

The mood on the Convention floor tonight is strangely desultory. This should be a happy lot—their man is in power and they are riding high. It can't be just the heat. (The Convention hall in fact is kept at what feels like a subfreezing temperature, and a number of people have already become ill from the sharp changes.) The mood seems to be one of contentment but not much excitement. Not everyone is content, of course; moderate and mainstream

Republicans are disturbed by the indications of where their party may be going. Some of the elected officials among this group have had no easy time of it in recent years treading between their own mainstream constituents and the strong Reagan supporters, and some have been challenged from the right in primaries. Some, like Maryland Senator Charles McC. Mathias, believe the Party is headed in a direction from which it cannot govern. (Mathias almost didn't get on his state's delegation, and was accused by a Maryland right-wing activist of being "a liberal swine.") Representative James Leach, of Iowa, a forty-one-year-old moderate, who made an attempt to offer a different voice here, said to me on the floor tonight, "This isn't my brand of Republicanism. It's anti-international-organization; this is a Party of a new nationalism, when any sensible American knows we have to be thinking internationally. The platform, the gold standard and all that—it's nutty pandering to the most unsavory groups in American politics: the New Right and the fundamentalists. But there are many Republicans who believe in arms control and the environment and sane monetary and fiscal policies—and I believe that we're definitely going to have life after death." Representative Olympia Snowe, of Maine, who is thirty-seven, said, "We'll have to get the moderates involved in the Party—and there's no question in my mind that if we don't do that, this is the irretrievable path of the Republican Party. This Convention has been an awakening. The platform committee wasn't even willing to acknowledge the existence of E.R.A. They wouldn't even consider compromise language Maureen Reagan and I supported. I came away with the impression that this Convention is being staged for the future, and courting the conservative constituency. I also believe that the conservatives, after four years, have become emboldened. I don't see what's in the Party platform that will reach a majority of the American people, and that concerns me deeply. Ronald Reagan will sustain himself based on his popularity; I think that's unrelated to the success of the Republican Party."

There is no confusing a Republican and a Democratic Convention. This one is virtually all white (fewer than five per cent of the delegates and alternates are blacks) and more affluent, and on the one hand more conservatively dressed and on the other more disposed to wearing funny hats and globs of buttons. (A deliberate attempt was made to have more women delegates than would have otherwise been the case.) The managers of this Convention—and many people were in on the act—have been struggling, against great odds, for ways to make it interesting and at the same time blanket out any notes of disharmony. (They considered cutting the Convention back from four days to three, since there is so little to do, but didn't want to give up a night of free television time.) The coopting of the Olympics continues tonight: several of the Olympic winners are here, and were introduced to the audience by Roosevelt Grier, the former professional-football star, who had been a great friend of Robert Kennedy and his family. Grier, who is now a preacher, has said that he switched allegiances because when he came to Washington earlier this year to lobby for the President's proposed constitutional amendment to allow prayer in the schools, friends did not support it. Tonight, Grier endorsed Reagan for "four more years." Political converts are in high favor here—Reagan needs Democratic votes in order to win—and so, for a number of reasons, Jeane Kirkpatrick, the United Nations Ambassador and a "neoconservative" Democrat, was given a featured place on the program. (Mrs. Kirkpatrick was even brought onstage to the tune of "Happy Days Are Here Again," which had been just about retired at the Democratic Convention.) Mrs. Kirkpatrick's place on the program tonight was of recent making, and the maneuverings that went into the decision signify some of the things going on in the Republican Party now. The congressional New Right members had wanted her to be the keynote speaker, but Reagan's more pragmatic managers considered her too controversial—her foreign-policy views too dogmatic and muscular for the picture of Reagan they wanted to present. (Besides, Mrs. Kirkpatrick had openly feuded with the White House staff in October, 1983, when she was blocked from becoming national-security adviser after William Clark was eased out and over to the Interior Department.) So the President's advisers finessed the situation by selecting as the keynote speaker Katherine Ortega, of whom few had heard except for the fact that, since she is Treasurer of the United States (an essentially honorific job), her signature is on our paper currency. The President's aides thought that picking Mrs. Ortega was quite a good move: a Hispanic woman from a large family, an American success story, would keynote the Convention. This maneuver also preempted Elizabeth Dole, whose ambitions (or her husband's) the Convention managers were not eager to promote, and who, they said privately, looked a little too—well, Republican. The Convention managers never made any pretense that Mrs. Ortega would write her own speech; they just hoped she would read one well. But, despite coaching lessons, the prospects didn't look good as the Convention approached.

Then, after the Democrats picked Ferraro, a scramble was made to put more women on the program, especially on opening night—among them Mrs. Kirkpatrick. She is a woman of high intelligence, with a debater's agility, and tonight she poured scorn on the Democrats to a degree that was somewhat startling. Clearly enjoying her new role as the heroine of the Republican right, she played to it, armed with simplifications and straw men. She praised her party's past leaders—Truman, Johnson, and John Kennedy (she didn't seem to know what to do about Hubert Humphrey, to whom she had been quite close, which also gave her a close association with Mondale)—but had nothing but contempt for what she termed "the San Francisco Democrats." And she moved in on the Carter Administration's record with a vengeance, calling it "indifferent to the subversion of others' independence or to the development of new weapons by our adversaries or of new vulnerabilities by our friends;" accusing it of exercising "unilateral restraint" while the Soviets built up their weapons systems (actually, almost every weapons system being built by the Reagan Administration was developed during the Carter Administration or earlier); blaming it for the coming to power of Ayatollah Khomeini. She distorted what she said were Soviet exploitations of the "loopholes" of the SALT I agreement—which was negotiated by the Nixon Administration—and misdescribed the nature of the strategic balance. "And then," she said, "feeling strong, Soviet leaders moved with boldness and skill to exploit their new advantages." This theory of history rests on shaky premises and overlooks Soviet ventures in the nineteen-fifties and sixties—in Europe, Africa, Asia, and Cuba. She listed a large number of countries in which "Soviet influence expanded dramatically" between the time of the fall of Saigon, in 1975 (during the Ford Administration), and January, 1981. The list included countries where "Soviet influence" grew before Carter came into office (and included both South Yemen and Aden, which is the capital of South Yemen), and, like the Reagan foreign policy, attributes all insurgencies, nationalist movements, and tribal rivalries around the world (many of which the Soviets took advantage of), as well as genuine Soviet efforts at subversion, to Soviet adventurism. She blamed the Democrats for the Soviet invasion of Afghanistan, and, of course, she cited the taking of the hostages in Iran. "We lost confidence in ourselves, and in our government," she said, and then, referring to a speech Carter would have been better off not having made, she said, "It was not malaise we suffered from, it was Jimmy Carter"—for which she was cheered strongly—and then she added, "and Walter Mondale," for which she was cheered even more strongly. Reagan, she said, had restored confidence— this is a major theme of the Reagan campaign—and she suggested that the release of the hostages on the day of his Inauguration had something to do with him. (The Republicans are far better at blaming Carter for the hostage crisis than at saying what they would have done about it; their proffered answer is that under them America would have been so respected that the crisis would not have happened.) She gave Reagan the credit for the installation of missiles in Europe, though this was a policy initiated by Carter to counter Soviet deployments—with the hope that it would lead to negotiated limits on the deployments. Then she set forth the proposition that "the same people who were responsible for America's decline have insisted that the President's policies would fail," and she said that whenever things go wrong "they always blame America first." She said, "They said that saving Grenada from totalitarianism and terror was the wrong thing to do. They didn't blame Cuba or the Communists for threatening American students and murdering Grenadians—they blamed the United States instead." (Actually, the Democrats were divided in their reaction to the Grenada invasion—in part on the merits of the case, in part because the invasion was so popular—and Mondale was criticized by some Democrats for not being critical enough. His criticism was tempered all along, and he actually ended up saying that he would have used force if he thought the students were in danger, and that he was impressed by the conclusion of Representative Michael Barnes, Democrat of Maryland and chairman of the Western Hemisphere Affairs Subcommittee, that the action was justified. Tip O'Neill at first said of the Grenada invasion, "It isn't the right thing to do," and then said it was "justified.") Then, going quite far, Kirkpatrick said that when the

Marines in Lebanon "were murdered in their sleep the 'blame-America-first crowd' did not blame the terrorists who murdered the Marines, they blamed the United States"—adding, in what became a refrain, "But then they always blame America first." Similarly for the breakdown of arms-control talks, or "when Marxist dictators shoot their way to power in Central America." She listed a number of things the American people know that Reagan isn't responsible for—as if someone had accused him of them—including "the repression in Poland" and "the obscene treatment of Andrei Sakharov" and "the re-Stalinization of the Soviet Union." Kirkpatrick's speech, devoid of much serious thought or sense of history, was a big hit.

Howard Baker, who also spoke this evening, did his best to appeal to a crowd that he must know does not favor him, with a strong attack on the Carter Administration. Of Mondale, the usually genial Baker said, "Misery has become very important to Walter Mondale. When he's in office, he creates it. When he's out, he invents it—because Walter Mondale has nothing to offer a successful America." He mocked Mondale's saying, in his acceptance speech, that the Democrats had learned from the 1980 election, and would know when to say no. Mondale, Baker said, didn't know how to say no to organized labor or to "the limousine liberals" or to raising taxes. "We don't have to wave the flag to prove we love this country," Baker said, in a reference to the San Francisco Convention. "We were waving the flag when some people were burning it." And, as if this were the issue between the two parties, Baker said, "We want America to be successful, not miserable." Some of Baker's harsher lines got a response from the crowd, but he didn't seem to win it over.

Now Mrs. Ortega can hardly capture the attention of the audience at all. She is an attractive and pleasant-looking woman, and is obviously trying, but she simply can't project. The important thing about her speech is that it was written for her by Presidential advisers, and therefore reflects their strategy. She, too, talks of Reagan's having restored confidence, and tears into "the Carter-Mondale years." She says, "We have come a long way in four years—from the shame of Teheran to the brave rescue of American students in Grenada." She says, "We have come a long way, and we are not going back to the Carter-Mondale years, when a weak leadership left the door open for Communist aggression—

from Afghanistan to our own hemisphere." Some of the President's advisers have been concerned that Reagan does not have foreign-policy successes to point to: policy in the Middle East is at a dead end; the Central American policy is highly controversial; and, despite an unprecedented arms buildup, there have been no arms-control agreements. But the Reagan people have taken the offensive and are saying, in speech after speech, that America is stronger, more respected, and, through its action in Grenada, has shown that it can beat the Communists. (In that instance, six thousand American ground troops, backed up by a ten-thousand-man Naval Force and eight hundred airmen, fought seven hundred Cubans, about a hundred of whom were military personnel—the rest were airport construction workers—plus a small local militia.) With the exception of Kirkpatrick, who put her own twist on the subject, the speakers don't talk about Lebanon. For good measure, they paint the Carter years as having produced nothing but reverses and humiliation. This is a simplistic and inaccurate picture, but, with repetition, may well be sinking in. Mrs. Ortega also attacks the economic record of the Carter Administration—another major refrain of the Reagan campaign. "Mr. Mondale's record, from the first day he entered public life," Mrs. Ortega says, "has been based on the idea of high taxes, big spending, more government regulation. And *promises, promises, promises.*" There's something surprising about all this. Some of the President's advisers had been telling me that this Convention was to be positive and offer a vision of the future. Attacking an opponent is fair game, but the relentlessness of it here, and the absence of much talk about anything else, and the repetition of the same points, give off the impression of a sledgehammer approach, and a certain emptiness. And not all of Reagan's advisers are convinced that attacking Mondale through his association with Carter is particularly fruitful. Perhaps this will be turned around as the week goes on, and especially when the President gives his acceptance speech.

Mrs. Ortega says that the other Democratic candidates were "shut out of their traditional Party home by the narrow interest groups in charge of last month's Democratic Convention"—an interesting way to try to appeal to Democrats—and, inevitably, cites Gary Hart's criticism of Mondale. The Republicans have long planned to use the criticisms of Mondale's primary opponents against him, and today Reagan, campaigning in Cincinnati, cited criticism of Mondale by Glenn. Reagan has been campaigning in the Midwest—Ohio, Missouri, and Illinois—yesterday and today, and will not arrive here until Wednesday. For all their confidence, the Republicans are concerned about the agricultural areas, which have been particularly hard hit by high interest rates. (Mondale, at the Iowa State Fair yesterday, called Reagan's economic and agricultural policies "a dagger in the heart of every farmer in America.") Mrs. Ortega describes "the Party that met in San Francisco last month" (San Francisco itself, with its large homosexual community and exotic style, is being given an invidious connotation) as "the Party of special interests, the Party of doomsayers, the Party of demagogues who look to America's future with fear, not hope." She adds, "To those millions of Democrats abandoned by their national leadership in San Francisco—Democrats who were *shut out* of their traditional Party home—we Republicans here in Dallas say, '*Nuestra casa es su casa*. Our home is your home.' "

AUGUST 21

Tuesday. The Doles, Kemp, and Ford spoke at the Convention tonight. Kemp, as he did four years ago, had a demonstration on his behalf. Boyish and enthusiastic, he is in great favor here, and if he decides to run for President in 1988 there is a network ready to go to work for him—in fact, it is already working for him. Kemp went through the now familiar criticisms of Iran, Afghanistan, and the Carter economic record. "Isn't it good to have a President who doesn't apologize for America?" he asked, and he accused the Democrats of offering "fear of the future, fear of growth, fear of global leadership." He said that the Democratic leaders "see no difference between the Soviet invasion of Afghanistan and the American liberation of Grenada." He said that the leaders of the Democratic Party are "soft on democracy." He praised Reagan's record and the Party platform. He said, "The first condition for peace is a superior national defense." He said that we must "give the world again a money it can rely on, a dollar 'as good as gold.' " Kemp delivered his speech with earnestness and crispness, and it went over well. He ended on an upbeat note of sweeping optimism.

Ford, in perhaps the harshest speech of the evening, attacked the Carter record and said, "The Democrats in San Francisco talked a lot about the future. Their theme seemed to be that America's future belongs to the wishers, the wasters, the wanters, the whiners, and the weak." Ford said, "Mondale has embraced fear as enthusiastically as he embraces his pre-Convention rivals. All he has to offer is fear itself." Mocking Mondale's saying in San Francisco that he had learned the lesson of the 1980 election, Ford said, "Where were you, Walter, when the taxpayers really needed you?" Ford is considered too moderate by many of the people here, and some boycotted his speech and attended instead a fund-raising party given by the National Conservative Political Action Committee (NCPAC) at the Circle T Ranch of Nelson Bunker Hunt, the oil billionaire. (Hunt ran into legal problems in recent years when he tried to corner the silver market.) The tickets cost a thousand dollars per person; Pat Boone served as master of ceremonies, and Bob Hope offered entertainment. The Democrats had their rounds of parties, of course, and their special events for their big donors, but the extent and the opulence of the partying here seems to outdo anything that has gone before. Yesterday, Phyllis Schlafly sponsored a luncheon/fashion show that was attended by thirteen hundred women and featured Cabinet wives and Republican women officeholders modelling elegant clothes. The door prize was a three-foot mink elephant. (There are some misgivings among Reagan's advisers about the fact that Bunker Hunt, Phyllis Schlafly, and Jerry Falwell are the subject of so much attention here, and at least one adviser is troubled that Falwell is on the Convention program. He says he does not believe that Falwell is a net plus for the ticket, even in the South.)

The big attention today was on Ferraro's press conference, in New York. The financial documents were released yesterday, but a few hours later than planned, and a briefing by the accountants had to be postponed until today. Spokesmen for Ferraro said that the delay had to do with problems in reproducing the documents, but the real problem was the last-minute discovery by the accountants of, among other things, the fact that Zaccaro had failed to list in his financial statement a hundred-thousand-dollar loan he had borrowed from an elderly woman's estate, of which he had been acting as a court-appointed conservator. (When the news of this transaction broke in the press over the weekend, Zaccaro's attorney said that Zaccaro did not know that there was anything wrong with the transaction, and also that he had repaid the loan, at a higher interest rate than the money had been earning.) It was learned from the Zaccaros' tax returns over the last six years, that the couple had been paying a high rate of taxes (about forty per cent)—one speculation had been that Zaccaro was reluctant to release his returns because he had sheltered a large amount of taxes—and that they owed slightly more than fifty thousand dollars in back taxes and interest, because of what was described as an accountant's error on their 1978 tax form (a mistake found by the Arthur Young accountants).

But the most important thing about Ferraro's press conference today was that she came off well: she took questions for nearly two hours (this was a deliberate strategy—she would sit there as long as the reporters had questions), with dignity, strength, good humor, apparent candor, and a lack of self-pity. Her argument for checking off the exemption was that once she entered Congress she wanted to keep her and her husband's financial affairs separate, and that she had become an officer in her husband's real-estate company, P. Zaccaro Company, in 1971, at the request of her husband, after his brother and father had died, so that someone could take over the business in case anything happened to him. (She also said that though she had received a small amount of income from it, and owned one-third of its stock, she never had any authority in the company; and she said that she would remove herself as an officer and as a stockholder, and hoped that her older daughter would take her place. The company is a real-estate-management company; Zaccaro's real-estate transactions are conducted through other companies.) She argued that the point of the ethics form is to ascertain whether there is any conflict of interest, and that there had not been any. Her case that she was entitled to check off the exemption was not entirely convincing to a lot of neutral observers, but neither did it seem that she had done it through any willful intent to deceive. (Some other members of Congress take the exemption, and several did not answer the question of whether they were entitled to the exemption at all.) Ferraro said today that she had not known until recently, after her husband's finances were reviewed by the Mondale people, about her husband's borrowing from the woman's estate, or about his having purchased the share of the building she had sold in order to pay back the campaign loans. (She said that her husband had told her this was legal, and that she had replied, "Sure it was, but it doesn't look so hot.") The picture that emerged was of some questionable judgment calls, less than tidy business practices on the part of her husband, and a rather poor choice of an accountant in the past—but not of venality or deliberate deception. And though the Zaccaros are wealthy—their net worth is estimated at about four million dollars—his business is not on a grand scale. (Most of his properties are in Little Italy and Chinatown.) One of the complications in all this—aside from the complications the Zaccaros brought on themselves—is that when a woman enters national politics the husband may be the main income earner, and in this case the husband's business was, even under the best of circumstances, a complicated one. Barring any further damaging disclosures—which could be all the more devastating, since Ferraro made so much of the thoroughness of the information that was being released (she said it was the most comprehensive disclosure ever made by an office-seeker)—Ferraro seems to have got through the worst of her crisis. Some investigative reporting will still go on, and some Republicans will still milk what they can from the situation—and there is no question that the whole episode, even if it gets no worse, has been costly to the Mondale ticket.

AUGUST 22

Wednesday. Reagan arrived in town today and was greeted by a tumultuous, and meticulously planned, welcome at the Loews Anatole Hotel. (Before Reagan's arrival, Mrs. Reagan attended a luncheon given by Republican women in her honor; the featured entertainer, at Mrs. Reagan's invitation, was Joan Rivers, who regaled the group with off-color jokes.) At Reagan's arrival ceremony, the packed atrium in which he stood magnified the sound of the cheers, and on the fourteen floors above him hand-lettered placards and bedsheets were hung from the railings. Behind him was an enormous American flag, and a large sign with the theme that the Reagan campaign has finally arrived at: "Bringing America Back. Prouder, Stronger, and Better." Arriving at this slogan took much doing, and was the result of a great deal of discussion and polling. Reagan has done his share of trying to appeal to various interest groups—Catholics, farmers, Hispanics, blue-collar workers, and so on (though somehow this kind of politicking doesn't get tied to Reagan)—but his campaign struggled before it came up with a central message. Robert Teeter says, "This is a central-message campaign—a big-issue campaign. We're not going to be arguing about housing and mass transit. This campaign is going to be about the changes Ronald Reagan has made and the future direction of this country." Teeter adds, "This campaign is a referendum on Ronald Reagan." A poll taken for the Republicans recently indicated that people believe Reagan has made some changes that needed to be made. This and other polling helped the Reagan people arrive at the theme.

Reagan looked cheerful and well pleased with his welcome, which he praised as "a Texas-sized welcome." He also praised the Dallas Cowboys. Tom Landry, the Cowboys' coach, and two Cowboy stars were seated with Reagan on the platform; Landry, one of Texas' heroes, has endorsed Reagan. In brief remarks, Reagan seemed to be trying to put a somewhat more positive tone on the week, saying that "by the time this Convention ends, the Republican Party will be on its way to being America's Party." He said, "Now, our opponents haven't had an easy time with our success. They've come up with an antidote—bring back the Carter-Mondale Administration." After the crowd shouted, "No," and booed, he continued, "We Republicans want to keep going forward." He said, "Our goal is to build an opportunity society for every man, woman, and child," and added that "G.O.P. doesn't just stand for Grand Old Party; it also stands for Grand Opportunity Party." And he said, "I happen to believe that helping people climb higher and make it on their own is a darned sight more progressive than keeping them down and dependent on government for the rest of their lives." He compared the Democrats as "the party of tax and tax and spend and spend" to the Republicans as "the party of growth and growth and jobs and jobs." Then, adhering himself to the Olympics once again, Reagan said, "Let's take our cue from our Olympic athletes. . . . Rather than raise taxes, let us challenge America in the next seventy-six days to raise her sights. . . . Let's go for growth, and let's go for the gold."

The philosophical divide between the Democrats and the Republicans seems to have widened since this Convention began— even despite the fact that the Democrats have tried to move toward the center. Republicans, even Reagan Republicans, used to refer at least to the fact that there were some in this country who needed help, and Reagan used to talk about the need to provide a "social safety net" for those who needed help. But the overwhelming theme that has been coming through here is: You're on your own. The corollary to this is: We'll cut taxes and cut spending, and there will be growth and everything will be fine. A parallel theme is that military strength is an end in itself, resolving all international problems; I do not believe that I have heard the word "diplomacy" here all week—not even from the Ambassador to the United Nations—or any suggestion that international questions might be complicated.

Tonight at the Convention, a totally liberated Barry Goldwater repeats the line from his 1964 acceptance speech which was considered so shocking at the time and was believed to have helped doom his campaign: "Extremism in the defense of liberty is no vice." Though Goldwater is credited with having founded the movement that is now supreme within the Republican Party (he may have been as much its instrument as its founder), the Party did go back to the mainstream after his defeat. But the Goldwater movement showed the promise of grass-roots activism, and the vulnerability of the establishment. And Reagan got his start in national politics through a television speech on behalf of Goldwater's candidacy. Yet Goldwater does not agree with some of the directions the movement has taken: he is a fiscal conservative and a libertarian—he has often spoken out against the social agenda. Goldwater, who is a courtly man, now utters one of the roughest litanies of the week: "Every war in this century began and was fought under Democrat Administrations." Going even further than Robert Dole did when he debated Mondale in 1976 and was criticized for taking a similar tack, Goldwater names each war, from the First World War through Vietnam, and the Democratic Presidents, from Woodrow Wilson through Lyndon Johnson, who were in office when they began. (Other speakers, earlier in the week, had praised Truman, Kennedy, and Johnson for being more willing to exercise a forceful foreign policy than the current Democrats seem to be.) Referring to Americans' reaction to the Olympics, he says, "Don't you Democrat leaders try to tell me that Americans don't love and honor America." Then, referring to Reagan and summoning up his own 1964 campaign slogan, Goldwater says, "In your hearts, you know he's right." Goldwater is cheered, but not thunderously. Still, the Convention seems to have come more to life; Reagan's arrival appears to have given it a lift, and now the grand old man of the movement has joined his followers and their political descendants in mutual vindication.

Senator Paul Laxalt, of Nevada, the President's close friend and the general chairman of the Reagan campaign, says some unusual things in his speech nominating Reagan. Laxalt, who is also a courtly man, says, "President Carter and his handpicked Vice-President—Walter Mondale—had this nation on its knees." Like the speakers before him, he says that Reagan has restored confidence, but then he goes back to attacking the Democratic Party and Mondale, and, in an odd turn, even takes on New York Governor Mario Cuomo for having recently got into an important debate with Archbishop John J. O'Connor over the proper role of the Church in politics. (Cuomo criticized Archbishop O'Connor for saying that he did not see how Catholics "in good conscience can vote for a candidate who explicitly supports abortion." Cuomo said that it was not the role of the Church to tell people whom to vote for, and Archbishop O'Connor later said that he was not telling Catholics how to vote.) Laxalt says, "You know, I can't help but wonder what's happened to the once great Democratic Party when the Democratic Governor of New York goes out of his way to attack the Catholic Archbishop of New York." And he adds, "Shame on you, Mario Cuomo!" Laxalt has taken one of the most sensitive issues around and turned it to partisan ends. (The White House, it is to be remembered, wrote or cleared just about all the speeches given this week.) Laxalt says, "The Democratic leaders have now made their party the Party of the left . . . The once great Democratic Party is now the home of the special interests, the social-welfare complex, the anti-defense lobby, and the glitter-set, lighter-than-air liberals—and it's getting worse every year." The Democrats, he says, "will raise your taxes and then they're going to forget all about reducing the deficit and go right back to paying off the special-interest groups and bigger and bigger and more and more wasteful federal programs." Laxalt says that the choice in November is "between Walter Mondale's fear of the future and Ronald Reagan's enduring, consistent optimism." Mondale's—and other Democrats'—attempt to make the case in San Francisco that economic and other problems lie ahead is being portrayed by speaker after speaker here as "doomsaying." Mondale's attempt to say that we must "face facts" is being derided here as "pessimism." Here there are no worries about the deficit or Central American policy or the arms race. The dichotomy, as it is defined here, is clear: Mondale is the Bad News Man and Reagan is the Good News Man. And so is the choice: Whom would you prefer as President?

Laxalt praises Reagan for offering leadership, character, optimism, and compassion. He praises him for having the courage to go on television in China and "tell the Chinese people, in plain language, that our system of self-government was better than theirs." (The Chinese censored those remarks, but Reagan's aides did not go to great pains to deny the suggestion that they were really aimed at the American audience.) He praises Reagan for his courage in proceeding with the attack on Grenada. He praises him for refusing to see Jesse Jackson after Jackson's trip to Central America and Cuba. He cites criticisms of Mondale that were made by Glenn ("Mondale has just promised everything to everybody"), Hart ("Mondale's mush—he's weak"), and Fritz Hollings ("Mondale is a good lap dog. He'll give them everything they want"). He turns the arms-control argument around by saying, "If anyone listening or watching tonight believes that we must at all costs have an arms treaty with the Soviets, no matter how unverifiable or irresponsible—I urge you to vote for Ronald Reagan's opponent." And then, perhaps inevitably, he says, "We've all witnessed what's happened to Bert Lance and Geraldine Ferraro these past few days." And he continues, "Let me ask—if Walter Mondale can't even run his own campaign, how in the world can we expect him to negotiate successfully with the Soviets?"

As the evening proceeds, Reagan and Bush are seen on television sitting together watching the Convention on television, both men tieless and with shirts open at the collar. There remains a certain joylessness in what ought to be a joyous Convention. Perhaps it is all the negative rhetoric, which can give the audience some kicks but doesn't lift the spirits. Perhaps it's the sameness of the rhetoric. Perhaps it's because the former outs are in, and confident, and there is little to get worked up about. The Convention gives off an air of complacency—and even a certain unpleasantness. The Democrats took their shots at Reagan, and went after his record hard, but they also talked of other things. This Convention seems to have turned into a contest as to who can slug the Democrats the hardest. One Reagan adviser tells me that he is concerned about not only the amount of attacking of Carter, and, through him, Mondale, that is going on here but also the nature of it. He says he thinks that the message has to be more subtle. He adds, "There's a lot of sympathy for Carter in this country—a lot more than we thought." He says, "And a lot of people say Mondale was just the Vice-President and he can't be blamed for everything." And there is something else that seems to have happened here: patriotism as a theme has slid over into a kind of nationalism, and even, on occasion, jingoism. What should be celebratory has taken on a slightly ugly tone. It's fun to think about America as a kind of athletic team beating the world—and a little dangerous.

Late this evening, Reagan and Bush were overwhelmingly renominated (jointly, on a single ballot)—with only two abstentions and with one vote each for Kemp and Kirkpatrick for Vice-President.

AUGUST 23

Thursday. This morning, at a prayer breakfast, Reagan went further then ever in asserting the role of religion in politics. (Reagan himself does not attend church; his aides say that this is because he does not want the security precautions taken for him to disturb the other worshippers.) He criticized the Supreme Court for its 1962 ruling banning state-sponsored prayer in the schools, and he said of those who oppose "voluntary" prayer in the schools, "The frustrating thing is that those who are attacking religion claim they are doing it in the name of tolerance and freedom and open-mindedness," and he continued, "Question: Isn't the real truth that they are intolerant of religion?" In March, the Senate rejected a constitutional amendment, backed by the President, that would have permitted organized, recited prayers in schools. Eighteen Republicans joined twenty-six Democrats in voting against the amendment. The Senate also rejected an amendment allowing for silent prayer. While any of these prayers would presumably be "voluntary," many senators worried that allowing them would bring pressures on schoolchildren who did not subscribe to the prayers. (One senator who argued strenuously against these amendments was John Danforth, Republican of Missouri, an ordained Episcopal minister.) More recently, the House voted overwhelmingly to allow for a moment of silent prayer in public schools, after defeating a Republican-sponsored proposal to allow spoken prayers (there was some division of opinion over whether this changed the status quo), and, also recently, both chambers approved a bill to allow students to hold religious meetings before or after school hours. The whole question of the proper role of religion in public life has taken on an unprecedented dimension, as certain religious leaders press for more involvement, certain politicians join in, or exploit, this pressure, and other politicians struggle against what they see as a tide—and find it increasingly hard to resist. (Though Reagan has continued to call for tuition tax credits for parents who send their children to private schools, the Republican-led Senate rejected the idea last year, and it has not been brought up again this year.) Reagan, in his speech this morning, dove right in—distorting history and questioning the morality of those who believe that religion and politics should be kept separate. He said, "The truth is, politics and morality are inseparable. And as morality's foundation is religion, religion and politics are necessarily related. We need religion as a guide." Whose religion he did not say, though he is careful to pay homage to all religions from time to time. He turned around the history of John Kennedy's emphasizing that he would separate his religion from his Presidency by saying that in those days certain religious questions—abortion, school prayer—were not issues. "The right of church schools to operate was not a political issue," he said. (Is it one now?) So some of those whom Kennedy had to assure, and their like-minded allies, and the President of the United States, who have helped fan those issues, are now saying that religion and government should be joined. In a veiled reference to Cuomo, Reagan said that in Kennedy's day religious leaders "held a place of respect and a politician who spoke to or of them with a lack of respect would not long survive in the political arena." He said, "We poison our society when we remove its theological under-pinnings"—which theological underpinnings he did not say. But Reagan may be underestimating the concern that this sort of speech could cause, and underestimating the divisiveness of it.

Tonight, Bush's acceptance speech is politely received. It's not just a question of politics: Bush is not a compelling speaker in a situation like this. His voice is nasal, and cannot fill a hall; Bush cannot belt it out. At times, he does receive warm applause—especially when he goes after the Democrats. He calls the Democrats the Party of "tax and spend, tax and spend," and refers to the Convention hall in San Francisco, as he has before, as a "temple of doom." He says, "Mr. Mondale calls [his] promise to raise taxes an act of courage. But it wasn't courage, it was just habit." He says, "The message the American people got from San Francisco was 'We'll raise your taxes.' " And he continues, "Our message from Dallas is: The American people want less spending and less regulation, not more taxes." He calls for the constitutional amendment mandating a balanced budget which Reagan has proposed and the platform has endorsed. In a reference to Jackson, he reminds the audience of "that speaker in San Francisco last month exhorting his fellow-Democrats with the cry 'Our time has come; our time has come.' " Then, addressing those he refers to as "the tax raisers, the free-spenders, the excess regulators, the government-knows-best handwringers, those who would promise every special-interest group everything," he says, "Your time has passed." He takes swipes at Jimmy Carter and Tip O'Neill, and says that, under Reagan, "forgotten is the Carter-Mondale era of vacillation, of weakness, of lecturing to our friends, then letting them down." He praises Reagan's record and cites more of Glenn's, Hart's, and Hollings' criticisms of Mondale. He says, "And I don't care what Walter Mondale and Tip O'Neill say about it, Grenada was a turning point for democracy in this hemisphere and a proud moment in the history of this country." This gets big cheers. (This morning's Dallas *Times Herald* had a banner story headlined "GRENADA VOTERS MAY UNDO U.S. INVASION." The story says, "As the unelected interim government that has ruled Grenada since October moves toward setting a date for elections to replace the Marxist regime deposed by the invasion, Grenadians and U.S. officials fear that the balloting may merely reinstate one of the extremist parties associated with the political turmoil of the past decade." It says that the Grenadian Hotel Association, among others, has asked for a postponement of the election.) Bush ends on an upbeat note; he quotes from President Eisenhower's second Inaugural Address (there has been little talk of Eisenhower here this week), and concludes, "May we continue to move forward in the next four years, on the high road to peace, prosperity, and opportunity, united behind a great American President, Ronald Reagan." Tonight, the delegates are holding red-and-blue placards that say "Reagan/Bush," and by the time Bush finishes the aisles of the hall have been filled by young people getting ready to put on a demonstration for Reagan. They don't seem very excited—just there to do a job.

Reagan's speech is preceded by an eighteen-minute film, over which much fuss was made this week between the Reagan-Bush committee and the networks—which expressed some concern about running a free advertisement. In the end, NBC ran the film, and ABC and CBS ran excerpts from it. It is, as is to be expected, a slick production, some of it carrying scenes that appeared in Reagan ads run earlier this year: bucolic scenes of families hugging each other and the like. Reagan narrates much of the film—sounding relaxed and folksy. Like most political commercials, it has people in the street ostensibly spontaneously praising Reagan. It shows Reagan at a church service with the troops in Korea, Reagan in China, Reagan at Normandy—all scenes we knew at the time were being filmed for campaign use. Reagan talks of his having been shot, and we see scenes of it, and he retells one of the one-liners that he got off at the time (that he had told the doctors he hoped they were Republicans). Reagan squirrels away his good lines and uses them again and again—like a performer who knows which lines work. In the film, he says, as he has said before, that the late Cardinal Cooke, when he came to see him during his recuperation, had told him that "God must have been sitting on my shoulder," and he adds, as he has before, "I told him that 'whatever time I've got left, it now belongs to someone else.' " (The audience in the Convention hall applauds.) Sometimes Reagan transfers his lines to another role: in the film, while we see him stroll with Mrs. Reagan past the graves at Normandy, Reagan asks, "Where do we find such men?" In the 1976 campaign, Reagan used this exact line—in that case, as one that he asked Mrs. Reagan after they had entertained some former Vietnam War P.O.W.s at the Governor's mansion in California. (He also gave the same answer. "The answer came almost as quickly as I'd asked the question: Where we've always found them in this country—on the farms, the shops, the stores, and the offices.") The film is brilliantly manipulative, which is what it is intended to be. We see scenes of Reagan at the ranch, looking robust and great. He says that a lot of people asked him whether he really wanted to serve in the Presidency for another four years rather than enjoy life at the ranch, and he says, "There are so many things that remain to be done."

As Reagan comes to the podium, there is, of course, a great deal of cheering, but there is no particular frenzy—not the excitement one would expect. Many of the young demonstrators wave their placards up and down expressionlessly. Reagan, who must know that this demonstration has been planned, modestly acknowledges it and acts as if he can't stop it and get on with his speech. From time to time, the crowd shouts, "Four more years," and gets to what might be described as a modified frenzy—but not nearly the excitement shown at the Convention in Detroit four years ago.

Reagan's speech is a surprise. One would have expected it to be Reagan at his best—upbeat and optimistic, vivid and gracious, and reaching out—and to offer a vision of the future. For months, his aides have been saying that Reagan would offer his own vision of the future, and Mondale had laid down the challenge for him to do so. But the first part of Reagan's speech—the great bulk of it, in fact—consists of an attack on the Democrats and a statistic-ridden defense of his own record. I was told today that there was quite an argument among the President's advisers about this speech, and that this was the tone the President wanted to strike. The Democrats, it seemed, got under his skin during their Convention— perhaps Reagan's equanimity is not so great as we have been led to think. He had always been a tough partisan campaigner; a striking change of tone occurred in his acceptance speech four years ago. Tonight, Reagan sounds more like the insurgent again; perhaps it is the role he is really most comfortable with. He attacks the Democrats for trying to "change their colors" in San Francisco, and says, "We didn't discover our values in a poll taken a week before the Convention. And we didn't set a weathervane on top of the Golden Gate Bridge before we started talking about the American family." (Mario Cuomo and Mondale had been talking about the family for some time, but Reagan might not be aware of this—and his resentment of the Democrats' trying to make off with his themes is clear.) He says that the choice this year is "between two different visions of the future, two fundamentally different ways of governing—their government of pessimism, fear, and limits, or ours of hope, confidence, and growth." He invites the audience to take the Democrats "on a little stroll down memory lane," and he attacks the Carter Administration's record. He says that the inflation during the Carter Administration "was a deliberate part of their official economic policy." (The inflation was obviously not deliberate policy. It resulted from a miscalculation at the beginning of the Carter Administration: an effort to overcome the Ford recession, through tax cuts, led to an overheating of the economy, and this was exacerbated by high oil prices and by high food prices as the result of a drought. In 1979, Carter appointed Paul Volcker to the Fed, to get confidence in the economy back, and inflation down. Volcker instituted a monetarist policy that led to high interest rates. Thus, it was Carter's misfortune, and miscalculation, that he didn't take his recession at the beginning, as some advised him to, and get it over with, and so he had a recession in an election year. Reagan, intentionally or not, did things the other way around. There are in fact statistics indicating that over-all economic growth during the Carter years was about as high as it has been in the Reagan years. But timing can be everything in politics.) Now, in his speech, Reagan attacks the Democrats for having raised Social Security taxes—a measure taken to shore up the Social Security system—and seems to overlook that Social Security taxes were raised during his Administration as well.

Reagan says that "for the twenty-six years prior to January of 1981 the opposition party controlled both houses of Congress," and "every spending bill and every tax for more than a quarter of a century has been of their doing." (The Republican Presidents of that period were presumably elsewhere.) He says that "by nearly every measure the position of poor Americans worsened under the leadership of our opponents"—and he cites teen-age drug use and crime, and even out-of-wedlock births. He says that the largest increase in the poverty rate took place between 1978 and 1981, and that that increase has been dropping in his Administration. (Reagan gets at this claim through an imaginative use of statistics, and in any event the poverty *rate*—the percentage of the population below the poverty line—has been higher in the Reagan years than in the Carter years. Inflation did hurt the poor during the Carter years, but during the Reagan years the poor are receiving fewer benefits.) He says that "1983 was the first year since 1978 that there was no appreciable increase in poverty at all." (The increase was nine hundred thousand people, despite the economic recovery.) Reagan says, "Pouring hundreds of billions of dollars into programs in order to make people worse off was irrational and unfair." He is beginning to sound increasingly like the Reagan who went around the country in the fifties and early sixties, after his movie career had floundered, making conservative speeches for General Electric—increasingly like the ideologue of his earlier Presidential campaigns. The soothing unifier has gone offstage.

"In the four years before we took office," Reagan says, "country after country fell under the Soviet yoke." And he says, as he often says, that under his Administration "not one inch of soil has fallen to the Communists." He is cheered for this, but the cheering has been neither very frequent nor very enthusiastic. He says, "America is on the move again, and expanding toward new areas of opportunity for everyone." He says, as he often has in campaigns past, "None of the four wars in my lifetime came about because we were too strong." It has never been clear what he meant by this. He refers to Grenada and to "Democratic candidates [who] have suggested that this could be likened to the Soviet invasion of Afghanistan." He says, "Today our combat troops have come home, our students are safe, and freedom is all we left behind in Grenada." He returns to the attack on the Democrats for spending. (Now he says that they have controlled both houses of Congress for forty-two of the last fifty years.) He attacks them for not passing a constitutional amendment mandating a balanced budget. (Even a number of Republicans are unenthusiastic about this idea, knowing that it has nothing to do with taking real steps to get the budget deficit down.) He attacks Mondale's record and says, "Was anyone surprised by his pledge to raise your taxes next year?"

The audience boos and hisses as Reagan continues attacking Mondale's record in the Senate, citing specific votes. This is not a very Presidential speech. It is as if Reagan got out of the hands of his trainers. He says, "If our opponents were as vigorous in supporting our voluntary-prayer amendment as they are in raising taxes, maybe we could get the Lord back in our schoolrooms and drugs and violence out." This is what is known as "vintage Reagan." (In his 1980 nomination campaign, he said, "If we can get the federal government out of the classroom, maybe we can get God back in.") He attacks the House Democratic leadership for holding up an anti-crime bill. (The House Judiciary Committee is concerned about provisions limiting defendants' rights. Reagan is making crime one of his big issues this year, and it obviously is one on people's minds, though it is also the case that most of the crimes people are concerned about do not come under the jurisdiction of the federal government.) He calls again for tuition tax credits. He says that the Democrats' "new realism"—a term Mondale used in San Francisco—is just "old liberalism." In one of the few passages in which he says what he is for, he says, "Our tax policies are and will remain pro-work, pro-growth, and pro-family," and, as he did in his State of the Union address this year, he promises a simplified tax system (a plan that is to be offered after the election). He says that the system will bring the tax rates of every American down, and that if this occurs growth will continue and the underground economy will shrink, and he continues, "The world will beat a path to our door." He adds, "No one will be able to hold America back; and the future will be ours." As the crowds at the Olympics did, the crowd here tonight now chants, "U.S.A.! U.S.A.! U.S.A.!" This is the new tone.

Reagan briefly refers to arms control and asks the Soviets, "who have walked out of our negotiations," to "join us in reducing and, yes, ridding the earth of this awful threat." He is applauded mildly. He asks the audience whether it doubts that the Democrats would do various bad things if they won in November ("send inflation into orbit again," "raise interest rates," "make unilateral and unwise concessions to the Soviet Union")—to all of which the audience, of course, shouts, "No." And when he adds, "And they'll do all that in the name of compassion," the audience boos and hisses. This is not a very pleasant, or happy, scene. Reagan reminds the audience, "In 1980, we asked the people of America: Are you better off than you were four years ago?" and he says, "We have every reason now, four years later, to ask that same question again, for we have made a change, and the American people joined and helped us." He points out that he began his political life as a Democrat, and says that he voted for Franklin Roosevelt in 1932 because the Democrats called that year for a reduction in the cost and size of government. (In his 1980 acceptance speech, he cited those parts of Roosevelt's first acceptance speech which called for the elimination of unnecessary government functions— but not those parts of it which called for an expansion of government activity.) He continues, "As the years went by and those promises were forgotten, did I leave the Democratic Party, or did the leadership of that Party leave not just me but millions of patriotic Democrats who believed in the principles and philosophy of that platform?" In other speeches, he has talked, movingly, of how the New Deal helped his father get through the Depression. Actually, Reagan left the Democratic Party and registered as a Republican in 1962, when some California Republicans approached him and asked him to campaign for the Party, and his earlier turn to conservatism has been ascribed to, among other things, his objection to the high tax rates after the Second World War—a time when Reagan was earning a good income in the movies. There are a lot of old Reagan lines in here: "Four years ago we raised a banner of bold colors—no pale pastels." (I heard Reagan use this line in 1976.) "We proclaimed a dream of an America that would be a 'shining city on a hill.' " Once again, he praises his record. Finally, he gets to his peroration. Now his cooption of the Olympics is complete. He says, "Holding the Olympic Games here in the United States began defining the promise of this season." (The decision to hold the Games here had nothing to do with him, of course.) The audience again chants, "U.S.A.! U.S.A.!" And then he goes through a long, vivid tracing of the path of the Olympic torch across the country, telling little anecdotes. ("There was Ansel Stubbs, a youngster of ninety-nine, who passed the torch in Kansas to four-year-old Katie Johnson. . . . In Richardson, Texas, it was carried by a fourteen-year-old boy in a special wheelchair.") What this has to do with him, or his plans for the future, is not clear, and the feel of what he was trying to get across is undercut by the audience's reaction—each state's delegation cheers when its state is mentioned.

Reagan ends on a note more typical of his more uplifting, and more successful, rhetoric. Referring to the Statue of Liberty, which he has linked to the Olympic torch, he says, "The glistening hope of that lamp is still ours. Every promise, every opportunity, is still golden in this land." America, he says, "will carry on in the eighties unafraid, unashamed, and unsurpassed." He concludes, "In this springtime of hope, some lights seem eternal. America's is. Thank you, God bless you, and God bless America." He is cheered, but not passionately. Nancy Reagan and the Bushes join him at the podium. Now a large flag has dropped behind them, and red balloons drop from the ceiling and white balloons rise from the floor (no blue balloons tonight). Some shimmering plastic confetti is dropped (this is a "Mylar drop") amid a play of lights.

(One of the tunes played during this demonstration is "Happy Days Are Here Again.") Some of the delegates are carrying small plastic American flags, like the ones at the Democratic Convention, and some wave them slowly—but no big thing is made of this here. Now Ray Charles sings his own version of "America the Beautiful." Then, after Reverend Criswell gives the benediction, asking God to "bless our President and our Vice-President," and reciting a paraphrase of "God Bless America," Vikki Carr leads the audience in singing "God Bless America."

XIX

MERRILL, WISCONSIN. The Mondale people, after much delibera-
tion, selected this picturesque small town (pop. 9,500) in north-
central Wisconsin as the site of Mondale's main Labor Day event
today. A large and cheerful crowd has turned out at the fairgrounds this afternoon to see Mondale and Geraldine Ferraro,
and Mondale is to make a speech laying out his themes for the fall
campaign. Though the general election has been under way for
some time now, the tradition that it "begins" on Labor Day is still
paid homage, and both the Reagan and Mondale campaigns have
put great effort into stepping out smartly. (Reagan is appearing at
a rally today in Irvine, California, in Orange County, the site of his
original, and lasting, political base.) One problem the Mondale
people faced in planning this day is that Labor Day has become,
almost everywhere, simply a day off: there are very few Labor Day
events for a candidate to attach himself to. (Democrats used to
open their campaigns in Cadillac Square, in Detroit.) For Ronald
Reagan, with the skills of the White House behind him, drawing a
crowd in Orange County should be no great trick. For Mondale,
the situation is more complicated. Merrill was chosen for a
number of reasons: Wisconsin is one of the Mondale campaign's
targeted states (Reagan carried it by four per cent in 1980, and
John Anderson, who got seven per cent, might have made the
difference between victory or defeat for the Democratic ticket
here); Merrill still celebrates Labor Day, with a parade and a picnic; and the town represents middle-class Middle America—and
an area close to Mondale's roots. This would present, the Mondale
people thought, a good picture for the television news programs
tonight, as well as help in Wisconsin.

Unfortunately, the day got off to a bad—if not calamitous, given
the attention it will get—start, when Mondale and Ferraro attended a Labor Day Parade in New York to which nobody came.

The scene of empty sidewalks on Fifth Avenue as Mondale and Ferraro and other dignitaries marched by (they were accompanied by New York Governor Mario Cuomo, Senator Daniel Patrick Moynihan, and A.F.L.-C.I.O. President Lane Kirkland) will inevitably make it onto tonight's news programs, and had a dispiriting effect on the Mondale entourage. Labor wanted Mondale to attend the parade, and the Mondale people felt that they had to include some labor event in their Labor Day activities, and agreed to be there. Labor had said it would do its best to have people there, but failed to deliver. To the extent that the parade draws crowds, it doesn't do it early in the morning. And certainly not at eight-forty-five in the morning. (In any event, in the past two years the parade didn't begin until 10 A.M.) The Mondale people wanted to start early, so that they could get on to Merrill by the early afternoon, and then to California by early evening. Their hope had been to do a labor Labor Day event without drawing great attention to it—to make Merrill the highlight of the day. When, over the weekend, they began to receive word that the event in New York might not come off so well, they were focussing on the subsequent events of the day, and went ahead. They probably had no choice at that point. (There had been alternatives—events that did not demand a crowd—as at least some of the Mondale people ruefully acknowledged later.) Thus, as can happen in politics, what should have been a minor incident became a major one—at least, temporarily; any campaign can misplan an event, but the Mondale campaign's doing so at this particular moment took on large proportions and was made into a metaphor for the state of the campaign itself. So, despite the good crowd that is here (people were brought in by the Mondale campaign from Eau Claire, Green Bay, and the university town of Madison), and that will provide good pictures, this morning's problem has already thrown a shadow over the day.

At this point, of course, Mondale cannot afford for many things to go wrong. Both he and Reagan have had a ragged month, but recent polls have had Reagan leading Mondale by from ten to fifteen points, and Mondale's own polls put him fifteen points behind—having lost a few points in recent weeks. The Mondale people know that the challenge for them is to narrow that gap within the next two to three weeks—to make the race be seen as truly competitive. (First, they realize, they have to stop the trend of the polls in Reagan's direction.) Analogies to other elections are much talked about these days: it is pointed out that Reagan's lead at this point is not as great as were Lyndon Johnson's in 1964 and Richard Nixon's in 1972—both landslide elections. Comparisons are made to other years, when leads were overtaken, or nearly overtaken. But it is also possible that the 1984 election has its own set of dynamics, and that there is no precedent for it. The Mondale people are pinning their hopes, and basing their strategy, on public and private polling data that indicate that Reagan is more popular than his policies are. Therefore, their challenge, as they see it, is to get people to focus on those policies—to "raise the stakes," as James Johnson, Mondale's campaign chairman, likes to put it—and get people to see the choice they will make in November in different terms. They concede that people have not reached that point yet. The other challenge, they say, is to show Mondale as fighting for those policies, as passionately committed to them, and also as doing unconventional things—thereby establishing him as a leader and overcoming his low ratings for leadership. Therefore, the plan is for Mondale to be aggressive on a variety of issues where, the Mondale people believe, the public agrees with Mondale's stands—on arms control, fairness, the environment—and to have him offer his own budget-reduction program. Like his saying in his acceptance speech that he will raise taxes (and that Reagan will, too, but won't admit it), this is to show Mondale as willing to "level with the people," to do things conventional politicians don't do.

Another adviser says about Mondale's "leadership" problem, "We have to make it clear that the question isn't salesmanship—who gives the best speech. We have to raise powerful questions: Who is best able to control nuclear weapons? People are not going to believe that Mondale can lead on these issues until they see him lead on these issues, and that will take a little time." He adds that Mondale wasn't able to talk about these things with any consistency until now, because of the intraparty primary fight he was involved in throughout the first half of the year, and the post-Convention difficulties. The Mondale people take heart from the polling that tells them the deficit issue has moved up in people's consciousness. One says, "That shows you how you can move issues up if you hammer away at them day after day." Richard Leone, a senior adviser who is responsible for "the message"—he coordinates the work on issues, advertising, polling, and speech-writing—says, "In this first phase of the contest, we have to get a lot of people who could potentially move to us to not tune out on the race—by being interesting and getting their attention. If we can get people to focus on what's our policy on the deficit, versus Reagan's, and on the idea that Reagan is a rich man's President, and on the question of where Reagan is taking us, then we could have a competitive race. If we get into October and people haven't paid attention to those things, then it's a *very* tough race."

Mondale's advisers know that with Reagan they are up against an unusual and (to everyone who has opposed him) a frustrating opponent. One adviser explains the gap in the polls as follows: "Reagan has leadership and communicates: he's a phenomenon that can't be looked at in the same terms as normally in a general election. It's not like anything I've seen; it's not like anything anyone has seen. Couple that with the fact that Fritz is probably not as well known or understood or defined as he should be." He concedes that Mondale's own polls indicate that people question Mondale's capacity for leadership, how tough he would be. He continues, "You have to think about whether conventional approaches are what you use, since it appears to be an unconventional situation. Our polls show us that on most of the issues we look pretty good. If we can focus on the playing field of the issues and point up that even with Reagan's great popularity the results aren't that great, and that people aren't being told everything, then we think we have a good chance—despite what the polls show, and despite the conventional wisdom, and despite the sadness with which people look at us and say 'Poor you.' "

Mondale's aides know that Mondale has yet to connect with large numbers of voters that he needs, and they say that the way to do that is to show him as a person of strong beliefs. Leone says, "We have to redefine the leadership issue in this campaign. It's not leadership to have no plan to deal with the deficit, and when we come up with one and they don't and just argue with ours, we'll be seen as leading. People will have to see that he is tough—mentally, emotionally, physically." I asked how this would be done, and he replied, "Showing him tough comes out of a fight—an underdog fighting against a huge operation, talking about things he feels strongly about, and stepping up to tough issues."

The Mondale people do have theories—on which they are operating—about how to pull Reagan into the fray, and about how to change the look and the definition of this election. They intend to try to make a major issue of the fact that Reagan has been vague about what he would do in a second term—to make it a "leadership" issue. Johnson says, "People don't understand very clearly at this point that Reagan's ability to run a campaign stringing together successful photo opportunities and big-screen events diminishes substantially as you get closer to the election." He is hoping that the debates will draw Reagan in, that the press corps will rebel against White House attempts to use it as a conveyor for only what it wants to convey (keeping Reagan well away from it most of the time), and that the press will start asking for Reagan's responses to the issues Mondale is raising. Johnson says, "The press will demand, Mondale will demand, the debates will require, that Reagan be closer to this election."

For any of this to matter, if it did occur, Mondale would have to become competitive with Reagan. Johnson agrees, and says that this could happen in two ways. The first part, he says, is "structural": there are more Democrats than Republicans; more people are being registered as Democrats (though the Republicans are conducting their own registration drive); Democratic senators, congressmen, and candidates for local office seem to be doing well in their own races, and the Democrats have the majority of state legislatures—and these factors strengthen the Democratic ticket's chances. He adds to the "structural" factors the debates and the dramatically increased coverage of the two candidates that will occur, and says, "There are seemingly very strong forces that will bring the race closer together." The second part, he says, "has to do with how compelling Mondale's issues are and how compellingly Mondale makes them." He says it is indisputably the case that people agree with Mondale on the issues, and adds, "As he makes his case aggressively and comes back from his current situation, that will spark interest." Johnson says the Mondale polls show that Reagan is seen as favoring rich people and not coming to grips with arms control or the deficit. While all these things may narrow the race, Johnson concedes that another set of things has to happen for there to be a Mondale victory. Mondale, he says, has to present his issues in a way that generates a very high degree of support from and turnout by Democrats—that makes Democrats see Reagan's reelection as a threat to what they believe in—and in a way that takes hold "beyond what we now see." A third factor, Johnson believes, is that Reagan is "mistake-prone." This is not the same thing as hoping that Reagan will make one big mistake; it simply assumes that, skilled as Reagan may be, he does make mistakes, and that these will become part of the picture. (Reagan mishandled Mondale's challenge to him to concede that taxes would have to be raised, and there is a body of thought that he mishandled his own Convention.)

Johnson says, "There are some aspects of the leadership fight that are moving a little bit at this point." He adds, "If you look at the aspects of leadership as walking on the beach of Normandy or standing on the Great Wall of China, Mondale will not compete at this. But there are other aspects of leadership where Mondale is measuring up and exceeding Reagan." Johnson says that this is showing up in the Mondale polling: that when people are asked about what aspects of leadership they consider important they name managing the relationship with the Soviet Union, and say that they believe that Mondale would be more successful at this than Reagan has been; that the idea of levelling with the American people as an aspect of leadership is catching on; that Mondale gets better marks than Reagan for unifying, rather than dividing, people, and also for the ability to see the future clearly. He also says that when people are asked by the Mondale pollsters what the key test of Presidential leadership is, and are given a variety of choices, the one that comes out on top, by far, is "investing in our future" (through education, job opportunities, increased competitiveness, insuring our economic future)—a result that surprises even the Mondale people. They are not yet sure that this can be turned into a powerful voting issue, but they take encouragement from the finding.

Johnson describes one line of analysis that he says is gaining a consensus within the campaign. It starts with the point that the election is now so dominated by Reagan as a personality that a lot of things are distorted—that if people are asked about Mondale versus Reagan, Mondale's negatives come out higher and stronger than they really are. It continues: some data suggest that if Mondale is seen in isolation from Reagan, people think highly of him; they feel that he is quite prepared to be President, that he is sincere, that he is ready to fight for justice and for the average family—in other words, that his "profile," out of the Reagan

shadow, is stronger and much more intact than had been anticipated. Therefore, according to this analysis, Mondale shouldn't
challenge Reagan head on over who is the stronger leader, or
attack Reagan (as Mondale began to do earlier this year) as inat-
tentive, or as presiding over an Administration touched by
"sleaze." Instead, Mondale should run at Reagan through the war/
peace issue, the rich/poor issue, and the issue of who has a better
vision of the future—through his values versus Reagan's values.
The theory is that Mondale has credibility on those issues, and
that this argues for a more patient strategy than some would
urge—for a strategy that is aimed at turning those issues into the
definition of the election. So, according to this theory, while people's affection for Reagan, or their view of him as a standup guy,
may not be seriously affected, it may be possible to move the
election to the point where those are not what the election is
about. (Moreover, there are a number of people within the Mondale campaign who remember that Jimmy Carter's attempts to go
at Reagan more personally failed, or even backfired.) There is an
increasing feeling among the Mondale people that the core of
Reagan's strength has to do with apparent decisiveness, personal
strength—characteristics that make him loom large. Therefore,
they conclude that the leadership issue must be redefined, and
that that will start to happen, as Johnson says, "if Mondale can get
the focus on the issues that concern people about their future."

For now, the Mondale people have targeted a large number of
states, because they are currently behind in so many states, and
also because they believe, as one important strategist puts it, "the
issues are running in our direction, even though we're behind in
the polls." They believe that what is changing, or might change,
the percentages in certain states is the presence of Ferraro on the
ticket (despite the recent problems over the financial affairs of
her and her husband, John Zaccaro), and the disjunction between
people's telling Mondale's pollsters that they like Reagan and a
majority also saying that they don't believe he "cares about people
like me." But to make what the Mondale people see as the para-
doxes in the polls work in their favor, they realize that Mondale
has to be seen as a real and desirable alternative. So at the same
time that states are being targeted the campaign is also concentrating on trying to move large numbers of people nationally, in order
to change the chemistry of the situation in general. Peter Hart,

Mondale's pollster, says, "As you move a lot of people in New York, you won't not move them in Michigan: if you do x per cent better nationally, you do x per cent better in one state or another." So in early October the Mondale people will see how they have done and narrow their targets and allocate their resources accordingly. While there is a great deal of focus on the electoral vote, Johnson argues that it's all very simple: "The electoral-vote challenge is likely to be solved by solving the popular-vote challenge." He adds, "We have virtually no states that are runaway states in our direction, and they have about fifteen to twenty states that, based on history, are likely to be heavily Republican. Deductively, if we get to fifty-one percent we should win most of the remaining states." Next week, the Mondale campaign will do its first national network advertising, and will also begin buying time for ads in certain targeted areas across the country (they're not telling where), to be followed up by polling, to test where their prospects are improving or might improve. The target voters for the Mondale and the Reagan people are the same: "soft Democrats" (blue-collar workers who voted for Reagan in 1980), and independents and young voters, many of whom supported Gary Hart in the primaries. (The Mondale people believe that independents care about the issues they are stressing: arms control, the environment, fairness, education.) The endorsement of Mondale by John Anderson, on August 28th, was seen by the Mondale people as at least symbolically important in trying to reach the independents and Hart supporters.

The squabbling between the blacks who had supported Mondale and those who had supported Jackson was put pretty much to an end during a series of meetings of fifty black leaders with Mondale and his aides in Minnesota in late August. Earlier in the month, Mondale had deliberately expressed frustration publicly with Jesse Jackson's continuing complaints and demands. (Jackson said that Mondale hadn't hired enough blacks—though a key former Jackson aide had been hired, and Charles Rangel, a black congressman from New York, who had supported Mondale, had been named national co-chairman of the campaign—and said that Mondale had to come out for a large jobs program.) Word was also conveyed to Jackson from the Mondale camp that such goings on had to end by Labor Day—that it was in neither Jackson's interests nor Mondale's that they continue. Following the Convention, the Mondale people had decided to be careful about reaching out to Jackson—to not be in a position of continuing to, and being seen as continuing to, give in to his demands. Jackson was in effect in the position he was in going into the Democratic Convention: there was no question that he would have to end up supporting the ticket, but he would extract all he could in the meantime. So at the end of the month blacks who had supported Jackson and blacks who had supported Mondale were gathered for a final (it was hoped) working out of things. Following a long session between Mondale and Jackson, and between the blacks and Mondale staff people, and then between Mondale and the black group, the matter was resolved about as well as could have been expected. Jackson announced that he would give Mondale support that would be "wide-based, deep, and intense," and the black group said it would support Mondale. Mondale's meeting with the blacks was said to have been tense and emotional—with Mondale resisting a demand that he back an expensive new jobs program while assuring the group about his concern for unemployment. Mondale insisted that his deficit-reduction program allowed for no additional expensive programs (nor does his current politics) and that the deficit-reduction program itself would lead to more jobs. Two additional prominent blacks—Mayor Coleman Young, of Detroit, a Mondale backer, and former Atlanta mayor Maynard Jackson, a Jackson supporter—were given major roles in the campaign. (Young was named head of voter-registration and Jackson a "senior policy adviser.") Andrew Young, the current Atlanta mayor, retreating from a remark he had made about the Mondale staff earlier in the month, said, "A lot of folk I thought were smart asses are a lot smarter than I thought they were."

What the net effect of Jackson's support will be on the Mondale ticket is the subject of some speculation—and disagreement—now, but the Mondale people are counting on a heavy black turnout to carry some Southern states, and believe that the combined black efforts to get out the vote—which will be joined with efforts by prominent whites—will be beneficial. And while the meeting with Jackson came out well enough from the Mondale people's point of view—as they expected it to—the public did get one more picture of Mondale seeming to be pleading for his support. One Mondale adviser thinks that the various problems the Mondale campaign had to deal with in August—Ferraro's problems, the resignation of

Bert Lance from the job of general chairman of the campaign (a job he never really assumed), the continuing efforts to get Jackson in line—cost the campaign about three weeks. (One adviser thinks that the thing that hurt Mondale the most during August was the Olympics—which affected the national mood in a way that redounded to Reagan's benefit. This person says, "If I could change one thing about August, I'd want to take out the Olympics.") One thing that cheers the Mondale people up about the past month is that they do not believe that Reagan made any political gains as a result of the Republican Convention, and think that in fact the Convention—the right-wing platform, the visible role of evangelist preachers, Reagan's speech about religion (in which he said that "religion and politics are necessarily related," and that those who oppose prayer in schools are "intolerant of religion"), the negative tone of Reagan's acceptance speech, and the obvious demoralization of the moderates—not only gave Mondale some material to work with but also gave him some ground. They feel that the Reagan people made a mistake at the Convention by allowing it to become so dominated by the social issues—thus potentially offending some "weak Democrats," independents, and young voters. (Some of Reagan's advisers felt the same way at the time.) They also feel—as do a few Reagan people—that too much time went into beating up on Jimmy Carter and on going back to the sixties for their attacks on Mondale. And they feel—as some Reagan advisers do—that the failure of the Republicans to talk about the future was a big mistake. They think that what they see as the Republicans' blundering at their Convention, as Leone puts it, "gave us another opportunity to explain what the election is all about." Now a key Mondale adviser says, "We have to get the contest going again." He adds, "I think you have to look at the campaign as starting all over again. Now the question is the same question we had after our Convention: Can we take the issues to Reagan?"

Ferraro's appearances with Mondale—here at the fairgrounds in Merrill, and at some other stops in these first few days—are the result of the Mondale staff's belief that Ferraro still stirs excitement, and adds strength to the ticket. They say that her popularity ratings are not as high as when she was chosen but that that would have been the case in any event; the polls indicate that people think she did well at her press conference dealing with her and her husband's finances a couple of weeks ago. While newspaper investigations into the Zaccaros' business dealings (mainly his) are continuing, the stories about them are diminishing, and the Mondale people are holding their breath, hoping that the worst is behind them. There is some uncertainty within the Mondale camp about how the gamble of choosing Ferraro will ultimately turn out. Meanwhile, Ferraro has been drawing large crowds as she has campaigned on her own, and has been going over well with them. There is a naturalness about her that people find appealing, and she lights up in front of a crowd. Moreover, Ferraro photographs well and, unlike Mondale, looks very good on television; it is a mysterious thing that has to do with the interaction of the camera and a person's features, and a chemistry between the camera and the person. (In Hollywood, there is an expression, "The camera loves him.") A television executive I know says, "Ferraro televises up; Mondale televises down." There are still large questions about both Ferraro's judgment and her depth. (She got the answer to a foreign-policy question wrong on a television program a couple of weeks ago, two days before her press conference, but people were so interested in her finances then that they didn't much notice.) A special effort is being made to brief her, but she has a lot to learn fast.

Now the sky has clouded over and it has begun to rain. This just might not be Mondale's day. Ferraro is greeted enthusiastically by the crowd as she comes to the podium, which is on a platform surrounded by blue molding—the molding draped in red-white-and-blue bunting. David Obey, the congressman from this district, and Anthony Earl, the governor—both Democrats—are here. Obey, a respected and important member of the House, gives Ferraro a warm introduction. ("She is bright, she is savvy, she can cut through the guts of an issue.") Ferraro, wearing a gray plastic raincoat, says, "I just have something to ask you before we start: Can we win?" The crowd shouts, "Yes." She continues, "Will we send Ronald Reagan back to his ranch?" The crowd shouts, "Yes." She knows how to get a crowd going. "I think so, too," she says. Her voice is full-volumed and a bit on the high side, with a touch of brass—particularly when, as here, she is talking to a crowd and enthusiastically. The Queens accent is apparent, and the people gathered here seem fascinated by her—something new and unusual has landed among them. They seem to like her, just as they seemed to like the idea of her before she began. Now, after praising Obey as "one of the most effective members of Congress, one of the dozen or so members who really make a difference on the issues," she adds, obviously referring to herself, "We all know who another one is, right?" She refers to Wisconsin and the Progressive movement and Robert La Follette—but mispronounces La Follette's name. (It comes out "La-Flat.") The crowd laughs, and there are some boos. Now, as she reads her speech, she dons a farmer's cap to keep the rain off her aviator-style reading glasses. She talks about the historic significance of Mondale's having chosen a woman as his running mate, and, making a slip, says, "You will also be making history when I stand in the Capitol and take the oath as the first woman President of this great nation." She praises Mondale as having "spent his whole public life fighting for middle-income families and working people," and says, "While Ronald Reagan was making movies, Fritz Mondale was making history as a champion of civil rights and social justice." The crowd laughs and applauds. She talks about "the special meaning for me" of what she says are Mondale's goals. When she mentions peace, she talks about rising tensions with the Soviet Union, the sending of troops to Central America, and adds, "And our young men have needlessly died in Beirut." She continues, "The question is, over the next four years, what will happen to my son, John, and to your children and your grandchildren? Will this President, unrestrained by the need for reelection, heighten the risk of war? I don't want to take that chance." She continues talking about the arms race, which she has been emphasizing in her appearances: "I want a President who believes in negotiation, not confrontation; who understands that an arms race does not lead to peace—it leads to an arms race; and who stops spending so much on the arms race and starts investing more in the human race."

Ferraro is effective at personalizing the issues and, though reading a text, at sounding as if she is talking from deep conviction. Her speeches are written for her, and they are well written (her speechwriter, Fred Martin, used to work for Mondale), and she delivers them with an apparent sincerity that reaches people. "We need a President who levels with us," she says—this is one of Mondale's themes—and, explicitly referring to her own recent experience, she says, "In the last three weeks, I have seen dramatic evidence in my own campaign of what I have known and practiced all my life: there's no substitute for levelling with the American people." She criticizes Reagan for the trade imbalance, which is having a bad effect on farmers, for the deficits and interest rates and the threat of diminished economic growth—and for his not talking about these things. "President Reagan won't tell us his plan for reducing deficits," she says. "We can bring down deficits and interest rates. But it takes strong leadership and straight talk. If deficits are bad—and they are—then let's reduce them. If taxes must go up—and they will, no matter who is in the White House— then let's do it fairly. And if our leaders won't level with us—then let's replace them." She is cheered. She talks about her own story of having grown up poor and of having put herself through law school at night while teaching school during the day. Her personal story was considered one of her assets when Mondale chose her— at least, this part of her personal story. She attacks the Reagan economic program as having been unfair to the middle class and the poor. She says, "I want our government to give full support to our schools, not to lobby for tax breaks for segregated academies."

Then, in what is a new addition to her standard stump speech, Ferraro says, "In the vision Fritz Mondale describes, government stays out of our private lives," and she goes on to make a strong statement about individual freedom on religious and moral questions. "Mr. Reagan talks about freedom, and he should," she says. "But there's no freedom more important than the liberty to think as you want, pray as you believe, and the liberty to be left alone. Mr. Reagan is for limited government—except when he wants government to affect our most private decisions and beliefs." At this, she is cheered strongly. Both candidates will be playing off the Republican Convention. Mondale is to give a major speech on the subject of religion and politics in Washington on Thursday, but he has already begun to talk about it. Yesterday, in a five-minute nationwide radio broadcast (Mondale, following Reagan's example, has been doing these every weekend, on Sundays, since early August), he said that the Republicans had "raised doubts whether they respect the wall our founders placed between government and religion." Mondale is said to feel that he must respond to Reagan on this issue, since it is so much in the air, and because he has his own strong views on the subject. His advisers have mixed feelings about his taking the subject on: those who are leery about his doing so realize that religion is a complex and sensitive subject, in which it is easy to be misunderstood, and they also realize that Mondale is opening himself up to counterattack. But stepping up to the issue is a way of getting attention, and, moreover, Mondale would undoubtedly be much criticized if he didn't deal with it. (And his aides say that he has been bothered for some time now by Reagan's playing to the religious right, and was quite disturbed by a speech Reagan gave early last year in Orlando, Florida, to the National Association of Evangelicals, in which he attacked "modern-day secularism" and government subsidizing of birth-control help to "promiscuous" teenage girls, repeated his call for a constitutional amendment "to restore prayer to public schools," and denounced abortion. And, talking about the Soviet Union and the fact that Communism does not accept the existence of God, Reagan said, "Until they do, let us be aware that while they preach supremacy of the state, declare its omnipotence over individual man, and predict its eventual domination of all peoples on the earth, they are the focus of evil in the modern world." It was in this same speech that Reagan referred to the Soviet Union as "an evil empire," and described the arms race as a "struggle between right and wrong and good and evil." In one sense, Reagan's talking about the subject of religion reaches into his foreign policy. Reagan's appealing to the religious right, and its effects on domestic politics, was on the table as a possible topic for Mondale's acceptance speech.) Polling done by the Mondale camp indicates that people as a whole are not quite clear about Reagan's having raised the issue at the Convention—but that they do feel strongly about the subject of personal and religious privacy (and about Jerry Falwell). Still, a large number of people are upset by Reagan's remarks—and Reagan himself has been backing away. (Yesterday, as he was leaving for California, Reagan said that he had only been referring to people who were opposed to such things as having chaplains in the military and "In God We Trust" imprinted on our currency, and added, "I'm not seeking to install a state religion in any way," and his aides have been saying that Reagan wouldn't be talking about the subject anymore. They added that Mondale would be making a mistake if he talked about it.)

Now Ferraro mocks the emphasis on patriotism at the Republican Convention (calling it "self-conscious patriotism that's made on Madison Avenue"), and says that when someone finds jobs for the eight and a half million unemployed in this country—"That will be a patriotic act." And she repeats this refrain in connection with providing teachers with the tools they need to educate children, stopping the nuclear-arms race, enforcing the civil-rights laws, and making the Equal Rights Amendment part of the Constitution. As she reaches her conclusion, she says, "Mr. Reagan preaches love of country, and I agree. But I say let's love our countrymen and women, too. Let's put people to work, let's enforce the laws, protect the planet, and keep the peace—that's the best way to honor the American flag." And she ends on a strong note, saying that the time to register new voters, the time "to seize our future," and the time for Mondale "is not later—it's *now*." She has got the crowd quite enthusiastic.

As Mondale is about to speak, the rain stops, and he removes his raincoat and his suit jacket, tossing them to the Zaccaros' two daughters, who are travelling with the candidates today. As he is introduced, Mondale strolls around the platform looking confident and relaxed. This may be deliberate: even though Mondale has had many relaxed and funny moments in the course of the campaign, his advisers and political supporters despair that he has come across as wooden and humorless, when they don't feel that he is that way at all. The Mondale that people who know him know and the Mondale that has come through in this campaign are very different—that is in part Mondale's failing, but it is also partly a question of what television news has chosen to show about him. Mondale himself is aware of his image as uninteresting, and, naturally, is bothered by it. However, Mondale can't be pushed into changing his style very much, and will go only so far in simplifying his speeches. One adviser says, "Walter Mondale is always going to be more complex than other speakers, because he feels strongly about certain issues and wants to talk about them. He can't be scripted the way their guy can." Then, as Mondale starts to speak, a light rain begins again, but he delivers his speech in his shirt-sleeves. This speech has been gone over and gone over until the last moment—a process that sometimes gives his speeches the feeling of having been written by committee, and takes the edge off what he says.

Mondale begins by setting forth the theme of his fall campaign.

"Today, the campaign for 1984 begins," he says, and he continues, "I want to tell you what I believe this race is all about. It comes down to this: in this election, we will decide what kind of people we are." He says, "Today, there are fifty thousand nuclear warheads on this planet. One false move and human history is over. What kind of people are we? Well, we're a strong country and we defend our freedom. But we're also a smart country that knows that those god-awful weapons must never go off." He says, "Mr. Reagan has a thing about arms control," and notes that Reagan is the first President since Herbert Hoover not to meet with a Soviet leader, and that he "opposed every agreement—by Kennedy, Johnson, Nixon, Ford, and Carter, every one of them—to control nuclear armaments." He says, "He has conducted an arms race on earth and now he wants to extend it to the heavens." He receives large cheers. He quotes John F. Kennedy's saying that we should never negotiate out of fear but that we should never fear to negotiate, and cites, as he did earlier this year, Kennedy's having called for a moratorium on atmospheric nuclear testing to prevent fallout and having challenged the Soviets to do the same, and points out that within two months the United States and the Soviet Union had negotiated a treaty banning such testing. He says that as President he will follow Kennedy's example. He calls, as he has for some time, for annual summit meetings between American and Soviet leaders and for a mutual, verifiable nuclear freeze. And he says that he will "challenge the Soviets with arms-control proposals to increase our security and to protect our future." Mondale has talked about these things before, but he does it better than usual here, with strong feeling. And the audience responds with applause and cheers. Mondale says, referring to Reagan and arms control, "That's one of the big issues that divides us and tests what the American people want."

Next, Mondale talks about the need for long-term economic growth, and refers to "an obscene trillion-dollar debt building up on our children's shoulders." He says, "We need a President who gets those deficits down, gets those interest rates down, restores American farm exports, strengthens those farm programs, and gives our farmers a chance." The audience cheers some more. It responds to him even more than it did to Ferraro. After talking more about the effects of the deficit, he returns to his refrain and asks, "Well, what kind of a people are we? I'll tell you what. We're a tough people; and this is a tough country. We're willing to see our problems as they are; we're willing to look them in the face, and we're a no-nonsense country that demands straight talk from our leaders." This is a major Mondale theme, which he began with his acceptance speech: that he is levelling with the American people and Reagan is not. He says, "Reagan has piled up the worst deficit in world history, and is running on a platform that would double it." (He is referring to the various tax cuts proposed in the Republican platform.) He says, "Let's tell the truth. Whoever is elected, this budget must be squeezed and revenues must be restored." And he says, "But the question is whether it will be done fairly: the question is who will pay." He is speaking with feeling here, even passion. He seems to have his themes down and be comfortable with them. He says, "In the Republican future, tax increases and program cuts will fall heaviest on working Americans of average means, just as they did before. And I don't think that's the kind of people we are." He says, "If there's one thing I'm sure of, it's that Americans are not selfish," and he cites budget cuts the Reagan Administration has made in programs for the poor. He had talked earlier in the year about what kind of people we are as a theme against Reagan, but then this got lost amid his fights against John Glenn and Gary Hart. Now he is using it as an overarching theme, working in the subjects—arms control, fairness, the deficit, levelling with the American people—that he intends to take against Reagan in the coming weeks.

The crowd chants "We want Fritz," and Mondale, smiling, says, "You're going to get him." He cites, as he has all year, Lincoln's saying we should have a government "of the people, by the people, and for the people." He says, "I don't believe a President should just serve all the people in his country club," and the crowd laughs, and he goes on to say, "I believe a President should serve all the people in our country, and that's what I'll do." That the polls indicate that people see Reagan as a rich man's President has encouraged Mondale all along, and this, plus a certain streak that is within him, something that comes from his roots, has led him to run something of a populist campaign. He attacks low corporate taxes, polluters, Pentagon contractors—as he did in his acceptance speech. Again he says, "What kind of people are we? Well, we're the most religious people on earth," and says that that is because "our faith is pure and unintimidated, because we practice our faith free from the intrusion of government." He says that when he grew up in Elmore, Minnesota, "just as you've grown up in these communities around here, we didn't need government to tell us that we believed in our God." He goes on, "And I think those who seek to inject government and the politicians into religion lack confidence in the wisdom and the decency and good sense of the American people." He says, "I want a future where government watches out for you and not over you. I want a government operating on your side, opening doors of opportunity, not looking over your shoulder, imposing dictates of conformity." He gets tremendous cheers. Clearly, this issue has struck a nerve. Now he refers to John F. Kennedy's last speech in the 1960 campaign: "Mr. Nixon, he said, had gone all over the country saying that we never had it so good, that our prosperity had never been greater at home and that our prestige had never been higher abroad. Mr. Nixon was saying in effect that Senator Kennedy, because he was focussing on the problems that Americans had to solve, was somehow gloomy and unpatriotic. The way that Kennedy answered that charge that night is the answer I give today. He said this: 'I run as a candidate for the Presidency with a view that ours is a great country but it must be greater.' And so it must. And so it must."

And now, becoming listy, as is his wont, Mondale talks about doing better on arms control, on human rights, on feeding people, on having young people serve in the Peace Corps. (All this is going over very well with the audience, however.) Then he sums up: "We are not a fragile people; we're a mature people." He says, "We can be the country who demands the truth about our economic future," and he reiterates some of his themes, speaking urgently. Then he adds, "Those are the stakes in this election. And before you make your final decision, I ask you to do exactly what you do when you approach the railroad tracks: stop, look, and listen. It's your choice, it's your country, it's your future. Let's go there together. If you will help us, we're going to win it." This is his hope: that he can get people to think about the implications of their decision, to look past Reagan's popularity to his policies—to, as Mario Cuomo said in his keynote address at the Convention, "separate the salesman from the product." And Mondale concludes by saying, "These pundits who say we're going to lose, they're wrong." He is given large cheers.

LONG BEACH, CALIFORNIA. At six-thirty Pacific Daylight Time, the Mondale-Ferraro entourage arrives at the Long Beach Airport, about thirty miles south of Los Angeles. A rally has been planned for Mondale's arrival, but since we are an hour behind schedule it will not make it onto the evening news programs, as had been hoped. The scheduling simply demanded too much: Merrill is about forty-five minutes from the Central Wisconsin Airport, and the trip also required a refuelling stop in Minneapolis. The Mondale people wanted to have Mondale in California on the same day as Reagan, and, having made the commitment to attend the Labor Day Parade, stretched the campaign, and the candidate, beyond the doable. Scheduling and reality were not in sync today, and the effects on the entourage—and on the candidate, who looks tired—are apparent. It's not just the long day; despite the evident success of the stop in Merrill, the unfortunate beginning of the day is still on the minds of the Mondale entourage. (And despite the fact that the speech in Merrill went over well with the audience, some of the people around Mondale feel that it lacked a certain punch.) While scheduling is a technical matter, it can affect the substance of the day as well as the morale of the entourage. Mondale is actually beginning this fall campaign tired; he never got the time to make up for the toll that the long struggle for the nomination took on him. He had little peace between the time he secured the nomination and the time of the Convention, or, despite a fishing trip, between the Convention and now. There were too many things going on; too many problems; too many diversions; too many demands on him. So, while he looks relatively rested (especially compared to the way he looked at the end of the primaries) and his face is tanned, it is clear that he is not really rested. And this fall Mondale's schedule will, of necessity, be more rigorous than Reagan's—whose aides take pains in any event not to tax him too hard in a campaign.

A crowd of about fifteen hundred is here to greet Mondale at the Long Beach Airport in the very warm evening—and Hart is here, along with Alan Cranston, Los Angeles Mayor Tom Bradley, and a host of other local officials. Hart, looking well, makes a brief, crisp, and strong speech to the crowd about the importance of defeating Reagan. Hart has committed himself to spending a substantial amount of time campaigning for Mondale, much of it in California. The Mondale people insist that they believe that Mondale has a chance of defeating Reagan in California—that Ferraro's presence on the ticket and Californians' attitudes about certain issues (arms control, the environment, fairness, the deficit, interest rates) could work to Mondale's advantage—despite Reagan's political roots here, and despite the fact that the Democrats haven't carried the state in a Presidential election since 1964. A poll taken by the Mondale people in California in midsummer showed Mondale trailing Reagan here by eight points—a fact they found encouraging. They have sent one of their top organizers here, and committed a fair amount of candidate time to the state, an expensive proposition (this is Ferraro's second trip to the West Coast since the Convention), and are trying to convince Californians that Mondale's campaign here will not be abortive, as Carter's was in 1980. Another factor in the Mondale campaign's thinking is that there are five and a half million unregistered voters here, of whom most are black, Hispanic, or lower-income whites. (One Reagan adviser—but only one, so far as I could find—has been concerned all along that the Democrats could win California, through increases in registration.) And still another factor here, the Mondale people say, is that the Democratic congressmen and members of the state legislature—who form the majority—are very concerned about a proposition that will be on the November ballot calling for a redistricting, and therefore will be working hard to increase the Democratic vote. The Long Beach area is a moderate one; with the exception of this morning, the Mondale campaign is deliberately not doing predictable things today, not going to stereotypically Democratic crowds. It has to walk a fine line between keeping its base fired up—or getting it fired up—and reaching out to persuade less committed voters. (Thus, though Mondale spoke to a white, middle-class audience this afternoon, he made a special point of emphasizing his commitment to helping the poor—a subject on which his advisers say he gets good marks in the polls.) A trip to California also gives the ticket a crack at Oregon and Washington, in which the Mondale people also think they have a chance. (Unemployment is high in both states—the lumber industry has been hit by the interest rates.) Ferraro will campaign in both states in the next couple of days, and Mondale will rejoin her in Portland on Wednesday. Today, the Los Angeles *Times* published a poll of its own which says that Reagan is twenty-seven points ahead of Mondale nationwide and that the Reagan-Bush ticket leads the Mondale-Ferraro ticket by twenty-three points. The Mondale people say that they are dubious about this poll, since it gives Reagan so much wider a margin than other polls do, but its publication in the Los Angeles paper on the day of their arrival here does not exactly cheer them up.

Now, addressing the crowd, Ferraro says many of the things she said in Wisconsin—and the crowd seems enthusiastic about her. Ferraro shows her pleasure at the response she receives: "You're wonderful, you're wonderful," she tells the crowd. Cranston introduces Mondale, praising him especially for his record on arms control, and then, after Mondale begins to speak, mysteriously, and almost incredibly, the sound system goes out. This is definitely not his day. He talks through a bullhorn until the sound system is restored, and then, spotting someone fainting, he calls for a medic. Through it all, he talks with more spirit than might be expected under the circumstances—about arms control, fairness—but his delivery is a bit ragged (any speaker would be jarred under these circumstances) and, seeming to sense that the audience is hot, tired, and distracted, he cuts his remarks short.

SEPTEMBER 4

COMPTON, CALIFORNIA. Tuesday. At shortly after noon in this Los Angeles suburb, Mondale is sitting on a lunch table talking to about three hundred people at the corporate headquarters and processing plant of Ralphs grocery chain, the largest in California. About half the audience is made up of meatcutters, dressed in long white coats, and the rest are management and clerical workers. Mondale is in his shirtsleeves, talking about the "unfairness" of the Reagan tax-cut program. One purpose of this event is to show Mondale talking about one of his issues against Reagan, another is to show him in relaxed, back-and-forth situations, the kind Reagan is very rarely seen in.

"In my opinion," Mondale says, "the stakes could not be higher for the ordinary people who are working in our country." He continues, "The test is what happens to people of average income in our nation—and that may be the greatest difference between Mr. Reagan and myself." He talks about the deficit: "Everyone who's looked at it who's honest knows that budget has got to be squeezed and revenues have to be restored." He tells them that ten cents on every dollar they pay in income taxes goes to pay interest on the debt. (Johnson says that in the Mondale polling, over seventy per cent of the people now believe that there will be a tax increase in 1985. A New York *Times*/CBS poll in August showed that fifty-two per cent believed this.) Mondale is to offer his deficit-reduction program next week—showing how he plans to carry out his acceptance-speech pledge to reduce the deficit by two-thirds. And he adds, "We've got to get those deficits down, and the question is: Are we going to be fair about it? I'm convinced that the case is overwhelming that Mr. Reagan will not be fair."

Now he goes over to a chart showing that low-income and moderate-income people paid more than before in taxes in 1982 through 1984, while upper-income people paid less. And he says, "I believe that's dead wrong. I believe it asks what kind of people we are." Mondale says, "Do we believe in work? Yes. Do we believe in being fair to working people? Yes. Do we believe in family and family life and giving families enough so their kids can have a decent life? Yes." Next, he shows a chart indicating some industries that pay no taxes or get tax refunds and saying that ninety thousand companies pay zero taxes, or get tax refunds, while a family earning twenty-five thousand dollars is taxed at a rate of nineteen per cent. "Now, I believe that's wrong," Mondale says. He continues, "Even though Mr. Reagan denies it, he's going to have to raise taxes. He doesn't want to talk about it, but he's going to do it. And he's going to wait until after the election to tell you how he's going to do it." He adds, "Now, why do you suppose he'd like to have you hear about it after you've voted? 'Cause if you do, you wouldn't vote for him, that's why." He says that the tax increase the Republicans have under consideration, a sales tax, would raise taxes on middle-income people. Referring to a comment Reagan made yesterday (Reagan said, "We do not appeal to envy and we do not seek to divide and conquer"), Mondale says, "Now, yesterday Mr. Reagan said when I talk this way I'm appealing to envy, and that I should shut up is what he's saying. If I were him, I'd want me to shut up, because people won't agree with him. I wouldn't blame you for being envious when you see that your taxes went up and the wealthy's went clear down." He continues, "But I don't think envy's the real word. I think it's anger. I'm mad. I'm angry. I'm damned mad, because I don't think it's right."

Now, sitting on the table again, Mondale takes questions, and he jokes with the meatcutters. In making a point about job safety, he asks them to hold up their hands if they had lost fingers on the job. A few do, and Mondale says to one "Did that go into a sausage?" amid laughter from the workers. As he talks with the workers, answering their questions, he seems increasingly relaxed. He says that Reagan "put a lot of people he put out of work back to work and he calls it full employment," and adds, "If you believe in jobs and full employment, you're looking at the candidate who will make a difference." He receives strong applause. Mondale says that he will get people back to work by getting deficits down, getting interest rates down, and causing exports to rise again, and also by rebuilding roads and ports. The "damned mad" line was deliberate—another attempt to catch people's attention. This has been a successful event in its own terms: the mystery of politics—much of the time—is what events, or sets of events, change impressions. One question is whether the negative impressions many people have of Mondale are so deeply ingrained that it is too late for him to change them.

SAN JOSE. At shortly after three-thirty, Mondale is speaking to a large audience at San Jose State University, a teaching-and-research center in Silicon Valley. (Reagan made his second stop of the day yesterday in this area. He said, among other things, "We believe in high tech, not high taxes.") Mondale is literally as well as politically chasing Reagan. Late last week, the Mondale people decided to accept an invitation for Mondale to address the American Legion tomorrow, in Salt Lake City; Reagan is speaking to the group today. Reagan had an enormous turnout at his first stop yesterday, and the contrast, on television, with Mondale's day—inevitably, the stories pointed up the Labor Day march fiasco—was unfortunate for Mondale. Mondale once again speaks in his shirtsleeves and begins by stating some of his themes—about the stakes in the election, about what kind of people we are, about arms control. And then he talks about education—a subject that he has been quite interested in throughout his public career—and his commitment to the subject, and his knowledge of it, shows, and the audience responds warmly.

The Mondale people think that the subject of education fits very neatly into their scheme of trying to get people to focus on the future under Reagan or Mondale, and hope to get Mondale a following on the campuses this fall. Leone says he doesn't accept the idea that young people will be heavily for Reagan. "Nobody's tried to tap their idealism," he says. Now Mondale says, "Without educational and scientific excellence, the billions we spend on the military are often wasted, because our security depends on our intelligence." He continues, "The hopes of millions of our young people seeking a better life and a better future will be destroyed, because education is the key to individual advancement in our society." He says, "Today, we have an Administration that simply doesn't understand the importance of education to our future," and "There has never been in modern American history a President who has tried to cut education more deeply or more insensitively than the current President of the United States." Referring to Reagan's efforts to identify himself with the Olympics, Mondale says, "As a nation, we all join the President in rejoicing at all those gold medals," and he adds that he wonders if Reagan "stopped to think a minute about what contributed to that outcome of which we're so proud"—the fact that the civil-rights laws, some of which the Administration has tried to reverse, had given minorities and women unprecedented opportunities. He says, "The commitment we make to education is a very clear test of the kind of people we are." So far, Mondale has been consistent in keeping up his main theme—this has not been one of his trademarks. He says, "We are not a people who steal from our children. We are a people who invest in our future. And the way we invest is to be sure that this generation is the best educated in our history. We can be the country that bolsters its schools, supports its scientists, unleashes our talents, and creates a future of excellence and jobs and opportunity."

Mondale mocks Reagan's proposal the other day that a teacher be the first "citizen passenger" launched into space. Mondale says, "He has given his answer to attracting talented teachers, and that is to launch a teacher into space." The audience laughs, and Mondale continues, "Well, that's O.K. But I want to launch an education corps to make teaching a valued profession again and achieve superb education here on earth." (Also last week, Reagan visited a school in Washington, D.C., and said, "I attended six elementary schools myself, and one high school. And in none of them was there a library. I think the facilities aren't nearly as important as the humanity in the facilities." Yesterday, in Merrill, Ferraro chided him for this.) Advancing one of the themes of his acceptance speech—that standards have to be raised—Mondale says, "I don't pretend that government can do it alone. We must do it together." He says, "Teachers must teach and restore discipline to the classrooms; students must do their homework, and parents must turn off those TV sets." He takes questions from the audience, and seems to loosen up as he goes along. Mondale is sufficiently confident of his knowledge that he doesn't worry about what kinds of questions might come up in these situations. He criticizes Reagan, as he has several times, for having joked recently (when he was testing the audio for a radio address) about launching the bombs against the Soviet Union. ("He cracks jokes about weapons that aren't very funny.")

Mondale's advisers say that he is more comfortable making the case against Reagan than he was making it against his fellow-Democrats—and this appears to be the case. In fact, it was the fight he wanted to have all along, and in part it was because he was making it early in the nomination contest that his opponents were able to gang up on him. Mondale talks privately as well as publicly about the importance of defeating Reagan, and seems to feel strongly—quite personally—about it. Last summer, he told a group of visitors to his home in North Oaks, Minnesota, that he would never forgive himself if he did not defeat Reagan. Now Mondale is asked what he would do about raising teachers' salaries, and, without making a specific commitment, he says, "I think the President can begin honoring teaching as a profession again, and honor learning and the product of learning."

Mondale likes to mention his travels throughout the country, and now he says he was told by a young man in New Hampshire that he couldn't stay in teaching because he couldn't afford to— and he smiles and remarks, "I don't think he voted for me, based on the returns, but we had a nice conversation." He cites the low salaries of teachers in Los Angeles, and says, "We're saying something about teaching when we give it this low status, and, of course, our kids will pay and our nation will pay." He continues, "As President, I intend to put a tremendous amount of attention on this. I've spent a lot of my life in it, and I don't think there's any way of getting it done except with leadership." Reagan couldn't put on this kind of performance, and Mondale knows it—but there are important things that Reagan can do that Mondale can't. That's part of what makes this such an unusual election: the candidates are so utterly different from each other—not just philosophically but also temperamentally, stylistically, in what they concern themselves with, in the way their minds work, and in their respective talents and weaknesses. It sometimes seems that they are operating in different universes. What Mondale is trying to do is get Reagan into his universe. Mondale now wraps up, saying, "Education is absolutely indispensable to the future of our country and to everything we want it to be." Again, trying to draw the contrast, and speaking with passion, he says, "You couldn't have a greater contrast between the two candidates." He criticizes Reagan's record on education, and says, "In the area of education, on policy, he's been uneducable. Our country needs a President that puts our kids first."

Mondale travels with a substantial entourage now, and his campaign is faced with having to do a lot of things at once, and quickly—having nailed down the nomination so late and then having lost so much time after the Convention. It is in fact still faced with organizational problems—with little time left. There are speeches to be written, events to be planned, scheduling decisions to be made, politicians to be soothed, Reagan's actions to be reacted to, state operations to be started up, money to be raised, and on and on. The Reagan-Bush campaign has had a luxurious time of it by comparison. The fatigue level within the Mondale campaign is still high. But now John Reilly, Mondale's law partner and close adviser, is travelling with Mondale again, and looking tanned and rested. James Johnson is back in Washington trying to put a lot of the pieces together—the planning of the campaign, reestablishing contact with various politicians and certain Washington figures who had become vocal critics of the campaign (in part because they hadn't been able to get Johnson's attention). He is meeting with fund-raisers and members of Congress this week, to reassure them that the race is winnable and that the members of Congress will be paid attention when the campaign goes into their areas. Mondale will meet with members of Congress when he returns to Washington later this week. All this fence-mending and hand-holding (like the meetings Mondale and his staff held with mayors and governors in Minnesota in late August) should not be necessary, but became so for two reasons: in part because Mondale had been based in Minnesota, the Mondale people were not sufficiently in touch with these people; and politicians tend to get very nervous when their party's nominee is not doing well in the polls. Democratic politicians are especially prone to talking about this out loud—and taking their criticisms to the press. (Mondale will base himself at his home in Washington this fall, which will solve several logistical problems; when he was in Minnesota, any time a member of his staff or an outsider wanted to see him, it was a major project.) Yesterday, Johnson flew to Ohio to talk with Governor Richard Celeste about the shape of the campaign there, and will hold meetings in Washington this week about the organization of the campaign in some other major states. Martin Kaplan, Mondale's chief speechwriter, is on the plane, looking almost dazed with exhaustion. His current obsession is with the speech on religion on Thursday. Leone, who is on the plane, is also keeping in touch with his operation back in Washington; a number of major figures from other campaigns are now helping out—including David Sawyer, who was Glenn's media adviser, and Patrick Caddell, who was Hart's pollster and adviser.

SEPTEMBER 5

SALT LAKE CITY. Wednesday. This morning, Mondale, wearing a Legionnaire's cap from the post in his home town of Elmore, is speaking at the Salt Palace, to the American Legion. This is a lion's-den appearance—this audience is naturally pro-Reagan. Moreover, in 1980 Reagan carried Utah with seventy-three per cent of the vote, and polls show him doing nearly as well here now. Yesterday, Reagan reaffirmed his support for prayer in the schools and said that "what some would do is twist the concept of freedom of religion to mean freedom against religion." He praised his own military buildup and reiterated his support for an anti-missile system in space. ("Now, some are calling this 'Star Wars;' I call it prudent policy and common sense.") He said that veterans' benefits will be protected, and he celebrated "The New Patriotism"— talking of the Olympics and of his visit to Normandy—and, as he is so effective at doing, he invoked the names of "MacArthur, Bradley, Patton, Ike," and he talked of his desire for peace. The Mondale people, of course, want Mondale's appearance here to be seen as a lion's-den appearance: Mondale going before the American Legion and talking about arms control. The large hall is not full, and some local Democrats have been added to the audience; yesterday, the Reagan people packed the hall. He tells the veterans that though he and they may not agree on all issues, they share certain values—that America must be strong, and that the world must be made safer—and he adds, "There is not one party that believes in family life and one that does not. There is not one party that believes in America's greatness and one that does not." And he interpolates in his prepared text, "There is not one party that believes in God and one that does not." For this he is applauded.

Mondale tells the Legionnaires several of the same things he has been saying all week—about the stakes in the election, about the danger of a world in which there are fifty thousand warheads. But now he makes the case for arms control in terms of what it means for security. He says, "We all want a strong defense. But the choice is over what kind of defense will make us secure, and how to use that strength to build a safer world." And he argues, as he has at other times this year, that the large amounts being spent on defense have not brought sufficient preparedness in conventional forces, or "readiness." (A report recently issued by the House Appropriations Committee's Defense Subcommittee has made the same point.) Mondale has talked about this issue particularly in the South—trying to show that he is not "soft" on defense but for a more sensible use of defense spending. He charges the Administration with having "refused to make choices between costly weapons systems," and argues that weapons procurement has taken such priority over operation and maintenance of the weapons we have that "we are dangerously dependent on nuclear weapons." He tells the Legionnaires that he opposes the B-1 bomber and the MX missile, because "they would be about as vulnerable as the weapons they replace," but that, as President, he would emphasize more survivable strategic systems—the Trident II (submarine) missile, the single-warhead Midgetman missile, and the Stealth bomber. He says that he would institute much tougher procurement practices.

And then Mondale makes a strong case for arms control. He says, "The atomic bomb has changed all the rules. World War III will be nothing like World War II. There will be no winners—we will all lose. There may well be no free world—only a poisoned, lifeless world." And he adds, "And to the veterans of World War II, of Korea and Vietnam, I say this: there will be no veterans of World War III." He says he knows that Soviet leaders "are cynical, ruthless, and dangerous," and he knows that "we must never negotiate with them on the basis of trust." And he is applauded as he adds, "We must insist that every agreement be specific, be mutual, and be verifiable." He argues that without the SALT I and SALT II agreements "we would have to plan on coping with thousands more warheads than are permitted by these agreements," and that the agreements help us monitor what the Soviet Union is doing, "prevent new and dangerous areas of competition," and enable us "to plan a more effective defense." He says that it is for these reasons that "every President from Eisenhower to Carter, regardless of political party, has negotiated arms-control agreements with the Soviets." He adds, "They didn't do it to make us weaker. They did it to make us stronger." He says, "The Joint Chiefs of Staff haven't consistently supported arms control in order to weaken our security. They did it in order to protect our security." And he continues, "But, unfortunately, Mr. Reagan appears not to share this understanding of arms control. He has failed this crucial test of leadership." Noting that yesterday Reagan "appeared before you and spoke of his desire for a world without war," he adds, "I do not challenge the sincerity of that desire." And he continues, "But that is not the issue. The issue is whether he has set us on a course toward peace and a safer world, and in my judgment he has not." This is an attempt to "separate the salesman from the product." Mondale criticizes Reagan's record on arms control, as he has done before other audiences this week. He says, "He has conducted an arms race on earth, and now he wants to extend it into the heavens, and even makes jokes about nuclear war. It's not funny." He gets fairly strong applause for this.

Then Mondale makes some specific arms-control proposals— some of them new, or variations on what he has said before. He says that he will "follow President Kennedy's example" and "declare a temporary moratorium on the testing of all nuclear weapons, and on the testing and deployment of all space weapons, and challenge the Soviets to join us." He says that this "pause" would be temporary and mutual, and that "I will use this temporary and mutual pause to challenge the Soviets" to negotiate agreements on these weapons. He does not say how long the pause would last, or how long it could be unilateral; his aides say that he would declare a moratorium—or pause—and call on the Soviets to make it mutual and to come to the bargaining table, and that if the Soviets did not make the moratorium mutual it would be discontinued; during the moratorium, negotiations would proceed. His aides say that in all cases the moratoriums would be temporary, and when Mondale has made this proposal in the past he has talked about a six-month moratorium in the case of some weapons and perhaps a shorter period in the case of others. His advisers say that the Soviets can't accomplish much within six months, and that what they do during that time can be monitored. They say that the point of this proposal is to try to break the logjam in negotiations over certain weapons as quickly as possible. They say that Mondale is deliberately using the word "pause" to differentiate it from a moratorium—to emphasize the temporary nature of it—and that the pause would be contingent on the Soviet Union's agreeing to negotiate mutual, verifiable treaties covering these weapons. Now he repeats his proposal for annual summit meetings with Soviet leaders, and announces, for the first time, "On my very first day as President, I will call upon the Soviet leadership to meet with me within six months in Geneva for fully prepared, substantive negotiations to freeze the arms race and to begin cutting back the stockpiles of nuclear weapons." He says, "We're determined enough never to lose an arms race. But we're also smart enough to know that in the nuclear world no one can win an arms race." He is applauded for this. He delivers the speech with strength and with feeling—but there remains the question of whether he can get through to people. He says, "The acid tests of leadership are honesty and action. A President must tell the truth about the future." He concludes, "I have come here today to launch this debate about the nature and purpose of American strength." That is his hope, at least. He tells the Legionnaires, "You, more than most, know the sacrifices that have been made to defend our right to have this debate." And he ends, "Thank you, and God bless America."

PORTLAND, OREGON. Early this afternoon, Mondale and Ferraro are addressing a rally—in the rain again—in a park. A large crowd is here, despite the rain. Representative Les AuCoin, of Oregon, is here, as is Representative Don Bonker, of Washington. Ferraro, wearing her gray plastic raincoat again, and a large rain hat, reads a speech that focusses on arms control—that is to be the subject of the day. She goes after Vice-President George Bush for some criticisms he made of Mondale yesterday. Bush said that Mondale wanted to make an absolute cut in defense spending (Mondale is calling for an increase of three to four per cent over inflation, and after his speech Bush said he was not aware of this), and also said that Mondale had prevented the Administration from reaching an arms-control agreement because the Soviet Union would rather deal with him than with Reagan. Last week, Bush said that Mondale "is so hot for an agreement right now that he will do almost anything to get it." After hitting Bush for his defense-budget remarks, Ferraro says, "He also blamed Fritz Mondale for causing the breakdown in arms talks with the Soviet Union." She adds, "Now, that's a good one. Mr. Reagan is the first President since Herbert Hoover not to sit down with his counterpart in the Soviet Union." She also says that "right now at least thirteen wars and civil wars are being waged around the world," and says, "Teddy Roosevelt made peace between Russia and Japan, and Jimmy Carter made peace between Israel and Egypt. But Ronald Reagan has done nothing to stop these conflicts. He's not had a single diplomatic success in three and a half years." This is a counterpoint to the Republican claims that Reagan has produced a more peaceful and stable world. She says, "We're not uninvolved just because we're at peace. In every one of the thirteen conflicts now raging, at least one of the superpowers is sending money, weapons, or both." She attacks the Reagan policy in Central America, and says that in Lebanon "our leaders made a mistake, and over two hundred and fifty young men paid with their lives." She adds, "A President must know when to use force and where, but he must also know when it should not be used. Let's send in the diplomats before the Marines." She receives big cheers, and presses on, reading her speech, through the rain, and the crowd stays.

The rain slows a bit as Mondale starts to speak, and once again he removes his raincoat and his jacket, and talks in his shirtsleeves. He jokes about the rain and says, "The rain is good. It makes things grow. And I'd like to see the Republicans try to get a crowd like we've got here today, who'll stand here and get wet!" Mondale is obviously buoyed by the crowd, and he is at his most relaxed and impassioned on this trip. There is a chemistry going between him and the crowd—and he is nearing the end of a long and difficult trip, and now Mondale is, as they say in politics, "hot." He says that "one of the reasons we're going to win is that at the Democratic National Convention we did what Americans do when at their best," and he refers to the "opening of doors" that the choice of Ferraro symbolized. He receives big cheers. Obviously, the Mondale people think Ferraro will be helpful in these West Coast states. Mondale says, "We have set aside this campaign day to talk about the most important issue on earth today, and that is controlling those god-awful nuclear weapons before they destroy us all." He continues, "In this election, there's much at stake, but nothing more important than getting control of those weapons and moving toward a safer world. It's a campaign which raises the question of what kind of people are we. Americans have always been peace-loving people. Today, most Americans understand how deeply these weapons threaten peace and our peace of mind. They hear their children talking about nuclear nightmares and they yearn for a safer world. That's the issue. All Americans want peace, Mr. Reagan." He is going strong now, as he says, "That's not the property of any political party. There's not one political party that believes in American greatness and one that does not. There's not one political party that is patriotic and one that is not. There's not one political party that believes in family and one that does not." And he adds, "And while we're at it, there's not one political party that believes in God and one that does not." He receives huge applause and cheers. He goes on, "So let's stop this nonsense that there is a party of weakness and a party of strength. To say that America is divided on the need for both peace and strength insults our people and encourages our enemies."

Mondale says, "We need you in Oregon. We need you in the Western United States to win this election—and we need you from this day right through to that election—and one of the key issues which divides us without any question is who would be best in moving this nation toward a safer world and getting control of those weapons." He attacks Reagan's record on arms control some more, saying things he has said all week—but now he is so familiar with what he wants to say that it comes out more naturally than before. From time to time, one can see a politician hit his stride, and that is what's happening here. Mondale says, "Mr. Reagan has a thing about arms control. He thinks it's weakness. Every President before him has understood. Every Joint Chiefs of Staff before him has understood that arms control is not weakness, it's strength." The crowd cheers him so loudly that his next words can't be heard. Then he says, "And we need a President who understands that." He repeats his intention, if he is elected, to, on his first day in office, "send a note to my Russian counterpart asking him to meet me in Geneva within six months to negotiate a mutual and verifiable treaty." This crowd cheers loudly; it is clearly more enthusiastic than the American Legion was. Mondale has to motivate these people to have any chance of winning out here, and he is clearly encouraged by the response he is receiving. He talks again about Kennedy's example, and, taking cognizance of the rain, which has become a downpour, and of the good nature of the crowd for sticking with him, he closes out his remarks. An experienced politician knows when to stop talking. He says, "I have been involved in every arms-control fight over the last twenty years. I understand it. I know it. I'm experienced. I've worked with the leaders of the world. My opponent has opposed every arms-control effort over the last twenty years. Let's elect a President who will lead us toward a safer world and get on with the business—" The cheering of the crowd drowns him out. "Let's go get it done. Give us your help and we'll win."

Toward the end of the long flight from Portland to Washington, I have a talk with Mondale. He is seated in the front compartment of the plane, with his staff. For much of the trip back, he has been working on the speech on religion that he will deliver tomorrow morning in Washington—and he has also been catching some sleep. Now Mondale—wearing faded jeans and a bright blue-green sweater, and shoeless (some sneakers are nearby), and finishing off a cigar as we begin to talk—looks fairly refreshed.

I begin by asking him what it was that so obviously affected his mood at the Portland rally, and he replies, "I liked the event. There were thousands of people there. I saw this crowd of people who could have left with dignity and they didn't."

Then, when I ask him how he accounts for the disparity between his standing and Reagan's in the polls, he replies, "Well, I think there are several things. Number one, I think there has been a belief that perhaps Reagan is not beatable, and the Reagan people are spreading that with all the strength they can. Then, there's the natural, I believe, pause after someone has been nominated, on the part of all the supporters of others, to get over their concerns and support someone who they had sort of agreed shouldn't be President. That takes a while. You've got Hart, Cranston, Jackson, Glenn, all those people out there, millions of them, that wanted somebody else. And it takes them a while to think things through and come around. And then we lost some time last month—we were on a tremendous high coming out of the Convention. Even though I think Ferraro has over the long run strengthened herself and our ticket by meeting the test, and I sensed that, it did lose us a couple of weeks when we couldn't get our message out. Those are some of the things that I think have been at work here."

I ask Mondale what he thinks he has to do to close the gap.

He replies, "First of all, speak clearly and with strength. Join the central issues. Bring the case home as hard as I can. Raise the stakes, so that people can see this is not a blur but a choice, and that our future is at stake. At least, the kind of future I describe is at stake. Show leadership."

"How do you do that?" I ask.

He replies, "Well, for example, Reagan is locked up—people can't get to him. I'm not protecting myself at all. I go to three hundred meatcutters sponsored by a major chain and let 'em throw anything they want at me. I go to a student body and take on all comers. I go to the American Legion and give a strong speech on arms control. I lay down my own budget with the good news and the bad news. And I think the contrast will become more apparent, and it comes down to leadership and strength, willingness to trust the public, and so on."

I ask Mondale if he plans to continue to use the over-all theme of "What kind of people are we?"

"Yes," he replies. "Because what I'm trying to show there is that this is about more than the individual you elect. This is also a test of what Americans believe and who we are. If we let Reagan become increasingly cruel toward the vulnerable, what kind of people are we? If we show arrogance toward the earth, the land, the water, the environment, what kind of people are we? Are we trustees of this earth or aren't we? If we fail this next generation in their education, learning, what kind of people are we? I think that's the way it should be put, because it engages everybody. Then we're all asking ourselves the same question. It's not what I see alone, it's what we as Americans see."

When I ask Mondale about the past month, he replies, "It was a frustrating August, because the key to an effective campaign is a clear message. And things kept happening to cut across our message. For example, I had three days when I was talking about defense reform—a very, very important issue. It wasn't totally lost, but mostly it was. But one of the things that just irritate the hell out of me is that here is this Reagan never holding a news conference, ducking totally from the press, sticking his head up like a gopher out of a foxhole once in a while, chirping and disappearing. That, and trying to make the national media sort of just a kept, unpaid outlet for his version of the news. And meanwhile someone like myself who is open gets his message cut across all the time, because in addition to my message there's always something around. Like today, I gave a speech on arms control, and a couple of the press tried to get from me what did I think of Tip O'Neill's comment that I should have been—I don't even know what Tip said today." (Today, O'Neill said that Mondale should stop "allowing himself to be punched around by Reagan," and should "come out slugging" against Reagan.) Mondale continued, "And here's the President trying to resist debates." (Mondale is pressing for six debates—a number he knows he won't get—and the Reagan people have so far agreed to one, and the expectation is that there will be two.) "He doesn't want to answer any of the questions. Here Regan comes out with a horror piece on my budget." (Yesterday, Treasury Secretary Donald Regan said that Mondale would raise taxes on every household by an average of $1,890—a prediction that was based on some faulty premises.) Mondale continues, "The President got embarrassed because he doesn't have one of his own. But I'm the one that's answering the questions. That's my job—but it's also Reagan's."

Mondale also says that the White House is "trying to use Secret Service as political security." He says, "Did you see all the signs today with sticks on them—you know, off on the edges—for Reagan and against abortion and so on? Well, at Reagan rallies they don't allow anybody in with sticks. Then when they get in they hand out sticks with Reagan signs on them." (This occurred at a rally in Cincinnati in August. Also, the Secret Service has kept reporters away from Reagan during campaign trips, in the name of security.) "All of it enforced. You know, I really admire the Secret Service, but they're being put in a position I'm sure they don't like—totally inappropriate."

I ask Mondale whether, now that he has moved from the primaries to the general election, he is planning to be more thematic.

"Have to be," he replies. "They have to know what my message is. The one thing that people keep saying is 'What is'—they don't put it this way—'What's your slogan?' And I've decided that that's not—now maybe I'll come out with one, but I've decided that this is not a campaign about a slogan. This is a campaign about what kind of people we are, and that comes up in a host of ways. And it's around that question that my campaign is being pressed."

As the plane circles to land in Washington, I ask Mondale whether he felt anything happening this week in terms of his getting himself across, and he replies, "Well, you know, I come back encouraged. I see more excitement, I see bigger crowds. I see people becoming engaged. I'm starting to hear snippets of hope. One test is when politicians show up—they can have reasons to be busy if they don't want to be there. But more and more they're around. That tells me that in terms of their careers they feel it's probably a good idea to be there."

As we land, I ask Mondale if he feels anything happening to his own stride and pacing as he tries out his fall campaign.

He replies, "Yes. I think it's coming. I really enjoy this a lot more than the primaries. I always hated fighting with my fellow-Democrats. I hated a divided Democratic Party. We've united that Party now. Now I have the chance to carry out what I've really wanted to do all along—the debate with Reagan about the future of our country. That's what we're doing now, and I find that a lot more fulfilling, and, of course, it's very challenging to figure out how to best make that case. And while I'm not satisfied yet, I think it's coming."

SEPTEMBER 12

WASHINGTON. In his speech on religion, given here last Thursday morning before the B'nai B'rith, Mondale took on both President Reagan and the religious right, which he said the Administration had "opened its arms to." He criticized Senator Paul Laxalt, Republican of Nevada and chairman of the Reagan campaign, for having sent a letter just before the Republican Convention to forty-five thousand ministers which opened, "Dear Christian Leader," told them that "as leaders under God's authority we cannot afford to resign ourselves to idle neutrality," and urged them to organize registration drives in their churches to reelect Reagan and Bush. Mondale said, "Most Americans would be surprised to learn that God is a Republican." He went on to say, "And if Senator Laxalt's letter were an isolated example, one might dismiss it as partisan zealotry." He offered as other examples Jerry Falwell's benediction at the Republican Convention on the night Reagan was nominated, in which Falwell referred to Reagan and Bush as "God's instruments for rebuilding America." Mondale attacked right-wing "Christian" report cards, which grade politicians on moral issues. One report card, Mondale said, "brands me as anti-family and unchristian." Saying that he does not "call for the suppression of these voices," he went on to say that he was "alarmed by the rise of what a former Republican congressman calls 'moral McCarthyism.' " (He was referring to former Representative John Buchanan, of Alabama.) Mondale said, "A determined band is raising doubts about people's faith. They are reaching for government power to impose their own beliefs on other people." He said he had been encouraged when he read that Reagan did not intend to speak more on the issue, and added, "But before he slips out the back door there are a few fires in the house worth putting out."

Mondale said, "I believe in an America that honors what Thomas Jefferson first called the 'wall of separation between church and state.' " He continued, "I believe in an America where government is not permitted to dictate the religious life of our people; where religion is a private matter between individuals and God, between families and their churches and synagogues, with no room for politicians in between." He said, "To ask the state to enforce the religious life of our people is to betray a telling cynicism about the American people." And he added, "Moreover, history teaches us that if that force is unleashed it will corrupt our faith, divide our nation, and embitter our people. Today, that force is being wielded by an extreme fringe poised to capture the Republican Party and tear it from its roots in Lincoln." He criticized the Republican Convention some more. Mondale went on to say, "Americans have only one President at a time. He must use his leadership to unify us. He must dispute his opponents with respect. The civility of our public debates depends on our willingness to accept the good faith of those who disagree. Our President must rejoice in the noise of public argument; it is the music of freedom." He added, "No President should attempt to transform policy debates into theological disputes." Noting that Reagan had said at the prayer breakfast in Dallas that anyone who opposes a constitutional amendment permitting school prayer is "intolerant of religion," Mondale pointed out that a number of church groups, as well as the B'nai B'rith, are also opposed to the constitutional amendment, and he added, "And they are also not intolerant of religion." (On the day before Mondale gave his speech, a group of Protestant, Catholic, Jewish, and Baptist leaders called on both parties to "reject categorically the pernicious notions that only one brand of politics or religion meets with God's approval and that others are necessarily evil.")

In his speech, Mondale said that he understood the "yearning for traditional values," and attributed this to the fact that "over the last generation, waves of change have swept our nation." He continued, "No institution has been untouched. Religion, marriage, business, government, education—each has been questioned, and each has struggled toward new foundations and new rules." He said, "By and large, it has been healthy for us. Our society is stronger, and not weaker, because women now have more opportunities and more choices. Our economy is stronger, and not weaker, because business must protect the environment. Our government is stronger because its leaders are accountable to a more skeptical public. Our churches and synagogues are stronger because they have struggled toward new ways to connect with their communities. Our schools and colleges are stronger because they opened their doors to the richness and diversity of America." Then he said, "But change is not easy. Many Americans have been upset to see traditions questioned. They have watched durable values give way to emptiness. And, too often, they have seen that void filled recklessly or self-indulgently." He said, "I join those Americans in their concerns," and he said that he stood with them in their outrage at the explosion of drug traffic, at child-molesting, at crime in the streets, at the growth of pornography, and at "low standards—whether they infect the classroom, the workplace, the government, or the street corner." He said, "From this turbulence and unease, a great yearning has been born in America in recent years. It is a quest for stable values. It is a search for deeper faith. And it deserves welcome and respect."

Mondale said this seeking of traditional values "is not a simple tide," and added, "It has undertows. And in the hands of those who would exploit it this legitimate search for moral strength can become a force of social divisiveness and a threat to individual freedom." He went on to say, "The truth is, the answer to a weaker family is not a stronger state. It is stronger values. The answer to lax morals is not legislated morals. It is deeper faith, greater discipline, and personal excellence." Mondale said, "Roosevelt said that the Presidency is preeminently a place of moral leadership. Our President sets the moral tone for our nation. He is a mirror in which we see what kind of people we are. And when he speaks of family, faith, and flag he must invoke such charged words to include Americans, not divide them; to inspire confidence, not arouse fears." And he added, referring to symbols Reagan has used heavily, "Family must not become code for intolerance. Religion must not become code for censorship. Neighborhood must not become code for discrimination. Law must not become code for repression. Work must not become code for callousness. Flag must not become code for jingoism. Peace must not become code for war." He ended by quoting President Eisenhower (who, he noted, had been little mentioned at the Republican Convention): " 'We—Republicans and Democrats alike—are motivated by the same loyalty to the flag; by the same devotion to freedom and human dignity; by the same high purposes for the nation's security and its welfare.' "

Reagan, in his speech before the B'nai B'rith, later that morning, stuck to more general topics, though he did say, "The United States of America is, and must remain, a nation of openness to people of all beliefs." And he added, "The unique thing about America is a wall in our Constitution separating church and state." He made a number of references to Jewish writers and Jewish history, and he reaffirmed his support for Israel.

Later in the day, Mondale spoke before the National Baptist Convention, U.S.A., where he was introduced by Jesse Jackson. In his speech there, Mondale made many of the same points that he had before the B'nai B'rith, but then also gave an impassioned call for those things he felt that government should take a role in— enforcing civil rights, and producing economic and social justice.

Also on Thursday, Mondale went to Capitol Hill to meet with Democratic senators and representatives, to reassure them that he was in fact taking the fight to Reagan and to urge them to direct their criticism at Reagan instead of him. He is said to have been greeted warmly by these members, with many of whom he has had long and close ties; afterward, O'Neill publicly praised him. Then Mondale went on to Atlanta, where, on Friday morning, he had a breakfast meeting with Bert Lance and with other leading Georgia Democrats who had managed to be busy elsewhere when Mondale wanted to hold an event in Macon in August.

On Monday, in Philadelphia, Mondale announced his program for reducing the deficit by two-thirds over four years—another gambit in his bid to be seen as levelling with the American people, stepping up to hard questions, and dealing with questions about the future, as well as being more "fair" than the Reagan Administration. Mondale had actually raised the challenge to himself by saying in his acceptance speech that he would reduce the deficit by two-thirds rather than by half, as he had been saying earlier in his campaign. Mondale began by using the deficit projected by the Congressional Budget Office—about two hundred and sixty billion dollars—rather than the one that the Administration recently projected, which is a hundred billion dollars lower. Many, if not most, of the things Mondale proposed he had proposed earlier in the year; he found the additional revenue needed for the two-thirds reduction by proposing some new (if in part unspecified) tax reforms, and by projecting larger savings as a result of lower interest on the national debt. Mondale would raise an estimated eighty-five billion dollars in taxes. Under his plan, families earning twenty-five thousand dollars or less (more than half the taxpayers) would pay no additional taxes, while those earning more than that would pay more, on a graduated basis. The provision of the 1981 tax-cut law which allows taxes to be indexed for inflation starting in 1985 would be modified for all those earning more than twenty-five thousand dollars to compensate for inflation of more than four per cent. (Mondale's original proposal would have deferred all indexing for this group. This change offsets the effect of higher inflation on other taxpayers but cuts the incentive to the government to permit inflation.) Mondale's plan would put a cap on the third year of Reagan's tax cut for those earning sixty thousand dollars a year or more; would impose a surcharge equal to ten per cent of the tax paid on family incomes of over a hundred thousand dollars and individual incomes of over seventy thousand dollars; and impose a fifteen-per-cent minimum tax on corporations. Mondale asserts that everyone making up to sixty thousand dollars would be better off, because interest rates would come down.

A new element in the Mondale plan is a proposal that all new taxes raised would be set aside in a trust fund that would go toward reducing the debt; this move is designed to shield Mondale from the charge of "tax and spend." Under the Mondale plan, there would be thirty billion dollars in additional spending—for education, environmental research, competitiveness in trade, rebuilding roads and bridges, and restoration of some of the Reagan cuts in social spending—and this would be offset by cuts in other spending. Some of these savings, such as cuts in health-care costs and in agriculture programs and defense, Mondale had talked about earlier. Whether all the numbers would withstand close scrutiny, whether all his economic assumptions would pan out, or whether all of Mondale's projected savings would be enacted can't be known now. But Mondale's was the most detailed proposal a Presidential candidate had made—and, in any event, had a larger point. Mondale had taken a big gamble, and no one, on either side, could be sure how it would turn out, but his is a campaign of big gambles now—to, as his aides say, get the attention of the American people and try to redefine what the election is about.

Other revenues would come from a presumed rate of growth to be stimulated by a presumed looser monetary policy of the Federal Reserve Board. Any additional spending, Mondale said, would have to be financed on a "pay-as-you-go" basis—by finding new revenues. One interesting aspect of Mondale's program is its recognition of limits; a leading Democrat from the New Deal and Great Society traditions is stipulating a new fiscal conservatism for the Democrats—an acceptance that, especially under present conditions, there are constraints on what government can do. In Philadelphia, Mondale said, of Reagan, "When it comes to the deficits, he is neither a moderate nor a conservative; he's a radical." He added, "There's no debt in the history of humanity that even compares to what he's been doing to our economy." He said that Reagan "whistles right along—'no problem'—when everybody knows there's a problem." He said Reagan was running a "happy-talk campaign." (One theory that the Mondale campaign has is that there is resentment "out there" of Reagan's painting things as more rosy than many think they are.)

Inevitably, the Administration landed on Mondale's plan on the day that it was announced. It was left to Bush, Regan, and others to offer more detailed critiques. Reagan, in a brief photo opportunity at the White House while he was meeting with the National Baptist Convention leaders, dismissed the plan as "nothing new." Reagan said, "He told us several weeks ago he was going to raise the people's taxes." When reporters asked Reagan if he would offer his own specific budget-reduction plans, he cut off the questioning, saying, "Now, this is a photo opportunity, and I'm going to stay with the business at hand."

Yesterday, Mondale got a strong dose of being up against an incumbent. Reagan announced that he would meet with Soviet Foreign Minister Andrei Gromyko in Washington at the end of the month, during Gromyko's annual visit to the United Nations. Mondale, who was trying to have the focus of the day be on the deficit, made the best of the situation, saying, "I'm glad it's occurring," but said that it was "pretty pathetic that an Administration, in the middle of its campaign for reelection, has its first meeting not with the Soviet counterpart of the President but with the Foreign Minister." Mondale said, trying to raise the ante for Reagan, "If they would come out with a significant arms-control agreement, I would be thrilled."

Today, the House ethics committee voted unanimously to investigate charges that Ferraro had violated the financial-disclosure laws when she claimed an exemption from disclosing the financial status of her husband. This action came as no great surprise: the conservative Washington Legal Foundation had brought a charge against Ferraro, and the Ethics Committee, protective of its image, couldn't not investigate it. Meanwhile, Ferraro had become embroiled in a dispute with the Catholic hierarchy, particularly New York Archbishop John J. O'Connor, over her position on abortion. Ferraro, like other prominent Catholic politicians, says that she is personally opposed to abortion but that, as a public official, she should not impose her religious views on others. Substantial numbers of anti-abortion picketers have been turning up at her appearances, and the whole issue is becoming a distraction from what she has been trying to say.

Also today, a Washington *Post*/ABC poll showed Reagan leading Mondale by sixteen points—this is a gain of nine points for Reagan since shortly before the two Conventions. A new Gallup poll has Reagan ahead by fifteen points, and a new Louis Harris poll gives Reagan a lead of thirteen points. The *Post*/ABC poll showed Mondale losing ground on the "leadership" issue; and it also said that while half the people feel that they are not better off financially than they were when Reagan took office, a majority of them feel that they would be better off under Reagan than under Mondale, and they tend to blame the Democratic Congress and previous Presidents for the deficit more than they do Reagan.

Mondale, meanwhile, has been campaigning in Wisconsin, Iowa, and Illinois, and will campaign in Mississippi tomorrow. Some of the events reflected questionable scheduling again, and Mondale is said to be unhappy about this. However, he drew a large crowd in Peoria today, and told it, "This deficit must be cut, but the question is which one of us will do it fairly." He attacked Reagan for having tried to cut Social Security, and said, "He took an axe, a sledgehammer out and tried to destroy help for our schoolchildren, our students who need to go on to college. He took an axe out and tried to destroy help for our handicapped children," and, Mondale said, Reagan tried to cut school lunches, help for pregnant mothers and newborn infants, and tried to cut money for protecting the environment. Mondale said that Reagan went so far "that even the Republicans wouldn't go along with his cuts." He continued, "There's a limit to what Americans will permit to happen in this good country of ours." He said, "This is a contest over what kind of people we are."

XX

The most important thing in politics, Stuart Spencer said to me last summer, is to control the agenda. Spencer, probably the man most responsible for Ronald Reagan's success in politics—other than Reagan himself—and now a key man in the Reagan-Bush reelection effort, said to me, "The premise is very simple: Control the agenda and focus the agenda, and make sure it's focussed on what we want to talk about, and don't get on side eddies; when Walter Mondale attacks, talk about things we want to talk about. It sounds simple, but it's very important." Spencer is a shrewd, affable man; as part of the then famous California public-relations company Spencer-Roberts, he managed Reagan's two campaigns for governor of California; in 1976 he helped Ford stave off Reagan's nomination challenge; in 1980, when Reagan's fall campaign got off to a shaky start, Nancy Reagan sent for Spencer. (Earlier this year, someone close to Reagan, speculating about who would serve in a second Reagan term, said the decisions would be made by Nancy Reagan, Stuart Spencer, and Reagan—"in that order.") The success of the Reagan team in controlling the agenda, while incomplete, of course, has been a major source of frustration to the Mondale camp.

The bombing of the new American Embassy in Beirut, on September 20th, was obviously not on the Reagan team's agenda—and the Mondale camp, after some hesitation about how to react, decided that this third truck-bombing of an American facility in Beirut (killing two Americans and many Lebanese) within seventeen months, and the evident lapses and delays in the protection of the Embassy, gave it a new issue against Reagan. (As did Reagan's remark to reporters in New York the following Sunday, on the eve of his United Nations speech: "Anyone that's ever had their kitchen done over knows that it never gets done as soon as you wish it would.") Now Mondale, who had heard a lot of similar talk from Republicans about the taking of the hostages in Iran during the Carter Administration, was saying that Reagan allows terrorists to "humiliate us and push us around and kill our people." (A difference between the hostage crisis and the events in Beirut is that the nation was reminded by television, every day, of the fact that the hostages were being held, for the full four hundred and forty-four days they were in captivity, whereas Beirut is brought back into national consciousness only when there is another disaster.) Vice-President Bush has been critical of Mondale's being critical of the Administration for not providing our facilities in Beirut with better protection, and says that Mondale is trying to turn the bombing to "political advantage." Reagan himself was quite critical of Carter for the hostage crisis during the 1980 campaign. The Reagan people I spoke with just after the bombing said they felt that this episode would go away, too, as had the prior ones—especially since it came on the eve of a week that had been carefully planned to put Reagan on display as a world leader and a peacemaker, with the speech at the United Nations, another to the International Monetary Fund, meetings with leaders of three nations, and a meeting with Soviet Foreign Minister Andrei Gromyko.

While the Reagan camp tries not to let itself become too satisfied with the polls—which have shown Reagan leading Mondale by from thirteen to thirty points in recent weeks—it is clearly, and understandably, very happy with the polls. And while the Mondale people have tried to not let the polls get them down, the polls are getting them, including the candidate, down. People at the Reagan-Bush committee say that, as of now, Reagan is ahead of Mondale in every state. (They say that Mondale leads only in the District of Columbia, and is even behind in Minnesota.) By the third week of September, the Mondale camp's own soundings were telling them that they were behind Reagan by from fifteen to twenty points. The Reagan-Bush committee's polling has Reagan twenty points ahead of Mondale. One Mondale aide said to me recently, "Let's put it this way: we've been on the road for about a month and we haven't exactly moved up." Another said to me last week, "Maybe it's just not there."

Lee Atwater, the deputy director of the Reagan-Bush campaign, said to me this week, "The single most consistent factor in this whole race is Mondale's negative rating. The flora and the fauna of the race may change—the issues may vary a little bit—but unless he gets that negative down he isn't going to go anywhere." Mondale is the first Presidential candidate since the Presidency of Franklin D. Roosevelt to be trailing in the polls who did not gain ground in September. A recent poll in West Virginia, one of the six states Carter carried in 1980, and one that the Republicans were saying at the time of the Dallas Convention that Mondale was ahead in, shows Reagan ahead of Mondale there by eighteen points. Even in Maryland, which the Democrats had been expected to win (they have a three-to-one lead in voter registration and Carter carried it in 1980), a recent poll by the Baltimore *Sun* showed Reagan beating Mondale by ten points. The Republicans not long ago were worried about the farm belt, but now Reagan leads Mondale in Iowa, where the candidates were neck and neck a month ago, by twenty-three points, and his leads in Illinois and Ohio are growing as well. (Taking no chances, Reagan announced new help for debt-ridden farmers shortly before leaving for a trip to Iowa last week.) Some Republican leaders have been emboldened to start thinking the magnitude of Reagan's sweep could be such that not only some of the half-dozen Republican senators who had been considered to be in trouble this year might be saved by the Reagan pull, thus maintaining Republican control of the Senate (Republicans now hold fifty-five of the hundred seats), but also there could be substantial Republican gains in the House, where the Democrats have a large majority. Several House members are finding themselves in unaccustomedly tough races. A House Democrat tells me that, while his colleagues are worried, general panic has not set in yet, but that if the polls don't look better in October it will. Recent soundings have indicated that people are jumping to the Republican Party in large numbers, and the only comfort some Democratic strategists take from this is the thought that the movement is so large and possibly "volatile" that these people might jump back. But there is little time, and Mondale is said to be aware that he could be leading the Party toward a big defeat. While the Mondale people talked about the debates as Mondale's big chance—he and Reagan will meet on October 7th and October 21st—there was some belief within this group that unless he started to gain ground before the first debate even the debate might not do him much good.

There remains a certain division of opinion within the Reagan campaign about how to talk about the election. In part, the Reagan people are promoting the view that Reagan is so strong that Mondale's cause is hopeless—this to keep Mondale's supporters from becoming energized, or potential supporters from thinking there is any point. But in part they are being very careful to take nothing for granted—this to avoid complacency among Reagan's supporters, and also to guard against the coming apart of what they have constructed thus far. The hardheaded realists among Reagan's advisers proceed on the theory that some combination of outside events and mistakes on Reagan's part could unglue their handiwork. By "mistakes," they mean that Reagan might say something that worries people about him. That he sometimes gets his facts wrong, his aides believe, has long since been accepted and discounted by the public, and is only of interest to Washington journalists and a few others. They recognize that though Reagan has always done well in debates, something could go wrong in those that are coming up. They decided to go ahead with the debates for two reasons: they did not think it would be politically acceptable to refuse to debate, and, when they were deciding on their strategy, late last summer, they considered it possible that the race would tighten sufficiently that Reagan might need a debate toward the end of October. Interestingly, the Reagan people, who wanted the 1980 debate to be held on Election Eve, and succeeded in having it held a week before the election, wanted the second of the two debates this year to be held further from the election. They solemnly make a good-government argument that no one event, such as a debate, should have an untoward effect on the election—which is a valid point (even if it did not concern them in 1980)—but they also concede that they want time to clear things up after the second debate, or change the subject, in case anything goes wrong. This, like the extremely tight control over press access to Reagan, conveys a heightened worry on the part of Reagan's advisers as to what he might say if he is allowed to be spontaneous.

Mondale began to argue on the stump that Reagan is "isolated" and is "travelling around the country in an answer-free zone," and the television reporters covering the Reagan campaign began to talk about the tight controls around the President. The Reagan people have become sensitive about this point, but their essential view is that nobody loves the press, so its complaints don't carry much weight. Jim Lake, the communications director of the Reagan-Bush committee, said to me not long ago, of the isolation question, "It doesn't bother me as a problem at all. People see him out there and delivering a message. It doesn't look like isolation to them." Another Presidential adviser says, "The world has long since seen and known that Ronald Reagan is isolated, and accepted that." He said that the public had "discounted for this," just as it has discounted Reagan's getting his facts wrong. When I asked him why, he replied, "What's wrong with it if the system works and people are happy? Ronald Reagan is part of the mythology of what America likes its leaders to be. If people are confident about the economy, are at peace, why should they want to attack the myth? That's what Mondale is up against." (Vice-President Bush, speaking at a rally in Ohio, pulled his wallet out of his pocket and slapped it on the podium and said, "Do you know what wins elections? It's who puts money into this and who takes money out.")

Reagan's advisers talk of Mondale's having offered a deficit-reduction plan as a gift from heaven. As they explain it, they had planned to spend a lot of time and money this fall making the case that Mondale would raise people's taxes, and then Mondale went and did the job for them. Through a careful direction of a chorus of Administration voices when Mondale unveiled his deficit-reduction plan earlier this month, and through subsequent statements, the Reagan campaign has, it believes, convinced people that Mondale's deficit-reduction plan is a tax-raising plan, period. (For a few days, Mondale tried to explain the plan with the aid of charts, which were indecipherable on television, and then the charts went away. One Reagan adviser says, "Mondale tried to educate people about something they don't want to be educated about." Other Democrats showed no great interest in embracing Mondale's plan—if he wanted to be "bold," he was on his own.) As for the polls indicating that most people believe taxes will be raised by whoever is the next President—a finding in which the Mondale people take comfort—the Reagan people say that people believe that Reagan is less likely to raise taxes. A Reagan adviser also says that although the Administration bobbled about a bit after Mondale challenged Reagan to admit that taxes would be raised, it managed to come out in a politically suitable place: by avoiding saying that they would never, never raise taxes, they avoided the trap they assumed Mondale was setting—a charge that in that case they would have to make large cuts in Social Security and Medicare. The White House was prepared to offer up some deficit-reduction plan—or apparent deficit-reduction plan—if the politics of the situation demanded it, but it never came to that. One Reagan adviser says, "What started out as a potential Mondale plus—a bold move to show that he is a strong leader—has become a Mondale liability, and we'll drive that home in the next thirty days."

Reagan's rhetoric against government spending has been so strong that people now believe, according to the polls, that he would be more likely than Mondale to cut the deficit. Moreover, his advisers say, people believe that Reagan *has* been laying out deficit-reduction plans over the past four years, and that Congress is responsible for the deficits. (In fact, Congress has agreed to most of Reagan's budget-reduction proposals; Reagan has simply never proposed sufficient budget cuts to offset his tax cuts and increases in military spending, and has never submitted anything resembling a balanced budget.) There is a line of analysis within both the Reagan and Mondale camps which holds that, by challenging Reagan to "level with the American people" about the need to raise taxes, Mondale played into two of Reagan's strengths: his reputation for fiscal conservatism, and the sense people have that he is a man of integrity. The Reagan people also say that Mondale made a mistake in taking Reagan on on the religious issue. They say the net effect of the argument was that Reagan was on television several times saying that he was a pluralist ("I'm not seeking to install a state religion in any way"), and this reassured many people, while Mondale's taking Reagan on got Reagan's fundamentalist base more fired up than ever, and pushed Mondale's ratings in the South still lower.

Reagan's campaign trips have not only been picture-perfect—sizable crowds, balloons, flags, just the right settings, just the right lighting, just the right blue coloring for the backdrops—but have had a very clear strategy behind them. Reagan may be managed, but he is very well managed. Reagan has concentrated on the farm belt, and on the Northeast and the Midwest, where he is trying to peel away, or hold, "soft Democrats." Reagan's itinerary usually allows him to make day trips and be back in the White House by early evening; he travels about two days a week. There was also one literally spectacular trip to Nashville, in mid-September, where Reagan appeared at the Grand Ole Opry with Roy Acuff and Minnie Pearl and celebrated Roy Acuff's eighty-first birthday, with a giant cake and a cascade of confetti. Roy Acuff endorsed Reagan. On this trip, Reagan kept up the theme that he is offering a positive message while Mondale (whom he never mentions by name) is simply offering negativism and gloom. At the Grand Ole Opry, Reagan, as he does in other appearances, saluted the "great resurgence of patriotic feeling sweeping the country" and referred to the Olympics and the new country-and-Western hit song by Lee Greenwood, "God Bless the U.S.A.," which is used in Reagan's ads and at his rallies.

The "new patriotism" was something waiting to happen, growing out of a natural desire to feel better about things after Watergate, Vietnam, and the hostage crisis, and it has been propelled by certain events, and also by some hucksterism—to the point where it is on the verge of, if not into, faddism. This endangers its authentic and attractive side; it also carries some dangers. Meanwhile, this new emotion and Reagan are perfectly suited for each other, and are furthering each other along. And Reagan told the audience at the Grand Ole Opry, as he does in other appearances, "I don't see why the other side keeps saying things are so terrible in this country." And he added, "So I hope you don't mind my asking, Do you feel better off than you did four years ago?" This line is greeted with applause, and it is essentially Reagan's case. He suggested to the Grand Ole Opry audience that it felt better off because of the expansion of the economy and the number of new jobs "in the past twenty months"—thus his story begins in 1983, after the recession—and because "you have a friend in the White House who doesn't believe that you're undertaxed." He added, "The other side keeps saying the answer to all this success is to start another old round of tax and tax and spend and spend." (Mondale's pledge to place revenues raised through new taxes in a trust fund seems to have got lost in the din.) Reagan asks audiences, "Do you want to go back to the old days of misery, misfortune, and malaise?" He told one audience recently, "It's springtime for America once again." Sometimes he puts a series of questions that invite the audience to respond, "U.S.A.!"—a chant that began at the Olympics and carried through to the Republican

Convention. By now, the audiences know how they are to respond. Reagan's speeches are well written for him, giving him the heroic prose that suits his style and his politics. He says, "We must continue . . . to make America great again and let the eagle soar." He tells an audience, "They see an America where every day is April 15th, tax day. We see an America where every day is the Fourth of July." He says, "Aren't you saying, 'We want to think big and aim high'? And aren't you saying, 'Don't hold us back, give us a chance and see how high we fly'?" Similarly, the Reagan campaign's commercials are soothing, bucolic, and optimistic. We see children at play, a couple getting married (this is a scene that was used in the eighteen-minute film about Reagan shown at the Convention— and shown in its entirety earlier this month on all three networks, and on cable as well, with some of the better parts of Reagan's acceptance speech added). One Reagan ad has a soothing voice saying, "It's morning again in America." His ads stress that America is "working" again. Mrs. Reagan, among others, was unhappy with Reagan's 1980 commercials—felt they used Reagan as a "talking head" too much—and so a group of commercial advertisers was assembled for this year's election. Reagan's ads come off like commercial commercials—soothing, pleasant, Miller time. They fit right in with what people who watch television are accustomed to seeing. Mondale's ads, by contrast, come off as political, didactic, and jarring—because they are intended to jar, to raise questions about nuclear war, the deficit, and so on. But they are no fun to watch. Moreover, it is not just the fact that Reagan himself is better on television than is Mondale but that Reagan is projecting many of television's prime-time values—toughness, heroism, the simple resolution of problems—and is thus reinforced by, and compatible with, the dominant culture. A friend of mine who is a close student of television says he thinks that perhaps the only person who could defeat Ronald Reagan is Clint Eastwood.

Reagan's play for the blue-collar voter has been quite determined and specific. At an appearance at a Polish Catholic shrine outside Philadelphia earlier this month, Reagan was introduced by John Cardinal Krol, of Philadelphia, who praised Reagan's policies, including his efforts to obtain tuition tax credits for private schools. This appearance by a cardinal was unusual. Reagan rang the chapel bell of the shrine, presented the shrine with a tapestry from Poland, and praised Pope John Paul II. At a rally near the shrine, Reagan said that the Democratic Party represents "defeatism, decline, and despair," and urged Democrats who felt "abandoned" by their party to support him. (Reporters noted that Reagan stumbled several times in the reading of his speech, as he has done on some other recent occasions.) A couple of days later, Reagan awarded a posthumous Congressional Gold Medal to Hubert Humphrey, presenting it to Humphrey's widow, Muriel, in a Rose Garden ceremony at the White House. Reagan praised Humphrey as "a liberal who was an internationalist." In mid-September, Reagan, wooing Italian voters in Buffalo, dedicated a housing project funded by a federal program his Administration had tried to cut. On September 19th, he made an appearance in Waterbury, Connecticut, at the site of a famous rally for John Kennedy late in the 1960 campaign, and invoked the memory of Kennedy—"I think John Kennedy would be proud of you and the things you believe in." (In 1960, Reagan was a spokesman for Democrats for Nixon.) He said, "I was a Democrat once," but "the Democratic leadership had abandoned the good and decent Democrats of the J.F.K., F.D.R., and Harry Truman tradition—people who believe in the interests of working people, who are not ashamed or afraid of America standing up for freedom in the world." And he added, "And if you see it as I do, I have to tell you—join us."

It was around the time Reagan was appearing with Cardinal Krol that Geraldine Ferraro was embroiled in a dispute with some members of the Catholic hierarchy over her position on abortion and was being met at many stops by anti-abortion hecklers, who sometimes tried to drown her out. (On September 21st, NBC reported that, "according to high Republican sources involved in the campaign," the Reagan-Bush campaign was coordinating these demonstrations by anti-abortion groups; was encouraging, through intermediaries, criticism of Ferraro by the Catholic clergy; and had got others to demand investigations of Ferraro's finances and orchestrated a series of damaging leaks to the press about her finances. The Reagan-Bush committee officials denied all this, but now further press investigations of these and other events are under way. Yet such things are hard to trace.) Mondale, too, was greeted by noisy hecklers on a few occasions. One incident that attracted attention was what appeared to be organized heckling of Mondale by hundreds of booing and jeering students at the University of Southern California, on September 18th—which led Mondale to shout, "We want to be heard, we will be heard, and we will win this election because we will be heard," and which CBS traced to a Reagan-Bush campaign official in California. The degree of political involvement of some members of the Catholic clergy in this election has caused some division within the Church. When New York Governor Mario Cuomo made a speech on the subject of politics and religion at Notre Dame in mid-September, Father Richard McBrien, the head of Notre Dame's theology department, interviewed on NBC, took issue with the activities of Cardinal Krol and also with those of Archbishop John O'Connor, of New York, and Archbishop Bernard Law, of Boston, who had been particularly outspoken about politics and the abortion issue. Father McBrien said that these clergymen represented a minority of American bishops. He said, "They're also looking for the rewards of political combat. I mean, rumors, for example, that if we support Reagan . . . we're going to get two Supreme Court appointments. That's typical political wheeling and dealing." (Mondale has made much of a claim by the Reverend Jerry Falwell that if Reagan is reelected "we will get at least two more appointments to the Supreme Court." Whether Father McBrien was referring to the same promise, or rumor, or claim, or whatever, is anybody's guess.)

Meanwhile, toward the end of the month there was unhappiness within the Mondale campaign with the quality of the television advertising, and, more important, concern about what was coming through of what Mondale was saying. Several of his events had gone well, but the problem was that whenever Mondale moved away from the original strategy of trying to make the issue of the campaign what kind of country this is—the issue of values—and moved closer to an attack on Reagan, it was the attack that inevitably was picked up in the brief "sound bite" on television, and in these instances Mondale came across as shrill and negative. The campaign was increasingly going at Reagan directly, thus playing to his strength as the dominant personality in the race, as opposed to going around him: getting people disturbed about his policies, stirring what is believed to be a latent anger about those policies, and raising questions about their effects now and in the future, and also putting Mondale forward as someone people might want to follow. The idea was to get back to an election over stakes, rather than over Reagan or Mondale. The major upshot of a rethink—a series of meetings last weekend that involved Mondale himself and went on into the week—was a speech on Tuesday at George Washington University, in Washington, in which Mondale tried once again to redefine, in his terms, what the election is about. And Mondale was to be seen more clearly, it was hoped, as someone who fought *for* things, not just against his political opponents. (This was emphasized in a five-minute ad the Mondale campaign ran on all three networks Thursday night.) A subsidiary purpose of the new approach was to meet Reagan's challenge for Democratic and young supporters by talking more about the right-wing and fundamentalist aspects of the Republican Convention. (There is a belief among some Democratic analysts that what may have stopped, or slowed down, a long-term realignment of voters with the Republican Party after 1980 were the social agenda and James Watt.)

Mondale had been scheduled to give a foreign-policy speech at George Washington, since this was the week that Reagan was to be so visible on foreign policy. (Mondale had already given a foreign-policy speech the previous week, before the latest bombing in Beirut, in which he said that the Administration's "swamp of policy confusion" in the Middle East had led to the death of nearly three hundred servicemen in Lebanon, and that if Reagan was reelected we would be "closer to the brink." He said Reagan was "essentially absent" from policy-making in the Middle East and was conducting "government by a smile button and leadership by isolation.") So, as a result of internal arguments, the speech at George Washington ended up beginning on the subject of foreign policy and then went on to the new points. (In the foreign-policy section, Mondale mocked Reagan for having given a conciliatory speech to the United Nations the day before, and said, "This Presidential sea-change raises a crucial question: How can the American people tell which Reagan would be President if he's reelected?") Speaking to the students, Mondale said, "I have been counselled to cut loose from my history—to desert the forgotten Americans I have always fought for," and he continued, "My answer is no. I would rather lose a race about decency than win one about self-interest."

In some respects, the speech was reminiscent of ones Mondale gave earlier in the year, in Tampa and at Emory University, in which he talked about "the soul of the Party" and told students that he did not accept the characterization of them as simply self-interested and materialistic. Those were among the very few speeches Mondale made during the primaries which took him beyond the cut-and-slash. Not mentioning Reagan, or the Republicans, Mondale said, "I do not know which is worse—the emptiness of [their] campaign, or the cynicism about the American people that it implies. I do not know which is more damning—their contempt for the issues, or their condescension toward our people." Referring to Reagan's attempts to woo Democrats, Mondale said, "Take a second look at the Republican home you're being sold, and the platform it's built on," and he continued, "Do you really want to join a party that intends to put government between you and the most private choices of your life?" After asking other such rhetorical questions, Mondale said, "This is a season for passion and principle." He continued—in a reference to a "surprise" dinner visit the Reagans paid last weekend to a black young man in Washington who had written to Reagan (there were pictures in the papers of the Reagans handing the young man a jar of jelly beans)—"This election is not about jelly beans and pen pals. It is about toxic dumps that give cancer to our children." He went on, "This election is not about country music and birthday cakes. It is about old people who can't pay for medicine. This election is not about the Olympic torch. It is about the civil-rights laws that opened athletics to women and minorities who won those gold medals. . . . This election is not about Republicans sending hecklers to my rallies. It is about Jerry Falwell picking Justices for the Supreme Court. . . . This election is about our values." He talked about the poor, and said, "The Republicans say they're for family values. But families don't disown their weaker children. What would we think of parents who taught their kids to think only of themselves, and not to care for their brothers and sisters? What would we say about parents who lived in high style—and left their children in debt as a result?" He added, "In this campaign, I will do everything I can to focus our nation on these questions—whatever the political consequences. It must never be said that in 1984 we did not know what we were doing. I won't permit this crowd to steal the future from our children without a fight. . . . They have a right to ask for your vote. But I'll be damned if I'll let them take away our conscience."

Then, as he had been doing in recent appearances, he turned one of Reagan's anecdotes about heroes back on him: at a recent dinner of Italian-Americans in Washington, Reagan had told a moving story about an Italian immigrant's son who became a milkman, and how the milkman had struggled and sacrificed so that his son could go to college and medical school, and that son became a prominent surgeon, who one day saved a President's— Reagan's—life. Mondale tells the story movingly, as Reagan did, and then adds the twist: that the surgeon, Dr. Joseph Giordano, wrote to the Los Angeles *Times* saying that the President had told only part of the story. He wrote that government programs of which Reagan had been so critical had helped make his story possible—that though his parents had sacrificed for him, he had been helped through medical school by government loans, that the medical technology with which he had saved Reagan's life would not have existed without federal research funds, and that now his parents are dependent on Social Security and Medicare. (Dr. Giordano later endorsed Mondale.) Mondale's speech got a strong response from the audience, and more than the usual amount of attention on television. Whether it was an event or a blip, or whether Mondale will continue along that path, can't be known yet.

On Wednesday, Reagan, in an appearance at Bowling Green State University, in Ohio, took a few questions from friendly students ("I've heard there's a fellow going around the country that says that I don't answer questions"). A large number of anti-Reagan students said that they had not been allowed into the hall, and they were kept quite a distance from it. Reagan blamed the latest truck-bombing on what he called "the near-destruction of our intelligence capability in recent years—before we came here." A Reagan aide told reporters it would not be incorrect to assume that he was referring to the Carter Administration. Senator Daniel Patrick Moynihan, of New York, vice-chairman of the Senate Select Intelligence Committee, said that Reagan's statement "is not only false, it's reckless," and other Democrats, including Carter, reacted angrily. The next day, Bush, who once headed the C.I.A., said he did not think the Carter Administration could be blamed, and Reagan, in a brief photo opportunity while he was meeting with the President of Peru, accused the press of distorting his remarks. He also phoned Carter to explain. Reagan also told the students at Bowling Green—two days after his United Nations address and two days before his meeting with Gromyko—that the Russians "really do have aggressive intent against us," and he joked, "Peace in America is such an attractive way to live that a war is a terrible interruption."

On Thursday, Mondale met with Gromyko—a session that was arranged after Gromyko had accepted Reagan's invitation to meet at the White House. Mondale's aides say that the meeting was decided upon in order to show that meetings with Gromyko are no big deal (Mondale had already met with Gromyko three times), and also to keep Mondale from being blanked out of the news during Reagan's big foreign-policy week. Mondale said that he would tell Gromyko that America has "only one President at a time" and that the Soviet Union has "nothing to gain from delay." Following the meeting, in New York, Mondale told reporters that he had urged Gromyko to go forward with negotiations with Reagan, and that "I was not negotiating." Nonetheless, he ran a danger of suggestions by surrogates for the President that he had interfered with Reagan's dealings with Gromyko, if those dealings did not go well, and that he had suggested to the Soviets that he would make them a better offer. A couple of Reagan's advisers told me shortly after Mondale announced the meeting that this was most likely to happen. On Friday, Reagan met with Gromyko, amid much picture-taking but no clear evidence that either country's negotiating position had changed, or that Reagan had resolved the disagreements within his own government. Secretary of State George Shultz said that the two governments had agreed to "stay in touch." Mondale branded the Reagan-Gromyko meeting a failure, saying there were arms-control steps that Reagan could have taken and that the events of the past two weeks showed that "we have a President who's not really in charge." Still, the fact of the meeting (Reagan's first with any Soviet leader) was widely considered a plus for Reagan.

Following that, both the Reagan and the Mondale camps began to clear their candidates' calendars and concentrate their efforts on preparing for the first debate.

XXI

The first three weeks of October will go down as the period when the Presidential campaign either did or did not turn around, but, while the answer is not in just yet, it will certainly go down as the period when the campaign began to take on a different look and the Republicans, for all their ostensible confidence, had a fright. The chemistry of the campaign had actually begun to change during the week before Mondale and Reagan met for their first debate, on domestic policy, on October 7th, in Louisville. But the aftermath of that debate, which Mondale was universally judged to have won—a judgment that fed on itself and, as often happens, grew more emphatic in the days following the debate—and the question that debate raised about Reagan's competence to handle his job (a question that was misnamed the "age issue"), began to change the atmosphere surrounding the race. But not, at least at first, the polls: though both sides agreed that their measurements showed that people had a better impression of Mondale following that debate, and both campaigns' polls showed Mondale picking up some over-all support, there was not much movement right away in the public polls. Then, as the second debate, tonight, approached, some of the public polls indicated that the race was tightening. The effect of tonight's debate, the candidates' last, on foreign policy, appeared less conclusive. The next, brief period, ending on November 6th, will tell us whether the public's negative attitudes toward Mondale and positive attitudes toward Reagan were so high all along, and certain currents that seem to be running in the country were so strong, that Mondale never had a chance. It will also tell us how much danger there was—there clearly was some—that the carefully constructed Reagan campaign could come apart.

Before the first debate, Mondale's situation, at least as the public saw it, was getting no better, if not deteriorating. An extensive

674

Washington *Post*/ABC poll, made public at the end of the first week of October, showed Reagan leading Mondale fifty-five per cent to thirty-seven, and indicated that Reagan was ahead everywhere except Rhode Island (where it found the two candidates even) and the District of Columbia (where Mondale was ahead). The poll found that Mondale's and Geraldine Ferraro's standings had slipped during the month of September, and that the margin of people who felt that the Republican Party was better able to solve the nation's problems was growing. On the day before the debate, a New York *Times*/CBS poll had Reagan leading Mondale by twenty-six points. Yet the polling by both the Mondale and the Reagan campaigns during the first week of October indicated that Mondale was gaining some ground. (And, though neither campaign had the Reagan lead as large as the *Times*/CBS poll did, both still showed Reagan with a comfortable margin.) And the Reagan-Bush campaign was finding, to its consternation, that Mondale was behind Reagan in California by only seven points; Reagan's lead had once been seventeen points. The investment in California by the Mondale-Ferraro campaign—in both candidate time and paid advertising—was apparently yielding results; and the Reagan-Bush Washington headquarters was worried about the status of its campaign in California. The Reagan-Bush campaign was also concerned during the first week of October that its lead in Ohio had shrunk from about seventeen points to twelve points, and its lead in Pennsylvania had gone from about eleven points to six points. For the most part, one Reagan-Bush official said, these were Democrats "going home," and not strong Reagan supporters or independents switching allegiance; but there were also signs of independents turning to Mondale.

All this occurred after—and was related by Reagan-Bush strategists to—the week following the bombing of the Embassy in Beirut, when Reagan likened the delays in providing more adequate protection for the Embassy to delays in getting a kitchen remodelled, and then tried to place the blame for the attack on cuts in intelligence-gathering capacity in past Administrations. But while there may have been slippage, such was Reagan's lead going into the debates that he would have to go into a steady free-fall in order to lose the election. Reagan's people were concerning themselves not with the possibility of a loss—though they remained on guard about the unthinkable happening—but with the magnitude of the victory, and its effects on the Republican Party. Nonetheless, they tried to cut off the subject of Beirut by having Reagan, on October 2nd, standing under an airplane wing in Brownsville, Texas, say that he "was responsible—and no one else" for the security arrangements in Lebanon. He had done a similar thing shortly after Christmas, in order to cut off debate on an adverse report by a special Pentagon-appointed committee about the successful truck-bombing of the Marine headquarters last fall. This time, Mondale, who had been keeping up the attack on Reagan about Beirut (and had said the day before, "What we have today is a President who gives us alibis"), said that Reagan's statement wouldn't "wash." Ferraro, in an appearance in Atlanta, asked whether, when Reagan took responsibility, "Does he mean he didn't heed the many warnings that preceded the attack?" And she asked whether he meant that he had approved the move into the new Embassy before it had adequate security. The Mondale people say that their polling found that the series of incidents surrounding the bombing was eating into Reagan's support among certain target groups, and was particularly hurting him among white males—a major source of Reagan support.

Reagan, meanwhile, was stepping up his attacks on Mondale, concentrating on the "Carter-Mondale" Administration and on Mondale's proposals to cut the deficit by, among other things, raising taxes. Reagan repeated the line of other Administration officials, saying that Mondale would raise taxes on the average family by eighteen hundred dollars. (The Reagan people are aware that this is not true—that taxes would be raised on a graduated basis, and would not be raised on any families earning twenty-five thousand dollars or less, and that the over-all figure is too high.) The Reagan campaign also began to run negative ads in early October (against "Carter-Mondale" and Mondale's tax increases, which are also the subject of an extensive ad campaign by the Republican Party). Some Reagan campaign advisers had been wanting to run these ads for some time, and finally got through when the numbers started to slip.

Reagan was having other problems as well. In the same plane-side news conference where he said he took responsibility for the events in Beirut, Reagan reacted to questions about the fact that, on the day before, Raymond Donovan, his Secretary of Labor, had been indicted. Donovan, the first sitting Cabinet officer to be indicted, had been charged by a Bronx grand jury with a hundred and thirty-seven counts involving grand larceny and fraud in connection with his previous activities as an officer and part owner of the Schiavone Construction Company, of Secaucus, New Jersey. (Nine other individuals and another company were also charged.) Donovan pleaded not guilty and charged that the prosecution was a "politically motivated hatchet job," and took a leave of absence without pay rather than resign his job. A number of the President's advisers, including James Baker, the White House chief of staff, believed that Donovan, who has had legal and political problems from the beginning, and particularly poor relations with labor, should have left long ago—but the President is reluctant to get rid of people, and Donovan had the backing of a number of conservatives in and out of the Administration. He got the job in the first place because he raised a great deal of money for Reagan in 1980—and at a time when few Eastern Republicans were interested in contributing to Reagan. In 1982, a special prosecutor appointed to investigate allegations that Donovan had ties to organized crime concluded that there was "insufficient credible evidence" to prosecute Donovan. (The recent indictment deals with state, not federal, law.) The indictment, of course, does not mean that Donovan is guilty, but it nonetheless came as an embarrassment to the Reagan Administration, which has had a large number of its members come under fire, or have to leave office, for misconduct.

Last month, an independent counsel who had been appointed to look into the financial dealings of Edwin Meese, counsellor to the President and Attorney General-designate, found "no basis with respect to any of the eleven allegations for the bringing of a prosecution against Mr. Meese for the violation of a federal criminal statute." The independent counsel, Jacob Stein, said that his assignment did not permit him to rule on the "propriety or the ethics" of Meese's conduct, or his "fitness for the post of Attorney General." However, to spare the Administration any more embarrassment the Republican-controlled Senate Judiciary Committee put off further consideration of Meese's nomination until after the election.

When Reagan was asked by reporters about the Donovan indictment, he replied angrily that his Administration officials faced a "lynch atmosphere." And in reply to a question about what some

Administration critics have come to refer to as "the sleaze factor," Reagan said, "The only sleaze factor that I've seen in all of the things that have been going on in these four years, if there is one, is on the other side, with their baseless charges of accusations that have all been proven false." Though Administration officials said at the time that they felt the Donovan matter would have little political effect, the campaign's polling indicated that the matter did have a negative effect for about six days, and then was overtaken by other matters—especially the first debate.

As Mondale headed into the first debate, he had a large, nearly fatal problem: his candidacy was being widely written off—dismissed as an embarrassment or a joke. He had become the subject of ridicule, which is a very difficult thing to reverse once it starts. (The same thing happened to Carter.) There is a cruel streak in the American system which leads people to ridicule someone who appears to be losing badly or to be falling from public favor. A kind of piling on occurs—to the point where the political figure is turned into a caricature, someone who can do nothing right. Everything he does is seen through a given lens. Mondale, before the debate, was reaching that point, if he had not reached it. A subsidiary of the cruelty is that the failing candidate's—or President's—"allies" become severe (though usually anonymous) critics, spreading the word about what a disaster he is. Members of his party walk away. This happened to Carter when his Presidency began to fail, and, though it is hard to remember, this even began to happen to Reagan in 1982, when the recession was threatening the Republican Party with large losses. Democrats, however, are far better at self-demolition than Republicans are. Everything about Mondale, it seemed, was wrong: his nose, his voice; he couldn't make an interesting speech; he was humorless; he was, to use the going word, a "wimp." That he could make a good speech, that he has a fine sense of humor (a trait not impossible to catch on television) went largely unrecorded, and unknown to the public. People were tuning him out. He was nearing the point where he was in danger of becoming—to use a phrase that James Johnson, his campaign chairman, used in a different context earlier this year—"politically dead."

Mondale cannot help his looks or his voice, of course, but some of the problem he had brought on himself. He had not made many inspiring speeches, and Mondale himself is aware that he is not a particularly effective speaker. He made no great effort to become more effective on television. There were a number of contexts in which Mondale did not come across as particularly strong or commanding—the way he handled his ties to the interest groups supporting him, the way he went about selecting a running mate, his appearing to appease Jesse Jackson, the Bert Lance bungle. Too often, he appeared to be caving in to pressure; his reluctance to displease, especially during the primaries, gave off a poor impression; the deals he made were costly. Beyond that, Mondale does not often project commandingness (Reagan does, no matter what is behind it), and there is in fact a kind of hesitancy to Mondale—born sometimes of seeing the complexities and mixed implications of things, sometimes of sheer indecision—which the public smells. Reagan is considered a leader because of the strength with which he holds—and, more important, conveys—certain convictions. One of Mondale's associates believes that part of Mondale's problem is that he sometimes seems to run his campaign as if he were governing: seeking a lot of expert opinion, and consensus, before making a move—making sure he knows all the implications. While this has its commendable aspects, it can also inhibit, even supplant, instinct, and come across as excessive caution. (Mondale's initial hesitancy over whether to criticize Reagan for the bombing of the Beirut Embassy last month was a case in point.) Some people, inside and outside the Mondale camp, think that much of the public made a judgment about Mondale during the primaries—a negative judgment that is hard to change. Another theory is that Mondale has been in public life so long, is such a familiar figure, that the public was willing to give him one look this year and if it didn't like what it saw would reject him. One of Mondale's advisers thinks that the stereotype of Mondale as simply an old-hat, dull politician is a consequence of "the juggernaut strategy." Late last year and early this year, Mondale's seemingly powerful, smooth-running, and unstoppable campaign acquired the nickname "the juggernaut." This man said, "We did politics for a year: our message was straw-poll winner, endorsee—not crusader for tax reform, or what have you." What people saw was a "politician." Mondale was, and still is, seen as Washington, government, while Reagan still runs against Washington (he still refers to the "puzzle palaces on the Potomac").

There are those who say that the strategy is what saved Mondale—
that and the deft use of rules that had been written to help him—
but it is now clear that something else was needed. Mondale's was a
tactical victory—but political tactics do not enrich the nation's soul.
So, while things were improving for Mondale, the stereotype, the
caricature, the dismissal of Mondale as a serious candidate, had
reached such a point that Mondale's candidacy going into the first
debate was, so far as the public was concerned, barely breathing.

There is also a theory that there are factors in this election which
go well beyond the personal attributes of either candidate, though
the Reagan campaign has been particularly adept at cultivating
them and taking advantage of them. There seems to be a kind of
brew of feelings and reactions in the land which, with his help,
plays right into Reagan's hands. The tradition that Mondale
comes out of—the New Deal and the Great Society—and seems to
personify, despite his efforts to indicate that his views have
evolved, is out of fashion. Beyond that, it still stirs resentments. I
can remember, during the Johnson Administration, at the time
the Great Society was being pushed through, that some people in
the Administration who fully subscribed to its philosophy felt that
it was overreaching—that blue-collar workers were beginning to
resent having their taxes go to help the poor. It was at that same
time that inflation was beginning to be a problem, because
Johnson was reluctant to raise taxes to pay for both the Great
Society and the Vietnam War. "Fairness" was an issue in the 1982
elections, but that was mostly fairness toward the middle class,
which was losing out in the recession. Many voters are still left
with—and reminded of—images that are hard to erase: student
protesters against the Vietnam War burning the flag (those were
the children of the upper-middle and upper classes; blue-collar-
workers' kids were fighting in Vietnam); the hostages in Iran. The
blue-collar workers were angry at the Vietnam protesters—to the
point of beating them up in 1970. Recently, when Ferraro demanded of an audience of United Auto Workers near Rockford,
Illinois, why so many of them were supporting Reagan, one of the
first responses she got was the hostages in Iran. (She pointed out,
to whatever avail, that the fifty-two hostages had all come home
alive, while two hundred and fifty servicemen had died in Beirut.)
A number of observers believe that there is a large element, if

largely an unspoken one, of race in this election. The civil-rights revolution, for all the good it said about this country, left a lot of bitterness in its wake and, as it has moved into such areas as busing, housing, and affirmative action, has, whatever the merits of the case, been more difficult and stirred anger among those whites directly affected—who tend to be the blue-collar workers. There are some who see the Administration as not only playing on that anger by trying to reverse past gains but, through a series of actions, having, intentionally or not, legitimized racism once again: through a series of court suits; through delaying its endorsement of an extension of the Voting Rights Act; by seeking to grant tax-exempt status to Bob Jones University; by its cultivation of certain individuals and groups clearly identified with the white backlash. (Reagan's one black Cabinet officer, Secretary of Housing and Urban Development Samuel Pierce, has virtually disappeared from view. Earlier in the Administration, Reagan, meeting with a group of mayors, greeted Pierce as "Mr. Mayor.") There are polling figures indicating that the Democratic Party is increasingly becoming the Party of blacks and women, while white males are heavily for Reagan. Another thing that is seen as bothering blue-collar men is the women's movement: recent figures indicate that, beginning in late 1983, the total percentage of white males in the work force has been below fifty per cent—the rest being women, blacks, and Hispanics and other "foreigners." And this trend has been continuing. Finally, the national Democratic Party has been seen as tolerant of, or soft on, other things that bother many people—homosexuality and crime.

All these things, a friend of mine here suggests, have given rise to a sort of nativist movement. "Nativist" is a term used by anthropologists to explain the reaction of a society that feels it has been pushed into too much change too quickly. (The turning of Iran to the Ayatollah Khomeini, he suggested, is a recent, and dramatic, example.) In America these days, it appears that helping the poor is out of fashion and an "I've got mine, Jack" attitude is in fashion. In a sense, Jerry Falwell is the ultimate American nativist leader (he goes on about homosexuality quite a bit), and he has a number of important allies. The fundamentalist-Christian movement has been deliberately sought out by the Republicans to counter Jesse Jackson's voter-registration drive. An absolutely liberal Mondale man tells me that he believes that one of the

things that is going on is that the Democratic Convention was seen
by the country as too beholden to blacks. The "diversity" that
Mondale kept celebrating at his Convention does not appeal to the
nativists. In recent years, there has seemed to be a new consciousness and fear—spoken and unspoken—that America is losing its white, English-speaking identity. The nativist movement, or
set of backlashes, also explains "the new patriotism." It is part of
our native religion that we are stronger and better than the rest of
the world. Suggestions that things are more complicated than
that, that there are events we cannot control, do not sit well with
the national psyche. Some people I have talked with about these
things think that this collective mood will pass; that the action-
reaction cycle that has governed our history will continue. But
meanwhile it is all working to Reagan's advantage. Reagan has not
only encouraged and benefitted from the new mood; his campaign has made him the personification of America. To suggest
that anything is wrong with him is to run down the country. In his
appearance at Bowling Green in late September, Reagan said,
"Uncle Sam is a friendly old man, but he has a spine of steel."

Actually, the Mondale campaign had been going through some
internal reevaluation of its strategy, and a fair amount of controversy, for some time before the debate. The first manifestation of
the reevaluation was the speech that Mondale gave at George
Washington University, in Washington, on September 25th, in
which he set forth in a sharper manner than before what he saw as
the stakes in the election. Essentially, by about mid-September
several of Mondale's campaign aides had become unhappy about
the way the campaign was going, and felt that Mondale still did
not have a message that was working. They subscribed to the
advice that Patrick Caddell, the pollster, had been giving: that the
stakes had to be made clearer, that Mondale had to stay on the
"high moral ground," and that such was Reagan's personal popularity that anything that came across as a personal attack on him
would work to Mondale's disadvantage. While the fact that Caddell—who earlier in the year had been advising Gary Hart and
may have done Mondale more damage than any other strategist,
and who has a history of tension with Mondale—was advising the
Mondale campaign emerged in the press only after the debate,
Caddell had actually been advising the campaign on an on-and-

off basis since August, and played a major role (including meeting with Mondale) in the rethink that led to the George Washington University speech. Some of the Mondale high command had felt it important to keep Caddell's role as secret as possible, for a mixture of reasons: some found it hard to admit that Caddell's advice might be needed; and Caddell, who can be temperamental, has a tendency to talk to the press about his role. So the deal was: Caddell would advise but the press wasn't to know. Yet such things are impossible to keep secret, and eventually the word was out. Caddell, sound as his advice may have been, would not have prevailed to the extent he did had he not had so many allies within the campaign; among them were some people who had initially had some misgivings about bringing him into the campaign at all.

But some key figures in the campaign were unhappy with the paid media, with what the campaign's polling was turning up (it did not square with other data they saw), with the fact that both Mondale's and Ferraro's "negatives" were rising, and, most important, with Mondale's failure to get his message across. Among this group were Bob Beckel, the campaign manager; Tom Donilon, the deputy campaign director and a longtime friend of Caddell's; John Reilly, Mondale's law partner and a key adviser; and Paul Tully, the national political director of the campaign. The resistance came from a very few people, who found it difficult to admit that a change was needed or that Caddell was needed, or who feared erosion of their own authority. Such things preoccupy campaigns—particularly campaigns in trouble—while the candidate is trying to get through the day. The object of much of the internal critics' unhappiness was Richard Leone, who had been brought into the Mondale campaign in the summer to be in charge of "the message"—and to supervise polling, speechwriting, advertising, and issues. This was a tall order, and Leone, an intelligent man who is a close friend of Johnson's and was brought in by him, had had little experience in national politics. Johnson, for all the campaign's troubles with Caddell in the past, had enough respect for his mind to invite him to advise the campaign—but the subsequent outbreak of near-war between some top campaign aides and Leone put Johnson in an uncomfortable position. It was a memorandum by Caddell that guided some of the initial thinking this fall—that Reagan should not be directly attacked and the stakes in the election should be made clear—but his advice was only sporadically followed. Mondale himself was aware that things were not going well for him in the early weeks of the campaign. A new memorandum, prepared by Caddell in mid-September, setting forth again what Mondale should do and what he should avoid, impressed several within the campaign—and also Mondale himself. It was essentially adopted—or so several people in the campaign thought—at a meeting, which Mondale attended, at Mondale's law offices on the Saturday before the George Washington University speech. But Leone kept resisting: thus, the first part of the speech was about foreign policy, which had been originally scheduled, and the second part was a setting out of the strong new themes as dictated by the new, or adjusted, strategy. This part of the speech was what several of Mondale's campaign aides had hoped his opening speech, in Merrill, Wisconsin, on Labor Day, would be more like. Bureaucratic arguments continued—through the first debate and up until the second one. After a large struggle, Beckel took over supervision of the paid media. Caddell played a large role in designing the media and the strategy for the first debate (the debates were under Leone's jurisdiction), but his involvement was resisted by some all along the way. And though many people in the campaign thought it was a settled matter that Caddell would play a major role in the second debate, there was a resistance to this, too, and roadblocks were erected, in the final days leading up to the debate. But Caddell ended up playing a large role in it after all. All this was going on while Mondale was getting ready for the most important, and potentially decisive, moment in his political career.

Meanwhile, Mondale, pleased with the positive response to his George Washington University speech, began to incorporate chunks of the new approach in his stump speech. ("This election is not about jelly beans and pen pals. It is about toxic dumps that give cancer to our children.") He continued to try to draw the contrast between the two parties, emphasizing the Republican platform, and he continued to talk about arms control. However, Mondale's natural inclination was to go after Reagan (he has always been a scrappy partisan), and sometimes the fancy advice he was being given—on how to go at Reagan without appearing to go at him—fell before the natural instincts of the man on the stump.

Thus, on Monday, October 1st, in a speech in New Brunswick, New Jersey, where Rutgers University is situated, Mondale, first stipulating that he was sure the President had "good intentions" about arms control, and that he did not doubt that "the President is for peace," went on to cite instances that have come to light indicating that Reagan both lacks a grasp of some important aspects of nuclear weaponry and is essentially uninvolved in the bureaucratic struggles that have paralyzed arms-control policy. (Reagan's disinclination to exercise leadership within his own government on important issues—his carrying the art of delegating to perhaps a new level—is at odds with the public's impression of him as a "strong leader." The leadership for which Reagan is so applauded has to do with his public presentation of his case, which is a different thing from how he conducts the Presidency.) Mondale, in his speech, said that Reagan "didn't bother to learn" such things as that submarine-launched missiles can't be recalled once they are launched or that most of the Soviet missiles are land-based (this had affected the United States' negotiating position), or that bombers and submarines carry nuclear missiles. Mondale said, "If a President doesn't know, if he doesn't decide, a President can't lead." The new idea was to stipulate Reagan's good intentions and attack his execution. Mondale's aides were at pains to explain that Mondale was not raising a question about Reagan's "competence"—which they considered dangerous territory—but was simply saying that Reagan didn't seem to have enough information to govern effectively; but the distinction was lost on a lot of people. Meanwhile, as part of the revised strategy Mondale wasn't talking as much as before about his plan to raise taxes in order to reduce the deficit, his campaign having concluded (as the Republicans had some time ago) that the tax-increase plan was not a winner for him. One of his advisers said to me recently, "I think the tax plan will go down as one of our mistakes." However, not all of Mondale's advisers agree: they point out that Reagan would have painted Mondale as a taxer anyway (Mondale had set forth a tax-increase plan in the primaries), and that Mondale's offering a specific plan to raise taxes by a specific amount (eighty-five billion dollars) helped to neutralize the issue; further, they think that Mondale got a lift out of the Convention, and afterward, by showing "leadership" on the issue—but that he would have got even more mileage if he had painted the deficit more as a moral issue, and not gone around explaining it with his charts. Mondale was also incorporating in his speeches a riposte to the Reagan campaign's attempt to tie Reagan to Democratic heroes—Franklin Roosevelt, John Kennedy, Harry Truman, and even Mondale's good friend Hubert Humphrey. Mondale said, "Why don't they leave our own heroes alone and honor their own—Hoover and Nixon and Agnew?"

The Mondale strategy going into the debate, as it was finally settled on, had several components, with two overriding and connected goals: to change the public's view of Mondale and to throw Reagan, as the Mondale people put it, "off his script." They believed that the Reagan people would assume, on the basis of Mondale's performance in the primary debates, that Mondale would be aggressive and programmatic—and, through a deliberate campaign of disinformation, the Mondale people encouraged the Reagan camp in those assumptions. And, according to an important Reagan adviser, "Most of us were expecting the primaries Mondale." But the Mondale people had decided against following their previous strategy of, as one aide described it, "Mondale coming on like a lawnmower"—a strategy that probably would not have worked anyway, since it did not provide the most attractive picture of Mondale and would have appeared unseemly against a popular President. The new strategy was to have Mondale reach for the high moral ground, be gracious, say that Reagan is an honorable man, but—and attack his policies. He was to show that he had strong convictions, and continue to try to get people to focus on the future. The key to it, they decided, was to have Mondale not savage Reagan but appear visionary and, as often as possible, make the question the stakes in the election. Mondale was to avoid arguments over facts and figures and correction of any Reagan mistakes (his staff would take care of that afterward), and, on occasion, suggest that Reagan does not understand the implications of his policies: in other words, take the issues to Reagan without appearing to be attacking him, or questioning his competence.

The two most important things that affected the outcome of the debate—and, more important, the interpretations of the outcome of the debate—were that both Mondale and Reagan did not match the expectations of them: Mondale made a better impression than people had expected, Reagan made a worse one. In part, each of them did things he had been doing for some time but that people hadn't seemed to notice; in part, Mondale turned in a better performance than he perhaps ever had before, while Reagan not only did not use his full talents but showed a faltering side that most people had not seemed to notice. Mondale showed some of the humor and conviction that he had been showing on the campaign trail but that had not been much noticed, and he also came across as a more commanding figure than he had before. He was aware that if he did not do well in the debate his campaign could collapse, and, though he is admittedly uncomfortable with television and was not particularly rested going into the debate, he reached (once again) for resources he had not called upon before. His performance was far from flawless, and he did not always seem at ease (especially at first), but he showed more ease with the medium than before, came across as in command of his material, and often had Reagan on the defensive. Yet Mondale still was not as thematic as he might have been, and though he called upon some of his more recent "high moral ground" rhetoric, he did not do it as much as some of his advisers had hoped. Nor, deft as he was at undermining Reagan's case, did he say many memorable things— the kinds of things that would move large blocs of voters to him. Mondale also did a lot more talking about the deficit than had been the plan, in part because it came up in the questioning, in part because he likes to talk about it (whatever his aides may think)—about its effects now and potentially in the future, and about the fact that he has offered a deficit-reduction plan and Reagan has not. He hammered at this point throughout the debate. And he slipped in a connection between the need for leadership on the deficit and the recent events in Beirut: "I believe that a President must command that White House and those who work for him. It's the toughest job on earth, and you must master the facts and insist that things that must be done *are* done." Toward the end, he said, "Well, we've just finished almost the whole debate and the American people don't have the slightest clue what President Reagan will do about the deficit. And yet that's the most important single issue of our time." At an earlier point, Reagan had said, "I'm running on the record. I think sometimes Mr. Mondale is running away from his."

Reagan's position in the debate, as it has been all along, was that a combination of economic growth and cuts in government spending will cure the deficit problem—a position with which few economists agree. He also said that "there is no connection" between the deficit and interest rates—a view espoused by his Secretary of the Treasury but not many others. And he said, flatly, that the deficit "is the result of excessive government spending." He said that economic conditions became so much worse in 1980 that "I was openly saying" that a balanced budget based on his tax-cut plan "was no longer possible." In fact, he said throughout 1980 that the budget could be balanced by 1983, and his plan, formally introduced in 1981, projected a balanced budget by 1984. Reagan did slip away from an answer in which he appeared to rule out absolutely the raising of taxes. Mondale made much of the Reagan Administration's early attempts to cut Social Security and Medicare, forcing Reagan on the defensive on this, and in his response Reagan made a tactical error. He said, "I will never stand for a reduction of the Social Security benefits to the people that are now getting them"—thus appearing to leave open the possibility, as he had before, that future retirees might receive reduced benefits. (His campaign moved to correct this two days later, having White House spokesman Larry Speakes issue a statement saying that future recipients would be protected as well, and Reagan himself told reporters that this is what he had meant in the debate.) Reagan also said that the cost of Social Security does not come out of the federal budget but is in a separate trust fund—but this is not the case. He also denied, erroneously, that he had tried to cut Social Security and Medicare by the amounts Mondale said. And he also claimed, erroneously, that "we have more people receiving food stamps than were ever receiving them before," and he got wrong the proportion of the defense budget that is for weapons. Reagan's defensiveness on the Social Security issue only served to emphasize it, and, in his defensiveness on other issues—fairness, the size of the defense budget—he went into long recitations of facts and figures.

And, while Reagan sometimes seemed testy and lacking in his usual public amiability, Mondale was unexpectedly gracious to Reagan. (This, too, was a deliberate effort to throw Reagan "off his script," as well as to show that Mondale is not simply a scrappy partisan.) Mondale conceded that Reagan had "done some things to raise the sense of spirit and morale—good feeling—in this country," and even went so far as to say, "I like President Reagan." (I am told that Mondale hadn't planned to go this far, but that when he saw that his graciousness to Reagan seemed to be disconcerting him he pushed on, and was even nicer.) In fact, though Mondale, as a practiced politician, understands partisan give and take, one gets the impression that he really does not like Reagan, because he so deeply disapproves of his policies.

Reagan collaborated in Mondale's success. Much of what he did, and what seemed to stun people, he had been doing for a long time: it seems that many people had missed, or forgotten, the difference between Reagan "the Great Communicator" reading to the television audience from a script and the Reagan of the press conferences, who often spouts facts and figures (some of them erroneous) in defense of a policy, who often loses his train of thought. It has seemed to many observers, however, that Reagan's reaction time has slowed in recent months, that he misses more opportunities to hit a question out of the park, that he loses his train of thought more often. So packaged, so sleek (for the most part) had his campaign been that people had lost sight of this less adept communicator. (Reagan has not held a press conference since July 24th, and has held fewer in his Presidency than any other modern President.) But the long debate—it was to be an hour and a half, and ran ten minutes longer—provided a striking picture of Reagan's fumbling, which, even to those who had been aware of it before, seemed especially marked. It raised again the question of why Reagan's aides have been so protective of him. Moreover, Reagan failed to summon forth the high rhetoric that has been so successful for him. Reagan, for all his easy-going public demeanor, is actually a very combative man, and it seems that the combination of being constrained by his aides from responding to Mondale's charges as the campaign went along (this was part of their strategy of trying to control the agenda), and being confronted in the debate with charges about his domestic policies, got under his skin, and got the better of his judgment. (He did much the same thing in his acceptance speech at the Republican Convention.) A closing statement of soaring rhetoric had been prepared for him, but instead he used the time to rattle off more facts and figures in rebuttal to various points Mondale had made, and then, at the end, reached, as if for a lifeline, for a quote from Thomas Paine. Reagan in the past has often come up with masterly verbal tricks, but increasingly he seems to fall back on old ones. This time, when he pulled out the line "There you go

again," which he had used to such devastating effect against Carter in 1980 (among other things, it put Reagan, the challenger, on
the same level as Carter, the President), Mondale was ready for
him and whanged the line back at Reagan with devastating effect.
In what will become the most memorable scene from the debate,
Mondale used this opportunity to turn to Reagan and say, "Now,
Mr. President, you said"—and Mondale repeated it slowly: "There
you go again." Reagan stared at his lectern. "Right?" Mondale
asked, driving it home. "Remember the last time you said that?"
Reagan said, "Umhum," still staring at his lectern, apparently
thrown and angered by this unexpected turn of events. Then, as
Mondale went on to say that Reagan had used that line when
Carter said that Reagan, if elected, would cut Medicare, and then,
after he became President, he had in fact tried to cut Medicare,
the expression on Reagan's face, as he looked at Mondale, was that
of a stricken man. The Mondale people had planned this, to
change the psychology of the debate—just as Reagan had in 1980.
(Reagan's fondness for stock lines extends to lines from the
movies. It was brought to my attention recently that a line Reagan
used in his Convention film—"Where do we find such men?"—
which, in the film, Reagan said that he had asked his wife, Nancy,
as they walked past the graves at Normandy, and which I recalled
him using in the 1976 campaign in connection with some former
Vietnam War P.O.W.s whom he and Mrs. Reagan had entertained
at the Governor's mansion in California, is actually a line from the
1955 movie *The Bridges at Toko-Ri*. The line was used, in a slightly
different form, in both the film and the book, by James Michener,
on which the film was based. Last year, it was brought to my
attention that Reagan's line in the 1980 debate in Nashua, New
Hampshire—"I am paying for this microphone, Mr. Green"—
bore a striking similarity to a line Spencer Tracy used in the movie
State of the Union.)

Reagan began his closing with a reference to the question he
had asked in debating Carter—"Are you better off than you were
four years ago?"—and moved on to ask, "Is America better off
than it was four years ago?" And gave his own response: "And I
believe the answer to that has to also be yes." (This was in the
prepared closing; it was from there that he veered off into the
statistics.) Mondale—after thanking the President for debating—
turned back on him the question: "Are you better off?" First, he

replied to the question: "Well, if you're wealthy you're better off. If you're middle-income, you're about where you were. And if you are of modest income you are worse off. That's what the economists tell us." (Reagan gets upset at this, but a welter of studies backs it up.) Then, turning, as he has been trying to do, the question about this election into what the future holds, and raising, as he has been trying to do, the stakes, Mondale asked, "Isn't the real question 'Will we be better off? Are we building the future that this nation needs?' I believe that if we ask those questions that bear on our future—not congratulate ourselves but challenge us to solve those problems, you'll see that we need new leadership." He continued, "Are we better off with this arms race? Will we be better off if we start this 'Star Wars' escalation into the heavens? . . . Are we better off when we load our children with this fantastic debt? . . . Can we really say that we will be better off when we pull away from sort of that basic American instinct of decency and fairness?" And he said, as he said at George Washington, "I would rather lose a campaign about decency than win a campaign about self-interest. . . . I believe that we will be better off if we protect this environment." And he concluded by saying, "We can be better if we face our future, rejoice in our strengths, face our problems, and by solving them build a better society for our children."

The immediate post-debate verdict by the commentators, backed up by the instant polls, was that Mondale had "won." Of course, what is important about these debates is not who "won," as if they were a sporting event (the more combative, the more the public seems to like it), but what they tell us about the contestants. These events have their drawbacks, and in some ways test the wrong things, but they also offer the most sustained view of the candidates, and therefore insights into them which the brief news clips do not.

The most important effects of the debate were that it caused people to see virtues in Mondale they had not noticed before (at once, his crowds, which had been getting better before the debate, got better still), and that the question of whether Reagan was too old to serve four more years—he is seventy-three—became an open subject. Among other things, Reagan visibly tired in the last third of the hour-and-a-half debate. Getting the debates to last an hour and a half was one of the Mondale negotiators' major strategic achievements, even though they held few cards; they figured that Reagan would not have sufficient stamina to last that full time in good form. The Reagan people wanted the debates to last an hour, but traded the extra half hour for a format that included a panel of questioners, which would slow things down and, they hoped, prevent Mondale from challenging Reagan directly. (Mondale may have actually won on both points: had he been going at Reagan directly, he might have looked too combative.) The issue is not, of course, Reagan's chronological age but whether he is in command of his job and whether, as many observers think, his grasp, attention span, and stamina have been decreasing of late. Reagan's debate performance legitimized the subject as one that could be discussed openly—and for the next few days there was quite a bit of talk about it in the newspapers and on television. Experts on aging were consulted. The Reagan Administration itself made some moves to head off the subject.

On Wednesday, Reagan remarked to reporters, "If I had as much makeup on as he did, I'd have looked younger, too." Mondale, inevitably, said, referring to the 1960 debates, "That's the same answer Nixon gave when he debated Kennedy. Mr. President, the problem isn't makeup on the face but makeup on those answers that gave you problems." On the day before, Reagan had quipped to reporters, "I'll challenge him to an arm wrestle." Mondale, speaking in Pittsburgh, replied, "Well, we had a little brain wrestle on Sunday night, didn't we? And in the next debate he'll find that the issue that concerns the American people is not arm wrestling but arms control." Also on Wednesday, White House aides brought out the President's physician, Dr. Daniel Ruge, to speak with reporters. Asked if Reagan had been tired Sunday night, Ruge said, "I think he was tired. Everybody was tired." Asked if the President had lost any stamina in recent years, the doctor paused, and said, "I don't know." Reagan's physical condition was not the question raised by the debate, of course; still, many people seemed to be going down the wrong trail. Reagan does in fact seem to be in remarkable physical condition, and we are constantly told that he enjoys clearing brush and riding horses at his ranch. Then, not long ago, there was the picture of the President on the cover of *Parade*, pumping iron. Yet we know that Reagan puts in a light workday, tends to be intellectually lazy, and proceeds from fixed ideas. So the question raised by the debate—

and his own people knew it—was whether Reagan had enough grasp of his job to perform it effectively. And how would he perform in a sustained crisis?

Reagan, for all his post-debate bravado, seemed quite dejected by his performance—one adviser says that on Monday he seemed depressed about it. On Thursday, Reagan said to reporters, "I look back now at the times when I wasn't the incumbent and never realized how easy it was to be on the other side." Immediately after the debate, Reagan's campaign staff began to pin the blame for his performance on the White House staff, saying that it had stuffed the man with facts and figures and had put him through too gruelling a preparation. Later in the week, Senator Paul Laxalt, Republican of Nevada and the Reagan campaign chairman, told a news conference that Reagan's debate performance stemmed from the fact that he had been "brutalized by a briefing process" that filled him with too many statistics, and not from "any physical or mental deficiency." (The fact that Reagan is fond of statistics, which he often tends to get wrong, was not mentioned.) These finger-pointing exercises were in part a way of trying to settle some scores: the main objects of the exercise were White House "pragmatists," with whom other elements of Reagan's entourage have been at odds for some time. (Laxalt and some others were present during the briefing process.) But one consequence, undoubtedly unintended, of these goings on was to suggest in another way that Reagan is not in charge.

Meanwhile, the debate was a strong tonic for the Mondale campaign: not only were his crowds larger than ever, but money, volunteers, and politicians started turning up. Mondale himself, clearly invigorated, and proceeding with renewed confidence, put on strong performances. His own camp thought that the debate was particularly damaging for Reagan with the young voters (the "yuppies") and the independents who, in large numbers, say that they would support Hart over Reagan but not Mondale. (This reaction is obviously in a vacuum, since Hart isn't running, but it does suggest to some that there is a sizable group of voters—concerned about the social issues and foreign policy—which may be movable.) The damage, the thinking goes, came from the emphasis Mondale placed on what he characterized as the extreme nature of the Republican Party and its platform. (The Mondale camp is now running an ad stressing this and Jerry Falwell's influence on the Party.) Reagan, in his response to a question about abortion, virtually suggested that anyone who has an abortion is a murderer, and told a bizarre anecdote about a man who beat a pregnant woman so badly that the child was born dead, which led the California legislature to pass a law making that act murder, and he said that that law "was signed by the then Democratic governor." In fact, it was Reagan himself who signed the bill into law. (When this was later brought up with Larry Speakes, Speakes said that he had no comment.) Mondale said that the question of abortion was such a sensitive one that the government should not decide it, and that if it did, such a law wouldn't work. He added, "Do we really want those decisions made by judges who've been picked because they will agree to find a person guilty?"

Mondale, in his appearances following the debate, continued to stress that "a leader has to know what's going on," and, at a large rally in Pittsburgh on Wednesday, October 10th—one of the largest rallies of his campaign so far—Mondale took the crowd through a litany, to which it replied, "But it just ain't so." He included Reagan statements that submarine-launched missiles could be recalled, that bombers and submarines are not equipped with nuclear weapons, that deficits do not result in higher interest rates. This was his way of raising the "age issue." He also now stressed more than before that the election was a referendum on such things as the Supreme Court, "Star Wars," and Central America—trying, as he has in various forms all fall, to get the voters to focus on the stakes and on the future.

Reagan, meanwhile, was attacking Mondale as being a taxer and weak on defense. And the Reagan-Bush campaign put additional negative ads on the air—stressing that in domestic policy Mondale's aim is to raise taxes and in foreign policy he would take us back to the Carter days. On Friday, Reagan took a colorful (and expensive) whistle-stop tour through part of Ohio using Harry Truman's special railroad car. In the six stops along the way, he hit at Mondale with new toughness. He said, "My opponent, Mr. Mondale, offers a future of pessimism, fear, and limits compared to ours of hope, confidence, and growth." He said Mondale "sees government as an end in itself" and that the Carter-Mondale Administration "took the strongest economy in the world and pushed it to the brink of collapse." He quoted Gary Hart's criticism of the Carter Administration's economic record in Ohio. He said of Mondale, "His philosophy can be summed up in four sentences: If it's income, tax it. If it's revenue, spend it. If it's a budget, break it. And if it's a promise, make it." The Reagan campaign is also using a tough ad in Ohio, drawing on anti-Carter Administration economic material that Hart had used.

However, much of the national attention that day was focussed on the debate that George Bush and Geraldine Ferraro had had the night before, and on its aftermath. The Reagan people had, in fact, had a tough week, and they felt that the Vice-Presidential debate, even if it did not do them a tremendous amount of good— Bush was generally, but not very decisively, agreed to have "won"—at least did nothing to contribute to the downward spiral some felt they were on, and gave their morale a needed boost. The Reagan people, who set so much store by setting the agenda, had lost control of it. The television coverage of the Mondale campaign that week was much more positive than before, and the coverage of Reagan more negative. The Reagan campaign's own measurements showed an immediate pickup in support for Mondale of about four points after the first Presidential debate, and showed Reagan's over-all lead dropping from eighteen points on the day before the debate to thirteen points by the end of the week. This was still, of course, a comfortable margin. However, according to a Reagan-Bush official, the margins had tightened in a few states, including New York, Pennsylvania, Massachusetts, Rhode Island, and Maryland; and, he said, California is definitely now a "battleground" state. The Republicans are planning to pour more resources into the state, and Reagan, who had not planned to return after he opened his campaign there, on Labor Day, is going there—and to Washington and Oregon as well—this week. And in the final days both candidates will, as expected, concentrate on the Midwest and the Northeast. According to the Reagan-Bush people, the South held firmly for Reagan after the debate. One Reagan-Bush campaign official said to me recently, "Reagan had enough in the bank to sustain something like this; now everything rides on the second debate." The Reagan people were beginning to give up their dream that this would be a major realigning election, making the Republicans the majority party, and their hopes of substantial gains in the congressional elections. They would be happy with—and many of them still expect—a Reagan victory of about fifty-five per cent of the vote. Nonetheless, some people within the campaign were concerned that things growing out of the first debate might take on a life of their own—by which they meant the question of whether Reagan is up to the job. One campaign official said toward the end of the week of the first debate, "We are not out of the woods yet." There was some concern within the Reagan camp that Reagan could not go all ninety minutes of the second debate without losing his train of thought or searching for a word—and that there would be even more attention to this the next time. But some Reagan advisers said that even if the "age issue" stayed around, or recurred in the second debate, they weren't worried. One said, "My feeling is if we stick to the high road and wrap ourselves in the best of American mythology and make the issue about America—which is Reagan versus an opponent—because of Reagan's likability, people will say, 'Yes, he is old, but we all get old and we can't throw him out.'"

One of Reagan's advisers told me several days after the first debate that the important thing was for the Reagan camp to keep its cool and to have a strategy. The strategy that developed was similar to the one followed after Mondale's apparently successful Convention: To "retag" Mondale with his negatives (that's why Reagan said after the Convention that the Mondale-Ferraro ticket was "so far left they've left America"), and retie him to the record of the Carter Administration. Now the strategy was, as one adviser put it, to "cut Mondale down to size"—thus Reagan's sharp attacks on him—and then have Reagan go back to the themes that had served him so well: optimism, the new confidence, the new patriotism. The belief was that Reagan couldn't take full advantage of his old themes until he had cut Mondale down to size. While there is some recognition within the Reagan camp that Reagan's basing his reelection on these vague themes—or what one adviser calls the "eagle soaring" rhetoric—is much criticized, there is also a belief that it is the way to win this election.

One Reagan adviser said that though Mondale may have won the first debate, it seemed clear that he failed to move large blocs of voters, and he did not see what Mondale could do to move large blocs of voters in the second debate. He added that if Mondale was judged to have "won" the second debate, and still did not pick up a substantial percentage in the polls, the Mondale campaign would collapse: people would see that even though Mondale had "won" two debates, the people still don't want him. And it was assumed within as well as outside the Reagan camp that Mondale would not have the same advantages going into the second debate that he did going into the first: he would not have the element of surprise; "expectations" of his performance would be higher; Reagan, a proud and competitive man, was bound to do better.

The most important thing about the debate between Bush and Ferraro, on October 11th, in Philadelphia, was that nothing terribly important seems to have happened, or to have registered on the voters. Ferraro's advisers insist that she met the most important test: Is she qualified to be the Vice-President? Some agree with that, some disagree. Going into the debate, Bush's ratings in some polls were twice as high as Ferraro's, and, though she was drawing large crowds, Ferraro was showing up in the polls as a drag on the ticket. Reagan-Bush campaign officials say that Bush met the key test: he stopped the Reagan campaign's downward drift. Ferraro neither committed any blunder nor gave a particularly compelling performance—the danger to the Reagan-Bush ticket was that she would. So worried were the Bush people about this that they very seriously considered avoiding a debate with her. Ferraro was in a bit of a box, and her discomfort there showed. She had been told so many times to drop her strong, "feisty," sometimes acerbic stump style that she seemed to be over-compensating. And many who had been seeing on television the clips of her rallies were surprised, and disappointed. But one doesn't perform in a debate the way one does on the stump, and this should have been no surprise. Still, Ferraro did not seem to find a pitch—with some exceptions—that she was at ease with. The impression was of a candidate on whom work was still in progress. She was understandably nervous going into the event, and her lack of confidence showed, especially when she talked about foreign policy.

Bush, on the other hand, came across as more knowledgeable about foreign policy, in part because he is more at ease with the subject. Before he was Vice-President, he was Ambassador to the United Nations, chief of the United States Liaison Office in Peking, and, for a year, Director of the C.I.A. Bush has a long résumé (he had also been a member of Congress), but he didn't stay in many of his positions long, and his depth is hard to get a fix on. He is usually a pleasant man, and seemingly an intelligent one, but he has always been a somewhat awkward campaigner—and the awkwardness showed up in the debate. (Several of the Reagan people do not have a high opinion of Bush's campaign skills.) Bush, too, sometimes has trouble finding the right pitch: his enthusiasm seems excessive, the voice goes into a whine. Sometimes his motions are herky-jerky. Simply, he does not seem a natural. In his campaigning this year, Bush has often been testy when questioned by reporters. (He gets particularly irritated when past differences between himself and Reagan—on, for example, abortion—are pointed out.) Inevitably, in the debate Bush defended Reagan's record, but he did it with such enthusiasm that he bordered on the comic. He even adopted one of Reagan's mannerisms—the slight pause and the tilt of the head.

Bush talked about "twelve-and-one-half-per-cent inflation" and "twenty-one-and-a-half-per-cent interest rates" during the "Carter-Mondale" Administration. These figures are a staple in the campaign against Mondale. But, a claim by Bush notwithstanding, the personal-savings rate—which the supply-side tax cut was supposed to boost—is now no greater than it was during the Carter Administration. Lately, the Reagan Administration has benefitted from the actions of the Federal Reserve Board, which has been loosening credit as a result of the slowdown in the rate of growth of the economy—from about ten per cent and seven per cent in the first two quarters of the year to about 2.7 per cent in the third quarter. Thus, the tightening of the money supply last fall and this spring, leading to increases in interest rates, which so irritated the Administration—and frightened the President's political advisers—has ended up working to Reagan's benefit, because interest rates are now being lowered. Individuals and industries are still being hurt by the interest rates, which in real terms (after inflation) are still higher than they were during the Carter years. Mondale tries to explain "real interest rates," and made a stab at it in his debate with Reagan, but the term tends to be an eye-glazer. As far as the general public is concerned, interest rates are going down; as far as the Reagan political advisers are concerned, it is the direction of the economic indicators that counts.

Similarly, Reagan and Bush talk about the "six million jobs" that have been created during their Administration; more jobs were created during the Carter Administration. It is true, as both Reagan and Bush said in their debates, that spending for food stamps has risen—but not to the extent that inflation and increases in food prices and in unemployment, as well as in the size of the population, would have required. By those measurements, spending for food stamps has dropped, as it has for other programs aimed at the same segment of the population. Bush also made claims of other increases in spending for the needy which turned out not to be true. Of Mondale, Bush said, "He goes around just saying every bad thing." He continued, "If somebody sees a silver lining, he finds a big, black cloud there. Whine on, harvest moon."

The fact that Bush seemed surer of himself in the foreign-policy section was probably what mattered. While some of the things he said were arguable—he suggested that terrorist actions were justified against governments that "don't believe in all of the values that we believe in"—Ferraro either did not argue against them as well as she has on other occasions (as in the case of Beirut) or seemed uncertain. At one point, when she was trying to explain Mondale's complicated proposal for temporary moratoriums on the testing and deployment of certain weapons, she was obviously struggling—staring down, as she did too often, at notes—and didn't get it quite right. On several occasions, she cited foreign trips she had taken, as credentials—these trips increased as she became more interested in the Vice-Presidential nomination. Whether Ferraro is any less informed about foreign policy than Reagan was when he became President is a valid question but, it seems, an irrelevant one. She is being held to her own test. And it is a valid test: the Vice-President has to be ready to step in. She was asked, as her aides expected, "the button question"—whether she would be willing to meet a direct challenge by the Soviet Union—and she replied, firmly, "If the Soviet Union were to ever believe that they could challenge the United States with any sort of nuclear forces or otherwise, if I were in a position of leadership in this country they would be assured that they would be met with swift, concise, and certain retaliation." And she went on to stress the importance of arms control. Yet Bush, when given an opportunity to ask Ferraro a question, said, "I'd sure like to use the time to talk about the World Series, or something of that nature," and he later passed up an opportunity for a rebuttal. Ferraro would have been landed on for similar things.

The scene that will be the most remembered from the debate, however, had nothing to do with substantive questions but, rather, with an exchange between Bush and Ferraro that seemed to raise the question of his—or his campaign's—attitude toward her: astonishingly, given the sensitivity of the situation, Bush said at one point, "Let me help you with the difference, Mrs. Ferraro, between Iran and the Embassy in Lebanon." One could sense backs going up all over the country, and Ferraro, quietly, responded, "Let me just say, first of all, I almost resent, Vice-President Bush, your patronizing attitude that you have to teach me about foreign policy." Then she took Bush up on his suggestion that she had just said that she "would do away with all covert action"—she had said she objected to the C.I.A.'s supporting a covert war in Central America—and she responded with dignified intensity to another statement by Bush regarding Beirut: that "for somebody to suggest, as our two opponents, that these men died in shame, they better not tell the parents of those young Marines." Ferraro replied, "No one has ever said that those young men who were killed through the negligence of this Administration and others ever died in shame. No one who has a child who's nineteen or twenty years old, a son, would ever say that about the loss of anybody else's child."

The next few days' discussion of the debate was marked by a running argument over the "shame" charge, and over the Bush entourage's increasingly strange talk about Ferraro. A few days before the debate, Bush's wife, Barbara, who has always come across as dignified, unburdened herself of some remarks about Ferraro to reporters. (Mrs. Bush said that she and her family like "to go rich," with "no poor-boy stuff like that four-million-dollar—I can't say it, but it rhymes with rich.") Mrs. Bush later indicated that the word she had in mind was "witch" and that she had thought her remarks were off the record, and in any event she called Ferraro to apologize. Then Peter Teeley, Bush's press secretary, told reporters before the debate that Ferraro is "too bitchy." The Ferraro camp concluded that the Bush people were trying to get under Ferraro's skin, or perhaps reinforce the idea that Ferraro, as a woman, wasn't ready, but it also felt that this talk represented a true attitude toward her—the Bushes are old money and class; Ferraro is new money, a sassy upstart. Then, the day after the debate, Bush, talking to some longshoremen, remarked to one of them, "We tried to kick a little ass last night." He later said that this was a private comment, not meant to be overheard, and was an old football expression. However, his staff later sported buttons saying " 'Kick Ass' George" and began passing them out. Bush, who must tire of being termed "preppy," sometimes seems to be overcompensating; and there is a theory that this is all a deliberate play for the male vote. Meanwhile, Mondale, who was said to be truly angry, demanded that Bush apologize for the "shame" remark, and, after a few days, Bush said that he could justify the remark because Mondale had said after the bombing of the Embassy last month, "Once again, we're humiliated in this region." He then cited one dictionary's definition of humiliation as including "shame," and, when that didn't work, cited another dictionary. Mondale replied in effect that Bush had an antecedent problem— that Mondale had been referring to Administration policy, not the men who died. He also called Bush a "political hit-and-run driver" who "doesn't have the manhood to apologize." On Thursday, Teeley commented to reporters, "You can say anything you want during a debate, and eighty million people hear it," and said that if the press reports that the statement is inaccurate, "So what? Maybe two hundred people read it, or two thousand, or twenty thousand."

On Monday, October 15th, Reagan, campaigning in the South, said that if Mondale was elected President he would "jeopardize the security of this nation." He criticized Mondale for having opposed several weapons systems in the past. He cited some of Mondale's primary rivals' criticisms of Mondale (including John Glenn's criticism of him for opposing certain weapons systems), and said, "His program of high taxes, sugar-coated with compassionate rhetoric, is a disaster in disguise that will destroy our economic expansion, increase unemployment, and reignite inflation." Reagan said that Mondale had "confused" the Soviet invasion of Afghanistan with the Reagan Administration's invasion of Grenada, "when we liberated Grenada from Communist thugs." This line, spoken at the University of Alabama, in Tuscaloosa, received big cheers. (Recently, the Washington *Post* reported that two newly founded tax-exempt foundations, which are barred from partisan political activity, are working with an arm of the Republican National Committee in planning to celebrate the anniversary of the invasion of Grenada, which took place last October 25th.) During

Reagan's Southern swing, he made an unusual stop at a McDonald's in Tuscaloosa. "What am I supposed to order?" he asked his aides. (The aides, as usual, took their meal on the plane, as Reagan usually does.) The following day, speaking in Illinois, Reagan said that the United States had been "unilaterally disarmed" during the Carter Administration, and criticized Mondale for praising Carter's handling of the Iranian hostage situation and for saying that it would be " 'a temporary problem.' " And, in a new line of attack, he criticized Mondale for failing to "repudiate" Jesse Jackson "when he went to Havana, stood with Fidel Castro and cried, 'Long live Cuba. Long live Castro. Long live Che Guevara.' " (Jackson's full quote, according to the Washington *Post*, was "Long live Cuba. Long live the United States. Long live Castro. Long live Martin Luther King, Jr. Long live Che Guevara. Long live Patrice Lumumba. And long live our drive for freedom.") Asked by a student at one stop in Illinois whether he thought he was too old to serve another term, Reagan joked, in something of a non sequitur, "The way I put it is, I'm not really this old. They mixed up the babies in the hospital."

Mondale, on Monday, a day that Democrats turned into an environmental day—having Mondale, Ferraro, and Hart, and also John Anderson, all addressing the subject—attacked the Administration's environmental record. At a toxic-waste dump near St. Louis, Mondale made a joke of the fact that late last week, apparently when Reagan officials heard he was going to visit the site, the Administration suddenly announced that it would seek funds to clean it up. He said a similar thing had happened when he visited a dump in Los Angeles earlier in the year. Mondale remarked, "If I only had seven hundred and sixty-one days to go in this campaign, I'd go to a dump every day and clean them all up." On Tuesday, Mondale decided to respond to Reagan's foreign-policy attack on him the day before, and, in a speech at Stanford University, said that for the past thirty years Reagan had had "a naive and primitive notion of national strength." Mondale said that Reagan had called President Kennedy "weak" for "not taking what he called 'the final step' in Cuba," had called Lyndon Johnson weak for "not threatening the use of atomic bombs in Vietnam," had accused Gerald Ford of "bowing and scraping" before the Soviet Union, and had criticized Richard Nixon for signing the SALT I and anti-ballistic-missile treaties. Mondale asked, "Did it strengthen America to put Americans in Lebanon, in a vulnerable spot, against the advice of the Joint Chiefs of Staff?" And he said that Reagan wanted to deploy an MX missile that would be a "sitting duck," and had spent twenty-five billion dollars on the B-1 bomber, which "the Soviets have spent fifteen years preparing to shoot down." He said Reagan's record on foreign policy was "a record of profound confusion," and he added that a President "must be in touch and in charge, a President must learn, he must listen, he must master, he must command, and he must lead."

Mondale then cleared his calendar of some other scheduled West Coast stops—after appearing, with Ferraro, at a celebrity-studded fund-raiser in Los Angeles—in order to prepare for the next debate. He also cancelled an appearance on Thursday at the Al Smith dinner, in New York, an event Presidential candidates traditionally attend. Mondale's aides said that Mondale felt that he had been "hot" in his recent appearances and actually had a chance at the Presidency if he did especially well tonight. (He was also feeling quite good about having defeated Reagan in the first debate, and pointing out to people that it had been said that Reagan had never lost a debate.) Some (but by no means all) of the aides were also of this view—in part it is what kept them going. The Mondale campaign's own polls indicated that Mondale trailed Reagan by about thirteen points this weekend, with Reagan's share of the voters at fifty-five per cent. (At one point, according to the Mondale polls, it had been at fifty-three per cent. The problem for Mondale has been how to get Reagan to below the at least fifty-per-cent rating he has held for months.) Public polls put Reagan's lead at from nine per cent to twenty-five per cent; the most recent *Times*/CBS poll cut Reagan's lead to thirteen per cent (from twenty-six), and today the *Post*/ABC poll cut it to ten per cent (from eighteen). The Reagan polls showed a lead of sixteen to eighteen points, and the Reagan people claimed that there was as yet no state where Reagan was behind. Still, there was a theory within the Mondale camp that the first debate had raised people's opinion of Mondale, and raised doubts in people's minds about Reagan, and that if there was anything like a repeat performance anything might happen. They agreed with the Reagan people that Reagan could "lose" the second debate and still win the Presidency: their view was that all was riding on the nature of the debate itself, and the fallout from that.

As the Presidential candidates headed into the last round of the election, some other things were happening that could affect or were affected by the politics of the year. In El Salvador on October 15th, President José Napoleón Duarte met with rebel leaders, and the two sides agreed to continue to meet. The move seemed to take the Reagan Administration by surprise, though it was on Duarte's stated agenda. The Administration has long been divided over the question of whether the rebels should be negotiated with. But Secretary of State George Shultz, who favors negotiations (as opposed to United Nations Ambassador Jeane Kirkpatrick, C.I.A Director William Casey, and some Pentagon officials), spoke positively of Duarte's move. Yet fighting resumed in El Salvador three days after the talks, and on Friday a plane carrying four C.I.A. agents crashed in El Salvador. Meanwhile, Nicaragua had thrown the Administration for something of a loop by agreeing to a draft treaty drawn up by the Contadora nations, but then the Administration insisted that the terms of the treaty be tightened. Detached observers think that there should be some tightening of some of the treaty's provisions—for verification, for example—but are concerned that, as in the case of arms control, the Administration might use this issue to sink the treaty. This week, a furor broke out over the discovery, by the Associated Press, of a manual written for the C.I.A., and distributed to rebels fighting in Nicaragua, about how to commit political assassinations and other terrorist acts. One of the things that Congress did as it adjourned, on October 12th, was to agree to temporarily cut off aid to the "contra" rebels fighting the Sandinista regime. It was agreed that Congress would provide funds next spring if the President submitted a report saying that the money was necessary and if neither chamber vetoed the request. Thus, a hard decision was postponed, and fudged. So was a decision on what to do about the MX: Congress finally decided that funds for the construction of the missile could be provided next year only if both the House and the Senate voted next March to release them. The House and the Senate finally agreed to authorize a five-per-cent increase, after inflation, in spending for the military budget. The House had voted for a three-and-a-half-per-cent increase and the Senate had approved an increase of seven per cent. (The Administration's original proposal had been for a thirteen-per-cent increase.) The bill to control illegal immigration across the southern border of the United States finally died in the cross-pressures that it encoun-

tered along the way. And the House, fingers to the wind, over-
came its previous misgivings and passed a strong anti-crime bill
just before Congress went home to face the voters.

The ultimate verdict about tonight's debate, in Kansas City, will be
made over the next few days, but it seemed at first that Mondale
did not do well enough, and Reagan did not do badly enough, to
alter the race in any dramatic fashion. The immediate verdict by
the commentators afterward was that Mondale had won on substance but Reagan had done well enough on style to mitigate, if
not eliminate, the "age issue." Therefore, it will come down to
what matters to the voters. (ABC's instant poll tonight had the
viewers about evenly divided, with a high percentage undecided.)
Reagan faltered from time to time, and committed some important substantive gaffes, and got lost in his closing, but people
seemed to be looking for—and the Mondale people were hoping
for—another stark, or even starker, picture of a faltering President. And, as there had been every reason to expect, Reagan
didn't make the verdict that easy. He put more force into his
performance (his aides had him attend a rally before the debate,
to get his spirits up), and started out talking with uncommon
speed; then he slowed down and gave an uneven performance
but, what was crucial, a better one than he had two weeks before.
Mondale didn't make the verdict particularly easy, either. While
he showed a strong grasp of the material, and worked in his theme
repeatedly—"A President must know what is essential to command"—he seemed to miss a couple of opportunities, and appeared tighter, more constrained, than he had two weeks earlier.
And, as before, he seemed to say nothing memorable—nothing
that would move masses. In a personality contest, Reagan wins.
    Mondale used an opening question about Central America to
criticize the Administration's policy there and go on the attack
about the C.I.A. manual for the Nicaraguan rebels as well as the
Administration's policy in Lebanon. He said that the Administration's policy in Central America "has strengthened our opponents," and that in Lebanon "we have been humiliated, and our
opponents are stronger." He continued, beginning the theme he
used throughout, "The bottom line of national strength is that the
President must be in command, he must lead," and he went on to
cite Reagan's statements that submarine missiles can be recalled

and that he hadn't realized that most Soviet missiles are land-based. "These are things a President must know to command," Mondale said.

Reagan blundered in his first answer, when, trying to explain away the C.I.A. manual, he said that "we have a gentleman down in Nicaragua who is on contract to the C.I.A., advising, sup-posedly on military tactics, the contras, and he drew up the man-ual," and that "a number of pages were excised by that agency head there, the man in charge," but that somehow some full cop-ies got away. Later in the debate, he corrected himself, saying, "There's not someone there directing all of this activity." Reagan denied that he had ever said the erroneous things Mondale said he had about nuclear missiles. (The record suggests that he did.) "I'm not going to continue trying to respond to these repetitions of the falsehoods that have already been stated here," Reagan said. He said that the Carter Administration had "tried the policy of unilateral disarmament," and, predictably, he attacked Mondale's past votes against certain weapons systems, and said that Mondale "has a record of weakness with regard to our national defense that is second to none." Mondale, ready for this, turned to Reagan and said, "Mr. President, I accept your commitment to peace, but I want you to accept my commitment to a strong national defense." But he didn't repeat his campaign argument about the number of Presidents Reagan has criticized for weakness. He cited several weapons systems he does back, and said, "My definition of na-tional strength is to make certain that a dollar spent buys us a dollar's worth of defense." Reagan, asked about the "age issue"— whether he could handle a lengthy crisis—was obviously ready, and joked, "I will not make age an issue of this campaign. I am not going to exploit for political purposes my opponent's youth and inexperience." Even Mondale was obliged to laugh. Reagan is very good at this sort of thing, and it may be the most remembered moment of the debate. On Lebanon, Reagan said, firmly, "I have no apologies for our going on a peace mission." After Mondale said that the Joint Chiefs had urged the President not to put the troops in the barracks that were subsequently blown up, and that "they went to him five days before they were killed and said, 'Please take them out of there,'" Reagan said, "The President of the United States did not order the Marines into the barracks. That was a decision made by the commanders on the spot." Mondale came back at this, quoting Truman's line "The buck stops here."

Inevitably, the two men argued over the Administration's record on arms control. Reagan, like Bush, said—contrary to a number of reports—that the Soviet Union had been the first to turn down a potential agreement on intermediate-range nuclear missiles in Europe. In the course of their argument over Reagan's proposal to develop a defensive anti-missile system—his "Star Wars" proposal—Reagan committed two gaffes. First, he said that he would give the Soviet Union a "demonstration" of such a system in order to persuade it to join in constructing one. He went on to say that all nuclear weapons could then be eliminated, because both sides would feel secure. Reagan is offering something that sounds visionary, but few people who have thought about it think it makes any sense. Reagan's statement about the demonstration raised questions about where such a test would be conducted, and how it could be proved that such a system could stop incoming missiles. (Most expert opinion holds that this is not possible.) The tests would also involve the breaking of the anti-ballistic-missile treaty. Mondale did not pick up on this. Reagan also said that he didn't know where such a weapons system would actually be placed, and Mondale replied, "Well, that's what a President's supposed to know." Mondale also attacked Reagan's proposal to share such a system with the Soviets, saying that it would amount to turning over our most sophisticated and sensitive technology. Mondale, as he has throughout the campaign, characterized the "Star Wars" proposal as an escalation of the arms race.

In his closing, Mondale made a wide-ranging case, talking about economic as well as foreign policy. He said, "I will keep us strong, but I think strength must also require wisdom and smarts in its exercise." He talked, as he had in the primaries, about the quick decisions a President might have to make in a crisis, and said, "Pick a President that you know will know, if that tragic moment ever comes, what he must know, because there'll be no time for staffing committees or advisers." He said that in this election the voters are "deciding the future of the world." And, trying to give Reagan a push out the door, he said, "We need to move on. It's time for America to find new leadership." Reagan, in his closing, said, "The meaning of this election is the future and whether we are going to grow and provide the jobs and oppor-

tunities for all Americans that they need," and then he wandered
into a long and rambling anecdote—one that he told at the 1976
Convention but in briefer and somewhat different form—about
having been asked to write something for a time capsule, and how
he thought about what he should say. He ended up saying, "Well,
what they will say about us a hundred years from now depends on
how we keep our rendezvous with destiny," and as he went on,
saying, "I want more than anything else to try to complete the new
beginning that we charted four years ago," and praising Bush,
and beginning to talk about the young people in this country, the
moderator had to cut him off, because he had run out of time.

Following the debate, the Reagan aides in Kansas City stressed
to reporters their view that Reagan had put away the "age issue"
and the election was in effect over. The Mondale people stressed
the substantive errors they felt Reagan had made, and said they
hoped to keep the story going on these while people continued to
make up their minds about the debate—and the election. But they
realized that they had a large gap to close, and only two weeks in
which to do it.

XXII

Ronald Reagan's overwhelming victory last night was above all a testimonial to the man as a political phenomenon. Reagan carried forty-nine states (losing only Walter Mondale's home state of Minnesota and the District of Columbia), and defeated Mondale fifty-nine per cent to forty-one per cent. The popular-vote margin was the second-highest in history (next to that of Nixon over McGovern, in 1972), and the electoral-vote margin, five hundred and twenty-five to thirteen, was the largest since Roosevelt's in 1936. Many people in both campaigns sensed that the race was effectively over either on the night of or a couple of days after the second debate, on October 21st, and the feeling that an avalanche was coming had been in the air for about the last ten days of the campaign. But despite its magnitude Reagan's victory affected races for the Senate and the House only marginally: the Democrats made a net gain of two Senate seats, and in the House the Republicans gained, as of the current count, fourteen seats (a few are too close to tell yet)—fewer than the twenty-six they lost in 1982. A few races, including the very narrow reelection victory of Senator Jesse Helms, Republican of North Carolina, over Governor James Hunt, were affected by the lopsidedness at the top of the ticket (Reagan carried North Carolina by sixty-two per cent, while Helms led by only about a point and a half), but for the most part Democrats held their own. Still, the Democrats had no great cause for comfort. Reagan's natural talents, his ability to help create and reflect the mood of the times, and also the good fortune that seems to follow his political career mowed down Mondale, as it had mowed down others who had gone up against him. The precise proportion of each of these factors in Reagan's victory—his most smashing one—is literally impossible to sort out.

The question has already arisen as to whether anyone other than Mondale could have defeated Reagan; all indications are

that, as the situation developed over the year, Reagan—with the
exception of one brief moment—became unbeatable. Mondale's
campaign was better than it was widely portrayed, but it was not as
good as it could have been, and though the nature of a race
between Reagan and any of Mondale's primary opponents might
have been different, there is no reason to believe that they would
have been able to defeat him, either. John Glenn was the pleasant,
"Eisenhoweresque" man who simply did not make a good candidate. The unsteadiness that marked Gary Hart's primary campaign, and the questions that arose about him, would likely have
continued into the fall. Perhaps another kind of persona than was
currently available to the Democratic Party might have done it, but
hypotheticals are of little purpose now. For what it's worth, some
Reagan people believed to the end that Mondale, despite his vulnerabilities, was the strongest candidate the Democrats could have
put up against Reagan. As the people went to the polls, the economy was in apparent good condition (the deficit was not something people wanted to think about), and people believed that they
were economically better off than they had been before (that
Reagan had presided over the greatest recession since the Great
Depression had been either forgiven or forgotten). There were no
upsetting international events—though the Administration clearly
was worried that there might be one in the closing days. Interest
rates were coming down (as a result of slower growth), inflation
was modest (by recent standards), and unemployment, at 7.4 per
cent, was just about where it was when Reagan came into office—
but so much lower than it was two years ago (when it reached
nearly eleven per cent) that people were convinced that things
were coming along nicely. (Even oil prices, the source of so much
misery during the Carter Administration, were dropping.) And
Soviet Foreign Minister Andrei Gromyko came calling. Those
Reagan aides who talked to me early in the year about the fact that
this could be a close election, or that Reagan could even lose, were,
as they now say, dealing with a lot of imponderables—all of which
broke right for them—and they also got some breaks they hadn't
counted on. Reagan had both helped create and capitalized on the
belief that America was "feeling better about itself." And Mondale
was saying things that a great many people simply didn't want to
hear, and was successfully portrayed by his opposition as a creature of a rejected past. Reagan is highly skilled not only at uplift-

ing rhetoric but also at the attack. There were some things that Mondale might have done about all this, but they went against qualities deep in his nature, and there were some things—exogenous circumstances—that would have presented a daunting challenge to anyone who opposed Reagan.

The combination of Reagan's politics of optimism, his winning personality, and, perhaps most important, his remarkable ability to project a posture of strength and decisiveness, along with relatively good times—or the appearance of them—produced a chemistry that was overpowering. The sunny disposition that Reagan presents, for the most part, to the public is a welcome thing— coming particularly as it did after a President who fretted aloud to the public—and as long as it doesn't seem too out of kilter with reality it works. Reagan does not go on about the burdens of office, or display them; he does not come across as a worrier. The fact that he was so packaged and managed in this campaign worked in his favor, because people liked the package they saw. And Reagan knows how to be packaged. Reagan knows how to look like a leader and talk like a leader and act like a leader. The greatest moment of peril to Reagan in the campaign was when he went unpackaged before the public in the first debate—and the question of whether he was up to the job (the "age issue") became an open one. But such was the reservoir of good will that so much of the public had for Reagan by then, and so strong was the desire to reelect him, that when he held himself together enough to perform passably in the second debate—proved, as it came to be said, that he was not "gaga"—the great majority of the public was satisfied. A great many people believed that his joking that he would not "make age an issue in this campaign," that he would not "exploit for political purposes my opponent's youth and inexperience," settled the "age issue," though it was irrelevant to it. And, as it turned out, there were negative attitudes toward Mondale which Mondale was never able to overcome—particularly as he was compared in the public mind to Reagan.

Reagan's persona, his packaging, his politics, and even his physique are all of a piece. Reagan not only says that America is "standing tall" but he stands tall as well. His confident (if self-conscious) stride gives off confidence. His snappy salute to the Marine guard when he alights from the helicopter on the White

House lawn is the salute of a commanding figure—a true commander-in-chief. The sheer physicality, even the masculinity, that
someone brings to a candidacy, or a Presidency, is a much overlooked factor—perhaps because we don't care to admit how much
it might matter. But the physical bearing that Reagan has brought
to the Presidency cannot be ignored as a political factor. (Consider
how he looked compared to Carter—and Mondale.) He looks the
way we want a President to look, and he offers to the public a
disposition that is amiable but capable of turning tough should the
need arise. His firing of the striking air-traffic controllers, breaking their union, in 1981 was a popular act, as was his invasion of
Grenada. Reagan doesn't dither in public. The indecision that has
marked his Administration on many of the big questions—the
deficit, arms control—has been largely kept from public view.
When Reagan makes a televised address, it seems that there is not
a doubt in his mind. His themes were, for the large part, positive
themes: America is great; we can become anything we want to be;
times are good and they are going to get better. Reagan's aides
counted on the theory that running a myth of what a President
should be like, and making Reagan equal America, would work—
though some acknowledged privately that it was a bit of a cynical
game. Voting against Reagan would be voting against America
itself.

Reagan is also a shrewd politician, with a special instinct for how
to appeal to the middle class—an instinct that has served him well
for many years. And someone here says that Reagan knows how to
slip a punch better than any politician since John Kennedy. And
he covers a retreat better than most: not long after he said that
taking the Marines out of Lebanon would amount to "surrender,"
the Marines were pulled out—or "redeployed." Often, Reagan will
publicly stand by an embattled aide—and then the aide is gone.
Reversals are never recognized. Put all this together with a man
whose powers of communication—under only certain, but the
most important, circumstances—rank with the best in the history
of American politics, and the result is a very formidable politician.

The picture of Reagan as a leader was carefully and
cumulatively built. Few politicians could have carried off the burial of the unknown soldier from the Vietnam War over Memorial
Day or the commemoration of the fortieth anniversary of the
landing at Normandy the way Reagan did. Reagan is very convinc-

ing when he looks moved, as he does on such occasions, and this undercuts the idea that he could be a hard-hearted man. Those scenes, plus the trip to China, built him up as a national and a world leader, yet even his own people noticed that at the time they did not particularly give him a boost in the polls, and wondered why. Bob Beckel, Mondale's campaign manager, says he felt at the time that all this was a setting of the stage for the fall campaign.

Shortly before the election, Richard Wirthlin, Reagan's pollster, said to me, "This has been an election that rode on two major issues—peace and prosperity. There has been considerably more focus on prosperity than there has been on peace, and that's been a tremendous advantage to Reagan. People feel things are better than they've ever been before, and are going in the right direction, and that has been more deeply felt in the last days of the campaign than in the early part: unemployment stabilized; inflation isn't what it used to be; interest rates are coming down; and, most important, people feel they have more money in their pockets." (Most do, as a result of the 1981 tax cut, the reduction in inflation, and the economic recovery.) Reagan aides say quite candidly that they tried to stay away from the subject of foreign policy in the campaign, since they considered it an area of political weakness for Reagan. Wirthlin said that in 1980 Reagan picked up the "nascent" theme of the new patriotism, and that that had grown, reinforced by the invasion of Grenada and reaching its apex in the Olympics.

Wirthlin described the 1984 election as "a megacampaign—not only in terms of mega-issues, but in terms of the broad philosophical underpinnings that transcend the issues." He said, "Ronald Reagan has been able to articulate, better than Walter Mondale, the more generic changes that have affected Americans: that they look at the decade of the seventies as a decade of crushed expectations—Watergate, OPEC, America on the defensive on many fronts—and they feel that there has to be a better way to deal with these things. I don't think people were expressing this very explicitly in 1980; I think 1980 was more of a rejection, first, of Carter and, second, of the Democratic agenda on how to deal with friends and foes and the economy." Wirthlin argues that in this election people were more certain of having voted for change, and that since 1980 Reagan has articulated more clearly the kinds of changes Americans have been seeking. In 1980, there was also something of a reaction to the loosening cultural mores of the nineteen-seventies—another wave Reagan caught—and this has grown since then. Wirthlin points out that though Mario Cuomo and Geraldine Ferraro and Mondale tried to identify the Democratic Party at its Convention with the basic values of family, the workplace, and patriotism, they were unable to preempt Reagan in this sphere.

Those Reagan political advisers who early in the year saw the election as potentially close, or even one that Reagan could lose, were, like others, accepting the idea that Mondale was the strong front-runner for the nomination, and there were a number of things they could not foresee. Wirthlin himself says that the public confirmation of the changes that Reagan had made in economic and foreign policy was not then that strong. Unemployment did not begin to fall rapidly until the spring and summer. All of Reagan's political advisers were worried that interest rates would be rising in the autumn, as the election neared. The Marines were still in Beirut, and the future course of events in Central America was unclear. Wirthlin said to me recently, "To say that the election is a referendum on the President's performance is pretty shallow. What this election is really about is confirmation of change and viewing government through somewhat different eyes. The bigger question has been: Are we comfortable as a people with the kinds of changes Reagan has tried to induce? The answer was very clouded in January." In mid-January, the Gallup poll had Reagan and Mondale tied, each with forty-five per cent of the vote, and a few days later the Washington *Post*/ABC poll had Reagan leading Mondale by only three points. (Other polls did have Reagan leading by more.) Even in early May, Gallup had Mondale down by only four points, and later in the month he was down by nine points.

Wirthlin says, "It was a much closer race earlier this year. What happened is that those issues that were in the balance and those elements that could affect it one way or the other came in Reagan's direction." He says that in January, 1983, only nineteen per cent of the people said that the economy was better than it had been a year before; that by January of 1984 about half the people felt that this was the case; and that shortly before the election sixty per cent felt so. He says that it took most Americans about a year and a half—until about the spring of 1984—to see that inflation really had come down. He adds, "Interest rates started coming down this fall. There was no foreign-policy crisis. So all of those things moved to us." Wirthlin also says, "Another thing we didn't see in January was the challenge Mondale would have in the primaries. Politics is a game of focussing your few resources on the imperatives, and his general-election strategy in January, before he was derailed, was a very strong one." This was when Mondale said that his three themes would be fairness, a more competitive economy, and arms control. Wirthlin, working with a mathematician from Palo Alto, actually did some simulations of the impact on an election of these issues, and, he says, "Mondale was right on target." But then Mondale, forced to develop the contrasts between himself and Hart, increasingly fell back on the traditional Democratic Party groups, thus intensifying his identification as a candidate of the "special interests" (as did his acceptance of political-action-committee funds for "delegate committees") and postponing his opportunity to move to the center. Then there was the Bert Lance matter, which, Wirthlin says, "took the bloom off his being 'courageous' in choosing Ferraro." Wirthlin says, "Those are the intervening events that changed what we thought might happen and what did happen." Meanwhile, Reagan had no primary opposition. Lee Atwater, the deputy director of the Reagan-Bush campaign, says that such challenges weaken the incumbent, by going at his leadership, and can even contribute to his defeat (Ford, Carter). Also, the combined resources of the Reagan-Bush campaign and the Republican National Committee and other groups were plentiful.

So Reagan, the pleasing persona, the self-defined successful President (Reagan is excellent at defining the terms of the situation), was running in what people felt were good times, and he cultivated and capitalized on currents in the national culture: the new patriotism; a "nativist" reaction, which had been developing for some years, against what many saw as excessive and unsettling social change; a sense that government should leave us alone and stop taking so much of our taxes. Anything is possible if you work hard and the government doesn't get in your way, Reagan told the country. Reagan bridles—and cites statistics—when it is suggested that this means that he has been less than fair to the poor, but the facts are that the less well off were the target of most of the budget savings, that the Administration would have gone further but for bipartisan opposition on Capitol Hill, and that the poverty rate has risen. Reagan restored the idea that America can whip anybody (Grenada, the Olympics), and persuaded the public that he had retrieved American defense policy from one of "weakness," even "unilateral disarmament." The fact that he misrepresented what had preceded him, and perhaps even his own achievement, was irrelevant. It sounded good, and Reagan is very convincing—in part because he is so convinced. The Reagan story was that he had cut taxes, slowed the rate of the growth of government, cut inflation and interest rates, restored our military strength and the respect with which we are held in the world. It's a good story, and the fact that it is more complicated than that didn't get in its way. By the time of the election, the Reagan-Bush polling indicated that sixty-five per cent of the people approved of the job Reagan was doing over all; sixty-five per cent approved of his handling of the economy; fifty-four per cent approved of his handling of foreign affairs; and sixty-three per cent felt that the country was headed in the right direction. And on the question of which of the two candidates was best described as "in touch and in charge"—a question Wirthlin watched very carefully throughout the campaign—Reagan ended up with a twenty-seven-point advantage over Mondale. Of the Mondale effort to paint Reagan as out of touch and not in charge Wirthlin says, "They couldn't make it stick; people just didn't believe it."

The deadliest problem for Mondale—other than Reagan's personal popularity—was the picture that the public had of him, and that he was unable to shake. With the exception of a brief period following the first debate, Mondale's approval rating, according to his own campaign's polls, never got above around forty per cent, while Reagan's rating hovered around fifty-five per cent. (The Reagan campaign had Reagan's approval rating in the sixties all fall. The lowest point of Reagan's popularity throughout his first term was in January, 1983, at the end of the recession, when his approval rating was forty-four per cent.) In mid-September, Mondale's rating was at its lowest—thirty-six per cent. His highest rating was forty-five per cent, after the first debate. Focus-group interviews conducted by the Mondale campaign showed that people believed that Mondale was weak, lacked leadership, was too beholden to the special interests—and these perceptions are, of course, related. These interviews suggested that Mondale could not shake the shadows of Carter and the hostages in Iran—that they were a large part of the picture of Mondale as "weak." And some of the actions of Mondale and his campaign reinforced that picture of "weakness." Mondale, unlike Reagan, sometimes appeared to dither. Reagan attacked Grenada; Mondale made a multi-part statement that raised questions about the invasion but left no clear position, and he later said it was justified. There were other examples—especially, even after he had the nomination sewed up, the appearance of his continuing to have to try to satisfy major interest groups, particularly women and blacks. People appear to admire decisiveness—as long as it doesn't get out of hand. But beyond Reagan's strapping shoulders and apparent clarity of views people, from what they saw, had some reason to question how decisive Mondale would be as President. And the Reagan campaign relentlessly tied Mondale to Carter.

There is no way to rewind the movie and make another one now—to know how, if Mondale, starting last year, had run a different kind of campaign, the outcome might have been different, or could have been decisively different. But there is the school of thought among some who were involved in the Mondale campaign that the campaign was focussed too much last year on the tactics of winning straw polls and endorsements, and failed to come up with a message. And it is now clear that the struggle to find a message for the Mondale campaign had gone on for a very long time. When Mondale announced his candidacy, in February, 1983, his essential message was "I'm ready" to be President—not a very exciting one, yet one that was carried through to the advertising for the New Hampshire primary, and was, by common consent, a dud, and it was eventually dropped. Thus, the "juggernaut" strategy—the strategy of making Mondale's candidacy seem so formidable that his nomination would be inevitable—was lacking one thing: something to say that would make people want to follow him. Mondale's aides knew that they were dealing with a candidate who is resistant to themes, and one premise of the "juggernaut" strategy was that if he did not sew up the nomination early his candidacy would collapse. (They appeared to have the Muskie model in mind—and also to underestimate Mondale's resilience.) But the campaign that Mondale waged last year, which impressed many people at the time, and which he carried through the primaries, served to accentuate his negatives: he was seen as simply a politician, and an old-hat one, too tied to the "special interests." He won by battering his opponents and by his campaign's making astute use of rules that had been written to favor him. His campaign was marked by tactical rather than strategic thinking. The argument over theme and message began last year, and continued right up to the end of the campaign. (In fact, it is still going on.) One Mondale aide said to me recently, "Every two or three months for two years, our campaign reached message gridlock."

By the spring of 1983, there was concern within the Mondale campaign about the fact that Mondale was not seen to have any message, and a feeling that this was feeding, or failing to offset, the view already developing that Mondale was a candidate of the "special interests." Mondale was advised from within the campaign to have a "the speech," with a concise message, that would fill the vacuum in which the special-interests charge was growing. It was also suggested to him that he stop giving speeches to conventions of interest groups tailored to their issues, and stop offering various groups, as a reason for supporting him, a list of issues on which he is on their side. He was advised, in other words, to develop a stump speech early, one that would have a national appeal—and have it be something he would be comfortable with. A speech suggested by Mondale's speechwriter, Martin Kaplan, stressed the theme of a return to discipline, standards, and excellence (Mondale used this on occasion and mentioned it in his acceptance speech, but never went very far with it); a season of rebuilding and retraining; of emphasizing the future through stressing education and skills. It called for reducing the deficit and returning to basic principles—the environment, justice, tax fairness. Though Mondale toyed with some of these ideas, he didn't accept the premise of the need for "the speech."

Around Labor Day of 1983, Mondale's campaign staff made another run at urging him to develop a unified national message: one that set forth a moral contrast with Reagan, one that showed Mondale as focussing on the future, and, most important, one that showed Mondale as a man of personal strength (the Mondale polling was already turning up problems in this area)—a man with backbone, and not just another "calculating politician." It was suggested that he keep to a minimum the number of events where he was seen surrounded by politicians and interest-group leaders; that he take unequivocal stands on tough issues; that he deliver the same message to different audiences—to defuse the "pandering" charge. He was urged to de-clutter his message, and not talk so much about things not germane to the average voter—about misalignment of currencies, about NATO, about the people worst off in this country. Another stump speech was proposed. There was a major argument within the campaign over Mondale's speech, on October 6, 1983, accepting the endorsement of the A.F.L.-C.I.O. This was seen by the Mondale campaign as the first major opportunity to launch a national message. A speech of general interest, and stressing excellence, was proposed, but Mondale, out of habit, gave an essentially red-meat labor speech that delighted the audience in the hall—and received a negative reaction in the press. His aides considered it an achievement that his speech to the National Press Club at the beginning of this year boiled his campaign message down to three themes, but he had trouble sticking to them, and after he was upended by Hart in New Hampshire he changed course. Mondale was embroiled in a dog-eat-dog intra-party brawl, in which he treated each state as a universe—and pitched his appeal to the subgroups in it—and in which both he and his opponents drove up his negatives.

The plain fact is that Mondale was not a thematic politician, and resisted attempts to make him one. A thematic campaign calls for a kind of repetition and discipline that are not in Mondale's nature: if there was something he wanted to talk about, he went out and talked about it. He has a curious and far-ranging mind, and if he thought something was important—and he thought a lot of things were important—he wanted to say so. He often talked about fairness and compassion—and did it passionately—but he talked about many other things as well. Mondale's suspicion of uplifting rhetoric—he called it "words" or "dawnism" (as in "the dawn of a new era")—lasted until almost the end of his campaign. He is a highly intelligent, well-informed, serious (but not humorless) man who believed to the end that the issues mattered. Mondale sees the complexity of things and talks about them in a complicated manner; Reagan sees simple truths and delivers a simple message.

When we talked shortly before Election Day, Beckel said, "They have the easiest positive message—a booming economy, peace—

and the easiest negative message—Carter, the hostages—and a guy who can deliver it." An effective message, Beckel said, needs a cadence, repetition, and simplicity, and he conceded that the Mondale campaign never arrived at this. He said that people don't want to face the fact of the deficit—"They don't want to hear it or think about it"—and that with so many people feeling well off, and the country at peace, they didn't want to change Presidents. "We couldn't go to the public and say the world is coming to the end and the President is a bad guy—people would shut you out. Finding a message has been the most frustrating part of the campaign—it's been like trying to probe through a very dense fog." I asked Beckel what Mondale's message was. He replied, "That there are two different ways to view how government involves itself in your life, and there are two different views on how to approach that, that Walter Mondale's is transitional: we will not go back to the way we were and we will not stay with the way we are—and the problem with the message is that it takes that long to say it. And he's trying to say a lot at a time when people are pretty content."

One of Mondale's aides said, "He was a victim of his strengths." And someone who worked with Mondale said that what he chose to talk about was another example of his running for the Presidency as if he were President: his idea was that a President deals with and talks about national security, agriculture, foreign policy, currencies, the poor—and in the end it all fits together as what the Presidency is. He viewed the citizens, one adviser said, as jurors who are listening. This adviser argues that Reagan, on the other hand, appealed to the voters not as jurors but as consumers and, drawing on the iconography of America, talked to them with a controlled, repeated message. Mondale was simply unwilling to accept the discipline of electronic politics—choosing one message per day and sticking with it, so that that is what gets on the air. Moreover, there is a side of him that likes political brawls, and he couldn't resist counterpunching Reagan when the plan had been for him to talk about something else. And the counterpunch was what was most likely to get on the air. Mondale often—far more often than the public seemed to know—moved the audience he spoke before. But television tends to pick up the "hot" line, the attack line, and what often came across was a partisan shouter; the moving lines, or passages, were not news. Mondale was described to me by one of his aides as "the last of the great stump orators;" the trouble is, stump oratory is not suited to a Presidential, television campaign. Mondale's and Reagan's respective political roots explain some of the differences between their styles: interest-group politics, pleasing the hall, and also serious addressing of the issues are the marks of the Minnesota politics in which Mondale was trained; television politics, mass-audience politics, and flair are the marks of California politics. Mondale was not a malleable candidate, which may speak well of his character but damaged his candidacy.

The fact that Mondale wove his nomination-acceptance speech into a more thematic and cohesive one than usual was considered a triumph by his advisers; however, some of the themes were seldom, or never, heard again. It did seem ominous at the time that the themes were being worked on up to the last minute. A particular triumph, some of his advisers thought, was Mondale's saying that the Democratic Party had learned from the 1980 election and would proceed with a "new realism." (He also talked about using the veto to hold the line on spending.) But it is now clear, as seemed possible at the time, that these things did not come from Mondale's bones; they were not heard again. The problem of settling Mondale down with a theme continued into the fall. The theme of his Labor Day speech in Merrill, Wisconsin—"What kind of a people are we?"—was the subject of a great deal of controversy within the campaign, and after a while it, too, went away. It turns out that the Merrill speech was the result of a struggle that lasted until virtually moments before Mondale gave it. The speech originally was an issue map for the fall campaign, dealing with the deficit, the religious issue, the strength of our conventional forces, and arms control. The day before Mondale was to give it, as he was flying to New York for his Labor Day parade kickoff, he read a memorandum by Patrick Caddell, the pollster, which said that the election should be made a referendum on national character and values and about the future, as a way to deal with the leadership problem, and had in it the phrase "What kind of people are we?" (Caddell wrote that his polling found that people were not particularly moved by Mondale's "courage" in saying he would raise taxes or by his choice of Ferraro.) Mondale asked for a rewrite of the speech, based on the memorandum, and Martin Kaplan stayed up the night before

Labor Day writing a new draft. It was a strong speech, placing the issues Mondale was talking about—fairness, the deficit, the poor, the environment, arms control—in moral terms, and asking, after he pointed to various things he objected to about the Reagan Administration's actions, "Is that the kind of people we are?" It also talked about the future in terms of choices the next President would have to make. On Monday morning, shortly before the Labor Day parade, Richard Leone, a senior Mondale adviser in charge of "the message," objected strongly to the new draft—both on its own terms and because of the change in strategy it represented, and, some thought, because he resented Caddell's intrusion into the campaign. Mondale that same morning decided that he didn't like some of the things in the overnight draft—he called it "too glum"—and so a new version was being hammered out just about until Mondale's plane landed in Wisconsin. The result was an amalgam of the old draft and the new one, plus a few other things; the phrase "What kind of people are we?" survived because Mondale liked it. Leone believed—and this was a view that came to be shared by some in the campaign who later did not agree with him on other matters—that the phrase was too reminiscent of Carter's "malaise" speech (which Caddell had inspired), that it suggested that the American people were guilty, and complicitous in the things Mondale was decrying. Kaplan had been careful to have the speech say that "we are a caring people," "we are a fair-minded people," and also that "we are a tough people . . . willing to see our problems as they are," but some aides thought that the nuances were too subtle. Beckel says that the message wasn't clear enough, and that the idea was hard to get across "in a climate where people feel that they are doing all right." Peter Hart, Mondale's pollster, who had urged that the Merrill speech be about straight talk, about hope and opportunity, and about standards and excellence, was mortified by the Merrill speech, and wrote a memo to James Johnson, the campaign chairman, that this was not the question for 1984, and even if it was people would not decide that the answer was Mondale.

The intra-campaign fight over whether Mondale should have continued to talk longer than he did this fall about his deficit-reduction plan—including a tax increase—continues until this day. The speech that Mondale gave at George Washington University, on September 25th, in which he talked about the stakes in the election, was along the lines of the undelivered Merrill speech (the second one), and was also heavily influenced by another Caddell memorandum. When this speech went over well—better than Mondale had expected—he incorporated parts of it into most of his speeches from then on. But he was also saying other things, in part as a result of the continuing argument within his camp over what he should say. Leone argues that Mondale's return to talking about basic Democratic values, and the turning away from dealing with the deficit, was a mistake, and was just the thing to drive away the "target groups"—"soft Democrats" and independents.

There were days this fall when it seemed that whatever strategy prevailed was the result of who had the loudest voice. The striking thing about all this is that the Mondale campaign of 1983 had been a far more disciplined creature, but the discipline seems to have fallen victim to the size and nature of the later battle, to fatigue, and to a considerable amount of battling over jurisdictions—which drained what energy the campaign had left. Leone argues that the talk about "new realism" in the acceptance speech was the establishing of a beachhead for getting back the target groups. He sees the Labor Day speech as a lost opportunity to continue the offensive. He believes that the campaign lost a fateful amount of time, and direction, in August, when it was preoccupied with the questions about the finances of Geraldine Ferraro's husband, John Zaccaro, and that Caddell's memorandum— the thesis of which he disagrees with—had excessive influence at a time of confusion. He argues that the campaign, having started down the path of "fiscal responsibility," should have stayed with it by building the case, and should have found a proper mix of "compassion" and "pragmatism," and that it was important for the campaign to maintain consistency. He says, "You don't go out with a tax plan and then back off; you have to have a very disciplined strategy, for the candidate, for the campaign." In his mind, the fiscal-responsibility message—that this is a tough world and we have to make tough choices—would have helped solve Mondale's "leadership" problem.

The argument within the campaign was not over which were the target groups—it was agreed that they were soft Democrats and independents—but over how to reach them. The theory of those who opposed Mondale's continuing to stress his deficit-reduction plan was that, aside from what they felt were its political negatives, there was evidence (turned up in Caddell's research) that there was plenty of anger and anxiety among voters, and not just among Mondale's base constituency, about the fact that many people were still hurting; and that there was a large question among independents as to what were Mondale's core beliefs. One campaign adviser said to me, "As long as the question of Reagan's leadership versus Mondale's leadership was sitting on top of everything, you had to show that your guy believed in some things, has a core, and what is at his core is that he believes that there are things government can do to alleviate pain." One of Mondale's political advisers says, "By the third week in September, we were at the point where the race was starting to disappear on us." As has been pointed out before, Mondale was the first trailing candidate to be losing ground in September; and the campaign was coming under a barrage of criticism from outside Democrats; so the decision was made that Mondale had to do something new, and *be seen* as doing something new, to give the campaign new life. The argument over how much emphasis to put on the tax proposal, it turns out, had been going on within the campaign for weeks. Some aides realized that Mondale was gaining credit for having "levelled" with the people, and that he had raised people's consciousness about the deficit, but they also realized that during September he was falling farther behind Reagan, and there was little time left. Moreover, they found that this was not an issue Mondale could raise without pounding Reagan, and the general view of Mondale's campaign was that pounding Reagan was getting Mondale nowhere—or was even hurting him. This was a subject of great frustration to Mondale: being told that he shouldn't go on the attack against someone about whom he felt there was so much to attack, and the attack mode being part of his political nature, made life difficult for him. The nuances of attack he was advised to follow did not sit easy with him, and often got left on the airplane when he departed it. Leone argued, and argues, that the reading of the polls that indicated people agreed with Mondale on the issues led some aides into trying to get Mondale to stress his "compassion," and that this, in turn, simply reinforced the idea that Mondale hadn't learned anything since 1980. Leone says that this took away from the "new realism" and buttressed the idea that Mondale's tax increases were for new spending. He argues that, as a result of press commentary that Mondale's cause seemed hopeless, the campaign had a tendency "to pull the strategy up by the roots to see if it was growing." Leone says that the Democratic Convention "was a package that made us look very different and interesting." He adds, "I feel strongly that the new realism and the lessons of 1980 are something we should have tried to stay with."

The tax gambit will go down as one of the great imponderables of the Mondale campaign. It had long been on the list of possibilities for the acceptance speech, as a part of an effort to have that speech portray Mondale as "bold." But two of Mondale's most important political advisers, Beckel and Paul Tully, the national political director, didn't know about it until shortly before Mondale gave the speech, and both thought it bad politics. Peter Hart, Mondale's pollster, didn't know about it until the day before the speech was given, and was alarmed. To some of Mondale's political advisers, the tax gambit was the product of the cloisteredness of the campaign's highest command for much of the summer at Mondale's home in North Oaks, Minnesota (the Lance problem was another example), isolated from the rest of the campaign and failing to check with key figures, the other message bearers, in the Democratic Party. One Mondale aide says, "Every Republican in the country knows how to make the case against it; every Democrat in the country had to deal with it." And it is a fact that a great many Democratic candidates had to defend themselves against Mondale's plan; as far as is known, no candidate endorsed it. A strategist for James Hunt in his campaign against Jesse Helms says that Mondale's pledge to raise taxes was a factor in Helms' victory. Republicans ran generic ads all over the country stressing the tax issue. There is the argument, as has been pointed out, that Mondale had said during the primaries that he would raise taxes, and that the Republicans were going to come at him on this anyway, so it was better for him to get out front, to lead on the issue. Others, in both the Mondale camp and the Reagan-Bush campaign, felt that what he did was lead with his chin: that the emphasis was too great; that it enabled the Republicans to portray Mondale as eager to raise taxes—thus confirming people's worst fears about "tax and spend" Democrats. Wirthlin says, "What filtered out to the electorate was that the Democrats hadn't changed. Soft Democrats and independents never accepted that he would use the taxes to pay off the deficit. Sixty-three per cent said they thought he'd use those taxes to pay for other things. So we came out ahead on who would handle the deficit better." Wirthlin says that if Mondale hadn't made his gambit "we wouldn't have been able to go after him with the same effect."

Moreover, when Mondale made a pledge in his acceptance speech to lower the deficit by two-thirds—he had promised to lower it by half during the primaries—he did it without the campaign's having a plan for carrying this out. This raised ante grew out of a meeting Mondale had with economic advisers at North Oaks, and, while it may have been responsible, it bogged the campaign down in figuring out how to carry out the pledge, and made Mondale's political position all the more difficult. Some advisers suggested that Mondale propose a freeze on spending as a sign of his new fiscal prudence (perhaps with cuts here to offset increases there), but Mondale rejected this approach as a violation of pledges he had made in the course of his campaign, and potentially phony. Some of his political admirers, concerned about the reaction of key constituencies, also objected. The Mondale campaign met the new deficit-reduction goal by finding some savings that may or may not have materialized, and by raising taxes from a total of sixty billion dollars to eighty-five billion dollars—but did not raise taxes on individuals any more than his previous plan had. The new plan actually lowered the amount by which the middle class would be taxed—by mitigating the effects of indexing, which Mondale had first proposed postponing entirely—but the politically devastating part of it was that all the middle class knew was that its taxes were being raised. One Mondale adviser says that had the Mondale campaign stuck with its original budget-reduction goal, a plausible tax program could have been worked out that did not touch the middle class—and that the politics of Mondale's plan was worse than the Mondale camp had anticipated.

Mondale never got across that his tax-increase plan was for the purpose of reducing the deficit—the Republicans helped see to that—or that his spending proposals were offset by "savings." Mondale didn't talk again about using the veto or about "pay as you go" for any new spending programs, and he didn't get across the fact that the tax increase was going into a trust fund. One Mondale aide says, "Yes, we raised people's consciousness about the deficit, but at enormous cost—something like three hundred thousand troops, or the Argonne Forest." Wirthlin's mathematical simulation of the campaign involved thirty variables, having to do with issues and personal traits of candidates. The simulation enabled him to determine how if certain things were stressed they would affect certain constituencies. Wirthlin says that a political campaign is like a symphony score: you can't stress all the instruments. He says, "You can be sure that our playing to effectiveness in getting things done, the future, and strong leadership meant that those parts of the symphony score pleased more of the audience than any others." Mondale's accentuating taxes in his own score, Wirthlin says, helped Reagan. In the end, the Reagan people felt that through a combination of Reagan's rhetoric and their paid advertising they made the point that Mondale wants to raise people's taxes in order to pay for his campaign promises.

Some of Mondale's aides had hoped that he would back some version of the Bradley-Gephardt "fair tax," to put him on the side of sweeping tax reform, and some argued strenuously for it, but this never came about. Peter Hart, one of the advocates for Mondale's making this part of his program, says that his polling indicated that it would go over very well. Meanwhile, tax simplification was one of the few specific ideas put forth by Reagan during the campaign (specifics not to come until after the election). Mondale's aides even held open the possibility of Mondale's backing a fair tax by including the gist of the idea, though not by name, in the platform. But the obstacles to his making such a proposal part of his campaign appeared to be several: a concern on the part of some of his advisers that the proposal would hurt the smokestack industries, which form an important part of the Democratic base, by withdrawing so many of their tax credits and so on; a concern on the part of some advisers that important contributors and fund raisers would not take kindly to the proposal; and Mondale's own sense, growing out of his having served on the Senate Finance Committee, that the proposal was politically unrealistic. Perhaps it is, but it points in the right direction, and would have painted Mondale as more visionary; but he surrendered the ground to Reagan.

Although a number of people in both the Mondale and Reagan campaigns felt that the election was over on October 21st—the night of the second debate—they also realized that, with two weeks left, anything could happen. The Reagan people were of course saying that the election was in effect over in order to put their "spin" on the event and to convince people that it was true, so as to let out whatever air was left in the Mondale campaign. But they also had some evidence on their side. Atwater said to me recently, "I thought it was over because of the general drift of the media commentary that night: they said that it was more or less a tie, and that Mondale didn't do what he had to do." (Much of the commentary was to the effect that Mondale had "won" but hadn't scored a "knockout.") Several of the Mondale people—and, according to someone close to him, Mondale himself—understood that though Mondale, as they believed, may have "won" the debate on the merits, his victory wasn't decisive enough to carry him to victory in the election. But the human reactions within the Mondale camp varied: some people were depressed, some were determined to give it all they had to the end—and pray for a break. The Mondale campaign had been at its point of maximum optimism, and the Reagan campaign at its point of maximum concern, going into the second debate. For the first time, Reagan's lead over Mondale was getting down toward, or into, the single digits. Peter Hart's polling for the Mondale campaign put Reagan's lead at thirteen points; an ABC poll had the two candidates ten points apart; the Louis Harris poll, which had been more optimistic (or less pessimistic) than other public polls about Mondale's standing all along, had Reagan's lead at nine points. The Reagan campaign had Reagan's lead at eleven points, the lowest it had been since the opening of the fall campaign. The Mondale people had, of course, hoped to cut Reagan's lead to single digits long before the second debate. Wirthlin says, "Mondale's best ride against us was in the five days preceding the second debate." Mondale's stump speeches had got better, and he was getting a better press—as a result of the first debate. The Administration was having a problem with the news that the C.I.A. had prepared a manual for the Nicaraguan rebels which appeared to advocate political assassination.

Meanwhile, the Reagan people had their own, frighteningly scientific measurement of what had happened during the second debate. Wirthlin, using a new technique, called TRACE, could measure at once the reaction of people to whatever happened in the debate. A group of forty were gathered in a market-research facility in a suburb of Kansas City, where the debate was held, and given a device that resembles a hand calculator, with five buttons; they were asked to push a button representing the degree to which they did or did not like something that was said or seen. A computer calculated the reactions from all forty participants every six seconds. The reactions were transposed onto a screen after the debate, so that the campaign could watch a replay of the debate and see how the test audience—which was a representative sample of Republicans, Democrats, and independents—reacted to each moment. According to Reagan-Bush officials of the Reagan-Bush campaign, every time Mondale attacked Reagan's leadership—his effectiveness, his grasp of the issues—which he did recurringly throughout the debate, Mondale's standing plummeted. They also said that when Reagan told his "age" joke his rating soared. Wirthlin says, "What came out was that Mondale's attacks on Reagan—on the grounds he attacked him on—backlashed."

The essential strategy behind Mondale's going directly at Reagan's qualities as a leader in the second debate was to try, once again, to throw Reagan off his stride and off his script. The Mondale people believed that now that the question of Reagan's competence was in the air Mondale had more leeway to do this. Leone says, "You had to do something about the mountain of Reagan's support and shake people about him personally in order to win." Caddell says—and he and Leone agree on very little, but they do on this—that the purpose was to knock Reagan off balance, to make it a debate not so much about the substance of foreign policy but about Reagan's competence to govern for four more years. I am told that the plan was for Mondale to engage Reagan more directly from the outset of the debate (and that Mondale had rehearsed doing this), but, for any number of reasons, he failed to do so. That Mondale was tighter than he had been in the first debate was recognizable from the outset. Some argue that the preparations for the second debate were not as good as they were for the first—in part because of squabbling to the end about who would be involved. In part, Mondale was being urged to do something very tricky, and also very high-risk. Moreover, Reagan did not cooperate by being thrown off balance. The evidence is that the people who had supported Reagan earlier simply didn't want to be told that they were wrong in their judgment. There is a school of thought among the Mondale people that if Mondale had been less intent on asserting that he was for a strong defense and that a leader should be smart as well as tough and had been more what he can be at his best in debates—fast on his feet, taking advantage of openings—he would have made a stronger, and better, impression on people. But by this time we are probably just talking about the margin by which Reagan would have won.

The phenomenon of Reagan's popularity was in part a result of a circular process. From the outset of his Administration, many Democrats were reluctant to take him on, because they believed him to be popular, and thus they insulated his popularity. They feared his communicative powers and, particularly if they came from states or districts that Reagan had carried in 1980, were inclined to tend to their own relationship with their constituents. Some voices spoke out, but it was generally considered safer not to. Thus the Democrats did not try to systematically build a case against Reagan over time—a behavior that contrasts with the way Republican oppositions have dealt with Democratic Presidents. So there had been very little "softening up" of Reagan before this year: he was popular, the thinking went, so do not attack him; and thus his popularity was undented. It is interesting to note that just after the Iowa precinct caucuses, in late February, after all the Democratic candidates had been criticizing Reagan, Reagan's popularity in the state took a considerable drop. After that, the Democrats turned on each other. However, by this summer economic conditions had taken a turn for the better, and Reagan had been allowed to get into a position where his presumed popularity was unshakably actual. How much difference a less fearful approach to him might have made can't be known.

This was the legacy that Mondale inherited, and the thesis behind the warnings to him that Reagan should not be gone at directly was based on the theory that what had not been accomplished in three and a half years could not be accomplished in three and a half months. But Mondale did not always heed the advice, since it went against his instincts, and in the end many people in his camp—but not all of them—felt that, particularly once the opening came as a result of the first debate, taking on Reagan, albeit in a complicated fashion, was all that was left to do. There were dissenting voices—who wanted Mondale after the second debate to return to the high thematic road he had eventually (for the most part) got on, but the overriding impulse of the campaign after the second debate was to take the substantive openings Reagan had offered, and see if Mondale could widen them—could convince people that Reagan didn't know what he was talking about.

On Monday, October 22nd, in Philadelphia, Mondale called Reagan "the most detached, the most remote, and the most uninformed President in modern history." In the debate, Mondale said, the American people "saw a President who cannot discuss any major issue without making a major mistake." He said, "They saw a Commander-in-Chief who is not commanding and who isn't a chief." He took Reagan to task for saying that the only alternative to the Marcos regime in the Philippines was Communism, and got in a shot at Bush (which it was obvious during the debate he had intended to take and had omitted) for having praised Marcos during a trip there in 1981, saying, "We love your adherence to democratic principles." He charged Reagan with having tried during the debate to pin the blame on the local commander for the placement of the Marines in the barracks that was bombed last fall, and he ridiculed—as he had failed to do in the debate—Reagan's suggestion that he would give the Soviets a "demonstration" of the Star Wars missile-defense system. The following day, campaigning in Ohio, Michigan, and Illinois, Mondale continued to attack Reagan as out of touch. Also, Mondale talked about a letter Reagan had written to Richard Nixon in the course of the 1960 campaign against John F. Kennedy. Among other things, Reagan's letter said, referring to Kennedy's program, "Under the tousled boyish haircut, it is still old Karl Marx—first launched a century ago. There is nothing new in the idea of a Government being Big Brother to us all. Hitler called his 'State Socialism' and way before him it was 'benevolent monarchy.'" Mondale had had the letter to use in the second debate, but he didn't do so; he said later that the opportunity hadn't arisen. Mondale had been accusing Reagan of political "grave robbing"—of appropriating unto himself Democratic heroes, including Kennedy. Now, speaking strongly, he said, "That's a big difference between the two of us. I believe that a President who cares, who leads—just as Kennedy did—can make and must make a difference in the lives of our country. That's not Karl Marx. That's not Adolf Hitler. That's America. That's America at its best." (Reagan, at a campaign stop in Ohio, said, "If you read the letter, you will find there is nothing wrong with it.")

Mondale also talked in his appearances about what he was for—

education, protection of the environment, civil rights, and fairness
in the tax system—but, inevitably, what made the news programs
was his attacks on Reagan, including a continuing attack on the
Star Wars program. Mondale was accompanied on Tuesday by
Gary Hart, who made many appearances with Mondale and on
his own. Hart is trying to get himself right with the Democratic
Party. Edward Kennedy, too, made a substantial number of appearances on Mondale's behalf. (Behind the ostensible support for
Mondale, the positioning for 1988 is on.) Jesse Jackson has
fulfilled his promise to try to get out the black vote in the South.
Mondale also told some steelworkers in Youngstown, Ohio, on
Tuesday, that he realized that the Carter Administration had not
done enough for the steel industry in Ohio—an issue Hart had
used against him and then Reagan used, drawing on what Hart
had said. (It also emerged in the news just after the debate that
there are three American hostages in Lebanon—a fact that the
American government had managed to keep pretty well under
wraps and that Mondale had considered using in the debate but
did not. Also, senators who examined the C.I.A. manual for the
guerrillas in Nicaragua said that the word "neutralize"—which
Sam Nunn, Democrat of Georgia, took to mean assassinate—was
still in the manual. In the debate, Reagan had said that references
to political assassination had been excised. Three Presidents, including Reagan, have signed an executive order barring the
C.I.A. from participating in political assassinations, or abetting
others in doing so.)
    One of the oddities growing out of the debate, which received a
bit of attention in the days following, was Reagan's talk about
Armageddon. According to the "Armageddon" theory, which is
widely held among the religious right, a passage in Revelation is
interpreted to mean that the world is rapidly approaching the
time when various nations, including the Soviet Union, Arab nations, African and European nations, and China will invade
Israel; that their armies will be destroyed in a limited nuclear war,
but a small number of Israelis will survive and will accept Jesus as
Christ—they will be physically lifted from the earth and will be
reunited in the air with Christ and then return to the earth and
punish the unbelievers and destroy Antichrist forces in the battle
of Armageddon. On the morning of the debate, a piece appeared
in the New York *Times* about the concern of some mainstream

religious leaders over the fact that Reagan has several times referred to the theory of Armageddon, suggesting that it may have some validity. Asked about this in the debate, Reagan said that his talking about the subject was "the result of just some philosophical discussions with people who are interested in the same things." Reagan continued, "And that is the prophecies down through the years, the Biblical prophecies of what would portend the coming of Armageddon and so forth. And the fact that a number of theologians for the last decade have believed that this was true, that the prophecies are coming together that portend that. But no one knows whether Armageddon—those prophecies—mean that Armageddon is a thousand years away or the day after tomorrow. So I have never seriously warned and said we must plan according to Armageddon."

The polls continued to show Reagan the "winner" of the debate, but by very narrow margins. It was also reported on Tuesday that American dependents were being removed from Lebanon and the personnel being reduced, and that the new Embassy is in effect shut down. The Administration was showing signs of concern that there might be another incident before the election.

Reagan, on Monday, was looking pleased about his performance—in contrast to the last time—and he kept up the attack on Mondale. Appearing at the Rockwell International plant in Palmdale, California, Reagan stood before a model of the B-1 bomber and a large banner saying, "Prepared for Peace," and said, "Mr. Mondale made a career out of weakening America's armed forces." (The Carter Administration had cancelled the B-1 bomber—a move that Congress approved.) Reagan said, "If it were up to my opponent, I'm afraid Rockwell might still be building the B-25—that is, if you were building anything at all." (The B-25 is a Second World War bomber.) Reagan's defense buildup has, among other things, helped fuel the economy and create jobs. On Tuesday, Reagan campaigned in Oregon and Washington. In Seattle, he compared Mondale's record on defense with that of the late Senator Henry Jackson, and said, "If you liked George McGovern's defense policies, you'll love my opponent's." (Jackson did, however, support cancellation of the B-1 bomber.) Reagan said nothing on Tuesday about its being the anniversary of the bombing of the Marine headquarters in Beirut. On the following day, he presided over a White House ceremony celebrating the anniversary of the invasion of Grenada. Before he returned to Washington, on Wednesday, Reagan made an appearance at Ohio State University, and repeated what had now become one of his standard lines—"If I could find a way to dress up as his tax program, I could scare the devil out of people on Halloween"—and continued to attack Mondale on defense policy. He also denounced the federal government for trying to "live our lives for us." At the White House ceremony (part of a two-day celebration), which was attended by medical students who were on the island when it was invaded, Reagan said that he felt that a "period of self-doubt is over" in America, and added that "history will record that one of the turning points came on a small island in the Caribbean where America went to take care of her own and to rescue a neighboring nation from a growing tyranny." He also mentioned the "courage and love of country" of the men who had been in Beirut.

On Wednesday, Mondale took a bucolic bus tour through Illinois, Missouri, and Iowa, and, invoking Harry Truman, urged members of the farm community to reject Reagan. (The farm vote had been an important ingredient in Truman's upset victory.) Mondale returned to giving more emphasis to his own values, and uplifting rhetoric, instead of continuing the attack of the last two days on Reagan.

The internal news both camps had been receiving since the debate was dramatic, and led to another controversial episode within the Mondale campaign. Both camps' polls indicated that Reagan's rating had taken a dramatic leap upward following the debate. By Monday night, Peter Hart's polling showed Mondale down by twenty points—from thirteen going into the debate and eleven points on the night of the debate—and Tuesday night it showed him down by seventeen. Caddell, on the other hand, was showing slightly better figures for Mondale. Within the Reagan camp, Wirthlin's numbers indicated that Reagan had gone to a seventeen-point lead by Monday night after the debate, and a twenty-point lead by Tuesday. On Wednesday, James Johnson, the Mondale campaign chairman, was facing not only these numbers but also the fact that Louis Harris, who had had Reagan's lead at nine points before the debate, was about to publish a poll putting it at fourteen points. Johnson was struck by Mondale's drop, in Peter

Hart's poll, from eleven points on the night of the debate to twenty points the next night—when the public polls were still calling the outcome of the debate roughly a wash. Mondale's approval rating was also dropping after the second debate.

On Wednesday, Peter Hart submitted a memo to the Mondale campaign saying that the only remaining question was the size of Mondale's defeat, and he recommended, among other things, that the campaign direct Mondale's energies and its own resources to saving other Democratic candidates, in particular some running for the Senate. Beckel was so angered by the tone of the memo, and fearful of its effect on the morale of the campaign, that he ordered its copies recalled and locked away. "The last thing we needed was to personally declare the race over," he told me later. Peter Hart says, "I thought it was important after the second debate to just level. I had put down on paper some other harsh things in the course of the campaign. This time, I said we were not going to win this election." Johnson was also struck by a phone conversation he had on Wednesday morning with Louis Harris, in the course of which Harris offered the theory that when Mondale started talking in the debate about Reagan's competence and knowledge people became very angry at Mondale. (This matches what Wirthlin says his TRACE study showed.) Harris also told Johnson that his data found that people, by substantial numbers, felt that Reagan was more likely than Mondale to keep us out of war, and to achieve an arms-control agreement, and was more knowledgeable on foreign policy. Harris also told Johnson that he thought that the Star Wars issue was a loser for Mondale: that Reagan's argument that we could build an impenetrable missile-defense system was very appealing to people. The evidence that Hart and Harris offered pointed to the conclusion that Mondale didn't have the standing with the public to be so critical of Reagan, and that people had decided to vote for Reagan, and had decided that they were going to lock in on that decision, and close off any further question—and even kick Mondale for continuing to raise the question of Reagan's competence and age. Johnson said to me shortly afterward, "When Peter walked into my office on Tuesday morning and said, 'I got twenty last night,' that was the moment I had to confront the fact that there was movement against us that was going to be big." Johnson was also aware that a new round of public polls was about to come, the first after Harris being the

New York *Times*/CBS poll, which usually had more pessimistic numbers for Mondale than Mondale's own polls.

So on Wednesday morning Johnson decided to go to Milwaukee, to meet Mondale and his travelling entourage to brief them on what he thought was happening—to prepare them psychologically for the new political atmosphere that he thought was ahead, and to talk about what was to be done. Johnson told me on the day after his trip to Milwaukee, "I went to Milwaukee because I believed there was a possibility—not a certainty—of an imminent avalanche." He wanted to warn the group that they might be headed for a political atmosphere in which all the talk was of a Reagan landslide, of a realigning election—and also to talk about what to do about the situation. Johnson told me that he had realized that the campaign's travelling party—referred to by campaign headquarters as "the road show"—might be becoming misled by the large crowds Mondale was attracting, and be unprepared for the ride that might lie ahead. At the meeting that night, in the Marc Plaza Hotel, in Milwaukee—after Mondale had taken his seemingly successful rural tour, and talked uplift talk—Johnson laid out before Mondale and the staff the data he had been receiving, and what he thought it meant in terms of reorienting the campaign, and explored options for the slightly less than two weeks that remained. He made the case that Mondale's slippage was probably related to the attacks on Reagan, and suggested that the campaign shift to a more positive tone. He discussed options for redeploying Mondale's time and the campaign's money, for helping other candidates, and for Mondale's ending the campaign with dignity and a respectable place in history. The reaction in the room was one of a good deal of anger. As several people in the room heard it, Johnson was telling them that it was over. (A couple of members of the Mondale campaign objected to his taking the trip; Beckel, the campaign manager, was out shooting commercials and did not even know that Johnson was going—and was not pleased.) Some felt that Johnson had unnecessarily brought a demoralizing message—a psychologically wounding one—to the candidate and the campaign when they had nearly two more weeks to do battle and were prepared to do so. It was suggested to him that the crowds were indicative of something that the tracking polls were not picking up. Mondale himself said, "Those aren't a loser's crowds." Moreover, Mondale and the high command were aware of what the tracking polls were saying, and Mondale that day had already shifted his campaign to a more positive one, and left off attacking Reagan on leadership. They said they had been through ups and downs in the polls before, and were ready for another psychological roller coaster, and they argued that even if the tracking polls were right Johnson should not bring such a demoralizing message to the campaign, which had to carry on. Besides, they argued, something might still happen. Some of the entourage remained angry at Johnson through the rest of the campaign. Some people argued later that the trip wasn't necessary: that all Johnson had to do was pick up the phone and talk to Mondale about the necessity for a change of message—a change that was in fact already under way.

"I'm a realist," one Mondale adviser said to me at about that time. "But you do the best you can, and you don't do that to a candidate at this point. And you don't go around saying we're going to lose." Mondale, his aides argue, is a political realist, but a candidate, in order to keep going, can't give up hope. One of Mondale's closest advisers, and a defender of Johnson, said a few days after Johnson's visit, "Mondale has a complete understanding of what's happening, but though you may understand reality, you don't give up."

One option that was discussed in the Milwaukee meeting was to cut back on the number of states Mondale would campaign in, and put more resources into them—an option that was rejected. Had Mondale visibly cut back on the states he would campaign in, the opponents of this strategy argued, it would be a sure sign that the campaign had given up; it was also said that the best way to help the Democratic Party was for Mondale to keep up an aggressive campaign to the end. There were two effects of Johnson's visit to Milwaukee which he apparently didn't calculate: one was that word of it would get back to the Washington headquarters and create further demoralization; the other was that word of it would get out to the press. Johnson was, after all, a highly visible person in the Mondale campaign, and when he suddenly turned up a number of correspondents wondered what was going on. On Friday, the Boston *Globe* reported that Johnson had told the Mondale entourage that Reagan had an insurmountable lead. (The campaign officially denied this.) The story was of national interest, of course, and was the cause of even more strain—and finger-pointing—within the Mondale campaign.

By the day after Johnson's trip to Milwaukee, when I spoke with

him, the size of Reagan's lead, as measured by Peter Hart, had
gone back to twenty points. Several Mondale people still considered it possible that something else could happen in the campaign—and believed that it would have to be a major Reagan
mistake to make any difference. (Johnson himself said to me that
day that there might still be "two or three generations of events"
before the election.) The grim truth was that with the exception of
one poll before the second debate (which showed a Reagan lead of
ten points), and the numbers of the past few days, neither Reagan
nor Mondale had moved up or down significantly in the Mondale
camp's tracking polls since mid-June, when Reagan led Mondale
by fourteen points. (The Mondale campaign did not do any tracking polls after the Democratic Convention, when Mondale got a
very brief jump in the polls.)

It was that fourteen-point gap in mid-June (Gallup had the
number at nineteen), after Mondale had nailed down the nomination, at a time when there should have been good will toward him,
that led the Mondale campaign to deliberately do some unconventional things—as the only hope of winning. Mondale and Johnson
talked specifically about the alternatives of running a conventional
campaign and nailing down a respectable, but insufficient,
number of electoral votes, or of taking a riskier path that might
offer the chance of winning. Johnson attributes four strategic decisions to that choice. The first was the selection of a woman as
Mondale's running mate. The second was the decision to be up
front and aggressive on the subject of taxes and the deficit.
(Johnson says that Mondale had no doubt that he had to do this;
he knew that he could not discuss the deficit and the economy and
trade without a credible plan of his own and that no credible plan
could exclude raising taxes.) The third was the decision to run a
national campaign—including in the South and the West, where
Mondale's chances had always been rated low—in the hopes of
garnering the necessary two hundred and seventy electoral votes.
The decision of the Mondale campaign to focus on the South and
the West early rather than concentrate on securing the Party's
"base" in the Northeast and Midwest has been cited as a blunder
by the Reagan-Bush campaign, and is criticized by some of Mondale's allies and aides. But Johnson and others argue that if they
hadn't tried early to peel away some Southern and Western states
there would have been no chance of winning them later. (More-

over, they say, they had to overcome indications that they had written some of these states off.) Beckel said to me shortly before the election, "With our base, you can't win an election. There is no particular base to begin with. If you just run in the East and Midwest, you lose, so we had to try to get some states in the South and the West, and we went to those states in August. If this race were a race with a six-point difference between the candidates, we'd be eight points ahead in Pennsylvania and we'd be fighting Reagan over the states we went to in August." The fourth decision, Johnson says, was the gamble, after the first debate, of going at Reagan on the questions of his competence and knowledge.

Whatever the staff thought of the effect of Johnson's visit to Milwaukee, Mondale showed no signs that he had given up. On the contrary, he threw himself into his campaign with as much vigor as ever—he urged that stops be added to his schedule—and he returned to talking about the themes he was most comfortable with. The picture that was conveyed of him was of someone who had finally "hit his stride" and was drawing large and enthusiastic crowds, but, of course, it was said, it was too late. Now Mondale was talking about compassion, and more than ever the things that government can do for people—talking from where his heart had been all along. (In early 1983, Mondale told his staff he wanted to make the role of government a major theme of his campaign—he said, "Let's have it out on this"—and he was dissuaded, on the ground this would portray him as mired in "the politics of the past.") He was now being credited with being an effective speaker at last, but the truth of the matter is that he had been effective before—but was now more consistent. Mondale once again showed that he had more resilience than most people had given him credit for—or perhaps than even he knew—and a large amount of dignity and pride that made him determined to have it recorded that he had done his best to the end. (Mondale's reversion to his true self also led him, on the weekend before the election, to pledge to a Hispanic audience, in McAllen, Texas, that if elected he would name a Hispanic to the Cabinet.) Mondale was now—at last, if a bit late—more conscious of how he came across on television, and his delivery, as seen on the medium, was better than ever. (He practiced for the first debate by using a videotape machine and watching the playback. One aide says that Mondale said later that he wished he had done that before.) Mondale, according to more than one adviser, had hardly watched television before, but now took an interest in watching the evening news programs, to see how he came across. Now his delivery seemed more measured and surer. And his campaign took more pains in the final days to give his events a good look—as one aide put it to me, "a more Republican look"—on television. Experienced advance people were brought in; there were more balloons—there was even a balloon expert.

From then on out, Mondale returned to his stump speech, based in part on the George Washington University speech, adding a section each day on a subject of importance to him— human rights, justice (including the possibility of Reagan's naming several Supreme Court justices), education, fairness. His campaign called it Mondale's "summation to the jury." On Thursday, October 25th—the day after the meeting in Milwaukee—Mondale, speaking to a large crowd in an arcade mall in Cleveland, cited Reagan's 1960 letter to Nixon again and Reagan's assertion that it was a good letter, and said that in this election "the choice is as clear, the differences as stark as they've been any time in this century." Referring to the letter, Mondale said, of Reagan, "No wonder he fought Social Security and Medicare. . . . No wonder he opposed student assistance and good education." Mondale said that he saw these things as "a commitment of one generation to another." He said, "No wonder he's turned his back on civil rights and women's rights, because he sees it as a step toward human bondage. I see it as opening doors toward liberty, toward freedom, toward hope, toward justice for all Americans." Mondale said, "We need a President who will stand tall, but we also need a President who stands for something. As President I want you to know my vision"—and he listed the things he wanted for his country: "I want an America where the economy grows. . . . I want the prosperity for us and our children. . . . I see an America where we put our kids first, where we invest again in them, in the human mind. . . . I see an America where we once again protect our air, our water, and our land. . . . I see an America of fairness where each generation understands its responsibilities to the other. . . . I see an America that stands before the world as a champion of human rights, of liberty and decency." He talked about the arms race, and then he turned Reagan's use of the image of America being a "shining city on the hill" back on him—differently from the way Mario Cuomo had at the Democratic Convention. Mondale pointed out that the line came from a sermon by John Winthrop to his fellow-pilgrims before their ship landed at the Salem Harbor, in 1630. He said that when Reagan talks about "a shining city on the hill" he overlooks an important part of Winthrop's sermon: "To be a city on the hill," Mondale said, paraphrasing Winthrop, "we must strengthen, defend, preserve and comfort one another. We must bear one another's burdens. We must look not only on our own things but also on the things of our brethren. We must rejoice together, mourn together, labor and suffer together. We must be knit together by a bond of love." Returning to a theme he had used at the very outset of his campaign, in 1983, Mondale said, "Let us be a community, a family where we care for one another," and he continued, "Let us end this selfishness, this greed, this new championship of caring only for yourself. Let's pull America back together again. Let's have new leadership. It's time for America to move on." The last line was the campaign's way of trying to, as some put it, "hand Reagan the gold watch." But they never found an effective way to do it.

On Friday, in Des Moines, in a speech criticizing Reagan for celebrating the anniversary of the invasion of Grenada and barely mentioning the anniversary of the attack on the barracks in Beirut, Mondale said, "Today, we have a happy-talk President who's only around for the good news." He added, "We need a President at all times, good and bad."

One of Mondale's closest aides said to me about that time, "Mondale feels that Reagan doesn't know anything, but if it's not there, it's not there. He feels that he took his best shot, and now he'll just go out and make his case. There's even a sense of relief." But there was also a side to Mondale that kept telling him—and in this he was reinforced by some of his aides—that the size and enthusiasm of the crowds he was drawing toward the end meant something. (Mondale even asked someone whether McGovern was drawing crowds at the end, and was told that he was, but not ones of such intensity.)

Meanwhile, the Reagan campaign, once the second debate was behind it and Reagan was looking strong in its polls, decided to return to a strategy of trying to win all fifty states and, in some cases, have Reagan and Bush try to help Senate and House candidates who were in tight races. Reagan went into West Virginia, traditionally a Democratic state, to nail down his lead there, and it was decided that he would concentrate on the Northeast and the industrial Midwest, and end up his campaign in California. As of midweek after the second debate, the Reagan-Bush people claimed that there was no state in which, in their own polling, Mondale was ahead. It was decided that Reagan would go to Massachusetts (the only state that McGovern carried in 1972, and normally a Democratic state); the Reagan polls indicated that Reagan was ahead there, and Raymond Shamie, the highly conservative Republican Senate candidate, was considered nearly even with John Kerry, the lieutenant-governor, who had headed the Vietnam Veterans Against the War. The election of Shamie, who had trounced Elliot Richardson in the primary, would give the Republicans an additional Senate seat, and one filled by a Reagan ideologue at that. As it turned out, Kerry won, though Reagan did carry Massachusetts. Despite the fact that Hawaii had gone Democratic in the 1976 and 1980 Presidential elections, and is presumed to be Democratic, the Republicans decided to try to take that, too—by putting a large amount (for Hawaii) of advertising money into the state. (This worked.) The Reagan-Bush campaign had more money to spend on advertising toward the end than the Mondale campaign did, the Mondale campaign having spent more at the outset (and the allied Republican committees were more flush than their Democratic counterparts). Moreover, the Mondale people were arguing to the end over which spots to put on, and had run several for only a few days—thus diminishing their impact. And the Reagan people decided to try to take even Minnesota from Mondale. William Roberts, the former partner of Stuart Spencer in the California public-relations firm Spencer-Roberts, was sent to Minnesota to work on it, and Reagan himself made a surprise stop there two days before the election. The Reagan campaign's efforts in the state forced Mondale to schedule an extra stop there himself at the end of October, and also to get there in time to hold a rally on Election Eve.

By Saturday, October 27th, the *Times*/CBS poll had Reagan ahead by eighteen points—a jump of three points since its poll taken after the first debate. In most of the important states that had been in question, the Reagan polls showed a double-digit lead. (The only one that was short of that was Pennsylvania, where Reagan was eight points ahead.) The South and Texas had long since been shut down for Mondale. Wirthlin says that by the end of September Reagan had the South and the West pretty sewn up, for a total of two hundred and eighty-seven electoral votes. The 1982 Texas model,where a moderate Democrat had been elected governor, with the support of blacks, Hispanics, and labor—a model that some in the Mondale campaign hoped would be followed in 1984—turned out not to be applicable. The key factors in 1982, it now seemed, were that the incumbent Republican governor was very unpopular and 1982 was during the recession. The way things developed in the South this year gave credit to the theory that had Carter not been on the ticket in 1980 the margins in many Southern states would not have been so narrow (as it was, he carried only Georgia). Several Democrats (and also Reagan-Bush officials) felt that Mondale had made a big mistake in not "balancing the ticket" with a Southern running mate, but this went against the high-risk strategy Mondale and Johnson thought was necessary to have any chance of victory. Stuart Spencer said to me recently, "If Mondale had chosen Sam Nunn"—a moderate Georgia senator—"I'd be sitting here a lot more worried." But the imperatives of Democratic politics at the time made this almost impossible for Mondale to do, even if he had wanted to. Spencer said, "Mondale ended up with a northern liberal-liberal ticket and in choosing Ferraro may have been four to eight years ahead of his time."

Despite the fact that things seemed to be going so well for the Reagan campaign, it did have one last fright, on Sunday, October 28th. On that day, Wirthlin's tracking polls indicated that Reagan had gone from a twenty-two-point lead on Thursday to a fifteen-point lead on both Sunday and Monday. A fifteen-point lead is a quite comfortable one, obviously, but no campaign likes to see movement in the wrong direction; moreover, the tracking indicated that Mondale was picking up the support of white males—the group Reagan had been doing best with—as well as of women and some young people. They attributed this shift to Mondale's effective campaigning and to the fact that the Mondale campaign was running ads stressing the dangers of nuclear war, about education and youth, and about senior citizens whose programs had been cut. One of the ads was a five-minute one that included shots of young children intercut with pictures of missiles rising out of silos. The background music to this scene was Crosby, Stills, Nash, and Young's "Teach Your Children." This part of the five-minute ad was also run as a separate thirty-second spot. It was one of the subjects of major argument within the campaign: some feared that it would backfire, others argued that since they were losing, they should not regret later that they had not tried it. After a struggle earlier in October, the Mondale campaign had got on the air an ad that depicted an invitation by Reagan and Jerry Falwell to join the Republican Party, and said, "Here's what you have to believe"—and then it listed a number of things in the Republican platform. But the ad was taken off and put back on, in a continuing struggle. Meanwhile, the Reagan campaign was running the most memorable ad of the campaign: it showed a bear stalking in the forest, and a voice said, "There is a bear in the woods. For some people, the bear is easy to see. Others don't see it at all. Some people say the bear is tame; others say it is vicious and dangerous. Since no one can really be sure who's right, isn't it smart to be as strong as the bear—if there is a bear?" At the end, the ad showed a man, armed with a rifle, facing the bear. The tag line was "President Reagan. Prepared for Peace." The ad was an unthreatening, nonfrightening allegory about the need to be strong, and even the Mondale campaign's focus-group interviewing showed that the ad was quite effective. The Reagan campaign also returned to the "feel good" ads, saying, "It's morning in America again."

In response to this one last fright, the Reagan campaign decided to run some negative ads in certain key states, such as Iowa and Pennsylvania, until the election. However, by Tuesday, Reagan's lead had risen back to the eighteen-point level. Wirthlin says, "The period from the twenty-fifth through the twenty-ninth was Mondale's last effective charge against our base, and it succeeded some." Two things that were believed to have stemmed any further erosion were that Reagan was highly active (for him) in the closing days of the campaign and the Reagan campaign greatly outspent the Mondale campaign on advertising.

On October 26th, Reagan, campaigning in New York, Connecticut, and New Jersey, appeared at a synagogue on Long Island, and criticized the Democrats for lacking "the moral courage or leadership" to pass a resolution at their Convention denouncing anti-Semitism. (Such a resolution had been proposed by some delegates, but the Mondale people got it set aside, out of concern that it would anger Jesse Jackson, at whom it was aimed, and open up the Convention to a rash of resolutions from the floor.) In the course of Reagan's appearance at the synagogue, members of the audience cheered and shouted, "Four more years," and White House advance workers handed out bright-blue yarmulkes with the Presidential seal inside, along with the words "The Visit of President Ronald Reagan to Temple Hillel." Reagan, in his remarks, also said that he favored the separation of church and state. (Reagan's political advisers say that the "religious issue" resulted in Reagan's getting nearly eighty per cent of the fundamentalist vote in the South but coming out with somewhat less of the Jewish vote than he had in 1980.) And, in his appearance at the synagogue, Reagan also drew an analogy between the United States action in Lebanon and the need to prevent another Holocaust: he said that the message of the Holocaust "should again be impressed on those who question why we went on a peacekeeping mission to Lebanon."

The Reagan Administration had got itself into a confusion over the subject of how it would respond to terrorism. After past attacks on American installations in Lebanon, American officials had warned that there would be retaliation, but there had been none—apparently, in some cases, because the targets were hard to find, and people not involved in the terrorist incidents might be killed, and the Department of Defense was reluctant to retaliate under such circumstances. In general, the military has been loath to get into actions that might not have public backing; in that sense, it has been "Vietnamized"—an accusation hard-liners usually make against Democrats. The form of the "Vietnamization" may be different, but the effect is the same. There was also concern that such actions would only inflame matters in the Middle East. But on October 25th Secretary of State George Shultz, speaking at the Park Avenue Synagogue, in New York, said that the United States must not become "the Hamlet of nations, worrying endlessly over whether and how to respond" to terrorist actions, and that retaliation might be taken "before each and every fact is known" and "we may never have the kind of evidence that can stand up in an American court of law." (Last April, the President signed a secret directive authorizing an "offensive" against terrorism.) Shultz said that the public must understand "before the fact" that the risks involved in combatting terrorism included "loss of life of some of our fighting men and loss of life of some innocent people." Following Shultz's speech, Vice-President Bush said that he did not believe that it represented American policy, and Reagan, campaigning in the Northeast, first told reporters, "There is nothing new in that speech that is not already policy," and then later said, "I don't think it was a statement of policy." Mondale later remarked that this confusion indicated that the White House was a "ghost ship" with no one in charge—a term borrowed from former Secretary of State Alexander Haig.

In his final week of campaigning, Reagan warned his audiences against "overconfidence," and said that he hoped to win not just the election but "a sympathetic Congress," and, in a reference to his famous role in the movie "Knute Rockne—All American," said, "And if you can, well, win those races for the Gipper." In a stump speech in Media, Pennsylvania, on October 29th, Reagan said that four years ago "we got out from under the thrall of a government which we had hoped would make our lives better but which wound up living our lives." He said, "Yet four years after our efforts began, small voices in the night are sounding the call to go back, back to the days of drift, the days of torpor, timidity, and taxes." He ridiculed (and misrepresented) Mondale's tax plan, and attacked him especially harshly on both domestic and foreign policy—going back over his record of several years, and throwing in the Carter Administration's record, Mondale's initial questioning of the invasion of Grenada, and Jesse Jackson's trip to Cuba. (This happens to have been the day after Reagan's poll first dropped to fifteen.)

After spending two days in Washington, Reagan left on October 31st for his last campaign swing—a trip that took him to eleven states. While he was in Washington, Reagan momentarily abandoned his characteristic caution about predicting victory and told a White House gathering of campaign aides that the Republican Party might be headed for "an historic electoral realignment." He also said that it was "no mere coincidence" that Democrats have long represented "the most blighted areas of the country" and "places of desperation."

As of October 31st, both the Harris and the Gallup polls gave Reagan a seventeen-point lead, and NBC News gave him a lead of twenty-four points. (Mondale's own polls also showed a Reagan lead of seventeen points, and Reagan's polls showed a lead of eighteen. Caddell and Hart were getting somewhat but not dramatically different numbers.) Mondale, in the face of these polls, kept telling audiences that the pollsters would be proved wrong, and said, "There's something stirring, the people are listening." Some of his own people continued to be puzzled by the "cognitive dissonance" between what the polls were saying and the size and enthusiasm of the crowds. Objective observers assumed that the crowds indicated that Mondale's base was getting activated, and that the intensity had something to do with a reaction to being told that Reagan was going to win—as well as with Mondale's consistently effective performances. People in politics proceed on some combination of empirical evidence, instincts, hope, and a certain amount of self-delusion—the ratio of these ingredients changing according to the circumstances. The self-delusion is important to keep people going—so it is functional—and the myths that feed it might always turn into facts. However, Mondale's closing days were accompanied by a drumbeat of commentary that Mondale was now doing wonderfully well as a campaigner but of course his case was hopeless. He was portrayed as the gallant loser—this is a favorite, and by now stock, figure in political commentary. Whether or not it affects the outcome of an election even marginally no one can know, but, over the years, people who work in campaigns have said that it does create a bandwagon effect, and does have an impact on the morale of the workers in the headquarters and in the field. And, in a circular way, the assumption about an outcome affects the nature of the journalism itself. One of my colleagues feels that this election was written off uncommonly early by several media outlets, and that this got in the way of people's hearing what Mondale was saying. It does seem that everyone was doing polls, and that this took over. We were surfeited by the news of them, and it seemed that they increasingly became the story of the election. Several people here feel there is a built-in problem in news organizations conducting polls—that this can color their coverage of the candidates, and, in the case of television, also takes precious time from other political coverage. But thus it shall probably ever be.

The boastful commentary by the Reagan-Bush people, who were now talking openly about taking all fifty states, suggests that they believed in the bandwagon effect. When Reagan appeared in Boston on November 1st, the crowd chanted "Fifty states" as well as "Four more years." It also shouted—as Reagan crowds had been doing since the Convention—"U.S.A.! U.S.A.!" Reagan quoted John Kennedy and urged Democrats to cross over and support him, and, drawing on a theme offered by Jeane Kirkpatrick at the Republican Convention, said that the current Democratic leaders had joined the "blame America first crowd." In Detroit on the same day, Reagan said, "We're better off than we were four years ago. We're more secure than we were four years ago." However, by November 1st the Reagan campaign was uncertain about the outcome in Pennsylvania, Massachusetts, Iowa, and Minnesota. There was also some nervousness about New York. A Reagan-Bush official said to me that day, "We had all fifty states won three days ago; we would have been better off if the election had been held then. We're now seeing some natural erosion of support among traditional Democrats." The issue was not whether Reagan would win, just the size of his victory, and the Reagan people joked about their seeming greediness in wanting to win it all. But the states that the Reagan people had considered that they had to win in order to preclude any possibility of Mondale's putting together a combination of industrial, border, and Western states—New Jersey, Ohio, and Connecticut—were comfortably in the Reagan column.

Michigan, ordinarily a Democratic state, had long been in Reagan's column. Reagan advisers believe that this is because, while unemployment in Michigan is still relatively high, the rate of unemployment was now dropping as a result of the recovery and, moreover, because Reagan has always run well among better-off blue-collar workers, which constitute a high proportion of the Michigan electorate. Ohio was considered a "tax sensitive" state, because the Democratic Governor, Richard Celeste, had raised taxes in 1983; Roger Stone, a campaign official who was in charge of the state (along with Northeastern states and the blue-collar voters), poured mailings into the state about the tax issue. Three million target voters—Democrats and independents—received mailings that said, "If you liked Dick Celeste's tax increase, you'll love Walter Mondale's," and included a direct-mail letter from Reagan on the subject.

Speaking to voters in upstate New York, Reagan urged Democrats to "come walk with us on this new path of hope and opportunity," and he continued to use the line he had used when he kicked off his campaign on Labor Day: "You ain't seen nothin' yet." To voters in the Midwest, Reagan said that the United States had become "a giant on the scene" under his Presidency, and he said, "The United States of America was never meant to be a second-best nation." He asked the various crowds "Are you better off now than you were four years ago?" and always got the answer he wanted. (To an outdoor rally in Cleveland, he said, "Thank you for the use of the hall.") And, as if he were replaying the role of George Gipp, the Notre Dame football hero who died young, he asked for a victory, and said, "Wherever I am, I'll know about it, and it'll make me happy." Reagan also told rallies to support Republican candidates, saying, "Don't send me back there alone." And he continued to attack Mondale for wanting to raise taxes and for "peddling doom and gloom." In the closing days of the campaign, Reagan made two trips to Illinois, in part to assure his own victory in the state, in part to help reelect Senator Charles Percy. (Percy lost, to Paul Simon, a liberal House member.) On Saturday, Reagan told voters that if Mondale was elected the nation would be left wandering "an endless desert of worsening inflation and recession" and said that Mondale had aided Carter Administration policies that "made America weak." In Arkansas, he responded to news reports that the Treasury Department was planning certain tax increases: "Over my dead body." He attacked Mondale's tax-increase proposal again, and said, "The principal difference is our vision for America will let the eagle soar. Theirs would return us to the days of the sore eagle."

Mondale, meanwhile, continued to draw large crowds, and stress his rhetoric of a compassionate, caring government. On October 30th, he participated in a torchlight parade in Chicago— a throwback to the time when there was a Chicago machine that could deliver—and made an emotional speech, evoking the memories of John Kennedy and Harry Truman and talking of the ideals that he said had made the Democratic Party great. The event may have been a throwback, but it buoyed Mondale and his entourage, and gave them some hope of carrying Illinois. Mondale went on to Baltimore, to Louisville, to Buffalo, talking about the issues of "decency" and "fairness." He compared the "fairness" of his own program with the effect of what he said Reagan's tax plan was likely to be, and said that under Reagan "the theory is that in America when you're in trouble you're on your own." On November 1st, Mondale and Ferraro addressed a huge rally in the

garment district of New York—there were red balloons gathered
in the shape of a giant apple—and Mondale said, as he had been
saying for some days, in various forms, "The pollsters are trying to
tell you the election is over. . . . But they forgot one thing: Polls
don't vote. People vote." He also responded angrily to Reagan's
charge that the Democrats were soft on anti-Semitism: "Mr. President, that charge says something about you. That is false and
contemptible. . . . I have fought anti-Semitism and bigotry many
times in my life . . . and I've stood up to those radical preachers
who are so close to this President, who've taken over the Republican Party."

That night, Mondale addressed a predominantly black Baptist
church in Cleveland, where, of his own choice, he made a flat-out
appeal for more help for the poor. Mondale had not been making
many appearances before black audiences, because the political
exigency of his campaign was to reach independents and "soft
Democrats"—blue-collar voters. Now another political exigency
was being met—stirring up the base. It was also one that Mondale
considered a personal imperative. He criticized the Reagan ads:
"Their commercials call it the new morning in America. It's all
picket fences and puppy dogs. No one's hurting, no one's old, no
one's hungry, no one's unemployed. Everybody's happy." He went
on, "These poor people can't hire any lobbyists. They can't pay for
any ads. They don't have fancy newsletters. They're not a power
bloc. They're not fashionable. Their voices aren't counted as
votes." And he added, "If we want to be a decent society, and we all
do, we must measure it not by how generous we are to the powerful but how just we are to the powerless." He quoted Hubert
Humphrey as saying, "The moral test of government is how it
treats those in the dawn of life, our children; those in the twilight
of life, the elderly; and those in the shadows of life, the sick, the
handicapped, and the unemployed." He added, "You don't hear
these words from this President." He said, "We all stand for independence. . . . No one's asking for dependence. But people want
education and training, so that they can stand on their own feet.
No one wants government to take the place of individual efforts,
but people do want government to get rid of discrimination.
That's what you're asking for: a chance for dignity, employment,
justice—so that it is possible for every American to have that indispensable dignity." And he attacked with passion the Administra-

tion's cuts in social programs, including, as he had talked about on other occasions this fall, its dropping of five hundred thousand people from the disability rolls, and he pointed out that a court had ruled that this action was illegal. (A federal appeals court in New York in August had ordered benefits restored to fifty thousand recipients and Congress in September passed legislation overturning the Administration's action, and the President signed the bill into law.) Referring to the termination of the disability benefits, Mondale said, "Of all the mean-spirited, inexcusable, cruel steps by this Administration, that takes the cake. Who are these people? They are the mentally ill, they are the handicapped, they are the broken, the sad, the dispirited, the helpless. . . . If there were ever a test of decency, surely giving them some minimal help would be that test." Referring to a line that Reagan had said at Bowling Green, in September, "Uncle Sam is a friendly old man but he has a spine of steel," Mondale said, "He misses something. We want him to be kindly with a spine of steel, but we want Uncle Sam to have a mind and a heart and a soul and a conscience." And on the following day he drew another large and enthusiastic crowd in Boston, where he attacked the Reagan Administration policies as dangerous and without "caring or compassion." Talking as he sometimes had earlier in the year, Mondale said, "If you're unemployed, it's too bad. If you're old, it's tough luck. If you're sick, good luck. If you're black or Hispanic, you're out of luck. And if you're handicapped you shouldn't be." He continued, "I don't believe in that a minute. I think this America has a human dimension. I don't think we're alone. I think we're together."

The theme that Mondale used toward the end—about an activist, caring, involved government, mixed with some caveats about prudent and careful management—was the one Mondale had wanted to go with from the beginning. Mondale is a liberal who believes in strong government, and other suits that people tried on him didn't fit. He was most comfortable—and most effective— when he put on the one that he was most accustomed to, and went out and said what he believed. Like any experienced politician, he knew how to play the angles, and had done his share of it, but he was at his best when he played it straight. It was then that he looked not like a conventional politician but like a man with a core of beliefs. In the end, when it was as clear to Mondale that he would lose as it could be, he decided to go out having talked about the things he believed in, so that people will have known where he stood.

Then Mondale went on to West Virginia—Massachusetts and West Virginia had voted Democratic in five out of the last six Presidential elections—and then, on Saturday, to Michigan, Illinois, and Tennessee. In a town just outside Detroit, he told a crowd that contained many union members, "Every time Michigan has asked for help, I've said yes. Every time the workers of this state have needed help, I've been there." (This sounded like the primaries Mondale.) He added, "When your kids have needed an education, I helped. When you've needed trade-adjustment assistance, I've been there. I love this state. We're fellow-Midwesterners. Give me this chance to be your President." He pointed out that he had supported the Chrysler bailout, which Reagan had opposed. And then he went back to the West Coast, via Texas. He had drawn a far larger crowd in Boston than the President had the day before—and there was always that chance that something might happen.

In most of the states where Reagan was campaigning on Friday and Saturday—in Illinois, Wisconsin, Arkansas, and Iowa—his margin was relatively low, and all but one of these (Wisconsin) had Republican candidates running for the Senate. (All lost.) Reagan said that Iowa's current agricultural hardships were the result of the "ineffective and totally wrongheaded grain embargo" imposed by Carter as a result of the Soviet invasion of Afghanistan. (Mondale, as Carter pointed out in his book, privately opposed the grain embargo—though he publicly defended it during the Iowa caucuses in 1980.) Reagan told his audiences, "America's best days are yet to come."

On Sunday, the *Post*/ABC poll had Reagan's margin at eighteen points, up from twelve shortly after the second debate, and Gallup gave Reagan an eighteen-point lead as well. There were more news reports of an imminent attack on an American facility in Lebanon, and trucks were blocking the access to the Capitol. Meanwhile, Geraldine Ferraro had been campaigning hard for the ticket, but the indications were, from the Mondale camp's own polling, that she wasn't helping it much. When she was chosen, there were people within the Mondale camp who believed that, for all the excitement of July, the real question was how she measured up in October as a possible President. Though George Bush's conduct of his campaign had been less than a smash hit (some of his rivals for the 1988 nomination think, or at least hope, that he has hurt himself for the future), he still maintained an edge over Ferraro in the polls. Ferraro showed a lot of strength—more than most people would have been able to under the circumstances she faced—and many of her problems were not of her own making. She could not help it that she was relatively inexperienced. She was bedevilled to the end by newspaper stories about her husband's financial dealings and stories, some of them cruel and quite controversial, trying to establish links between her husband, or her husband's parents, and organized crime, and one story, in the New York *Post*, said that her parents had been indicted for running a numbers game, and that her father died shortly afterward. Ferraro was eight years old at the time. Ferraro, who clearly is deeply attached to her mother (as well as to the rest of her family), broke down when an aide told her about this one, but maintained a strong presence when she faced a press conference shortly afterward. The stories never linked Ferraro herself to organized crime—though they reported that, unsurprisingly, she had received campaign contributions from a couple of people with connections to it; the contributions were relatively small, and these people also contributed to other New York politicians, and one of the contributors had held respectable public positions—though he was shot, gangland-style (and survived). The stories indicated that whatever connections her husband had were tenuous (some of them were inherited from his father's real-estate dealings, and cut off). There seemed to be a pattern to these stories—the suggestion of a concerted effort by her opponents—and we may not have heard the end of this. (The House ethics committee never got around before the election to ruling on whether she had validly claimed an exemption from disclosing her husband's financial status on a financial-disclosure form.) In the closing days of the campaign, Ferraro was concentrating on the industrial states, and also made one last swing to California, where she had made six previous trips.

Ferraro drew good crowds, and made spunky presentations, but there are people quite friendly to her candidacy who think that she was damaged by spending so much time on the attack—a role she enjoyed but one that did not present her as something she was

supposed to represent: the future. Because she drew crowds, her
schedule was heavily concentrated on rallies; but her feisty crowd-
pleasing style was not universally appealing. She did not do as well
as had been hoped in winning over the Hart constituency, and, in
the end, she, like Mondale, focussed on core constituencies—in
her case, the women's vote. Her speeches made a more blatant
appeal to vote for her because she was a woman. And, in line with
this effort, she appeared in late October on the Phil Donahue
show, a program widely watched by women at home. (The Mondale campaign's polling indicated that it was doing better with
working women than with housewives.) On the show, she said, as
she had said elsewhere, that because of the attacks on her family
background she was "going to spend the rest of my life" making it
up to her family. She also said, as she had said before, that if she
had known what would lie ahead in terms of pain to her family she
probably would not have run for the Vice-Presidency.

On Sunday, Reagan made his surprise stop in Rochester, Minnesota—an aide told me that only Iowa and Minnesota now stood
in the way of a fifty-state victory—and then went on to stops in
Chicago and St. Louis (where he appeared with Bob Hope), and
then headed home to California. Along the way, at every stop,
Reagan told audiences, "You ain't seen nothin' yet." And in California on Monday he stood on the steps of the Capitol, in Sacramento (where he was accompanied by Frank Sinatra), and recalled
that when he first took office there, in 1967, he had told the
people of California that "all of us together had an opportunity to
start a prairie fire that would sweep across this country." Reagan
has been a movement politician from the start, and that has been
part of his appeal, and his success. That the nation is, in general,
more conservative now than when Reagan came on the scene
cannot be denied. How much of a role Reagan had in igniting that
"prairie fire" and spreading it cannot possibly be assessed, but that
he had one is a certainty. Timing also undoubtedly played a role.
Reagan knew, and still knows, how to give voice to what is bothering people, and he has a clear sense of direction. These things
have made him an effective public leader and politician.

In a paid half-hour Election Eve television broadcast, Reagan
said that the election was about "whether we go forward together
with courage, confidence, and common sense, making America
strong again; or turn back to policies that weakened our economy,
diminished our leadership in the world, and reversed America's

long-revered tradition of progress." (The Mondale campaign had no money for such a broadcast, and used what it had for five-minute ads leading up to the election, figuring that if the gap remained wide by Election Eve a half-hour broadcast would be of little use anyway.) Reagan recalled that four years ago "I asked you to join us in a great national effort to free America from leadership that said we suffered from a malaise, that told us we must learn to live with less . . . and the steady loss of freedom and respect for America abroad were all beyond our control." He said, "The greatness of America doesn't begin in Washington . . . Only by trusting you, giving you opportunities to climb high and reach for the stars, can we preserve the golden dream of America as the champion of peace and freedom among the nations of the world." He criticized "the professional politicians of Washington," and talked about how he, working with the people, had prevailed over them to get change. As he had on Election Eve four years before, he referred to John Wayne's saying, just before he died, "Just give the American people a good cause, and there's nothing they can't lick." He said that it was the people of America who "brought America back," and continued, "And you're making us great again. All we did was get government out of your way." He criticized his (unnamed) opponent as wanting to "knock opportunity" and tax the people. "They do everything they can to save us from prosperity," Reagan said. (Once again, he misrepresented Mondale's tax plan.) "Our work is not finished," he said. He mentioned some of the very few specific things he has said he wants to achieve in a second term: simplification of the tax code, a constitutional amendment requiring a balanced budget (which has nothing to do with the deficit problem), and a line-item veto (which even Republicans in Congress resist, on the ground that it shifts the balance of power excessively). Another proposal was for tax incentives for businesses that invest in "enterprise zones" in rundown areas (this is at odds with his talk of simplifying the tax code). Another was lowering the minimum wage for teen-agers. He pointed out again that in the last four years "not one inch of soil has been lost to Communist aggression," and expressed a desire to banish all nuclear weapons from the face of the earth. He said, "We have always been a new world, and, yes, a shining city on a hill where all things are possible." He concluded, "America's best days lie ahead, and—you ain't seen nothin' yet."

To the end, the Mondale people were searching for a line that would sum up his candidacy—one that he could use over the final weekend—but didn't come up with one. The main story remained that Mondale was drawing good crowds, and doing well, but, of course, would lose. On Monday, Mondale told a crowd in downtown Los Angeles, "Tomorrow . . . we can make history by giving them the biggest upset in history." And he did have his own message: "The choice is clear. If you let them make history, they'll turn your vote into a future you never wanted." He talked of the importance of cleaning up the environment and "making sure that no James Watt or Anne Gorsuch ever gets their hands on the environment again," and of launching "a renaissance in education, science, and learning." He talked of tax fairness and of human rights. Mondale said, "Starting tomorrow, we can stop the politicians from writing prayers for our children and sticking their noses in our home." He said, "Do you really want them to tell women and minorities that the march toward justice is over?" And he asked, "Do you really want to give them a mandate to turn their back on suffering in America?" And he repeated his line "I believe that America should not only stand tall but should also stand for something." He asked, "Do you really want to tell them to extend the arms race into the heavens?" Then, having made his case, Mondale went on to a rally in Mason City, Iowa, where he had begun campaigning in February, 1983, and then arrived in Minnesota for one final rally at the Twin Cities airport.

On Election Night, the networks, which were under pressure not to give the results before the polls were closed in many states, though they had their own exit polls, signalled the fact of the Reagan landslide early, and the big question became whether Reagan would carry all fifty states. This was a new sort of Election Night question. CBS called Reagan's reelection at 8:01 P.M. and ABC and NBC did it within a half hour. All the networks showed many states falling into Reagan's column early: first the South and the border states and then some of the industrial states—Illinois, New York, Ohio, and on, relentlessly. In the end, Reagan carried Illinois by fifty-six per cent, New York by fifty-four per cent, and Ohio by fifty-nine per cent. Reagan carried Texas by sixty-four per cent and West Virginia by fifty-five per cent. Later in the evening, it became clear that Reagan was carrying Iowa (though the Democratic Senate candidate, Thomas Harkin, defeated the incumbent, Roger Jepsen). And it became clear that Reagan was carrying Massachusetts. Eventually, the networks gave Minnesota to Mondale—but he carried it by only about fifteen thousand votes (for a near fifty-fifty tie), and the incumbent Republican senator, Rudy Boschwitz, was reelected.

At eleven-twenty, Mondale was on the air to concede. (The candidates had agreed that neither would make a statement about the outcome until the polls had closed across the country; in 1980, Carter conceded before the polls closed in the West.) Appearing with his family and supporters, Mondale seemed collected and dignified, though tired. He said that he had called Reagan to congratulate him, and continued, "We are all Americans. He is our President, and we honor him tonight." Mondale paid tribute to the electoral process, and said, "Although I would rather have won, tonight we rejoice in our democracy, we rejoice in the freedom of a wonderful people, and we accept their verdict." He thanked Minnesota for not letting him down, and said to his young supporters, "I know how you feel because I've been there myself. Do not despair. This fight didn't end tonight." He continued, "It began tonight. I have been around for a while, and I have noticed in the seeds of most every victory are to be found the seeds of defeat, and in every defeat are to be found the seeds of victory. Let us fight on." And he said, "My loss tonight does not in any way diminish the worth or the importance of our struggle. The America we want to build is just as important tomorrow as it was yesterday." At times it did seem he was having trouble getting the words out. "Let us continue to seek an America that is just and fair," he said, and he added, "Tonight, especially, I think of the poor, the unemployed, the elderly, the handicapped, the helpless, and the sad, and they need us more than ever tonight." He talked, one more time, about jobs and fairness and education and arms control. "That has been my fight," he said. He concluded, "I'm at peace with the knowledge that I gave it everything I've got. I am confident that history will judge us honorably."

Reagan, appearing at the Century Plaza, coming onstage to "Hail to the Chief" and speaking to a crowd waving flags and shouting "Four more years," looked quite good, as well as understandably happy. He had not just won, he had triumphed. Reagan mentioned that Mondale had phoned him to concede—the crowd booed at the mention of Mondale's name—but he had no words of praise or consolation for Mondale. He thanked his aides and supporters, and said, "So we began to carry a message to every corner of the nation, a simple message. The message is, here in America the people are in charge." He said, "To the extent that what has happened today reaffirms those principles, we are part of that prairie fire that we think still defines America, the fire of hope that will keep alive the promise of opportunity as we head into the next century." He praised his own record, and then said, "The credit belongs to the American people—to each of you. And our work isn't finished." He concluded, "We're united again, and now let's start building together and keep that prairie fire alive and let's never stop shaping that society which lets each person's dreams unfold into a life of unending hope. America's best days lie ahead, and you know—you'll forgive me, I'm gonna do it just one more time—you ain't seen nothin' yet."

There has been a lot of talk suggesting that the voters deliberately split their tickets so that Reagan would not have too much of a mandate. But that makes the process more intellectualized than there is reason to believe that it is. Similarly, much of the polling of voters' attitudes suggests that a political judgment is a more deliberative one than it often is: a voter who likes a certain candidate, for whatever reason, is likely to find in him the virtues the pollster asks about. As has been pointed out, senators and congressmen—especially congressmen, who have smaller constituencies—have long since learned the art of tending their own gardens, building their own relationships with their constituencies, often on matters that have little or nothing to do with ideology. For example, Reagan carried New Jersey by sixty per cent, but Bill Bradley, the Democratic senator, won with a vote of sixty-five per cent. In some states, as has been noted, particularly North Carolina, the Reagan pull affected races down the line—resulting in the election of some new Republican House members as well as the reelection of Jesse Helms. (The Helms-Hunt race was arguably the second-most important one this year, because of Helms' ideological influence. Money poured into the race from all over, and Helms ended up spending, to date, at least thirteen million dollars and Hunt at least nine million. In general, more money was spent on congressional races than ever before.) Paul Simon, a liberal, squeaked through over Charles Percy for a number of reasons that had nothing to do with ideology. So, though the country may have moved to the right, it is less ideological than many analyses would make it seem.

The factors that went into the Reagan victory—Reagan's persona, his themes, the times, the various reasons people found him preferable to Mondale—contributed to the landslide, but the landslide also built upon itself, as landslides do. Mondale is a good man who could have waged a better campaign, but he went out with a kind of integrity and even courage that raised his standing in the eyes of many people. He is undoubtedly the last of a type to run for the Presidency: the last of the New Deal, non-television candidates. (He was actually a transitional figure, but didn't get that across.) The younger breed of Democrats is cooler and more trained in the medium, and whether it is a good thing that effectiveness on television counts for much in politics is irrelevant—it is a fact. (However, being "good on television" is a quality that eludes definition, and a decent and well-informed candidate could be as effective as a packaged one. Mondale's difficulty with television was to a large extent self-inflicted.) Mondale was widely considered a bore, and he knew it, because he wanted to talk about "issues." He may have tried to talk about too many of them, or in too much detail, but that is a different point. Reagan's success at running an essentially substanceless, carefully controlled campaign has been much criticized, but it will undoubtedly also be emulated, since it worked. But not everybody could pull it off.

There are some things about the returns that are noteworthy and not a little worrisome, the most important one being that sixty-six per cent of white voters supported Reagan while ninety per cent of black voters supported Mondale. White males supported Reagan sixty-eight to thirty-one. For all of the efforts made by both parties to increase turnout, it was up only very slightly (and the black vote did not increase by any dramatic amount); the exit polls suggested that new voters supported Reagan by a somewhat higher margin than those who had voted before. The Republicans out-organized the Democrats as well as out-spent them. The turnout was without question affected by the drumbeat of predictions of the outcome. As for income groups, Mondale carried only those earning under twelve thousand five hundred dollars (by fifty-three per cent to forty-six per cent). Reagan carried all age groups, and did extremely well among the youngest voters—those eighteen to twenty-four—carrying them by sixty per cent to forty per cent (Reagan had done worst among this group four years ago); the baby-boom voters—those twenty-five to thirty-nine—supported Reagan by fifty-six to forty-four. No one, not even among key Republicans, is certain that the allegiance of the young voters will remain permanently Republican. As it turned out, women supported Reagan by an even higher percentage than they had in 1980; and the exit polls indicated that Ferraro's candidacy cost the Party more votes among women than it gained. Reagan did substantially better among Hispanics than he had four years ago, and he did better among blue-collar voters than he had in 1980—receiving the votes of about fifty-three per cent of them, as opposed to about forty to forty-five per cent four years ago. The lesson was that the labor and teacher organizations can be helpful in terms of mechanics, logistics, and money in the primaries but they can't necessarily deliver their members. The other lesson that became clear to the Mondale people before the election was that their theory that Mondale could win the election by putting together a coalition of blacks, Hispanics, labor, teachers, environmentalists, and independents presumably upset with Reagan's policies on arms control and fairness fell before the feeling of too many of these people that they were well off under Reagan and, for this or other reasons, preferred him to Mondale.

Many of the Democrats are taking comfort from having pretty well held their own in Congress against the Reagan onslaught and emerged with thirty-four of the governorships. However, many other House races were extremely close, and nearly as many people voted for Republicans as for Democrats for the House, and Republicans took most of the seats not held by incumbents. It is true that there is a lot of strength—and also a lot of talent—in the Democratic Party, but it clearly has a problem with the electorate when it comes before it as a national party trying to win the Presidency. It is probably no accident that the only two Democrats to win the Presidency since John Kennedy (who did so by the narrowest of margins, and having put a Texan on the ticket) were Southerners—Johnson in 1964, in the wake of Kennedy's death, and Carter in 1976 (again, barely), in the wake of Watergate and Reagan's nearly upending Ford for the nomination. It seems clear that the Party needs to work out some new equation with its interest groups, and has to develop a coherent message. There are some signs of a temptation to wait for things to go wrong in the second Reagan term, even while there is yet another round of soul-searching.

The Republicans are facing a different set of dangers: one is hubris as a result of the landslide; the second is that the various factions will now break into open warfare, and that the right wing will go farther than the public will accept. Reagan is now a lame duck, and it is generally assumed, by his own advisers, among others, that he will not have long to put through whatever he wants to put through.

Washington and politics being what they are, the speculation about the 1988 election is already in full sway—in fact, has been for some time. Among Democrats, the talk has long since switched from which Mondale people would have what jobs to who will be the nominee in 1988. The Republican contest for the 1988 nomination had been openly under way for some time. It is now becoming fashionable among some Democrats to say that the problem with Mondale's nomination was that he was a product of the Washington "insiders." It had been said that the problem with Carter's being nominated was that he was an "outsider." The questions that the Party faces are deeper than this.

Now, of course, comes the hard part for Reagan. The deficit, which is absorbing an increasing amount of the national wealth and limiting long-term growth, as well as exposing the country to other dangers, is sitting there. Though the President says he wants to emphasize arms control in his second term, the jockeying within his Administration over arms control continues. The future direction of Central American policy and events is uncertain—and still the subject of controversy within the Administration. There is no real reason to expect Reagan to change long-standing work habits.

This morning, Mondale held a press conference, which he opened in good humor, saying, "Based on incomplete analysis of the returns, I think there's a good chance that I won't win this election." He went on to say, talking with a candor that is unusual in politics, and with a natural composure that would have stood him well in earlier days, if more people had been able to see him this way, "From the very beginning of my campaign for the nomination, I seemed to have trouble convincing young Americans and others that I had that vision of the future that I believe I have. I was unable to appeal to independents who were necessary and moderates who were necessary for my victory even though I thought my message was a moderate, practical, sound, and solid one. It didn't take." He added, "I was unable to make the case, which I thought was a strong one—and from all my experience is absolutely right—that the long-term, tough problems of our nation can only be solved by a President who masters the essential details and who is in command. . . . I was unable to make effectively the case that new leadership was needed to achieve that objective." He went on to say that he was running against a popular incumbent President, who "is very well liked, in the midst of what is perceived as good economic times and with diminished international tensions—I think of a temporary nature, but perceived as such—and with an electorate that was understandably anxious for some continuity." He defended his choice of Ferraro and his telling the people that he would raise taxes. He said, "I feel very, very strongly that I went before the American people and I told them the truth before the election about the need to bring that deficit down and about the necessity of having new revenues to bring it about, and in my opinion doing it in a fair way so that middle- and moderate-income Americans did not have to pay more taxes. I believe that one of the biggest meals of crow that this Administration will eat—and there will be several—will be this one concerning revenues. The American people were left with the impression that this deficit can be brought down to the extent that it must without tax increases. That has never been possible. It will be clear that that's not possible." He added, "And they will have to explain what they do now to the American people in light of what they implied to them in the election."

Mondale continued, explaining what he meant when he had said the night before that the seeds of defeat are sown in victory. He said that he believed the Reagan Administration would have to go after Social Security and Medicare and other social programs, and said, "I believe in the main they've left the impression with the American people that they don't intend to do that." He continued, "I believe that there's a very strong instinct in the American life for fairness. If they retreat on civil rights, as they have been, if they retreat on women's rights, as they have been, if they don't turn around and start enforcing the laws that protect the environment, if, by failing to deal with this deficit, unemployment starts rising again, as I think is a very likely prospect, I think the American people are going to be very angry. But this is the day after the election. I don't want to go into that." He talked of his doubts about the Administration's commitment to arms control and ability to plan for it, and its coherence in managing foreign policy. He said, "I hope I'm wrong in every one of those things. We wish the President well today. But if what we've seen is what we're going to see, I believe that we are going to see a strong revival of the Democratic Party in this country."

Asked about when he thought he might lose, Mondale said, "I knew it was tough from the very beginning. No one who campaigned around the country and saw the reality of what was going on could have doubted that." He said that he felt his Convention "may have been the most successful in history," and that "for a while I thought that that had changed the landscape," but "in a few weeks we were back to about that tough level." He said that he thought he had a chance after the first debate, but "I would say that my chances of winning probably disappeared at the end of the second debate. My feeling was that if you had the same kind of growth, which I doubted we'd have in the second debate, that I then had a chance to win."

Asked what advice he would give other Democrats, Mondale candidly said, "I think that, more than I was able to do, modern politics today requires a mastery of television." He said, "I think you know I've never really warmed up to television." He continued, smiling, "And in fairness to television, it's never really warmed up to me." He said, "I like to look someone in the eye and say it and listen, and there's something about that that I've never been comfortable with and I think it's obvious. I don't believe it's possible anymore to run for President without the capacity to build confidence and communications every night. It's got to be done that way." But Mondale added, "The thing that scares me about that, the thing that's held me back, is that I think more than we should American politics is losing its substance. It's losing the debate on merit. It's losing the depth that tough problems require to be discussed. And more and more it's that twenty-second snip, the angle, the shtick, whatever it is, and we need—I hope we don't lose in America—the demand that those of us who want serious office must be serious people of substance and depth and must be prepared not just to handle the ten-second gimmick that deals, say, with little things like war and peace, but what are you going to do in Lebanon, in Central America, in Nicaragua, in China, in Afghanistan, in Poland. That's one thing I really worry about. So we've got to find people that can handle it at both levels. And I would give that very, very strong emphasis." Asked if any of his primary opponents might have done better against Reagan, Mondale laughed and said, "Oh, you know, I did my best. And I worked my heart out. And I was the nominee for the Democratic Party and I made my case with all the strength I could. I believe that I made a strong case. I think history will deal kindly with this campaign and with the record that it made."

Reagan held a press conference a couple of hours later in which, responding to Mondale, he said, "My position is solid—we're not going to try to deal with the deficit problem by raising taxes," and he also said, incorrectly, that the tax-reform plan under discussion by his Administration "would not result in any individual having his taxes raised by way of a tax reform." (At the least, those who are taking more deductions than would be offset by the lower rates would be paying higher taxes.) Talking about arms control, he said, "We don't have a conflict within the Cabinet . . . and I don't know where all this talk came from." He added, "We're prepared to go forward with the arms-control talks, and I have to believe that the Soviet Union is going to join us in trying to get together." When he was asked where his Administration would find budget cuts, he referred, as he has before, to the "two thousand four hundred and seventy-eight recommendations submitted by the Grace Commission," adding, wisely, "and we know that we probably won't be able to do all of them." (Many of the Grace Commission proposals are simply politically impossible, and some suggest inflated savings.) Reagan added, "We've made a number of steps that have revealed that the government is still larded with a lot of fat and still doing things in an old-fashioned way." When he was asked whether he had received a mandate, in light of the congressional results, Reagan said, "Well, I feel that the people of this country made it very plain that they approved what we've been doing, and we're going to continue what we've been doing, and, if need be, we'll take our case to the people."

Index

Aaron, David, 129
ABC, 756
  see also Polls
Abortion, 588
  see also individual candidates
Abrams, Mike, 377–78
Acid rain, 267–68, 306
Acuff, Roy, 666
Addabbo, Joseph, 111
Adelman, Kenneth, 12, 61, 93, 98
Affluence, and voting, 398, 411, 759
Afghanistan, 141–42
Alabama
  Democratic conference, 231
  general election, 254–60
  polls, 176
  primary, 176, 231, 254–61, 357–70,
    388, 393–7
  straw poll, 176
Alaska
  caucuses, 480
Albert, Carl, Rep., 372
Albosta, Donald, Rep., 120, 129, 138
Alexander, Bill, Rep., 95, 239, 245, 249
Allain, William, 234
Allen, Richard, 58, 128–30, 132
American Civil Liberties Union
  (A.C.L.U.), 292
American Defense Education Act, 321
American Federation of Labor-Congress
  of Industrial Organizations (A.F.L.-
  C.I.O.), 22, 33, 34, 247, 340, 476
  Mondale endorsed by, 178, 182, 198,
    204, 231, 273–74, 312, 318, 326, 386,
    476–77, 719
  see also Kirkland; Labor
American Federation of State, County,
  and Municipal Employees (AFSCME)
  338, 341

American Federation of Teachers (A.F.T.),
  199, 231
American Political Science Association, 20
American Society of Newspaper Editors,
  449
Anderson, John, Rep., 122, 359, 431, 617
Andrews, Mark, Sen., 54–56, 160
Andropov, Yuri, 14, 29, 58, 142, 301, 340
Angola, 63
Argentina, 277
Ariyoshi, George, Gov., 490
Arizona
  caucuses, 417
Arkansas
  caucuses, 238–54, 398–99
  general election, 749–52
Armageddon, 732–33
Arms control, 11–15, 74, 95, 98–101,
    103–6, 111–14, 206, 580–81
  anti-satellite weaponry, 460–61, 643
  build-down, 106–10
  nuclear freeze, 83, 93–94, 104
  plutonium ban, 367
  SALT I, 73–74, 702
  SALT II, 15, 76–77, 83, 98–100, 142,
    188, 190
  Scowcroft Commission, 87, 99
  START, 48, 97–98, 100–1, 103, 108,
    216
  Vladivostok agreement, 99
  zero-zero, 12, 13, 15
  see also Missiles; "Star Wars"; *individual
    candidates*
Arms Control and Disarmament Agency,
  11–12, 61, 93
Arrington, Richard, Mayor, 257–58, 396–
  97
Askew, Reubin, Gov., 26, 37, 167, 247,
    312, 504

abortion, on, 167, 267
  campaign funds, and, 34
  candidacy announcement of, 18
  Hart, and, 373, 375
  nuclear freeze, on, 167
  polls, and, 177, 201, 233, 347
  primary campaign, 177, 201, 233, 350–
    51
  withdrawal from race, 372
Aspin, Les, Rep., 82–83, 110, 113–16
  MX, and, 82–86, 92–95, 101–2, 452
Atari Democrats, 9, 322, 367–68, 414, 541
Atwater, Lee, 571, 661–62, 715, 728
AuCoin, Les, Rep., 95, 111–14, 452, 646

Baby-boom voters, 323, 760
  see also Young voters
Bacharach, Burt, 473
BAKER Howard, Sen., 7, 52, 55, 112, 145,
    150–51, 160–64, 206, 215
  Republican Convention, and, 586–87,
    597
Baker, James, 57, 60, 120–21, 124–25,
    130, 134, 138, 158–59, 210, 217–18,
    296, 575, 677
Ball, George, 61
Baltimore Sun, 662
Barnes, Michael, Rep., 596
Barrett, Laurence, 119–23
Baxley, Bill, 482–90
Bayh, Birch, Sen., 166, 186
Beach Boys, 69
Beatty, Warren, 409, 473
Beckel, Bob, 234, 509
  Democratic Convention, and, 511, 513,
    529, 531, 534, 547, 552
  general election, and, 549, 713, 719–20,
    722, 725, 735, 736
Bentsen, Lloyd, Sen.
  Vice-Presidential candidate possibility,
    500, 511
Berman, Michael, 508, 584
Bernstein, Carl, 130
Biden, Joseph, Sen., 252, 324, 450–51
Bishop, Maurice, 154, 195
  see also Grenada
Black vote, 26, 170, 289, 529, 681–82
  general election campaign, and, 519,
    624–25, 732, 750, 759
  primary campaign, and, 40–41, 169–73,
    177, 226–27, 258, 288–89, 315, 331,

398, 407, 411, 415–16, 432, 444–48,
    456, 503
Blackwell, Unita, 234
Blakley, Ronee, 473
Blanchard, James, Gov., 399
Blue-collar vote, see Labor
Bob Jones University, 46, 544, 681
Boggs, Thomas, 186
Bograd, Paul, 458–59
Bond, Julian, 171
Bonker, Don, Rep., 646
Boone, Pat, 600
Boschwitz, Rudy, Sen., 757
Boston Globe, 302, 311, 347, 737
Bradley, Bill, Sen., 33, 324, 540–41, 758
  see also Taxes
Bradley, Tom, Mayor, 170–71, 474, 477,
    520, 635
  Vice-Presidential candidate possibility,
    503
Brady, Nicholas, 82
Breen, Jon, 16
Brennan, Joseph, Gov., 315
Bridges at Toko-Ri, The (film), 690
Briefing papers, 117–23, 129–38, 147,
    218, 578
Brown, Harold, 32, 77, 82, 90–92
Brown, Jerry, Gov., 418, 457
Bryan, Richard, Gov., 481
Bryan, William Jennings, 533
Brzezinski, Zbigniew, 81, 129
Buchanan, John, Rep., 653
Budget, see Defense; Economy; Taxes;
    individual candidates
Bumpers, Dale, Sen., 26, 36–39, 107, 324,
    433, 500–1
  Presidential candidate possibility, 18,
    168
  Vice-Presidential candidate possibility,
    500–1
Bureau of Land Management, 65
Burford, Anne Gorsuch, 65–67, 210–11,
    526, 576–77, 756
  see also E.P.A.
Burford, Robert, 65–66
Burris, Roland, 482, 496
Burt, Richard, 110
Bush, Barbara, 700
Bush, George, V.P., 8, 69, 82, 124, 127,
    416–17, 518, 586, 661, 746
  campaign (1980), 16, 586

campaign (1984), 130, 132–33, 290
campaign (1988), 586, 753
C.I.A., and, 133, 697
debate, and, 695, 697–701
defense, on, 157–58, 201
domestic policy, on, 698–99
foreign policy, on, 697–99
MX, on, 108
polls, and, 586, 637, 753
renomination, and, 607
renomination speech of, 608–10
taxes, on, 698
Vice-Presidential role of, 586
Bushkin, Kathy, 371, 403, 468–69
Byrd, Robert, Sen., 112, 140, 142, 163–64
Byrne, Jane, Mayor, 40, 375

Caddell, Patrick, 139–40, 550, 734
  Carter pollster, as, 20, 119, 121
  Hart campaign, and, 323, 327–28, 352–
    54, 358–59, 362, 365, 370, 375–77,
    381, 409, 411, 419, 427–28
  Mondale, and, 323–24
  Mondale campaign, and, 382, 643,
    682–84, 721–23, 729, 746–47
California
  general election, 457, 635–43, 675, 733,
    742, 754, 756
  polls, 28, 175–76, 675
  primary (1972), 465
  primary (1984), 20, 21, 28, 175–76, 436,
    454–59, 471–89, 491–92
  straw poll, 28, 175–76
Campion, Charles, 316–17
Carr, Vikki, 616
Carter, Jimmy, Pres., 5, 37, 98, 130, 318,
    322, 364, 429, 454, 489, 509
  Afghanistan, and, 141–42, 199, 247,
    448
  arms control, and, 99, 277
  candidacy (1976) of, 17, 21, 23–24, 269,
    316, 405
  candidacy (1980) of, 512, 743, 757
  defense, and, 15, 51, 76–77
  deficit, and, 294
  Democratic Convention, and, 522
  economic policy, and, 189, 612
  F.B.I. and C.I.A., and, 133
  Iowa caucuses (1976), and, 19
  Iran hostages, and, 131–32, 190, 595–
    96
  New Hampshire primary (1976), and,
    19, 22, 166, 310
  taxes, and, 367
  see also Arms control; Briefing papers;
    SALT
Carter, Rosalynn, 522
Casey, William, 120–21, 124–26, 131–32,
    134, 136–37, 158–59, 218, 704
Castro, Fidel, 154
Catholics, 570
Caucuses, 18, 20
  see also individual states
CBS, 113, 408, 491–92, 669, 756
  see also Polls
Celeste, Richard, Gov., 20–21, 427, 643,
    748
Central America, 62–65, 145–46, 422–23,
    451
  see also individual countries
Central Intelligence Agency (C.I.A.), 125–
    28, 130–36, 158, 218
  Nicaragua, and, 423–24, 704, 706, 732
Charles, Eugenia, 154
Charles, Ray, 616
Chicago Council on Foreign Relations, 401
Childers, W. D., 372, 378
China
  Reagan's visit to, 290, 452, 578, 713
Chrysler Corporation bailout, 399, 413–
    14, 419, 436
Church, Frank, Sen., 418
Churchill, Winston, 62
Cisneros, Henry, Mayor, 521, 541
  Vice-Presidential candidate possibility,
    503–4
Civil Rights Commission, 160, 210, 243–
    44
Clark, William, 13, 49, 50, 57, 59–61, 80,
    124–25, 158–59, 217–18, 594
  Central America, on, 62, 64, 146
  environment, on, 306
  Lebanon, on, 145
  MX, on, 85
Clements, William, 82
Cline, Ray, 131, 134
Clinton, Bill, Gov., 238
Coelho, Tony, Rep., 511
Cohen, William, Sen., 106–7
Coleman, Milton, 416

Collins, Martha Layne, Gov., 480, 491
  Vice-Presidential candidate possibility,
    503
Commission on Presidential Nominations.
  See Hunt Commission
Commission on Strategic Forces, 80–81
Comprehensive Employment and
    Training Act (CETA), 191
Congressional Budget Office (C.B.O.), 97,
    294, 298, 589
Connecticut
  general election, 668–69, 675, 748, 756
  primary, 408
Conservative Opportunity Society, 590
Coors, Joseph, 66
Corbin, Paul, 136
Costa Rica, 451
Council of Economic Advisers, 206, 296
Cox, Archibald, 14
Cranston, Alan, Sen., 26–29, 268, 329,
    635
  arms, on, 167
  campaign funds, and, 166, 253
  candidacy announcement of, 18
  nuclear freeze, on, 27, 167, 329
  polls, and, 28, 175–77, 266, 347
  primary campaign, 21, 28, 166–67,
    175–77, 200, 221–22, 312, 329–30,
    350–51, 456
  strategy of, 27–28
  taxes, on, 167
  unemployment, on, 329–30
  withdrawal from race, 351
Crawford, Charles, 135
Criswell, W. A., 586, 616
C-SPAN, 591–92
Cuomo, Mario, Gov., 168, 188, 200, 331,
    410, 433, 495, 501–2, 524, 538, 605,
    618, 669, 714
  Democratic Convention, and, 520, 523–
    28, 551
  Vice-Presidential candidate possibility,
    501–2
Cutler, Lloyd, 82

Dailey, Peter, Amb., 14
Daley, Richard M., 40, 375
Dallas *Morning News*, 586
Dallas *Times Herald*, 609
Dam, Kenneth, 104, 217
Danforth, John, Sen., 607
Darman, Richard, 124–25, 296

Darr, Carol, 135
Deaver, Michael, 60, 69, 124, 158–59, 567,
    573, 575
Debates
  Democratic, 188, 337–38, 352, 386–87,
    408, 410, 412–13, 430
  Presidential, 621–22, 662, 674, 678,
    686–97, 705–8, 727–31
  Republican (1980), 16
  Vice-Presidential, 697–701
Defense, 47–48, 142
  budget, 7, 51–53, 207, 577
  Carter administration, and, 51, 52, 76–
    77
  weapons, 50, 54
  see also Arms control; Missiles; *individual
    candidates*
Democratic Convention, 310, 493, 498–
    565
  ballot of, 540, 545–48
  blacks, and, 529–31, 536–40
  brokered, possibility of, 22–23, 425
  Cuomo, and, 522–28
  Ferraro, and, 508, 552–55
  Hart, and, 514–16, 529–31, 541–47
  Hispanics, and, 538–39
  Jackson, and, 493, 512–20, 530–38
  Jews, and, 532–33, 536, 539
  Mondale, and, 521–22, 545, 559–64,
    721, 726
  nominating rules, and, 399, 418, 442,
    445
  nomination, and, 547–48, 559, 565
  participants in, 540–41
  platform of, 495, 512–17, 528–38, 541–
    45
    arms control, 530–31
    Fairness Commission, 521, 528–31,
      540, 552
    Persian Gulf/Central America, 521–22,
      528, 530, 533
    quotas, 528, 531–32
    runoff primaries, 529–30, 532
  superdelegates to, 514–15, 532
  voter registration drive (general
    election), and, 530, 538, 550
  see also Lance
Democratic National Committee, 22, 167,
    499, 511
  credentials committee, 495–96
  fundraising, 510–11
  platform committee, 495

Democratic Party, 540–41, 603–4, 662, 746, 760–61
  factionalism in, 25, 491, 495
  goals of, 25–26
  identity, and, 591
  Mid-term Conference of, 250
  national campaign, and, 166
  unity, and, 483–85, 487, 512, 559–60
Des Moines *Register*, 266, 312
Deutch, John, 82
Dicks, Norman, Rep., 95, 101–2, 104–5, 108, 110, 114
A Different Kind of Presidency, 369
Dioxin, 210
Disability benefits, 751
District of Columbia
  general election, 709
  polls, 675
  primary, 444, 546
Dodd, Christopher, Sen., 64, 372, 467
Doe, Samuel, 11
Dole, Elizabeth, 581, 594, 599
Dole, Robert, Sen., 7–9, 338, 581, 585, 599, 604
  Republican Convention, and, 585, 587
Domenici, Pete, Sen., 52–54, 56–57
Donilon, Tom, 480, 482–83, 490, 491–92
  Democratic Convention, and, 511, 516, 521, 529, 531, 540, 545–47
Donovan, Raymond, 676–78
Donovan, William, 125
Downey, Thomas, Rep., 95, 102, 109–10, 155
Drake, Tom, 254, 257
Duarte, José Napoléon, 451, 578, 704
  see also El Salvador
Dukakis, Michael, Gov., 200, 258, 583
  Vice-Presidential candidate possibility, 503–4
Dye, Brad, 482, 546

Eagleton, Thomas, Sen., 481, 484
Earl, Anthony, 627
Eastwood, Clint, 667
Economy
  consumer spending, 71
  deficits, 3, 4, 7, 10–11, 50–51, 53, 139, 449, 571, 720, 725
  inflation, 71, 208, 589, 612, 710, 714
  interest rates, 3, 70, 449, 589, 710, 714–15
  oil prices, 710

recession, 71, 710
recovery, 10, 70–71, 117, 147, 208, 523
soup kitchens, 207–8
see also Unemployment; *individual candidates*
Education, Department of, 199, 416
Edwards, Edwin, Gov., 444
Eidenberg, Eugene, 22
Eisenhower, Dwight D., Pres., 30, 609, 643, 655, 710
Election, 1984
  election day, 756–58
  popular vote, 709
  results, 709, 756–60
  split tickets, 758
  state and congressional election results, 758–61
  see also individual candidates
Electoral College, 569–70, 624, 709, 746, 756
Elkhart (Ind.) *Truth*, 122–23
Ellsberg, Daniel, 137
El Salvador, 63, 451, 578, 704
  death squads, 216–17
  House action, 451
  see also Reagan
Enders, Thomas, 63
Entitlement programs, 53, 56
Environment, 26, 760
Environmental Protection Agency (E.P.A.), 65–69, 210–11, 268, 306
  Superfund, 67, 459
Equal Rights Amendment (E.R.A.), 68, 187, 588
Ethics in Government Act, 120

Fahrenkopf, Frank, 510
Falwell, Jerry, Rev., 585–86, 600, 630, 653, 681, 693
Farrakhan, Louis, 416, 447–48, 517–18
Fauntroy, Walter, Rep., 529
Fazio, Vic, Rep., 95, 101
Federal Bureau of Investigation (F.B.I.), 133, 138
Federal Election Commission (F.E.C.), 415, 464
  delegate committees, 438–42, 465–66
  Ferraro, 581–82
Federal Reserve Board, 41, 299, 449, 589
Feldstein, Martin, 10, 206–7, 296, 299, 449–50
Feinstein, Dianne, Mayor, 474, 506–7

Vice-Presidential candidate possibility,
    503–4
Ferraro, Geraldine, Rep., 498–500, 503,
    505–8, 549, 551, 553–54, 623, 625,
    627–28, 697, 714–15, 743, 752–54
  abortion, on, 658–59, 668
  debate, and, 695, 697–701
  deficit, on, 629
  endorsements of, 504
  financial problems, and, 581–84, 600–2,
    658, 723, 753
  foreign policy, on, 627, 699
  Labor Day events, and, 617–18, 626–31
  labor vote, and, 507
  Lebanon, on, 628, 676
  nomination of, 552
  polls, and, 626–27, 637, 752, 754, 760
  Reagan, and, 508
  speeches of, 753–54
    acceptance, 552–55
    Labor Day, 627–31
    Long Beach, 637
    Portland, 646–47
  women's vote, and, 760
  see also Zaccaro
Field, Mervin, 457, 491
Fletcher, Norman, 491
Florida
  general election, 233–34, 570
  polls, 175, 177
  primary, 19, 177, 201, 233, 261, 371–80,
    383–84, 387–90, 397, 431
  straw poll, 177, 201
  uncommitted delegates, 398
Flynn, Raymond, Mayor, 353
Foley, Thomas, Rep., 86, 94–95, 101
Folsom, Jim, Jr., 257
Food stamp programs, 191
Ford, Gerald, Pres., 125, 130, 469, 585,
    599–600
  arms control, and, 99
  Republican Convention, and, 585
Ford, Michael, 251
Ford, Wendell, Sen., 480
Frank, Barney, Rep., 103
Friedan, Betty, 505
Friedman, Milton, 293
Fundraising, Democratic, 8, 22, 175, 473,
    703
  general election, 584
  registration drive, 538–39
  telethon, 510

"unity" party, 483–85
  see also Political-Action Committees
Fundraising, Republican, 600, 758
Futrell, Mary, 481

Gambino, Robert, 133
Gambling with History, 119
Garn, Jake, Sen., 77
Garrick, Robert, Adm., 131–32
Gemayel, Amin, 150, 153, 213–14, 302–3
  see also Lebanon
Gender gap. See Women's vote
General Advisory Committee on Arms
    Control, 81
Georgia
  general election, 743
  primary, 260–61, 384–89, 395, 397
Gephardt, Richard, Rep., 33, 95, 324
  see also Taxes
Gergen, David, 120, 124–25, 129–30, 134
Gingrich, Newt, Rep., 590–92
Giordano, Joseph, 672
Glenn, Annie, 180, 182, 269
Glenn, David, 270
Glenn, John, Sen., 18, 26, 29–32, 180–81,
    185, 193, 271–72, 275, 286, 516, 710
  arms control, on, 31–32, 187–90, 224,
    229–30, 274–78
  campaign funds, and, 166, 186–87, 223,
    253, 266, 278–80, 337, 397, 539
  candidacy announcement of, 174
  defense, on, 201–2, 274–75
  domestic policy, on, 191
  economic policy, on, 188–89, 224
  endorsements of, 200, 273–74, 427
  energy policy, on, 282–84
  environmental policy, on, 267–68
  E.R.A., on, 187
  foreign policy, on, 193–95, 224, 228
  Glenn: The Astronaut Who Would Be
    President, 182
  Grenada, on, 194
  Hart, and, 387
  Lebanon, on, 193–94, 226, 263–64
  polls, and, 174–77, 218, 221, 233, 261–
    62, 266, 311, 336, 338, 347, 353, 355
  primary campaign, 20–21, 31, 165–67,
    174, 176–78, 185–90, 198, 202, 204–
    5, 233–34, 251, 260–86, 312, 314,
    336–38, 350, 352, 356, 361, 397, 432,
    710
  Right Stuff, The, 180, 182, 200, 261, 349

Senate career of, 184
special interest groups, and, 191–93
Social Security, on, 187
strategy of, 178–84, 263, 270–71
taxes, on, 190, 240, 274–75, 314–15
withdrawal from race, 397–98
Glenn, Lyn, 270
Glickman, Dan, Rep., 95, 101
Goldsmith, Judy, 481
Goldwater, Barry, Sen., 53, 77, 150, 424, 556, 604
Goode, Wilson, Mayor, 315, 415–16
  Vice-Presidential candidate possibility, 503
Goodman, Robert, Lt., 222, 225, 241, 330
Good Morning America, 89, 108, 382–83
Gore, Albert, Jr., Rep., 84–86, 95–98, 101–4, 108, 110–11, 114
Gorsuch, Anne. *See* Burford
Gorton, Slade, Sen., 54
Grace Commission, 298–99, 764
Grace, J. Peter, 298
Graham, Bob, Gov., 481, 490, 496
Grassley, Charles, Sen., 54–55
Gray, Robert, 131, 135
Grenada, 149, 154–57, 160–64, 194, 609, 701
Grier, Roosevelt, 594
Gromyko, Andrei, 658, 673, 710

Hagan, Tim, 21, 234
Hahn, Kenneth, 474
Haig, Alexander, 12–13, 59, 746
  Central America, on, 62–63
  Lebanon, on, 144
  MX, on, 48, 82
Halper, Stefan, 130–31, 133–34
Hamer, Fannie Lou, 535
Hamilton, William, 182, 262–63, 337
Harkin, Thomas, Sen., 756–57
Harris, Fred, 166
Hart, Andrea, 473
Hart, Gary, Sen., 33, 168, 360–61, 364, 366, 370–71, 374, 377, 383, 398, 405, 411–12, 431, 459, 462–63, 489–90, 544, 550, 550, 591, 693
  acid rain, on, 453
  age, and, 32, 321
  arms control, on, 35, 168, 363, 367, 388, 401, 460–61
  budget, on, 374, 385

campaign funds, and, 321, 328, 365, 426, 439, 464, 467, 473, 539
campaign, internal dissension in, 461–62, 514–15
candidacy announcement of, 18, 255
concession of, 443, 464, 493–96, 514–16, 529–30
debates, and, 352, 386–87, 408, 410, 412, 430
defense, on, 33, 35, 321, 368–69, 376
delegates, and, 417, 434–35, 439–41, 454, 467, 480, 489, 492, 493, 516, 539–40, 546–47
Democratic Convention, and, 512, 514–17, 530–31, 541–45, 547
domestic policy, on, 320–21, 367, 376, 378–79, 399, 472
economic policy, on, 367–68
endorsement of Mondale, 546
endorsements of, 371–72, 399, 427, 467
environment, on, 453, 459–60
foreign policy, on, 374–75, 401–2, 406–8
general election, 418, 431, 550, 591, 635, 693, 710, 732
Iran, on, 430
Israel, on, 379–80, 402–5, 430
Jewish vote, and, 405
labor, and, 322, 326, 398, 412–16, 428, 465, 476
Mondale, and, 326–28, 351–52, 365–66, 387, 470, 487–88, 494–95
name, and, 322–23
Navy commission of, 35, 373
New Democracy, A, 356, 366–67, 413
nuclear freeze, on, 35, 168, 363, 460–61
oil, on, 417
polls, and, 36, 176, 311, 314, 327, 347, 355, 400, 408, 410–11, 426–27, 456–58
primary campaign, 22, 26–28, 32–36, 166–67, 176, 198, 221–22, 266, 312, 314, 317, 322–23, 350–81, 389, 391–99, 400–5, 408–21, 425–32, 434–37, 448, 453–60, 467, 469–74, 480, 491–92, 546–47
Senate career of, 363–64, 373, 542
strategy of, 328–29, 360–63, 377, 409–12, 417–20, 430–31, 435–36, 464–65
taxes, on, 33, 321, 324, 363, 367, 408, 413
themes of, 378, 387, 401

Vice-Presidential candidate possibility, 484, 502–3
young voters, and, 33, 323
Hart, John, 373, 473
Hart, Lee, 373, 375, 458, 473
Hart, Peter, 429, 547, 560, 624, 722, 725, 727–28, 734–35, 738, 746–47
Hartman, David, 383
Hatcher, Richard, Mayor, 529
Hawaii
general election, 742
primary, 397, 546
Hawn, Goldie, 473
Hazardous-waste dumps, 66–69, 702
Helms, Jesse, Sen., 143, 585, 709, 725, 758
Helms, Richard, 82
Henkel, Oliver, 365, 410, 412, 418–20, 427, 435–36, 461–62, 495, 515, 533, 545
Hart, on, 405
Hennessy, William, 547
Heritage Foundation, 54
Himmelman, Harold, 361
Hispanic vote, 169–70, 173, 288, 426, 456, 521, 760
Democratic Convention, 538–39
general election, 570, 739
Hodsoll, Frank, 123
Hogan, Mark, 463–64
Holliday, Jennifer, 565
Hollings, Fritz, Sen.
candidacy announcement of, 18
economic policy, on, 319
polls, and, 176–77, 347
primary campaign, 26, 166–68, 221–22, 312, 318–20, 347, 350–51, 399, 467
withdrawal from race, 399
Holman, Carl, 445–48
Honduras, 451
Hope, Bob, 600, 754
House of Representatives
Budget committee, 186
Intelligence committee, 424
Judiciary committee, 119
Post Office and Civil Service committee, Human Resources subcommittee, 120
see also specific issues
Hugel, Max, 126
Humphrey, Hubert, V.P., 39, 243, 316, 334, 345, 402, 465, 556, 668
Humphrey, Muriel, Sen., 668

Humphrey, Skip, 481
Hunt Commission, 18–21
Hunt, James, Gov., 18, 725, 758
Hunt, Nelson Bunker, 600
Hyland, William, 58, 63

Idaho
caucuses, 454, 546
Illinois
delegates, 398
general election, 659, 662, 680, 734, 749, 752, 756
polls, 407, 662
primary, 19, 171, 331, 375, 398, 400–1, 405, 407
Immigration, 521, 704–5
see also Simpson-Mazzoli
Independents, 398, 410, 431, 549, 550, 624, 750, 760, 762
India, 277
Indiana
primary, 425, 427, 430–31, 448
Ingram, Carroll, 234
Inouye, Daniel, Sen., 162
Interior, Department of, 65–66, 267
Iowa
caucuses, 18, 19, 22, 28, 166–67, 177, 198, 260–86, 311, 337–38, 350, 361, 402
general election, 659, 662, 734, 744, 748, 752, 754, 756
polls, 22, 175, 177, 662
straw poll, 22, 177
Iran
hostages, 131–32, 651
intelligence, 190
Isaacs, Maxine, 247, 389, 507
Israel, 213–14
Jerusalem as capital, 379–80, 402–3, 405

Jackson, Henry, Sen., 75, 79, 85–86, 91, 98, 146, 150, 186, 304, 402, 733
Jackson, Jesse, Rev., 331–32, 416, 518–20
black vote, and, 398, 411, 415–16, 444–48, 455–56, 519, 732
candidacy announcement of, 168, 222
Central America, and, 518
concession of, 444, 493–94, 535
Cuba, and, 517–19, 606, 702
delegates, and, 434, 445, 454, 516, 539, 546–47

Democratic Convention, and, 467, 512–20, 530–38, 545, 547, 552
endorsements of, 331, 375
general election, 517, 570, 679, 681, 732
Goodman's release, and, 225–26, 330
Jews, and, 354, 416, 447, 456, 517–18
Mondale, and, 442–43, 496, 517, 519–20, 624–25
polls, and, 174, 233, 311, 338, 347, 355
primary campaign, 41, 167, 169–74, 227, 233, 239, 241–42, 257–58, 330–36, 350, 354, 397–99, 403–4, 411, 415, 417–18, 426, 430–31, 444–48, 455–56, 483–84, 491–92, 503–4, 519–20, 546, 744–45
security, and, 416
social justice, and, 332–34
Syria, and, 225–26, 330
taxes, on, 413
Jackson, Maynard, 625
Jackson, Michael (radio personality), 485
Jackson, Michael (singer), 550–51
Jefferson-Jackson Day dinner, 22, 177, 188
Jennings, Jerry, 130
Jepsen, Roger, Sen., 757
Jewish vote, 181, 331–32, 354, 405, 407, 416, 447, 456, 517–18, 570, 744–45, 750
see also individual candidates
Jewish Defense League, 354
Johnson, James, 25, 41, 198, 200–1, 233–34, 249–52, 254, 264, 314–16, 339–40, 359, 375, 380–81, 394–95, 406, 419, 429, 434, 436, 479–82, 491, 509
delegate committees, and, 440
Democratic Convention, and, 531, 539, 548–49
general election, and, 510–11, 550, 584, 619, 624, 642–43, 722, 734–38, 743
Hart, on, 405, 431
Reagan, on, 621–23
Vice-Presidential nominee, and, 504
see also Mondale, strategy
Johnson, Katie, 615
Johnson, Lyndon, Pres., 12, 73, 182, 243, 310, 619
Joint Chiefs of Staff, 190, 260
Lebanon, and, 150, 225, 302
MX, and, 76–77, 79, 91
Jones, David, Gen., 260
Jones, James, Rep., 186
Jordan, Hamilton, 17

Jordan, Vernon, 445
Justice, Department of, 125, 128, 136, 217–18

Kantor, Mickey, 457, 474
Kaplan, Martin, 258, 532, 551, 643, 718, 721–22
Kassebaum, Nancy, Sen., 112
Kasten, Robert, Sen., 589
see also Taxes
Kean, Thomas, 458
Keefe, Robert, 186, 337–38
Kefauver, Estes, Sen., 310
Kelley, Paul X., Commandant, 163
Kemp, Jack, Rep., 8–9, 586, 589, 590, 599
see also Taxes
Kennan, George, 110
Kennedy, Edward, Sen., 135–36, 153, 163, 180, 209, 433, 514, 523, 557
candidacy (1980) of, 24, 178, 311, 316, 378, 512
candidacy (1984), possibility of, 21, 25, 168
Democratic Convention, and, 557–58
Kennedy, John F., Pres., 17–18, 35, 136, 548, 632, 634, 686
arms control, and, 347
Glenn, and, 179–80, 183, 272, 279
Hart, and, 328–29, 360, 369–71, 379, 412, 544
Reagan, and, 608, 668, 692, 731, 740, 747
Kennedy, Robert F., Sen., 136, 180, 272, 457
Hart, and, 329, 459, 544
King, Carole, 320
King, Coretta Scott, 41, 389
King, Martin Luther, Jr., Rev., 333
King, Martin Luther, Sr., Rev., 389
Kirkland, Irena, 475
Kirkland, Lane, 204, 280, 312, 318, 455, 475–77, 509, 511, 618
see also A.F.L.-C.I.O.; Labor
Kirkpatrick, Jeane, Amb., 159, 747
Central America, on, 63–64, 704
Republican Convention, and, 594–97
Kissinger, Henry, 74, 81, 159
Central America, on, 146, 304
MX, on, 82, 85
Knute Rockne—All American (film), 746, 749
Koch, Edward, Mayor, 410
Korean airliner, 139–40, 142–43, 157

Krol, John, Cardinal, 667–69

Labor
  general election, and, 422, 507, 570,
    573, 618, 624, 667, 681, 750, 752, 760
  Primary campaign, and, 26, 288, 291,
    318, 342–43, 346, 398, 411–16, 428,
    465, 475–79
  see also individual candidates and
    individual labor unions
Laffer, Arthur, 48
La Follette, Robert, 628
Laird, Melvin, 76, 82
Lake, Jim, 568, 664
Lance, Bert, 499, 508–11, 515, 529, 539,
    583–84, 626, 656, 679, 715
Landry, Tom, 603
Lavelle, Rita, 68, 211
  see also E.P.A.
Law, Bernard, Archbishop, 669
Laxalt, Paul, Sen., 8, 292, 605–6, 652–53,
    693
Leach, James, Rep., 593
League of Conservation Voters, 268
League of Women Voters debates, 337–
    38, 352, 386–87, 412, 430
Lebanon, 143–46, 149–53, 160–61, 163,
    193–94, 206, 213–15, 217–18, 422,
    660–61, 672, 675–76, 680, 706, 752
  House action, 150–51
  Senate action, 149–50
Legal Services Corporation, 210
Lehrman, Lewis, 136
Leone, Richard, 619–20, 626, 640, 643,
    683–84, 722–23, 729
Levitas, Elliott, Rep., 109
Lewis, Ann, 510
Long, Gillis, Rep., 95, 491, 496
Long, Robert L. J., Adm., 225
Los Angeles Herald Examiner, 485
Los Angeles Times, 5, 174, 176, 473, 486,
    672
Los Angeles World Affairs Council, 50
Lott, Trent, Rep., 590
Louisiana
  Primary, 444
Love Canal, 67
Lyons, John, 82

McBrien, Richard, Father, 669
McCarthy, Eugene, Sen., 168–69, 200,
    310, 312

McCarthy, Joseph, Sen., 146
McCarthy, Leo, Lt. Gov., 200
McCone, John, 82
McCreight, Rex, 273–74
McDonald, Wesley, Adm., 156
McEvoy, John, 464, 516
McFarlane, Robert, 80–82, 108, 159, 211,
    302
McGovern, George, Sen.
  arms control, on, 168
  campaigns of (1972, 1976), 200, 316,
    323, 457, 465
  candidacy announcement of, 167
  Hart, and, 33, 35, 329, 387
  Mondale, and, 330, 484
  polls, and, 175, 347
  primary campaign, 17, 25, 39, 167,
    221–22, 318, 330, 350, 397, 470,
    483–85, 516, 545
  withdrawal from race, 397–98
McGrory, Mary, 61–62
Mackay, Kenneth, 372
McNally, Antoinette, 318, 320
McNamara, Robert, 83
McWherter, Ned, 238
Magnuson, Warren, Sen., 104
Maine
  caucuses, 19, 200, 315–16, 359, 546
  polls, 176–77
  straw poll, 176–77, 315
Manatt, Charles, 342, 445, 499, 508–11,
    529, 583
Mann, Thomas, 20
Martin, Fred, 628
Maryland
  general election, 662, 749
  polls, 652
  primary, 425
Mason, Marsha, 473
Massachusetts
  general election, 546, 747–48, 757
  polls, 36, 176
  primary, 36, 176, 198, 355, 397–98
  straw poll, 36, 176
Mathias, Charles McC., Sen., 145, 152,
    160–61, 190, 593
Matsui, Robert, Rep., 109
Medicare and Medicaid, 50, 53
  see also individual candidates
Meese, Edwin, 5, 60, 124, 131, 141, 159,
    208–10, 218, 238, 238, 305, 509
  attorney general, nomination as, 292,
    421, 677

confirmation hearings of, 421
Meet the Press, 7, 240, 268
Metzenbaum, Howard, Sen., 183
Michel, Robert, Rep., 587, 591
Michener, James, 690
Michigan
    caucuses, 21–22, 201, 399, 401, 546
    general election, 748
Mikulski, Barbara, Rep., 532
Miller, Zell, Lt. Gov., 238
Milwaukee *Sentinel*, 176
Minnesota
    general election, 709, 748, 754, 756–57
    primary, 251–52, 398
Missiles, 76–77
    Anti-Ballistic Missile System (ABM), 75–
        76, 78, 87, 89–90
    Big Bird, 78
    cruise missiles, 74, 155, 189–90, 215
    Europe, and, 14–15
    ICBM, 101, 103
    Midgetman, 85, 87, 95, 99, 102–3, 105–
        6, 110
    Minuteman, 74–75, 87–88
    Multiple Independently Targeted
        Reentry Vehicles (MIRVs), 73–74, 76,
        106
    Pershing, 189, 215
    throw weight, 99–101, 108, 157
    see also MX
Mississippi
    caucuses, 232–38, 399, 546
Missouri
    caucuses, 426
    general election, 734, 749
Mitchell, George, Sen., 315, 481
Mitchell, John, 126
Moe, Richard, 491
Mondale, Joan, 317, 505
Mondale, Walter, V.P., 26, 39–44, 180–81,
    185, 195–97, 224–32, 255, 298, 312–
    14, 322, 326, 349, 352–53, 361, 380–
    81, 383, 392–93, 404, 408, 411, 474–
    75, 478, 490, 500, 507, 521–22, 545,
    556, 559–60, 569, 571, 622–23, 631,
    678–79, 716–18, 739, 741, 747, 759,
    761–62
    agriculture, on, 247–48
    arms control, on, 41, 188, 224, 229–30,
        257, 277, 281, 340, 347–48, 385, 401,
        644–46, 648, 707
    black vote, and, 40–41, 171, 173, 222,
        226, 241–44, 258, 315, 407, 517,
    624–25, 700, 759
    budget proposal, and, 339, 562, 632–
        33, 638, 656–59, 726
    campaign ads, 743–44, 755
    campaign funds, and, 34, 40, 166, 251,
        253, 312, 321, 415, 426, 439–41, 462,
        466–67, 510, 539, 556, 715
    candidacy announcement of, 18, 42–43
    Carter, and, 41, 199, 247, 408, 429–30,
        717
    Chicago Mayoralty race, and, 40, 171
    civil rights, on, 243–44, 396, 483
    concession of, 757
    debates, and, 188, 337–38, 352, 386–
        87, 408, 410, 412–13, 430, 621–22,
        662, 674, 678, 686–94, 696–97, 705–
        8, 727–31
    defense, on, 199, 201–2, 561, 644, 702–
        3, 706
    deficit, on, 239–40, 246, 485–87, 562–
        63, 620, 632–33, 637–38, 656–59,
        726
    delegate committees, and, 415, 438–42,
        465–67, 495
    delegates, and, 417, 434–35, 438–41,
        454, 466, 479–82, 490–93, 496, 516,
        533, 546–47
    domestic policy, on, 230–31, 264, 345–
        46, 385, 399, 671–72
    economic policy, on, 188, 224, 235–36,
        239–41, 247, 255–56, 258–59, 561
    education policy, on, 44, 244, 640–42,
        756
    elderly, on the, 389–90
    Electoral College, and, 569–70, 624
    endorsements of, 171, 200, 231, 258,
        315, 338, 342, 353, 364, 375, 382,
        386, 389, 410, 415–16, 427, 474, 514,
        557, 624, 719
    environmentalists, and, 267–68, 760
    environmental policy, on, 230, 267–68,
        702, 756
    fairness issue, and, 237, 248
    farmers, and, 245–49, 339, 662
    foreign policy, on, 224, 227–29, 231,
        281, 343–44, 347–48, 401–2, 406–7,
        670–71
    general election, 287–88, 418, 431, 434,
        488–89, 510, 546–47, 556, 570, 591,
        617–52, 656–59, 662–64, 669–70,
        675, 683–86, 694, 703, 709–10, 717,
        723–31, 734, 738–39, 749–52, 756–
        57

Glenn, and, 394

Grenada, on, 194–95, 596

Hart, and, 326–28, 351, 380–85, 387, 391–94, 398, 400–2, 406–15, 417–21, 425–38, 444, 454–55, 487, 496–97, 499, 511–12, 520, 529–30, 714

Hispanic vote, and, 426, 456, 521, 739, 760

homosexuals, and, 40, 483

independents, and, 750, 760, 762

industrial policy, on, 258–59

Jackson, and, 442–43, 446, 455–56, 475, 487, 496–97, 499, 509, 511–13, 517, 521, 529–30, 624–25

Jewish vote, and, 407, 456, 750

Labor Day events, 617–18, 626–37

labor vote, and, 256, 342, 343, 346, 395–96, 398, 413, 426, 453, 476–79, 624, 750, 752, 760

leadership qualities of, 555–57, 619–22, 724, 762

Lebanon, on, 225–26, 344, 660–61, 676, 702–3

Medicare, on, 260, 382, 396, 688

nomination of, 360–61, 393, 492–94, 547–48, 559–65

nuclear freeze, on, 340, 347, 388, 632, 645–46, 649

nuclear power, on, 453

oil, on, 417

Olympics, on, 626

polls, and, 174–77, 196–97, 200, 218, 221, 233, 261, 266, 309, 311, 338–39, 347, 355, 388, 398, 400, 407–9, 428–29, 455–57, 491, 499, 548–50, 555, 566–67, 584, 618, 620–21, 636–38, 649–50, 659, 661–62, 674–75, 691, 703, 714, 716–17, 725–26, 728, 734–35, 738, 744, 746–47, 752

poor, on the, 750

press conference (post-election), 761–63

primary campaign, 21, 165–67, 171, 174–78, 185–86, 188, 198, 200–5, 221–22, 231–60, 263–66, 269, 275–76, 287–88, 309–18, 338–56, 359, 381, 383–400, 403, 406–21, 425–32, 434–40, 448, 454–59, 474–90, 491–92

religion, on, 633–34, 652–56

Social Security, on, 342, 382, 390, 394–96, 477, 659, 688, 740

Soviet Union, on the, 228, 281, 340, 564, 632, 649, 673

special interest groups, and, 40, 43–44, 178, 198–99, 204, 230, 312–14, 340, 346, 349, 351–52, 478, 558, 715, 718

speeches of, 719, 762–63
  acceptance, 559–64, 721, 726
  A.F.L.-C.I.O., 719
  American Legion, 643–46
  Boston, 751
  Cleveland, 740–41, 750–51
  Compton, California, 637–39
  concession, 757
  George Washington University, 652–55, 684, 722–23, 740
  Labor Day (Merrill, Wisc.), 631–34, 721–22
  Los Angeles, 756
  National Press Club, 223–32
  New Brunswick, New Jersey, 684–86
  New York City, 750
  Pittsburgh, 694
  Portland, 647–49
  San Jose, California, 639–42

strategy of, 178, 197–201, 243, 246, 249–52, 258, 382, 393–95, 406, 412–13, 418–21, 428, 435–36, 479–83, 549, 555–56, 619–24, 650, 652, 682–83, 686, 723, 729–30, 738–39

taxes, on, 237–38, 240, 313–14, 339–41, 413, 562–63, 633, 638, 651, 656–57, 685–86, 721, 724–27, 746, 749, 762

teachers, and, 760

television, and, 185, 259, 393–94, 493, 627, 669, 695, 739, 759, 763–64

themes, of, 232, 348–49, 385–86, 488, 507, 556, 561–64, 624, 633, 718–21, 739, 751–52, 755–56

toxic waste, on, 702

trade balance, on, 247, 259, 485–87

Vice-Presidential role, and, 41–42, 193, 203, 419, 429

Vice-Presidential selection, 484–85, 496, 498–507, 762

vulnerabilities of, political, 313, 357–58, 430, 478, 716–17, 720–21, 759

white vote, and, 743, 759

women's vote, and, 743

young voters, and, 384, 398, 416, 550–51, 759–60

see also Democratic Convention
Mountain States Legal Foundation, 66
Moynihan, Daniel Patrick, Sen., 155, 162, 200, 405, 410, 618, 672
Muskie, Edmund, Sen., 17, 39, 200, 254, 310
MX, 32, 41, 72–116
  Air Force, and, 76–78, 85
  criticism of, 88–91
  Deep Underground Missile Basing (DUMB), 78
  Dense Pack, 78–79, 83, 86, 106
  "fratricide," 78
  funding of, 79, 109, 112, 142
  House action, 79–80, 94–95, 102, 108–16, 142, 451–52, 704
  Joint Chiefs of Staff, and, 76–77, 79, 91
  Multiple Protective Shelters (MPS), 76–78, 86
  Peacekeeper, 85, 103
  Scowcroft Commission, 80–103, 108, 114
  Senate action, 79, 92–94, 112, 142, 704
  shell-game system, 87, 91
  shelter system, 77–78
  silos, 87–88, 91–93
  "window of vulnerability," 75, 87, 89
  see also Arms control; Missiles

National Association of Evangelicals, 46
National Conservative Political Action Committee (NCPAC), 341–42
National Education Association (N.E.A.), 33–34, 178, 199, 204, 231, 321, 385, 481
  Mondale endorsed by, 178, 231
National Organization for Women (N.O.W.), 187, 231, 481
  Mondale endorsed by, 231
  Vice-Presidential candidate selection, and, 504–6
National Religious Broadcasters, 292
National Security Council (N.S.C.), 58–59, 61, 64, 81, 129–30, 135, 159, 211
National Women's Political Caucus, 178, 387
Nativist movement, 681–82, 715
NBC, 668, 756
Nebraska
  primary, 425, 437

Nevada
  primary, 397
New Democracy, A, 356, 366–67, 413
New Federalism, 3
New Hampshire
  primary, 18–19, 127, 166–67, 261, 267, 270, 273, 309–11, 316–20, 329–30, 336–56, 359, 381, 397, 431, 546
New Jersey
  general election, 546–47, 684–86, 758
  polls, 176
  primary, 176, 453–60, 491
  straw poll, 176
New Jersey (U.S.S.), 213, 303
Newman, Paul, 320
New Mexico
  primary, 491
New patriotism, 643, 666, 682
New Right, 585, 590–91, 593–94
Newsweek, 48, 159, 360
Newton, Wayne, 69
New York
  general election, 660, 744–45, 748–50, 756
  polls, 407, 410
  primary, 405, 410–11, 431, 547
New York magazine, 360, 387–88
New York *Post,* 753
New York *Times,* 119, 121, 130–32, 136
  see also Polls
Nicaragua, 63, 146, 158, 451, 578, 704, 732
  mining of harbor, 423–24, 451
Nicholson, Jack, 473
Nightline, 129–30, 132
Nitze, Paul, 12–13
Nixon, Richard, Pres., 39, 73, 76, 119, 125, 130, 137, 167, 244, 407–8, 437, 449, 559, 585–86, 619, 634
  arms control, and, 89–90
  domestic programs, and, 191
  Pentagon Papers, and, 136–37
Nofziger, Lyn, 127
North Carolina
  general election, 709, 758
  primary, 425, 432, 546
Nuclear freeze. *See* Arms control *and individual candidates*
Nuclear Nonproliferation Act of 1978, 274, 277
Nuclear power plants, 453

Nuclear weapons. *See* Arms control;
  Defense; Missiles
Nunn, Sam, Sen., 106–7, 112, 153, 732,

Obey, David, Rep., 627–28
O'Connor, John J., Archbishop, 605, 658,
  669
Office of Management and Budget
  (O.M.B.), 10, 57, 296
Office of Science and Technology Policy,
  130
Office of Strategic Services (O.S.S.), 125
Ohio
  general election, 30, 672–73, 675, 694–
    95, 734, 747–48, 750–51, 756
  polls, 426–27, 675
  primary, 20–21, 31, 234, 425–32, 436,
    448, 480
Oklahoma
  primary, 397
Oldaker, William, 582
Olympics, 571–72, 594, 603, 615, 626,
  640, 643, 666, 716
O'Neill, Thomas P., Rep., 86, 95, 138, 145,
  149, 151, 160, 195, 215, 302, 493, 511,
  591, 596
  Mondale, and, 315, 455, 651, 656
  Vice-Presidential candidate, and, 504–5
O'Neill, William, Gov., 315
Oregon
  general election, 636, 646–49, 733
  primary, 425
Organization of Eastern Caribbean States,
  195
Ortega, Katherine, 594–95, 597–99
Ottolini, Joseph, 346

Pakistan, 277
Panetta, Leon, Rep., 113
Parade, 217
Paxton, Jane, 481, 491
Payment-in-Kind Program (PIK), 248
Pearl, Minnie, 666
Pell, Claiborne, Sen., 545
Pennsylvania
  general election, 656–58, 667–68, 675,
    694, 739, 744, 746, 748
  polls, 411, 675, 739
  primary, 405, 411–16, 546
Pepper, Claude, Rep., 389–90
Percy, Charles, Sen., 106, 749, 758–59

Perle, Richard, 90–101, 104, 106, 107, 110
Perry, William, 82, 91
Phipps, Whitney, 538
Pierce, Samuel, 681
Pipes, Richard, 58
Political-Action Committees (PACs), 34,
  38, 40, 321, 415, 439, 441–42
Polls, 586, 716–17
  general election, 499, 518, 548–50,
    566–67, 569, 571–72, 579, 584, 618,
    626–27, 630, 638, 661–62, 674, 691,
    703, 714, 725–26, 728, 738, 744,
    752–54, 760
  primary, 46, 117, 148, 261, 292, 314,
    327, 358, 398, 400, 407–8, 410–11,
    426–29, 455–57, 491, 511, 550, 555,
    620–21, 732
  specific polls
    Baltimore *Sun*, 662
    Boston *Globe*, 311, 347
    Des Moines *Register*, 266
    Gallup, 174, 218, 221, 261, 338, 566,
      659, 714, 738, 746, 752
    Harris (Louis), 174, 567, 659, 728,
      734–35, 746
    Los Angeles *Times*, 174, 176, 636–37
    Milwaukee *Sentinel*, 176
    New York *Times*/CBS News, 174, 273–
      74, 353, 355, 432, 499, 567, 638,
      675, 703, 736
    Washington *Post*/ABC News, 6, 174,
      218, 355, 400, 408, 659, 675, 703,
      714, 728, 752
  see also Hart (Peter); Caddell; Wirthlin;
    individual candidates
Poverty, 612, 681–82, 716
Powell, Jody, 119
Pritchard, Joel, Rep., 101, 110
Puerto Rico
  caucuses, 399
PUSH-Excel program, 334, 416
  see also Jackson (Jesse)

Quaddafi, Muammar, Col., 449
Quayle, Dan, Sen., 153
Quinn, Jack, 495

Race issue, 40–41, 226–27, 444–48, 456,
  503, 519, 624–25, 679–81, 759
Rangel, Charles, Rep., 624
Reagan, Maureen, 588, 593

Reagan, Nancy, 69, 566, 573, 602, 660, 667

Reagan, Ronald, 4–8, 15–16, 55–56, 69, 117, 142, 147, 160, 287, 291, 306–8, 488–89, 524, 567–69, 571–74, 579, 593, 602–8, 620–23, 679, 711–13, 715, 730
  abortion, on, 292, 630, 694
  administration of, 4–5, 301, 576
    internal tensions in, 59–61, 123–25, 217–18, 577, 587–88, 761
  age, and, 573–74, 694, 696, 702, 705–8, 729
  agriculture, on, 752
  Armageddon, on, 732–33
  arms control, on, 13–15, 46–48, 50, 97–98, 101–9, 112–14, 157, 206, 216, 301, 440, 448, 580–81, 707, 761, 764
  baby boomers, and, 550, 760
  birth control, on, 46, 630
  black vote, and, 170, 289, 759
  budget of (1982), 11, 577
  budget of (1984), 295–300, 577, 589, 755, 764
  campaign (1980), 30, 128–33, 136, 288, 290–91, 405, 548
    funds, and, 415, 422, 677
  campaign (1984), 256, 287–89, 421–24, 457, 545, 550, 568–70, 581, 617, 639, 643, 651, 662–77, 695–97, 701–3, 709, 733–34, 741–42, 744, 746–50, 752, 754, 756–59
    ads, and, 744, 754–55, 610, 750
    funds, and, 424
    themes, and, 556, 589, 602, 755
  candidacy (1984), possibility of, 70–71, 92, 147, 217
  Central America, on, 62–65, 158, 304, 425, 705–6, 761
  China, on and visit to, 290, 452, 578, 713
  civil rights, and, 46–47, 160, 170, 210, 243–44, 291, 544, 640, 681, 751
  Congress, and, 6, 51–53, 55, 69–71, 206, 210
  Constitutional amendments, and, 300, 588–89, 755
  crime, on, 613–14
  debates, and, 686–97, 705–8
  defense, on, 9–10, 46–57, 71, 207, 215–16, 298, 577, 733

  deficit, on, 292–95, 664–65, 687–88, 761
  domestic policy, on, 56, 147, 206–9, 750–51
  economic policy, on, 3, 7–10, 70, 287, 291–95, 306, 523, 714
  election of (1980), 288
  election of (1984), 709–64, 756
    press conference (post-election), 764
  Electoral College, 569–70
  El Salvador, on, 64–65, 158, 216–17, 304, 424, 450
  endorsements of, 666
  environmental policy, on, 67, 306
  fairness issue, and, 46–47, 208–9
  Ferraro, and, 508, 581
  foreign policy, on, 157–58, 160, 164, 211, 300–4, 422, 714
  Grenada, and, 149, 154, 156, 161–63, 211–12, 734
  Hispanic vote, and, 292, 760
  Honduras, on, 304
  Iran and Iraq, on, 486
  Jewish vote, and, 518, 744–45
  Kennedy, John F., and, 608, 668, 692, 731, 740, 747
  Korean airliner, and, 140–42
  Labor Day event, 617
  labor vote, and, 273, 280, 288, 291–92, 573, 667, 748, 769
  leadership qualities of, 620–23, 685, 712–13, 729
  Lebanon, on, 144, 150–52, 161–62, 206, 211–15, 225, 287, 301–3, 422–23, 675–76, 706, 712, 745
  Medicare, 207, 297, 579, 762
  military strength, and, 51, 77–78, 88, 99–103, 106–10, 157, 216, 580–81, 613–14, 643, 716, 733–34, 755
  minimum wage, on, 755
  missiles, on, 46, 103, 107
  movie scenes, and,
    Bridges at Toko-Ri, The, 690
    Knute Rockne—All American, 746, 749
    State of the Union, The, 16, 690
  MX, on, 77–78, 96, 101–2, 107–9, 207, 577
  New Hampshire primary (1980), 127
  Nicaragua, on, 422–24, 451, 728
  Nixon, letter to, 731, 740
    Normandy, at, 492, 610, 643, 690, 712

nuclear war, on, 566–67, 579
Olympics, on, 571–72, 615, 640, 643, 671
polls, and, 46, 175, 206, 218, 261, 293, 499, 518, 549, 566–67, 569, 571–72, 579, 618, 630, 636–37, 659, 661–62, 674–75, 714, 716, 728, 732, 734–35, 738, 741, 743–44, 746, 752
poverty, on, 612
press, and, 5–6, 45, 49–50
religion issue, on, 291–92, 626, 630, 745
renomination of, 607
security, and, 651–52
"sleaze factor," and, 421–22, 509–10, 678
"Social Darwinism," and, 524
Social Security, on, 46–47, 50, 207, 579, 612, 688, 762
Soviet Union, on, 46–49, 58, 60, 141–42, 157, 216, 300–1, 448–49, 579–80, 614, 658, 673
space program, on, 305
special interest groups, and, 178–79
speeches of, 422, 719
  acceptance, 611–16
  Boston, 747
  Cleveland, 749
  Detroit, 747
  election night, 757–58
  Grand Ole Opry, 666
  Labor Day (1984), 748
  "mirrors," 52, 240
  New York, 744–46
  Pennsylvania, 746
  "Star Wars," 46–48, 53–54, 59–60, 305, 440
  State of the Union Message (1982), 3–4, 300
  State of the Union Message (1983), 9–10
  State of the Union Message (1984), 287–308
strategy of, 288–90, 307–8, 421, 568–71, 574–75, 592, 660–69, 675, 696, 713–15, 725–28, 734–35, 741–44, 747–49
style of governing, 4–6, 11, 45–47, 69–71, 106–7, 112–13, 141, 147, 207, 222–23, 295, 297, 304, 450, 761
taxes, on, 206–8, 293, 296–97, 523,

566–67, 574–79, 614, 676, 746, 748–49, 755, 764
unemployment, on, 164, 748
veto, line-item, and, 755
vulnerabilities of, political, 5, 117, 290–91, 300, 579, 621–23
white males' vote, and, 743, 759
women's vote, and, 305, 743, 760
young voters, and, 550–51, 759–60
see also Republican Convention
Reconstruction Finance Corporation, 29
Redford, Robert, 473
Reed, Thomas, 82, 89, 93
Regan, Donald, 206, 296, 299–300, 449–50, 651
Reilly, John, 249–50, 498, 502, 504, 539, 584, 642
Republican Convention, 566–616, 626
  delegates to, 587
  film at, 610
  internal conflicts, and, 587–88
  keynote speaker at, 594–95
  nomination, and, 586
  platform of, 585, 588–90
    abortion, 588
    budget, 589
    school prayer, 588
    taxes, 588–89
  Reagan speech at, 611–16
Republican Party, 3, 8, 50, 289, 299, 603–4, 716, 761
  campaign (1988), 586–87
  identity, and, 591
  moderates in, 587
  Right-wing of, 585–87
Rhode Island
  polls, 675
  primary, 397
Richardson, Elliot, 125
Right Stuff, The, 180, 182, 200, 261, 349
Rivers, Joan, 602
Robison, James, 586
Rockefeller, Jay, Gov., 456
Rockefeller, Nelson, V.P., 585
Rodino, Peter, Rep., 119, 138
Rogers, Kathi, 317
Rohatyn, Felix, 29
Roosevelt, Franklin D., Pres., 396, 614, 662, 686
Rostow, Eugene, 11–14, 93
Rowny, Edward, Gen., 98

Rubenstein, David, 120
Rubin, Miles, 467
Ruckelshaus, Jill, 68, 210
Ruckelshaus, William, 68, 210–11, 306
  see also E.P.A.
Ruge, Daniel, 692
Rumsfeld, Donald, 82, 225, 306

"Sagebrush rebellion," 76
Sager, Carole Bayer, 473
Sakharov, Andrei, 519
Sarbanes, Paul, Sen., 481
Sasser, James, Sen., 496
Sawyer, David, 180, 185, 261, 265, 275,
  337, 643
Sawyer, Grant, Gov., 480
Schlafly, Phyllis, 585, 600
Schlesinger, James, 82, 260
Schneiders, Greg, 261–62, 265, 267–69,
  280–81
Schroeder, Patricia, Rep., 489
Scowcroft, Brent, Gen., 81–82, 85–86,
  90–93, 97, 108
  see also MX
Scroon, Paul, 195
Sears, John, 127
Senate
  Appropriations committee, Defense
    subcommittee, 54–55, 104
  Armed Services committee, 54, 75, 83,
    91, 110, 153
  Budget committee, 46, 49–50, 52–55,
    57
  Foreign Relations committee, 31, 61,
    106, 152, 450
  Intelligence committee, 126, 162, 424,
    450
  see also specific issues
Shaheen, Jeanne, 317
Shannon, James, Rep., 112
Shaw, George Bernard, 272
Sheinbaum, Betty, 483
Sheinbaum, Stanley, 483
Shriver, Sargent, 166
Shultz, George, 13–14, 61, 145, 159, 211
  Central America, on, 146, 303, 423,
    704, 745–46
  Grenada, on, 155, 303
  Lebanon, on, 302–3
  MX, on, 108
  Persian Gulf, on, 486

terrorism, on, 745–46
Siegel, Mark, 19–20
Simon, Paul, Rep., 749, 758–59
Simpson-Mazzoli Immigration bill, 521,
  704–5
Sinatra, Frank, 754
Skutnik, Lenny, 307
Small, Donna, 481, 491
Smith, Gerard, 73–74
Smith, Levering, Adm., 82
Smith, Mary Louise, 210
Smith, Tim, 135
Snowe, Olympia, Rep., 593
Social Security, 115
  see also individual candidates
Somoza, Anastasio, 63
  see also Nicaragua
Sorensen, Theodore, 17, 33, 360, 369
South
  general election, 233–34, 701–3, 738–
    39, 743, 745, 756, 760
  polls, 174
  primary, 19, 20, 177, 198, 232–60, 262,
    267, 337, 359, 365, 370, 395, 427, 511
  see also individual states
South Carolina
  caucuses, 399
South Dakota
  primary, 491
Soviet Union, 156
  arms control, and, 75, 85, 88–89, 97–
    99, 105, 110, 580
  Lebanon, and, 152
  Missiles, and, 90, 97
  Olympics, and, 448
  U.S.-Soviet relations, 157, 448–49
  see also Andropov; Gromyko; Korean
    airliner; Mondale; Reagan
Speakes, Larry, 49–50, 140, 688, 694
Spence, Roy, 197
Spencer, Stuart, 550–51, 571, 660
Spinney, Franklin, 54
"Star Wars," 46–49, 53–54, 59–60, 305,
  440, 691, 694, 707, 735
State of the Union, The (film), 16, 690
Stein, David, 582
Stein, Jacob, 677
Stockman, David, 57, 120, 123–24, 296,
  298–99, 305
  see also O.M.B.
Stone, Roger, 573, 587, 748

Strategic Air Command, 75
Strauss, Robert, 25, 251, 315, 442–43, 480–81, 484
Stringfellow Acid Pits, 68, 211
Strother, Ray, 371, 375
Stubbs, Ansel, 615
Syria, 213–14

Taft, Robert A., 585
Taxes, 3, 7, 11, 57, 70, 139, 148, 296, 589, 725–27
   see also individual candidates
Teachers, 178, 415, 760
   see also A.F.T.; N.E.A.
Teeter, Robert, 571, 602–3
Teller, Edward, 48
Tennessee
   general election, 666
   primary, 426, 431
Terrorism, 215, 745–46
   see also Lebanon
Texas
   caucuses, 426–27, 481–82
   general election, 288, 569–70, 739, 743, 756
Thatcher, Margaret, Prime Min., 155–56
Time magazine, 6, 48, 360
Times Beach, 67
Today Show, 119
Tower, John, Sen., 91
Townes, Charles, 77–79
Townes Commission, 77, 82, 85
TRACE, 728–29, 735
Trujillo, Stephen, Sgt., 307
Truman, Harry S, Pres., 238, 248, 310, 449, 477, 561, 668, 686, 694, 707, 734, 749
Tsongas, Paul, Sen., 200
Tully, Paul, 529, 725
Turner, Stansfield, 133

Udall, Morris, Rep., 24, 166, 491
Unemployment, 191, 208, 571, 710, 714
United Auto Workers (U.A.W.), 26, 247, 399
United Mine Workers (U.M.W.), 231
Urban Coalition, 445
U.S. News & World Report, 360
Utah
   general election, 643–46

Valis, Wayne, 134–35

Van Cleave, William, 130
Van Riper, Frank, 182–84
Vento, Jerry, 337
Vermont
   primary, 354, 359
Vice-Presidential candidate selection, 496, 498–507, 510–11, 583, 721, 743
   see also Ferraro
Viguerie, Richard, 125
Virginia
   caucuses, 480
Volcker, Paul, 41, 299–300, 612
Voter registration, 530, 538, 550, 625
Voters (1980), 288–89
Voters (1984), 288–89, 549–50, 759
Voting Rights Act, 46
Vrdolyak, Edward, 375, 400

Walinsky, Adam, 136
Wallace, Chris, 567
Wallace, George, Gov., 39, 255, 291, 357
Wall Street Journal, 302
Warner, John, Sen., 163
War Powers Act of 1973, 143–45, 149–50, 162, 211, 303
Washington
   general election, 636, 733
   primary, 397
Washington, Harold, Mayor, 40, 171, 331, 375, 516
Washington Legal Foundation, 581
Washington Post, 6, 119–20, 128–31, 159, 211, 354, 375, 387, 408, 416, 491, 701–2
   see also Polls
Watt, James, 66, 69, 158, 211, 267–68, 282, 292, 756
   see also Interior, Department of
Wayne, John, 755
Weber, Vin, Rep., 590
Weicker, Lowell, Sen., 163
Weinberger, Caspar, 48–50, 55–57, 60–62, 159, 207, 211, 216
   arms control, on, 104, 108, 301
   Lebanon, on, 145, 150, 153, 163, 302–3
   Midgetman, on, 87
   MX, on, 78, 85, 89, 91–92, 108, 110
   Nicaragua, on, 423
West
   general election, 738–39, 743
   polls, 174
West Virginia

general election, 662, 741–42, 756
polls, 662
primary, 456, 491
Wheeling-Pittsburgh Steel Corporation,
    413, 436
White, Mark, Gov., 197, 481–82
White, William, 186
White male voters, 681, 743, 759
White voters, 759
Wilkie, Curtis, 268
Winger, Debra, 473
Winter, William, Gov., 234–35
Wirth, Timothy, Rep., 467
Wirthlin, Richard, 47, 118, 212, 218, 288–
    91, 420, 569, 713–15, 725–27, 729,
    734–35, 743–44
Wisconsin
    general election, 617–34, 659, 736, 752
    polls, 176, 200
    primary, 176, 198, 200

straw poll, 176
Women's vote, 170, 178, 398, 570, 681,
    743, 760
Woolsey, James, 81–82, 84–86, 90–91, 99
Wright, Jim, Rep., 95
Wyoming
    general election, 354–55

Young, Andrew, 41, 331, 389, 496, 532,
    583
Young, Coleman, Mayor, 170–71, 399, 625
Young voters, 322, 398, 411, 550–51,
    569–70, 590, 759–60
    see also individual candidates

Zaccaro, John, 507, 581–84, 600–2, 627,
    723
    see also Ferraro
Zhao, Ziyang, Premier, 452

About the Author

Elizabeth Drew is a staff writer for *The New Yorker* and is a panelist on "Agronsky & Company." She also participates in other public affairs programs. She is the author of five other books: *Washington Journal: The Events of 1973-1974; American Journal: The Events of 1976; Senator; Portrait of an Election: The 1980 Presidential Campaign;* and *Politics and Money: The New Road to Corruption.*

Born in Cincinnati, Ohio, Elizabeth Drew graduated Phi Beta Kappa from Wellesley College, where she majored in political science. She then worked as an associate editor for *The Writer* in Boston. From 1959 to 1964 she was a writer and editor for *Congressional Quarterly* in Washington, and in 1964 began writing for such journals as *The Atlantic Monthly* and *The New York Times Magazine.* From 1967 until 1973 she was Washington editor for *The Atlantic Monthly.*

Ms. Drew has received many awards for her work and holds honorary degrees from six universities, including Yale, Reed, and Williams. She has been described as "the American Boswell" and as "the Samuel Pepys of Washington."